Berni Organ Company

"The Excelsior"---96 Key

With bass and snare drums and cymbal set on detachable wings.
Representing a regimental band of about 40 musicians, specially constructed
for large parks and carnival companies, for parading through cities.
The success attained with these organs for this purpose has
been enormous.

A magnificent facade with moving statues as band leaders.

DESCRIPTION

Dimensions: 15 feet long, 10 feet high, 6 feet wide.

INSTRUMENTATION

Basses:	12 Bottom stopped pipes.	**Trumpets:**	22 Wooden trumpets.
	24 Open pipes.		18 Brass Clarinets.
	36 Open mixed pipes.	**Clarinets:**	18 Stopped pipes.
Trombones:	12 Wooden reed trombones.		54 Open pipes.
	30 Open pipes.	**Violins:**	140 Open pipes.
Accompaniment:	15 Stopped pipes.	**Flutes:**	44 Open pipes.
	45 Open mixed pipes.		22 Stopped pipes.
Saxophones:	44 Open pipes.	**Mixtures:**	60 Open pipes.
Barytones:	22 Wooden reed pipes.		

Total, 618 pipes.

Prices: $5,000, including 100 yards of music.

TREASURES OF
MECHANICAL MUSIC

A compilation of hundreds of tracker bar,
key frame, and note layouts for automatic music
machines, together with historical and technical
information and a collector's portfolio of
outstanding mechanical musical instruments.

By Arthur A. Reblitz and Q. David Bowers

The Vestal Press, Ltd.
Vestal, New York 13850 USA

Library of Congress Cataloging in Publication Data

Reblitz, Arthur A.
    Treasures of mechanical music.

    Subtitle: A compilation of hundreds of tracker bar, key frame, and note layouts for automatic music machines, together with historical and technical information and a collectors' portfolio of outstanding mechanical musical instruments.
    Bibliography: p. 621
    Includes index.
    1. Musical instruments (Mechanical) I. Bowers, Q. David. II. Title.
ML1050.R4   789'.7   81-461
ISBN 0-911572-20-1   AACR2

First printing: April 1981

SPECIAL CREDIT NOTE

The authors acknowledge the extensive assistance with proofreading the final manuscript and many helpful suggestions made by Claes O. Friberg.

FRONTISPIECE: Advertisement circa 1912 for a 96-key band organ imported to America by the Berni Organ Company of New York City.

DEDICATION:

To the late Charlie Bovey, whose wisdom, energy, and foresight made possible the restorations of Virginia City and Nevada City, Montana, and the saving of the equipment and archives of the B.A.B. Organ Company. Arthur Reblitz spent much time in Montana visiting the Bovey enterprises and studying the information so generously made available for his use.

To the late Eugene DeRoy, who in the 1960s travelled with Dave Bowers throughout Europe in the successful quest for large orchestrions and organs and the historical information associated with these magnificent musical instruments of yesteryear; and to his only daughter, Els, who gave the DeRoy archives of catalogues and scale sticks to Dave because "my father wanted you to have them."

ABOUT THE AUTHORS

Arthur A. Reblitz

Arthur A. Reblitz has been interested in all facets of music machines and their music for most of his life. During his college years he spent his vacation time working at the original Svoboda's Nickelodeon Tavern in Chicago Heights, Illinois. There he gained valuable experience working on over 100 music machines, including nearly every major brand of American instrument. In 1968 he graduated with high honors with a B.S. in Music Education from the University of Illinois.

Art is the owner of Art Reblitz Player Pianos in Colorado Springs, where he lives with his wife Jeannie. He specializes in repairing automatic pianos, orchestrions, and band organs and in arranging new music rolls for these instruments. Some of his past customers include Bellm's Cars & Music of Yesterday Museum (Sarasota, Florida), the Bovey Restoration (Virginia City and Nevada City, Montana), House on the Rock (Spring Green, Wisconsin), Knott's Berry Farm (Buena Park, California), the Vestal Press Collection (Vestal, New York), as well as many private collections. Instruments have ranged from simple player pianos and organettes to the complex Hupfeld Super Pan Orchestra. He has also made rolls with advertising jingles for Coca-Cola, McDonald's, Anheuser Busch, and other national firms.

A "Registered Craftsman" member of the Piano Technician's Guild, Art is the author of Piano Servicing, Tuning, and Rebuilding. *This fully illustrated volume was published in 1976 and was in its fourth printing by 1980. It is used as a text by several dozen colleges, universities, and schools of piano technology, and it has been translated into Braille. Art has contributed many articles to the bulletins of the Musical Box Society International and the Automatic Musical Instrument Collectors' Association.*

Q. David Bowers

Q. David Bowers, a 1960 graduate of the Pennsylvania State University, received in 1976 the Alumni Achievement Award from that institution's College of Business Administration. Over the years he has been involved with several different businesses in the field of collectors' items, including Hathaway & Bowers, Inc. (1967-1972), a firm which imported many large band organs and orchestrions from Europe in the days when few others cared for them, the Mekanisk Musik Museum (with Claes O. Friberg in Copenhagen, Denmark), and American International Galleries (with Bonnie Tekstra and Claes O. Friberg in Irvine, California).

He is the author of over a dozen different books, several of which have achieved prominence in the music field. Put Another Nickel In, *written in 1965, told the story of the Rudolph Wurlitzer Company via hitherto unpublished information from the Wurlitzer archives.* The Encyclopedia of Automatic Musical Instruments, *published in 1972, was designated by the American Library Association as "one of the most valuable reference books of the year," an honor conferred on only a handful of the more than 15,000 books published in that year. This 1008-page volume was made possible with in-depth interviews with many of the personalities who originally comprised the automatic musical instrument business, including Messrs. Bacigalupo, Bruder, Bursens, DeRoy, Frei, Hupfeld, Imhof, Link, Perlee, Rand, Rockola, Seeburg, Weber, Whitlock, and Wurlitzer, thus preserving much information which would have otherwise been lost to history.*

Dave has contributed articles to the Musical Box Society International, the Automatic Musical Instrument Collectors' Association, the Musical Box Society of Great Britain, the Fair Organ Preservation Society, and other organizations.

TABLE of CONTENTS

ACKNOWLEDGEMENTS

The authors express appreciation to the many collectors, dealers, museum officials, and others who contributed to the present volume. We are grateful for the help and cooperation of many individuals without whose help the book would not be a reality.

The following made major contributions to the book in the manner indicated:

Charlie and Sue Bovey (making available the B.A.B. Organ Company scales and archives), J. Brink (fair organ, dance organ, and street organ scales), Jerry Doring (orchestrion scales), John Ellingsen (copying B.A.B. Organ Company scales; checking details of orchestrion scales), Carl Frei, Jr. (band organ scales), Claes O. Friberg (European orchestrion and reproducing piano scales; editorial suggestions; proofreading), Frederick Fried (band organ scales), Roy Haning (proofreading of band organ and dance organ scales), Terry Hathaway (contribution of his personal collection of scales, including those from the Hathaway & Bowers files as gathered 1967-1972; technical interpretation of the Hupfeld Pan and other sophisticated scales), Dr. Jan Haspels (European organ scales), John Hovancak (band organ and orchestrion scales), David Junchen (pipe organ scales; music roll arranging information), P.M. Keast (recollections of his experiences as a music roll arranger, as presented in an interview), Mike Kitner (article on roll perforating; Seeburg tubing diagram; many tracker scales for coin pianos, orchestrions, band organs, reproducing pianos, and the Mills Violano-Virtuoso; technical consultation); Doyle Lane (Wurlitzer factory scale sticks and blueprints for band organs, pipe organs, and orchestrions), Mel Locher (Mills Violano-Virtuoso information and wiring diagram; European orchestrion scales), John Malone (photographs and data pertaining to the Play-Rite Music Roll Company), Arthur W.J.G. Ord-Hume (article concerning the tuning and musical aspects of certain automatic musical instruments), Arthur Prinsen (European dance organ scales), Dave Ramey (orchestrion and band organ scales; technical consultation and advice), Harvey and Marion Roehl and the staff of the Vestal Press (Q.R.S. photographs; Seeburg scales; Rolmonica scale; proofreading; preparation of illustrations; technical assistance and advice), Ken Smith (band organ scales; proofreading of band organ information), Tom Sprague (coin piano and orchestrion scales; technical advice), Wilda Looff Taucher (Looff photographs), Marcel van Boxtel (European band organ scales), and Graham Webb (music box scales).

Appreciation is also expressed to the following individuals who diligently answered letters and inquiries, spent time on the telephone, and in other ways helped to make the book more complete:

Mr. and Mrs. Byron Akers, Mike Ames (Mills Violano-Virtuoso and Mortier information), Durrell Armstrong (American coin piano and orchestrion scales), Norman Arnold (pipe organ information), Robert Baker (Skinner pipe organ scale), Richard Barnes (Wurlitzer pipe organ scale), Robert Baumbach (Marquette S roll scale), Tom Beckett (Duo-Art pipe organ scale; other help), Robert Billings (Recordo scales), Dr. William Black (photography), Dr. Ron Bopp (Seeburg HO scale), Terry Borne (detailed information concerning Seeburg H and MSR scales), Christine Bowers (graphics), Herb Brabandt (band organ scales), James Bratton (reproducing piano scales), Larry Broadmoore (reproducing piano scales), Arthur Bronson (dance organ scales), David Burke (Imhof & Mukle scales), Noel Burndahl (Resotone Grand information), Ron Cappel (Bruder 94-key "Selection" organ scale), Dick Carty (reproducing piano information), Durward Center (Moller Artiste scale; Welte pipe organ and orchestrion scales), Francis Cherney, Dr. George Coade (European orchestrion scales), Jerry Cohen (Wurlitzer Solo Violin Piano information), Wilber Comings (Robert-Morton organ scale), Jim Crank (pipe organ scales),

Warren Dale (American orchestrion scales), Dr. Harold Davis (Mills Violano-Virtuoso information), Jerry DeBacker (Solo Art Apollo information), Bob Dumas (pipe organ scales), Paul and Laura Eakins (coin piano and orchestrion scales), Bill Edgerton (Bernhard Dufner information), Kurt Elbers (Weber orchestrion scales), Dr. John Field, Dr. Howard and Helen Fitch (organette information), Ed Freyer (Link, Regina Sublima, and other scales), Allen Galpin (Wellershaus organ scale), Dr. Robert Gilson (European orchestrion scales; photography), Larry Givens, Ron Goldstein (organettes), Glenn Grabinsky, Cliff Gray, Leonard Grymonprez (many European organ and orchestrion scales), Ed Hattrup (European orchestrion scales), Ralph Heintz (organette scales), Jack Hewes (band organ scales), Frank Holland (European orchestrion and reproducing piano scales), Judith Howard (fair organ scales), Robert Jensen (band organ scales), Dana Johnson (band organ and orchestrion scales), Robert Johnson (Welte 100-hole orchestrion scale; Welte pipe organ scales), Jim Knudtson (Nelson-Wiggen Selector Duplex Organ information), Larry Leonard (Estey pipe organ scale), Pete Levine (Limonaire scale), Alan Lightcap (Hupfeld Phonoliszt-Violina scale), Ed Link (Link pipe organ scale), Gordon Lipe (Wurlitzer Pianino scale), Richard Lohr (North Tonawanda Musical Instrument Works Mando-Orchestra scale; Berry-Wood scales), Mel Luchetti (pipe organ scales),

Tom Marshall (North Tonawanda Musical Instrument Works barrel organ scale), Hayes McClaran (orchestrion scales), Claude Marchal, Jim Marke, Francis Mayer, Marvin Merchant (Bruder organ scale), George Messig (band organ scales), Bruce Miller (Bruder band organ scale), Jim Miller, Dr. Robert Miller (European band organ scales), Robert Moore (Kimball electronic organ scale), Mike Naddeo, Don Page, Stan Peters (organette scales), Bill Pixley (reproducing piano scales), Gerald Planus (music box information), Bill Pohl, Ed Purdy, Gordon Ralph (Seeburg-Smith BH scale information), Don Rand, Wesley Reed (organette and Tel-Electric scales), Frank Rider (coin piano and orchestrion scales), Fred Rieger (Estey pipe organ scale), Marty and Elise Roenigk, Gary Sage, Art Sanders, Ed Schmidt (band organ scales), Joseph Schumacher (organette scales), Mike Schwimmer, James Spriggs (Gavioli Meloton scale; organette and music box information), Staples & Charles (historical information), Allan Stafford, Gary "Chip" Statler (Decap information), Robert Steeves (Unified Reproduco scale), Noble Stidham, Marshall Stone, David Stumpf (band organ scales), Al and Flo Svoboda, Dr. Ramsi Tick (Q.R.S. historical information), Verbon Waggoner (music box scales), Jim Wells (Wurlitzer 180 band organ scale), Craig Williams (Roesler-Hunholz and Clark organ scales), James Williams, George Willick (Apollo piano scale), Oswald Wurdeman (American orchestrion and band organ scales), Marvin Yagoda (Peerless Trio scale), and Peter Ziegler (Unified Reproduco scale).

Note: Picture credits are given in the photograph captions.

The corner of a collector's music room. The colorful "nickelodeon" near the center is a beautiful Seeburg Style J Solo Orchestrion which uses type H rolls. Originally used in a tavern in Montana, the Style J was rescued by a Utah collector in the 1960s. The Style J is very rare; fewer than a half dozen examples of this style are known to exist. To the extreme right is a foot-pumped Gulbransen home player piano, circa 1925, and an impressive library of music rolls for it.

PREFACE BY THE AUTHORS

ART REBLITZ: The first music machine I can remember was a Seeburg KT Special with a plain glass window in front of the drums. The time was 1954, and I was seven years old. It had a sign on top which read: "The Old Nickelodeon - See and Hear It Play - Lousy But Loud - 10 Tunes - 10c." "Lousy" was an understatement, but "Loud"? It was on its last legs and could barely be heard above the clanging pinball machines and general racket of the amusement arcade in which it was located in Daytona Beach, Florida. I was intrigued with seeing the mechanisms work, devices which actually *produced* music.

Not satisfied until I learned how it worked, I spent many hours searching through the Chicago Public Library until I found two or three old books by Dolge and White, which contained information about player pianos. This was before the days of the Vestal Press library of instant knowledge about music machines; the information really had to be searched out, and when it was found the facts were often contradictory and inaccurate. By studying these early books and an article in the *Encyclopaedia Britannica* I learned how pneumatic actions worked, but I still needed to know what sort of roll it was which could play the piano and all those percussion instruments at the same time. I wasn't aware that the KT Special had a xylophone, because it was hidden inside the lower compartment of the cabinet and wasn't working. The few available books said little about coin-operated pianos. The *Readers' Guide to Periodic Literature* steered me toward some magazine articles about the Sanders family's Musical Museum in Deansboro, New York, the Bornand Music Box Company in Pelham, New York, and some of the other long-established places, but I still needed more technical information to satisfy my curiosity.

Then in 1961 came Harvey Roehl's landmark *Player Piano Treasury,* and then in 1963 Larry Givens' *Rebuilding the Player Piano* made its appearance, the latter including several tracker scales which answered some of my questions but generated many more. A letter was quickly fired off to Larry Givens, a very busy man, who nevertheless took the time to answer such questions as "how does the mandolin work in a Wurlitzer Mandolin Quartette?," "how can the Nelson-Wiggen Style 8 piano play mandolin, xylophone, *and* bells from a style A roll?," and "how can a style O roll play flute or xylophone solos and a different piano accompaniment at the same time?"

During one of my first visits to Svoboda's Nickelodeon Tavern, Chicagoland's great old collection of mechanical wonders, where public enjoyment had priority over pristine restoration, I noticed an "O" tracker scale taped inside the cabinet of a Coinola model SO orchestrion. I was fascinated as I watched the holes in the roll pass over the tracker bar, causing catchy music to be produced. My curiosity lead to the discovery that in those days many of the piano lids and front doors were unlocked. During this and later visits to the Svoboda establishment I enjoyed peeking inside the cabinets while the mechanisms played their music. Years later, after working for Al, Flo, and their sons Allan and Corky for several years, Al told me, "I remember when you used to come here before you worked for me; you were always opening the doors of the pianos while they played. I never bothered you because I knew you were *learning.*"

From fourth grade through college, and then during four years of mandatory military service, I played flute and piccolo in various bands and orchestras. Sitting in the first row of a band or in the middle of an orchestra for that length of time enables one to hear every detail of a great variety of music. I spent a lot of time imagining myself to be hearing a huge music machine and wondering how a machine could be constructed which would have the finesse, subtlety, versatility, and power of a human ensemble. This same question was pondered by every orchestrion and band organ designer, and their attempts to solve the problem in an economical and practical way are illustrated by their tracker bar and key frame scales.

As those who know me will testify, I have never stopped asking one question after another about how music machines work. The scales and layouts in this book are the result of 25 years of these questions. Assembling the book took several years longer than anticipated, because every time it was "done" whole bunches of additional information turned up, right down to the last few weeks before publication. Most of the useful scales are listed in this book. Most have been verified, when possible, by checking original machines, rolls, books, and music arrangers' scale sticks. Nevertheless, the distribution of this book will undoubtedly generate more information—additional scales, variations, and corrections—and we welcome such information. After all, we're still not done asking "how do they work?"

Arthur A. Reblitz

DAVE BOWERS: I first met Art Reblitz back in the mid 1960s. After exchanging some letters, I invited him to accompany me on a searching expedition during my next visit to Chicago. We had a grand time visiting and photographing the old factories of the Operators Piano Company, Seeburg, Nelson-Wiggen, Marquette, and the Mills Novelty Company. The day was topped off by a behind-the-scenes tour of Svoboda's Nickelodeon Tavern, which to Art was what heaven must be like.

As the years went by I intensified my interest in historical research. When *The Guidebook of Automatic Musical Instruments* (in two volumes) came out in the late 1960s it contained many suggestions by Art. Likewise, *The Encyclopedia of Automatic Musical Instruments*, published in 1972, contained some of his contributions. As an author of quite a few books I am used to people saying "I liked your book." Did they actually *read* the book? An author never knows for sure. Well, with Art's case there was never a doubt. He would not only read each book I wrote, but he would go over it with the literary equivalent of a scanning electronic microscope. "Did you notice in your book that Welte and Peerless, two unrelated firms, both used the same exact wording in one of their advertisements?" No, I hadn't noticed, and a new avenue for research was opened.

The present volume is a combination of Art's interests and mine. The tracker scales, key frame layouts, and technical data are the result of his tireless searching. The photographs, historical information, and captions are my contributions. The object was to create a reference book which would contain useful technical information not already in what Art has described as the Vestal Press "library" of books, and at the same time to provide pictures and historical information which, hopefully, will be *interesting* to the reader. Only you can judge the result.

To me, automatic musical instruments represent a tangible link with a romantic bygone era. These instruments actually were there, were alive, and often were the center of attention. That these *animate* objects can come to life again to entertain the present generation is truly marvelous. Imagine how the student of political history would react if George Washington, Abraham Lincoln, Theodore Roosevelt, Winston Churchill, Josef Stalin, Queen Victoria, and Will Rogers could come to life today to be studied and interviewed in person. Well, the fact that Ruth Style 36, Seeburg KT Special, Nelson-Wiggen Selector Duplex, Wurlitzer Mandolin Quartette, and other piano and organ styles exist today and actually are alive is precisely the equivalent for the student of automatic musical instrument history. How fortunate we are!

And yet there are some things which have gone before and which are seemingly lost forever. The immense and impressive Apollonicon barrel-operated organ which entertained Londoners 150 years ago, Michael Welte's first orchestrion (1849) with over 1100 pipes, the curious Imhof & Mukle orchestrion which entertained visitors to New York's Jockey Club around 1907, the several dozen (that's right, *several dozen)* Style 38 Ruth organs which Charles I.D. Looff used on his carousels in America around 1910, the precocious and remarkable Electromagnetic Orchestra which played for visitors to the Centennial Exhibition in 1876, P.T. Barnum's Welte orchestrion . . . these and many others survive only via written records, just like George Washington, Abraham Lincoln, and Theodore Roosevelt, and can no longer be studied in the flesh.

Pictures represent a way to appreciate the instruments of years gone by. Each time I acquire a previously-unseen catalogue of old instruments, a faded time-worn snapshot of a Wurlitzer band organ in a traveling show which visited Newport, Kentucky in 1915, or a postcard showing a beer garden with a large glass-fronted orchestrion looming over the proceedings, I experience a thrill. It is almost like being there. Not quite, but almost. Among the pages to follow are hundreds of photographs which I have collected over the years. Some, like the Electrova piano in a Connecticut candy parlor in 1915, are from the days of long ago. The instruments pictured probably no longer exist in such instances. Others show Ampicos, Hupfelds, Wredes, and Reginas in collections today; instruments which have survived and which are now appreciated. As the picture credit notes in the captions demonstrate, this has not been a solo effort. Many generously helped.

Picture collecting is a challenging pursuit. Photography was popular in 1876, but did anyone capture the likeness of the Electromagnetic Orchestra then? Did anyone take pictures of the Operators Piano Company orchestrion-building activities? What about the Philipps or Welte production facilities in Europe? The dream is sometimes fulfilled. What a thrill it was when a motion picture of the interior of the Seeburg Piano Company factory came to light a few years ago in, of all places, a Swedish film archive! Mr. J.P. Seeburg himself could be seen with freshly-minted KT Special orchestrions and roll-operated pipe organs. Some pictures have surfaced, like a trout on a hook, but have slipped away. About ten years ago a gentleman showed Terry Hathaway a photograph, circa 1920, of a disastrous flood. Piled against a bridge was a thicket of debris, including a Cremona Orchestral J orchestrion which had washed up in all of its art glass glory. "I'll send you a copy of the picture," Terry's visitor said. The picture never arrived, and, unfortunately, the man's name was not recorded.

A recent addition to my personal collection of instruments is a Wurlitzer Style 16 Mandolin PianOrchestra. This specific instrument, which was once used in a Minneapolis restaurant, is mentioned in the book. Now, I enjoy the instrument's music—the piano, pipes, and percussion effects—but even more, or at least equally, I enjoy its history and specifications. Perhaps you, too, will come to "like" this particular instrument when you read about it. I know I have developed an affection for many different types of instruments just by seeing their pictures. So far as I know, there are no examples of the Hupfeld Helios II/36 "Rococo" orchestrion which still exist. The original catalogue picture, reproduced in this book, is charming. After seeing the picture and reading about Helios orchestrions, would you drive 100 miles on a Sunday afternoon to hear one of these play a concert, should one be discovered? I would. And, I think you would too. Such is the charm of old-time instruments—not only the instruments themselves, but their pictures, their specifications, and, to focus on Art Reblitz' specialty, their tracker bar scales or key frame layouts.

You have the book in your hands. Art and I both hope it will help you to *learn*, just as we learned when we assembled the information. Life is short. Time marches inexorably onward. While learning is fine, just great in fact, do take the time also to *enjoy*.

Chapter 1
INTRODUCTION

Wurlitzer Archives photograph of the Style 16 Mandolin PianOrchestra.

INTRODUCTION

It's hard for me to remember the different Wurlitzer models, but I do recall the Style 16 PianOrchestra. What an orchestrion it was! You would put a nickel in it and it would light up like a Christmas tree! There were two of them in Minneapolis. One was in a restaurant, the Shanghai Cafe, downtown. I used to service it. The Shanghai was like something out of a fairy tale, all in the Oriental style. The inside of the place was full of carved teak furniture, vases, live trees, and other decorations. Birds flew around in the air as you ate dinner. It was quite an attraction at one time, although not many remember it now. The orchestrion later went to the Stagecoach Inn in Shakopee, not far from Minneapolis. Perhaps you've seen it there.

The other Style 16 in Minneapolis once belonged to me. I took it in on trade on a Violano-Virtuoso. You may be interested to know that pianos and orchestrions usually didn't stay for long in a particular tavern. As soon as they were paid for, and that usually only took two or three years at the most, the owners got rid of them and got something different, just like jukeboxes are changed frequently today. Anyway, I took this Style 16 in on trade. It must have been around the middle of the 1920s, for at the time it wasn't worth much. Most places wanted the smaller machines like the Western Electrics and Seeburgs. I took out the motor and some of the instruments and then junked it, except for part of the front of the case which I used to build a toolbox. I still have the box in my shop back home in Minneapolis.

Rolls were very important. You had to have the right kind of music. Mostly the people liked the new music they heard when shows came to town or on phonograph records. This was before the radio was popular. I used to tell the owners to throw away the rolls after a few months, except for certain songs which were old favorites and were always popular. I made a lot of money selling rolls. We never patched or fixed them. If a roll tore, it was thrown away.

Recollection by Oswald Wurdeman

This is a book about old-time mechanical music machines, specifically about the discs, rolls, and other "programmed music" they use. While the subject can be viewed as being technical, the authors have added quite a bit of spice and romance, mainly in the form of hundreds of illustrations, many of which have never before appeared in a publication intended for collectors. As such, the present volume promises to be a useful, and we hope *interesting*, companion to *The Encyclopedia of Automatic Musical Instruments, Player Piano Treasury*, and other Vestal Press reference books.

An old-time automatic musical instrument can be likened to a modern data processing machine. Information is stored on a tape (piano roll) or disc and is retrieved in logical order, resulting in a program, in this case, of music. It is significant to note that the Univac, the first large-scale modern computer, introduced in the 1940s, was made by a firm which long ago incorporated into its structure the North Tonawanda Musical Instrument Works, a well-known maker of self-playing pianos and organs.

But the North Tonawanda Musical Instrument Works, founded in 1906 and active until about 1922, was a late entry in the game, relatively speaking. Four hundred years earlier, in 1502, the large pinned cylinder organ still on exhibit today in the ancient castle overlooking Salzburg, Austria is said to have sounded its first note. And this instrument, large in size and fairly complex in musical ability, was obviously preceded by others.

In the self-playing organs of antiquity, each musical note was represented by a protruding pin, usually made of metal, on a wooden cylinder. As the barrel turned, the pins came into contact with a series of levers which opened valves and released air which, in turn, caused the desired musical notes to sound. The system employed over 400 years ago in Salzburg was essentially the same as that used today in Switzerland and Japan for small novelty music boxes. As the tiny pinned cylinder, in this case made of metal, turns, tuned metal teeth in a *music comb* are plucked, and *Lara's Theme* or *Carousel Waltz* fills the air with its tinkly melody.

The basic cylinder or barrel system was used for many different types of automatically-played instruments, including music boxes, pianos, church organs, orchestrions, organettes, and even circus calliopes.

Perhaps the *creme de la creme* of the cylinder type of instrument was the immense Apollonicon built in London during the early 19th century by Flight & Robson. This device was equipped with multiple sets of barrels programmed with complete overtures and operatic scores which would be played on hundreds, perhaps thousands, of organ pipes and other effects.

In the same vein was an instrument presented to the public in 1849 by Michael Welte: an automatic pipe organ on which he had worked for several years. A later account reprinted in the catalogue of M. Welte & Sons noted:

"The public nicknamed the instrument 'orchestrion' because it successfully imitated a many-voiced orchestra of artists in Karlsruhe. It was a marvel of mechanical skill, containing eleven hundred pipes, which were actuated by thousands of small pins set on drums. These represented musical melodies and harmonies, which might be said to be 'written' upon three large wooden cylinders which rotated with a precision such as had been supposed unattainable before."

Despite the acclaim given to cylinder-operated instruments it was eventually realized that this system had many limitations. A musical selection could only be of a fixed length equal to the time required for the cylinder to make one revolution, or, in the instances of cylinders with special spiral programming, the length of several revolutions. Thus an opera or overture would have to be shortened to just a mere fragment of the whole composition, while a simple tune like *Dixie* would be lengthened and embellished or, more usually, repeated several times.

The cylinders used on many large music boxes, organs, and orchestrions were interchangeable, but the great expense of making cylinders, plus storage problems, made the acquisition of a large number of cylinders impractical.

The solution for music boxes was the disc, and for pianos, orchestrions, and organs the answer was the music roll or music book.

Music Boxes

The music box disc was invented in the mid 1880s. By the time the 1890s had ended, the cylinder music box was obsolete. The reason was money. In 1895 the Pittsburgh firm of Heeren Brothers offered for sale an Ideal Sublime Harmonie Piccolo cylinder music box, made in St. Croix, Switzerland by Mermod Freres, a model with a cylinder measuring 24½ inches long and containing a program of six tunes. The price of the box was $775.00, and extra cylinders cost $165.00 each. A few years later the Regina Music Box company offered an instrument which used steel discs measuring 27 inches in diameter, which stored 12 of the discs, and which played them automatically in succession. The Regina, housed in a handsome glass-fronted cabinet measuring about six feet high, cost just $350.00, and a virtually unlimited supply of extra discs could be purchased for just $2.00 each.

At the same time small 8½-inch Regina discs for the Style 21 (a music box which sold for only $10.00) retailed for just 25c each. Discs could be produced in quantity at low cost. A large collection of music could be obtained cheaply, including popular new tunes as they appeared on the market. Still, discs had the disadvantage of having a fixed playing time, usually less than a minute per selection.

Discs appeared in many formats. Some had projections on the underside, like a cheese grater. These came into contact with a star wheel which, in turn, plucked a metal music comb similar to that used on a cylinder box. Other discs, the Stella type for example, had punched holes which actuated a special mechanism which plucked the comb. Disc sizes ranged from about 4 inches for a tiny Thorens or Helvetia model to a huge Komet box which used sheets measuring 33 inches in diameter. Generally, the larger the disc was, the longer the playing time would be. Certain rare disc-shifting boxes had a mechanism which permitted a program which lasted for two revolutions of the tune sheet.

Unlike an organ pipe, which could be sounded many times in quick succession, a note on a music comb required a brief moment to come to rest after it had been plucked, even if the comb tooth was equipped with a damper device. For this reason, music combs usually had several adjacent teeth each playing the same note, particularly in the instance of notes which were used frequently in musical arrangements. In this way, if note C was required several times in succession, it could be played first on one tooth, then next on the tooth beside it, and then on a third tooth. By that time the first tooth would be still, and it could be plucked again.

The present volume gives musical scales for many different types of disc music boxes. The "big three" in the industry, Polyphon, its American offspring, Regina, and Symphonion are represented as are several other trademarks. Of all the musical scales researched by the authors, those of music boxes were found to be the least standard. Tuning of a music box comb seems to have been an art, not a science, with the technique passed from craftsman to craftsman and from generation to generation. The result is that two Polyphon music boxes of the same type, for example, when calibrated on an oscilloscope or stroboscopic device today are apt to be found to be tuned slightly differently.

Pianos and Orchestrions

Mechanical pianos which were operated by a pinned barrel were popular in the 19th century. Such instruments were usually of the upright style and contained a large cylinder on which many tunes, often eight, nine, or more, were programmed. By means of a lever on the side of the case the barrel could be shifted slightly so as to bring another set of pins, and thus another tune, into play. Most of these pianos were ruggedly built and were designed to be moved from place to place. Dozens of such instruments were once carted around the streets of New York City, London, and other metropolises. Changing the program on an existing cylinder or making a new cylinder was very time consuming and expensive. It was far easier to keep the piano moving to new locations and new listeners.

During the 19th century many experiments were made with other systems. Alexander DeBain perfected a device which employed pin-studded wooden shingles, called *planchettes*, each of which had a fragment of a melody programmed on it. The planchettes were fed into a reading device which actuated the desired piano or organ notes.

The Jacquard loom, first publicly exhibited in France around 1801, revolutionized the weaving industry by using a series of interlinked punched cards to reproduce elaborate designs on woven fabric. This undoubtedly acted as the inspiration decades later for the many types of pianos, pipe organs, and band organs which were operated by folding cardboard music books.

However, it was the paper music roll which was to achieve the greatest popularity for use on pianos, organs, and orchestrions.

The holes in a paper roll were "read" as they passed over a tracker bar. Made of wood or metal, the tracker bar had a series of closely spaced holes arranged in a row perpendicular to the path of travel of the roll. Each hole was connected via tubing to a pneumatic apparatus. When a tracker bar hole was uncovered by a corresponding opening in the roll, the pneumatic apparatus would be actuated, and by means of vacuum or compressed air a bellows would cause a piano note to strike or a valve would be opened to admit air to an organ pipe. Early piano rolls had one hole for each musical note in the scale.

Soon, *control perforations* were added so that the instrument could perform different operations such as rewinding automatically after the end of a selection or the operation of the soft pedal or sustaining pedal. By the early 1890s, M. Welte & Sons, the world's leading builder of orchestrions at the time, had converted its production from barrel instruments to those which used paper rolls. A single roll could contain the program to actuate hundreds of pipes as well as drums, bells, and other orchestral effects.

In 1898 the Peerless Piano Player Company of St. Johnsville, New York introduced the first paper-roll-operated coin-controlled piano to be extensively marketed in America. Still, there was time for the barrel piano to breathe a few more gasps, so the Wurlitzer Tonophone, a barrel instrument first sold in 1898, achieved a production run of about 2,000 from then until 1908.

By 1904, many different styles of roll-operated pianos and orchestrions were to be found in places of public amusement and accommodation. "Wurlitzer has just the right instrument for your business," that firm advertised, and noted that its pianos were ideal for amusement parks, billiard halls, beer gardens, bowling alleys, boats, cafes, confectioneries, cigar stores, clubs, dance halls, drug stores, department stores, groceries, hotels, lodges, lunch rooms, merry-go-rounds, news stands, post card studios, railroad depots, and restaurants.

In the same year, 1904, the Welte-Mignon, a piano which not only played the various keyboard notes but which also re-enacted the tonal expression and shading of the human artist, was introduced for use in the home. Prior to that, the push-up piano player, which used a 65-note roll, represented the ultimate musical enjoyment in sun parlors and living rooms in thousands of homes. Later, the 65-note player was to evolve into the inner-player, with mechanisms built inside the piano case, and, still later, into the standard 88-note home player piano.

Via the Welte-Mignon the keyboard artistry of the pianist could be recorded for posterity, just as the camera in a different way could record the action of an express train or the tranquility of a New England landscape. Within a decade the *reproducing piano* had secured a niche in the world of serious music. In America the Duo-Art and Ampico gave the Welte-Mignon strong competition. By the end of the 1920s there was scarcely a single famous concert pianist who had not recorded his work for future generations through the medium of the paper roll. The performances of Rachmaninoff, Paderewski,

Hofmann, Carreno, Busoni, and other immortal pianists could be heard at the same time in Louisville, London, Leipzig, or Los Angeles. Why, you could even buy a Duo-Art roll of composer George Gershwin playing his own *Rhapsody in Blue*.

By 1915 orchestrion manufacturers had learned to use the music roll's great versatility and potential. Hurley, Wisconsin, a town of 3,700, including many Italian, Polish, Finn, and Swedish immigrants, had 111 saloons, or one tavern for every 33 inhabitants! A worker seeking pleasure after a day in the nearby iron mines could stop at various taverns and bordellos and, provided he had a pocketful of nickels, hear a beautiful Seeburg G or H orchestrion play the latest ragtime tunes, or he could listen to a Cremona Orchestral J, a mammoth Wurlitzer Mandolin PianOrchestra, or any one of dozens of other mechanical pianos and orchestrions which filled the smoky rooms and the streets outside with marches, Stephen Foster melodies, drinking songs, and other tunes. In Butte, Montana, in Leadville, Colorado, and in the Barbary Coast district of San Francisco the scene was similar. Music, merriment, and money were a powerful combination.

In Germany the firm of Ludwig Hupfeld, which grew to become the world's largest manufacturer of automatic musical instruments and which eventually employed 6,000 people in several factories, introduced the Pan Orchestra, a marvelous orchestrion which had a tracker bar with 124 holes. "The music of the Pan Orchestras lets you discover that these are neither organs nor orchestrions. Rather, they form a special class which can only be compared with a live orchestra. The musical parts of the Pan are entirely independent from each other. At any time a given voice or rank of pipes or particular instrument can be brought out tonally above the others. The Pan comprises all degrees of tonal power from the hushed piano to the thundering fortissimo. The drum and trapwork is recorded from a man's hand and imitates it exactly as it ranges from tender gracefulness to strong and intense rhythm. The connoisseur of music has at his call the wonderful strains from Tristan, Parsifal, an entire symphony, a violin concert with the accompaniment of an orchestra, or, yes, even a duet. Solo performances on the cello, flute, xylophone, organ, and other instruments are possible as are trios and chorales," noted a Hupfeld catalogue.

Not to be outdone, the Rudolph Wurlitzer Company proclaimed that its top-of-the-line orchestrion, the PianOrchestra, "is without question the most wonderful self-playing musical instrument ever built. It is a combination of all the different instruments used in a full symphony orchestra, assembled in a single magnificent case, and arranged to play in solo and concert work, exactly the same as a human orchestra."

As development of the orchestrion continued and competition increased, attention was focused on musical arrangements. The success of a particular instrument could depend as much on the skill of the music roll arranger as on the construction of the orchestrion itself. A particularly enlightened firm, Gebr. Weber (Weber Brothers) of Waldkirch, deep in Germany's Black Forest, had two music arrangers, Otto Weber (a principal of the company) and Gustav Bruder, design two marvelous instruments, the Maesto, which was introduced in 1926, and the Elite, which made its debut about two years later. By participating in the design of the orchestrions, the musical arrangers produced instruments with potential matched perfectly to the skills of the arrangers who produced music for them.

In the 1970s, Harvey Roehl, author of *Player Piano Treasury*, would write:

"There is little doubt that the Weber Maesto orchestrion is the most life-like of anything in its class of instrument ever perfected by man ... Many connoisseurs of automatic musical machines agree that there is simply nothing else that can equal it. It was built very late in the game, and every known device was incorporated to insure that it would resemble as closely as possible a human orchestra. To say that the designers succeeded well would be a gross understatement! Nothing can compare with the artistic renderings of the Maesto."

Reed Organs and Pipe Organs

During the period from 1775 to about 1850 dozens of different builders were engaged in the production of barrel-operated organs in England. One of these, George Astor of London, was a relative of John Jacob Astor, the famous American fur trader. For the small church or chapel the barrel organ, often furnished with several interchangeable cylinders, afforded the possibility of hearing expertly-arranged hymns and other melodies.

The 19th century saw the production of many large barrel-operated organs, the previously-mentioned Apollonicon perhaps being the most outstanding example. The mechanically-operated organ for use in churches, private homes, and concert halls was very popular.

In the 1880s and 1890s organettes, small automatically-operated reed organs, became a nation-wide fad. Popular magazines and newspapers were filled with puffery and ballyhoo concerning them. An 1886 advertisement for the Dulcimer Organette, an instrument which used perforated paper strips, is typical:

"Dulcimer Organette! This extraordinary instrument has been designated the 'wonder of wonders.' It distances all comparison, unquestionably surpasses in every desirable quality, every mechanical musical instrument ever invented . . . It lends itself to the most pathetic equally to the most lively music. It is at once the musician and the music . . . It plays such an anthem as 'America' with all its grand, solemn melody and effect, and the next instant will play 'Yankee Doodle' in lively, mirthful measures. It will bring cheerfulness to the most dismal home, and add redoubled pleasures to an already cheerful home. A piano or organ requires a finished performer to bring music out of them, but the Dulcimer Organette is complete in itself and needs no knowledge of notes or cunning accomplishments in fingering . . . Nor does the Dulcimer Organette alone please the ear by the rising harmony and infinite variety of its matchless music. It likewise gratifies the eye by its beautiful form and the exceeding elegance of its general appearance . . ."

Organettes came in many forms, shapes, sizes, and musical systems. Many used perforated heavy paper strips, others used paper rolls, and still others used pinned wooden cylinders or perforated metal or cardboard discs. The success of the organette industry gave rise to a generation of larger instruments. The Aeolian Company, which had its inception as a maker of organettes, produced the Aeolian Organ, then the Aeolian Grand, then the Orchestrelle, and, finally, the ultimate player reed organ, the Solo Orchestrelle. Examples of the latter instrument cost up to $5,000 each and were of immense size. The Wilcox & White Company, of Meriden, Connecticut, also an organette maker, put on the market the Symphony, a keyboard-style reed organ which used paper rolls. And, in Europe and America there were many other styles as well.

Although many different types of paper-roll-operated pipe organs were made, only a few achieved success in the marketplace. The Aeolian Company produced over 2,000 large pipe organs for home installation, a record unequalled by any other manufacturer. Early models used Aeolian Pipe Organ rolls. Later styles used the more sophisticated (with automatic control of the various pipe registers) Aeolian Duo-Art Organ rolls. M. Welte & Sons produced several types of player organs, of which the Welte Philharmonic Organ, made in different sizes,

was the most popular. The Rudolph Wurlitzer Company likewise marketed several types of player pipe organs. One installation in a Denver auditorium featured two different rolls: one for the playing notes and a separate roll for the register changes.

Band Organs

Band organs, called fairground organs in Europe, and their indoor cousins, dance organs, have long furnished the spirit for carousels, skating rinks, dance halls, and similar places. The Wurlitzer 146-A, 153, or 165 organ playing *Over the Waves, The Stars and Stripes Forever,* or *The Blue Danube Waltz* would make a merry-go-round irresistible.

The barrel organ, operated by a pinned wooden cylinder, was the standard in the 19th century. The products of Bruder, Ruth, Gavioli, Frati, Limonaire, and other European makers were imported into America and sold by the thousands. In 1893 Eugene DeKleist, a German who earlier worked with Limonaire Freres, established the North Tonawanda Barrel Organ Factory in New York state, thus founding an enterprise which would later evolve into the Rudolph Wurlitzer Manufacturing Company.

In America, the paper roll became standard after the 1905-1910 period of transition. Wurlitzer, which standardized most of its thousands of band organs to use rolls of three types, styles 125, 150, and 165, led the market, but competition was mounted by the North Tonawanda Musical Instrument Works (founded in 1906), the Artizan Factories (founded in 1922), Niagara, and a few scattered others.

In the 1890s most European manufacturers shifted emphasis from pinned cylinders to folding cardboard music books. Paper rolls were also used, but only in limited situations, for it was learned that the folding books were more durable for outdoor use in changing climatic conditions. The music book used a special *key frame,* a series of spring-loaded levers, to read the musical program perforated on the heavy leaves. Each time a hole appeared in the cardboard, a lever or key would pop up through the hole, thus causing another hole to open at the end of a tube connected to a valve which controlled a pipe or other function. The pipe would then sound the desired note. Certain types of organs used cardboard books which were held against a tracker bar by a grooved metal pressure roller. This was known as the *keyless frame* system.

The decade from 1905 to 1915 saw the production of some of the most elaborate organs ever to grace the earth. Ruth, Bruder, Gavioli, Marenghi, Limonaire, and others each tried to outdo the others. Some of the facades of the larger organs were so ornate that they would have been right at home in the Palace of Versailles!

Most large-scale band organs used in America were imported from Europe. At Cleveland's Euclid Beach Park, on the south shore of Lake Erie, vacationers skated to the music of a 110-key Gavioli organ. On Feltman's Carousel in America's playland by the sea, Coney Island, the horses went up and down and around and around to thrilling melodies provided by an immense 94-key Gebr. Bruder organ. Charles I.D. Looff, prominent American carousel builder, imported large Ruth organs by the dozens, including many of the large Style 38s. Alas, many of these magnificent organs are gone. But, fortunately, many are still with us. When Euclid Beach Park closed down, no buyer could be found for the skating rink Gavioli. Dr. Robert Miller, a distinguished Connecticut surgeon, learned of it, and rescued the classic instrument from oblivion. Today it plays once again to delight collectors and other enthusiasts who care to listen to its melodies of yesteryear. The 94-key Bruder from Coney Island was similarly rescued, but not before it fell into great disrepair. Sadly, most of Charles I.D. Looff's Style 38 Ruth organs are gone. More happy was the fate of a large Style 165 Wurlitzer organ which was shipped on December 31, 1918 from North Tonawanda, New York to Playland-at-the-Beach in San Francisco. It was carefully preserved and maintained over the years and entertained hundreds of thousands, perhaps millions, of carousel riders with its 20-tune programs. When the park was razed to make room for a low-cost public housing project, the Style 165 organ went to an appreciative collector.

In the 1950s the Wurlitzer 146-A band organ which had delighted visitors to Endicott, New York's Enjoie Park stopped working. A local collector was notified, and soon the instrument had a new home, where it remains to this very day.

Perhaps it is not quite right that a visitor (as of 1980) to the carousels located in Disneyland in California or Disney World in Florida, huge carousels which are triumphs of the woodcarver's art, has to listen to *tape recordings* of band organs, rather than the real thing. But perhaps it is also right that the collectors who own the Wurlitzer, Bruder, Ruth, Gavioli, and other organs of yesteryear appreciate them in a way that insures their posterity. Today the history and music of these instruments are being studied more carefully than ever before. It is a fact that in this book you have access to more information concerning the musical scales of these organs than did the most accomplished musicians and

engineers at the original factories in North Tonawanda, Waldkirch, or Paris decades ago! Certainly this bodes well for the future generations of collectors, yet unborn, who someday will want to know what the instruments sounded like.

In 1913, Jonas Riggle, a skating rink owner in Vandergrift, Pennsylvania, wrote to the North Tonawanda Musical Instrument Works to say:

"We find that since we installed your organ our business has increased splendidly, in fact has taken on new life. A banquet and dance was held last week in our rink, and the dancers insisted on having the organ play one piece for them. The orchestra was a special one from Pittsburgh and it was inclined to poke fun at the 'grind organ,' but after hearing it play, they commented upon the beauty of its music; and all the people wanted it to play more, as the time was so perfect and the music was so good."

What did the music sound like? How were the organs of the North Tonawanda Musical Instrument Works constructed? What were their musical scales and abilities? Thanks to the collecting fraternity this information is now readily available to those interested.

The Importance of Musical Scales

Why should you learn about tracker bar layouts, music box scales, key frame specifications, and related musical scales? There are several reasons . . .

First of all, the relationship between a musical instrument and the rolls, discs, or other music it uses is symbiotic. One needs the other. One is of no use without the other. By studying the tracker bar layout of a Wurlitzer 65-Note Automatic Player Piano roll, for example, you can discover what an instrument which uses that type of roll is *theoretically* capable of doing. By reading the accompanying editorial commentary we give, you can learn what *actually was done*. So it is likewise with the rolls used on instruments made by Hupfeld, Marquette, Seeburg, Welte, Weber, Popper, Imhof & Mukle, and a host of others.

By studying the musical scales you can appreciate the old-time instruments to a greater extent. Just like the classic car enthusiast might like to look under the hood of a fine Packard, or the horologist might want to know what makes a particular Eli Terry clock tick, the collector of automatic musical instruments desires to know how various pianos, organs, orchestrions, and music boxes produce their music. The musical scales give many valuable insights.

For the repairer, information concerning musical

scales is not only interesting, it is essential. For the arranger of new music it is likewise.

In 1965 one of the authors interviewed Farny Wurlitzer, who from 1909 until his death in 1972, was in charge of the Rudolph Wurlitzer Company's large factory in North Tonawanda, New York. He was there when it happened; he was there during the golden age of organs and orchestrions during the early 20th century. He not only knew his own products, but he was also familiar with the competition. "Of all the automatic musical instruments you've ever heard, which one impressed you the most?" he was asked. His answer: "The Phonoliszt-Violina," an instrument not made by Wurlitzer, but made by a competitor, Ludwig Hupfeld, thousands of miles away in Leipzig, Germany. Why did the Phonoliszt-Violina impress him? This book may help explain the reason.

Although nearly all of the automatic musical instruments discussed in this book are from the past, music discs, rolls, and folding cardboard books are still being made for many of the models today. If Gustav Bruder, music arranger for Gebr. Weber in the 1920s, can be considered the Leonardo da Vinci of orchestrion music roll arrangers, is there another artist, perhaps the musical equivalent of a Rembrandt, Monet, Picasso, or Bierstadt, whose talents exist right now and remain to be developed? In recent times such famous pianists as Roger Williams and Liberace have made the journey to an obscure brick building located on Niagara Street in Buffalo, New York, far from the limelight of Broadway or Las Vegas, to sit down at the keyboard of an antiquated piano to record their melodies for use on Q.R.S. 88-note home player piano rolls, much in the same way that Scott Joplin, for instance, sat down years ago to record his impressions of how to play his own ragtime compositions. In Europe, Arthur Prinsen, Marcel van Boxtel, Carl Frei, Jr., Keith Pinner, and others have committed their talents to arranging new melodies or reproducing old tunes for use on Mortier, Bruder, Ruth, Gavioli, and other organs from the past. In America, Arthur Reblitz, Mike Kitner, Dave Junchen, Terry Borne, Harold Powell, John Malone, Ramsi P. Tick, and others have been active arranging new music or perforating new copies of old piano and organ rolls.

A music roll plays the *real instrument.* The best hi-fi or stereo system, even a custom-made one costing tens of thousands of dollars and employing the latest advanced technology, can only approximate what a piano sounds like. An Ampico, Duo-Art, or Welte is the real thing; it not only is what a piano sounds like, it is a piano, and it plays an actual human performance! The bass drum in a Seeburg KT Special is the real bass drum sound, the xylophone in a Hupfeld Helios orchestrion is the real xylophone sound, and the gleaming brass piccolo on the front of a Wurlitzer Style 125 band organ is the real piccolo sound. The instruments exist. The *real* instruments with *real* sound. Now, it is the roll (or disc or music book or whatever) that determines how great the music will be. The difference between a cub scout playing *Chopsticks* with two fingers on a piano and a concert by Sergei Rachmaninoff is solely a matter of what can be recorded on a music roll. The instruments have the potential, and this book describes it. Add artistry in music roll arranging, and the result may well be what Wurlitzer described in one of its advertisements years ago when it said that a particular orchestrion "will not only make good under the most exacting conditions, but it is no exaggeration to say that it will *carry the most critical audience by storm.*"

A VISIT TO CHARRIERE & CO., Bulle, Switzerland, in 1926. On this and the next three pages (also see page 202) are photographs from the salesrooms and other areas of Charriere & Co., a distributor for Gebr. Weber, Hupfeld, M. Welte & Sons, Popper & Co. and other manufacturers of automatic musical instruments. (Charriere photographs courtesy of the late Otto Weber)

On this page is a view of the music roll room of Charriere & Co. Rows of neatly boxed Weber (to the right), Hupfeld, Popper, and other rolls awaited prospective purchasers.

The top illustration shows a Popper & Co. coin piano in a corner. In the left-hand salon are several Weber and Popper instruments. To the right is a gallery of Welte reproducing pianos.

The picture to the right shows Storage Room No. 1 with rows of electric pianos, a tall Popper orchestrion, and, against the right side wall, two Weber Styrias, a Weber Violano, and two Weber Brabo orchestrions.

Below is an exterior view of the Charriere & Co. building. Otto Weber said that during the 1920s Charriere was second only to G.J. Gerard (Brussels, Belgium) in terms of the number of large Weber instruments sold.

Above is shown part of the sales area of Charriere & Co. The large instrument partially concealed behind the wall at the left side of the picture is a late-style Weber Solea orchestrion, a model of which just two specimens are known to exist today (in the collections of Steve Lanick and Bellm's Cars & Music of Yesterday Museum). It uses Maesto rolls. To the right of the Solea, against another wall, is a Hupfeld Violina Orchestra (also see page 202 of this book for additional information about this instrument). Above it is a framed photograph of the Hupfeld factory in Bohlitz-Ehrenburg, near Leipzig, Germany.

To the left is a photograph of a Weber Unika piano with violin pipes being unloaded from a service door in Gebr. Weber's Waldkirch (Germany) factory.

In the room illustrated above, the visitor to Charriere & Co., Swiss distributors of pianos and orchestrions, could hear, from left to right, a Popper Welt Piano (orchestrion), a Weber Grandezza (piano, mandolin, and xylophone), another style of Popper Welt Piano, and, to the far right, a mirror-fronted Weber Violano ("artistically-played piano with registers of violins [pipes]"). The Popper orchestrion models display front panels with animated "motion picture effects."

To the right is a view of one of the Charriere workshops. In the background is a rare Hupfeld Model II Violina Orchestra with front panels removed. The five-tier pneumatic stack construction differs markedly from that of the standard Phonoliszt-Violina. In the center of the three instruments is a Weber Styria orchestrion. In the foreground is a Popper Violin Piano.

GENERAL COMMENTARY
Concerning
MUSICAL SCALES AND LAYOUTS
In This Book

The old cliche "music is a universal language" may apply to the audible sound which reaches our eardrums and to printed music manuscripts. Remarkably, people around the world agreed long ago to use Italian descriptive words in most manuscripts, so anyone anywhere in the world understands music printed anywhere else. This universality *does not* apply, however, to the world of mechanical music terminology.

The individuals who devised automatic musical instruments in Italy, France, Germany, Belgium, England, Holland, Switzerland, the United States, and other countries were often partly musicians, partly mechanics, partly engineers, but mostly individuals, each with unique ideas about the way a music machine should be constructed. The study of old scale sticks and charts involved in the preparation of this book uncovered a wide array of colorful terms coined on the spur of the moment by designers and technicians who needed to communicate with each other within their own factories but nowhere else. Few of these terms are found in any dictionary, and those which are often have different meanings from those used by innovators in the world of automatic musical instruments. A listing of many of these terms is given at the end of this book. Now, many decades after most instruments were made, collectors, restorers, and historians around the world can equate different terms to a common meaning or understanding.

Every attempt has been made to include the most accurate and complete information, but some scales, particularly European orchestrion and band organ scales, lack some details or contain minor errors due to the difficulty of transcribing original scale sticks. Readers are encouraged to submit additional details, corrections, and scales for inclusion in future editions.

The scales in each section of this book are listed in order of increasing size, relationship, or alphabetically, whichever is more appropriate or traditional. In the coin piano and orchestrion section all manufacturers of instruments using rolls are listed alphabetically. The standardized A and G rolls, which were used by more than one firm, have their own sections. Under the various firms the rolls are listed in order of increasing complexity or in another appropriate way.

It is important to note that many band organs, table top organettes, and other instruments were made in various keys other than the ones indicated by the printed scale sticks or the pitches marked on the pipes or reeds. For example, a small Wurlitzer band organ such as a Style 103 which uses Style 125 rolls plays in a different key than a Style 125 organ using the same Style 125 rolls. Some Wurlitzer 157 organs play in a different key than others. Some Gem roller organs play in a key other than the one given in this book, and other Gems are tuned "in the cracks" between the keys on a piano or organ. Numerous other examples of inconsistencies and variations exist.

IMPORTANT NOTICE: An instrument should never be tuned until the original tuning pitch is known. It should never be necessary to remove wood or metal from organ pipes (unless they are of the fixed pitch variety, and then material should be removed only in tiny amounts and with the advice of a competent expert). No attempt should be made to tune a music box comb unless the original temperament is understood. During the writing of this book the authors were cautioned by every leading music box restorer that tuning should not be tried by an amateur. Once metal is removed from a music box comb or an organ pipe it cannot be replaced, and the unit may be severely damaged or ruined.

When an instrument name or function is listed by itself it stays on only as long as that hole is open. An example is hole 64 (mandolin) in the American G orchestrion roll scale. The term "chain perforation" refers to a hole which holds its instrument or function on only as long as it is open, whether or not the hole pattern actually looks like a chain. If a function is listed with "on" and "off" it is controlled by a lock and cancel mechanism. An example is hole 27, "flute pipes off," in the G orchestrion scale. Many band organ scale sticks do not indicate whether a certain function is a chain perforation or a lock and cancel; the mechanisms in the organ must be examined to ascertain the correct function.

In orchestrion scales with only one snare drum hole it is for a reiterating (repeating or roll) beater. In European band organs and some orchestrion scales with two snare drum holes, they are usually for two single stroke beaters. In any case where one beater is single stroke and the other is reiterating (as in the Operators Piano Co. "Coinola" O roll scale) that is noted on the scale. Unless otherwise indicated, "bass drum" usually refers to bass drum and cymbal, while "tympani" refers to a smaller beater on the bass drum, without cymbal.

German instruments use different note names for the English A sharp and B, calling them B and H respectively. When tuning an instrument to a printed scale or note stamped on the instrument, care must be taken to determine whether the English or German terminology is being used. In this book the English system is used exclusively. All black notes are indicated as sharps instead of flats, except in the music box section.

Care should be taken to observe any clues, such as original tubing layouts or markings, on an instrument which will help to establish the correct tracker scale. Most American instruments used rubber tubing for the tracker bar. When this has decomposed and fallen to the bottom of the cabinet it is nearly impossible to figure anything out. Fortunately, American manufacturers usually standardized their instruments so that all rolls of a given style use the same tracker bar layout, but there are exceptions. On the other hand, some European makers of large orchestrions (examples are Imhof & Mukle, Popper, and Welte) seem to have made frequent changes in their roll scales, with the result that an instrument discovered today is likely to be slightly different from other similar instruments. Fortunately, most European makers of orchestrions used high quality metal tubing to connect the tracker bar with the various mechanisms, and this is usually intact today. If the original metal tubing in an instrument is intact it is probably safe to assume that it is correct, even if it varies from a tracker scale printed in this book. It is important to be sure, however, that the connections are original. Often band organs, orchestrions, and other instruments were converted years ago from one layout to another to permit the use of a cheaper or more easily available type of music roll. As an example, hundreds of beautiful Bruder, Ruth, Gavioli, and other classic organs were converted from music book operation to roll operation, usually with a great loss to the musical potential and ability of the instruments involved. Wurlitzer and B.A.B. organ rolls were often used for such conversions. Enlightened collectors and connoisseurs today will often re-convert such instruments to their original and more musically elaborate scales.

The Wurlitzer Company obtained instruments from several manufacturers, including DeKleist, Philipps, Whitlock, and Bruder. Many early DeKleist coin pianos and band organs use tracker bars and rolls which are spaced 10 holes per inch, while instruments imported from Philipps used a spacing of 4 holes per centimeter. These two hole spacings are almost the same, and the difference is noticeable only when a wide span of holes is measured. A roll of one hole spacing will not work on an instrument of the other spacing.

As noted in the comments preceding the B.A.B. roll section, many of the band organ scales in this book were taken from B.A.B. scale sticks. The B.A.B. company transformed many European organs from one style of music to another, and then B.A.B. labeled the new music rolls with the name of the original organ. Thus an 89-key Gavioli organ might have been reduced in musical abilities to 82 or 80 keys by B.A.B. and given, for example, an "80-key Gavioli" label. Or, in another instance, a Bruder key frame might be switched to a Ruth organ with the result that new music for it would be labeled "Ruth," even though the scale was Bruder. This explains the presence of "Gavioli," "Bruder," "Ruth" and other scales which differ widely from what the original factories intended!

Perhaps the outstanding example of organ scale confusion is that represented by an instrument in the Bovey Collection in Nevada City, Montana. Originally a barrel-operated organ made by Bruder or Ruth, the original open-front cabinet has been modified, and a carved front, possibly of American origin, has been added. The barrel and its keys have been replaced with a valve chest similar in design to Gavioli equipment. The organ plays cardboard music books of an unknown scale, possibly of Ruth origin. When this organ was obtained by Charles Bovey from Andy Antoniazzi of the B.A.B. Organ Company it was designated as a Marenghi organ!

In the same vein, Dutch street organs often were made by converting Mortier, Gavioli, and other organs to new scales. In England many fine large-scale organs such as

110-key Gaviolis were sharply reduced in scale so that cheaper music books could be used on them. American organs of the North Tonawanda Musical Instrument Works, Artizan, and Niagara were often converted to play Wurlitzer 125 or 150 rolls once original music was no longer readily obtainable for them.

The band organ scales in this book have been listed alphabetically by maker, with exceptions being Artizan, B.A.B., and North Tonawanda Musical Instrument Works scales (which are listed in the same section because of their interchangeability in many instances) and the scales of unknown makers. If an unknown scale bears a close resemblance to a scale of a specific maker, or if the scale seems incongruous but the scale stick, for example, is marked "Gavioli," then mention of this is made, such as "Gavioli?," or some similar notation.

As some of the most wonderful organs ever to grace the earth were made by Bruder, Ruth, Gavioli, and other European manufacturers, the authors of this book encourage restorers to rebuild such instruments to their original glorious musical specifications whenever possible. To play Wurlitzer 150 or 165 rolls, for example, on a large Bruder or Ruth organ is to waste a good portion of the organ's musical potential.

Chapter 2
DISC MUSIC BOXES

THE CRITERION

Disk labels shown: THE BULLY SONG · HOME SWEET HOME · LOUISIANA LOU · "EL CAPITAN" MARCH · WASHINGTON POST MARCH · THE STARS AND STRIPES FOREVER · STAR SPANGLED BANNER · AULD LANG SYNE · LOST CHORD · MONASTERY BELLS

MUSIC BOX

WAGSTAFF & CO. N.Y.

ALL THE WORLD'S BEST MUSIC FOR A CHRISTMAS PRESENT

"PERPETUAL MELODY IN A SINGLE GIFT!"

A peerless combination of everything most desirable in music-box invention. The culmination of life-long study and experience. Simple, durable, never out of tune. Endless variety of interchangeable tune-sheets. Entrancingly harmonious and sweet. Artistic cases in mahogany or oak:

Style	I.	44 Keys,	Case 12¼ x 10 x 8 inches, including one tune-disk,		$14.00 ;	tunes,	$0.25
"	II.	58 "	" 15¾ x 14¾ x 9 "	"	"	"	25.00 ;	"	.40
"	IV.	77 "	" 22 x 20 x 10 "	"	"	"	45.00 ;	"	.60
"	V.	154 "	" 22 x 20 x 10 "	"	"	"	70.00 ;	"	.60
"	X.	92 "	" 28 x 25 x 13 "	"	"	"	75.00 ;	"	1.40
"	XV.	184 "	" 28 x 25 x 13 "	"	"	"	120.00 ;	"	1.40
"	XVI.	184 "	" in upright cabinet "	"	"	"	175.00 ;	"	1.40

TIME PAYMENTS IF DESIRED   M. J. PAILLARD & CO., 680 Broadway, New York   (THE OLDEST HOUSE IN THE BUSINESS)

A Criterion advertisement of December 1898. The decade of the 1890s saw the rise of the disc music box. By 1900 the Swiss cylinder box, which could not offer inexpensive interchangeability of music, was nearly obsolete.

Many of the tuning scales for disc music boxes were provided to the authors by Graham Webb. They are in some instances corrections and revisions of the scales listed in his *The Disc Musical Box Handbook*. Graham Webb advises that these scales, together with other information previously found in *The Disc Musical Box Handbook* and *The Cylinder Musical Box Handbook*, will be combined into a single volume to be issued in the future.

Experts and specialists consulted by the authors all strongly advise that tuning a music box comb is something that should not be undertaken by an amateur. In view of this, we mention that the following data is given as general information only, and we do not recommend the tuning of a comb except by an experienced professional. Further, it has been the observation of the authors that tuning is apt to vary from one instrument to another, even among such "standard" boxes as Polyphon, Regina, and Symphonion products. For this reason, the scales we list may not necessarily match those on another given box. Note: While flats have been converted to sharps, to facilitate comparison of scales, in other portions of this book, in the music box section we adhere to the flat and sharp notations as provided by Mr. Webb.

POLYPHON AND REGINA MUSIC BOXES

The tuning scales for Regina and Polyphon are interchangeable up to and including the 15½" (39.8 cm.) size. The scales given for the 11- and 15½-inch sizes are for those instruments with single combs or with double combs which are plucked simultaneously. When using the scales for certain types of double-comb upright instruments in which the teeth are plucked alternately, start with the lowest note, which is located in the upper comb. This tooth will be number 1 of the scale, the first tooth of the lower comb will be number 2, and so on. For Polyphon instruments the comb scale for the 14 1/8" box is the same as that for the 11" size, and the 22½" comb scale is the same as that for the 19 5/8" size.

The Polyphon Musikwerke was established shortly before 1890 by Gustave Brachhausen and Paul Riessner, both of whom were earlier associated with Symphonion. By 1895 many different styles were being produced, ranging from small hand-held models to tall upright instruments which were eight feet or more high. Within the next few years Polyphon became the world's largest manufacturer of disc music boxes. At one time over 1,000 persons were employed at the factory in Wahren, a suburb of Leipzig, Germany.

The height of Polyphon's business was in the 1895-1905 decade. During this time the automatic disc-changing music box made its appearance, many musical clocks and furniture items with musical mechanisms were made, and other items were developed. Most popular of all was the 15½" table model box, of which tens of thousands were sold.

In the early 1890s Gustave Brachhausen came to America to found the Regina Music Box Company. In 1892 and 1893 preparations were underway. By 1894 the business was incorporated, and soon thereafter a factory site was found in

Rahway, New Jersey. Under Polyphon's direction and financial control, Regina produced a wide variety of its own distinctively-styled instruments, some of which were interchangeable scale-wise with Polyphon products. Most famous of all were the Regina automatic disc changing music boxes made in 15½", 20¾", and 27" diameter formats. A disc-operated mechanical piano, the Concerto, was also sold. From 1894 until 1921, approximately 100,000 disc boxes were shipped by Regina. The main years of activity were prior to 1905.

Today, a good number of Polyphon and Regina disc boxes of various sizes, styles, and appearances survive and are favorites with collectors.

6½" (16.5 cm.) POLYPHON DISC; 30 TEETH

1 F
2 F
3 Bb
4 Bb
5 C
6 D
7 Eb
8 F
9 G
10 A
11 Bb
12 C
13 F
14 F
15 G
16 A
17 Bb
18 Bb
19 C
20 C
21 D
22 D
23 Eb
24 Eb
25 E
26 F
27 F
28 G
29 A
30 Bb

8¼" (20.7 cm.) POLYPHON DISC; 40 TEETH
8½" REGINA DISC

1 F
2 G
3 C
4 F
5 F
6 G
7 A
8 A
9 Bb
10 C
11 C
12 D
13 E
14 F
15 F

16 G
17 A
18 Bb
19 B
20 C
21 C
22 D
23 D
24 E
25 E
26 F
27 F
28 G
29 G
30 A
31 A
32 Bb
33 Bb
34 B
35 C
36 C
37 D
38 E
39 F
40 G

9 5/8" (24.3 cm.) POLYPHON DISC; 46 TEETH

1 F
2 Bb
3 Bb
4 C
5 F
6 F
7 G
8 Bb
9 Bb
10 Middle C
11 D
12 D
13 Eb
14 F
15 F
16 G
17 A
18 Bb
19 Bb
20 C
21 D
22 Eb
23 E
24 F
25 F
26 G
27 G
28 A
29 A
30 Bb
31 Bb
32 B
33 C
34 C
35 D
36 D
37 Eb
38 Eb
39 E
40 F
41 F
42 Gb
43 G
44 A
45 Bb
46 C

11¼" (28.1 cm.) POLYPHON DISC; 54 TEETH
(Or 108 teeth if double comb with simultaneous plucking)
11" REGINA DISC

1 G
2 C
3 C
4 D
5 E
6 G
7 G
8 A
9 B
10 C
11 C
12 D
13 E
14 E
15 F
16 G
17 G
18 A
19 B
20 Middle C
21 Middle C
22 D
23 E
24 F
25 F#
26 G
27 G
28 A
29 A
30 A#
31 B
32 B
33 C
34 C
35 C
36 C#
37 D
38 D
39 E
40 E
41 F
42 F
43 F#
44 G
45 G
46 G
47 G#
48 A
49 A
50 B
51 C
52 C
53 D
54 E

15½" (39.8 cm.) POLYPHON DISC; 76 TEETH
(Or 152 teeth if double comb with simultaneous plucking)
15½" REGINA DISC

1 G
2 G
3 C
4 C
5 C
6 D
7 E
8 F
9 G
10 G
11 A
12 B

No. 2525. Billard-Automat

in Verbindung mit 104er Polyphon-Musik-Werk.

118 Stahlstimmenzungen, vertheilt auf 2 Stimmenkämme,

mittelst auswechselbarer Noten spielbar.

Gehäuse in Eiche oder Nussbaum fournirt.

Das Billard wird geliefert mit:

6 Bällen, 6 Queues, Queueshalter, Schreib-
tafel, geätzte Glasscheibe und mit 1 Noten-
scheibe.

Extra-Notenscheiben in mehreren Hundert verschiedenen
Stücken zu haben.

Auf der Seite des Billards zum Ab-
stoss des Balles befinden sich zwei Geldeinwürfe; wirft man 20 Pfg. in den Einwurf links, so kann man den Kasten mit den 3 Bällen heraus-ziehen und eine Parthie bis 500 spielen, wirft man rechts in den Ein-wurf 30 Pfg., so kann man eine Parthie bis 1000 spielen und ist durch Record festge-stellt, dass eine Parthie bis 500 ca. eine halbe und bis 1000 ca. eine volle Stunde beansprucht.

Länge 200 cm, Breite 90 cm, Höhe 200 cm.

Above: Polyphon 24½" (62.5 cm.) disc changing music box. It is believed that only a few hundred of these large and impressive instruments were ever made, for they are far rarer today than are, for example, automatic disc changing Regina instruments.

Right: This curious billiard table, advertised in H. Peters & Company's 17th catalogue, features a 19 5/8" Polyphon movement. Apparently it was not a commercial success.

Below: View of the gigantic Polyphon Musikwerke, which at one time employed 1,000 people.

13 C
14 C
15 D
16 E
17 E
18 F
19 G
20 G
21 A
22 B
23 Middle C
24 Middle C
25 D
26 E
27 E
28 F
29 F#
30 G
31 G
32 G
33 A
34 A
35 B
36 B
37 C
38 C
39 C
40 C#
41 D
42 D
43 D#
44 E
45 E
46 F
47 F
48 F#
49 G
50 G
51 G#
52 A
53 A
54 A#
55 B
56 B
57 C
58 C
59 D
60 D
61 E
62 E
63 F
64 F
65 F#
66 G
67 G
68 G
69 A
70 A
71 A
72 B
73 C
74 C
75 D
76 E

19 5/8" (50 cm.) POLYPHON DISC; 60 TEETH
UPPER COMB SCALE

1 F
2 F
3 A
4 Bb
5 Bb
6 C
7 D
8 Eb

9 F
10 F
11 G
12 A
13 Bb
14 Bb
15 C
16 D
17 D
18 Eb
19 F
20 F
21 Gb
22 G
23 A
24 Bb
25 Bb
26 C
27 C
28 D
29 D
30 Eb
31 E
32 F
33 F
34 Gb
35 G
36 Ab
37 A
38 A
39 Bb
40 Bb
41 B
42 C
43 C
44 D
45 D
46 Eb
47 Eb
48 E
49 F
50 F
51 Gb
52 G
53 G
54 A
55 A
56 Bb
57 B
58 C
59 D
60 Eb

LOWER COMB SCALE (58 TEETH)
1 Bb
2 F
3 G
4 Bb
5 Bb
6 C
7 D
8 Eb
9 E
10 F
11 G
12 Ab
13 A
14 Bb
15 C
16 Db
17 D
18 Eb
19 E
20 F
21 G
22 Ab
23 A
24 Bb
25 B

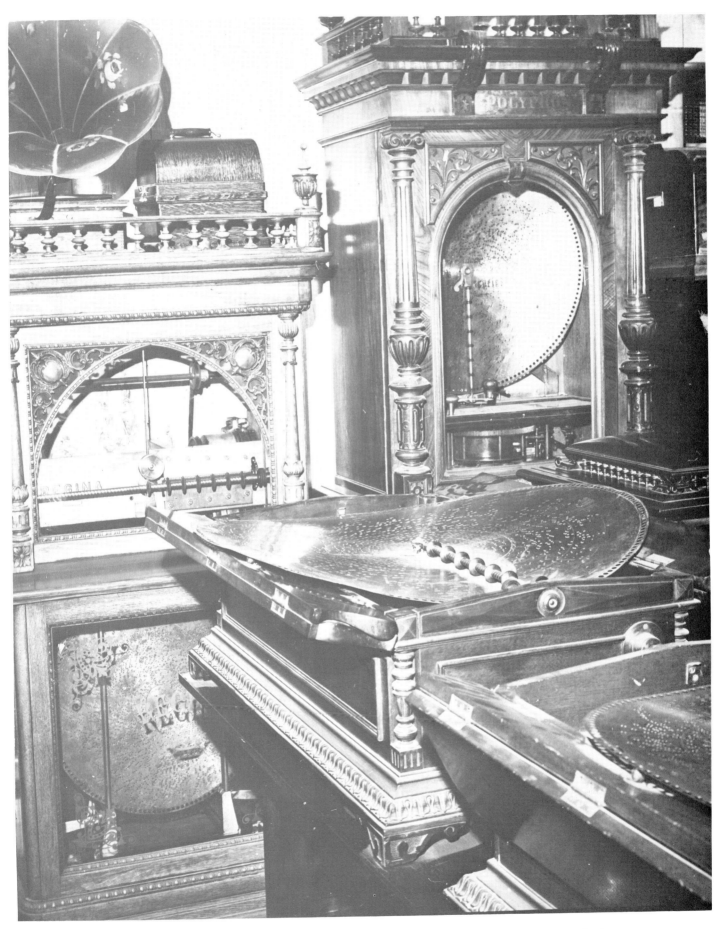

A music box collector's idea of what heaven must be like! (Collection of Roy Haning and Neal White)

26 C
27 Db
28 D
29 Eb
30 Eb
31 E
32 F
33 F
34 G
35 G
36 A
37 A
38 Bb
39 Bb
40 C
41 C
42 Db
43 D
44 D
45 Eb
46 Eb
47 E
48 F
49 F
50 G
51 G
52 Ab
53 A
54 Bb
55 Bb
56 C
57 C
58 D

22½" (56 cm.) POLYPHON DISC WITH BELLS

This scale is the same as the 19 5/8" (50 cm.) Polyphon scale but with the following notes added for the bells: F, G, A, Bb, Bb, C, C, D, D, Eb, E, F, F, G, A, Bb. Another original Polyphon scale is for an instrument tuned to a different key. The bell notes are as follows: G, A, B, C, C, D, D, E, E, F, F#, G, G, A, B, C.

24½" (62.5 cm.) POLYPHON DISC
UPPER COMBS; 60 teeth on large comb; 20 teeth on small comb

1 Bb
2 F
3 G
4 Bb
5 Bb
6 C
7 Db
8 D
9 E
10 F
11 F
12 Gb
13 G
14 A
15 Bb
16 Bb
17 C
18 C
19 D
20 D
21 Eb
22 Eb
23 F
24 F
25 Gb
26 G
27 G
28 A
29 A

30 Bb
31 Bb
32 C
33 C
34 D
35 D
36 Eb
37 E
38 F
39 F
40 Gb
41 G
42 G
43 A
44 A
45 Bb
46 Bb
47 C
48 C
49 Db
50 D
51 D
52 Eb
53 Eb
54 E
55 F
56 F
57 G
58 G
59 A
60 Bb
61 F
62 G
63 A
64 Bb
65 B
66 C
67 C
68 D
69 D
70 Eb
71 Eb
72 F
73 F
74 Gb
75 G
76 G
77 A
78 Bb
79 Bb
80 C

LOWER COMBS; 59 teeth on large comb; 20 teeth on small comb
1 Bb
2 F
3 F
4 A
5 Bb
6 Bb
7 C
8 D
9 Eb
10 E
11 F
12 F
13 G
14 Ab
15 A
16 Bb
17 Bb
18 C
19 Db
20 D
21 D
22 Eb
23 E
24 F
25 F
26 G

It is necessary to see these machines to realize their mechanical perfection and the absolute ease with which they are operated, and you cannot, without hearing them, form a just idea of the fine music they produce. Their execution of the most difficult pieces as well as of popular airs is good enough to satisfy the most critical. The two large machines on upper part of page have piano sounding boards, making the tones loud and clear. The great feature of these instruments, however, is the fact that they are equipped with nickel-in-the-slot attachment, so that the machine will not only pay for itself in a very short time, but will also make a good revenue producer. Neither of these machines require any attention, as they are thoroughly automatic in every respect, the tune-sheets being changed mechanically by simple regulating dial on outside of machine.

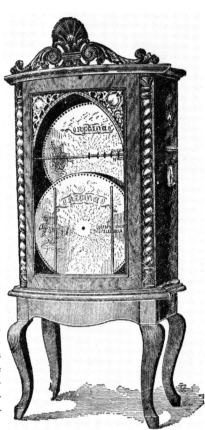

Orchestral Corona, Nos. 33 and 34.
With Piano Sounding Board.
Automatic tune-changing device. Long-running movement. No. 33 for parlor use. No. 34 with slot attachment.
Two large Combs, with 172 Tongues, tuned in chromatic scale, embracing over 7 octaves. Dimensions of Tune Sheets, 27 inches diameter. Case in Oak or Mahogany, highly polished; dimensions, 72 x 39 x 24 inches. **Price** **$350.00**

Sublima Corona, Nos. 37 and 38.
With Piano Sounding Board.
Automatic tune-changing device. No. 37 for parlor use. No. 38 with slot attachment. Long-running movement.
Two large Combs, with 130 Tongues, tuned in chromatic scale, embracing over 7 octaves. Case of No. 37 in Oak or Mahogany, oval front. Dimensions, 75 x 34 x 26 inches. Case of No. 38 same as No. 37, except the front is of square design instead of oval. Dimensions, 78 x 30 x 23½ inches. **Price** **$187.00**

Regina Corona No. 36. With Piano Sounding Board.
Automatic tune-changing device. Long-running movement. No. 36 with slot attachment Duplex arrangement.
Two Combs, with 156 Tongues. Dimensions of Tune Sheets, 15¼ inches diameter. Case of No. 36 in Oak or Mahogany. The front is of square design. Dimensions, 68 x 25½ x 21 inches. **Price** **$175.00**

Regina Nos. 14 and 15.
Musical Automaton, with penny or nickel slot attachment. If ordered with nickel drop, unless otherwise stipulated, the tune will play twice for one coin. No. 14. Single Comb, 78 Steel Tongues. No. 15. Duplex, 156 Steel Tongues. Dimensions, 22¼ x 20¼ x 12¾ inches. Tune Sheets, 15½ inches in diameter. Case in Mahogany and Oak.

No. 14.	**Price**	**$55.00**
No. 15.	**Price**	**$80.00**

Regina disc boxes were marketed by jewelry stores, department stores, restaurant supply houses, and other outlets. Above is shown a page, circa 1905, from an Albert Pick & Co. (restaurant and hotel suppliers) catalogue.

Overleaf: View in the Regina factory, circa 1905. (Courtesy of Murtogh Guinness)

27 Ab
28 A
29 Bb
30 Bb
31 B
32 C
33 Db
34 D
35 Eb
36 Eb
37 E
38 F
39 F
40 G
41 G
42 Ab
43 A
44 Bb
45 Bb
46 B
47 C
48 C
49 D
50 D
51 Eb
52 Eb
53 E
54 F
55 Gb
56 G
57 Ab
58 A
59 Bb
60 Gb
61 A
62 Bb
63 Bb
64 C
65 C
66 Db
67 D
68 D
69 Eb
70 E
71 F
72 F
73 G
74 G
75 A
76 A
77 Bb
78 C
79 D

27" REGINA DISC
UPPER COMB SCALE; 86 TEETH

1 F#
2 D
3 D#
4 F#
5 F#
6 G#
7 A
8 A#
9 B
10 C#
11 C#
12 D
13 E
14 F
15 G
16 G
17 A
18 A#
19 B

20 B
21 Middle C
22 D
23 D
24 D#
25 E
26 F
27 F#
28 G
29 G
30 G
31 A
32 A
33 B
34 B
35 C
36 C
37 C#
38 D
39 D
40 D
41 E
42 E
43 F
44 F#
45 F#
46 G
47 G
48 G
49 G#
50 A
51 A
52 A#
53 B
54 B
55 B
56 C
57 C
58 C#
59 D
60 D
61 D# (tuned same as 66)
62 E
63 F
64 F#
65 G
66 D# (tuned same as 61)
67 F
68 F#
69 G
70 A
71 A
72 A#
73 B
74 B
75 C
76 C#
77 D
78 D
79 D#
80 E
81 E
82 F#
83 F#
84 G
85 A
86 A#

LOWER COMB SCALE; 84 TEETH
1 B
2 D
3 D#
4 F#
5 G
6 G
7 A
8 B
9 B
10 C

This 20¾'' Regina table model music box displays prominently the grain characteristics of its quartered oak finish.

"Parlor model" Regina disc-changing music box which holds 12 discs, each measuring 15½" (39.8 cm.) in diameter, and plays them automatically in succession, one for each time a nickel is deposited. Or, if desired, by means of a lever the same tune can be played repeatedly. Above is shown a close-up view of the duplex music comb in an instrument in the Gilson Collection. (Top photograph courtesy of Dr. Robert Gilson)

The above Regina letterhead, used in 1904, is a virtual advertisement for various Regina music boxes. The firm's officers, listed at the top right, were located in Leipzig, Germany and were affiliated with Regina's parent firm, Polyphon.

The REGINA MUSIC BOX.

A HOME ORCHESTRA PLAYING OVER 1,000 TUNES.

A New Departure in Music Boxes, wonderfully brilliant in tone, far surpassing any Swiss Box made. Simple in construction, without any intricate parts to get out of order. It is unrivalled as a Social Entertainer and is a source of delight to all who hear it. Plays Classic and Popular Music, runs about 30 minutes with each winding, and has indestructible metal tune discs. **A GRAND HOLIDAY GIFT** and a most acceptable present, being a constant reminder of the donor. These Boxes last a lifetime and never require tuning like a piano. Handsomely cased in all modern woods, and an ornament to **NEW ORCHESTRAL REGINA,** the largest Music Box made. A wonderful instrument arranged with any room. The **NEW ORCHESTRAL REGINA,** money drop attachment for Hotels and Public Places. Send for handsome illustrated catalogue. Boxes from $14 to $200. Sold by all music dealers. **REGINA MUSIC BOX CO., Rahway, N. J**

November 1896 advertisement for the Regina disc music box. The enticing advantages of owning a Regina are enthusiastically presented. Instruments could be purchased through local music stores, department stores, or jewelers who stocked them, or they could be ordered by mail directly from the Regina Music Box Company in Rahway.

11 D
12 D
13 E
14 F
15 F#
16 G
17 G
18 A
19 B
20 B
21 Middle C
22 C#
23 D
24 D
25 E
26 F
27 F#
28 F#
29 G
30 G#
31 A
32 A#
33 B
34 B
35 C
36 C#
37 D
38 D
39 D
40 D#
41 E
42 E
43 F#
44 F#
45 G
46 G
47 G
48 G#
49 A
50 A
51 A
52 A#
53 B
54 B
55 C
56 C
57 C#
58 D
59 D (tuned same as 64)
60 E
61 E
62 F#
63 G
64 D (tuned same as 59)
65 E
66 F#
67 G
68 G#
69 A
70 A
71 B
72 B
73 C
74 C
75 C#
76 D
77 D
78 E
79 E
80 F
81 F#
82 G
83 A
84 A

SYMPHONION MUSIC BOXES
—Monopol Music Boxes—

Symphonion and Monopol scales are interchangeable in instances in which the disc sizes are similar. Some of the scales given are for single-comb movements, some are for the type of movement which uses opposed combs which are plucked simultaneously, and some are for the sublime harmonie style with combs at each end of the bedplate.

Symphonion/Monopol scales, provided by Graham Webb, are included for general information only. As noted in the introduction to this section, individual instruments are apt to differ. Tuning of a music comb should be done only by an experienced professional music box craftsman.

In 1885 or 1886 Symphonion music boxes, the first practical disc-type boxes to be marketed, were introduced. From then until the late 1920s the firm sold a wide variety of products. The height of Symphonion's disc music box business was during the 1890s and the first few years of the 20th century. Around the turn of the century, an American subsidiary, the Symphonion Manufacturing Company (with offices in New York and a factory in New Jersey), was established. Music boxes were made in America under the Imperial Symphonion trade name.

Paul Lochmann, the principal figure of the Symphonion firm, left around 1901 to form the Original Musikwerke Paul Lochmann, which made Lochmann "Original" disc boxes and other products.

The Symphonion factory turned out a wide variety of instruments in nearly two dozen disc sizes over the years. Particularly interesting were the famous three-disc "Eroica," which featured three discs playing at the same time, a number of ornate musical clocks, and several varieties of disc-changing devices.

Together with Polyphon and Regina, Lochmann was one of the "big three" manufacturers of disc music boxes.

The Leipziger Musikwerke, later Paul Ehrlich & Co., distributed a wide variety of music boxes under the Monopol label. Many of these had mechanisms and discs interchangeable with Symphonion products, indicating a connection between the two firms.

11¾" (30 cm.) SYMPHONION DISC
Comb nearest pressure-bar hinge

1 D
2 A
3 D
4 E
5 F#
6 G
7 A
8 A
9 B
10 C#
11 D
12 D
13 E
14 F#
15 F#
16 G
17 G#
18 A
19 A

LIST
of
Music-discs
suitable to the
Symphonion No. 2, 4, 6.

When ordering state numbers
as given below.

—◄■►—

New numbers are continually
added to present list.

Sizes:

No. 2. $10^3/_4 \times 10^3/_4 \times 7$ in. = 60 tongues.
4. $12 \times 12 \times 7$ in. = 72 „
6. $13^3/_4 \times 13^3/_4 \times 7^1/_2$ in. = 84 „

Sizes:

No. 2N. $15 \times 11^1/_2 \times 8$ in. = 60 tongues.
4N. $16^1/_4 \times 12^3/_4 \times 9^1/_2$ in. = 72 „
6N. $18 \times 14 \times 9^1/_2$ in. = 84 „

Kr. 10 I 93

2	4	6	Title	Composed by
1	1001	2001	God save the Queen. English National Anthem	Henry Carey
2	1002	2002	Vienna temper. Waltz	Joh. Strauss
3	1003	2003	Oberländler dance No. 2	J. Gungl.
4	1004	2004	Oh, so sweet, from the opera: „Martha"	F. v. Flotow
5	1005	2005	Woman's heart. Mazurka	J. Strauss
6	1006	2006	March of the Cadets	O. Métra
7	1007	2007	Holy night, tranquil night. Christmas-song	*
8	1008	2008	Gavotte dedicated to the Princess Stephanie	Alph. Czibulka
9	1009	2009	Bridal Chorus from the opera: „Lohengrin"	R. Wagner
10	1010	2010	„Oh, azure lake" from the operette: „The fairy Castle"	C. Millöcker
11	1011	2011	Yankee-doodle. „A Yankee boy is trim and tall." American popular air	*
12	1012	2012	My Queen. Waltz	C. Coote
13	1013	2013	O sanctissima, o piissima. Christmas-song	*
14	1014	2014	Agathe's Prayer from the opera: „Robin Hood"	C. M. v. Weber
15	1015	2015	Maritana-Waltz from the operette: „Don César"	R. Dellinger
16	1016	2016	Nuptial-March from: „A midsummer-night's dream"	F. Mendelsohn-B. Härtel
17	1017	2017	Fire brigade-Galopp	Fr. v. Suppé
18	1018	2018	Devils March	C. M. v. Zichrer
19	1019	2019	Flowershow-Polka	*
20	1020	2020	The last rose of summer. Irish popular song	*
21	1021	2021	Russian National Anthem. „God protect our noble Czar"	A. Lwoff
22	1022	2022	Oh du lieber Augustin. German popular song	*
23	1023	2023	Polka from the operette: „Madame Angot"	Ch. Lecocq
24	1024	2024	„And winding you the bridal wreath". Chorus from the opera: „Robin Hood"	C. M. v. Weber
25	1025	2025	Lagoon-Waltz from the operette: „A night at Venice"	Joh. Strauss
26	1026	2026	March from the operette: „Boccaccio"	C. Millöcker
27	1027	2027	Carlotta-Waltz from the operette: „Gaparone"	C. Millöcker
28	1028	2028	Treasure-trove. Waltz from the operette: „The Gipsy-baron"	Joh. Strauss
29	1029	2029	Dream-Waltz, from the operettes „The field-preacher"	C. Millöcker
30	1030	2030	March from the operette: „One night at Venice"	Joh. Strauss
31	1031	2031	March of the Volunteers, from the operette: „The field-preacher"	C. Millöcker
32	1032	2032	J'y pense! Fillipeen. Gavotte	R. Eilenberg
33	1033	2033	The fortune teller. Polka Mazurka from the operette: „The Gipsy-baron"	Joh. Strauss
34	1034	2034	The Bride-show. Polka from the operette: „The Gipsy-baron"	A. Stolpe
35	1035	2035	Electricity Polka	W. A. Mozart
36	1036	2036	Papageno's air, from the opera: „The magic flute"	
37	1037	2037	The page's air, from the opera: „Figaro's wedding"	
38	1038	2038	Chorus: „Too kind you are" from the opera: „The Barber of Sevilla"	G. Rossini
39	1039	2039	Duetto: „My shop is here" from the same opera	"
40	1040	2040	Kiss-waltz from the operette: „The merry war"	Joh. Strauss
41	1041	2041	You and you. Waltz from the operette: „The bat"	"
42	1042	2042	Duetto: „In our country" from the opera: „Il Trovatore"	G. Verdi
43	1043	2043	Chorus: „May echo give the sound of songs" from the opera: „Zampa"	F. Herold
44	1044	2044	Air: „Sole I am but not alone" from the opera: „Preciosa"	C. M. v. Weber
45	1045	2045	Light Cavalry. Galopp	Richter
46	1046	2046	Spunge out! Galopp from the operette: „The beggar-student"	C. Millöcker
47	1047	2047	Galopp from the operette: „One night at Venice"	Joh. Strauss
48	1048	2048	Cossak's Ride. Galopp from the operette: „The field-preacher"	C. Millöcker

Above: As was the practice of many other music box disc manufacturers, Symphonion used a common key number for the same tune in various disc sizes. For example, "The Last Rose of Summer" is disc number 20, 1020, or 2020, depending on the diameter.

Right: A typical 13 5/8" (34.5 cm.) Symphonion disc box from the 1900 period. Like other Symphonions of its genre, it has two diametrically opposed music combs arranged in what is called the sublime harmonie configuration.

20 B
21 C#
22 D
23 D
24 E
25 E
26 F#
27 F#
28 G
29 G
30 G#
31 A
32 A
33 A#
34 B
35 B
36 C
37 C#
38 D
39 D
40 E
41 F#
42 G

Comb most distant from pressure-arm hinge
1 D
2 A
3 A
4 D
5 D
6 E
7 F#
8 A
9 B
10 C#
11 D
12 D
13 E
14 F#
15 F#
16 G
17 G#
18 A
19 A
20 B
21 C#
22 D
23 D
24 E
25 F#
26 F#
27 G
28 A
29 A
30 A#
31 B
32 C#
33 D
34 D
35 D#
36 E
37 F
38 F#
39 G
40 A
41 B
42 C#

13 5/8" (34.5 cm.) SYMPHONION DISC
2 combs nearest pressure bar hinge; 50 teeth

1 Bb
2 F
3 Bb
4 Middle C
5 D
6 Eb
7 F
8 G
9 A
10 Bb
11 C
12 D
13 D
14 Eb
15 E
16 F
17 F
18 Gb
19 G
20 Ab
21 A
22 Bb
23 Bb
24 B
25 C
26 C
27 Db
28 D
29 D
30 Eb
31 Eb
32 E
33 F
34 G
35 F
36 F
37 F
38 F
39 Gb
40 G
41 G
42 G
43 Ab
44 A
45 A
46 Bb
47 Bb
48 Bb
49 C
50 D

2 combs most distant from pressure bar hinge; 50 teeth
1 Bb
2 F
3 F
4 Bb
5 Bb
6 C
7 D
8 Eb
9 F
10 G
11 A
12 Bb
13 Bb
14 Middle C
15 D
16 D
17 Eb
18 E
19 F
20 F
21 G
22 A
23 Bb
24 Bb

Above: The duplex music combs, arranged sublime harmonie style, of a Symphonion Style 25St musical clock made circa 1895. The instrument uses 11¾" (30 cm.) diameter metal discs.

Right: The Style 25St Symphonion musical clock. The original catalogue described it as having a "beautifully carved walnut case with first class Lenzkirch clock. Runs 14 days. Silver dial about 8 inches in diameter. The clock with gong movement strikes every hour or every second hour, according to order, and sets the musicwork running after striking fully. During the night the music works can be silenced. The music can be played independently of the clock."

The Symphonion 3-disc "Eroica" music box is one of the most curious instruments ever produced. To the left is shown a case style variation of Style 38B, an instrument discovered in England and later sold in the United States by Vicki Glasgow. Three discs, each identified by the letter A, B, or C, are played simultaneously on six music combs comprising a total of 300 teeth. The discs measure 14" (35.5 cm.) in diameter. Symphonion's catalogue, circa 1898, noted that "the unexcelled capacity of modulation possessed by this instrument produces effects which never have been heard before in any mechanical music box." Most "Eroica" models were made in tall rectangular cases; a lesser number were made as part of hall clocks. The instrument pictured to the left is nearly 10' high.

25 C
26 D
27 Eb
28 F
29 F
30 G
31 A
32 Bb
33 C
34 D
35 F
36 F
37 G
38 A
39 Bb
40 Bb
41 Bb
42 B
43 C
44 C
45 D
46 D
47 D
48 Eb
49 Eb
(50 E?)

14¾" (37.5 cm.) SYMPHONION DISC; 76 TEETH
(Or 152 teeth if double comb with simultaneous plucking)
(Note sequence is similar to 15½" Polyphon but is in a different key)

1 Eb
2 Eb
3 Ab
4 Ab
5 Ab
6 Bb
7 C
8 Db
9 Eb
10 Eb
11 F
12 Ab
13 Ab
14 Ab
15 Bb
16 Middle C
17 C
18 Db
19 Eb
20 Eb
21 F
22 Ab
23 A
24 A
25 Bb
26 Db
27 Db
28 D
29 Eb
30 E
31 E
32 E
33 Gb
34 Gb
35 Ab
36 Ab
37 A
38 A
39 A
40 Bb
41 B
42 B
43 C
44 Db
45 Db

46 D
47 D
48 Eb
49 E
50 E
51 F
52 Gb
53 Gb
54 G
55 Ab
56 Ab
57 A
58 A
59 B
60 B
61 C
62 C
63 D
64 D
65 Eb
66 E
67 E
68 E
69 Gb
70 Gb
71 Gb
72 Ab
73 A
74 A
75 B
76 C

19 1/8" (48.5 cm.) SYMPHONION DISC
Comb nearest drive wheel; 53 teeth

1 D
2 E
3 G
4 G#
5 A
6 C
7 C#
8 D
9 E
10 F
11 F#
12 G
13 A
14 A#
15 B
16 C
17 C#
18 D
19 D#
20 E
21 F
22 F#
23 G
24 G#
25 G#
26 A
27 A
28 A#
29 B
30 C
31 C#
32 D
33 D#
34 E
35 F
36 F#
37 F#
38 G
39 G#
40 G#
41 A

The Symphonion Manufacturing Company's American factory at Bradley Beach, New Jersey as it appeared circa 1900. Music boxes made in America were often given the Imperial Symphonion designation. (This and other Symphonion factory photographs courtesy of Murtogh Guinness)

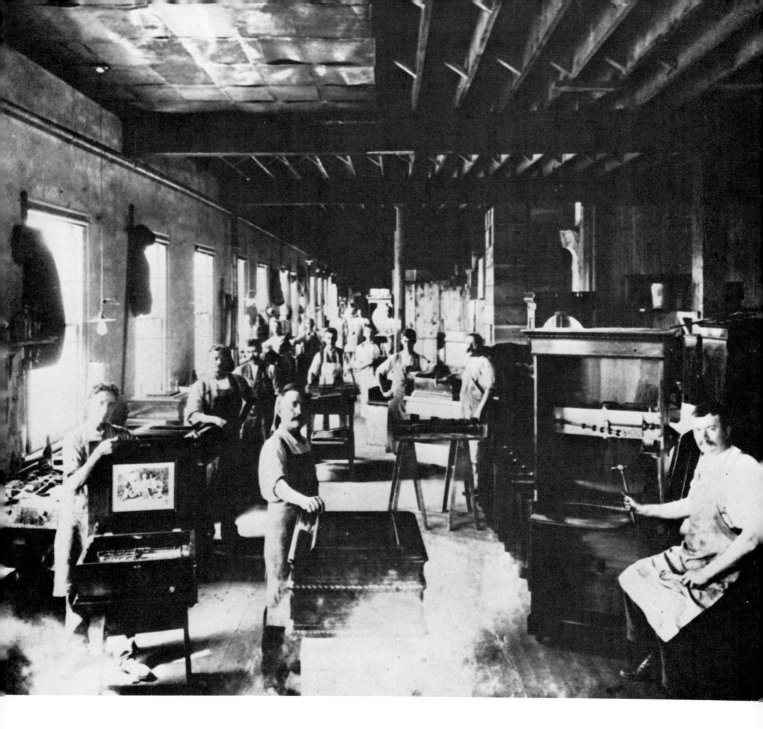

Workmen in an assembly area of the Symphonion Manufacturing Company's New Jersey factory pose for the photographer in this circa 1900 view. At one time Symphonion disc boxes were marketed extensively in America, but by the early 20th century the competing Regina Music Box Company had captured most of the market, leaving the Symphonion, Criterion, and other makes with sharply reduced sales. Although great things were envisioned for Symphonion's American factory, in actuality it seems to have been unprofitable.

This section of Symphonion's American factory was devoted to handling and storing music box discs.
The impressive pile of discs in the right foreground must have weighed many hundreds of pounds.

42 A#
43 B
44 B
45 C
46 C#
47 C#
48 D
49 D
50 D#
51 E
52 F#
53 G

Comb most distant from drive wheel; 53 teeth
1 D
2 A
3 A
4 B
5 C#
6 D
7 D
8 E
9 F#
10 G
11 A
12 A
13 B
14 C#
15 D
16 D
17 E
18 F#
19 F#
20 G
21 G#
22 A
23 A
24 B
25 C#
26 D
27 D
28 E
29 E
30 F#
31 F#
32 G
33 G
34 A
35 A
36 B
37 B
38 C#
39 C#
40 D
41 D
42 D
43 E
44 E
45 F#
46 F#
47 G
48 G
49 A
50 A
51 A
52 B
53 B

25¼" (64 cm.) SYMPHONION DISC
Upper and lower comb; 60 teeth each
(Opposed combs only)

1 D#
2 D#
3 G
4 G
5 G
6 A
7 B
8 C
9 D
10 D
11 E
12 F
13 F#
14 G#
15 G#
16 A
17 C
18 C
19 C#
20 C#
21 D
22 D#
23 D#
24 F
25 F
26 F#
27 G
28 G
29 G#
30 G#
31 A
32 A#
33 A#
34 Middle C
35 C
36 C#
37 C#
38 D
39 D#
40 D#
41 D#
42 E
43 F
44 F
45 F#
46 G
47 G
48 G#
49 G#
50 G#
51 A
52 A#
53 A#
54 B
55 C
56 C
57 C
58 C#
59 C#
60 D

A scene in Symphonion's American factory, circa 1900. Arranged on display panels at the back of the room are different components which go into various Imperial Symphonion models. To the left is a very large Imperial Symphonion with 12 saucer bells in addition to the musical comb. This type was designated as the Symphonion Orchestrion.

OTHER DISC MUSIC BOX SCALES

20.6 cm. KOMET DISC

1 G
2 C
3 C
4 D
5 E
6 F
7 G
8 G
9 A
10 B
11 C
12 C
13 D
14 E
15 F
16 F#
17 G
18 G
19 A
20 Blank
21 A
22 B
23 B
24 C
25 C
26 D
27 D
28 E
29 E
30 F
31 F
32 F#
33 G
34 G
35 G
36 A
37 A
38 B
39 C
40 D
41 E

    Preceding scale courtesy of James Spriggs

4½" THORENS DISC

1 C
2 G
3 C
4 D
5 E
6 G
7 G
8 A
9 B
10 C
11 D
12 F
13 G
14 A
15 B
16 C
17 C
18 D
19 D
20 E
21 E
22 F
23 F
24 F#
25 G
26 G

27 A
28 A
29 B
30 C

    Preceding scale courtesy of James Spriggs

**11" THORENS DISC
"EDELWEISS II"**

1 C
2 D
3 G
4 C
5 C
6 D
7 E
8 E
9 F
10 G
11 G
12 A
13 B
14 C
15 D
16 E
17 F
18 G
19 G
20 A
21 A
22 B
23 B
24 C
25 C
26 D
27 D
28 E
29 E
30 F
31 F
32 F#
33 G
34 G
35 G
36 A
37 A
38 B
39 C
40 D
41 E
42 Blank
43 Blank

    Preceding scale courtesy of James Spriggs

Chapter 3
PLAYER PIANOS

HOME PLAYER PIANOS
Various Manufacturers

The home player piano began its popularity in the late 1890s when Wilcox & White (of Meriden, Connecticut), the Aeolian Company, the Peerless Piano Player Company (of St. Johnsville, New York), and others began to aggressively market a line of push-up piano players for the home.

Typically, such a push-up piano player contained two foot pedals for providing vacuum, a pneumatic apparatus, and a row of tiny felt-covered "fingers" which were located at the front. The push-up player, known as a "vorsetzer" (literally: "sitter in front of") in Germany, would be pushed up to the keyboard of a regular upright or grand piano and would play upon the keys.

By the first few years of the 20th century the marketing of piano players became big business. The Aeolian Company, with headquarters in New York, ran multiple-page advertisements in Collier's, McClure's and other magazines extolling the virtues of the Pianola, its trademark for the player. "Pianola" became incorporated into the American idiom as a term representing piano player or, later, player piano, irrespective of the make—just as such trademarks as Scotch Tape, Kleenex, Xerox, Frigidaire, and Victrola are often used to designate products of other manufacturers, much to the dismay of corporate patent and trademark attorneys.

The Cecilian piano player, made by the Farrand Company, was another leading entry in the field, and the term "Cecilian" also came to have generic use. Thus, an early writer, circa 1905, described a trip to the end of the trolley car line, to the "electric park," where he spent part of the afternoon sipping beer and "listening to a cecilian." The trademark had its origin in St. Cecilia, patron saint of music.

Some particularly fancy push-up players had one or more ranks of organ reeds in addition to the piano "fingers." Included in this category were some deluxe models made by Wilcox & White, Chase & Baker, and Peerless.

Most push-up piano players used 65-note rolls with pinned ends, with the roll measuring 11¼" wide, spaced 6 holes per inch. The scale contained 65 playing notes in order from the bass to the treble.

The familiar type "A" coin piano roll used by Seeburg and others is adapted from this format. Years later, after 65-note rolls for home use became a part of history, the A rolls, of the same width and hole spacing, were still being made for "nickelodeon" pianos.

65-NOTE HOME PLAYER PIANO ROLL
11¼" wide; spaced 6 holes per inch

1 to 65, 65 notes in order, A to C#

From the late 1890s to about 1910 the 65-note roll dominated the home market. There were, to be sure, some variant scales, including 58, 70, 82, and 88 notes.

Around the end of that period, the built-in player mechanism, or "inner player" as it came to be known, became popular. The clumsy push-up player became an anachronism, and instruments were marketed with all of the mechanisms within the case; the player piano as we know it today. Some of these built during the first decade of the 20th century were of the 65-note specification, but after 1908 the industry shifted toward the 88-note scale, which had the advantage of being able to play the entire keyboard (although it was logically argued that many of the keys at the extreme treble and bass ends would not be used for most music). During the transition period, some instruments were made with combination 65-note and 88-note tracker bars,

actuated by a shifting device. Melville Clark, a DeKalb, Illinois manufacturer, was one maker who produced these in quantity.

Meantime in Europe, the push-up piano, and then the inner-player or player piano was enjoying the same vogue. Ludwig Hupfeld gained a foothold on the market in the very early years with its 73-note Phonola. The "ola" suffix to Phonola had a catchy ring, so when the Aeolian Company pirated it for use in its Pianola trademark, Hupfeld sued, alleging that Aeolian simply took the Phonola name and translated it into English.

As Harvey Roehl relates in his book, Player Piano Treasury, a gold mine of information on the subject, the "ola" suffix proved irresistible to others as well, with the result that such names as Technola, Aeriola, Autola, Convertola, Concertola, Marveola, Vacuola, Tone-ola, Pistonola, Playernola, and Combinola made their appearance! And, of course, in the field of coin-operated pianos there was the famous Coinola. The trend, so it seems, hasn't stopped, for in modern times we have Motorola radios and TV, and, lest we forget, secret payoffs for favors, or "payola." Then there's Rock-Ola, but, interestingly enough, this is a coincidence. The well-known maker of juke boxes and other devices was named after its founder, Dr. David Rockola.

During the 'teens the 88-note player piano achieved immense popularity, and the 65-note scale in America (and in Europe, Hupfeld's 73-note Phonola scale) was forgotten.

88-note players were made by the tens of thousands yearly, then by the hundreds of thousands, and then in the 1920s, by the millions. The Pianola, made by the Aeolian Company, was probably the best seller, although strong competition was mounted by the Autopiano (which, its advertisements noted, was especially useful on board battleships of the U.S. fleet!), Gulbransen, Wurlitzer, Angelus, Story & Clark, and others. All in all, there were literally hundreds of different player piano trademarks, many of the "stencil piano" type, consisting of instruments made by leading manufacturers and then sold through local department stores or music shops which affixed private labels to them. Harvey Roehl quotes figures which indicate that 1923 may have been the height of the market, at least in America. During that year 347,589 pianos of all kinds were made in the United States, of which more than half were players (20,661 reproducing pianos and 170,549 player pianos). By way of comparison, in 1909 364,545 pianos of all kinds were made, of which just 34,495 were upright player pianos. In 1931, in the midst of the Depression, 51,370 pianos of all kinds were made, including only 1,692 upright player pianos.

While public interest waned sharply after the 1920s when other types of entertainment, notably the home phonograph and, even more appealing, so it seemed, the radio, the player piano never died. In the 1950s the Aeolian Company continued to make a small number of players. By the 1960s several other makers joined the arena, and by the 1970s business had improved to the point at which the Aeolian Company had several strong competitors, including the Universal Piano Company. Around the same time, in 1978, the Superscope Company, a maker of audio equipment, introduced the Pianocorder, which by means of digital encoding on a cassette-type tape played a piano with expression. Interestingly enough, a return to tradition was made when, among other styles, a vorsetzer or push-up model of the Pianocorder was marketed.

88-NOTE HOME PLAYER PIANO ROLL
11¼" wide; spaced 9 holes per inch

0 Sustaining pedal
1 to 88, 88 playing notes in order, A to C

This beautiful walnut Smith & Barnes foot-pumped 88-note home player piano from the 1920s has been restored and delights listeners once again with its melodies. Literally hundreds of different makes of 88-note players were marketed during the 1920s. Many were so-called "stencil pianos" and bore the name, or stencil, of a local department store or music outlet. Others bore the names of leading manufacturers such as Jacob Doll & Sons, Aeolian, Smith & Barnes (as above), Autopiano, Gulbransen, Bush & Lane, and others. (Tom Beckett Collection)

THEMODIST (or SOLODANT) HOME PLAYER PIANO ROLL

These were made to the same specifications as regular 65-note and 88-note player piano rolls but with the addition of accent holes in the left margin for the bass and right margin for the treble. They are used by the Aeolian Themodist and Solodant player pianos which have a divided pneumatic stack and which have vacuum control regulators which lower the vacuum to a level determined by a manual control on the keyslip until an accent hole comes along, making the appropriate notes stand out tonally from the accompaniment. Certain Angelus pianos (made by Wilcox & White) may have used these theme rolls as well.

The Themodist or Solodant rolls represent one step toward the later-developed Aeolian Duo-Art and Artrio Angelus reproducing pianos which use theme holes in the same place on the tracker bar to bring out bass or treble accented notes.

The Solodant name was also registered by Hupfeld. 73-note Hupfeld Solodant rolls have the accent holes in the middle of the roll. The Solodant name appears on certain makes of French and British rolls and probably represents a licensing of the trademark.

Makers of Home Player Piano Rolls

Literally hundreds of different trademarks appear on player piano rolls. *Player Piano Treasury* gives a brief history of a number of makers, including Altoona, Atlas Player Roll Co., Billings Player Roll Co., Bennett & White, Columbia Music Roll Co. and the Capitol Roll & Record Co. (both owned by the Operators Piano Co.), Connorized Music Co. (especially prominent in the first decade of the 20th century), Globe Co., Gulbransen, Imperial Player Roll Co., International Player Roll Co., I.X.L. Co., Mel-O-Dee, Mel-O-Art, National Music Roll Co., QRS, Recordo Player Roll Co., Republic Player Roll Corp., Rhythmodik, Standard Music Roll Co., United States Music Co., Universal, and Vocalstyle.

The QRS firm, known today as QRS Music Rolls, Incorporated, was the dominant firm in the field in the 1920s. Founded around 1900 by Melville Clark, the firm acquired a number of its competitors in the field, so that by 1926, the peak year of the business when nearly 10,000,000 rolls were sold by the company, the enterprise included the assets of nearly a dozen earlier roll makers. J. Lawrence Cook, Lee Roberts, Victor Arden, Max Kortlander, and several others produced many thousands of different roll titles.

In the 1930s the player roll business fell on hard times. QRS was reorganized under the name of the Imperial Industrial Company under the aegis of Max Kortlander. In April 1966 Ramsi P. Tick, formerly manager of the Buffalo (N.Y.) Philharmonic Orchestra, formed a new corporation, the QRS Music Rolls Inc. firm we know today. Now located in Buffalo, QRS produces new arrangements of currently popular tunes and has enlisted the talents of Liberace, Roger Williams, and others to produce "artists' rolls," which feature distinctive arranging styles. The current QRS catalogue lists several thousand different selections, including most of the best-selling favorites from the "good old days."

The Aeolian Company produced rolls during the 1960s and 1970s, but production was considerably below that achieved by QRS. MelOdee rolls were made for several years during the late 1960s by Givens-Gourley, Incorporated. Later, much of the Givens-Gourley apparatus was acquired by Harold Powell (Klavier Music Rolls) of North Hollywood, California. As the decade of the 1980s began, Klavier was producing 88-note home player rolls as well as recuts of reproducing piano rolls such as Ampico, Duo-Art, and Welte (Licensee). The Play-Rite Music Roll Co., of Turlock, California, which began making 88-note rolls in the 1970s, was also an entry in the 88-note home player roll market, using a very sophisticated electronic recording apparatus to make the masters. Play-Rite also supplied recut rolls of many different types of coin piano, orchestrion, and band organ rolls.

Today, the home player piano stands as one type of instrument which almost but never quite became obsolete. New instruments and new rolls are being produced to delight still another generation of appreciative listeners.

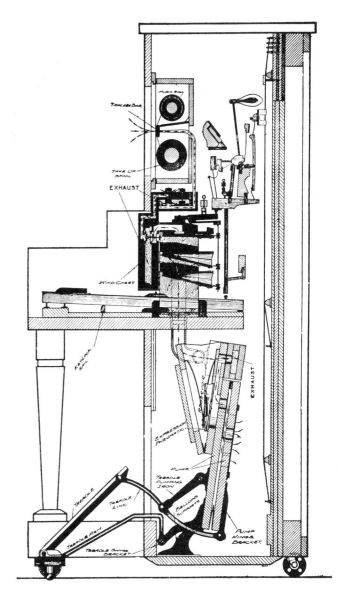

The inner workings of an 88-note home player piano. (From an Autopiano catalogue)

This Aeolian 65-note piano player was made circa 1900 by Aeolian's branch in England, the Orchestrelle Company.

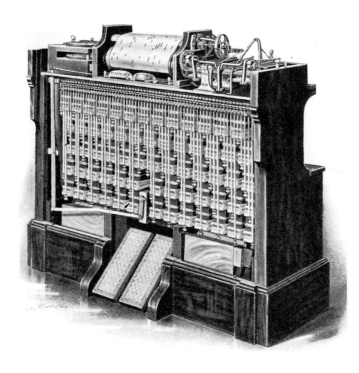

The Krell Auto-Player

Style 18

Dimensions

Height	.	.	.	3 feet
Width	.	.	.	3 feet 10 inches
Depth	.	.	.	1 foot 4 inches

Weight, 225 lbs. Boxed, 325 lbs. Export, 23 cubic feet

The push-up piano player was especially popular during the 1900-1905 years. Above is shown the Krell Auto-Player, Style 18, interior and exterior views. This instrument used 65-note player rolls. Below is a scene of the Hupfeld factory, circa 1904, showing push-up piano players in production. Most used 73-note Phonola rolls, the German counterpart to the American 65-note format.

The PIANOLA IN THE SUMMER HOME

OWING TO the recent establishment of our "Exchange Department," we have a new plan by which Pianolas may be obtained for Summer Homes on exceptionably favorable terms.

Persons who are interested and reply at once, mentioning this magazine, will be given full details.

What the Exchange Department Is

The Exchange Department has been organized in order to afford an outlet for the Pianolas and pianos which are constantly being taken in exchange for the Metrostyle Pianola and the Pianola Piano, the latest productions of The Aeolian Company.

The Aeolian Company   Aeolian Hall, 362 Fifth Avenue, New York
124 East Fourth Street, Cincinnati, Ohio

Genesis: this picture, taken decades ago, shows what is believed to be one of the first buildings used by the Peerless Piano Player Company in St. Johnsville, New York. Peerless was in on the doorstep of the push-up piano player industry, and by 1905 the firm had grown to be one of America's largest. (Photograph courtesy of Carlo Polidori)

Singing is Half the Joy
of Owning a Gulbransen

The songs you like best to hear, sung by some loved voice, to *your own* softly-accented, perfectly-timed accompaniment on a Gulbransen. There's genuine enjoyment for you!

Select your song rolls from the hundreds upon hundreds available, with the words already printed on them. The key they are pitched in doesn't matter. Too high? Too low? Just turn a knob. The Gulbransen instantly transposes.

An ordinary song roll may be played as a splendid and correct accompanying number, on the Gulbransen. The difficult fingering is taken care of by the roll. Through the pedals you *register* your touch, your time, your expression, following exactly the interpretation given the song by the vocalist.

Four simple Instruction Rolls—exclusive with the Gulbransen —show a method of correct playing. Bear this in mind, too: you can play *any* make of roll, *even electric reproducing rolls*, on your Gulbransen.

Every piano and player-piano needs tuning at least twice a year. Don't neglect your Gulbransen.

GULBRANSEN-DICKINSON COMPANY, *Chicago*

Canadian Distributors:
Mutual Sales Service, Limited, 79 Wellington St. West, Toronto

© 1923 G·D Co

Gulbransen
Trade Mark

Nationally Priced
Branded in the Back

White House Model
$**700**
Country Seat Model
$**600**
Suburban Model
$**495**
Community Model
$**420**

Count the
Pedal Strokes on
the Gulbransen

*Fewer Pedal Strokes
and More Music*

Send This Baby for a Baby
CHECK COUPON

☐ Check here if you do *not* own a piano.
☐ Check here if interested in having player action installed in your piano.

Write name and address in margin. Mail to GULBRANSEN - DICKINSON COMPANY, 810 N. Kedzie Avenue, Chicago, Ill.

(Pronounced Gul-BRAN-sen)

GULBRANSEN
The *Registering* Piano

Registers YOUR TOUCH • *Registers* YOUR TIME • *Registers* YOUR EXPRESSION • *Registers* YOUR INDIVIDUALITY

The card on the player illustrated above is meant to giv the impression that the present price of the instrument in the window is $212. As a matter of fact, it does not refer to the Pianola in the window, but to an old-style 65-note player in some out-of-the-way corner of the store. Note also that the card reads, "Reduced $212," and not, "Reduced to $212." Many Wrong Method dealers make constant use of this means of securing prospects.

This is the Old Style Pianola referred to on the price card in the window.

PIANOLA PIANO NEW		
Original Price - -		$675
Reduced - - -		212
Price NOW - -		$463

There was lots of competition in the player piano business years ago, as this page from a circa 1920 buying guide shows. So what else is new?

Your Dream
z Ballad
ck Watson

9886
WHAT KIND OF FOOL AM I
from: "Stop the world I want to get off"
Played by Dick Watson

10-342
Good Morning Starshine
Played by Brian Williams

Word Roll
8713
MOCKIN' BIRD HILL
(Tra-La Twit-tle Dee Dee)
Played by J. Lawrence Cook

Wo
9
WHEN YOU'R
(The Whole World I
Played by J. L

S
7
MOON
AGAIN
nce Cook

Q·R·S
Word Roll
9067
In The Chapel In The Moonlight
Played by Max Kortlander

Q·R·S
Word Roll
9819
ALICE BLUE GOWN
Marimba Waltz Ballad
Played by Scott & Watters

Q·R·S
Word Roll
9529
Far Away Places
Waltz
Played by Ted Baxter

Q·R·S
1-53 WORD RO
992
A FOGGY
N LONDON
Played by Dick

Roll
26
OLD SMOKY
z
ck Watson

Q·R·S
Word Roll
10-339
With Pen In Hand
Played by Gene Hale

Q·R·S
Word Roll
1186
WHISPERING
Fox Trot
Played by J. Lawrence Cook

Q·R·S
Word Roll
9214
The Shifting Whispering Sands
Played by J. Lawrence Cook

Q·R·
Word R
845
CALIFOR
(Here I Co
Played by J. Law

·S
55
ISE
lad
ck Watson

Q·R·S
WORD ROLL
8312
HAPPY BIRTHDAY TO YOU
Happy Birthday To You, He's A Jolly
Good Fellow, Hail, Hail, The Gang's
All Here, How Dry I Am, Happy Birth-
day To You, Auld Lang Syne.

Q·R·S
Word Roll
9823
YELLOW BIRD
Played by Walter Redding

Q·R·S
8-26 WORD ROLL
Q-183
(ORIGINAL QRS-3560)
WHEN THE RED RED ROBIN
COMES BOBBIN' ALONG
Played by Arden & Kortlander

Wo
3
Show Me T
Played by

1
CARDY
nd
Watters

Q·R·S
Word Roll
9399
ROCK-A-BYE YOUR BABY
WITH A DIXIE MELODY
Played by J. Lawrence Cook

Q·R·S
Word Roll
9927
I GOT RHYTHM
Gershwin
Played by Hi Babit

Q·R·S
Word Roll
5906
The Rose Of Tralee
Waltz
Played by Harold Scott

Q·R·
8-38 WORD
6
LONDON
Played by

ll
3
BALL
Scott

Q·R·S
10-55 WORD ROLL
9218
IT'S THE TALK
OF THE TOWN
Played by Max Kortlander

Q·R·S
Word Roll
1510
I Love To Tell The Story
Church Hymn
Played by Phil Ohman

Q·R·S
Imperial
"SONGRECORD
Q-124
THE ORIGINAL IMP.-07079
THERE'S A RAINBOW
'ROUND MY SHOULDER

Q·R·
Word
797
TICO-
Samb
Played by J. L

A Visit to Q.R.S. Music Rolls, Inc.

Ramsi P. Tick, owner of Q.R.S., at the front door of the factory. Following the death of the previous owner, Max Kortlander, in 1961, Ramsi P. Tick purchased the enterprise. It was moved from Brooklyn to Buffalo in 1966.

Front of the Q.R.S. building, a structure which decades earlier was used as a power distribution station for the local trolley car system.

A Visit to Q.R.S. Music Rolls, Inc.

. . . being a tour of the factory premises located at 1026 Niagara Street, Buffalo, New York. Q.R.S., established in 1900 as a subsidiary of the Melville Clark Piano Company, is the oldest and largest manufacturer of player piano rolls in the world today. (Photographs by Harvey and Marion Roehl of the Vestal Press)

Factory wall showing, among other vehicles parked there, the large "Roehl Road Car" home on wheels.

Directly behind the factory is the New York Thruway extension which goes northward to Niagara Falls. Beyond the bridge to Canada lies Lake Erie.

Tours of the Q.R.S. premises by visitors are encouraged. Weekdays at 10 a.m. and 2 p.m. anyone can see how music rolls are produced. Above is shown the reception area.

View of the room where visitors to the Q.R.S. factory are treated to a slide show telling the history of piano rolls in general and the Q.R.S. business in particular.

These scenes of the main factory floor give an idea of the many different steps and processes which comprise the perforating of home player piano rolls.

Harvey Roehl sits at the bench of the special "marking piano" which records a live performance by making pencil marks on a strip of paper. Who knows, Fats Waller may have perched on the same bench in a bygone day.

The recording head of the marking piano. A blank paper roll is drawn steadily across the drum while the pianist plays. In recent years such luminaries as Roger Williams and Liberace have made recordings here.

However, the above piano is the one on which most roll arrangements are recorded. A pianist can directly produce a master roll by playing the piano slowly, one note or chord at a time.

A technician carefully checks a master roll (recorded on the piano shown to the left) to locate stray notes, errors, and other irregularities.

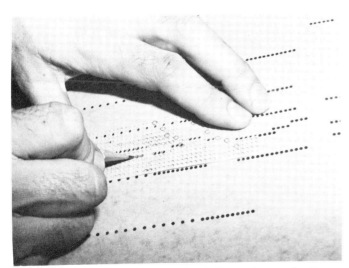

A handy perforated gauge is used to indicate where perforations in the heavy master roll should be or shouldn't be. Even the most careful recording is apt to need a few corrections.

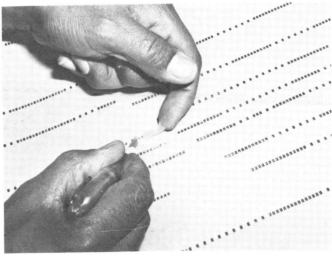

Adhesive tape is used to cover a series of holes which have been punched in error on the master roll.

At the left, Rudy Martin checks the work of the machine which makes production master rolls using original masters made on the recording piano. Above is shown another view of this large and intricate device.

Tunes currently being produced by Q.R.S. range from the latest hits to "oldies but goodies" from the turn of the century. Although visitors can buy rolls at the factory, most sales are accomplished through a worldwide dealer network. Over 3,000 tune titles are currently available.

Above: The business end of the perforator which makes master rolls. Note the pin-feed alignment holes along the margin. These insure proper tracking and feeding of the master.

Bob Berkman searches in the basement vault for a master of a roll scheduled to be put into production.

Right: One way to store a bunch of master rolls.

Rolls being made: Rick Sensabaugh works the second shift at a production roll perforator. Sometimes it is hard to keep up with the demand. Player pianos are popular once again, and in a big way.

Another view of a production perforator. Note the many rolls of paper to the left which feed into the machine. Rolls are made today with the same equipment used many decades ago!

Paul Miller operates a perforator which spews forth a double set, each many layers thick, of piano rolls.

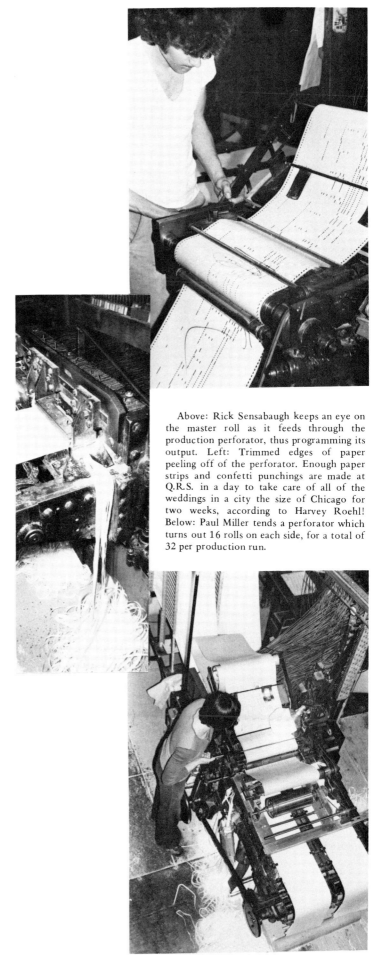

Above: Rick Sensabaugh keeps an eye on the master roll as it feeds through the production perforator, thus programming its output. Left: Trimmed edges of paper peeling off of the perforator. Enough paper strips and confetti punchings are made at Q.R.S. in a day to take care of all of the weddings in a city the size of Chicago for two weeks, according to Harvey Roehl! Below: Paul Miller tends a perforator which turns out 16 rolls on each side, for a total of 32 per production run.

The versatile Ms. Murray affixes end tabs to a bunch of new rolls. At this point the rolls are still together, 16 plies, just as they came off the production perforator.

Marcia Murray stamps the title on the end of a music roll which has been freshly perforated.

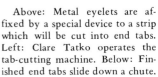

Above: Metal eyelets are affixed by a special device to a strip which will be cut into end tabs. Left: Clare Tatko operates the tab-cutting machine. Below: Finished end tabs slide down a chute.

Ms. Murray shows how the end of a stack of rolls is neatly cut at a 90-degree angle by means of two manually-operated paper knives.

In addition to making the rolls themselves, many other related operations take place at Q.R.S. Included are end-tab making, spool end molding, and the making of cardboard roll spools or cores.

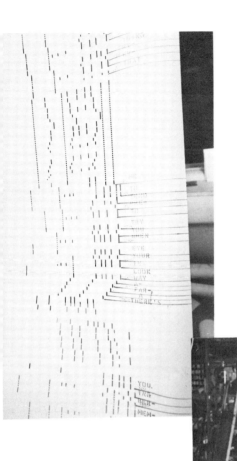

David Snyder prepares a stencil for marking the words on a music roll. Q.R.S. rolls are just the thing for "sing along" parties!

Above: Guidelines help to figure out where the words should go on a roll. Right: Felix Klempka with a machine intended to make full-face stencils on the Q.R.S. "Educator" roll set. Below: Diane Shakoor stencils a roll.

Close-up view of the narrow stencil as it emerges from the die plate.

"The stencil is a long continuous loop which has a length equal to that of the roll to be imprinted. One pass of the roll from a rack at one end to a bin at the other, with a big 'swoosh,' and the words are on!"

Stacks of specially printed decorative leaders for Q.R.S. "Celebrity" rolls and reproducing piano rolls.

Walter Gibbs checks the operation of the injection molding machine which makes spool ends for piano rolls.

The output of the automatic injection molding machine, a handful of spool ends.

This machine makes cardboard cores from four paper strips which are fed onto a mandrel. The formed tube comes continuously off of one end and is cut into 11¼" lengths.

In this operation the left spool end is stapled to the cardboard core. Making a single piano roll involves many different operations, all of which are done at the Q.R.S. factory.

It's handy to have a player piano right in the middle of the production floor to check rolls. Felix Klempka, production supervisor of the plant, listens to a newly-cut tune.

Liesa Ritchie uses a special machine to wind piano rolls on spools.

In the above view Hugh Johnson, at the left, operates a machine to fasten the paper cores of music rolls to the left spool end, as shown earlier. The operator to his right is putting the completed rolls into boxes and labeling the box ends. The disc overhead is a large Q.R.S.-label record which was used in a theatrical production years ago. To the right about 1,001 spooled rolls await boxing.

"The meaning of the three Q.R.S. initials has been lost with the passage of time. The best explanation we can discover is the motto 'Quality, Real Service' or 'Quality Roll Service' — as printed in some of our old catalogues."

Above: Fitting the rubber stamp for imprinting the box end. Right: Genie Reilly stamps box ends and loads the boxes with rolls.

Genie Reilly packs a bunch of rolls together. Next step: by conveyor belt to the shipping room.

Eleanore Chmura prepares a shipment for a customer's order. In the background are shelves full of reference books, which are also popular with player piano owners.

Doreen Czosek picks stock from shelves. "Way Down Yonder In New Orleans," "The Old Piano Roll Blues," "Try to Remember," "Turkey in the Straw," "Does Your Chewing Gum Lose Its Flavor on the Bedpost Overnight?," or whatever else you want to hear, she can find if Q.R.S. cuts it!

The final packing operations. Frank Brewster prepares shipping documents, while Robert Lang operates a scale to determine shipping charges.

Postal trucks full of cartons await shipment to the postoffice, where they will be sent all over via the economical "special rate for sound recordings."

Meanwhile, back at the office . . . Ramsi Tick's desk is the same one used for many years by Max Kortlander, the previous owner of Q.R.S., which he styled as the Imperial Industrial Company.

Ramsi Tick and Bob Berkman check "Variety" to determine which new tunes have potential for piano roll sales.

Above: Production schedule for a Q.R.S. periodic bulletin and other activities. Above right: Opening the morning mail. Right: June Caputi, who manages the office where orders are received and bookkeeping is done.

Susan Caputi operates a bookkeeping machine. In the far right picture she is shown at a special sink made from, of all things, an old Victor phonograph cabinet!

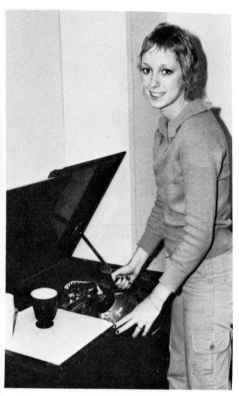

Marlene Hartz does graphic arts work for Q.R.S. and the related Q.R.S. Arts Foundation (which sponsors concerts). Typesetting is done on an IBM Composing Typewriter.

Piano fallboard from an old Melville Clark instrument. Clark owned Q.R.S. in the early years. On this page are shown some Q.R.S. rolls from years ago, including ethnic rolls, children's rolls, and the famed "Educator" set.

"During the 1920s Q.R.S. sold as many as ten million rolls per year and maintained factories in Chicago, New York, San Francisco, Toronto, and Sydney. After World War II sales declined to a low point of under 200,000 annually. Today, player pianos and player rolls are staging a strong revival."

A photograph in the Q.R.S. archives shows a banquet from over a half century ago.

Portrait of Max Kortlander, owner of
Q.R.S. before Ramsi P. Tick acquired it.

This Dictaphone ad from the 1920s
features Q.R.S. as one of the firm's best
customers. Thirty Dictaphones were used in
various Q.R.S. departments.

*As the piano roll business waned, Q.R.S. sought to diversify by selling all sorts of related items
such as radio tubes, phonographs, and records. Within a few years, the selling of anything would have
helped. In the early 1930s Wurlitzer, in an effort to stay liquid, sold refrigerators and furniture in its
outlets. Q.R.S. went through bankruptcy and was acquired by Max Kortlander. The production of
rolls remained continuous, although in sharply reduced amounts.*

Q.R.S. today produces a colorful variety of advertising brochures, bulletins, and other sales aids, even including T-shirts! Will bulletins such as those shown above become collectors' items in the future? Unless we miss our guess, yes!

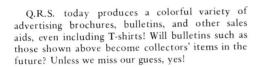

WINTER 1977-78

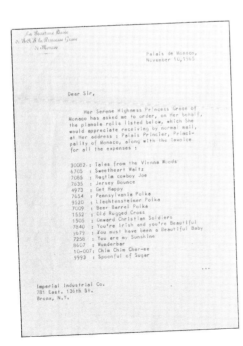

Among the thousands of Q.R.S. customers are numbered Princess Grace of Monaco (letter to the left) and Jackie Gleason. Her Highness requested "Ragtime Cowboy Joe," "Beer Barrel Polka," "Onward Christian Soldiers," "Wunderbar," "Spoonful of Sugar," "Jersey Bounce," "Get Happy," and "Old Rugged Cross," among other tunes, while Jackie Gleason asked for a wide selection of popular Christmas melodies.

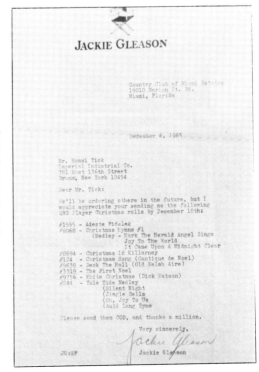

Jeannie Reblitz, Art's wife, pedals an 88-note Monarch player piano. (Photo courtesy of the Colorado Springs Gazette-Telegraph)

A Visit to PLAY-RITE MUSIC ROLLS, INC. of Turlock, California

This 5,000-square-foot building houses the office and main production facilities for Play-Rite Music Rolls, Inc. Another location is maintained as an auxiliary facility. The photographs to illustrate this section were taken in November 1979.

On the next several pages you will go on a photographic tour of Play-Rite Music Rolls, Inc., located in Turlock, California. The founders of the business, John and Bill Malone and their mother Jeanne, who began their enterprise around 1960, have incorporated modern technology with traditional methods of manufacturing. In 1974 Elwood Hansen joined the firm, and in 1977 Robert Kolsters became a part of it.

Play-Rite makes on a regular basis standard 88-note home player piano rolls; Ampico, Duo-Art, and Welte (Licensee) reproducing piano rolls; styles A, G, and O orchestrion rolls; and styles 125, 150, and 165 Wurlitzer band organ rolls. Styles M, OS, NOS, Welte Philharmonic Organ, Wurlitzer Style R Pipe Organ, Hupfeld Phonoliszt-Violina, Hupfeld Helios orchestrion, Welte 75-note orchestrion, Wurlitzer Mandolin PianOrchestra, and Wurlitzer Concert PianOrchestra rolls have been or can be made on special order using existing equipment, according to John Malone. "Basically, Play-Rite can produce any type of music roll on a custom basis," he noted.

An example of a Play-Rite innovation is the digital one-to-one mastering system. For the production of music rolls traditionally a drafting board master two or three times longer than the finished roll is made. This mastering process normally requires many hours of work. The Play-Rite one-to-one digital electronic mastering system, which was assigned United States patent no. 4,143,807 on March 13, 1979, makes it possible to use any existing old piano roll as a master, thus eliminating the old-style method.

The office and reception area greets visitors to the Play-Rite enterprise. Rolls are sold by mail and by a distribution network of dealers.

Staff artist Walter Erickson records a new "live performance" 88-note home player roll on an Ivers & Pond piano which has been specially adapted for the purpose. The recorder in the background digitally encodes the performance for later computer processing.

Walter Erickson uses the electronic editing control box during the recording of an 88-note home player roll. Note the sensing devices attached above the piano action.

A close-up view of some of the solid-state electronic sensing devices used to record an artist's musical interpretation. Another set of sensors is under the keys of the same instrument.

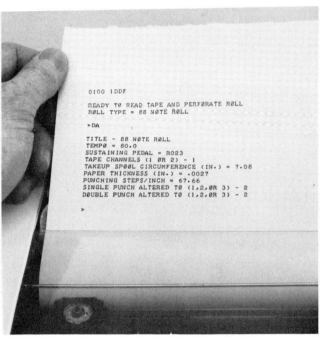

```
0100 1DDF

READY TØ READ TAPE AND PERFØRATE RØLL
RØLL TYPE = 88 NØTE RØLL

>DA

    TITLE - 88 NØTE RØLL
    TEMPØ = 80.0
    SUSTAINING PEDAL = RO23
    TAPE CHANNELS (1 ØR 2) - 1
    TAKEUP SPØØL CIRCUMFERENCE (IN.) = 7.08
    PAPER THICKNESS (IN.) = .0027
    PUNCHING STEPS/INCH = 67.66
    SINGLE PUNCH ALTERED TØ (1,2,ØR 3) - 2
    DØUBLE PUNCH ALTERED TØ (1,2,ØR 3) - 2

>
```

The magnetic tape recording of an artist's rendition is used via a Teletype machine to program a computer which, in turn, punches out the first paper music roll of a particular performance. From the initial keyboard performance by the pianist to the playback of the first roll can be accomplished in just a tiny fraction of the time previously used by music roll manufacturers.

In the distance Jeanne Malone uses an adapted computer-controlled Acme perforating machine to make a "production master" roll.

First, the "production master" is hand annotated with "sing along" words, as shown to the right. Then, as shown above, the words are transferred from the production master to the word stencil belt.

Walter Erickson uses a typewriter-like keyboard to punch out the word stencil belt. Later, the stencil is used to transfer the words to the right-hand margin of an 88-note or other player piano roll.

Susie Robinson operates the Play-Rite high speed perforating machine, a device which incorporates many refinements. The perforator uses a production master to make 22 identical copies in less than five minutes. The crankshaft speed is 4,000 rpm, and the music rolls advance at a speed of seven feet per minute. Innovations incorporated into the machine include a micro-processor, intermittent drive, dynamic balancing, and pressure lubrication. It has interchangeable dies which enable Play-Rite to make rolls up to 18 inches in width.

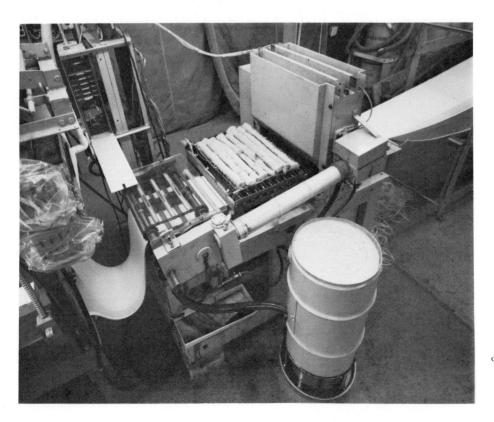

An overall view of Play-Rite's high speed one-to-one perforating machine.

The title, tempo, and other pertinent information is printed on the leader of each roll by this Multigraph machine. Shown is the leader, tempo 80, for "Five-Foot-Two," which is noted as being a "Live Performance Recording."

The word printing machine, which utilizes a stencil belt, prints the song lyrics on the music roll. The lyrics must be positioned properly in relation to the music so that the user can sing along as the music is played.

Darla Baxter spools an 88-note roll onto a cardboard tube with plastic flanges. In the background is part of the roll inventory awaiting order filling and shipment.

Jeanne Malone operates a vintage 1928 Acme perforating machine which was formerly used by the Staff Note Player Roll Company of Milwaukee, Wisconsin. Being produced when the photograph was taken were Wurlitzer 165 band organ rolls. The machine operates one-to-one and pneumatically reads the master roll. In the foreground is a mechanical reader which permits the copying of old original rolls which are too badly damaged to use with the pneumatic reader.

Darla Baxter spools a 15-tune Wurlitzer 65-Note Automatic Player Piano roll. Note the ladder rung arrangement of the spooling rack. This reduces friction on the copy being spooled and permits a 260-foot roll to be spooled nearly as easily as a short 30-foot roll.

This transcribing device transfers information on a perforated paper music roll to a magnetic tape for storage. The tape can then be played back on the Play-Rite recording piano or fed into the computer attached to the roll perforator.

As of early 1980 there were three main firms in the United States which produced 88-note home player piano rolls. Q.R.S., of Buffalo, New York, in business since 1900, was approaching the million-rolls-a-year mark with its sales. In North Hollywood, California the Klavier Music Roll Company (Harold Powell) produced player rolls as well as rolls for Ampico, Duo-Art, and Welte reproducing pianos using equipment which included perforators once located in the Ampico factory. And, as shown in the present section of this book, Play-Rite produced 88-note home player rolls as well as other types. In addition, several persons produced recuts of special rolls. Ed Freyer made styles A, G, and Link coin piano rolls, Tom Wurdeman produced several types of coin piano and band organ rolls, and a contributor to the present book, Mike Kitner, punched rolls of many types.

PLAY-RITE MUSIC ROLL
P. O. BOX 1025
TURLOCK, CALIF., U.S.A. 953

AUTOMATIC ROLL NO. G-754

"GENUINE JAZZ GEMS"

1. Just A Little Drink, Fox Trot
2. Collegiate, One-Step
3. I'm Always Thinking Of Someone, F
4. Sing Loo, Fox T
5. Shirley, Fox Tr
6. In The Purple
7. Miss You, Wal
8. By By The Light

Military Band Orga
STYLE 125
ROLL NO. 3151
STANDARD WALTZ ROLL

1. On The Beautiful Blue Danube, Waltzes
2. Over The Waves, Waltz
3. Wedding Of The Winds, Waltzes
4. Estudiantina, Waltz
5. Dream Of Heaven, Waltz
6. Faust, Waltz
7. Skaters, We

AY-RITE MUSIC ROLLS,
P. O. BOX 1025
TURLOCK, CALIF., U.S.A. 95380

CAPITOL N.O.S. ROLL NO. 58
POPULAR VARIETY ROLL

't You Hear Me Say "I Love You" Waltz
s That Pretty Baby, Fox Trot
Haunting Waltz
ttle Nest Fox Trot Ballad
On, Fox Trot Ballad
One Night Of Love In Spain, Ballad
wilight Rose, Waltz Ballad
oronado Nights, Spanish Fox Trot Ballad
der The Moon, Fox Trot Ballad
ritz, Viennese Waltz
-La Hawaiian Fox Trot Ballad
Dance, Novelty Haning & White
© 1978 - Play-Rite, Inc.

WURL
Military Ba
STY
ROLL N
SOUTHERN M

1. My Old Kentucky
2. Silver Threads Am
3. Auld Lang Syne
4. Listen To The Mock
5. Darling Nellie Gray
6. Old Black Joe
7. Turkey In The Straw
8. Swanee River
9. Massa's In The Cold Cold C
10. Dixie Land

Mfd. By
PLAY-RITE MUSIC ROLL'
TURLOCK, CA 95380

AMPICO
PLAY-RITE MUSIC ROLLS INC.
TURLOCK, CALIF. U.S.A.
53886
HUNGARIAN RHAPSODY NO. 15
LISZT
Played by Arthur Loesser
© 1979 - Play-Rite, Inc.

Y-RITE
130

KENNY RODGERS MEDLEY

1. Lucille (Bowling/Bynum)
2. The Gambler (D. Schlitz)
3. She Believes In Me (S. Gibb)
1 © 1976 ATV Music Corp.
2. & 3. © United Artists Music and
Records Group, Inc.
Played by Louis Anderson
WORD ROLL
© 1979 - Play-Rite, Inc.

ROLLS, INC
1025
., U.S.A. 95380

LL NO. O 1980

e A Yellow Ribbon
Lucille
The Gambler
4. Still The One
5. Bad, Bad Leroy Brown
6. Music Box Dancer
ight Up My Life
elieves In Me
es You
rtainer
ELECTRIC PIANO

RO LL NO. A-2500

1. Raindrops Keep Fallin' On My Head, F
2. Tennessee Waltz
3. Hello Dolly, Waltz
4. Seventy Six Trombones, March
5. Alley Cat, Fox Trot
6. Old Piano Roll Blues, Fox Trot
7. Music, Music, Music, Fox Trot
8. Cruising Down The River, Waltz
9. Beer Barrel Polka
10. Crazy Otto Rag, Rag

HIGH GRADE

PLAY-RITE MUSIC
P. O. BOX
TURLOCK, CALIF

ROLL

1. Ain't We Go
2. Stumbling
3. Runnin'
4. I'll Build
5. Barney G
6. You've
7. Last Ni
8. Linger
9. Peggy
10. When Iris

WURL
Military Band
STYLE 165
ROLL NO. 6516

1. American Patrol
2. Battle Hymn Of The Republic
3. Hail Columbia
4. Onward Christian Soldiers
5. America
6. Battle Cry of Freedom
7. Tenting Tonight On The Old C
8. El Capitan, March
9. Just Before The Battle Mother
10. Star Spangled Banner

Mfd. By
PLAY-RITE MUSIC
TURLOCK, CA

LL NO. A-658

"SONGS OF YESTER-YEAR"

1. Three O'Clock In The Morning
2. Good Bye Dolly Gray
3. When You And I Were Young Maggie
4. The World Is Waiting For The Sunrise
5. My Wild Irish Rose
6. It's A Long, Long Way To Tipperary
7. Pack Up Your Troubles In Your Old Kit Bag and Smile,
Smile, Smile
8. Barney Google
9. Put On Your Old Gray Bonnet
10. Iowa Corn Song

HIGH GRADE MUSIC ROLLS FOR ELEC
ELECTRIC

DUO-ART
PLAY-RITE MUSIC ROLLS INC.
TURLOCK, CALIF. U.S.A.
3000
"THE STING" PART 1
1. The Entertainer
2. Solace
(Scott Joplin)
Played by William Flynt
© 1979 - Play-Rite, Inc.

IC ROLLS, IN
1025
U.S.A. 95380

J ROLL
UT'N RYTHYM

The Garden
Whispering Hope
Haven Of Rest
4. What A Friend
5. Sweet Hour Of Prayer
6. Old Rugged Cross
7. Battle Hymn Of The Republic
8. Church In The Wildwood
9. Old Time Religion
10. Silent Night
11. Rol O

© 1979 - Play-Rite,

LEABARJAN MENTOR—"STYLE 3"

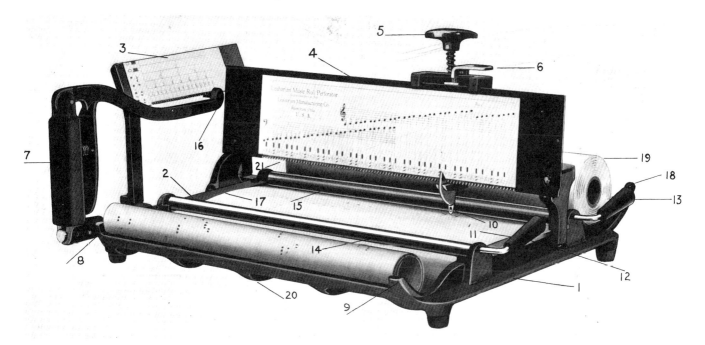

Names of Machine Parts

1. Base
2. Cross Slide
3. Time Scale
4. Note Scale
5. Punch Button
6. Note Scale Index
7. Cross Slide Handle
8. Left Front Paper Guide
9. Right Front Paper Guide
10. Punch
11. Right Paper Guide
12. Front Nipper
13. Rear Nipper
14. Front Paper Fastener
15. Rear Paper Fastener
16. Time Scale Index Pin
17. Left Paper Guide
18. Right Paper Guide, Rear
19. Paper Supply
20. Front Roll Holder
21. Notches in Note Scale

Note—Place a drop of oil on moving parts occasionally

The Leabarjan Perforator in the Schools

DO IT YOURSELF ROLLS: In the 1920s the Leabarjan Company manufactured a wide variety of roll perforators, mostly of small sizes intended for individual (rather than factory production line) use. Apparently these achieved a modest measure of popularity. Today, the arranging and perforating of music rolls is a very popular subject with collectors.

The above illustration shows one of the Leabarjan Perforators, Style 5, being used for educational purposes in a public school room. The music teacher is demonstrating the use of the machine to a group of students.

The Leabarjan Perforator affords a very interesting and successful method of teaching the time values of notes and rests, the position of notes on the staff, the piano key-board, different scales, and all the fundamental principles of music. The science of music is a separate and fundamental subject, the problems of which should be mastered, if possible, before the instrument of expression is chosen. This is possible where the student learns to make a perforated music roll—with the Leabarjan Perforator genuine music study will be a pleasure and the student will be anxious to accomplish a greater task each day.

The Leabarjan Perforator will give the music student a tangible record of his knowledge of music; a record that will not only be a book of notes that he has written or from which he has played or studied, but a roll of perforated music that will immediately reveal the accuracy of his musical understanding.

Chapter 4

EXPRESSION and REPRODUCING PIANOS

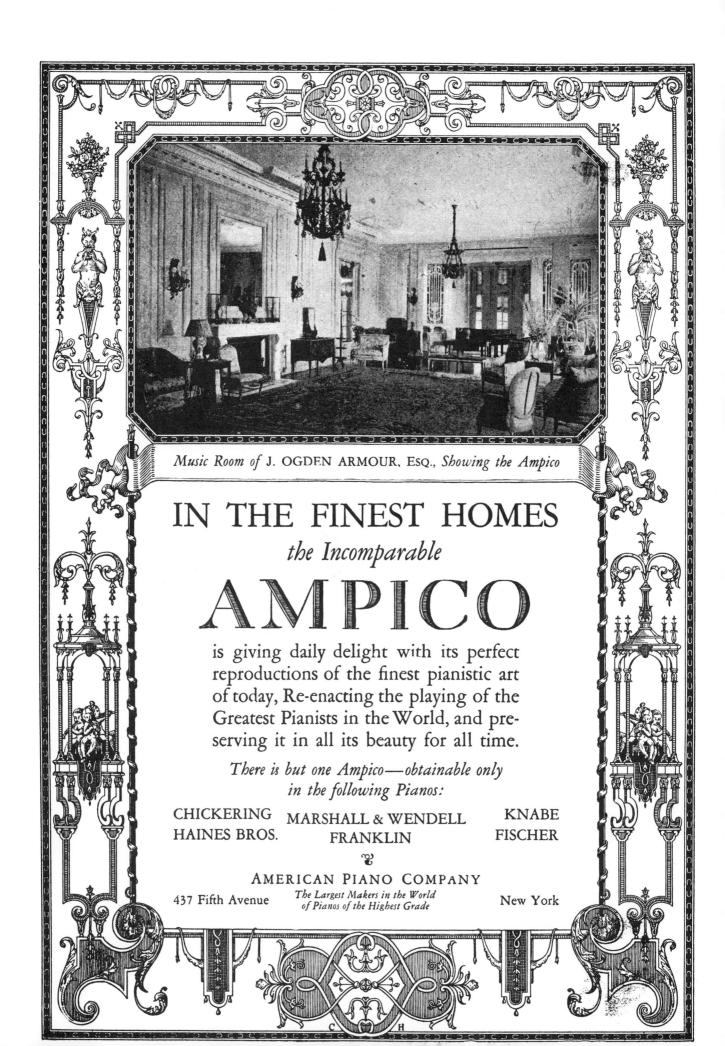

Music Room of J. OGDEN ARMOUR, ESQ., Showing the Ampico

IN THE FINEST HOMES

the Incomparable

AMPICO

is giving daily delight with its perfect reproductions of the finest pianistic art of today, Re-enacting the playing of the Greatest Pianists in the World, and preserving it in all its beauty for all time.

*There is but one Ampico—obtainable only
in the following Pianos:*

| CHICKERING | MARSHALL & WENDELL | KNABE |
| HAINES BROS. | FRANKLIN | FISCHER |

AMERICAN PIANO COMPANY

*The Largest Makers in the World
of Pianos of the Highest Grade*

437 Fifth Avenue   New York

AMERICAN PIANO COMPANY
Ampico Reproducing Pianos

The Ampico reproducing system marketed by the American Piano Company (of which AMPICO is an acronym) was introduced around 1914. The invention of Charles F. Stoddard, the earliest models were known as Stoddard-Ampicos. By means of this mechanism an upright or grand piano could re-enact the playing of famous pianists, complete with pedaling and varying degrees of keyboard expression. Around 1920 the Model A Ampico mechanism, which incorporated some refinements, was introduced.

In 1929 a redesigned Ampico system, the Model B, the work of Dr. Clarence Hickman, made its debut. The Model B system utilized some expression refinements and also permitted the use of large-diameter "jumbo" rolls of longer playing time.

Ampico systems were installed in a number of different piano makes, including J. & C. Fischer, Marshall & Wendell, Haines Brothers, Chickering, Knabe, and (after 1925) the top-of-the-line Mason & Hamlin.

Additional information concerning the Ampico system (as well as others) can be found in *The Encyclopedia of Automatic Musical Instruments, Player Piano Treasury*, and *Re-enacting the Artist* (Ampico information only).

During the 1920s the Ampico was probably the best selling reproducing piano in America, with Duo-Art being a close second, and with the Welte (Licensee) third. Many thousands were sold.

AMPICO MODEL A ROLL
11¼" wide; spaced 9 holes per inch

1 Slow bass crescendo (decrescendo when released)
2 Bass intensity 1
3 Sustaining pedal
4 Bass intensity 2
5 Fast bass crescendo/decrescendo
6 Bass intensity 3
7 Cancel bass intensities
8 to 90, 83 playing notes, B to A
91 Rewind
92 Cancel treble intensities
93 Treble intensity 3
94 Fast treble crescendo/decrescendo
95 Treble intensity 2
96 Hammer rail
97 Treble intensity 1
98 Slow treble crescendo (decrescendo when released)

AMPICO MODEL B ROLL
11¼" wide; spaced 9 holes per inch

0 Amplifier
1 Blank
2 Bass intensity 1
3 Sustaining pedal
4 Bass intensity 2
5 Blank
6 Bass intensity 3
7 Cancel bass intensities
8 to 90, 83 playing notes, B to A
91 Rewind
92 Cancel treble intensities
93 Treble intensity 3
94 Fast crescendo/decrescendo

95 Treble intensity 2
96 Hammer rail
97 Treble intensity 1
98 Slow crescendo (decrescendo when released)
00 Sub intensity

Holes 2 to 93 and 95 to 97 are the same as the Ampico Model A scale. Hole 00 provides an intensity level softer than the normal setting for extremely soft playing. Holes 0 and 98 are multiplexed to control three levels of pump vacuum (normal, 1st amplification, and 2nd amplification). The single crescendo mechanism in the Model B controls both bass and treble. For a complete understanding of the mechanisms of the Ampico reproducing system and its competitors refer to the service manuals published by the Vestal Press.

Marshall & Wendell grand piano equipped with a Model A Ampico reproducing system. (Courtesy of Ellsworth O. Johnson)

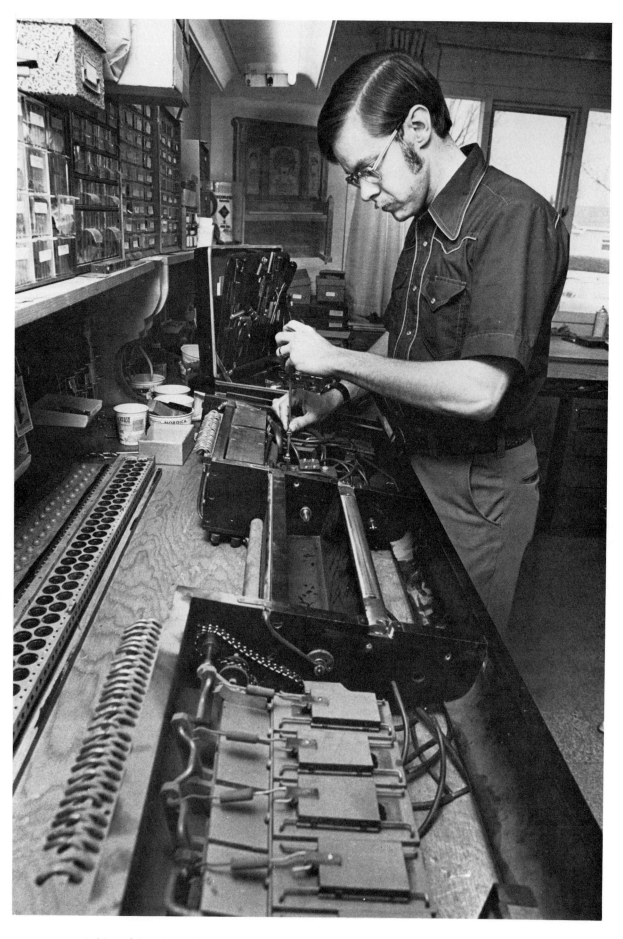

In his workshop Art Reblitz works on a drawer from an Ampico reproducing piano. (Photo courtesy of the Colorado Springs Gazette-Telegraph)

Although most Ampico pianos were made in standard cases, there were some exceptions. A notable example in this regard is the magnificent Chickering Ampico grand piano in a hand-carved ornate case shown above. Often a custom case such as this would take a year or two to complete. (Tom Beckett Collection)

AMPICO
RECORDINGS
DECEMBER — 1925

NOCTURNE

Chopin, obliged to pass the night at a wayside inn, was impelled to play the piano found in the public room. Upon this occasion the guests and stragglers in the hotel were enraptured with the composer's playing of his famous NOCTURNE in E Flat, Op. 9, No. 2—*The painting is by Balestrieri.*

New Ampico Recordings
December, 1925

Played by Moriz Rosenthal

65313H Carnaval de Vienne (Carnival of Vienna), Humoresque on Themes of Johann Strauss — *Rosenthal* 2.00

WITH incredible skill Rosenthal has taken snatches of the waltzes of Johann Strauss and wrought them into a piano piece of the utmost brilliancy, and he plays it with a facility unbelievable until heard. At times several of the waltz themes are played simultaneously, and that each shines clear and distinct is one of the marvels of that piano technique which has made Rosenthal a supreme master of the keyboard. That he colors each with precisely the sentiment and lyric beauty its dulcet phrases demand discloses the poetry which lies in the soul of this colossal figure amongst the pianists of all time.

Let us think of the melodious snatches of waltzes of which this dazzling piece is made as the fantastic figures in a carnival crowd, and let us imagine that we are surveying the spectacle from the vantage-point of a balcony overlooking the scene. It is a riot of color and movement. Gaily dressed masques come into view, exciting our interest and admiration, only to disappear quickly in the ever moving surge of gaiety and festival.

Every now and then the crowd thins out as it were and in the music one hears a waltz tune ringing out clear and defined as an isolated figure in the carnival is seen in relief; but in an instant the street is full again and the bewildering, dazzling spectacle is once more at full tide.

Played by Mischa Levitzki

65321H Etude, Op. 8, No. 12, D Sharp Minor, "Pathetique" — *Scriabine* 2.00

THIS study is touched with the divine fire that burned when Chopin gave to the world his famous "Revolutionary Etude." The same patriotic ardor and protest are alight in the splendid eloquence of Scriabine's work, lacking only a little of the heart-breaking appeal of Chopin's noble music of the same character.

This Bulletin with the January 1925 Catalog supplies a COMPLETE LIST of all Ampico Recordings to date.

Concert Appearances of Ampico Artists
Where You May Hear Them in Person

Dec.			Dec.		
1	BRAILOWSKY	St. Louis, Mo.	9	SCHMITZ	Denver, Colo.
1	LEGINSKA	Montreal, Can.	10	BRAILOWSKY	Troy, N. Y.
2	RACHMANINOFF	Washington, D. C.	10	LEGINSKA	Concord, N. H.
3	BRAILOWSKY	Joplin, Mo.	12	BRAILOWSKY	New York City
3	LHÉVINNE	San Francisco, Cal.	13	LEGINSKA	Boston, Mass.
3	RACHMANINOFF	Baltimore, Md.	14	LEGINSKA	Brooklyn, N. Y.
3	SCHMITZ	Leavenworth, Kans.	14	LHÉVINNE	Portland, Ore.
4	RACHMANINOFF	Brooklyn, N. Y.	15	BRAILOWSKY	Springfield, Ohio
4	SCHMITZ	Mt. Vernon, Iowa	16	LHÉVINNE	Seattle, Wash.
7	SCHMITZ	Fremont, Neb.	27	LEGINSKA	Fall River, Mass.
8	BRAILOWSKY	Chicago, Ill.			

✠ ✠ ✠

Accompaniment Recordings from Previous Bulletins

No.	Title Composer Played by Price
30361G	AH, LOVE, BUT A DAY! A Flat, Soprano or Tenor (with words)— *Beach* .... Browning 1.75
30371G	AH, LOVE, BUT A DAY! F Major, Contralto or Baritone (with words)— *Beach* .... Browning 1.75
65281G	ARLESIENNE, L', *Adagietto* (Violin Accompaniment)— *Bizet* ...... Browning
30401G	AWAKENING, B Flat, High Soprano (with words)— *Golde* ....
30411G	AWAKENING, A Flat, Mezzo-Soprano (with words)— *Golde* .... Golde
30423G	BOHÈME, LA, "Michiamano Mimi" (My Name is Mimi), D Major, High Soprano (with Italian words)— *Puccini*.... Golde 1.75
65141G	CAPRICE VIENNOIS, Op. 2 (Violin Accompaniment)— *Kreisler* ...... Browning
64541F	CAVATINA, Op. 85, No. 3, Key of D (Violin Accompaniment)— *Raff*.Browning 1.50
30201G	DO NOT GO, MY LOVE, F Sharp Minor, Soprano or Tenor (with words)— *Hageman* .... Browning
30211G	DO NOT GO, MY LOVE, D Minor, Alto or Baritone (with words)— *Hageman* .... Browning
30161G	DOWN IN THE FOREST, "A Cycle of Life," E Flat, Soprano or Tenor (with words)— *Ronald* .... Browning
30171G	DOWN IN THE FOREST, "A Cycle of Life," Key of C, Alto or Baritone (with words)— *Ronald* .... Browning
30181G	DUNA, D Flat, Soprano or Tenor (with words)— *McGill* ...... Browning
30191G	DUNA, B Flat, Baritone (with words)— *McGill* .... Browning
30141G	GIVE A MAN A HORSE HE CAN RIDE, B Flat, Baritone (with words)— *O'Hara* .... Pollock
30151G	GIVE A MAN A HORSE HE CAN RIDE, Key of D, Tenor (with words)— *O'Hara* .... Pollock 1.75
64771G	HUMORESQUE, Op. 101, No. 7, Key of G (Violin Accompaniment)— *Dvořák* .... Browning
30381G	JEAN, E Flat, Tenor (with words)— *Burleigh* .... Browning 1.75
30391G	JEAN, D Flat, Baritone (with words)— *Burleigh* .... Browning 1.75
30321G	LAST SONG, THE, Key of A, Soprano or Tenor (with words)— *Rogers*.... Wille 1.75
30331G	LAST SONG, THE, Key of F, Alto or Baritone (with words)— *Rogers*.... Wille 1.75
30301G	MAH LINDY LOU, E Flat, Soprano or Tenor (with words)— *Strickland*.Browning 1.75

No.	Title Composer Played by Price
30311G	MAH LINDY LOU, Key of C, Contralto or Baritone (with words)— *Strickland* .... Browning 1.75
30271G	MA LITTLE BANJO, G Flat, Tenor or Baritone (with words)— *Dichmont*.Browning 1.75
65291G	MELODY (Violin Accompaniment)— *Dawes* .... Browning 1.75
64911G	OLD REFRAIN, THE (Viennese Popular Song) (Violin Accompaniment)— *Trans. by Kreisler* ...... Browning 1.75
63793G	ONE FINE DAY, "Madame Butterfly," G Flat, Soprano— *Puccini*... Steeb 1.75
30241G	PAGLIACCI, "Vesti la Giubba" (On with the Play), E Minor, Tenor (with words)— *Leoncavallo* .... Browning 1.75
65011G	POÈME (Violin Accompaniment)— *Fibich-Kubelik* ...... Browning 1.75
30341G	REQUIEM, Op. 15, No. 2, B Flat Major, Tenor (with words)— *Homer*. Browning 1.75
30351G	REQUIEM, Op. 15, No. 2, G Flat Major, Baritone (with words)— *Homer*.Browning 1.75
65023G	RONDE DES LUTINS, LA (The Dance of the Goblins), Op. 25 (Violin Accompaniment)— *Bazzini* ...... Browning 1.75
64551F	SOUVENIR, Key of D (Violin Accompaniment)— *Drdla* ...... Browning 1.50
65153G	SPANISH DANCE, Op. 26, No. 8 (Violin Accompaniment)— *de Sarasate*.Browning 1.75
30281G	SPIRIT FLOWER, A, G Flat, Soprano or Tenor (with words)— *Campbell-Tipton*.... Suskind 1.75
30291G	SPIRIT FLOWER, A, Key of E, Mezzo-Soprano or Baritone (with words)— *Campbell-Tipton*.... Suskind 1.75
30251G	STAR, THE, D Flat, Soprano (with words)— *Rogers* .... Browning 1.75
30261G	STAR, THE, B Flat, Mezzo-Soprano (with words)— *Rogers* .... Browning 1.75
64781G	THAÏS, "Meditation," Key of D (Violin Accompaniment)— *Massenet, Trans. by Marwick* .. Browning 1.75
30221G	TOMMY, LAD! Key of F, Tenor (with words)— *Margetson* .... Browning 1.75
30231G	TOMMY, LAD! Key of D, Baritone or Bass (with words)— *Margetson*.Browning 1.75
30121G	WHO IS SYLVIA? Key of F, Alto or Bass (with words)— *Schubert*... Lamson 1.75
30131G	WHO IS SYLVIA? Key of G, Mezzo-Soprano or Baritone (with words)— *Schubert* .... Lamson 1.75
64903G	ZIGEUNERWEISEN (Gypsy Airs), Op. 20 (Violin Accompaniment)— *de Sarasate* ...... Browning 1.75

This Bulletin with the January 1925 Catalog supplies a COMPLETE LIST of all Ampico Recordings to date.

This December 1925 publication was mailed to Ampico owners, usually by the music stores where the instruments were originally purchased. This was at the height of popularity of the Ampico. Each issue of the magazine featured new roll releases and a story about each, usually a listing of previously-issued rolls as well, and timely information—in this issue a schedule of concert appearances of Ampico recording artists. Sergei Rachmaninoff in particular was very popular with the public.

Mason & Hamlin Ampico Model B reproducing grand piano in a Louis XVI art-style case. Built in 1930, the instrument was once used in a Bethlehem (Pennsylvania) home.

MELVILLE CLARK PIANO COMPANY
Apollo Expression and
Reproducing Pianos

This system, introduced in the 'teens by the Melville Clark Piano Company of DeKalb, Illinois, was popular for about a decade. The Apollo system, made in several variations, was featured by the Rudolph Wurlitzer Company, and it is believed that most sales were through that firm. The J.P. Seeburg Piano Company used Apollo rolls on certain of its instruments, the Style X coin piano and the Phono-Grand being examples.

The name "Apollo" was used on many instruments over the years, including thousands of Melville Clark non-expression players of the early years. Detailed information concerning the various firms involved with the Apollo system can be found on page 292 of *The Encyclopedia of Automatic Musical Instruments*.

In its various forms the Apollo system was also called Art Apollo, Artecho, Apollo X, and QRS Autograph Automatic.

APOLLO X ROLL
ART APOLLO ROLL
QRS AUTOGRAPH AUTOMATIC ROLL
PRICE & TEEPLE ART SYMPHONOLA ROLL
(Expression rolls)
11¼" wide; spaced 9 holes per inch

1 Full vacuum to stack
2 Sustaining pedal
3 Expression soft, 4-step ratchet
4 Expression loud, 4-step ratchet
5 Rewind
6 Shutoff
7 to 92, 86 playing notes, B to C
93 Bass hammer rail
94 Treble hammer rail
95 Accent
96 Play

This scale is the same as that used on Seeburg XP rolls sold by the Automatic Music Roll Company.

SOLO ART APOLLO ROLL
SOLO APOLLO ROLL
(Expression rolls)
15¼" wide; spaced 9 holes per inch

1 ?
2 Expression soft (in steps)
3 Expression loud (in steps)
4 Expression soft (in steps)
5 Expression loud (in steps)
6 to 31, solo stack notes 1 to 26
32 to 102, main stack notes 1 to 71
103 to 128, solo stack notes 27 to 52
129 Solo stack note 53?
130 and 131, Lock and cancel?
132 Rewind
133 ?
134 Sustaining pedal?

Holes 2-3 and 4-5 seem to operate expression stepping ratchets (which go from loudest to softest in steps as in the Apollo X) for the two stacks, respectively. The main stack notes (on which most of the music is played) are located toward the center of the roll, with the bass and treble sections of the solo stack located to the left and right sides. This piano theoretically could play any note or group of notes at one volume level simultaneously with any other note or chord played at a second different volume level, unlike any other known reproducing or expression piano, but with its cumbersome two stacks, sluggish expression system (when compared to a full reproducing piano), wide roll, and lack of automatic tracking device it was never very popular, judging from its extreme rarity today.

APOLLO ARTECHO ROLL
ARTECHO ROLL
(Fully reproducing rolls)
11¼" wide; spaced 9 holes per inch

1 Bass intensity 1
2 Bass intensity 2
3 Bass intensity 3
4 Sustaining pedal
5 Cancel bass intensities
6 Bass diminuendo
7 Bass crescendo
8 Bass hammer rail up
9 to 91, 83 playing notes, B to A
92 Short perforation: cancel pianissimo, hammer rails down
   Long perforation: rewind
93 Treble hammer rail up
94 Pianissimo
95 Treble crescendo
96 Treble diminuendo
97 Cancel treble intensities
98 Treble intensity 3
99 Treble intensity 2
100 Treble intensity 1

The Artecho (or Art Echo) system is fully reproducing, unlike the Apollo X and Solo Art Apollo, which are expression pianos (similar to the Recordo).

A modified version of the Art Echo roll was used on the Wurlitzer Autograph coin-operated piano.

AEOLIAN COMPANY
Duo-Art Reproducing Pianos

The Duo-Art reproducing piano, a product of the Aeolian Company, was formally introduced in 1913. At the time Aeolian was the premier manufacturer of home player pianos, mainly under the Pianola trademark. In addition, Aeolian's large player reed organs, the Orchestrelle and Solo Orchestrelle, as well as a series of home pipe organs found ready acceptance in the marketplace at the time.

The Duo-Art, a full reproducing piano, was incorporated into various types of upright and grand pianos, including Aeolian, Stroud, Wheelock, Steck, Weber, and, most expensive of all, Steinway. While most models were electrically-operated, foot-pumped Duo-Arts achieved some measure of popularity, especially in Great Britain, where it was considered an advantage to be able to add individual expression (via pumping intensity and by hand manipulation of the auxiliary controls near the keyboard) to that recorded by the artists.

In the early days most Duo-Arts were sold under the Duo-Art Pianola name. Later, Pianola was dropped from the nomenclature. The Duo-Art system remained constant from 1913 until after the 1932 merger between the American Piano Company (makers of the competing Ampico reproducing piano) and the Aeolian Company. Around 1935 a redesigned Duo-Art system, which incorporated certain mechanical design changes which gave the technician easier access to the piano action, was made for use in grand pianos, but due to the depressed market at the time only a few were sold. Duo-Art rolls remained of the same scale and layout throughout the entire production period.

Duo-Art rolls were perforated in America and in England. Some very elaborate rolls, with illustrations and stories printed across the entire width of the paper, were made as part of the Audiographic series. Duo-Art rolls were made of varying lengths ranging from just a few minutes of playing time to over ten minutes.

Together with the Ampico, and to a lesser extent the Welte-Mignon, the Duo-Art system was a leader in the American market. Many thousands of instruments were sold, including thousands of the top-of-the-line Steinway models.

DUO-ART ROLL
11¼" wide; spaced 9 holes per inch

1 Rewind
2 Sustaining pedal
3 Bass theme
4 Accompaniment intensity 1
5 Accompaniment intensity 2
6 Accompaniment intensity 3
7 Accompaniment intensity 4
8 to 87, 80 playing notes, C# to G#
88 Theme intensity 4
89 Theme intensity 3
90 Theme intensity 2
91 Theme intensity 1
92 Treble theme
93 Shutoff/replay
94 Hammer rail

A beautiful Steinway Duo-Art piano in a Spanish Mediterranean case. Steinway and other piano makes using the Duo-Art system were offered in a wide variety of period or art cases, including Louis XV, Louis XVI, Queen Anne, Sheraton, William & Mary, and Jacobean, to mention just a few. (Courtesy of the University of Illinois)

Detail of a Steinway Duo-Art reproducing grand piano of the 1920s.

THIS music-roll is my interpretation. It was recorded by me for the Duo-Art and I hereby authorize its use with that instrument.

NUMBER 6099

The DUO ART PIANOLA
The Authorized Medium of the Great Pianists

THE illustrations at the top of these pages reproduce, in part, the labels on Duo-Art music-rolls. The statements these labels contain are signed by Ignace Jan Paderewski and Josef Hofmann and chronicle a new and revolutionary development in musical art.

The statements which are similar are without qualification. "My interpretation" embraces the talent and genius in pianism for which Paderewski and Hofmann are famous. It means that these rolls when played upon the Duo-Art Pianola, reproduce Paderewski and Hofmann at the pianoforte—reproduce their technique, their rhythm, their dynamics, their pedaling, and as Hofmann has stated elsewhere in a published letter, their "very personality with all that implies."

The World's Greatest Pianists

Paderewski and Hofmann have made many such Duo-Art music-rolls. Every owner of a Duo-Art Pianola has access to these rolls—access to the magnificent piano-playing of the greatest pianists that ever lived. What such a privilege means in enjoyment for the music-lover, in education for the music-student, is beyond computation.

Bauer · Ganz · Friedheim · Byrd · Lambert · Beebe · Berumen · Henry · Brard · Shattuck · Oottlow · Rubinstein · Cortot · Gabrilowitsch

Duo-Art, Ampico, and Welte each tried to outdo the others in their lists of featured pianists as this Aeolian Duo-Art advertisement indicates.

Steinway Duo-Art reproducing grand piano in a Louis XV art-style mahogany case. This instrument, once owned by the Fisher family in Michigan (of Fisher Body Works), was sold by Wallace Donoghue in the early 1970s. Now restored by the Carty Piano Company, it entertains once again with the melodies of Gershwin, Paderewski, and other Duo-Art artists.

EMPECO EXPRESSION PIANOS

The Empeco system, popular in Europe but virtually unknown in America, was used by Philipps, Kastner, and several other European manufacturers in the same manner that the Recordo system in America was installed in different piano makes. While most Empeco pianos were made for home use, some Empeco systems were installed in coin-operated instruments for use in public locations.

EMPECO ROLL
(Expression roll)
11 1/8" wide; spaced 9 holes per inch

1 Mezzoforte
2 Decrescendo
3 Mandolin off/on
4 Sustaining pedal
5 Bass accent
6 to 91, 86 playing notes
92 Rewind
93 Shutoff
94 Treble accent
95 Crash decrescendo
96 Treble crash
97 Cancel
98 Mezzo piano

Hole 3 has three vertical holes in the tracker bar which are multiplexed to turn the mandolin on and off.

RECORDO EXPRESSION PIANOS

The Recordo trademark, originally used to designate a specific type of piano, came to be widely used to indicate an expression (not fully reproducing) system incorporated in a wide variety of pianos. Some popular makes of rolls with Recordo coding are: Aria Divina Reproducing Roll, Imperial Automatic Electric, International for Expression Pianos, MelOdee Expression Roll, Pianostyle for Expression Pianos, QRS Recordo, Recordo, Rose Valley Recording Roll, U.S. Auto-Art, Vocalstyle Home Recital Series, Vocalstyle Reproducing, and Vocalstyle Reproduco.

A number of different Recordo expression mechanisms were made by widely separated manufacturers. While all Recordos use the same tracker scale format, there are at least three different types of Recordo rolls, each with its own system of intensity coding. Each of the many different expression systems will work best with one specific type of these three variations.

Recordo "A" rolls (about 1915 to late 1923) are coded to accommodate a mechanism capable of 10 intensity levels, using various combinations of the four perforations. Recordo "B" rolls (late 1923 to January 1926) are used by mechanisms having only five levels, each level overriding any lower level. Recordo "C" rolls (February 1926 to February 1930) are used by rare expression mechanisms having full binary control providing 16 different levels. (Note: the designations A, B, and C were originated by Recordo researcher Robert Billings and were not used in original terminology.)

Pianos using the Recordo system were made in large numbers and achieved a wide popularity.

RECORDO ROLL
ARIA DIVINA REPRODUCING ROLL
IMPERIAL AUTOMATIC ELECTRIC ROLL
INTERNATIONAL FOR EXPRESSION PIANOS ROLL
MELODEE EXPRESSION ROLL
PIANOSTYLE FOR EXPRESSION PIANOS ROLL
QRS RECORDO ROLL
RECORDO RED LABEL ROLL
ROSE VALLEY RECORDING ROLL
U.S. AUTO-ART ROLL
VOCALSTYLE HOME RECITAL SERIES ROLL
VOCALSTYLE REPRODUCING ROLL
VOCALSTYLE REPRODUCO ROLL
  and others
11¼" wide; spaced 9 holes per inch
(Expression rolls)

1 Bass hammer rail
2 Mandolin
3 Sustaining pedal
4 Play
5 Rewind
6 to 88, 83 playing notes, B to A
89 4th intensity
90 3rd intensity
91 2nd intensity
92 1st intensity
93 Treble hammer rail

LUDWIG HUPFELD, A.G.
Reproducing Pianos

In 1904 the firm of Ludwig Hupfeld, located in Leipzig, Germany, introduced the Phonoliszt, a piano with expression. The Phonoliszt system was continued in production for over two decades, during which time it was installed in dozens of different upright and grand pianos. In addition, it was incorporated into the famous Phonoliszt-Violina violin player. The Phonoliszt pianos found wide use in hotels, restaurants, and other public locations where they were operated by means of coins deposited in nearby wallboxes.

In 1905 the Hupfeld Dea (often written as DEA, in capital letters) was developed. It was Hupfeld's answer to the Welte-Mignon, the initial reproducing piano system which had astounded the musical world.

The Dea system attracted acclaim. Today, collectors consider the finely-crafted systems to be among the best ever constructed. The musical performance of the Dea was excellent, and an illustrious roster of pianists recorded for Dea rolls. But, the Dea existed in the shadow of the Welte-Mignon, and despite the Dea's attributes, the instruments were never sold in large quantities.

After World War I Hupfeld introduced the Triphonola reproducing piano. Using the standard 88-note roll size format (11¼" wide, holes spaced 9 per inch), the system was made in two ways: the Duophonola, which was electrically operated, and the Triphonola, which was electrically operated but which also had an auxiliary foot pump (in response to the sentiment, especially prevalent in England, that it was desirable to foot-pump a reproducing piano in order to add one's own interpretation to the music expression). Today, Hupfeld reproducing systems of all types are highly prized by collectors.

HUPFELD DEA ROLL
40.5 cm. wide; 26+ holes per 10 cm.

1 to 6, six bass expression levels from PP to FF
7 to 49, Notes in order A to D#
50 Sustaining pedal on
51 Playing note E
52 Sustaining pedal off
53 Playing note F
54 Single punch: shutoff; longer perforation: rewind
55 Playing note F#
56 Hammer rail up/down
57 Playing note G
58 Crash valve on/off; also motor resistance lower/higher
59 to 96, Notes in order G# to A
97 Bass expression accelerator
98 Blank
99 Blank
100 Treble expression accelerator
101 to 106, Six treble expression levels from FF to PP

Each expression mechanism, one for the bass and one for the treble, has six levels or intensities. When one of the six expression holes is punched (holes 1-6 for bass and 101-106 for treble), the expression mechanism moves slowly to that intensity level and stays at that level until another expression hole is punched.

The slow movement of the expression mechanism causes a slow crescendo or decrescendo, depending on whether it is moving to a higher or lower setting. When a fast crescendo, fast decrescendo, or quick intensity level change between notes is desired, the bass or treble expression accelerator hole (97 or 100) is punched together with the expression hole.

The soft pedal is turned on and off by the same track in the roll; a single punch is "off," and a longer perforation is "on." The crash valve is turned on and off in the same way. When it is "on" the motor resistance is also lowered, causing the pump speed to increase.

HUPFELD PHONOLISZT ROLL
(Rolls marked "Pt.")
11 5/8" wide; 26+ holes per 10 cm.

1 Playing note F
2 to 34, G to D#
35 Sustaining pedal
36 E
37 Soft
38 F
39 Mezzo forte
40 F#
41 Crescendo
42 G
43 Bass hammer rail
44 to 77, G# to F

37+39+41 = Shutoff
37+39+41+43 = Rewind

HUPFELD DUOPHONOLA ROLL
HUPFELD TRIPHONOLA ROLL
HUPFELD ANIMATIC T ROLL
11¼" wide; spaced 9 holes per inch

1 Hammer rail
2 Accompaniment MF-PP
3 Theme MF-FF
4 Sustaining pedal
5 Bass theme
6 to 93, 88 playing notes, A to C
94 Treble theme
95 Accompaniment expression accelerator
96 Theme MF-PP
97 Theme expression accelerator
98 Accompaniment MF-FF

1+95 = Rewind
1+97 = Shutoff

Each pneumatic system, theme and accompaniment, has two bellows which can move from open to closed either slowly or quickly. The zero position is MF, with the PP-MF bellows closed and the MF-FF bellows open.

Features of the Triphonola system were incorporated into the piano part of the Hupfeld Pan Orchestra orchestrion, to which refer.

View of the roll mechanism of a Grotrian-Steinweg grand piano equipped with a Hupfeld Dea reproducing mechanism. Although the Dea system was devised in 1905, it was not until 1907 that instruments were available for public sale. When Hupfeld applied for the Dea trademark on January 10, 1907, the firm, to be fully protected, noted that the Dea term could be applied to "piano-playing devices and built-in players for pianos, harmoniums, and organs, self-playing pianos, self-playing harmoniums, organs and orchestrions, reproducing pianos," and other types of roll-operated instruments. (Siegfried Wendel Collection)

An interior view of a fine keyboard-style Hupfeld Dea reproducing piano originally sold, probably circa 1910-1914, by Hupfeld's agent in Stockholm, Sweden. (Mekanisk Musik Museum, Copenhagen, Denmark)

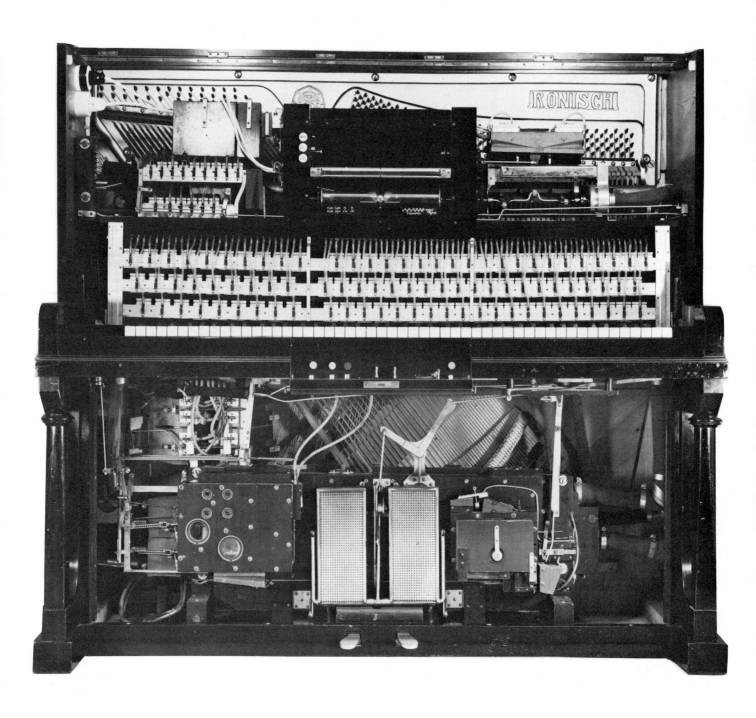

Interior view of an upright Hupfeld Triphonola reproducing piano built in the 1920s. The instrument can be foot-pumped or, by means of a separate pump, be electrically-operated. The pneumatic stack features aluminum unit valves attached by springs. These can be removed easily for servicing. (Daniel Fibbi Collection)

J.D. PHILIPPS & SONS
Reproducing Pianos

J.D. Philipps & Sons of Frankfurt-am-Main, Germany made the Duca, a reproducing piano, from about 1908 until the late 1920s (with advertisements continuing until 1931). The system achieved moderate sales success, mainly in Europe (although Wurlitzer imported a few to America), but in a European market dominated by the Welte-Mignon, the quantities made were relatively small. Case designs of the Duca were varied and included keyboardless models, styles with automatic roll changers, a vorsetzer (push-up model), and coin-operated types. Over 2,000 different rolls were made for the Duca.

PHILIPPS DUCA ROLL
(Marked "PD" on leader)
10 3/8" wide
Holes spaced 4 per centimeter

1 Bass sforzando
2 Bass mezzoforte off
3 Bass mezzoforte on
4 Bass decrescendo
5 Bass crescendo
6 Bass fast soft
7 Bass fast loud
8 Hammer rail down
9 Hammer rail half up
10 Shutoff
11 to 91, 81 playing notes, C to G#
92 Hammer rail up
93 Rewind
94 Sustaining pedal on
95 Sustaining pedal off
96 Treble fast loud
97 Treble fast soft
98 Treble crescendo
99 Treble decrescendo
100 Treble mezzoforte on
101 Treble mezzoforte off
102 Treble sforzando

The Philipps Duca II and III had all of the above functions, with separate bass and treble expression mechanisms. The Duca I apparently had only one incomplete expression unit, providing sforzando, crescendo, and decrescendo.

PHILIPPS DUOLA ROLL

1 Mezzo forte
2 Hammer rail up
3 Soft bass
4 Sustaining pedal
5 Bass accent
6 to 91, 86 playing notes, A to A#
92 Rewind
93 Shutoff
94 Treble accent
95 Hammer rail up fast
96 Fortissimo
97 Forte
98 Melody soft

The Philipps Duola piano was primarily made for use in commercial locations. Typically, the Duola was in an upright keyboard-style case, ornamented with lamps and/or mirrors. Coins were dropped into one or more wallboxes which were electrically connected to the piano. Note the similarity of this to the Empeco scale.

PHILIPPS P.A. ROLL
8 7/8" wide

1 Blank
2 Crescendo
3 Decrescendo
4 Blank
5 Sustaining pedal off
6 Hammer rail down
7 Playing note
8 Blank
9 to 12, playing notes
13 Sustaining pedal on
14 Fast loud
15 Fast soft
16 Mezzoforte on
17 Mezzoforte off
18 Blank
19 to 27, playing notes
28 Rewind
29 to 50, playing notes
51 Shutoff
52 to 78, playing notes
79 Blank
80 Blank
81 Blank
82 Hammer rail up
83 Blank
84 Blank (or harmonium on)
85 Blank
86 Sforzando
87 Blank
88 Blank

The preceding scale has 63 playing notes. Its main use was probably on coin-operated instruments for commercial purposes. Holes 6 and 82 in the preceding scale may be transposed.

TEL-ELECTRIC COMPANY
Expression Pianos

The Tel-Electric Company of Pittsfield, Massachusetts produced two different types of solenoid-operated expression pianos: the Tel-Electric and the Telektra. The rolls consisted of thin brass sheets (5" wide for the Tel-Electric; 6¾" wide for the Telektra) which were read by a series of metal fingers. The devices were offered as attachments which could be fitted to nearly any upright or grand piano. A console or control box contained the roll mechanism and could be located at any distance from the piano. A bank of solenoids mounted under the front of the piano was connected by cable to the console and a power unit.

Formed in 1905, the firm's corporate offices were located at 12 West 23rd Street, New York City, in 1915. The Tel-Electric Company's products seem to have enjoyed about a decade of popularity.

TEL-ELECTRIC ROLL
Thin brass roll
5" wide; spaced 15 holes per inch

1 to 65, 65 playing notes A to C#
66 Hammer rail
67 Accent
68 Sustaining pedal
69 Expression loud
70 Expression normal
71 Expression soft
72 Hammer rail
73 Latch release

In one example reported by Wes Reed, holes 66 and 72 are connected together, possibly to split the electrical load of a very large solenoid.

When hole 73 is opened, power is cut to everything but the roll motor, and the roll rewinds automatically.

TELEKTRA ROLL
Thin brass roll
6¾" wide; spaced 15 holes per inch

(Additional information needed)

WILCOX & WHITE COMPANY
Reproducing Pianos

The Artrio-Angelus reproducing system (sometimes called Angelus-Artrio, and often just Angelus in original sales literature) was made by Wilcox & White of Meriden, Connecticut, a famous maker of player pianos, reed organs, and organettes.

Introduced around 1915, the Artrio-Angelus was offered primarily in pianos made by Mehlin & Son. Financial difficulties overtook the firm around 1920, causing bankruptcy a year later. The Simplex Player Action Company acquired the Artrio-Angelus business and continued to make units through the 1920s. The era of greatest popularity of the system seems to have been from about 1915 to 1920. Production and sales were modest in comparison to the "big three," Ampico, Duo-Art, and Welte, but nevertheless quite a few were sold.

A recording studio was maintained in Meriden, Connecticut. The Artrio-Angelus repertoire includes many well-known pianists.

ARTRIO-ANGELUS ROLL
11¼" wide; spaced 9 holes per inch

1 Accompaniment intensity
2 Leaker closed, raises general vacuum level
3 Rewind
4 Sustaining pedal
5 Bass theme
6 Accompaniment intensity
7 Accompaniment intensity
8 to 92, 85 playing notes, A# to A#
93 Theme intensity 5
94 Theme intensity 4
95 Treble theme
96 Theme intensity 3
97 Theme intensity 2
98 Hammer rail
99 Theme intensity 1

M. WELTE & SONS
Welte Reproducing Pianos

In 1904 the world was thrilled with the introduction of a hitherto-unknown device: the reproducing piano. After several years of effort, Karl Bockisch, of M. Welte & Sons, and Hugo Popper, Leipzig music merchant and manufacturer, produced the Welte-Mignon. Edwin Welte provided assistance as well. In America an example of the device was shown at the St. Louis World's Fair in the same year.

The Welte-Mignon featured mechanisms which would not only play the recorded notes (in the manner of a player piano) but which would also re-enact or reproduce the playing intensity of the left and right hands and the pedaling. By 1906 the Welte-Mignon was being offered for sale in music showrooms all over Europe.

An idea of the impact of the instrument can be gained from the testimonial given by Josef Hofmann, who was one of many pianists who recorded for Welte-Mignon rolls:

"The incomparable Welte-Mignon art piano has opened an eventful future before the musical world. Henceforth the piano player will be on a level with the productive artist in regard to the imperishability of his work, since he will live for all time in his work. What a loss it means to us not to have had the Welte-Mignon long ago! But what a blessing it will prove to future generations!

The Welte-Mignon acquired a formidable reputation. While other leading makers (notably Ludwig Hupfeld, who introduced the Dea in 1905) worked on or made reproducing systems, M. Welte & Sons early developed an insurmountable lead. Hugo Popper, who at the time may have been the leading musical merchant in Germany, had the exclusive agency in that country. Popper, a connoisseur and a gentleman with refined tastes, had entree into the musical world and was able to enlist prominent pianists' support for the project. At the outset there were many artists who feared that the Welte-Mignon either would not reproduce their playing correctly or, equally bad, would lessen the demand for their in-person services at concerts. Popper allayed these concerns and imbued the artists with the thought that the Welte-Mignon would immortalize their playing, as indeed it did.

Welte-Mignon systems were installed in a variety of case styles, including upright and grand pianos, cabinet-style (keyboardless) players, and vorsetzers (designed to be pushed up to a piano keyboard).

Early Welte-Mignons used red or white paper rolls. These are familiarly known as "red Welte" instruments by collectors today. The red Welte rolls measure about 12 7/8" wide. Later variations and evolutions of the Welte-Mignon system include the "green Welte" rolls, predominantly made on green paper, and with 11¼" width and 9-holes-to-the-inch spacing, and, especially popular in America, the Welte (Licensee) rolls, which were used on a redesigned system and which were 11¼" wide with 9 holes per inch. Additional information concerning Welte-Mignon can be found in *The Encyclopedia of Automatic Musical Instruments* as well as various other Vestal Press publications and reprints.

In America, Welte-Mignon pianos were first sold to the public in 1906, during which year Welte set up a new firm in the United States for this purpose. From that point until about 1914-1916, Welte was predominant. Following the introduction of the Duo-Art and Ampico systems, the aggressive marketing of the Aeolian Company and the American Piano Company, progenitors of these two competitors, the sales of the Welte-Mignon declined. Within a short time after that, the American properties of Welte, including a factory in Poughkeepsie, New York, were seized by the Alien Property Custodian as reparations for the war. After that point few if any "red Welte" instruments were sold in America.

Under complex licensing arrangements the Auto Pneumatic Action Company of New York acquired the right to use the Welte name in connection with reproducing pianos. The word "Licensee" in parentheses was added to the trademark, and instruments sold under this arrangement were known as Welte-Mignon (Licensee) or, as shortened in collectors' terminology today, Welte (Licensee) pianos. These featured a completely redesigned system. Made in large quantities, these (Licensee) pianos achieved a strong sales volume in the 1920s. Over 100 different makes of upright and grand pianos featured this system.

WELTE-MIGNON "Red Welte" ROLL
12 7/8" wide; almost 8 holes per inch

1 Bass mezzoforte off
2 Bass mezzoforte on
3 Bass crescendo off
4 Bass crescendo on
5 Bass sforzando off
6 Bass sforzando on
7 Hammer rail down
8 Hammer rail up
9 Motor resistance valve off (slower)
10 Motor resistance valve on (faster)
11 to 90, 80 playing notes, C to G
91 Rewind
92 Blank
93 Sustaining pedal on
94 Sustaining pedal off
95 Treble sforzando on
96 Treble sforzando off
97 Treble crescendo on
98 Treble crescendo off
99 Treble mezzoforte on
100 Treble mezzoforte off

WELTE-MIGNON (LICENSEE) ROLL
11¼" wide; spaced 9 holes per inch

1 Bass mezzoforte off
2 Bass mezzoforte on
3 Bass crescendo off
4 Bass crescendo on
5 Bass sforzando off
6 Bass sforzando on
7 Hammer rail down
8 Hammer rail up
9 to 88, 80 playing notes, C to G
89 Rewind
90 Blank (shutoff on some)
91 Sustaining pedal on
92 Sustaining pedal off
93 Treble sforzando on
94 Treble sforzando off
95 Treble crescendo on
96 Treble crescendo off
97 Treble mezzoforte on
98 Treble mezzoforte off

The replay hole in the tracker bar is positioned between holes 1 and 2.

GREEN WELTE ROLL
11¼'' wide; spaced 9 holes per inch

1 Bass sforzando off
2 Bass mezzoforte
3 Sustaining pedal
4 Bass crescendo
5 Bass sforzando on
6 to 93, 88 playing notes
94 Treble sforzando on
95 Treble crescendo
96 Hammer rail
97 Treble mezzoforte
98 Treble sforzando off

Unlike the Red Welte and Welte (Licensee), which use lock and cancel perforations for most expression functions, the Green Welte primarily uses chain perforations. "Crescendo" holes 4 and 95 produce slow crescendo; when released, slow decrescendo occurs. "Sforzando on" holes 5 and 95 produce fast crescendo. "Sforzando off" holes 1 and 98 produce fast decrescendo. Holes 2 and 97 control bass and treble mezzoforte hooks as in the other Welte systems, but the hooks stay engaged only as long as the holes are punched, requiring no cancel perforation.

All Green Welte rolls play at tempo 70. Rewind is activated by a long perforation at hole 1.

The Welte Vorsetzer, or push-up piano player, enabled the owner to utilize the Welte-Mignon reproducing system on any grand or upright piano. These devices were extremely popular, and it is believed that thousands were sold.

Detail of a Steinway grand piano which incorporates an original Welte-Mignon reproducing system.
(Claes O. Friberg Collection)

FACTORY PHOTOGRAPH
STYLE 169 $3600.°°

This photograph of the 1920s shows a fine Stieff piano (made in Baltimore) equipped with a Welte (Licensee) mechanism in a drawer. This type of Welte device was available in over 100 different piano brands.

IGNACE J. PADEREWSKI RECORDING
HIS PLAYING FOR THE WELTE·MIGNON

M. WELTE & SONS, Inc.

FREIBURG i/B GERMANY   FOUNDED 1832   POUGHKEEPSIE NEW YORK

Manufacturers by Special Appointment to Imperial and Royal Courts

THE WELTE·MIGNON PIANOS AND THE WELTE PHILHARMONIC ORGANS

STUDIO 273 FIFTH AVENUE, N.Y.

February 18, 1915.

Peter Bacigalupi & Sons,
908 Market St.,
San Francisco, Calif.

Gentlemen:-

      We wish to call your attention to the new "1915" model Welte-Mignon, for we believe you fully appreciate that the day of the Reproduction Piano has arrived. And now that it is here you should know what is going on, so that you can supply your customers with "<u>THE ONLY PLAYER PIANO IN THE WORLD</u>" that automatically reproduces the actual playing of the "<u>GREATEST PIANISTS</u>" just as if they were personally seated at the key-board.

      <u>"NO PUMPING OR PERSONAL MANIPULATION REQUIRED."</u>

      A small noiseless motor running on either direct or alternating current, and attached to any convenient electric light fixture, furnishes the motive power. There are no foot-pedals to tax your strength, or intricate levers to try your science. With the introduction of the music-roll, and the impetus to the motor, the rendition of a composition becomes complete.

      Our new 1915 models are as near trouble-proof as it will ever be possible to build such an instrument. The mechanism has been simplified to a minimum, so that any reliable piano mechanic can adjust it easily.

M. WELTE & SONS, INC. Feb. 18, 1915.

Peter Bacigalupi & Sons. - 2 - CONTINUED

"WELTE-MIGNON AT $1000."

We are now producing a Welte-Mignon that can be retailed at $1000, and pay the dealer a handsome profit. Our greatly increased output and up-to-date factories have made this price possible. Also, for the same reason, we have reduced the prices of Welte-Mignon music from 25% to 50%. This brings our artists' rolls recorded by Paderewski, Hofmann, Lhevinne, de Pachmann, etc., within the reach of everyone.

Let us send you our 1915 Upright Models that retail for $1000, $1150, $1250, $1500 and $1800, with our Cabinet Attachment for grand pianos at $800. Set aside a special room in your building for a "WELTE-MIGNON STUDIO," and we can assure you that you will not only build up a very profitable and exclusive patronage for the Welte-Mignon, but you will add dignity to your store.

"STUDIO RECITALS."

No form of publicity will create instantaneous interest in the Welte-Mignon so satisfactorily as frequent "STUDIO RECITALS" by world renowned pianists, all of whom record their playing for the "MIGNON." These recitals bring to your warerooms the most desirable clientele, and in addition to their constructive value in developing the Welte propaganda, will prove of inestimable benefit to your general business.

"LET US TELL YOU HOW TO EDUCATE YOUR PEOPLE TO BETTER MUSIC."

Trusting we may have the pleasure of an early response, together with your valued order, we are

Cordially yours,

Burton Collver

Vice Pres. & Gen. Mgr.

BC/EH

Peter Bacigalupi & Sons, the main retailer of coin pianos, orchestrions, and related items (such as Edison phonographs) in San Francisco during the early 20th century, received many solicitations from makers of various types of automatic musical instruments, the Welte letter shown here being typical.

Interior view of an original "Red Welte" upright reproducing grand piano. All of the various Welte systems operate on the same basic principles, but various designs, layouts, and configurations will be found. The above instrument operates on DC current by means of a rectifier. The original DC motor is used in order to utilize the perforation on the roll which will speed up the motor under certain conditions when extra demand is put on the pump for vacuum, such as a loud fortissimo passage. This piano was manufactured in Welte's Poughkeepsie, New York factory, probably around 1915. (Courtesy of Ellsworth O. Johnson)

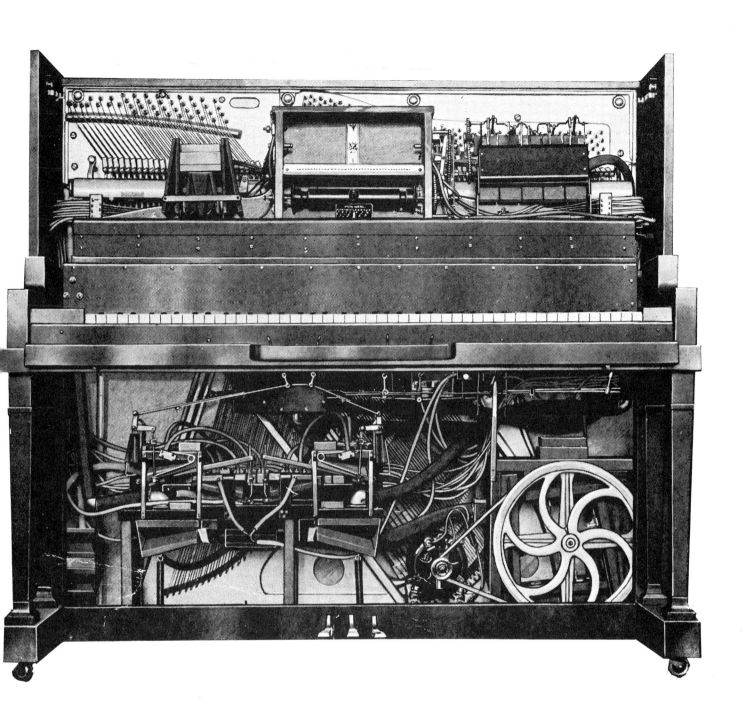

Original Welte instruction diagram showing the Welte-Mignon (Licensee) reproducing action installed in a typical upright piano. At one time the Welte (Licensee) action was available in over 100 different piano brands. Whereas the Aeolian Company and the American Piano company installed their Duo-Art and Ampico systems in their own "house brands" of pianos for the most part, the independent manufacturers of pianos often used the Welte (Licensee) system.

FOLLOWING PAGE: Underside view of a Welte-Mignon (Licensee) reproducing action installed in a typical grand piano. From a Welte instruction manual of the 1920s.

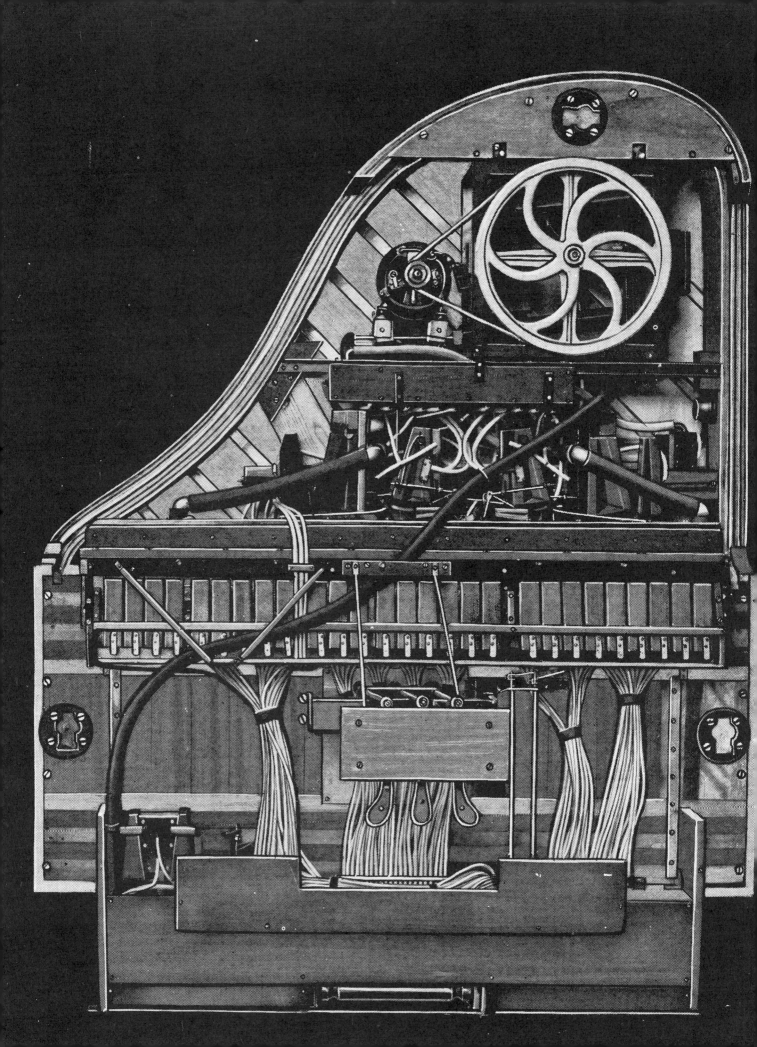

ALLAN HOOVER
ROOM 2740
420 LEXINGTON AVENUE
NEW YORK, N.Y. 10017

April 13, 1970

Mr. Warren Dale
Crest Player Pianos
934 W. Foothill
Azusa, California 91702

Dear Mr. Dale:

Your letter of April 4 has been awaiting my return to town.

In regard to the history of the Chase Piano: It was presented to my mother in the White House many years ago and was placed in the upstairs Oval family sitting room. This has passed down through my side of the family to my son. Ignace Paderewski, the pianist who was also President of Poland, was a great friend of the family. He particularly enjoyed manipulating the controls manually, after having shut off the automatic reproduction. The musical effects he could thus bring out of the rolls were truly phenominal to the pleasure of us all. He seemed to take great delight in putting his own expression into the music.

We have enjoyed this instrument for many years.

I trust this provides the information you are seeking.

Sincerely,

Allan Hoover

AH'lc
P.S. In regard to the piano bench, various members of the family--none of us--can remember having seen it for years.

Allan Hoover furnishes some details concerning a beautiful A.B. Chase Welte (Licensee) grand piano which was once used in the White House during Herbert Hoover's administration. (Courtesy of Warren Dale)

Norwich Town,Connecticut April 14 1950

Mr. Richard C. Simonton,
The Pacific Network,
6906 Santa Blvd.
Los Angeles, California.

Dear Mr. Simonton:

        Your name first came to my attention in an article of The
New York Times, March 26th, entitled: Record, Piano Rolls, Per-
formanes by Outstanding Composers Virtuosos Restord Form; also in
Time Magazine, issue of April 3rd.

        Was particularly impressed in that you visted Freiburg,
Baden, Germany and called upon my cousin Edwin Welte and his
brother-in-law Karl Bockisch. Having visited there myself seven
times since 1901, am taking the literty of writing to you in the
hope of sharing some reminiscenes. The old firm was known as
M.Welte & Soegne G.m.b.H. (Ltd.) and was located on Lehener Strasse
between Clara and Wensinger Strassen. Mr. Edwin sent me a picture
of the factory showing the walls which were all that remained of
the factory after the air raids of Nov.24th, 1944.

        My uncle Berthold Welte (Edwin's father), Uncle Michael jr.
and Emil Welte (my father) were brothers, sons of the founder,
Michael Welte sr. who was born in Voehrnbach, Black Forest in 1807
and died 1880 in Freiburg.

        Enclosed is an article that appeared in our local paper,
the Norwich Record of April 2nd, 1950 and that gives a full des-
scription of the Welte family.

        The old firm was founded in 1832 by Michael Welte and
later he admitted his three sons. In 1901, the grandsons, Edwin
and Carl were admitted into the firm plus Karl M. Bockisch who
had married Edwin's sister. Karl Bockisch was born 1878, Edwin
1876 and Carl 1872, so I am the oldest survivor of the firm.
The Preferred Shares, or assets of the German firm was divided
amongst the older Weltes and the surplus after the 5% for Preferred
Shares was paid out, was divided as follows: 3/12 to K.Bockich,
4/12 to Edwin Welte and 5/12 to Carl M. Welte.

        Whenever I visited Freiburg, my visits lasted several
months at a time, enjoying the hospitality of the Weltes, among
them my father's married sisters. The surrounding countryside is
very beautiful. Remembering this, I thought best to get in touch
with Mr. Simonton and get some first hand information as to just
what happened on his visit to Freiburg, how he happened to pick
out Mr. Edwin and what he thinks of the grandeur of the scenery
around Freiburg and the cheerful inhabitants.

        Incidentally might mention I was in Freiburg 1901 when
Mr. Edwin was working on the device, later known as the Welte-Mignon,
which reproduced the exact interpretation of the pianist when he
recorded his playing. Mr. Edwin brought the first Player to New
York City in 1904 where it was exhibited at our New York studio and

and later, at the St. Louis World Fair 1904.

My father, Emil Welte, came to the United States in 1866 and opened a store on East 14th Street, New York City, opposite Steinway Hall. The American branch was known as M.Welte & Sons Inc., and later opened a studio at 557 Fifth Ave. until World War I, when the assets of the firm were taken over by the Alien Property Custodian. The holdings of Mr. Edwin Welte and Mr. Karl Bockisch were sold at public auction- my father and I having retired earlier from the business. Some prominent people took over the American branch, but by that time, 1920, interest in Player pianos was on the wane and the Weltes went out of business. The same thing happened to the mother house in Freiburg which went bankrupt in 1933.

The Welte factory was completely destroyed by the American flyers in two devastating raids on Freiburg in Nov. 1944 when 75% of the old city of Freiburg was destroyed. Mr. Bockisch did repair a part of the buildings and is contiuing in the trade of repairing organs and pianos.

My cousin Edwin is working on a new model Lichttonorgel as he calls it. His first successful model was destroyed by air raids while on exhibit in Leipzig. I believe a better title for his new style organ would be the Photo-Cell Organ. Perhaps he explained the new organ to you. According to the reports I read after it was exhibited at the Philharmonie in Berlin 1938, it must be a marvelous instrument, far superior to any electronic organ yet produced since it actually reproduces the photographed tones (from disks) of the finest organs in Europe. I hope you did get the opportunity to hear it so I can get your valuable point of view.

Mr. Edwin sent me sketches and descriptions of his latest invention in the hope I could revise the text for American comprehension. Mr. Edwin, though born in Germany, has an excellent knowledge of English and the changes I made in the text he sent were but minor ones. But what puzzles me, is Mr. Edwin's contention that his Lichttonorgel is unique. I have found similar patents here and in France; meaning, the ideas Mr. Edwin uses do not seem new but have been used and patented by others. Mr. Edwin asked me to give his organ an English name. Licht (light) Ton (Tone) Orgel (Organ). Light-Tone-Organ does not make sense. Considering the idea involved, I thought Photo-Electric Organ would be more comprehensible here. But such a title is not new and has been used.

Now I have placed my cards on the table and what I would like, is to get a full report from you about your visit to Freiburg. What were your impressions of Mr. Edwin Welte and of Mr.Bockisch, who also is a distinguished technician in the musical instrument field.

Undoubtedly you have many remembrances to cherish in the years to come of your trip to Germany. Let me hear from you.

Sincerely

Carl M. Welte

CARL M. WELTE

P.S.You may keep the newspaper clipping which I enclosed.

Norwich Record april 27 1950

RUDOLPH WURLITZER COMPANY
Expression Pianos

The following scale, taken from an original Wurlitzer scale stick, is apparently from some type of piano with expression or reproducing abilities.

UNKNOWN (WURLITZER?) EXPRESSION PIANO
(From original Wurlitzer scale stick)

1 Blank (if present)
2 Blank (if present)
3 Blank (if present)
4 ?
5 Rewind
6 Shutoff
7 Hammer rail up
8 Hammer rail down
9 Sustaining pedal on
10 Sustaining pedal off
11 No. 3 P off
12 No. 3 F off
13 No. 3 FF off
14 No. 3 P on
13 No. 3 F on
16 No. 3 FF on
17 to 96, 80 playing notes, C# to G#,
97 No. 2 P off
98 No. 2 F off
99 No. 2 FF off
100 No. 2 P on
101 No. 2 F on
102 No. 2 FF on
103 No. 1 P off
104 No. 1 F off
105 No. 1 FF off
106 No. 1 P on
107 No. 1 F on
108 No. 1 FF on

One end of the original Wurlitzer scale stick has the following combinations noted: 1st = 1; 2nd = 2; 3rd = 1+2; 4th = 3; 5th = 1+3; 6th = 2+3; 7th = 1+2+3.

Listening to the Hupfeld Dea.

Chapter 5
MUSIC ROLL MAKING

(Photo courtesy of the Colorado Springs Gazette-Telegraph)

Above: Art Reblitz, shown in his workshop-office in Colorado Springs, Colorado, arranges a music roll. Over the years he has produced many new orchestrion rolls, including styles G, 4X, O, and others. A special Wurlitzer Mandolin PianOrchestra roll was made for Knott's Berry Farm, a leading California attraction, who used it on their Style 29-C orchestrion. For Bill Edgerton a new 4X roll with popular tunes was arranged, to be used as a sales aid for reproductions of the famous Seeburg KT Special. When Dave Bowers and his wife Christie were married, Art's wedding gift was a Coinola O roll arrangement of "I Love You Because," one of the Bowers' favorite songs.

Left: Art Reblitz with veteran music roll arranger P.M. Keast, photograph taken about 1970. Elsewhere in the present book Mr. Keast gives his recollection of his employment years ago as an arranger of coin piano and orchestrion rolls for Q.R.S., Clark, and Capitol.

ARRANGING MUSIC ROLLS

by Art Reblitz

A music roll arrangement, like any other artistic creation, begins in the mind of the arranger and is then put down on paper. The process of arranging a roll can be broken into these two basic parts: arranging the music, and notating it on paper.

The first part of the job, arranging the music, is exactly the same as arranging for human-played instruments. The available notes, acoustical qualities of the instrument, and the abilities and limitations of the human or mechanical player must be considered. Then the music is arranged with these factors in mind.

Classical piano or organ music which is available in printed manuscript form is already suitable for the reproducing piano or organ, so it can be put on a roll for one of these instruments with no further arranging. Band and orchestra music is too complex for a music machine, so it must be reduced to a simpler texture to sound good. Popular sheet music, as available in music stores, is arranged for the limitations of the average home pianist, so it is too simple for music machines and must be rearranged to a more complex form in order to produce the desired result.

One either has the basic musical ability to arrange music or one does not. Although music theory, harmony, counterpoint, composition, and arranging are all taught in college music programs, and much useful information can be learned from these courses, the best composers and arrangers have always been those individuals who had a certain knack or talent and who picked up most of what they knew by listening to music.

In planning a musical arrangement for a certain music machine, all the usual musical qualities must be considered: harmony, chord structure and voicing, ornamentation, orchestration (or variety of registration), rhythmic variety, voice leading of countermelodies and bass lines, and all the other factors which go into a fine arrangement. In addition, mechanical qualities such as the note scale of the music machine, its acoustical characteristics, and technical limitations have to be considered during the planning stage of the musical arrangement.

The second part of making a roll, putting the arrangement down on paper, is completely different from arranging for human musicians. Manuscript music, or printed music for humans, is graphically notated in a way which transmits the composer's or arranger's ideas to the performer visually. A lot of music can be condensed into a small space because the human eye is capable of moving from one note to the next, from beginning to end of each line, from one line to the next, and from one page to the next. One note symbol or combination of symbols conveys enough information to the performer to enable the movement of all ten fingers, both feet, and in the case of wind instruments, to vary the air pressure and simultaneously vary the amount of muscle tension in the lips, among other physiological factors. A roll-operated music machine, on the other hand, is not nearly as efficient at assimilating complex information, so its music must be notated in a much more spread-out format. A tracker bar or key frame can have just so many holes or keys because of the practical limitations of paper or cardboard width. The total number of holes or keys must include all notes, expression functions, percussion instruments, and mechanical functions (such as shutoff and rewind). While the entire score, including all the orchestral instrumental parts, for all of the Beethoven symphonies can be printed in a few pocket-size books, no one has ever figured out a way to put all of that information on a roll for even the most sophisticated orchestrion. Indeed, a basic condensed version of the notes, with limited expression perforations, would take up a whole shelf full of rolls for the full unabridged symphonies!

The main difference between manuscript notation and roll notation is the "real time" element built into the rolls. In manuscript music the time value of each note and space is indicated by a visual code which is meaningful to humans (although subject to the performer's interpretation). In a roll, the time value of a note is determined by the length of the hole. Once an arranger gains the concept of time being built into paper travel and hole length, roll arranging becomes very logical. Most arrangers of human music find music machines to be too limiting to be of more than superficial interest, and they are willing to put up with human unpredictability introduced into their music by conductors and performers to gain the human versatility and excitement which music machines lack. However, to the rare music arranger who likes the sound of an automatic piano, orchestrion, band organ, or other machine, roll arranging is extremely fascinating. Music machines do not introduce any human subjectivity into the music, so the arranger of music rolls can depend on hearing his or her music exactly as it was conceived, with 100% reliability.

There are two basic methods of plotting lines on a piece of blank music roll paper. Each requires its own equipment: the keyboard-operated recording piano or the drawing board.

As a recording piano is played, signals from the keys are transmitted electrically or pneumatically to a recording machine which draws lines on a moving roll of blank paper, or to a computer which stores the information for future use. Making rolls by this method is based on the assumptions that suitable equipment is available and that the person who wants to make a roll has the keyboard technique to play the piece. The playing can be done either in real tempo in one playing, or in slow motion in several playings, overdubbing as in a sound recording studio (if the recording piano is capable of this function). No special knowledge of music roll notation is necessary on the part of the keyboard artist, but after the roll is recorded, it must be edited carefully on a drawing board to delete mistakes and to make changes. The quality of the final product is as dependent on the skill of the editor as on the talent of the recording artist and accuracy of the recording machine. The most common uses for a recording piano are for making player piano and reproducing piano rolls. (Interestingly, some reproducing piano rolls are *not* made this way, but are "drafting board music," so to speak.) A recording pipe organ is used similarly to produce reproducing pipe organ rolls. Many excellent rolls have been produced by this method, including nearly all of the old reproducing rolls.

A variation of the usual recording piano was the machine used by the late J. Lawrence Cook for many years at QRS. His piano keyboard was connected directly to a master music roll perforator through a control pedal, and it punched rolls one punch space at a time. After selecting a note or chord, Cook would depress the pedal, the selected note or notes would be punched once, and the paper would advance by one space, ready for the next punch. When he wanted to punch more notes simultaneously than he could reach on the keyboard, he could lock those notes "on" with latching key tabs. Since a quarter note on a word roll might take 12 punches, his process was extremely slow and demanded the unusual talent of mentally subdividing music into extremely tiny increments and then playing it in equally extremely slow motion. For example, at a given moment he might be on the third punch of a four-punch bass note, the 27th punch of a 48-punch sustained melody chord (with one of the inner voices of that chord ready to be changed to a new note a few punches later), the middle of a space between accompaniment chords, some other punch number in a tenor countermelody, and yet another number in an ornamentation figure!

Cook's unusual ability enabled him to arrange and punch rolls simultaneously with no need for further editing. Since he could hear the notes being played as he went along, he could hear and correct any note mistakes before punching them. Since actual punching was controlled by the pedal, everything could be done with precision, eliminating the need for the rhythmic "cleaning up" of recordings which was always necessary when the stylus recording machine was used. Cook's musical output on his recording machine was remarkable, especially considering the fact that he was responsible for nearly all QRS roll arrangements produced over a span of about 40 years after 1927, including most rolls issued during that time under other artists' names such as Kortlander, Wendling, Laney, Scott, and Watters.

A drawing board, in its simplest form, need consist of no more than a transparent grid with vertical note lines and horizontal rhythm lines placed over a light source, with the roll moved over the top surface of it. The grid shows the exact placement of all possible notes within a given section of roll paper. The arranger draws lines where he wants specific notes to occur. This system requires a different note grid for each tracker bar spacing, and a different rhythm grid for each tempo desired. It is used with excellent results by roll arranger David Junchen, for example.

Another setup, used by the author after he saw the picture of Eugene DeRoy on page 623 of *The Encyclopedia of Automatic Musical Instruments,* consists of a slanting board with two roll spools, a tracker scale stick, and a rhythm scale. The tracker scale stick is inter-

changeable and is mounted horizontally over the top edge of the board. The rhythm scale, which is also interchangeable, extends down the length of the roll, slides to the left and right, and has a pointer riding over the tracker scale. To make a roll, the appropriate scale stick and rhythm scale are inserted, a roll of blank paper is wound on the spools, and everything is aligned carefully. Lines indicating the beginning of each measure are drawn on the margin of the paper. These lines are used as reference points in positioning the paper along the rhythm scale for the correct rhythmic placement of notes. To draw the position of a hole, the paper is moved up or down until the beginning of a measure corresponds to the appropriate mark on the rhythm scale. The rhythm scale is then slid sideways until the pointer indicates the desired note or function on the scale stick, and the note is then drawn with a pencil line extending from one line on the rhythm scale to another. This process is repeated for every single hole in the entire roll. After all the hole positions are drawn, a straightedge is installed horizontally on top of the paper, and cross lines or T lines are drawn to connect the beginnings and endings of all notes which are to be sounded simultaneously. These T lines make it possible for the person who punches the roll to do so more accurately.

Using a drawing board is much more time consuming than using a recording piano for some rolls, such as reproducing piano rolls. But for other types of rolls it is often a desirable method. Also, there are many types of rolls which are impractical to make on a recording piano, including band organ rolls, orchestrion rolls, and specialty rolls such as those for the Encore Automatic Banjo. The idea of building a recording device which will record a pianist, drummer, and xylophonist (or flutist) for making style O orchestrion rolls sounds interesting, but the practical fact of the matter is that there are no dance combos having this instrumentation, and if there were such combos of sufficient musical excellence, it would cost more to hire them and then edit their rolls on a drawing board than to have the rolls arranged on a drawing board in the first place. It is interesting to note that Hupfeld advertised that the percussion effects on the Pan Orchestra roll were "recorded from a man's hand," so perhaps such a recording device did exist at one time. The Mills Novelty Company recorded many Violano-Virtuoso rolls by means of a keyboard device laid out to represent different violin notes. In spite of this, many collectors consider the finest Violano-Virtuoso rolls to be the early ones which were done drafting-board style without benefit of the keyboard.

Many excellent rolls have been made on the drawing board, including the Duo-Art and Ampico "reproducing" rolls "played" by Frank Milne. Gustav Bruder's extraordinarily imaginative and musical Weber orchestrion rolls which feature some of the most wonderful arrangements the field of automatic musical instruments has ever known were done on a drawing board, as were many snappy Link coin piano rolls arranged by Ray Deyo. There are many other examples.

Making rolls by this method does not require any keyboard technique, but it does require a great deal of patience and the ability to hear what music will sound like by looking at lines on paper, just as a composer can hear what music will sound like by reading a musical manuscript.

The drawing board roll arranger must also have a complete grasp of the technicalities of how holes in a paper roll cause a music machine to play, including the following concepts: tracker scale of the instrument; tracker bar hole size; punch size; paper speed; relation of paper speed to tempo; paper buildup on the take-up spool and its effect on tempo; proper length of each hole; the amount of longitudinal space between consecutive holes; the use of silence between notes; the power of the machine (how many notes can it play at once); which notes, if any, are octave-coupled; in an orchestrion or band organ, the acoustical qualities of each rank of pipes and of the percussion instruments; which percussion instruments, if any, are of the reiterating or repeating type; how fast each note on each instrument is capable of repeating; and the speed of operation of lock and cancel devices. The arranger of band organ music, for example, has to know how long it takes for the large bass drum beater to actually strike the drum head. The delay between the start of the drum signal and the production of the drum sound must be taken into consideration so that the drum will not lag behind.

The best way for a prospective music roll arranger to become familiar with the medium, given a certain amount of musical and mechanical ability, is to learn the technicalities by studying rolls, to watch rolls play until the function of each hole is understood, and to memorize the sounds of various hole patterns. The arranger should then construct a simple drawing board, arrange a short piece of music, punch it out, listen to it, and compare it to other rolls. With much trial and error, careful observation, patience, and practice, the arranger will experience the thrill of creating a new musical arrangement and then having it brought to life by a non-living music machine. A good roll arrangement is like a fine piece of art; it reflects the creator's own abilities, ideas, and techniques and is different from the same melody arranged by another.

Above: The music manuscript or "sheet music" for the first four measures of "The Carnival of Venice," a tune known the world over, as it would appear in a typical mediocre printed arrangement. There are no embellishments, and the simple chords are within the ability of the average home pianist.

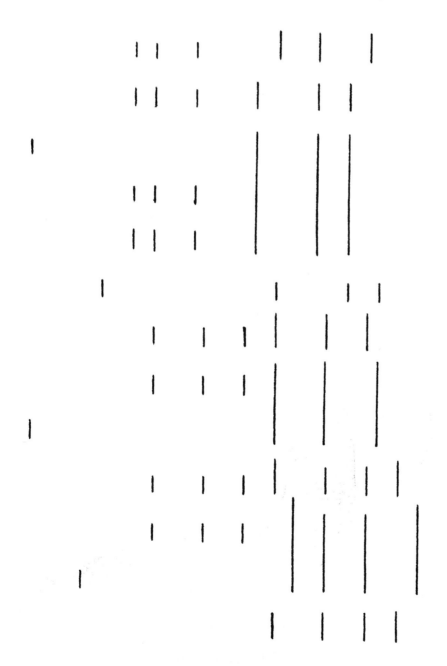

"THE CARNIVAL OF VENICE," as arranged by Arthur Reblitz for several different automatic musical instruments, illustrates how sheet music can be adapted for use with different tracker scales and instrument potentials.

At the left is shown "The Carnival of Venice" arranged exactly like the sheet music. The bass notes and accompaniment chords are to the left, and the right hand melody chords are to the right. A player piano playing this roll would sound just like a person playing the sheet music.

On the following pages are to be found an embellished arrangement for the 88-note home player piano, an arrangement for the Wurlitzer Style 125 band organ, and a simple arrangement for a 14-note Mechanical Orguinette organette. In each instance the notes only are shown; the blank paper sections and roll margins are not indicated.

Clever and interesting arrangements make the difference between a roll which is, to put it simply, boring, and one which is fascinating enough to listen to again and again. Just as the aficionado of New Orleans jazz knows that "Just a Closer Walk With Thee," when played by a jazz combo, can be quite different from the same tune played on a church organ at a funeral, the collector of automatic musical instruments knows that while the tune title serves to spark the initial interest in hearing a roll, it is the arrangement which ends or sustains the curiosity.

Start Here

Start Here

The above shows "The Carnival of Venice" as arranged by Arthur Reblitz for a typical 88-note home player piano roll. Two of the bass notes are punched an octave lower than in the simple sheet music arrangement. The right hand melody chords are moved up an octave, played in full octaves with various embellishments. A new tenor countermelody part has been added in the form of a rolling octave tremolo, with the accompaniment chords now falling between the octave countermelody notes. This is only one of the many styles of player piano roll arranging. There are, in fact, as many styles as there are arrangers. The above example is representative of a typical way of converting a plain arrangement into a more interesting one.

G C D E F g a b c c'd e f f'a'g a b c c'd e f f'g a b c E F F'G A B C C'D E F F'G

Above is a scale, approximately actual size, for the Wurlitzer 125 band organ roll. Below is Art Reblitz' arrangement of "The Carnival of Venice" for the same scale. The 125 scale is non-chromatic, which means only those notes which are absolutely necessary are present. With "unnecessary" bass notes and sharps eliminated from the scale, the roll is very compact, having greater hole density (or more holes per given area of paper) than the same general arrangement would have on a fully chromatic roll. The bass and accompaniment chord section on the left side of the roll is squashed together. The trumpet notes on the right side of the roll begin in the lower octave of the trumpet pipes, but when the melody goes too low in the 2nd full measure, the trumpet part jumps up to the higher trumpets. The melody section is arranged simply in block chords with a few simple embellishments during long sustained notes, as in the 3rd full measure. In this example, the bass drum is played on the first beat of each measure by the extreme right hand hole, and the snare drum plays on the second and third beats by the extreme left hand hole, which looks like another accompaniment chord hole.

Start Here

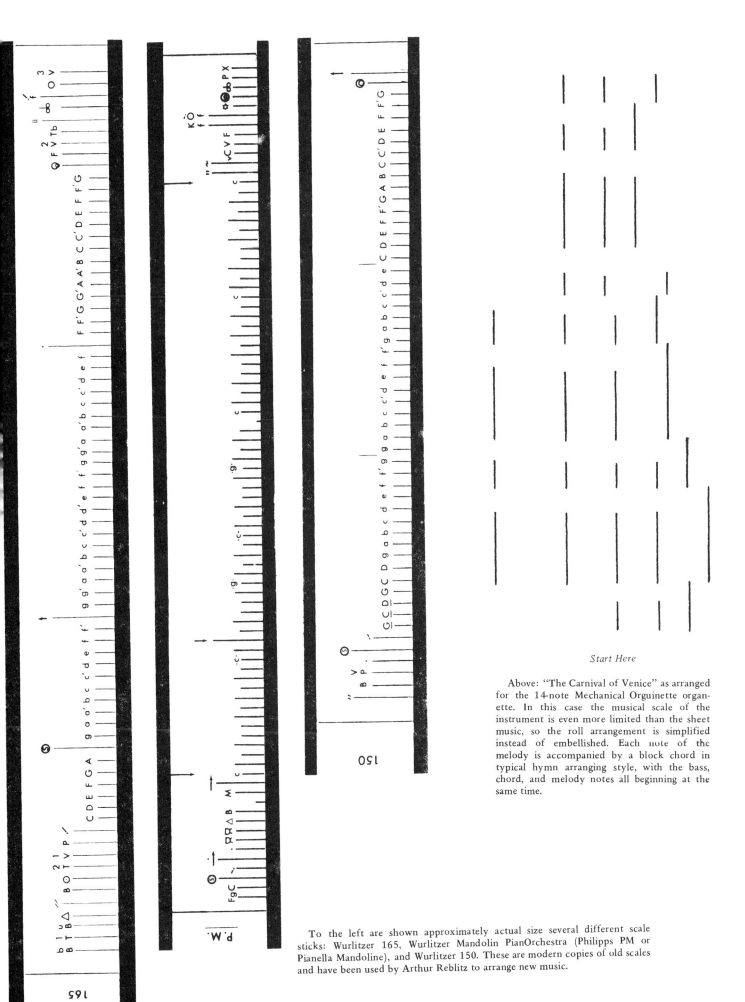

Start Here

Above: "The Carnival of Venice" as arranged for the 14-note Mechanical Orguinette organ-ette. In this case the musical scale of the instrument is even more limited than the sheet music, so the roll arrangement is simplified instead of embellished. Each note of the melody is accompanied by a block chord in typical hymn arranging style, with the bass, chord, and melody notes all beginning at the same time.

To the left are shown approximately actual size several different scale sticks: Wurlitzer 165, Wurlitzer Mandolin PianOrchestra (Philipps PM or Pianella Mandoline), and Wurlitzer 150. These are modern copies of old scales and have been used by Arthur Reblitz to arrange new music.

RECOLLECTIONS
of a
MUSIC ROLL ARRANGER

by P.M. Keast

P.M. Keast, born in 1888, was active in the coin piano and orchestrion roll arranging business from 1917 through 1930. As a child he played the violin, and his brother played the clarinet. When P.M. decided to play in a city band in which there was no demand for the violin, he learned other instruments; first, the clarinet, then the brass instruments, the woodwinds, and finally the drums. While playing the drums in a dance band he developed a friendship with Roy Rodocker, who was superintendent of the coin-operated music roll division of the QRS Music Roll Co., then (1917) located in DeKalb, Illinois. In the fall of the same year Mr. Keast went to work at QRS, where he began by adding percussion effects to style O roll arrangements. He worked at QRS until 1921, when he went to work for the Clark Orchestra Roll Company, in which situation he remained until 1924. He then worked for the Capitol Roll & Record Co. in Chicago until 1930 when his job was curtailed.

After selling band instruments to schools for the C.G. Conn Co. he became active in the school band programs in Elmhurst and Park Ridge, Illinois. This continued from 1930 until his retirement in 1954. At that time he opened the Keast School of Music in Elmhurst, which included a small music store and studios for several teachers. Sometime in the late 1960s Harvey Roehl, founder of the Vestal Press, met Mr. Keast's son who was dean of liberal arts at Cornell University (and later president of Wayne State University in Detroit) and who informed Harvey about his father's connection with the music roll business. After visiting with the Keasts, Harvey suggested to Art Reblitz that further contact might turn up some interesting details. A condensation of Mr. Keast's correspondence with Art Reblitz may be found on pages 721-722 of The Encyclopedia of Automatic Musical Instruments, to which the reader is directed for additional background details. Following this correspondence, Art Reblitz, Dave Junchen, Dave Ramey, and Tom Sprague had an extensive interview with Mr. Keast. Rather than reprint the interview in conventional form, we give a synopsis by Art Reblitz of the pertinent material in the interview, as related by P.M. Keast.

The QRS Years

We never knew what "QRS" stood for, but there have been some opinions. One was "Quality Roll Service," [or "Quality Real Service"], and that's the one that seems to stick the most. You can make up your own, because it didn't mean anything that I ever heard of.

Roy Rodocker brought me over to QRS. We used to play dance orchestra work together in DeKalb. He was a clarinet and sax player and I played the drums. Harry Hamilton was also a drummer, and he was working for QRS, adding drum parts to G and O rolls. He was drafted [into World War I] and I was in town, and Rodocker persuaded me to come over there and take Hamilton's job. I didn't know any more about that than a pig does about Latin. I suppose if I hadn't been a drummer I wouldn't have been at QRS.

The only help I had in learning the job was from Hamilton. He was there for a day or so before he had to take off, and in the meantime he came up and showed me a few things. Other than that, I didn't know anything about it.

The QRS Company did their recording in Chicago, under the direction of Lee S. Roberts. The recording

artists at QRS were tops. That was one reason why QRS was so successful; they had the best they could get in the way of performers. The recording was done on a recording piano connected to a machine with a set of fingers. As the pianist played, the blank paper rolled over the fingers which would press a carbon, and as long as the keys were held, there would be marks. [Ed. note: This is the same recording piano which was used by QRS, relocated in Buffalo, N.Y., in the 1970s to make the QRS "Celebrity Series" rolls.] Max Kortlander, who was the real work horse, then took the pencil recordings and corrected mistakes. Max might have come out to DeKalb in the early days, but I never saw any of the recording artists out there.

I remember hearing that once when Rudolph Ganz made a recording they cut the slots out and played it back to him, and he swore that it wasn't him because there were too many mistakes. What happened was that the pianist frequently touched the wrong keys, actuating the recording mechanism without sounding the notes. These would turn up as mistakes in the master music roll. Those were the things that Max would eliminate. However, he tried to preserve the individuality of the artist as much as possible. Each artist was different, and we could tell out in DeKalb when we heard a roll who was doing the playing most of the time.

After Max edited the master rolls they were hand punched in Chicago. They sent light weight paper rolls to us in DeKalb, made of paper like the finished rolls, all punched out. On a semiclassical recording like "Nola," we left the rhythm as it was, but on all the word rolls our arrangers went to work arranging them according to strict tempo according to the rhythm scales. I had two rhythm scales, each having two faces on one side. The back was flat, with each long side of the top surface bevelled. One was 2/4, another 3/4, another 4/4, and another 6/8. Each measure was broken into half notes, quarter notes, eighths, sixteenths, and so forth. We used those four scales for everything we did. They were made in the metal department.

When the rolls came out from Kortlander they couldn't be in scale because the artists couldn't play in strict rhythm by hand. That's where the responsibility of the arrangers came in. Fred Phillips was the chief arranger, Roy Lauer was next, then Zig Swanson, and then myself. Lauer and Phillips and Swanson just worked on 88-note piano rolls; they had nothing to do with the coin-operated rolls. Rodocker worked mostly on organ rolls, and Mike Kommers and I worked on coin-operated rolls. I used a black pencil for all my marking. My rolls and Lauer's looked about the same when we were through with them; Phillips had a different style. No credit was ever given to an arranger on a roll label.

I had two pianos in my arranging room. One was a straight piano and the other was a correcting piano with a kind of push-up device that fit on the front of the keyboard. With a roll like "Nola," in which we didn't want to change the rhythm at all, we ran it on this machine and left the rhythm just as it was.

To convert an 88-note roll into a coin-operated roll we would run the 88-note roll on a machine and it would imprint a pencil master roll according to the coin-operated roll scale. We could reset it and use it for any different kind that we might want. Then we would arrange the imprinted master roll down to the smaller note scale of the coin-operated piano, rearrange it for solos, and so on, always keeping in mind the limitations as far as the power of the instrument was concerned. If we'd load it up too heavy with octave tremolos and that sort of thing, some of the instruments could not handle it and would die. [The reference here is to Coinola instruments with reiterating xylophone or bells; there was not much vacuum reserve. —Ed.] We had to take that into consideration all the time; we didn't use as much octave tremolo with some rolls as with others.

We were always careful not to let the notes run out of the range of an instrument. When we arranged the music down to the coin-operated scale, if the notes went out of the range we brought them back in some way or other.

We worked directly on the imprinted rolls, changing the marks to fit what we wanted on the finished rolls. We didn't use an intermediate copy and didn't copy anything down onto manuscript paper.

My drawing board had a ratchet on the side representing one punch. [Ed. note: Mr. Keast uses the term "one punch" in referring to the increment of paper between one punch and the next down the length of the paper; "one punch" equals one advance step on the perforator.] Everything in our operation was geared to that single punch; the ratchet, the sprocket holes in the master paper, our tempo scales, Norberg's punching machine, the perforators, etc. Art Norberg was a cracker jack puncher; he was the original and was the better of the two by far.

Since QRS was owned by the Melville Clark Piano Company, most of our equipment such as our arranging boards was made of wood in the experimental part of the company. Melville Clark wasn't active in the operation except to oversee the whole thing. He was the kind of guy who liked to hang around in the experimental shop of the piano company, always fussing around with a couple of guys who were fine mechanics in wood.

We had gadgets like a correcting device for 88-note rolls. Down in another room, a large one, we had a Seeburg G orchestrion, a Coinola, and a Seeburg H organ [possibly a photoplayer, or was it an H orchestrion? - Ed.] and instruments like that so we could take a roll over and play it on the instrument itself. That was a big help. We didn't do much correcting, however; we had it pretty well worked out in our room before the rolls were made.

Roy Rodocker was the superintendent of the factory, completely in charge of the coin-operated division. I didn't have much opportunity to hear the orchestrions because I kept busy making rolls; sometimes I would hear them and sometimes I wouldn't. So I never had any

preference for any certain type of orchestrion. Rodocker's offices were in the room where they had the G and Coinola and big [Seeburg] organ and so forth. When I got through with the master roll, it would go to the machine room and come out as a production roll, and then they'd take it down to Rodocker. He always checked one of each roll; I didn't check them.

When I started at QRS I got 25c per hour, until QRS went to Chicago; then I got a dollar an hour. I wasn't in charge until I went back to DeKalb [to the Clark Orchestra Roll Co.]. I don't know how much the artists were paid. The arrangers got more money than the punchers and cutters, but it didn't amount to much.

When I first went to QRS in DeKalb, their arrangement for putting words on the side of word rolls was a very crude thing. They had a long table, a stencil, a bunch of rolls, and a man at one end of the roll and another man way down at the other end. They laid the stencil on one copy of the roll and then ran from one end to the other with an inked roller. They carried that on even after they moved to Chicago; they had a large room with several apparatus like that. All of a sudden somebody invented the automatic stencil machine which required only the push of a button, and they eliminated the whole thing. That was probably inside of a year of the time they moved to Chicago.

According to stories I have heard, Mr. Gulbransen was a foreman in the Melville Clark piano factory when he had an idea for a simple player piano action. The Clarks wouldn't listen to him, so he built and perfected it after hours in the basement of his home in Sycamore, so Clark couldn't claim the rights to it.

Melville Clark sometimes drove me in to Chicago in his air-cooled Franklin. Once when he was driving me in, he told me about a lawsuit which was brought against QRS. A couple of fellows who thought they were real smart brought Clark to court because they said piano rolls could be read like sheet music. They trained a couple of guys to read the notes in the roll. It only took Clark a few minutes to knock that on the head; he scrambled the tubing on a perforator and brought in a roll with the notes scattered all over the place! I don't know who masterminded the job, but when Clark got through with it he made monkeys out of those two guys.

Melville had a son, Bayard, who wasn't interested in the business in the early days but who had a print shop in the same building.

I don't know exactly when Melville Clark died; it might have been in the 1920s. After he died, Tom Pletcher came in with some financial interest from St. Louis. They came out to DeKalb, looked it over, bought the whole thing, and went out to the South Side of Chicago. Pletcher had nothing at all to do with making the rolls; he was the top man financially. It was Kortlander who kept doing the actual work. I went to Chicago with them and stayed about six months. Then Ernest Clark bought the coin-operated part of the business and took it back to DeKalb. I went back to DeKalb with him and had charge of the arranging department. Rodocker went to Chicago at the same time I did. I don't know how long he stayed there with QRS before he went over to Capitol.

The Clark Orchestra Roll Years

Clark's building was a low two-story frame structure right next to the railroad tracks. The old Lincoln Highway [U.S. Route 30] is the main street of DeKalb. Just a block south of that is the Northwestern Railroad, running up at an angle. Clark was located in there.

Everything at Clark was also on the single punch basis, with the drawing board ratchet, the rhythm scales, and the punching machine all based on that single punch. The master rolls were practically the same length as the production rolls.

I don't remember that we had the instruments over there at Clark, like they had at QRS, while I was there. So we had to make sure that the rolls were right before we sent them out. For example, we had to make sure the flute turned on and off when it should. But then, that was our responsibility; we knew they were right.

In the picture in Harvey Roehl's book [Player Piano Treasury —Ed.], Phil Oberg was running the punching machine. He was the person who determined the beginning and the end of each slot from the marks which I made. The cutters would then cut the slots in between. It required pinpoint accuracy all the way because the rhythm depended on the beginning of those holes.

When Ernie Clark bought the coin-operated part of the business he had the stipulation that he could use the QRS rolls. [Ed. note: Between 1921 and 1923 about half of the Clark Orchestra Roll Co. arrangements were different from the standard QRS word rolls; after 1923 all Clark arrangements were the same as QRS arrangements.] The rolls which you couldn't find on QRS were arranged by us on the drawing board, during the time that I had charge of the arranging department. I always liked the playing of the QRS artists better than our own original drawing board work, but I honestly thought that some of the drawing board work was better adapted to coin-operated machines, because the 88-note word rolls had to be revised extensively and sometimes didn't work so well. When the rolls were arranged specifically for the coin-operated instruments to begin with, I could stay within the range from the start. Our drawing board arrangements wouldn't be as complicated as four-hand work because there wasn't so much of that stuff in the high treble. That sounds great on the word rolls, but a lot of it is lost on coin-operated rolls. It was easier to arrange down the two-hand rolls such as those played by Zez Confrey or the ones Kortlander played by himself.

I thought I could duplicate the arranging of the various artists at the arranging board, and some of the work I did at the drawing board was patterned after theirs. They used certain combinations or procedures, such as a rolling melody or countermelody, which they usually used in four-hand arrangements. Kortlander played the top part and Roberts played the bottom; Arden played the low part and Ohman played the high part. Each had his own ideas, and if you worked on those for a few years you got so you could do them yourself. When you work on something like that day after day, if you don't absorb some of it, you're screening it all out some way or another.

I suppose I could still do it to an extent. I doubt if I could arrange on a piece of blank roll paper, but if you gave me the master paper, the drawing board with the ratchets and the scales, I could make a roll. Whether or not I would get the correct combinations of notes, I don't know. That was their big secret; they would each get their own effects with certain combinations of notes, combined with certain rhythmic ideas.

My one regret is that I never learned to play the piano. I learned all those other instruments, but the one that I could enjoy now I can't play. My training in music was sufficient that I could handle the arranging, and I knew the keyboard, but I never learned to do it with my fingers. Maybe the fact that I couldn't play the piano was a good thing; if I had been able to play I'd have tried and the results wouldn't have been as good.

When I was working at Clark, I used to come into Seeburg once a month and meet Mr. Kazecki for a music selection conference. He had charge of that program. We would make up the content of the rolls, and then I'd go back and we'd work them out. I don't remember any instance of a publisher bringing us sheet music like they bring it to a band leader to have a new song plugged. We never put anything on the rolls that wasn't already reasonably popular. Ten songs per roll was a limited number, and when Mr. Kazecki and I made up the list we chose the ten that we thought were the most popular and would "sell" on a coin-operated machine. That's the name of the game, I guess.

I don't know who took my place when I left Clark in 1924. If they used QRS rolls for all of their masters after that time, they were just readapting them. Ernest Clark didn't know anything about it. He didn't do any arranging. NEVER! As a matter of fact, he was a kind of a joke out at DeKalb; everybody there felt that if it hadn't been for his brother Melville being a businessman, Ernie would have been digging ditches or something like that. He just sort of fell into it. He was a kind of good-time Charlie all over town. I heard that after we left he got in with a promoter who tried to get him elected mayor. They also developed the "Coin Slot" [magazine] after I left. [Ed. note: When Mr. Keast learned of the "Coin Slot" issue excerpts which are reprinted in The Encyclopedia of Automatic Musical Instruments, he thought they contained more advertising hokum than factual material. He had no memory of them being published during the time he actually worked at Clark. He also had no memory of 4X, XP, Empress L, M, Nelson-Wiggen Selector Duplex, C or other rare types of rolls. He remembered the National changer rolls but said his work did not include these.]

About the same time that I left, the other boys left too. Harry Hamilton became the city clerk. Marion Wright left, but I don't know when. He was a very good piano player and played professionally. My brother went into the food business; he ran an A&P store. He is living [at the time of the interview in 1970] in Gibson City, Illinois. As far as I know, there was no political reason for anyone leaving. I haven't any idea where the rest of the people are. At QRS, Phillips and Lauer were both older than I was. Zig Swanson was about four years older than I was, and he is the last one I knew of; he was living in DeKalb, but I'm 82, so if he's alive he'd be about 86.

The Capitol Years

When I joined Capitol [a division of the Operators Piano Co.] they were at 22 South Peoria Street in Chicago. They had built a new place over on North Kedzie, just south of Chicago Avenue, and we went into there about three or four months after I joined them. The rolls and pianos were made in the same building, as had been done at the other address. At Kedzie they had a long, low building, and the arranging rooms were in the front, facing Kedzie. My room was in there. I think it was on the second floor, but I'm not sure.

My entire job was arranging. I'd come in and go up to work and possibly be there all day without seeing anybody. I never took breaks. My job was so fascinating that I would start at 8 o'clock in the morning and never get out of my chair until noon. I had excellent eyes before that, but it got so I'd look out the window and everything was all foggy, so I had to wear glasses from then on. It was very fascinating work, just like an architect or draftsman who has a building planned in his mind and stays at the drafting board until it's all down on paper. First thing you know, you're beginning to get hungry. My only problem was keeping awake after playing a dance job until two or three in the morning.

There were four of us: Roy Rodocker, who did all the organ work [Ed. note: It is probable that many of the sprightly OS and NOS Reproduco rolls were his work], myself, Gullman (who died approximately a year after I got there), and another fellow who did a little bit of everything. He didn't do much arranging but did a lot of other work for Rodocker.

I don't remember anything at all about hand-played rolls at Capitol; they escape me. Most of the work that I did was on the drawing board. The only recording I remember being done was when Rodocker occasionally had a couple of black fellows around the plant who played rolls in their own typical style. Roy liked their music and he was the one who worked on their rolls. [Ed. note: Mr. Keast didn't remember any of the artists whose names commonly appear on Supertone player piano rolls.] Capitol made Sears (Supertone) rolls. Sears used to beat the price down until about all their rolls were good for was to help meet the payroll over at Capitol. We didn't put any extra work into them at all. Normally we would clean up mistakes, but for Sears the rolls went right through, mistakes and all!

We used a different system at Capitol. The master rolls were much longer than the production rolls. I never liked arranging there as well because I couldn't see the music, because it was stretched out so far. At Clark it was right in front of me all the time.

We sometimes got a whole group of songs in from South America, and they wanted rolls made with those songs. That was a challenge. They just sent the fiddle parts, and we were supposed to make them into coin piano rolls. I didn't know any more about South America than the man in the moon. It was always a shot in the dark as far as we were concerned, trying to be careful that we didn't Americanize the rolls!

The only fellow in the factory that I knew was Louie Severson. He was the mechanical genius behind the operation, but he didn't have the money. That was another man who lived up in the Moraine Hotel on the North Side, who didn't do anything except walk around the plant in a big flat-footed way. [Ed. note: Louis M. Severson is listed in early trade directories as the president of the Operators Piano Co.]

The trouble with Operators was that when radio came in, these things went out. Seeburg was in the same boat, but Seeburg had what it took to convert over. [Ed. note: In the early 1930s Seeburg went through bankruptcy proceedings.] Even though Severson and his brother at the plant tried many different ideas to incorporate the radio idea into their boxes, it just didn't go. Another thing where Operators made their biggest mistake was that when they were over on Peoria, most of their output was absorbed by the Jenkins Company of Kansas City, so they didn't have much of a wide outlet. Jenkins took carloads of their machines, practically all of them, so when Kansas City went out, they had nothing to go back on.

One Thursday I was told that I was through Saturday. Rodocker had the best job in the place, and I suppose they did about the same thing with him not too long after I left. That's how it worked.

Occasionally I drive within a block of the Operators factory on the way to one of my musical accessory supply houses, but I've never driven past the actual factory itself since 1930. I never talked with anyone about the music roll business from 1930 until Harvey Roehl contacted me.

Collectors of today wonder why I didn't save some of the equipment, why I didn't gather some of the rolls, and why I didn't do this or that. Well, as far as we were concerned, that business would just keep going on forever, just like anything else. We never thought for a minute that we would be out of business overnight. Imagine QRS selling something like 10 million rolls in one year, and then four years later being practically out of business. The piano business was just about gone, and the coin-operated piano business was entirely gone, as far as the instruments and rolls were concerned. It wasn't just the Depression, of course, it was the radio [and the electronic amplification of phonograph records, which gained popularity beginning in 1926-1927]. I give J Lawrence Cook and Max Kortlander a great deal of credit for keeping the QRS Company going all through the years. And I think the comeback of the player piano and the collector activity of today is just great.

PERFORATING MUSIC ROLLS
BY HAND

by Mike Kitner

Mike Kitner, a Pennsylvanian, has custom-perforated music rolls for clients all over the United States. Wurlitzer Mandolin Pian-Orchestra rolls featuring new arrangements (by Art Reblitz), recuts of Seeburg H orchestrion rolls (composite rolls selected and in some cases edited by Terry Borne), and other products have been enthusiastically received by collectors. In the following article Mike Kitner shares many valuable insights and experiences.

Readers of this book will undoubtedly be amazed at the large number of different types of rolls which were made over the years. It seems hard to believe that all of these types were ever available in sufficient quantities to meet the needs of the machines which played them, even in the heyday of mechanical musical instruments. It should come as no surprise, then, that many of them are very rare today.

The demand for the universally popular 88-note home player piano rolls has been sufficient to keep factories busy turning them out in huge quantities over the years. To a lesser extent, the more popular varieties of the coin piano, band organ, and reproducing piano rolls are also in demand, and individuals with the money and ingenuity necessary to build and operate production roll perforators find a steady market for their products.

Perforation of rolls by machine has not been possible in recent years for the majority of roll types, due mainly to the limited market for them. It is economically impractical to invest thousands of dollars in a production perforator which could turn out more rolls in a few hours than there are instruments in the world to play them. Since there is a substantial demand for scarce music rolls of all types, I suggest that hand-produced rolls might fill this demand.

At the time of this writing there appears to be only one practical way of making paper music rolls: by punching them mechanically with a punch and die. Much talk is bandied about concerning exotic schemes involving lasers, high pressure air, gas flames, whirling knives, sandpaper, etc., but nothing substantial in this area has come along yet. Therefore, for purposes of this discussion, roll perforating can be divided into two basic methods: production perforating and hand perforating.

A "production perforator" is a completely automatic machine in which the punching of the roll is directed by some sort of a program, usually in the form of a perforated master roll or, in a few modern instances, by magnetic tape. Hypothetically, a production perforator could consist of a single punch and die which roams from side to side of the roll, but all machines in practical use contain one punch and die for each hole position on the roll. This type of machine is capable of producing a large quantity of rolls in a fairly short time and with a minimum of human involvement. Most music rolls are produced in this way. The disadvantages of this system, however, are the high cost of the machinery and the difficulty and expense involved in changing the

perforator from a roll of one hole spacing or hole size to another. Most production perforators are limited to producing rolls of one spacing and one hole size.

Hand punching in its simplest form consists of merely knocking the holes into the paper with a punch and mallet. Certain refinements can improve this method. The advantage is that any type of roll can be made, regardless of hole spacing or size. The obvious disadvantage is the amount of human labor required to produce a roll. Nevertheless, because of its versatility this is the system which I decided to use. The following discussion describes some of the refinements which I have developed.

The hand-operated perforator itself is a single punch and die mechanism, constructed with a very heavy steel frame to insure rigidity. The entire frame which carries the punch and die is mounted on wheels which roll on tracks that run perpendicular to the length of the paper. The punch and die are commercially made units. The die is mounted in a holder on the lower part of the frame directly beneath the paper. The punch is carried in a movable quill which runs in a guide mounted on the top of the frame directly above and aligned with the die. The quill is driven down by an air-operated diaphragm which is controlled by an electric solenoid valve. A pedal-operated switch actuates the solenoid.

The perforator frame is positioned across the width of the roll by an indexing system consisting of an accurately made index bar. This bar is drilled with holes that are spaced the same as the roll being produced. The index bar is mounted on the frame, and a stationary pin can be dropped into any hole on the bar to hold the perforator frame in any of the hole positions on the roll. The roll paper is guided through the machine by paper guides which allow free longitudinal movement of the paper but which prevent it from moving sideways.

The machine is set up and adjusted for the type of roll to be made. The correct diameter punch and die are installed, and the appropriate index bar is installed and carefully positioned.

The roll to be made will be either a new arrangement or a copy of an existing roll. In the case of new arrangements, the arranger supplies the unperforated paper with all the hole positions marked in pencil.

To copy an existing roll, first a length of blank paper equal to the length of the finished roll is cut. The original roll is then laid on top of the blank paper. All the hole positions are marked in pencil by drawing lines over and through the holes in the original. The original is laid with the side which touches the tracker bar facing up, and the far edges of the original and the blank sheet are carefully aligned. The width of the blank paper is usually greater than that of the finished roll in order to facilitate stapling the copies. After the pencil-marked master is completed it is rolled up, and 10 or 11 additional sheets, also wider than the finished roll, are measured and cut. The master is laid on top of these sheets, and the far edges of all the sheets are aligned carefully. This aligning is very critical and is a time-consuming procedure, because the far edge of each sheet will be the true edge of the finished roll. As the far edges are aligned, all the sheets are stapled through the excess margin of the near edge of the roll. Many staples are used, because they must prevent the individual sheets from moving during the perforating process.

In cases in which the original roll is of no value, perhaps due to excessive damage, and in cases where a perforated copy from a previous run is to be re-copied, the copying of the master can be done much faster by stippling ink over the holes with a foam rubber applicator. This takes only a fraction of the time required to pencil-mark a master, but it results in the destruction or damage of the original copy.

When all the copies are stapled with the marked master on top, they are hung on a series of rods near the ceiling and allowed to drape back and forth between ceiling and floor. This is the only practical way of handling great lengths of stapled copies, because rolling them up would result in buckling and tearing at the staples.

The beginning of the roll is fed through the perforator's paper guides, which are then adjusted for zero clearance, to prevent any lateral movement of the paper. The operator of the perforator then proceeds to punch out all the marked holes, usually working each hole track for about two feet down the length of the paper. The paper is slid back and forth through the guides by hand. After two feet of a given track is punched, the machine is moved to the next hole position and locked in that position by the index bar. Chaining of long holes is accomplished by repeatedly operating the punch while pulling the paper at the correct speed to obtain chains with just enough paper between the holes to give the roll strength, without causing the note to stutter.

As the roll is perforated it is allowed to fall in folds into a box beneath the perforator. When the entire roll is perforated it is drawn back through the guides and folded into another box. Attached to the perforator frame is a clamp designed to hold a single-edge razor blade. A blade is then inserted into this clamp, and its position is adjusted to coincide with the untrimmed near edges of the roll. The paper is drawn through the guides once more, and the razor blade slits the excess margin from all the copies at once, staples and all. Depending upon the width of the roll, it is sometimes possible to save the margin and use it for making some sort of a narrower roll at a future time.

Once trimmed, the now-unstapled copies are again pulled back through the guides and again hung on the ceiling rods and draped as in the beginning. Starting with the top copy, each roll is then pulled off and wound up, from beginning to end. The rolls can then be spooled easily on whatever cores or spools they require.

This perforating process is obviously very slow, but I feel that it is one of the best ways to reproduce obscure rolls for which the cost of an automatic perforator with the same versatility would be prohibitive. The speed and quality of production of the finished rolls is directly dependent upon the skill of the operator. Some types of rolls are more difficult to perforate than others. In general, organ arrangements take longer than piano arrangements of a given number of hole positions. Band organ arrangements are among the most time consuming rolls to produce due to the large amount of hole space. The rolls being produced usually have a spacing measurement of between four and ten holes per inch. Rolls which I have recut have required the fabrication of about 20 different index bars. Punch diameters range from .062" to .120". Five sizes have been suitable for all rolls produced to date. The punch-die clearance must be near zero to give a sharp hole in all copies. This necessitates a very rigid frame to hold them.

Some rolls present special difficulties. Although the transverse position of the holes is fixed by the indexing system, the longitudinal position is determined by the operator. Slight errors in longitudinal position are not noticeable on notes or most control functions, but the theme holes in Duo-Art reproducing piano rolls and the picker holes in Encore Automatic Banjo rolls must be positioned very accurately. Very slight misalignment of these holes produces noticeable errors in the music. Mills Violano-Virtuoso rolls are extremely difficult to make by hand for a number of reasons. The holes must be punched out absolutely clean, since even the tiniest bridge of paper will cause a note to stutter, due to the electrical reading system in these machines. Some holes in Violano rolls can be three feet or more in length, producing severe structural weakness which makes the unspooled rolls very hard to handle. The hole diameter in Violano-Virtuoso rolls is almost equal to the spacing of the holes, so two adjacent holes have only the tiniest thread of paper separating them.

My own perforating machine can handle rolls up to 16" wide. It can punch round holes only. It is possible to punch cardboard book music on it as well.

In summary, I feel that this approach to perforating is the most practical for making obscure music rolls. The initial cost of the equipment is modest compared to a production machine, but great patience and considerable skill are required of the operator if quality rolls are to be made.

During the 1920s Eugene DeRoy's Symphonia music roll factory, which was located at several different addresses in the Antwerp, Belgium area, cut dozens of different types of rolls. In particular demand were rolls for Hupfeld, Popper, Weber, Philipps, and other German-made orchestrions and pianos. DeRoy, being highly competitive and very energetic, produced current popular tunes faster and cheaper than did the original instrument makers. Many of the tracker scales in the present book are from the archives of the late Eugene DeRoy, which passed to Q. David Bowers after Mr. DeRoy's death.

July 4. 1966

Mr. Q. D. Bowers

Dear Mr. Bowers :

Thanks for your letter of 23 th which enclosing the IO Dollars
to copied the Weber instruments.
Some one offer me a big orchestrion Hupfeld Helios for 55,000.- Fr
= + I.IOO Dollars, with two trackerbar (two music rolls actions)
I have not seen this instrument and don't know which model ? nor the
the state, so when I have a moment time I will look after and send you
all details. Also I know a big Pepper for sale, I also send you detail
when I have seen it.
The catalogus are not for sale for the present, but I will send copies
of any instruments you like.
Keith, Prowse & C°. in London only sell Hupfeld imported from Germany.
they did not sell Poppers, I have been working 4 years by them.
I can cut you any kind of Popular Tunes ; Price from I July 66
IOO.- Fr per meter + ± 2 Dollars. if you take only one roll, but
I cant cut 8 a 9 Rolls at the time, than the price will be cheaper,
Can you use more then one roll ?
I must cut a Weber Maesto rol for a another persoon with the follo-
wing tunes : American Medley : Entertainers Rag & I could have danse
all night & Seventy six trombones & Should I & Bleue Tango &
Tennessee Waltz & Entrée des Gladiators & Way down Jonder in New -
Orlean & Can Can . If you like I make one for you a the same time
for the Price of 75.- Fr per meter = ± I,50 dollars
and another Weber Maesto roll " DIE FIDELER BAUER " (The jolly pea-
sant) from L. Fall. price XXX 2.500.- Fr = ± 50. dollars.
Find enclosing list of Original Germain Type of Weber Maesto Rolls
I can cut for you at the price of IOO.- Fr per meter = ± 2.- dollars
List of Weber Waesto Types of Popular tunes I have already made,
You can choise the tunes you like and make a roll with 4 popular
tune on one roll. Price par meter 75.- Fr; per meter
Also list of Philipps Pianella (226 mm.) Hupfeld Helios (296 mm
popular tunes I have in stock, at the price of 75.- Fr per meter.
Awaiting your answer;
I remain
Yours sincerely

Eug De Roy.

This July 4, 1966 letter from Eugene DeRoy tells of the services he offered at the time. This was near
the end of his roll-cutting career, and despite the quotations and interest expressed, he cut no more rolls
after this time. The Weber Maesto roll with the American Medley (which had been ordered by Leonard
Grymonprez, although the letter does not mention this) was never made.

FOURNISSEUR POUR PIANOS

"Symphonia"

49, Avenue Te Boelaer Lei, 49
BORGERHOUT-ANTWERPEN

H. Reg. : 197.49 – Tel. 35.00.73
C.C. : 40.15.71

NAMES OF ROLLS I CAN CUT :
PRICE PER METER FOR POPULAR TUNES ;
100.– Fr. = ± 2 Dollars

WEBER UNICA.	PAPER	WIDE	273	mm.
WEBER GRANDEZZA	"	"	325	"
WEBER BRABO & STYRIA & OTTERO		"	325	"
WEBER MAESTO		"	361	"
WEBER VIOLINA	"	"	432	"
PHILIPPS PIANELLA	"	"	226	"
" DUCA (DUCA)	"	"	265	"
" PAGANINI	"	"	346	"
POPPER , Piano & Orchestrion	"	"	350	"
" SUPERBA	"	"	350	"
KUHL – KLATT	"	"	340	"
" " ACCORDEON JAZZ	"	"	340	"
FRATINOLA	"	"	390	"
" MELODICA	"	"	317	"
" HYMNIA	"	"	317	"
NIZZA ACCORDEON JAZZ	"	"	286	"
LOSCHE (LOSCHE) Piano & Orchestrion			350	"
HUPFELD CLAVITIST	"	"	296	"
" PHONOLISZT	"	"	296	"
" HELIOS	"	"	296	"
" ANIMATIC	"	"	286	"
" SYMPHONICA JAZZ	"	"	286	"
PIANOLA 65 T.	"	"	286	"
AEOLIAN 58 T.	"	"	260	"
P.E. SOLOPHONE	"	"	325	"
P.E. JAZZ	"	"	325	"
BURSSENS ARBURO	"	"	350	"
DE CAP Piano & Orchestrion			350	"

Typed in 1966, this listing was sent to Q. David Bowers by Eugene DeRoy. At the time the Symphonia company was located at 49 Avenue Te Boelaer Lei in Borgerhout, a district of Antwerp. The demand for music rolls had long since passed its peak, and Mr. DeRoy's store was mainly devoted to supplying piano action parts and other musical instrument components to local technicians and others.

To the best of the authors' knowledge, Eugene DeRoy was the only music roll manufacturer in the world to cut rolls for dozens, perhaps even hundreds, of different orchestrions, pianos, and related items. In addition, he cut music books for fairground organs and dance organs.

Gustav Bruder, music roll arranger. (Leonard Grymonprez, photo)

Chapter 6
COIN PIANOS and ORCHESTRIONS

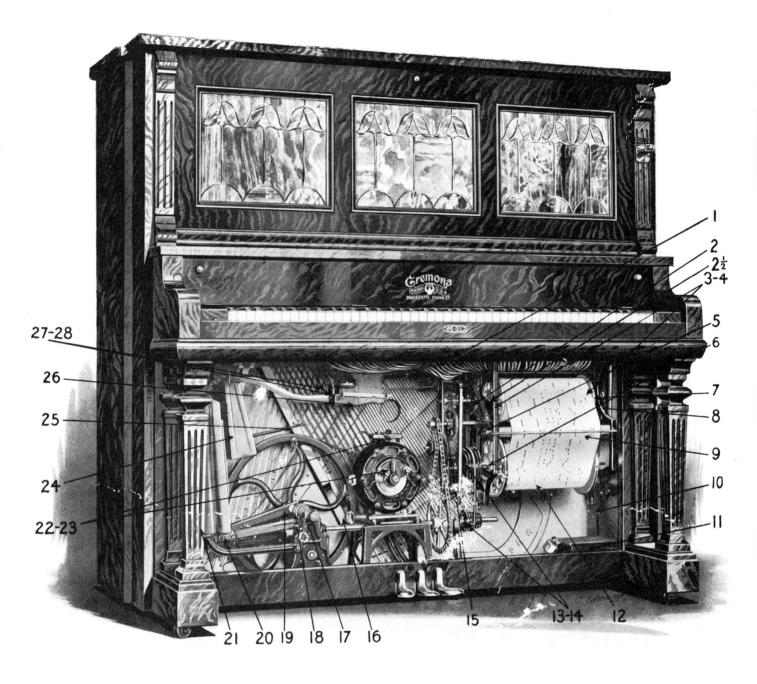

Specifications

1	Rubber tubes leading from pneumatic action to tracker.	15	Shifting sprocket wheel and pin.
2	Drag spring, upper spool.	16	Thumbscrew for shifting motor base.
3-4	Metal flanges, music spool.	17	Brass bearing.
5	Screw knob for shifting tracker.	18	Worm and gear.
6	Position of set screw for adjusting lower spool.	19	Shafts connecting bellows.
7	Thumbscrew holding pin.	20	Pins connecting shafts to bellows.
8	Round pin holding music roll in place.	21	Main bellows.
9	Tracker-bar (or mouthpiece)	22-23	Oil cups on motor.
10	Magazine slot and iron box.	24	Equalizer bellows.
11	Iron money box.	25	Tension spring to regulate bellows.
12	Music roll winding on take-up spool.	26	Shifter bellows.
	Spool pulleys.	27-28	Two regulating screws back of small rubber tubes leading from shifter bellows to tracker-bar.

Interior components of a Cremona A-roll coin piano are shown in this hand-painted illustration from the 1908-1910 period. Not all of the specifications (see left) are still readable, due to flaking of the paper, but enough are so you can get a general idea of how the Cremona worked. With chains, belts, pulleys, and shafts, the Cremona mechanisms were unnecessarily complicated. Still, Cremona instruments were well known for their ruggedness and dependability. The late Joseph Bacigalupi, who furnished this illustration, related that his father, Peter (of the firm Peter Bacigalupi & Sons), used to order Cremona pianos (as well as North Tonawanda Musical Instrument Works Pianolins) by the freight car load.

STYLE "A" COIN PIANO ROLLS
Used by Seeburg, Marquette, and Many Others

The type "A" roll, first introduced shortly after the turn of the 20th century and produced for commercial use until the early 1940s, was the most widely-used roll style for coin-operated pianos. Literally thousands of different melodies were arranged for use on these rolls, Typically, an A roll contains 10 tunes, although some rolls with fewer or more were also made.

In the early years of the coin piano industry in America, most Chicago-area makers used the A roll on pianos with mandolin attachment and on pianos with mandolin and one additional instrument (usually a rank of pipes or a xylophone). Thus the J.P. Seeburg Piano Co. used the A-roll on its styles A (keyboard piano with mandolin), B (keyboard piano with mandolin), C (keyboard piano with mandolin, art-style case; later used to designate a cabinet type keyboardless piano with mandolin and repeating xylophone), E (piano, mandolin, one rank of pipes [most early models] or xylophone [most late models]), F (piano, mandolin, one rank of pipes), K (cabinet style piano with mandolin and one rank of pipes [early] or xylophone [late]), L (cabinet style piano with mandolin; the most popular style of coin piano ever made by any manufacturer; many thousands were sold), P-G-A (circa 1919 piano with mandolin in phonograph-style case), and others. Seeburg, formed in 1907, featured the A roll as its basic type on smaller models (i.e., non-orchestrions) from then until the late 1920s. The Automatic Music Roll Company, a branch of Seeburg, sold A rolls made by the Clark Orchestra Roll Co. of DeKalb, Illinois. Clark also sold rolls under its own label.

The Marquette Piano Co. (founded in 1905, active until about 1920, maker of "Cremona" pianos) was a leading user of A rolls as was the Operators Piano Co. (founded in 1904, active until the 1930s, maker of "Coinola" pianos). The Nelson-Wiggen Piano Co. and the Western Electric Piano Co. (a subsidiary of Seeburg), both especially active in the 1920s, produced thousands of pianos which used A rolls.

The availability of a wide variety of music, the low cost (many A rolls originally sold for $2.50 to $3 each for a ten-tune roll), and the excellent musical arrangements on many of the rolls led other piano manufacturers and sellers to adopt the A roll. Many would buy a "kit" from the Monarch Tool & Manufacturing Co. or another supplier to convert an upright piano to a coin piano, and then a distinctive trademark would be added. In addition, certain manufacturers who in the early days used their own distinctive rolls later converted their designs (especially in the early 1920s) to use the inexpensive and readily available A rolls. National (Peerless) and the North Tonawanda Musical Instrument Works are two of several firms which did this.

The list of coin piano trademarks which used the A roll also includes such names as Anderson, Ariston, Armstrong, Billings, Capitol (a sales arm of the North Tonawanda Musical Instrument Works), Carleton, Chicago Electric, Colonial, Concertrola, Cote, Decker Brothers, Eberhardt, Engelhardt (related to Peerless), Empress (mechanisms made by the Operators Piano Co.; sold by Lyon & Healy), Evans, Haines, Harwood (Seeburg under a different label), Howard, Ideal, Jewett, Kibby, King, Kreiter, Lehr, Monarch, National (Peerless; not to be confused with National of Grand Rapids, Michigan, which uses a different roll), Netzow, Originators, Pianotainer, Presburg, Price & Teeple (also sold Carleton), Rand (North Tonawanda Musical Instrument Works), Reed, Regina (made by the Marquette Piano Co.), Reichard, Schaeffer, Schultz, Seltzer (made by the Operators Piano Co.), Starr, Victor Coin, Waltham, Watson, and William A. Johnson.

Early distributors of A rolls included the Automatic Music Roll Company (a division of the Seeburg Piano Co.), the Columbia Music Roll Co. (name changed in 1924 to the Capitol Roll and Record Co.; a division of the Operators Piano Co.), the Marquette Piano Co., and the U.S. Music Roll Co. In the 1920s the Clark Orchestra Roll Co. was dominant in the A roll market.

In the early days QRS masters were often used for A roll arrangements. While many variations exist, typically an A roll tune lasts for about 2½ minutes. Selections are mostly of a popular nature, including many melodies which by today have been long forgotten. Occasionally a composite roll of old-time favorites, saloon songs, patriotic melodies and marches, ethic music of Poland, Mexico, or Ireland, or some other theme would be made.

Today many of the finer arrangements on A rolls are available in recut form so that a large library of music can be obtained for fairly low cost.

STYLE "A" COIN PIANO ROLL

11¼" wide, holes spaced 6 per inch. Early designation: S (not to be confused with the Solo S roll used on large Cremona photoplayers). Note: While most A rolls bear the letter prefix (such as A-305), many are labeled only with the roll number and do not have the prefix A.

Scale:
1 Soft pedal
2 Sustaining pedal
3 Play
4 to 61 C-A, 58 playing notes
62 Extra instrument (such as xylophone or a pipe rank)
63 Rewind
64 Mandolin
65 Shutoff

The extra instrument, if present, is usually either a rank of flute or violin pipes or a xylophone (of either the single-stroke or reiterating type). Some A rolls are specially arranged with many short holes in the treble for a single stroke xylophone. These rolls are frequently identified as "xylophone specials" or have the word "xylophone" incorporated into the roll title, the Clark Orchestra Roll Co. roll Clark 898 "Xylo-Pep" being an example.

In some Seeburg pianos hole No. 1 operates a vacuum regulator, and the hammer rail works together with the mandolin from hole 64. In Seeburg A-roll coin pianos having a soft-medium-loud volume control, hole 1 operates in conjunction with the control knob in determining various combinations of setting of the soft pedal (hammer rail) and regulator pneumatics on the vacuum distribution box. Refer to the Seeburg tubing diagram and accompanying text.

The Seeburg Style L cabinet piano has only 54 playing notes for the 58 note holes in the roll. The lowest bass note is B, and it is coupled to the next higher B on the stack so that both

CLARK ORCHESTRA ROLL COMPANY

MANUFACTURERS OF
MUSIC ROLLS FOR REPRODUCING, AUTOMATIC PIANOS AND ORCHESTRIONS.

Roll-Makers For 40 Years   Telephone 492

DE KALB, ILLINOIS

Jan.7,1939.

Imperial Industrial Corp.
728 E. 136th St.
New York City.   Attention Stuart R.Fraser.

Gentlemen:

Your letter with inclosure from Tufts College,received,and in reply can only say,that we never had any of the masters from the Q.R.S. library,comprising many of the great compositions referred to by Mr.Lewis.

In fact,all I originally bought from the above company was the automatic lay-out and the popular masters of general character. The old and well known symphonies were not in demand for our style of roll,and if arranged for the Electric,would not be very convincing of it's merits,for the lack of expression.

I thought that Mr.Kortlander bought up the whole music cutting plant from the wreckage,when he took it over;and that the entire inventory of masters were his for the taking; but when I stop to think of the terrible waste,and wanton destruction of machines that prevailed under the Pletcher-Page management,I can easily see where the masters may have gone to,---the boiler room where the fire is the hottest.

I believe that will give you my answer for Mr.Lewis.   Now to change the subject.

I have felt very much embarrassed in not being able to settle for the last bunch of masters,for I dont like to have bills,unpaid,lying around.

The last bulletin brought very little return for the efforts made to put new numbers into the hands of piano owners,and we still owe ourselves a good "kick in the pants" for trying I guess.

As you know,I did'nt ask for masters for Dec.-Jan.and for two reasons;-1 I still owed for the last ones and,2- I did'nt have the heart to try,at this time of year,to take on the expense of putting out the new bulletin.

Will inclose a check for $10.00 to apply on invoice,and may I submit the correct status of account,as I understand it?

Yours as ever,

"The Shop Where Harmony Reigns"   Clark Orchestra Roll Co.

E.G.Clark

As the final several paragraphs indicate, the coin-operated piano roll business was breathing its last around 1939 when this letter was written. (Courtesy of Larry Givens)

notes play at once from hole 15. The second bass note, C, plays from hole 4. The last 5 treble notes are missing in this piano, so the 5 highest note holes in the tracker bar are coupled down an octave on the piano. In this piano the lowest three piano notes, B, C, and C#, play from roll holes 15, 4, and 5 in that order. The upper 13 piano notes, in order E, F, F#, G, G#, A, A#, B, C, C#, D, D#, and E, are played from holes 44 through 56 inclusive, in order. Holes 57 through 61 are coupled to holes 45 through 49 in order as follows: 57 to 45, 58 to 46, 59 to 47, 60 to 48, and 61 to 49.

The Nelson-Wiggen Style 8 cabinet piano has two extra instruments, xylophone and bells, both of the reiterating (repeating) type. Some Style 8s were originally tubed to play A rolls, and others were tubed to play G rolls. In the A roll version, each time hole 62 calls for an extra instrument, one instrument plays. At the end of hole 62 an alternating mechanism pushes a switch valve over so the other instrument will play next time.

The Western Electric "Selectra" tune selecting device depends on hole 61 to "find" a certain song. Special Selectra A rolls were cut with a long hole 61 between songs.

Large keyboardless pianos such as the Seeburg K and Western Electric X use the same standard piano back (made by the Haddorff Piano Co. of Rockford, Illinois) as the Link 2E, which has 61 playing notes tuned from G to G. Because the A roll has only 58 playing notes, the lowest three piano notes have no pneumatics, and the piano is tubed as follows: Lowest notes: G (inoperative), G# (inoperative), A (inoperative), A# (hole 4), B (hole 5), C (hole 6) . . . Highest notes: F (hole 59), F# (hole 60), G (hole 61).

The 43-note Tangley Calliaphone CA-43 has a note range from F to B. The two highest notes, A# and B, are not played automatically. This leaves 41 notes which are played from the 58 notes of the A roll. These are coupled in the bass as follows: F (lowest note) (roll holes 9 and 21), F# (10 and 22), G (11 and 23), G# (12 and 24), A (13 and 25), A# (14 and 26), B (15 and 27), C (4, 16, 28), C# (5, 17, 29), D (6, 18, 30), D# (7, 19, 31), E (8, 20, 32), F (33; not coupled from there to the end of the treble, which is note A, hole 61).

The 53-note National calliope has a note range from C to E. Unlike the Tangley CA-43 in which the extra notes are coupled in the bass, the National has them coupled in the treble. For this reason, an A roll which sounds pleasing on a CA-43 might not sound so on a National 53-note, and vice versa. In the National 53-note scale coupling begins in the treble, as noted. The higher notes in the National scale are coupled as follows: E (not coupled), F (coupled 45 and 57), F# (46 and 58), G (47 and 59), G# (48 and 60), A (49 and 61); end of coupling), A# (not coupled from here, hole 50, to end of range, E, hole 56).

A Guide to Better Electric Piano Service

Your electric piano is a good sized investment. That same amount of money in the bank would require some attention from you. An automatic instrument should have at least as much care if it is to give the maximum of service. We have found that the majority of complaints about the operation of electric pianos are caused by neglect of their owners, therefore we have issued this leaflet for the purpose of instructing our customers in some of the elementary points of electric piano operation.

Any piano should be tuned at least twice a year. A public instrument, which receives much more abuse that the home player, needs more attention.

If your player stands exposed to sudden temperature changes or moisture, it is certain that the tuning will have to be more frequent.

A piano out of tune drives away trade.

The electric motor and all moving metal parts should be oiled occasionally. Follow the directions of the manufacturer in doing this. **Never oil wooden bearings.** Oils will cause wood to swell and bind. Graphite alone should be used to lubricate wood.

Purchase a good tracker bar pump from your dealer and clean out the appertures in the tracker bar. Lint, dirt and small pieces of paper will be sucked into the holes and if not removed will eventually get into the player action and cause trouble.

Examine the motor belt at times. A loose belt will slip and retard the action of the player. Too tight a belt will result in excessive friction and wear.

Temperature changes, if too violent, will cause the finish of the case to "check". A good piano polish (not a cheap furniture oil) will bring out the lustre of the grain. If in doubt about the finish of your player, consult with your dealer.

Little need be said about the placing of the player. A prominent position will of course result in greater use of the piano by your patrons. Keep chairs and tables away from the front of the case so that patrons will be able to reach the coin slot easily.

The most important part of the piano is of course the music. No matter how much your instrument may have cost, without music it is worthless. The proper music will bring out the full value of the piano.

CLARK ORCHESTRA ROLLS are built especially for your instrument. Their use will increase your income materially and build prestige for your house. Your patrons already know that CLARK ORCHESTRA ROLLS contain the best arrangements and the latest music.

Electric piano owners often believe that one new music roll a month is sufficient. Consider this. The average patron of your house spends a half hour with you. During that time he can hear every tune of a ten-tune roll. Once played, it does not offer his nickels the temptation a new roll would. One new roll per week at least will cause that same patron to spend just four times as much money and people will begin to talk of your up-to-date methods.

We maintain a modern repair shop in which any necessary electric piano repairs can be made quickly and well. Our tuning facilities are at your disposal. Our shelves contain a good selection of the latest and best CLARK ORCHESTRA ROLLS. You are welcome to make use of this store to the utmost.

Some hints and suggestions for the coin piano owner as given by the Clark Orchestra Roll Company in one of its periodic bulletins.

STYLE E VIOLIN
MADE WITH FLUTE OR VIOLIN PIPES

Seeburg Style E coin piano with violin (or flute) pipes, a popular style made circa 1910-1915. The instruments on this page use standard type A coin piano rolls.

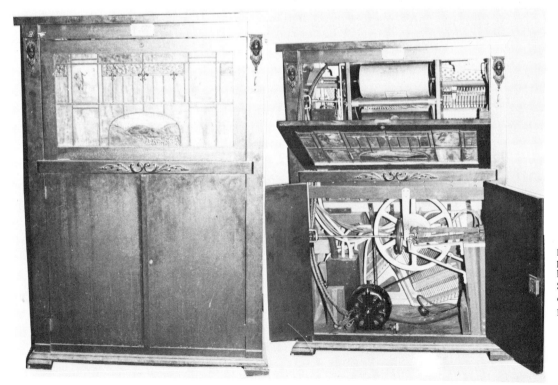

This unusual Seeburg A-roll piano has the interior of a Style L piano and a cabinet which is a hybrid between the standard Style L case and the rare PGA cabinet. (Mike Kitner Collection; photograph by Dr. William Black)

IMPORTANT—Read Carefully

To assist you in obtaining the latest music for your piano with the slightest delay, we would suggest that:

In ordering from this Bulletin, be sure to state the Manufacturer's name and style of your piano or orchestrion, OR THE LETTER BEFORE THE NUMBER ON THE PROGRAM ON THE ROLL WHICH IS NOW IN YOUR INSTRUMENT.

For your information, we are listing herewith the names of the styles of 65-note rewind electric pianos which use the rolls listed in our Bulletin with the letter A before the number.

STANDARD 65-NOTE REWIND COIN-OPERATED ELECTRIC PIANOS
USING 3½-INCH CORES

American	National 20R
Carleton	Nelson-Wiggen
Casino	Style 1-2-3-4
Chicago Electric	Originators
Coinola A,C, & Cupid	Operators, A, C
Colonial	and Cupid
Cote	Presburg
Cremona	Price & Teeple
Eberhardt	Rand
Electra	Regina
Empress 65-note	Reichard
Engelhardt	Schaeffer
Eusymphonic	SEEBURG A, B, C, E,
Harwood	F, K, L & PGA
Heller	Starr
Howard	Tangley Calliaphone
Jewett	Tangley Calliope
Lehr	Victor
Marquette	Violophone
Midget Orchestra	Western Electric
Monarch	A, C, X and J

And All Styles of
SEEBURG Organs, Orchestrions and Pianos

USING 3-INCH CORES

Anderson	Evans	Netzow
Ariston	Haines	Reed
Armstrong	Ideal	Rhapsodist
Autoelectrola	Wilson	Schultz
Billings	Wm. A. Johnson	Standard F and GR
Concertrola	Kibby	Waltham
Decker Bros	King	Watson
Electratone	Kreiter	

We would ask that you be careful when ordering, as rolls shipped according to order cannot be exchanged.

We reserve the right to discontinue without notice any numbers here listed.

Rolls listed in this Bulletin will be ready for shipment the first of the month.

For All Standard 65-Note Rewind Coin Operated Pianos
Also SEEBURG Styles A, B, C, E, F, K, PGA and L

A-1359 NATURAL MELODY HITS
1. Highways Are Happy Ways, Fox Trot.
2. A Night In June, Fox Trot.
3. Roam On My Little Gypsy Sweetheart, Fox Trot.
4. Good News, Fox Trot.
5. Miss Annabelle Lee, Fox Trot.
6. Baby Feet Go Pitter Patter, Fox Trot.
7. The Calinda, Fox Trot.
8. Someday You'll Say "O.K.!", Fox Trot.
9. O! Ya! Ya! Fox Trot.
10. Who's That Pretty Baby? Fox Trot.

A-1360 FLASHES FROM SONGLAND
1. Baby Your Mother, Fox Trot
2. Swanee Shore, Fox Trot.
3. She Don't Wanna! Fox Trot.
4. Under the Moon, Fox Trot.
5. After I've Called You Sweetheart, Waltz.
6. Lucky In Love, Fox Trot.
7. Barbara, Fox Trot.
8. Love and Kisses, Fox Trot.
9. Sweet Someone, Fox Trot.
10. Vo-Do-Do-De-O Blues, Fox Trot.

A-1361 FUNNY! SMART! DISTINCTIVE!
1. She's Got "It," Fox Trot.
2. I Walked Back From the Buggy Ride, Fox Trot.
3. When the Work's All Done This Fall, One-step.
4. Red Lips—Kiss My Blues Away, Fox Trot.
5. Things That Remind Me Of You, Waltz.
6. Yes She Do—No She Don't, Fox Trot.
7. My Sweet Yvette, Fox Trot.
8. I Call You Sugar, Fox Trot.
9. Do You Love Me? Fox Trot.
10. Just Once Again, Fox Trot.

A-1362 IT'S GOT "IT"
1. The Old Gray Mare, Fox Trot.
2. America Did It Again, One-Step.
3. Nanette, Fox Trot.
4. Lady Do, Fox Trot.
5. I've Lived All My Life Just For You, Waltz.
6. Wy-Lets, Fox Trot.
7. Oh, Dem Golden Slippers, Fox Trot.
8. That Pretty Little So and So Of Mine, Fox Trot.
9. Gid-ap, Garibaldi, One-step.
10. Who-oo? You-oo! That's Who! Fox Trot.

A-1363 ALL HIT REVIEW
1. I Wonder How I Look When I'm Asleep, Fox Trot.
2. Captain Lindbergh, One-Step.
3. Ain't That a Grand and Glorious Feeling? Fox Trot.
4. You Don't Like It—Not Much, Fox Trot.
5. Positively-Absolutely, Fox Trot.
6. Wasn't It Nice? Fox Trot.
7. The Same Old Moon, Fox Trot.
8. Just Call On Me, Fox Trot.
9. No Wonder I'm Happy, Fox Trot.
10. Bye Bye Pretty Baby, Fox Trot.

For All Standard 65-Note Rewind Coin Operated Pianos
Also SEEBURG Styles A, B, C, E, F, K, PGA and L

A-1364 SPECIAL XYLOPHONE ARRANGEMENT
1. Under the Moon, Fox Trot.
2. Who-oo? You-oo! That's Who, Fox Trot.
3. She's Got "It," Fox Trot.
4. I've Lived All My Life Just For You, Waltz.
5. Who's That Pretty Baby? Fox Trot.
6. My Sweet Yvette, Fox Trot.
7. Baby Your Mother, Fox Trot.
8. Things That Remind Me Of You, Waltz.
9. Someday You'll Say "O. K." Fox Trot.
10. She Don't Wanna! Fox Trot.

A-1365 HOT STEPPIN' BLUES
1. Cow Cow Blues.
2. Back Water Blues.
3. Falling Rain Blues.
4. The Texas Wail.
5. One Sweet Letter From You.
6. Lonesome Road Blues.
7. Mean Old Bed-Bug Blues.
8. Uncle Sam Blues.
9. Black Snake Blues.
10. Arkansas Blues.

A-1366 ANOTHER GOOD ONE—MEXICAN
1. Serenata Mexicana.
2. La Higuerita, Couplet.
3. La Revolcado, Polca.
4. Reliquia de Amor, Valse.
5. Ingratitud, Valse.
6. Te Imploro, Tango.
7. El Pagare, Paso Doble.
8. Vals del Rialto.
9. Al Pie De Tu Ventana.
10. Yo Amo A Una Mujer Que Es Todo Amor, Cancion.

A-1367 GERMAN
1. Whisky und Soda, One-step.
2. Bist du glucklich, Schatz, One-step.
3. Es gibt im Leben manches Mal Momente, Fox Trot.
4. Waltzertraum, Waltz.
5. In der Nacht, One-step.
6. Eine kleine Freundin hat doch jeder Mann, One-step.
7. Ja, weil die Susi, Fox Trot.
8. Untreue Liebe, Waltz.
9. Puppchen, One-step.
10. Ach konnt ich noch einmal so lieben, Song.

A-1331 BIG HIT REVIEW
1. Ain't She Sweet, Fox Trot.
2. I Love You, But I Don't Know Why, Fox Trot.
3. I Never See Maggie Alone, Fox Trot.
4. Crazy Words—Crazy Tune, Fox Trot.
5. High-High-High Up in the Hills, Fox Trot.
6. I'm Looking Over A Four Leaf Clover, Fox Trot.
7. Moonbeam, Kiss Her For Me, Fox Trot.
8. Everything's Made For Love, Fox Trot.
9. Black Snake Moan, Fox Trot.
10. You Can't Cry Over My Shoulder, Fox Trot.

This list, issued by Seeburg in the late 1920s, features a selection of 10-tune A rolls, including one honoring America's greatest hero of the time, "Captain Lindbergh, One-Step." It was the policy to assign program titles to rolls, so "Flashes from Songland," "Hot-Steppin' Blues," and others undoubtedly helped to stir up buyer interest. A contemporary Clark Orchestra Roll Co. catalogue featuring xylophone-oriented arrangements has such program titles as "Xylophonic Clicks," "Xylaratin' Xylophone Hits," "Xylo Ripples," "Zillo-Phone Hits," "Xylo-Pep," "Xyloette," "Xylo-Flash," "Splittin' Kindlin,' " "Ticklin' the Xylophone," "Xylographical Hits," and "Xylophobia," the last one being particularly interesting, for it means "fear of wood," or perhaps "fear of xylophones"!

BULLETIN

CLARK ORCHESTRA ROLLS

September-1925

65-note rewind

ELECTRIC PIANO MUSIC

CLARK ORCHESTRA ROLLS
are made for the following Automatic Instruments

If your piano is listed here, CLARK ORCHESTRA ROLLS may be obtained to operate it.

STANDARD 65-NOTE REWIND ELECTRIC PIANOS
Using 3 inch Cores

American	Nelson-Wiggen
Carleton	Style 1
Casino	Banj-O-Grand Style 2
Coinola A and C and Cupid	Banjo X Style 3
Colonial	Style 4
Cote	Originators
Cremona	National 20R
Eberhardt	Presburg
Empress 65-note	Price & Teeple
Engelhardt	Rand
Eusymphonie	Regina
Harwood	Reichard
Heller	Schaeffer
Howard	Seeburg A, B, C, D, E, F, K, L.
Jewett	Starr
Marquette	Tangley Calliaphone
Midget Orchestra	Tangley Caliope
Monarch	Victor
Western Electric A, C, X	Violophone

Using 3 ◼ inch Cores

Anderson	Kibby
Ariston	King
Armstrong	Kreiter
Autoelectrola	Netzow
Billings	Reed
Concertrola	Rhapsodist
Decker Bros.	Schultz
Electratone	Standard F and GR
Evans	Waltham
Haines	Watson
Ideal	Wilson
Wm. A. Johnson	

Music for these pianos is always in stock and your orders will be promptly filled.

Rolls for Credit Must be returned within 5 days from receipt of order.

Rolls Shipped as ordered cannot be returned.

See other page for styles 4x, 5x, 5

---

578   **Review of Irresistible Hits**
1 Oh, Katharina, One-step
2 When I Think Of You, Fox trot
3 The Midnight Waltz
4 Ukulele Lady, Fox trot
5 On the Way To Monetrey, Fox trot
6 In Shadowland, Waltz
7 Isn't She the Sweetest Thing? One-step
8 Lady, Be Good, Fox trot
9 Fascinating Rhythm, Fox trot
10 Keep Smiling At Trouble, Fox trot

577   **All Hit Waltz Roll**
1 The Midnight Waltz
2 Oh, How I Miss You To-Night
3 At the End Of a Winding Lane
4 Only a Weaver Of Dreams
5 Pal Of My Cradle Days
6 The Melody That Made You Mine
7 In Shadowland
8 I'm So Ashamed
9 A Waltz In the Moonlight
10 One Stolen Kiss

575   **"The Big Ten" Conference Winner**
1 Who Takes Care Of the Caretaker's Daughter? Fox trot
2 Isn't She the Sweetest Thing? One-step
3 The Midnight Waltz
4 Ukulele Lady, Fox trot
5 Pretty As a Picture, Fox trot
6 Oh! Those Eyes, One-step
7 My Mother's Humming Lullaby, Waltz
8 Lady Of the Nile, Fox trot
9 When My Sugar Walks Down the Street, Fox trot
10 You Gave All Your Kisses To Somebody Else, Fox trot

574   **A "Hot Roll" From the Musical Bakeshop**
1 If I Ever Cry You'll Never Know, Fox trot
2 Yes Sir, That's My Baby, Fox trot
3 In the Purple Twilight, Fox trot
4 Pal Of My Cradle Days, Waltz
5 If You Knew Susie, Fox trot
6 Mighty Blue, Fox trot
7 Twilight Shadows, Waltz
8 Sweet Georgia Brown, Fox trot
9 Stop Your Ticklin' Me, One-step
10 Charleston, Fox trot

Excerpts from the Clark Orchestra Roll Company's bulletin of September 1925. Above is a list of some of the different trademarks of instruments which used the type A coin piano roll. Some, such as Eusymphonie, Presburg, and Violophone were obscure, while others such as Seeburg (in particular), Cremona, Nelson-Wiggen, and Western Electric were well known.

One contemporary Clark bulletin recommended that coin piano owners burn their old music rolls so that they would not offend their customers by playing out-of-date music!

Note the imaginative program titles such as "A 'Hot Roll' From the Musical Bakeshop" and " 'The Big Ten' Conference Winner."

579   **The Musical "Vamp"**
1 Seminola, Fox trot
2 I'm Always Thinking Of Someone, Fox trot
3 Miss You, Waltz
4 Dainty Miss, Fox trot
5 If You Knew Susie, Fox trot
6 If You Hadn't Gone Away, Fox trot
7 Twilight Shadows, Waltz
8 In the Purple Twilight, Fox trot
9 Sing Loo, Fox trot
10 On the Oregon Trail, Fox trot

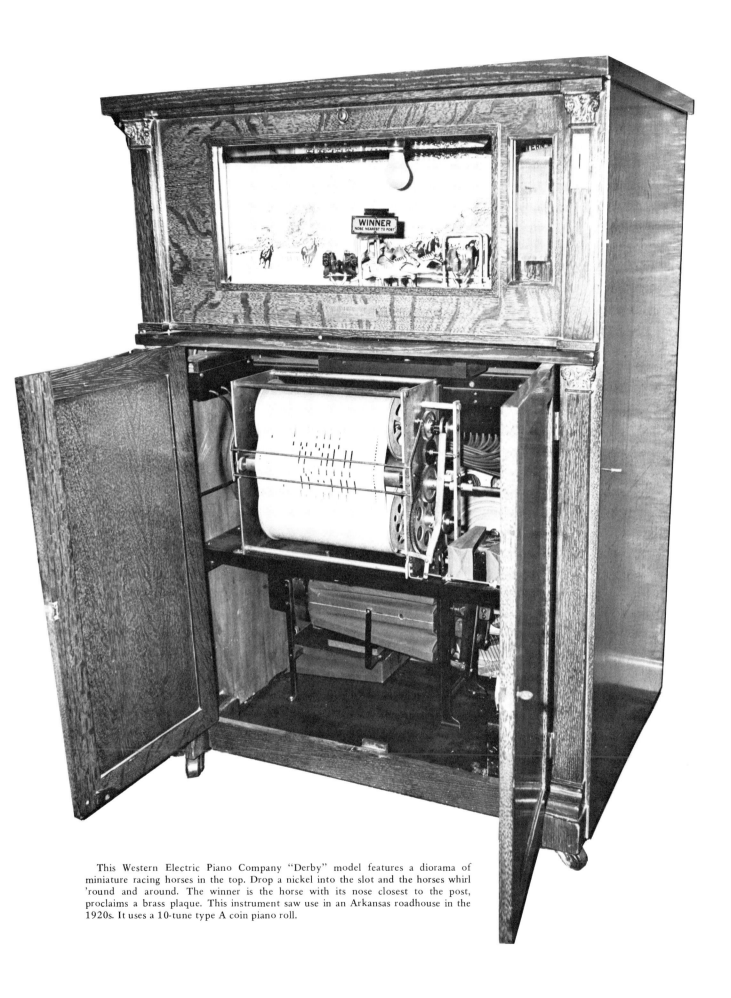

This Western Electric Piano Company "Derby" model features a diorama of miniature racing horses in the top. Drop a nickel into the slot and the horses whirl 'round and around. The winner is the horse with its nose closest to the post, proclaims a brass plaque. This instrument saw use in an Arkansas roadhouse in the 1920s. It uses a 10-tune type A coin piano roll.

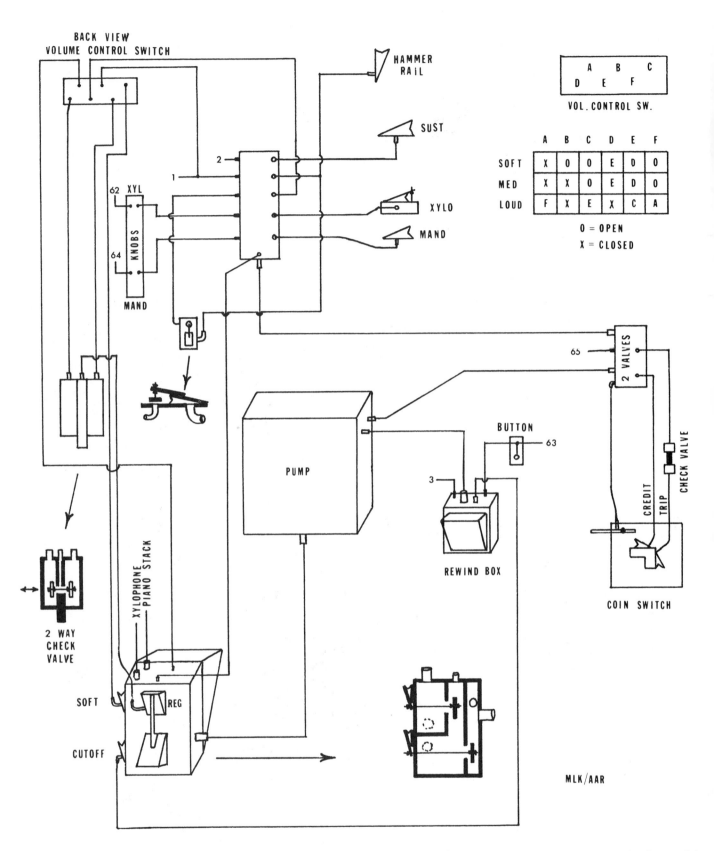

The above tubing diagram was devised by Mike Kitner from a Seeburg Style K piano with xylophone, serial number 165,200.

Functions of the soft-medium-loud switch used in some Seeburg A-roll coin pianos:

The regulator pneumatic, labeled REG, has no effect while open. When it closes, it pulls on the soft level regulator, providing a stack vacuum level between normal and soft.

When the knob is set on "soft," the hammer rail is moved up and the stack vacuum is shunted through the soft regulator, providing the softest possible playing level. Tracker bar hole 1 has no effect. In the "medium" mode, with hole 1 closed, the hammer rail is down and the stack receives vacuum through the soft regulator. The regulator pneumatic is closed so the stack vacuum is higher than in the soft mode. When hole 1 is open, the hammer rail moves up and the regulator pneumatic opens, providing the softest playing level. In the "loud" mode, with hole 1 closed, the hammer rail is down, and the soft regulator is bypassed, providing the loudest possible playing level. When hole 1 is opened, the hammer rail moves up and the stack receives vacuum through the soft regulator, with the regulator pneumatic closed.

BARREL PIANOS

There seem to be nearly as many barrel piano scales as there are barrel pianos, a situation similar to that of barrel organs. The typical barrel piano has an incomplete non-chromatic bass octave with as many as or a few more bass notes in proportion to the total number of notes as there are in the typical band organ scale. The accompaniment octave usually has 10 or 12 notes, with the rest of the main piano scale devoted to the melody section. In pianos having a separate reiterating mandolin section, the section usually occupies the treble portion of the instrument.

Large barrel piano orchestrions have a key for bass drum, another for cymbal, two keys for snare drum, one for triangle, and 10 or 12 more keys toward one end of the barrel for xylophone notes. Some barrel pianos have a completely chromatic melody section, while others are limited to playing in one or two different keys. The tuning scale is marked on the pinblock of many instruments.

During the 19th century, most automatic upright pianos were of the barrel type. After the advent of the music roll's popularity in the early 20th century, barrel pianos were still made for use in locations with sharp climate changes (such as Belgium, which in many areas is very damp) or for especially hard or rugged use. In the latter category, barrel pianos were popular on the streets of New York and other American cities, as a musical accompaniment for merry-go-rounds and carnivals (C.W. Parker sold hundreds for this purpose), and similar activities. The music was repetitious (although some instruments had interchangeable cylinders to obviate this problem), but this was not important if the instrument moved from place to place.

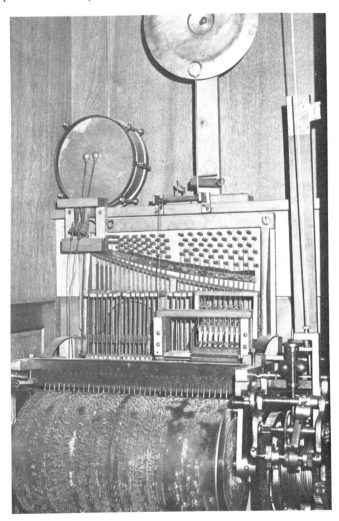

Above and right: Interior and exterior views of two different barrel pianos made during the early 20th century. Barrel pianos and orchestrions were popular in Belgium, France, Italy, and Spain as late as the 1920s. Their use in America practically ceased with the widespread popularity of the roll-operated piano in the first decade of the 20th century.

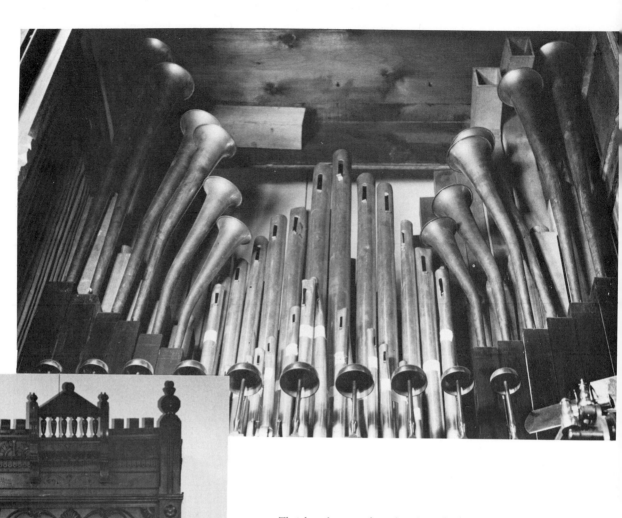

The barrel-operated orchestrion shown on this page was made in Buffalo, New York during the late 19th century by Bernhard Dufner. The cabinet measures 10'6" high by 5'6" wide by 3'8" deep and uses barrels which are 2'10" long and 8" in diameter. The instrumentation consists of 120 pipes arranged in four ranks, including 12 brass trumpets. Ten saucer bells are displayed in front of the pipes. The barrel frame comprises 58 keys, including 10 separate keys for the bells.

Dufner, who came to America in 1867 from Germany's Black Forest district, moved to Buffalo in 1868 and remained in that city until his death in January 1898. In 1873 a directory listed him as a "Manufacturer of Orchestrions, Hand Organs, and all Sorts of Automatic or Self-Playing Instruments. Cylinders Made on Short Notice. 795 Washington Street." The city directory of 1887 lists him at 224 Goodell Street. William Edgerton, who described Dufner in an article in the Autumn 1978 Musical Box Society "Bulletin," estimates that Dufner made about three or four dozen orchestrions during his career, the most outstanding being a $12,000 instrument with 60 barrels made around 1878 for a Mr. Powers, who was a Rochester art dealer.

During the late 19th century the making of barrel-operated orchestrions was done by a number of different craftsmen and shops, including Frick in Louisville, Kentucky (this apparently was an extensive operation, according to the late Farny Wurlitzer, who visited the Frick factory in the 1890s) and Schoenstein (who was very active in the San Francisco area and who made and/or imported many very large orchestrions for residences and commercial locations).

(Bernhard Dufner information and illustrations courtesy of William Edgerton)

BERRY-WOOD PIANO PLAYER COMPANY
Pianos and Orchestrions

The Berry-Wood Piano Player Company, headquartered in Kansas City, Missouri, was a small but important force in the coin piano and orchestrion field in the early 20th century. Its main period of activity was from about 1907 to 1914. Instruments produced included several different types of keyboard-style pianos with mandolin attachment (some with an additional instrument as well, such as a 25-note set of orchestra bells [Style C-B], or a rank of flute or violin pipes [Style F]) as well as several large orchestrions (called "Auto Orchestras"). The most elaborate instrument was the Style A.O.W. (Auto Orchestra W) which contained a piano, 34 flute pipes, 34 violin pipes, 25 orchestra bells, 25-note xylophone, kettle drum effect, castanets, crash cymbal, bass drum, snare drum (with additional rim beater), tambourine, and mandolin effect.

Rolls were made in two formats: endless and rewind styles. Early instruments were of the endless style, then instruments were made with the buyer's choice of either format (with the designation being "R" for rewind during this period; for example, orchestrion Style A.O.H. used endless-type music, and A.O.H.R. used rewind-type music), and, finally, later styles were made in the rewind format (without mention of the "R"; the A.O.W. orchestrion, which uses rewind-type music, being an example).

Additional information concerning Berry-Wood rolls is solicited.

BERRY-WOOD ORCHESTRION ROLL
15¼" wide; holes spaced 6 per inch

1 Rewind
2 Shutoff
3 Bass drum, cymbal, triangle
4 Snare drum
5 to 86, 82 notes in order C to A
87 Sustaining pedal on
88 Cancel pedals
89 Soft pedal on
90 Play

The Berry-Wood orchestrion roll given above was probably for use on Styles A.O.H.R. and A.O.S.R. The Style A.O.W. may use a more complex roll for it contains effects not provided for on the preceding scale.

BERRY-WOOD STYLE F ROLL
15¼" wide; holes spaced 6 per inch

1 Rewind
2 Shutoff
3 Pipes off
4 Pipes on
5 to 86, 82 notes in order C to A
87 Sustaining pedal on
88 Cancel pedals
89 Soft pedal on
90 Play

BERRY-WOOD PIANO ROLL
11¼" wide; spaced 6 holes per inch; endless

1 Shutoff
2 to 59, Playing notes
60 ?
61 Sustaining pedal on?
62 Cancel pedals?
63 Soft pedal on?

This scale is based on examination of roll 6557 which is punched with boat-shaped holes.

The Berry-Wood Style A.O.W. ("Auto Orchestra, Style W) was the largest orchestrion made by the firm. Apparently only a few were ever produced.

EQUIVALENT TO 10 PIECE ORCHESTRA

BERRY WOOD

New York
141st Street and
Canal Place

AUTO-ORCHESTRA—STYLE AOW

**Kansas City
Mo.**

...PROGRAMME...
ROLL NO. 9053

Silver Bell,

Percy Wenrich

Haunting Rag,

J. Lenzberg

Hula Hula Intermezzo,

P. Wenrich

Lemon Drops,
Rag Two step   M. Bernard

Ring Ting-a-Ling,

Jean Schwartz

The Oyster Rag,

Tom Lyle

Oriental Maidens,
Intermezzo   P. Wenrich

The Round Up Rag,

Jerome Shay

...PROGRAMME...
ROLL NO. 9218

Auntie Skinner's Chicken Dinner,
One-Step, Two-Step   Theo. Morse

Roll Them Cotton Bales,
Fox Trot   J. Rosamond Johnson

Saskatoon,
Rag   Phil Goldberg

Goofer Dust,
One-Step   Chris. Smith

December Morn,
Fox Trot   Harry Lincoln

My Ziegfeld Midnight Girl,
One-Step   Dave Stamper

Starlight and You,
Waltz   Charles Quick

Keep It Up,
Fox Trot   Chris. Smith

Two different program cards, shown actual size, issued by Berry-Wood circa 1910. Such cards were made for display at various places around a place of business, including on the piano itself, to entice nickels.

FRONT VIEW
BERRY-WOOD 88 Note Automatic Piano
Note the Artistic Appearance

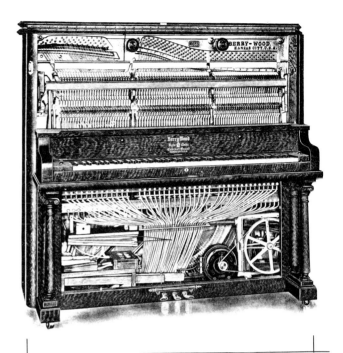

INTERIOR VIEW
BERRY-WOOD 88 Note Automatic Piano Showing Player Construction
Note the Compactness and Extreme Simplicity

These views of a Berry-Wood coin piano circa 1908-1910 show the roll mechanism mounted on the back of the instrument, an arrangement used by several other manufacturers as well, notably by Peerless. While the endless-type roll had the advantage of simplicity in operation (no rewinding mechanism was necessary; patrons did not have to endure silence as they had to with pianos which rewound rolls at the end of the last selection), the roll was awkward to change, and the instrument had to be positioned well out from the wall.

J.P. Seeburg claimed to have introduced art glass in the American coin piano. Until art glass became popular, shortly before 1910, nearly all instruments had plain glass, as did the Berry-Wood shown here.

BACK VIEW
BERRY-WOOD 88 Note Automatic Piano Showing Automatic Music
Tracking Device
Note the Rigid Construction of Piano Frame

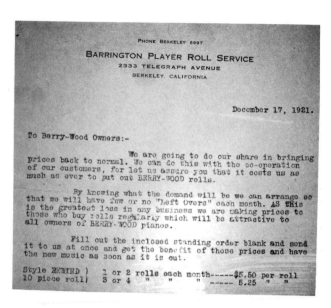

By December 1921 Berry-Wood rolls were rare. Some of the demand was filled by the Barrington Player Roll Service, which apparently perforated new tunes on a monthly subscription basis.

Style 15

THIS beautiful instrument is built exclusively for use with our *Hand-Played* Music Rolls and is beyond a doubt the finest production ever offered to the trade. The music rendered by this player is an exact reproduction of the interpretation of the artist, and all mechanical effects are eliminated completely. Made as a plain Automatic Piano or with Flute or Violin Pipes. Music rolls are exactly as played by an artist and contain from four to eight selections. Eighty-eight Note Scale. Rewind Music. Magazine slot.

In ordering state whether wanted as Piano alone or with Flute or Violin Pipes.

The Style 15 Berry-Wood coin piano was available as a piano alone or with one rank of pipes.

Style F.
In Rewind Music Only

CONTAINS Celebrated Berry-Wood Eighty-eight Note Player Action, Thirty-seven wood Flute or Violin Pipes. All mechanism contained in a rich Teakwood finished case, Beautiful Swell front center Art Glass Panel, Two Oval Side Panels of Harp Design, Double Veneered Case, Full Iron Plate, 7⅓ Octaves. Full Extension Automatic Music Desk, Three Strung Unisons; imported German Wire, Full Copper Wound Bass Strings, Built-up Pin Blocks of Rock Maple Double Repeating Action, Billings Brass Flanges, Best Ivory Keys, Fourteen Pound Hammers.
Magazine Slot
In ordering state whether Flute or Violin Pipes are wanted

The Style F Berry-Wood piano featured a rank of violin or flute pipes in addition to the piano.

One of several suggested form letters supplied by Berry-Wood to its dealers and distributors, circa 1912.

BLESSING PIANOS AND ORCHESTRIONS

The Blessing family, of Unterkirnach, in Germany's Black Forest, was active in the field of automatic musical instruments from the 1790s until the second decade of the 20th century. Although factory production of instruments had ceased, some family members continued custom building of orchestrions and other units, and repair of instruments, until the 1960s.

Production of Blessing instruments was limited, with the result that only a few pianos, orchestrions, and related instruments survive today.

52 Mandolin off
53 Xylophone on
54 Bells and harmonium on
55 Cello (harmonium reeds) on
56 Mandolin on

The hole which turns the xylophone off is unknown. Holes 4+7 in combination = rewind. The scale stick is marked "Mandoline + xylophone = tremolo," which probably means that these two instruments are of the reiterating type. The piano range is holes 9 to 48, F to F; the pipes and harmonium range is 21 to 41, B to A; the range for the bells is 30 to 41, A to A. This particular scale is from the archives of the late Eugene DeRoy and is marked "Weisser Blessing."

BLESSING ORCHESTRION ROLL
11 9/16" wide; spaced approximately 5+ per inch

1 Castanets
2 Bass drum and cymbal
3 Snare drum
4 Shutoff
5 Sustaining pedal on
6 Soft pedal on
7 Sustaining pedal off
8 Pipes and harmonium off
9 F
10 G
11 A
12 B
13 C
14 D
15 E
16 F
17 F#
18 G
19 A
20 A#
21 B
22 C
23 C#
24 D
25 E
26 F
27 F#
28 G
29 G#
30 A
31 A#
32 B
33 C
34 C#
35 D
36 E
37 F
38 F#
39 G
40 G#
41 A
42 A#
43 B
44 C
45 C#
46 D
47 E
48 F
49 2nd violin (pipe rank) on
50 1st violin (pipe rank) on
51 Triangle

BLESSING POLYVOX ROLL
Approximately 11 7/16" wide; 5+ per inch

1 (if present): Blank
2 Wood block
3 Wood block
4 Cymbal
5 Bass drum
6 Snare drum
7 Sustaining pedal
8 Normal
9 Soft pedal
10 Rewind
11 Play
12 to 62, 51 playing notes, G to A
63 Shutoff
64 Xylophone on
65 Mandolin on
66 Cancel xylophone and mandolin
67 (if present): Blank

The first 12 notes are bass, G to F#; the second 12 notes are accompaniment, G to F#. The highest 27 notes are melody and mandolin, G to A. The highest 15 notes are xylophone, G to A.

JACOB DOLL & SONS
Electrova Coin Pianos

Electrova pianos were made circa 1905-1920 by Jacob Doll & Sons of New York City. In addition, the Electrova trademark is sometimes seen on instruments (with different roll types than listed here) made by the Peerless Piano Player Company (of St. Johnsville, N.Y.) and by the Electrova Company (44-note cabinet style).

Today, Electrova instruments are quite scarce and are encountered only in specialized collections.

ELECTROVA STYLE 65 AND 66 ROLL
11¼" wide; 9 holes per inch

1 Mandolin on
2 Sustaining pedal on
3 Sustaining pedal off
4 Soft expression on
5 Cancel soft expression
6 Blank
7 to 92, 86 notes in order A# to B
93 Blank
94 Shutoff
95 Rewind
96 Hammer rail up
97 Hammer rail down
98 Mandolin off

Note: Holes 4 and 5 control a pneumatic choker device; they seem to work as listed for some rolls, but other rolls seem to have the functions reversed.

Views of a fine Electrova piano which uses Style 65 and 66 rolls. (Mike Kitner Collection; photographs by Dr. William Black)

Far in the back of the Candy Kitchen (Main Street, Danbury, Connecticut) in this circa 1915 view can be seen (behind the gentleman sitting on the stool) an Electrova coin piano. At the time a nickel could buy a dish of ice cream, all the candy you could eat in fifteen minutes, or the latest ragtime tune. (Photograph courtesy of Dr. Robert Miller)

PIERRE EICH
Coin Pianos
and Orchestrions

Pierre Eich, of Ghent, Belgium, produced instruments from the early 20th century until the inception of World War II in 1939. Very popular during the 1920s and 1930s were such Eich instruments as the Solophone (a piano with 3 to 6 ranks of pipes, depending upon the model), the Super Violin (a piano with violin pipes), the Piano-Jazz, and the Accordeon-Jazz. Many of the Eich products of the 1930s were in Art Deco style cases.

PIERRE EICH HARMONICA JAZZ ROLL

1 Bass F#
2 General cancel
3 Bass G#
4 Temple block
5 Triangle
6 Saxophone on
7 Jazz flute on
8 Wood block
9 Mandolin on?
10 Blank
11 Bass drum
12 Rewind
13 to 22, Bass C, D, E, F, G, A, A#, B, C, C#
23 to 39, Accompaniment notes, D to F#
40 to 51, Countermelody, G to F#
52 to 81, Melody, G to C
82 Shutoff
83 Soft
84 Blank
85 Blank
86 Snare drum
87 Blank
88 Snare drum brush
89 Tambourine
90 Loud
91 Cymbal

PIERRE EICH HARMONICA JAZZ ROLL
(Variant of the preceding)
As preceding, except for these differences:

2 Blank
4 Blank
5 Blank
6 Blank
7 Blank
9 Blank
10 Blank
88 Snare drum, reiterating beater
89 Castanets or triangle

PIERRE EICH SUPER VIOLIN ROLL

1 Bass F#
2 Blank
3 Bass G#
4 Blank
5 Piano melody section off, violin pipes on
6 Tremolo
7 Blank
8 Mandolin on
9 Blank
10 Blank
11 Swell shutter(s) closed?
12 Rewind
13 to 22, Bass C, D, E, F, G, A, A#, B, C, C#
23 to 39, Accompaniment D to F#
40 to 51, Blank
52 to 81, Melody, G to C
82 Shutoff
83 Hammer rail up
84 Blank
85 Violin pipes on
86 Swell shutter(s) open, chain perforation
87 General cancel
88 Blank
89 Blank
90 Sustaining pedal, full vacuum
91 Blank

PIERRE EICH SOLOPHONE ROLL

1 Bass F#
2 Lowest 12 clarinet pipes on
3 Bass G#
4 Lowest 12 violin pipes on
5 Blank
6 Tremolo
7 Switches 2 to lower 12 cello pipes on
   and hole 4 to low 12 saxophone pipes on
8 Blank
9 Cancel 7
10 Cancel 2 and 4
11 Blank
12 Rewind
13 to 22, Bass C, D, E, F, G, A, A#, B, C, C#
23 to 39, Accompaniment D to F#
40 to 51, Counter melody F to F#, 12 lower pipes, no piano
52 to 81, Melody G to C, 18 upper pipes, continuation of piano scale from 39
82 Shutoff
83 Piano muffler on (piano hammers 9 to 46), swell shutters open
84 Upper 18 clarinet pipes on
85 Upper 18 violin pipes on
86 Blank
87 Cancel 84, 85, 88, and 89
88 Low 12 saxophone pipes on (there are no upper sax pipes)
89 Upper 18 cello pipes on
90 Sustaining pedal, swell shutters open
91 Blank

The preceding scale is from an instrument examined by Ed Hattrup. This particular Solophone has three ranks of pipes (clarinet, cello, and violin) divided into 12 lower and 18 upper notes, and 12 saxophone pipes. The lower and upper pipes may be turned on and off independently, for contrasting melody and counter melody.

Right: This beautiful Pierre Eich Solophone is in a light golden oak case with decorative wood carvings applied as trim. Made circa 1915-1925, the instrument contains a piano (made by J. Herrburgher, Paris) and six ranks of pipes representing flute, clarinet, saxophone, violin, viola, and cello. Swell shutters for expression are in the top of the instrument. The case measures 7'6" high by 5'8" wide by 2'9" deep. The Solophone was originally used in Belgium, where Eich instruments were made and where nearly all were sold. (Jim Prendergast Collection)

Below: Although Pierre Eich is known today for its pianos and orchestrions, during the early 20th century the firm made some very ornate fairground organs, two examples of which are shown below. Little is known about these instruments.

PIERRE EICH SOLOPHONE ROLL

(Variant of the preceding)
As preceding, except for these differences

2 Saxophone on
4 Violin on
5 Triangle
7 Cello on
8 Wood block
9 Clarinet on
10 Cancel
11 Bass drum
83 Soft pedal
84 Flute pipes on
85 Violin pipes on
86 Snare drum
87 Cancel
88 Soft
89 Oboe pipes on
90 Sustaining pedal
91 Cymbal

9+4 = Violin pipes on
7+4 = Cello pipes on
9+2 = Clarinet pipes on
7+2 = Saxophone pipes on
9+4+2 = Clarinet and violin pipes on
7+4+2 = Saxophone and cello pipes on

PIERRE EICH VIOLIN PIANO ROLL

Approximately 334 mm. wide; spacing is 21+ per 100 mm.

1 Violin pipes on
2 Shutoff
3 General cancel
4 Sustaining pedal
5 to 65, Notes C to C
66 Hammer rail
67 Mandolin on
68 Rewind

ENCORE AUTOMATIC BANJO

The Encore Automatic Banjo was popular from the late 1890s through the first several years of the 20th century. The instrument consists of a four-string banjo mounted vertically in a glass cabinet, with four metal "fingers" which pluck the strings, and with leather-covered buttons which stop the individual strings at the desired frets.

Encores were manufactured by two different firms, both interrelated. In Cambridgeport, Massachusetts, the Auto-Manufacturing Company (and its forebears, the New England Automatic Banjo Co. and the Eastern Specialty Co.) produced about 350 to 400 instruments. The American Automusic Company of New York produced even more, perhaps several thousand totally.

Rolls are of the endless type and are usually perforated with punches shaped like the letter D. Typically, several tunes were pasted together to form a program of several pieces. Each tune is about one minute in length.

ENCORE BANJO ROLL
9 5/8" wide; 5 holes per inch

1 Shutoff
2 C string pick
3 to 12, C string buttons, C# to A#
13 G string pick
14 to 23, G string buttons, G# to F
24 B string pick
25 to 34, B string buttons, C to A
35 D string pick
36 to 45, D string buttons, D# to C
46 Shutoff

In some instruments the roll feeds in the direction of front to back as it crosses the tracker bar; in others it feeds in the opposite direction.

Above: Encore Automatic Banjo, circa 1900, manufactured by the American Automusic Company of New York. (Bellm's Cars & Music of Yesterday Museum)

Left: This placard dates from the first few years of the 20th century and was designed to be affixed to the front of an Encore Automatic Banjo. It notes "music changed every day," which must have kept someone busy attending to the instrument! The program of five tunes comprises "Fare Thee Well Molly Darling," "Violets," "Alagazam," "Rosalie My Royal Rosy," and "Oh! Didn't He Ramble." Detailed information is given concerning each selection, a very unusual feature seen on few other program cards of any type. The card was once used on a route owned by the American Automusic Company. (Photograph courtesy of Larry Givens)

THE ≈ ENCORE

10 REASONS WHY ✧ ✧

THE AUTOMATIC BANJO IS THE KING OF SLOT MACHINES

✧ ✧ ✧ ✧

1. Because it is the Greatest Mechanical Marvel of the Century.

2. Because it is the only Automatic Musical Instrument wherein mechanical operation can be detected only by visual proof.

3. Because in range and brilliancy of execution, it surpasses the highest skill of the greatest manual experts.

4. Because it is the only Automatic Musical Instrument that reproduces absolutely by mechanical means the manual method of execution and rendition.

5. Because it is not a Music Box. It is a Banjo picked by Fingers and includes the essential musical effects of the Mandolin and Guitar.

6. Because there are no concealed effects. The whole operation is exposed and it is, therefore, a delight to the eye as well as the ear.

7. Because there is no musical instrument more popular than the Banjo.

8. Because it has an automatic Register that counts each nickel that is dropped in the slot, and is a mechanical Cashier of unquestionable honesty.

9. Because its operation involves no element of chance, and, therefore, violates no law. It can be used in all public places without risk of suppression.

10. And for all of the above reasons; BECAUSE IT IS THE GREATEST MONEY-EARNING SLOT MACHINE OF THE AGE.

For full information as to terms, address

American "Automusic" Company.

TRADE

MARK

New York Offices: No. 53 Broadway.

The Encore Automatic Banjo, marketed around the turn of the 20th century, featured a four-string banjo housed in a glass-fronted case. The rolls were endless and usually consisted of several different tunes pasted end to end. Despite glowing expectations, the Encore was not a commercial success. The story of this fascinating instrument can be found in a special chapter, "Ordeal by Letter," in "The Encyclopedia of Automatic Musical Instruments."

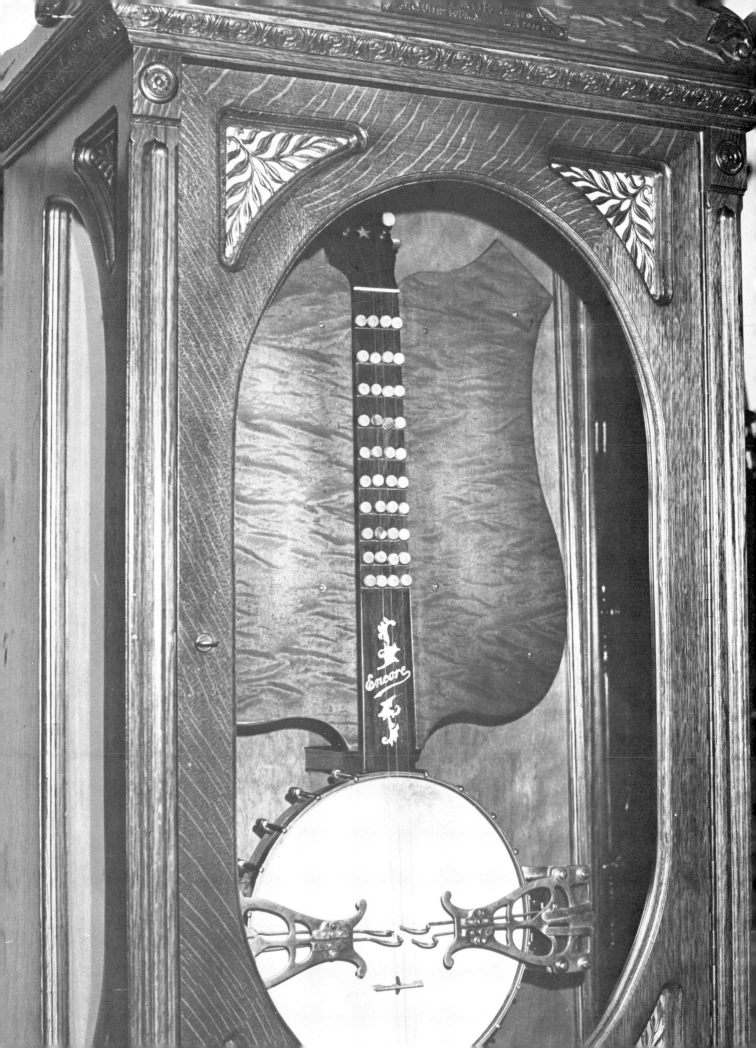

FRATI & CO.
Coin Pianos and
Orchestrions

Frati & Company, a Berlin, Germany firm, produced roll-operated pianos and orchestrions beginning in the late 19th century. From then until the 1920s many different designs were made, most of which were sold under the Fratinola name. In later years the firm was acquired by J.D. Philipps & Sons (of Frankfurt-am-Main), and certain Frati pianos and orchestrions were made with Philipps roll mechanisms.

During the period from about 1910 to 1914 very large orchestrions, called Fratihymnias, were made. Containing extensive instrumentation, these were competitive with the gigantic orchestrions being made at the time by Hupfeld, Philipps, Popper, and others. Apparently Frati orchestrion production was limited in comparison to these other makes, for few exist at the present time.

FRATI PIANO/ORCHESTRION ROLL
39.5 cm. wide; spacing approximately 22+ per 10 cm.

1 Xylophone off
2 Xylophone on
3 Shutoff
4 Sustaining pedal off
5 Sustaining pedal on
6 to 37, Notes E to B
38 Rewind
39 to 77, Notes C to D
78 Mandolin
79 Mandolin
80 Hammer rail
81 Hammer rail

The scale stick from which the preceding notation was taken gives no indication of which mandolin and hammer rail holes are on or off. The xylophone and mandolin have 32 notes and are played from holes 46 to 77. Some instruments may have been made with two additional holes in the tracker bar, both blank, preceding hole 1.

FRATIHYMNIA ORCHESTRION ROLL
Approx. 31.6 cm. wide; spacing approx. 20 holes per 6 cm.

1 Oboe on
2 Mandolin on
3 Cello pipes on
4 Contra bass on
5 Harmonium I (or bassoon) on
6 Accompaniment off
7 Harmonium IV(?) (or cello) on
8 Bass coupler on
9 Xylophone on
10 Melody off
11 Clarinet on (or solo violin pipes on)
12 Sustaining pedal
13 Solo violin pipes on
14 Flute on
15 Baritone on
16 to 45, Playing notes?
46 Castanets
47 Piccolo (or flute) on
48 Forte register off
49 General cancel
50 Triangle
51 Forte register
52 Piano on
53 Shutoff
54 Tremolo
55 Rewind
56 Swell shutter(s)
57 Violin pipes on
58 to 91, Playing notes
92 Orchestra bells on
93 Drum control?
94 Tympani soft
95 Snare drum soft
96 Bass drum
97 Horn
98 Cymbal
99 Snare drum
100 Tympani
101 Crescendo on
102 Tambourine
103 Tambourine

FRATI MELODICA (SYMPHONICA) ROLL
12½" wide; spaced approximately 17 holes per 3"

1 Clarinet on (variant scale: Bass coupler on)
2 Flute on
3 Sustaining pedal
4 Violin pipes on
5 Bass drum and cymbal
6 Soft pedal
7 Cymbal
8 Shutoff
9 to 20, Bass E, F#, G# to F
21 Rewind
22 General cancel
23 to 43, F# to D
44 Xylophone on
45 to 63, Notes D# to A
64 Mandolin on
65 Snare drum
66 Castanets
67 Snare drum, loud
68 Tremolo

Holes 3 and 4 together may turn the mandolin off in some models; in others, hole 64 may be a chain perforation.

„Fratihymnia"

No. 7.

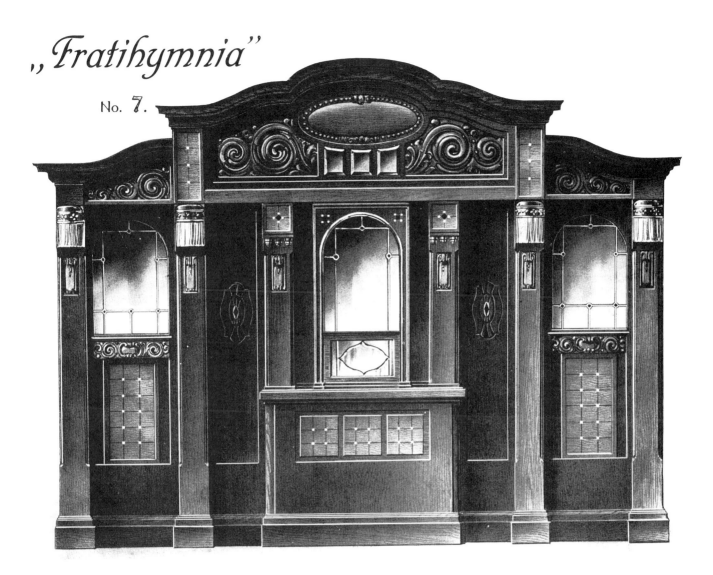

Artistic Playing Orchestrion „Fratihymnia"

No. 7.

In contradistinction to the preceding instrument of the same type, this Fratihymnia 7 contains all instruments of a **complete military band**, with trombones, trumpets, horn, saxophone, tuba, cornet-à-pistons, piccolo, cornets, clarinets, flutes. bassoon, oboe, forte and piano beatiug big and little drum, with cymbals, kettledrum, castanets, anvil, triangle, chimes, etc. etc.

A tremendous volume of sound is produced by this orchestrion, the demand for a substitute for a military band is excellently met. The playing produces an enthusiastic effect and the percussion is of an excellent precision. Even the largest room is filled with music by this monster-ensemble.

The instrument is adapted like the preceding one for **concert and ball rooms**.

It can be supplied in natural oak, stained in any colour. If desired, the front spaces or squares can be filled with animated pictures or with any other desired equipment, the extra price for which to be specially agreed upon.

Height about 3,15 m	Width about 4,15 m
Depth about 1.30 m	Weight about 1200 Ko.

Frati produced catalogues in the English language in order to take advantage of the market in England, America, and other English-speaking areas. Sometimes translations had a few rough edges, as the term "monster-ensemble" above illustrates. To keep tabs on what the competition was doing, Farny Wurlitzer collected catalogues of German orchestrion makers during the 1910-1914 period. The above illustration is a page from one of these. (Courtesy of the late Farny Wurlitzer)

STYLE "G"
ART STYLE—ORCHESTRION

HEIGHT, 6 ft. 5 in. Length, 5 ft. 6 in. Depth, 2 ft. 4 in. Contains 2 sets of pipes, violin and flute, bass and snare drum, Cymbal, Triangle, Tympani. Mandolin, loud and soft effect piano, giving the effect of an Orchestra of 6 men. Can be regulated and shut off any one instrument not desired to play. New and original scale of seven and one-third octaves, overstrung bass and three unisons throughout. Ornamental full iron plate. Nickeled tuning pins. Imported music wire and copper-wound bass strings. Brass flange action, highest grade imported wool hammers. Best grade ivory keys and ebony sharps. Double veneered hardwood case. Roll fall-board with continuous nickeled hinges. Double casters. Early English mission finish. Magazine slot registering 20 coins. Roll contains from 10 to 20 selections on rewind system.

J. P. SEEBURG PIANO CO.   MANUFACTURERS, CHICAGO

The Seeburg Style G orchestrion, sold from about 1911 until the mid 1920s, was one of the most popular large styles of the era. Several different case design variations were made, the most popular of which is shown above. Although it is stated that the music rolls contain up to 20 selections, in practice nearly all were of 10-tune format.

STYLE "G" AND "4X" ORCHESTRION ROLLS
Used by Seeburg, Nelson-Wiggen, and Others

The Style G roll (which was later made in a variation, the 4X) was introduced circa 1911 as the SS roll by the J.P. Seeburg Piano Company of Chicago. Containing percussion effects, the G roll was designed for use on large orchestrions such as the Seeburg styles G (piano, mandolin effect, bass drum, tympani effect, snare drum, triangle, cymbal, violin pipes, flute pipes), L Orchestra (same as the Style G orchestrion but with just one rank of pipes, usually flutes), the early KT (cabinet style orchestrion), and on several photoplayers. In later years a variation of the G roll, the 4X, was devised for orchestrions featuring a xylophone (see detailed text below).

Rolls of this type were distributed in the early years by the Automatic Music Roll Company (a division of Seeburg) and, like contemporary A rolls, were made by the coin-operated division of the QRS Music Roll Co. In the 1920s the Clark Orchestra Roll Company made many 4X rolls. Capitol (a division of the Operators Piano Company) also made G rolls.

While the note range of the Style G roll is limited, many of the musical arrangements are quite excellent. For this reason the early Style G orchestrion, its exterior decorated with colorful art glass (including two three-dimensional torches) and its interior filled with various pipes and percussion effects, is a favorite with collectors today. About three dozen are known to exist.

In the 1920s the market turned its direction from large ornate keyboard-style instruments such as the Style G and the Style L Orchestra to small compact cabinet-style (keyboardless) types. To simplify construction, pipes were eliminated and the xylophone became prominent as the featured extra instrument (pipes required a pressure system in addition to the vacuum system; the xylophone was operated on vacuum and did not require pressure). The Seeburg KT, KT Special, and to a lesser extent, the E Special, became very popular. Nelson-Wiggen manufactured a series of instruments which included styles 4X, 5 (rare), 5X, and 6, which were of somewhat similar conception. Western Electric Piano Co., a subsidiary of Seeburg, did likewise. To fill the demand, 4X rolls, which featured intermittent xylophone perforations, were made in a wide range of selections in the 1920s. Most Automatic Music Roll Company G rolls of the 1920s have xylophone arrangements. Many Capitol G rolls of the same period have pipe arrangements.

As different instruments were tubed slightly differently, several variations are given below. Refer to the supplementary text for additional details.

Early G-roll instruments such as the Seeburg styles G, L orchestra, and early KT use pipes as their extra instrument(s). Early Automatic Music Roll Co. and some Columbia/Capitol rolls have elongated treble notes at appropriate places to play the pipes effectively.

Later instruments such as the late KT, Nelson-Wiggen 4X, 5X, and others, have a single-stroke xylophone. 4X rolls, introduced by the Clark Orchestra Roll Co. in the year 1923, are similar to the G rolls but have many short alternating holes at appropriate places in the treble to make the single-stroke xylophone "busier." From that time on, most Automatic Musical Roll Co. and many

Capitol G rolls also have the 4X-style xylophone arrangements. Most collectors prefer to use Automatic and Columbia/Capitol G rolls with pipe arrangements on their instruments with pipes, and reserve their xylophone-arrangement Capitol G rolls and all Clark 4X rolls for instruments having single-stroke xylophones.

G AND 4X ORCHESTRION ROLLS
11¼" wide; spaced 6 holes per inch
(As tubed on the Seeburg G orchestrion)

1 Hammer rail
2 Sustaining pedal
3 to 14, notes in order G#. to G, octave coupled
15 to 26, continuation of note scale, G# to G
27 Flutes off
28 Rewind
29 Flutes on
30 Snare drum
31 Normal vacuum for piano and drums
32 Low vacuum for piano and drums
33 Shutoff
34 Tympani
35 Bass drum and cymbal
36 Tympani
37 Violin pipes off
38 Play
39 Violin pipes on
40 to 63, treble notes in order G# to G
64 Mandolin
65 Triangle

Keyboardless Orchestrions

Seeburg, Nelson-Wiggen, and Western Electric cabinet-style (keyboardless) G-roll orchestrions use the same piano back as the Link 2E which has three extra bass notes. The lowest three piano notes in these non-Link orchestrions have no pneumatics and are not used. Because the lowest G-roll note is G# and because of the three unused notes there are only 10 octave-coupled notes, beginning at A# and ending at G. Holes 3 and 4 (notes G# and A) are not coupled.

The notes, from the bass to the treble in chromatic order, are connected in the following manner: G (lowest note; not used), G# (not used), A (not used), A# (hole 5 in the roll), B (6), C (7), C# (8), D (9), D# (10), E (11), F (12), F# (13), G (14), G# (3), A (4), A# (5), B (6), and on in chromatic sequence to the top treble note G, which is tubed to hole 63.

Seeburg KT Orchestrion

Most KTs do not have a lock and cancel for piano expression, so holes 31 and 32 are blank. In KTs with one primary valve controlling both tambourine and castanets, they play together from hole 30 (snare drum). In KTs with two separate valves, the tambourine plays from 30 and the castanets from 35 (bass drum). The xylophone has 22 notes, from G to E. In general, early KT instruments had one rank of pipes (violin or flute) as the extra instrument; later KTs featured a xylophone.

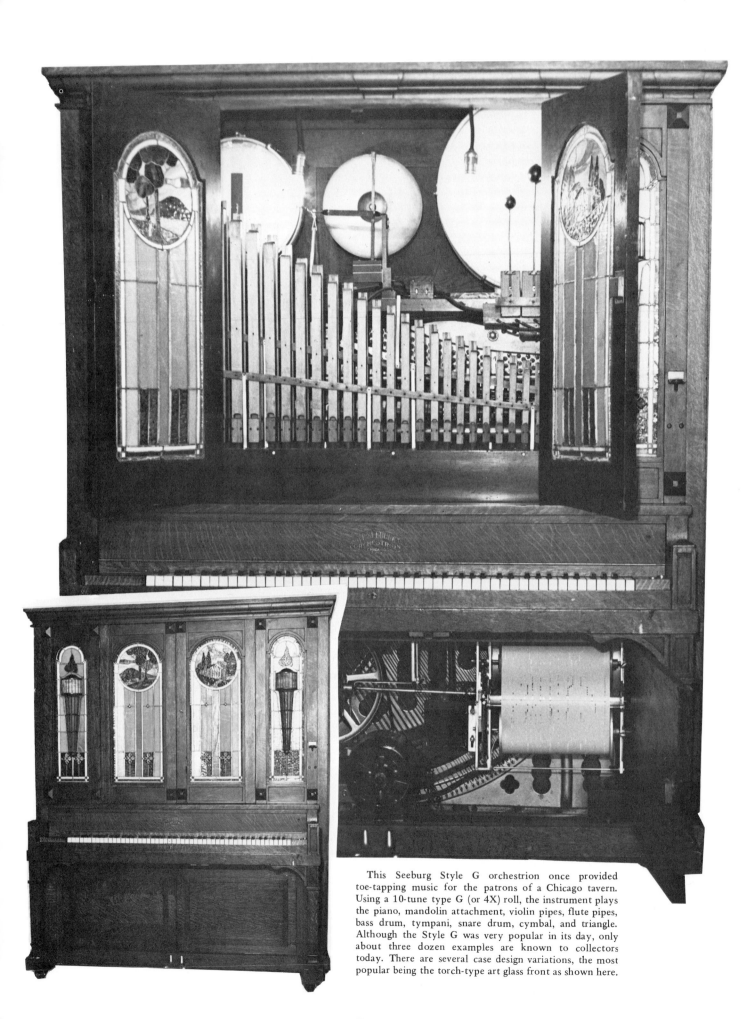

This Seeburg Style G orchestrion once provided toe-tapping music for the patrons of a Chicago tavern. Using a 10-tune type G (or 4X) roll, the instrument plays the piano, mandolin attachment, violin pipes, flute pipes, bass drum, tympani, snare drum, cymbal, and triangle. Although the Style G was very popular in its day, only about three dozen examples are known to collectors today. There are several case design variations, the most popular being the torch-type art glass front as shown here.

G AND 4X ORCHESTRION ROLLS
(As tubed on the Seeburg KT orchestrion)

1 Hammer rail
2 Sustaining pedal
3 to 14, notes in order G# to G (see text above)
15 to 26, continuation of note scale, G# to G
27 Extra instrument (pipe rank or xylophone) off
28 Rewind
29 Extra instrument on
30 Tambourine or castanets (see text above)
31 Blank
32 Blank
33 Shutoff
34 Blank
35 (See text above)
36 Blank
37 Blank
38 Play
39 Blank
40 to 63, treble notes in order G# to G
64 Mandolin
65 Triangle

Seeburg KT Special (and E Special)

The KT Special and E Special have more percussion instruments than there are holes in the G roll to play them, so several instruments are coupled together, while others alternate with each other, depending upon the setting of a multiplex switch which is controlled by the hammer rail perforation (hole 1). Although all KT Specials have the same basic instrumentation, several different ways of connecting the instruments to the tracker bar apparently were used.

Some very early KT Specials were housed in the standard eagle-art-glass-front KT-style cabinet with a flat top. The interior of this rare early style has the cymbal mounted on the left side of the cabinet with its own pneumatic and beater, the wood block has a single stroke beater, and each percussion instrument has its own separate valve. The multiplex switch switches a tube going from the tracker bar from one percussion instrument to another instrument whenever hole 1 is punched. No KT Special of this type with its undisturbed original tubing has been encountered by the authors. A logical way to connect the tubing is as follows:

1 Hammer rail and percussion multiplex switch
2 Sustaining pedal
3-14 Playing notes G#-G in order
15-26 Continuation of playing notes G#-G
27 Xylophone off
28 Rewind
29 Xylophone on
30 Snare drum
31 Normal vacuum
32 Low vacuum
33 Shutoff
34 Tympani and tambourine
35 Bass drum and cymbal; 35+1 wood block and castanets
36 Tympani
37 Drum lights off
38 Play
39 Drum lights on
40-63 Treble playing notes G#-G
64 Mandolin
65 Triangle

All of the above functions except the percussion multiplexing are known to be correct. The percussion tubing scheme seems to be what Seeburg intended, but a more musical way of controlling the multiplexing is to connect the multiplex switch to the mandolin or drum light switch. This way, the wood block will play the bass drum part for more extended musical passages instead of erratically alternating with the bass drum whenever the soft pedal hole is punched.

Apparently the next development in the evolution of the KT Special was the standard larger cabinet with a rectangular stained glass window (with a theatre-curtain design in the glass) and a bulky top trimmed with dentil molding. The cymbal is mounted over the bass drum and is played by an extension of the bass drum beater, but each of the other percussion instruments has its own separate valve. The wood block has a reiterating beater instead of a single stroke beater. This would seem to suggest that Seeburg intended to tube the wood block to play the reiterating snare drum part alternately with the snare drum, as controlled by the multiplex switch. The castanets would then logically be tubed to some other single-stroke instrument, perhaps one of the tympani or the tambourine. The bass drum and cymbal would always play from hole 35.

What was apparently the final version of the KT Special, and the style which is probably the most common today, has a dual-purpose multiplex switch, switching two separate tracker bar holes from two instruments to two other instruments. The snare drum, wood block, tambourine, one tympani, and the bass drum-cymbal beater each have their own separate valves, but the other tympani, triangle, and castanets are all connected to the same valve. Enough instruments in existence are tubed to the following scheme to suggest that it might be the way Seeburg originally tubed them.

30 Snare drum; 30+1 = wood block
34 Tympani
35 Bass drum and cymbal; 35+1 = tambourine
36 Tympani, triangle, and castanets
65 Tympani, triangle, and castanets

Many collectors who read the original catalogue descriptions of the KT Special as reproduced in *Player Piano Treasury* and *The Encyclopedia of Automatic Musical Instruments* and who put this instrument on their "most wanted" list are disappointed when they finally acquire one which is tubed to the above scheme and discover that it sounds like an entirely insane drummer! The musical output of a KT Special of this type will be improved if several modifications are made; this is a case where making minor changes in the originality of an instrument will greatly enhance its musical enjoyability. To do this, add separate valves—preferably reproductions of original Seeburg valve boxes—to the triangle and castanets. Add a reiterating mechanism to the tambourine, and disconnect the wood block slide valve to make it play single stroke. Then tube everything to the following scheme:

30 Snare drum; 30+1 = tambourine and castanets
34 Tympani
35 Bass drum and cymbal; 35+1 = wood block
36 Tympani
65 Triangle

Seeburg apparently wasn't very concerned with the correct tubing of the KT Special; at least this was the situation shortly after its introduction. A rather amazing letter dated May 7, 1925, from K.R. Craft of the Seeburg Service Department to the Dixie Music Co. of Tampa, Florida, notes: "As for the Style 'KT' Special we do not have a blue print showing the tracker bar connections, but we are enclosing herewith a blue print for the Style 'G' and we trust you will be able to follow up the rest."

Any reader having additional information concerning the original tubing of the several KT Special variations is encouraged to communicate with the authors.

Miscellaneous Orchestrions

Large Nelson-Wiggen and Western Electric orchestrions with more drums and traps than related holes in the roll have a shifter which functions like the one in the Seeburg KT Special. The Nelson-Wiggen 5X has 20 large marimba bars, from G to D, playing at the same pitch as the piano. Other Nelson-Wiggen, Seeburg, and Western Electric orchestrions have 22 or more xylophone bars pitched an octave higher than their corresponding piano notes.

General note: The competition between Clark/Automatic and Columbia/Capitol, in combination with a large market for G and 4X rolls, resulted in an exceptionally wide variety of music being produced. Many excellent arrangements exist today on these rolls, and, hence, they are favorites with collectors. Most rolls are of 10-tune length and contain tunes which play about 2½ minutes each. Often G/4X and A rolls with the same programs (same listing of tunes) were marketed at the same time.

Interior view of a Seeburg KT orchestrion. This instrument, which has an eagle-motif art glass front, was one of Seeburg's most popular during the 1920s. It uses style G or 4X rolls. (Roy Haning and Neal White Collection)

For SEEBURG Styles G, KT, KT Special, E Special, Orchestrions, and Styles P, Q, and W Motion Picture Players. Also adapted for Western Electric Style A and G Orchestrions

G-907   NATURAL MELODY HITS
1. Highways Are Happy Ways, Fox Trot.
2. A Night In June, Fox Trot.
3. Roam On My Little Gypsy Sweetheart, Fox Trot.
4. Good News, Fox Trot.
5. Miss Annabelle Lee, Fox Trot.
6. Baby Feet Go Pitter Patter, Fox Trot.
7. The Calinda, Fox Trot.
8. Someday You'll Say "O. K.!" Fox Trot.
9. Oh! Ya! Ya! Fox Trot.
10. Who's That Pretty Baby! Fox Trot.

G-908   FLASHES FROM SONGLAND
1. Baby Your Mother, Fox Trot.
2. Swanee Shore, Fox Trot.
3. She Don't Wanna! Fox Trot.
4. Under the Moon, Fox Trot.
5. After I've Called You Sweetheart, Waltz.
6. Lucky In Love, Fox Trot.
7. Barbara, Fox Trot.
8. Love and Kisses, Fox Trot.
9. Sweet Someone, Fox Trot.
10. Vo-Do-Do-De-O Blues, Fox Trot.

G-909   FUNNY! SMART! DISTINCTIVE!
1. She's Got "It," Fox Trot.
2. I Walked Back From the Buggy Ride, Fox Trot.
3. When the Work's All Done This Fall, One-Step.
4. Red Lips—Kiss My Blues Away, Fox Trot.
5. Things That Remind Me Of You, Waltz.
6. Yes She Do—No She Don't, Fox Trot.
7. My Sweet Yvette, Fox Trot.
8. I Call You Sugar, Fox Trot.
9. Do You Love Me? Fox Trot.
10. Just Once Again, Fox Trot.

G-910   IT'S GOT "IT"
1. The Old Gray Mare, Fox Trot.
2. America Did It Again, One-Step.
3. Nanette, Fox Trot.
4. Lady Do Fox Trot.
5. I've Lived All My Life Just For You, Waltz.
6. Wy-Lets, Fox Trot.
7. Oh, Dem Golden Slippers, Fox Trot.
8. That Pretty Little So and So Of Mine, Fox Trot.
9. Gid-ap, Garibaldi, One-step.
10. Who-oo? You-oo! That's Who! Fox Trot.

G-911   ALL HIT REVIEW
1. I Wonder How I Look When I'm Asleep, Fox Trot.
2. Captain Lindbergh, One-Step.
3. Ain't That a Grand and Glorious Feeling? Fox Trot.
4. You Don't Like It—Not Much, Fox Trot.
5. Positively-Absolutely, Fox Trot.
6. Wasn't It Nice? Fox Trot.
7. The Same Old Moon, Fox Trot.
8. Just Call On Me, Fox Trot.
9. No Wonder I'm Happy, Fox Trot.
10. Bye Bye Pretty Baby, Fox Trot.

To the left is a Seeburg listing of new G rolls released around 1927. Above and below are views of a Seeburg E Special orchestrion. The E Special, which contains the same instrumentation as the KT Special, was made in limited numbers and is quite rare today. (Roy Haning and Neal White Collection)

A rarity among large Seeburg orchestrions is the Style L Orchestra, which saw limited production in the 'teens. The instrumentation is similar to that of the Style G, except that the L has one rank of pipes instead of two. It uses a type G (or 4X) roll of 10-tune length. The above instrument was originally sold by the Sanders-Dreyer Music Company and was used in St. Louis, Missouri.

LUDWIG HUPFELD, A.G.
Coin Pianos, Orchestrions, etc.

The firm of Ludwig Hupfeld A.G. (Ludwig Hupfeld, Inc.) was in its day the world's largest manufacturer of automatic musical instruments. Products encompassed nearly the entire spectrum of the field and included such diverse items as organettes, disc music boxes (via an ownership interest in Symphonion), home player pianos (mostly sold under the Phonola label), expression pianos, reproducing pianos, orchestrions, violin players, theatre photoplayers, and theatre pipe organs.

Founded near Leipzig in 1880 (or 1872, according to some catalogues), the firm in the early years was known as J.B. Grob & Co. By 1886 the company was the sole distributor for the Ariston organette, the most popular style (in terms of unit sales) ever made. In addition, the firm made or sold barrel-operated pianos and related instruments. In 1892 Ludwig Hupfeld took over control, and shortly thereafter the name was changed to the Hupfeld Musikwerke (Hupfeld Music Factory), although the Grob name was used in advertising until about 1900.

In 1899 Hupfeld moved to a newly-built factory at Apelstrasse 4 in Leipzig-Eutritzsch. Production grew at a record rate, and soon Hupfeld became Europe's premier maker of player pianos, both the push-up and the interior type, most of which were sold under the Phonola trademark. In addition, electric pianos and orchestrions became popular, and Hupfeld at an early time established a firm foothold in that market.

Soon, production grew to the point at which a new factory was necessary. In 1909 a new facility costing 2,000,000 gold marks was commenced in Bohlitz-Ehrenberg, near Leipzig. This immense structure measured 275 meters long and had a tower 63 meters high. The floor space was 100,000 square meters (about a million square feet). By 1912 about 1200 workmen were employed. Within a few years the number had risen to about 2000. In the following years Hupfeld acquired several other firms. By the 1920s Hupfeld had four large factories, many sales outlets, and a work and sales force of about 6000 people. By the late 1920s the market for automatic instruments had diminished to almost zero, so Hupfeld turned to the making of furniture, radios, and other items for the home, in addition to regular (non-player) instruments. Today the main factory at Bohlitz-Ehrenberg still stands and is used for the production of regular household pianos.

Types of Hupfeld Instruments

Hupfeld player pianos: The early Phonola piano players (push-up style) and player pianos were of a special 73-note scale. After 1908, when the 88-note system was standardized, Hupfeld built Phonolas with the 88-note mechanisms as well. Some of these (as well as later 73-note instruments) used theme perforations devised by the Aeolian Company and were named "Solodant." At various times in Hupfeld history there was extensive cross-licensing of patents with other manufacturers, notably the Aeolian Company.

Universal pianos: The Universal was a simple orchestrion with piano, mandolin, and a 10-note section of bells or xylophone bars. Those in deluxe cases were sometimes called Concert Universal models. Larger models with 30-note xylophones were designated as Concert Universal Grand and Concert Clavitist Universal. Some of these latter models could play Clavitist and Phonoliszt piano rolls as well as orchestrated rolls. Another Universal type with percussion effects was designated as the Universal Orchestra.

Expression pianos; reproducing pianos: Several types of expression and reproducing pianos were made under the Phonoliszt, Dea, and Triphonola names. Refer to the reproducing piano section of this book for additional information and scales.

Helios orchestrions: The Helios orchestrions were made in many interior designs and case configurations. Using special Helios rolls, these instruments could play a wonderful range of effects. In terms of the quantities originally manufactured, the Helios models were the most popular classic orchestrions of the early 20th century. Today, several examples survive of Helios Style Ic/31 and II/25. Scattered specimens exist of certain other models of classes I, II, and III.

Pepita orchestrions: The Pepita orchestrions used a special roll, usually of 10-tune length, and were in many instances compact versions of Helios orchestrions. Only a few were made.

Pan Orchestras: The Pan Orchestra used a 124-hole tracker bar (spaced 9 holes per inch) which enabled it to combine various instruments and registers in many, many ways. This was the most sophisticated and expensive automatic musical instrument ever built by Hupfeld. Pan Orchestras were made in several standard styles, including models O, I, II, III, and IV, and in a photoplayer format known as the Kino-Pan.

Animatic orchestrions: Especially popular during the 1920s were Animatic orchestrions which contained a piano, mandolin, and sometimes a 10-note xylophone. Some elaborate models also had percussion effects. Later variations included the Hupfeld Sinfonie-Jazz, an orchestrion with saxophone and lotus flute pipes which used a special Animatic-SJ roll with solo effects.

Hupfeld violin players: Early models, of which none survive today (so far as the authors know), were the Violina, which featured real violins; the Clavitist-Violina, which featured a piano which used Clavitist arrangements, in combination with a Violina; and the Dea-Violina, which featured Dea reproducing piano roll arrangements in combination with four real violins played by two rotating bows. This experimentation was consolidated into a single product, the Phonoliszt-Violina, which combined a Phonoliszt expression piano with ee violins, each of which had a single string played by a rotating rosined "bow" composed of about 1350 real horsehairs. The Phonoliszt-Violina was immensely successful, and thousands were sold. In later years, a variation which included additional instrumentation and percussion, the Violina Orchestra, was marketed in limited numbers.

Other Hupfeld instruments: Over the years many other Hupfeld instruments were made, mostly in small numbers in comparison to those just enumerated. In addition, various barrel-operated pianos and orchestrions were made from the 1880s until about 1914. Other types of early players used heavy manila or cardboard strips. Some of these varieties are enumerated in the detailed Hupfeld history which begins on page 430 of *The Encyclopedia of Automatic Musical Instruments*.

HUPFELD CLAVITIST ROLL
11 5/8" wide; 26+ holes per 10 cm.

1 to 5, Orchestra bell notes, B, C, C#, D, D#
6 Mandolin and xylophone
7 to 34, Playing notes C to D#
35 Sustaining pedal
36 E
37 Snare drum
38 F
39 Hammer rail
40 F#
41 Bass drum
42 G
43 Shutoff
44 to 72, Notes G# to C
73 to 77, Orchestra bell notes: E, F#, G, G#, A

39+43 = Rewind

The scale for the mandolin and xylophone is G to C, holes 42 to 72, or in some, F# to C, holes 40 to 72.

HUPFELD CLAVITIST ROLL
(Variant of preceding, with differences as noted)

1 Violin pipes on
2 Xylophone on
3 Blank
4 Blank
5 Blank
73 Blank
74 Blank
75 Rewind
76 Blank
77 General cancel

The first Clavitist scale listed is from an original Hupfeld factory scale stick. The second is from the archives of the late Eugene DeRoy.

HUPFELD ANIMATIC S ROLL
11¼" wide; spaced 9 holes per inch

1 Cymbal
2 Mandolin
3 Wood block
4 Sustaining pedal
5 Bass accent
6 to 81, 76 playing notes, A to C
82 to 93, 12 solo xylophone notes, C# to C
94 Treble accent
95 Shutoff
96 Snare drum
97 Bass drum
98 Hammer rail

The hammer rail (98) is turned on by a long hole and off by a single punch. Rewind is activated by holes 4, 95, and 1 in that order. In most models the twelve corresponding piano notes could also be added to the solo note section. Some Animatic S models did not have a xylophone, and the owner could choose between shutting these notes off or letting the piano play them. Nearly all Animatic S rolls are arranged for this solo section. Ordinary Animatic rolls (without the S suffix) do not have solos or percussion holes.

HUPFELD SINFONIE-JAZZ ORCHESTRION ROLL
(HUPFELD ANIMATIC-SJ ROLL)
11¼" wide; holes spaced 9 per inch

1 Hi-hat cymbal
2 Mandolin
3 Loud wood block
4 Sustaining pedal
5 Bass accent
6 Fox trot bells on and saxophone off
7 Crescendo for piano
8 Triangle
9 Soft wood block
10 Snare drum damper
11 Bass drum damper
12 Tap cymbal
13 Lotus flute on
14 to 81, 68 playing notes, F to C
82 Tympani roll
83 Crash cymbal
84 D or B
85 D# or C
86 E or C#
87 F or D
88 F# or D#
89 G or E
90 G# or F
91 A or F#

92 A# or G
93 Solo note switch
94 Treble accent
95 Shutoff
96 Snare drum
97 Bass drum
98 Hammer rail

Holes 84 through 92 play notes D through A# on the saxophone and lotus flute when hole 93 is not punched, and notes B through G when 93 is punched. According to one scale, there are 9 fox trot bells which play the following notes from holes 84 to 92: D, D#, E, F, F#, G, A, A#, and C.

The Sinfonie-Jazz (also called Symphony Jazz) was made in several different styles. The rolls are of the Animatic series, numbered in the 50,000 to 61,000 serial range. Animatic rolls with percussion effects (but without pipe registration) have an S prefix; those with pipe registration, as given in the preceding scale, have an SJ prefix.

The Hupfeld Sinfonie-Jazz, introduced in the late 1920s, represented the last major orchestrion type to be made by that firm. The largest model, Style 19, was made in Art Deco and traditional style cases.

Rewind is activated by holes 4, 95, and 1 in that order.

HUPFELD PEPITA ROLL
Approx. 20.5 cm. wide; 26+ holes per 10 cm.

1 ?
2 ?
3 Triangle
4 Bass drum
5 Xylophone on
6 Sustaining pedal?
7 Shutoff
8 D#
9 F
10 G
11 B?
12 C?
13 D
14 F
15 G
16 G#
17 A
18 A#
19 B
20 C
21 D
22 D#
23 E
24 F
25 G
26 G#
27 A
28 A#
29 B
30 C
31 D
32 D#
33 E
34 F
35 G
36 G#
37 A
38 A#
39 B
40 C
41 D
42 D#
43 E
44 F
45 Rewind
46 Soft (hammer rail?)
47 Violin pipes on

48 Mandolin
49 Snare drum
50 Castanets
51 General cancel

The largest Pepita orchestrion contained bells and cymbal in addition to the instruments enumerated in the preceding scale. Holes 1 and 2 might be used for these functions.

The Pepita seems to have been most popular circa 1910-1914.

HUPFELD HELIOS I ORCHESTRION ROLL

11 5/8" wide; 26+ holes per 10 cm.

1 Oboe (or clarinet) on
2 Cymbal
3 Bass drum
4 Cello and violin pipes on
5 Snare drum
6 Xylophone and (in later models) lotus flute on
7 Snare drum
8 to 12, Bell notes B, C, C#, D, D#
13 to 34, Piano notes E, F#, G# to D#
35 Sustaining pedal
36 E
37 General cancel
38 F
39 Piano soft (low vacuum), swell closed, expression crescendo speed
40 F#
41 Piano off
42 G
43 Shutoff
44 to 69, Piano notes G# to A
70 to 74, Bell notes E, F#, G, G#, A
75 Mandolin on
76 Aeoline or viola pipes on
77 Flute on

39+43 = Rewind

Positions 4, 76, and 77 on the tracker bar each have 3 holes in a vertical row. In one instrument these have the following functions:

4 Short perforation = violin pipes on, or
4 Long perforation = violin and cello pipes on
76 Short perforation = viola pipes on, or
76 Long perforation = viola and aeoline pipes on
77 Blank

One original Hupfeld scale stick observed by the authors is marked with all of the playing notes one whole step lower than in the preceding scale.

Hupfeld Helios orchestrions were divided into several classes, each one of which had different instrumentation. The style numbers consisted of a class number following by a case design number. Thus, a Helios orchestrion with Class I instrumentation housed in case design number 22 would be known as Helios I/22.

It is believed that Helios classes I, II, and III used one style of roll, and that the larger classes IV and V used another style with more registers (although the rolls for I, II, and III would play on them). It is presumed that in the very large models, additional registration was accomplished, at least in part, by extensive multiplexing; the use of holes in combination with each other.

Below is given a synopsis of the various Helios classes and representative instrumentation for each. In practice, instrumentation was apt to vary slightly.

Helios Class I orchestrions: Overstrung piano with mandolin effect (the mandolin effect in most instruments consisted of a "harp effect" apparatus with vibrating wooden hammers that strike below the regular piano hammers); registers of pipes for the voices of violin and violoncello; orchestra bells; bass drum; snare drum; and expression effects. Xylophone available on special order. Variations: Class Ib, as preceding, but with flute pipes in addition. Class Ic, as Class I but with clarinet reed pipes and large bass pipes in addition.

The buyers of Helios orchestrions, all classes I through V, were offered several options of tonal character. An instrument could be voiced softly for use in a drawing room or salon, or it could be voiced loudly for use in a skating rink or amusement part. This was done by adjusting the wind pressure and voicing the pipes appropriately before the instrument left the factory.

Helios Class II orchestrions: Helios II orchestrions were available in regular or "concert" specifications. The concert type had extra expression controls on the piano. Instrumentation: overstrung piano with automatic pedal and expression effects; mandolin effect; pipe registers for aeoline, violin, flute, piccolo, clarinet, viola, cello, bass cello (in concert instruments) or bass flute (regular instruments); orchestra bells; trapwork, including bass drum, Chinese cymbal, and snare drum. The trapwork can play with expression effects. Xylophone optional.

Helios Class III orchestrions: overstrung piano with separate expression controls for bass and treble sections; mandolin effect; pipe registers for violin, aeoline, flute, piccolo, clarinet, oboe, horn, bassoon, viola, cello, double bass, and bass violin; orchestra bells; percussion consisting of bass drum, Chinese cymbal, and tenor drum, each with expression. Xylophone optional. "Provides finely modulated music of powerful fullness of tone corresponding to a full orchestra. Suited for recitals even in the largest halls."

Helios Class III orchestrions, "concert" specifications: piano as preceding; mandolin effect; pipe registers for violin, horn, flute, piccolo, clarinet, trumpets, cello, bass horn, principal, double bass, bass viol, and trombone; orchestra bells; percussion as preceding. Xylophone optional. "Tonal character corresponds to a wind orchestra. Especially suited for dance and concert music in halls."

Helios Class IV orchestrions: piano with expression effects; pipes representing violin, tenor violin, violoncello, concert flute, piccolo, flute, clarionet, gamba, aeoline, saxophone, oboe, bugle, Vienna flute, bass, bass viol, cello, bassoon, trumpet, and double bass; harp effect; xylophone; orchestra bells; castanets; chimes; triangle; kettle drum; cymbals; bass drum; tenor drum; several bird whistles; other effects.

Helios Class V orchestrion: about 1500 pipes controlled by 49 registers on a multiplexed roll. Hupfeld noted that "the 49 registers consist of 7 for bass, 9 for accompaniment, 22 for melody, 11 for solo. Represents 100 to 120 performers. The effects of the music are stupendous, reproducing all the charms of an orchestra, full of harmonies and tone shadings."

Like other types of Hupfeld instruments, there were several different types of roll mechanisms available for Helios orchestrions, including the single tracker bar, 6-roll automatic changer, duplex system (two tracker bars side by side), and the duplex roll changer (two roll changers, side by side).

Helios roll catalogues list hundreds of different melodies in all types of categories from popular to classical, from ragtime to religious. The numbering system runs from 1 to at least 2345 (released in November 1933), but others may have been made. The abbreviation "Hs" (for Helios) appears on many of the roll labels.

The very rich variety of the music played and the interesting and ornate case designs have made Helios orchestrions favorites with collectors today.

Hupfeld-Kunstspiel-Instrumente

Lfde. Nr.	Modell	Für Vortrag und Tanz	Höhe in cm etwa	ohne Mandoline	mit Mandoline	mit Mandoline und Xylophon	Jazzband
		Animatic-Clavitist-Pianos		Bei Bestellung ist der Modellnummer noch hinzuzufügen (z. B. I X)			
				°/o	M	X	J
601	1	* nußbaum	132	3300	3450	3750	4400
607	6	eiche	144	3600	3750	4050	4700
608	7	mahagoni . . .	144	4000	4150	4450	5100
609	4	eiche	194	4500	4650	4950	5400
610	4	mahagoni . . .	194	5100	5250	5550	6000

Lfde. Nr.	Modell		Höhe in cm etwa	Preis RM.
		Animatic-Phonoliszt-Pianos		
611	1	eiche Grunert	139	4500
612	2	* nußbaum	143	4500
614	4	* eiche	150	5000
618	5	* nußbaum	140	4700
616	10	dunkelmahagoni Rönisch . .	139	5600
617	15	eiche Grunert, ohne Klaviatur, Büfettform	162	4100
		Animatic-Phonoliszt-Flügel	Länge	
625	I	** schwarz poliert Hupfeld . .	180	7700
626	III B	** schwarz poliert Rönisch . .	200	8800
		Phonoliszt-Geigenpfeifen-Piano	Höhe	
631	—	* eiche	240	7000
		Phonoliszt-Violina mit autom. Stimmhaltung		
636	B	* nußbaum Rönisch	245	13000
		Violina-Orchestra		
751	I	eiche, ohne Klaviatur, Rönisch	300	21000
752	II	** nußbaum, mit Klaviatur, Rönisch . . .	260	23000
		Mehrpreis für:		
641	—	Elektrische einarmige Leuchter		60
642	—	Elektrische Doppel-Leuchter		100

* Auch mahagoni oder nußbaum-rot, mahagoni-artig gefärbt, lieferbar; Mehrpreis 5 °/o.
** Preis einschl. Ferngebläse in Kiefergehäuse mit 3 m Zuleitung.
Mehrrollen-Einrichtungen siehe Seite 4.

778

Preisliste Nr. 5

gültig ab 1. April 1926

über

Kunstspiel-Instrumente

für

gewerbliche Zwecke

The student of automatic musical instrument history will find much information in this April 1926 Hupfeld brochure. At the time the German mark was worth between 20c and 25c in United States funds, so a Phonoliszt-Violina, for example, cost about $3000. This was the twilight era of Ludwig Hupfeld's automatic musical instrument empire, and very few large Helios or Pan instruments were being sold. Wouldn't it be wonderful to be able to order from this list today! (Information from Gunther Hupfeld via Claes O. Friberg)

Hupfeld-Kunstspiel-Instrumente

Lfde. Nr.	Modell	Für Vortrag und Tanz	Höhe in cm etwa
		Helios-Piano mit Klaviatur	
731	—	nußbaum	192
		Helios-Orchestrions	
661	I/22	eiche	280
663	I/34	eiche	280
665	I/30	eiche, einfache Ausführung, ohne Holzeinlegearbeit	280
671	Ib/37	eiche	270
677	Ic/31	eiche	300
685	II/25	eiche	315
688	—	Modell II/25, eiche, ohne Sockelfigur, ohne Seitenspiegel mit Kronen und ohne beleuchtete Opale weniger RM. 900.—	
695	II/26	eiche	305
698	—	Modell II/26, eiche, mit schlichter Front, also ohne Spiegelnischen und Figur, ohne Blumenschmuck und ohne plastische Lichtwechselbild in der Mittelfront weniger . . . . RM. 1100.—	
705	II/33	eiche	335
711	III/42	eiche	315
716	III/39	eiche	325
		Mehrpreis für:	
720	—	Tanzbesetzung f. alle Helios-Orchestrions	
721	—	Xylophonbesetzung für alle Helios-Orchestrions	
		Konzert-Werke Pan	
737	I	eiche	300
738	II	eiche, mit Xylophon und Schlagzeug . .	292
739	III	eiche	300
740	IV	eiche	345

Mehrrollen-Einrichtungen siehe Seite 4.

Hupfeld-Kunstspiel-Instrumente

Lfde. Nr.	Modell	Für Vortrag und Tanz	Höhe in cm etwa	Preis RM.
		Mehrpreis für:		
		Mehrrollen-Einrichtungen		
		Zwillingsrollen-Einrichtung nur in:		
755	—	Animatic-Clavitist 6, 6 M, 6 X, 6 J . . .		
757	—	Animatic-Phonoliszt 2		
758	—	Helios-Orchestrions		1000
759	—	Konzert-Werke Pan 1, 2, 3, 4 . . .		
		Sechsrollen-Magazin nur in:		
765	—	Animatic-Clavitist 4, 4 M, 4 X, 4 J . . .		
766	—	Animatic-Phonoliszt 4		
767	—	Phonoliszt-Geigenpfeifen-Piano . . .		800
768	—	Phonoliszt-Violina B		
		Zehnrollen-Magazin nur in:		
776	—	Konzert-Werke Pan 1, 2, 3, 4 . . .		
777	—	Violina-Orchestra, Modell I . . .		1500
		Für Lichtspiel-Theater		
		Mit Zwillingsrollen-Einrichtung und Schaltung am Instrument		
		a) für Klaviervorträge:		
780	6	Animatic-Clavitist, eiche	144	4600
782	2	Animatic-Phonoliszt, nußbaum . . .	143	5500
		b) für Violinvorträge mit Klavierbegleitung:		
786	—	Phonoliszt-Geigenpfeifen-Piano in Kinoausstattung, Piano eiche, Geigenpfeifengehäuse kiefer	153	8000
787	—	Phonoliszt-Violina in Kinoausstattung, Piano Rönisch nußbaum, Geigengehäuse kiefer	147	14000
		c) für orchestrale Vorträge:		
792	Ia	⊛ Kino-Pan, kiefer	175	20000
793	IIa	⊛ Kino-Pan, kiefer	175	24000
794	IIIa	⊛ Kino-Pan, kiefer	175	27000

805 ** Preis einschl. Ferngebläse in Kiefergehäuse mit 3 m Zuleitung.
807 ⊛ Auch lieferbar mit 2×10 Rollenmagazin und Fernschaltungstafel einschließlich 5 m Kabel; Mehrpreis RM. 3000.

Hupfeld-Notenrollen

(Allgemeines hierüber siehe Seite 6)

Lfde. Nr.	Art und Verwendungsmöglichkeit	Gruppe I RM.	Gruppe II RM.	Gruppe III RM.
834	**Animatic-S** . . . . Für alle Animatic-Clavitist-Pianos: 88töniger von pianissimo bis fortissimo gut-nuancierter Klaviervortrag, je nach Instrumentenbesetzung mit bzw. ohne Begleit-Instrumente.	3.50	5.75	8.—
	Automatische Rollen mit 3 Stücken RM. 9.—			
836	**Animatic-T** . . . . Für alle Animatic-Phonoliszt-Instrumente und Violina-Orchestra: 88töniger Klaviervortrag — vollkommenste Nuancierung, besondere Melodieführung.	4.50	7.50	14.—
	Schlagernoten Spezialgruppe Ia RM. 3.— Automatische Rollen mit 3 Stücken RM. 9.—			
837	**Violina** Für Violina-Orchestra 88er Skala: Für Phonoliszt-Violina und Geigenpfeifen-Phonoliszt 73er Skala: Violinsoli mit Klavierbegleitung.	7.—	10.50	14.—
838	**Phonoliszt** Für Geigenpfeifen-Phonoliszt und Phonoliszt-Violina: 73töniger Klaviervortrag.	3.50	5.75	8.—
841	**Helios** Für Helios-Piano u. alle Helios-Orchestrions: Orchester-Musik.	3.50	5.75	8.—
843	**Pan** Für alle Konzert-Werke Pan u. Kino-Pan: Orchester-Musik.	9.—	13.50	18.—
845	**Violina-Orchestra** Für Violina-Orchestra-Instrumente: Orchester-Musik.	9.—	13.50	18.—
	Alle Preise einschl. Lizenz.			
847	Rollen für elektrische Kunstspiel-Instrumente mit Magazin-Einrichtung, Mehrpreis . .	—.50	—.50	—.50

Above: This composite photograph was put together by Hupfeld's publicity department. It shows the Leipzig factory (which still stands today), pictures of several different Hupfeld pianos and orchestrions (taken from catalogue illustrations), and tiers of Hupfeld employees seated on benches and standing. (Photograph courtesy of Claes O. Friberg)

Right: This 1916 photograph shows rolls being perforated in the main Hupfeld factory. Hupfeld was continental Europe's largest manufacturer of music rolls.

Above: Ron Cappel is shown in his Whittier, California workshop in a scene which hasn't been duplicated since Hupfeld stopped making Helios orchestrions in the 1920s. Lined up and awaiting restoration are three Hupfeld Helios Ic/31 orchestrions, representing about half of the total number known to exist! Destined for the collections of their owners, Jens Carlson, Jerry Cohen, and Dr. Robert Gilson, the orchestrions each will have the cloth, leather, and rubber parts renewed, the piano actions redone, and other restoration work performed. Once done, they should be good for another several decades of good music.

Left: Ron Cappel and Art Reblitz are shown in front of a large Style F Aeolian Solo Orchestrelle with its external cabinet removed. The Orchestrelle, reported Ron, was one of the most challenging restorations he and his associate Rex Anderson ever did. It's not that it is complicated, it is just extensive. There are 1001 different reeds, or so at least it seems.

Hupfeld Helios Ic/31 orchestrion

Above: Hupfeld Helios II/36, the Rococo style as designated by the catalogue. In 1912 this model sold for 11,600 marks, the most expensive instrument in the Class II series.

Below: This duplex automatic roll changer combined two 6-roll devices, for a total repertoire of 12 rolls.

Above: Hupfeld Helios III/42 orchestrion in a large banquet hall as shown in a 1927 photograph. This particular instrument survived the ravages of time and was located by Claes O. Friberg in 1974. It was probably one of the very last large Helios orchestrions to be made by Hupfeld.

Right: Tens of thousands of rolls for Hupfeld coin pianos, player pianos, and other instruments were stored in this section of the Leipzig factory.

Below: Rows of music roll perforators punch out a cascade of melodies for different Hupfeld instruments.

Notenstanzsaal.

Blick in das Notenrollenlager.

This is a really perfect production in the art of Orchestrion building, where experience and technical progress combined with the highest musical intelligence, have created an instrument that is almost overwhelming in its effect, both musically as well as with regard to its splendid exterior. The rich fulness of its tone, rising at full power to a mighty fortissimo, the perfect tone-graduation, the exactness of the rhythm, and the unique effect of the drums and cymbals, all combine to give the wonderful resemblance to the performance of a living orchestra. This model, in its artistically designed case, with an allegorical figure and several brilliantly illuminated lamps in the centre, is most ========================= impressive and effective. =========================

The exceedingly rich specification comprises :— First-class Overstrung Piano, Violin, Tenor Violin, Violoncello, Concert Flute, Piccolo Flute, Clarionet, Gamba, Æoline, Saxophone, Oboe, Bugle, Vienna Flute, Bass, Bass Viol, Harp, 'Cello, Bassoon, Trumpet, Double Bass, Xylophone, Bells, Castanets, Chiming Bells, Triangle, Kettle Drum, Cymbals, Bass Drum and Military Drum, several Bird Whistles ======== and other musical accompanying effects.========

Dimensions :—Height, about 10 ft. 7 in., with the top points about 12 ft. 4 in. Width, about 13 ft. 2 in. Depth, about 4 ft. 6 in.

This case design, known as the Helios III/39 or Helios IV, was one of the most elegant ever made. The same basic style was used for several varieties of very large Hupfeld Pan Orchestras.

Hupfeld Pan Orchestra Rolls

Hupfeld considered the Pan Orchestra (this type of instrument was referred to as an "orchestra" rather than an "orchestrion" in Hupfeld literature, with the inference that an orchestrion was somehow "mechanical" in character, whereas the Pan Orchestra was not; admittedly an interesting distinction) to be its finest accomplishment.

Using an extensively multiplexed 124-hole roll, the Pan Orchestra had the capability of playing several different orchestral voices, each one playing different notes, at the same time! This was accomplished by the use of several different musical scales which did not overlap. The piano of the Pan was of the reproducing type, with the same basic concept as used in the Hupfeld Triphonola, and could re-enact artists' rolls. In fact, Hupfeld produced some piano-only rolls for the Pan; a curious waste, so it would seem, of the extensive orchestral effects. Perhaps such rolls were made to lend variety to a long program.

With its extensive instrumentation, solo capabilities, and other features the Hupfeld Pan Orchestra ranked with the Weber Elite (to which refer) in the capability for musical dexterity and versatility. As no examples of the Weber Elite survive today, the several Hupfeld Pan Orchestras which remain furnish the opportunity to study the summit of ingenuity in automatic musical instruments.

Hupfeld advertised the Pan Orchestra as follows:

"The Concert Pan Orchestras have a pneumatic action of highest quality. The cabinets of each model are chosen by using artistic considerations, as are the orchestral voices within the case.

"The music of the Pan Orchestras lets you discover that these are neither organs nor orchestrions. Rather, they form a special class which can only be compared with a live orchestra.

"The musical parts of the Pan are entirely independent from each other. At any time a given voice or rank of pipes or particular instrument can be brought out tonally above the others. The Pan comprises all degrees of tonal power from the hushed piano to the thundering fortissimo. The drum and trapwork is recorded from a man's hand and imitates it exactly as it ranges from tender gracefulness to strong and intense rhythm.

"The connoisseur of music has at his call the wonderful strains from Tristan, Parsifal, an entire symphony, a violin concert with the accompaniment of an orchestra, or, yes, even a duet. Solo performances on the cello, flute, xylophone, organ, and other instruments are possible as are trios and chorales.

"Max Bruch, Hubert Cuypers, Julius Pruwer, Richard Strauss, and other masters of music have participated in the actual recording or directing of Pan music rolls and have given their art to them so that the full orchestral performance as played by the Pan leaves no desire unsatisfied. The noble and rich modulation, the artistic instrumentation, the charming harmony and blending of the tones, the piquant rhythm, and the realistic delivery give fully the illusion of an orchestra of live performers.

"All Pan Orchestra models include a reproducing piano. This is available exclusively in the Pan instruments and makes possible the reproduction of actual performances from over 200 of the foremost pianists of the world.

"The music produced is in keeping with the elegant exteriors of the Pan Concert Orchestras which, in all styles and models, can suit the best rooms. Also, we frequently install Pan instruments without cases. These are secluded in a niche or separate room and play into a room through lattice work . . .

"Because of its outstanding musical performances the Pan is very popular. Pan Orchestras are found in castles, manor houses, villas, spas, restaurants, theatres, drawing rooms, and on finely appointed boats. All over the world the Pan has come to be appreciated and valued as a work of art . . ."

The Pan Orchestra was made in several basic models, from the Model O through the I, II, III, IV, and Kino-Pan. The first, the Model O, had a keyboard and was the only Pan model so equipped. So far as is known, none of these exist today, although one survived in Germany until the late 1960s, when it was inadvertently destroyed just one week before a collector learned of it and came to acquire it. The Kino-Pan, made in several variations, was a cabinet-style low-profile instrument made for use in motion picture theatres. In addition, some Hupfeld theatre pipe organs were equipped with mechanisms to play Pan Orchestra rolls.

At least two large styles of Pan Orchestras were made by Hupfeld. Designated as the Super Pan Orchestra and the Excelsior Pan Orchestra, these were made in exceedingly limited quantities. The only known Excelsior Pan Orchestra was completed in 1926 and sold to the Postzegel Hotel in 's Hertogenbosch, Holland, where it remained until it was acquired by Eugene DeRoy and sold to Q. David Bowers in 1966. Later it was sold into the San Sylmar Collection, where it remains today. This instrument was sold by Duwaer & Naessens, the Amsterdam agency for Hupfeld, who fitted two accordions in separate cases to the left and right. Another Pan Orchestra, also sold by Duwaer & Naessens, served for many years in the Casablanca, a night spot in Amsterdam's Zeedyk district. This model, a Super Pan Orchestra, is presently in the collection of Q. David Bowers, who acquired it in the 1960s. This, too, was later equipped with accordions, which have since been removed. In the 1930s, when orchestrions were becoming technologically obsolete, Duwaer & Naessens added accordions to many different models in order to "update" them for further use. It is from these two instruments, the Excelsior Pan Orchestra and the Super Pan Orchestra, that the information given in the following scales was taken.

In 1929 Hupfeld issued a large 53-page catalogue containing all of the Pan Orchestra roll titles which had been issued up to March of that year. The first roll was numbered 90001, the *Alessandro Stradella Overture*, by von Flotow. The catalogue continued through 90942. Additional rolls were made through the first several years of the 1930s. These were described in periodical printed supplements. The last roll number seen in a printed supplement by the authors is 91024. In later years additional music was cut by Euterpe (of Borgerstraat 89, Amsterdam), and by Eugene DeRoy's Symphonia Music Roll Co., located in Hoboken, a district of Antwerp, Belgium.

For the convenience of Pan Orchestra patrons the music was divided into various categories, including operas and operatic music, concert and classical music, salon music, songs and chorales, dances and marches (subdivided into fox trots, marches, one-steps, shimmys, two-steps, waltzes, and so on), and special music for accompanying films.

A perusal of the 1929 catalogue shows such varied entries as: *Ave Maria* (90035), *Wedding of the Winds* (90037), *Silent Night* (90045), *Alexander's Ragtime Band* (90062), *Brahms' Hungarian Dance No. 5* (90087), *Peer Gynt Suite* (on a set of 6 rolls, nos. 90118a, b, and c, and 90019a, b, and c), *The Marseillaise, French National Anthem* (90123), *Liszt's Hungarian Rhapsody, No. 11* (90134), *William Tell Overture* (90144), *Orpheus in the Underworld* (90191), *Dardanella, Foxtrot* (90384), *Violin Concerto, Opus 64, Andante, F. Mendelssohn-Bartholdy* (90469), *Swanee* (90567), *My Isle of Golden Dreams* (90597), *I Never See Maggie Alone* (90836), *Estudiantina Waltz* (90839), *Light Cavalry Overture* (90871), *Doll Dance* (90884), and *Charmaine* (90898).

For the lover of classical music the works of Beethoven, Mozart, Wagner, Brahms, Verdi, Tschaikowsky, Chopin, and others were available, often in sets or series of rolls. For example, Beethoven's *Fifth Symphony* was available on five large rolls.

Rolls with other musical characteristics were also available in sets and series or, in the instance of more popular numbers, in composite or potpourri rolls. For example, roll no. 90318 was titled *Christmas Fantasy* and featured 10 different selections. In the same vein was roll no. 90716 with 17 different Christmas melodies. Roll 90651 contained 24 popular college songs.

Depending upon the length of the roll, it was classified into Price Group I, II, or III, with the latter being the most expensive. Many, if not all, Hupfeld Pan Orchestras were equipped with either the 10-roll automatic changer or the duplex roll system, so a concert of several hours' duration could be programmed on the instrument.

To further appeal to varying musical tastes, Hupfeld catalogued the Pan Orchestra rolls into the following categories according to the featured solo instrument(s): cello and flute solos with orchestra; flute solo with orchestra; orchestra music; orchestra with cello solo; orchestra with harp; orchestra with harp and xylophone; orchestra with harmonium (sometimes called "organ"); orchestra with harmonium and lotus flute; orchestra with lotus flute; orchestra with violin solo; orchestra with violin and cello solos and harmonium; orchestra with violin and flute solos; orchestra with violin solo and harmonium; orchestra with xylophone; piano solo (reproducing piano arrangements recorded by famous pianists); piano solo with orchestra accompaniment; piano solo with xylophone and harp; piccolo solo with orchestra; violin solo with piano; violin and cello solos with piano; violin, cello, and flute solos with orchestra; violin and cello solos with harp or piano accompaniment; violin and cello solos with harp and orchestra; violin and cello solos with orchestra or piano; violin and flute solos with piano; violin solo with harp or piano; violin solo with harmonium and piano; violin solo and harmonium with orchestra and piano; violin solo with orchestra or piano; xylophone solo with orchestra; and xylophone solo and harp with piano. The first instrument(s) listed were featured. For example, in an arrangement with a xylophone solo with orchestra accompaniment, the xylophone would be the featured instrument and would play many solo passages, with the orchestra accompanying. In an arrangement with orchestra and xylophone, the orchestra (or "full orchestrion") components would predominate, with xylophone accents or occasional solos.

HUPFELD EXCELSIOR PAN ROLL

14 1/8" wide; spaced 9 holes per inch
(Numbering is from right to left in this instance)

1 Piano accent (normally slow; fast with hole 96)
2 Piano expression accelerator for holes 3 and 4
3 Piano expression MF (normally slow; fast with hole 2)
4 Piano expression MP (normally slow; fast with hole 2)
5 Piano treble theme expression
6 Piano 1 register on (piano melody section notes 21-44 off; see holes 99 and 100)
7 Bells on (countermelody section)
8 Xylophone on (melody section)
9 to 20, Countermelody notes
21 to 44, Melody notes
45 to 81, Bass notes
82 Piano bass coupler (couples lower octave piano notes to holes 70-81) and trigger for MF hammer rail lift (see hole 113)
83 Swell modulator MP (modulates or increases all swell shutter settings; normally slow; fast with hole 85)
84 Swell modulator MF (modulates or increases all swell shutter settings; normally slow; fast with hole 85)
85 Swell shutter accelerator; affects 83, 84, and countermelody swell shutters, hole 102
86 Trapwork coupler (affects 87, 88, and 91)
87 Snare drum
87+86 = Jazz cymbal
88 Tympani
88+86 = Tambourine
89 Snare drum
90 Tympani
91 Triangle
91+86 = Castanets and wood block
92 Crash cymbal, soft striker; soft and loud strikers if bass swell is on
93 Cancel bells, xylophone, mandolin, lotus flute, piano 1 register, MF hammer rail lift (98), and MP hammer rail lift (113)
94 Piano bass theme expression
95 Sustaining pedal
96 Piano accent accelerator (see hole 1) and trigger for shutoff and rewind (see hole 98)
97 Lotus flute on (also cancels countermelody cello)
98 (lower hole): trigger only for rewind and piano soft register
98+98T MP hammer rail lift register on
98T+96 Shutoff
98+98T+96 Rewind
99 Uncoupler 2 (turns on piano notes, holes 33 to 44, overrides piano 1 register, shifts melody pipe notes, holes 33-44, to countermelody section, holes 9-20)
100 Coupler 1 (turns off piano and xylophone notes, holes 21-32, and shifts holes 21-32 to top range of pipe ranks in melody section)

101 Melody tremolo
102 Countermelody swell half open (register on)
102+102T Countermelody swell fully open (normally slow; fast with hole 85)
103 Melody swell half open (register on)
103+103T Melody swell fully open (normally slow, fast with holes 105+105T)
104 Bass swell half open (register on)
104+104T Bass swell fully open (normally slow; fast with holes 105+105T)
105 Register cancel for swell shutters (countermelody, melody, and bass half open and fully open)
105+105T Melody and bass swell accelerator (see holes 103 and 1
106 Countermelody note section 6 coupled to holes 15-20
107 Countermelody note section 5 coupled to holes 9-14
108 Countermelody note section 4 coupled to holes 15-20
108+120 Countermelody note section 10 coupled to holes 15-20
109 Countermelody note section 3 coupled to holes 9-14
109+120 Countermelody note section 9 coupled to holes 9-14
110 Countermelody note section 2 coupled to holes 15-20
110+120 Countermelody note section 8 coupled to holes 15-20
111 Countermelody note section 1 coupled to holes 9-14
111+120 Countermelody note section 7 coupled to holes 9-14
112 Piano 2 register on (piano countermelody notes 9-20 off), countermelody cello on
113 Piano 3 register on (piano bass notes 45-81 off)
113+82 Piano MF register on (the MF register will not turn on if the "piano/forte" switch is in the "forte" position)
114 Register cancel for piccolo, violin, flute, clarinet, oboe, countermelody clarion, bass horn (horn event mellow and bright), piano register 2 and piano register 3
115 Oboe on (melody section)
116 Countermelody clarion and bass section violin on (cancels countermelody cello); with the top hole the clarinet (melody section) also turns on
117 Flute on (melody section)
118 Violin pipes on (melody section)
119 Piccolo on (melody section)
120 Countermelody coupler (see holes 108-111)
121 Mandolin on (melody section, holes 21-49)
122 Bass horn on ("horn event"). Bottom hole in tracker bar = mellow horn; bottom and top holes together = bright horn also
123 Countermelody tremolo
124 Blank

The large bass section foundation bourdon and vox turn on when the melody section violin, flute, clarinet, and oboe registers are on together.

The countermelody section clarion and cello play together when the melody section violin, flute, and oboe registers are on together.

The accordions, chimes, and bird whistle (as arranged in the San Sylmar specimen of the Excelsior Pan Orchestra) are turned on by their respective solenoid-operated valves, operated by remote pushbuttons.

The five-octave countermelody note section plays from twelve note holes in the roll, holes 9-20. The five octaves are divided into ten half-octave sections; when a certain note is desired, the half-octave encompassing that note is connected to the tracker bar by countermelody couplers 106-111 and coupler multiplex hole 120.

The technical information for the Pan Orchestra was provided by Terry Hathaway, who supervised rebuilding of the San Sylmar Collection (J.B. Nethercutt) Excelsior Pan Orchestra, and who rebuilt certain portions of Q. David Bowers' Super Pan Orchestra.

The Hupfeld Excelsior Pan Orchestra as it appeared in the restaurant of the Postzegel Hotel, 's Hertogenbosch, Holland, before it was acquired by Q. David Bowers, who subsequently sold it into the Nethercutt Collection.

Left: This photograph is of a Pan Orchestra Model VI and was taken in 1928 as the instrument was being set up for exhibition at the Nuremburg Trade Exhibition. The unit is equipped with a duplex automatic roll changing device. According to Max Deffner, who once worked extensively with Hupfeld instruments, this particular Pan was sold from the exhibition to the owner of an establishment known as the Cafe de la Rhocee. The Pan Orchestras, of great complexity and musical ability, were the ultimate Hupfeld orchestrions.

Right: Original Hupfeld Pan Orchestra tracker bar scale, shown reduced in size to permit reproduction here. The lines are spaced nine to the inch. This scale, made by the Hupfeld factory, was done in multiple colors and was intended for use in servicing the instrument. The multiple musical scales are visible at the bottom.

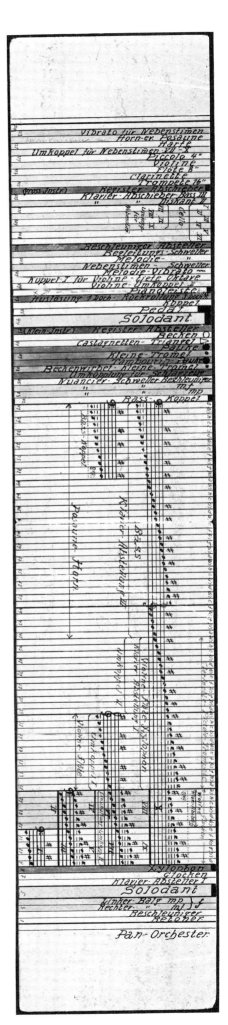

No.	Preis-Gruppe	Be-setzung	Titel	Komponist
90001	III	O.V.Hm.	Alessandro Stradella. Ouverture.	Fr. v. Flotow
90002	III	O.V.	Der Bajazzo. Prolog.	Rugg. Leoncavallo
90003	II	V.C.Hf.	Tannhäuser. Lied an den Abendstern.	Richard Wagner
90004	II	O.	An der schönen blauen Donau. Walzer.	Johann Strauß
90005	II	O.	Espagnole. Grande Valse.	A. Mascheroni
90006	I	V.O.	Vogerl fliagst in d' Welt hinaus. Lied.	Alex. Hornig
90007	I	O.	Das Farmermädchen. Banjo-Ständchen.	Georg Jarno
90008	II	O.	Japan. Brautzug. Charakterstück.	A. Tellier
90009	I	O.	Spanischer Tanz.	M. Schmeling
90010	II	V.Hm.	Ständchen. (,,Leise flehen deine Lieder".)	Franz Schubert
90011	I	O.	Les Millions d'Arlequin. Valse boston. (Tanz-walzer.)	Richard Drigo
90012	II	O.	Der Obersteiger. Grubenlichter-Walzer.	Karl Zeller
90013	I	O.	Rakoczy-Marsch.	. . . .
90014	I	O.	Schwindelmeier & Co. Wahrheits-Marsch.	Rudolph Nelson
90015	II	O.	Hochzeitsständchen.	Oscar Klose
90016	I	O.	Große Rosinen. Mädel jung gefreit. Rheinländer.	Walter Kollo
90017	I	O.	Freiweg. Marsch.	C. Latann
90018	I	O.	Puppchen. Puppchen, du bist mein Augenstern. Twostep.	Jean Gilbert
90019	I	O.	Filmzauber. Untern Linden Marsch.	Walter Kollo
90020	I	O.	Toboggan. Schottisch.	Louis Fremaux
90021	I	O.	Kirschblüte. Twostep.	L. Albert
90022	II	O.	In Treue fest. Marsch.	Carl Teike
90023	I	O.	Deutschlands Ruhm. Marsch.	M. Schröder
90024	I	O.	Unter dem Grillenbanner. Marsch.	Wilh. Lindemann
90025	II	Fl.O.	Turteltäubchen. Charakterstück.	E. Demaré
90026	II	O.	Deutschmeister-Regiments-Marsch.	W. A. Jurek
90027	II	Picc.O.	Plappermäulchen. Charakterstück.	H. Ikker
90028	II	X.O.	Haide und See.	G. H. Geldard
90029	I	V.Hm.	Es ist bestimmt in Gottes Rat. (3 Verse.)	F. Mendelssohn-Bartholdy
90030	I	V.Hm.	Wie sie so sanft ruh'n. Choral. (2 Verse.)	
90031	I	V.Hm.	Weh, daß wir scheiden müssen. (3 Verse.)	Johanna Kinkel
90032	II	V.Hm.O.	Altniederländisches Dankgebet (,,Wir treten zum Beten".)	Eduard Kremser
90033	II	V.Hm.	Der Trompeter von Säkkingen. Behüt dich Gott. (5 Verse.)	V. E. Nessler
90034	I	V.Hm.	Der Freischütz. Leise, leise. (2 Verse.)	C. M. v. Weber
90035	II	V.C.O.	Ave Maria. (2 Verse.)	Franz Schubert

Excerpts from a Hupfeld Pan Orchestra catalogue of the 1920s. For each roll (see upper right panel) the following information is given: (1) serial number, (2) price group [smaller rolls are in the I category and are cheaper; most expensive are large III category rolls], (3) musical characteristic of the roll; the instruments or solo sections featured, (4) title of the melody, and (5) composer of the original music.

At the bottom right is an explanation of the abbreviations used for the different musical characteristics.

90841	I	O.	Du! Wann bist du bei mir? (Who.)	Jérome Kern
90883	I	O.L.	Eine hat mich geküßt. (Blue skies.)	Irving Berlin
90446	I	O.	Eine kleine Freundin hat doch jeder Mann, aus: ,,Die blaue Mazur".	Franz Lehár
90872	II	O.L.	Einmal ist keinmal. (Lonesome and Sorry.)	B. Davis u. C. Conrad
90922	I	O.L.	Eis! Eis! Eis! (Ach Brigitte, bestell' dir doch bitte Eis!) (Ice cream.)	H. Johnson, B. Moll u. R. Kind
90588	II	O.	Eldgaffeln. (Feuerzauber.)	Einar Landén
90781	I	O.	Es geht die Lou lila.	Dr. Rob. Katscher
90754	I	O.	Fleur d'amour. (Wenn blüht die rote Rose.)	José Padilla
90509	I	O.	Fox Macabre.	Fr. Hollaender
90596	I	O.	Foxtrot della nostalgia.	V. Vitaliani
90609	II	O.	Georgette.	Ray Henderson
90418	II	O.	Glocken-Foxtrot. (Fox-Trot de las Campanas.)	Pastallé u. Viladomat
90876	I	O.L.	Hallelujah.	Vincent Youmans
90425	I	O.	Harem.	Maurice Yvain
90900	I	O.L.	Heut' geh'n wir morgen erst ins Bett! Heut' tanzt Mariett'!	Rudolph Nelson
90878	I	O.L.	Heut' war ich bei der Frida.	Jim Cowler
90686	I	O.	Honey love.	Percy Wenrich
90586	I	O.	Ich hab' ein Stübchen im fünften Stock, aus: ,,Drunter und Drüber".	Walter Kollo
90806	I	O.	I miss my Swiss. (My Swiss miss misses me.)	Abel Baer
90323	II	O.	Indianola.	Henry u. Onivas
90836	I	O.	I never see Maggie alone.	Everett Lynton
90835	I	O.	I Wonder where my Baby is To-Night. (Wo steckt die Melanie seit gestern Nacht?)	Walter Donaldson
90766	I	O.	Ja der Sonnenschein. (Yearning.)	Joe Burke

Erläuterung
der Bezeichnungen für die Besetzung

C.Fl.O. = Cello- und Flöten-Soli mit Orchester-Begleitung.

Fl.O. = Flöten-Solo mit Orchester-Begleitung.

O. = Reine Orchestermusik.

O.C. = Orchester mit Cello-Solo.

O.Hf. = Orchester mit Harfe.

O.Hf.X. = Orchester mit Harfe und Xylophon.

O.Hm. = Orchester mit Harmonium.

O.Hm.L. = Orchester mit Harmonium und Lotosflöte.

O.L. = Orchester mit Lotosflöte.

O.V. = Orchester mit Violin-Solo.

O.V.C.Hm. = Orchester mit Violin- und Cello-Soli und Harmonium.

O.V.Fl. = Orchester mit Violin- und Flöten-Soli.

O.V.Hm. = Orchester mit Violin-Solo und Harmonium.

O.X. = Orchester mit Xylophon.

P. = Piano-Solo (Künstlerrollen).

P.O. = Piano-Solo mit Orchester-Begleitung.

P.X.Hf. = Piano-Solo mit Xylophon und Harfe.

Picc.O. = Piccolo-Solo mit Orchester-Begleitung.

V. = Violin-Solo mit Piano-Begleitung.

V.C. = Violin- und Cello-Soli mit Piano-Begleitung.

V.C.Fl. = Violin-, Cello- und Flöten-Soli mit Piano-Begleitung.

V.C.Hf. = Violin- und Cello-Soli mit Harfen- oder Piano-Begleitung.

V.C.Hf.O. = Violin- und Cello-Soli mit Harfe und Orchester-Begleitung.

V.C.O. = Violin- und Cello-Soli mit Orchester- und Piano-Begleitung.

V.Fl. = Violin- und Flöten-Soli mit Piano-Begleitung.

V.Hf. = Violin-Solo mit Harfen- oder Piano-Begleitung.

V.Hm. = Violin-Solo und Harmonium, abwechselnd mit Piano-Begleitung.

V.Hm.O. = Violin-Solo und Harmonium, abwechselnd mit Orchester- und Piano-Begleitung.

V.O. = Violin-Solo mit Orchester- oder Piano-Begleitung.

X.O. = Xylophon-Solo mit Orchester-Begleitung.

X.Hf.P. = Xylophon-Solo und Harfe mit Piano-Begleitung.

A glimpse of part of the interior of the Hupfeld Excelsior Pan Orchestra in J.B. Nethercutt's San Sylmar Collection. Made in 1926, the orchestrion originally saw service in an elegant Dutch restaurant.

This huge Hupfeld Super Pan Orchestra was once located in a cafe in Zeedyk, a district of Amsterdam. It was originally sold circa 1926 by Duwaer & Naessens, Holland distributors for Hupfeld products. In the 1960s it was purchased by Eugene DeRoy, who sold it to Q. David Bowers. In this view the center front panels are removed to permit a view of the complex interior.

HUPFELD SUPER PAN ORCHESTRA ROLL
14 1/8" wide; spaced 9 holes per inch
(Standard Pan Orchestra roll)

The Hupfeld Super Pan Orchestra contains instrumentation which is different in some respects from that in the Excelsior Pan; one aspect being the substitution of harmonium reeds for some of the pipe ranks. All functions are the same as those in the Excelsior Pan Orchestra except for the following differences:
91+86 = Castanets
114 Cancel violin, flute, oboe, bass horn, piano register 2
　　 and piano register 3
116 Blank
119 Blank

Violin+flute+oboe = bass harmonium
Countermelody sections 1-5: harmonium
Countermelody sections 6-10: violin celeste

Hupfeld Phonoliszt-Violina Rolls

In the field of automatic musical instruments there were many experiments with violin players. Only two models were commercially successful: the Mills Violano-Virtuoso and the Hupfeld Phonoliszt-Violina. Both used real violins in combination with a piano.

The Phonoliszt-Violina, which consisted of three real violins (each with one active string and three unplayed ones) which were played by means of a rotating aluminum bow, on the inside of which were strung about 1350 real horsehairs. To play, the violin which was mounted in an inverted vertical position, was pressed forward against the bow. The speed of the bow could be varied from fast to slow, tremolo could be used, and other expression effects were possible. Accompanying the violin music was a Phonoliszt expression piano.

An original advertisement noted:

"The self-playing Violina is provided with real violins operated by a horsehair bow and means the solution of a problem that has been vainly sought for centuries.

"It can be easily understood what difficulties had to be overcome from a technical point of view to solve this problem, as contrary to the piano, where the production of tones is based on the already provided keyboard in connection with the inside mechanism, on the violin some way or method had to be found to produce the tone.

"The violins are placed inside of a rotating horsehair bow with 1350 horsehairs, with which they are brought in touch during the playing. The bow, same as with hand playing, comes in contact with the violin under different grades of pressure to produce the tone graduation either soft or loud or any shading required for artistic violin playing. Also, all other effects and finesses in playing are provided for, such as staccato, legato, glissando, vibrato, as naturally as by hand playing, and where the sordino effect is necessary it certainly will surprise you, as it works without any noise as by human hand.

"Violin virtuosos and great band leaders after hearing the Phonoliszt-Violina have been astounded at the faultless technique and marvelous interpretation.

"The most admirable quality of the Phonoliszt-Violina is its soul, thus the most important factor in violin playing has been accomplished to give soul to this only self-playing violin.

"The Phonoliszt-Violina consists of three violins and the self-playing Phonoliszt Autograph Player which accompanies the violin in the most artistic manner. Imagine hearing a Josef Hofmann, Arthur Friedheim, Ferruccio Busoni, Harold Bauer, Wilhelm Backhaus, or Eugene d'Albert playing the piano as a solo instrument or accompanying a Zimbalist, Kubelik, or Sarasate. For this is the Phonoliszt-Violina.

"The Phonoliszt-Violina repertoire has been compiled on the same principle as for other instruments, so that all the different tastes are duly considered. Not only are there folksongs, marches, waltzes, and the latest hits in light opera, but also violin concert pieces and even duets. This repertoire is constantly growing by new and selected additional pieces."

The typical Hupfeld Phonoliszt-Violina played special Phonoliszt-Violina rolls, but by means of a lever, it could be switched to play Phonoliszt (expression piano only) rolls as well. A few instruments were equipped with the ingenious duplex roll changer which stored 6 rolls on each changer (6x2=12 rolls totally) and played each side alternately, thus eliminating a pause during roll rewinding. This type of instrument played the Phonoliszt-Violina rolls on one changer and the Phonoliszt rolls on the others, thus giving a concert alternating between violin and piano selections and piano solos.

On April 5, 1912, noted violinist Efrem Zimbalist wrote that "Certainly the Phonoliszt-Violina is the eighth wonder and marvel of our time." Today, collectors consider the Phonoliszt-Violina to be one of the most marvelous of all self-playing instruments from years gone by. Their sentiment often echoes what two prominent musical personalities, Eugene DeRoy and Farny Wurlitzer, said during interviews in the 1960s: of all the self-playing instruments with which they were familiar, the Phonoliszt-Violina impressed them the most. While surviving specimens of the Phonoliszt-Violina aren't common, there are over 50 represented in collections around the world, so that the opportunity exists to hear these play their violin pieces once again.

HUPFELD PHONOLISZT-VIOLINA ROLL
11 5/8" wide; approx. 26+ holes per 10 cm.

1 D violin note switch
2 Open D string
3 D#, with switch - C
4 E; with switch - B
5 F; with switch - A#
6 F#; with switch - A
7 G; with switch - G#
8 to 34 Piano notes C# to D# (keys 17 to 43 on the keyboard)
35 Sustaining pedal
36 Piano note E
37 Piano vacuum low (180 mm. of water)
38 Piano note F
39 Piano MF (280 mm.)
40 Piano note F#
41 Piano crescendo
42 Piano note G
43 Bass hammer rail
44-50, Piano notes G# to D
51 Piano treble coupler (notes play unison or 8' pitch)
52 Treble separator (piano notes play octave higher, or 4')
53 A violin note switch
54 Open A string
55 A#; with switch - G
56 B; with switch - F#
57 C; with switch - F
58 C#; with switch - E
59 D; with switch - D#
60 E violin note switch
61 Open E string
62 F; with switch - G#
63 F#; with switch - G
64 G; with switch - F#
65 G#; with switch - F
66 A; with switch - E
67 A#; with switch - D#
68 B; with switch - D
69 C; with switch - C#
70 Violin slow crescendo
71 Violin soft - bow turns 7 r.p.m.
72 Violin fast crescendo
73 Violin MF - bow turns 14 r.p.m.
74 Violin on strongly
75 Violin accent - bow turns 32 r.p.m.
76 Violin tremolo
77 Violin mute

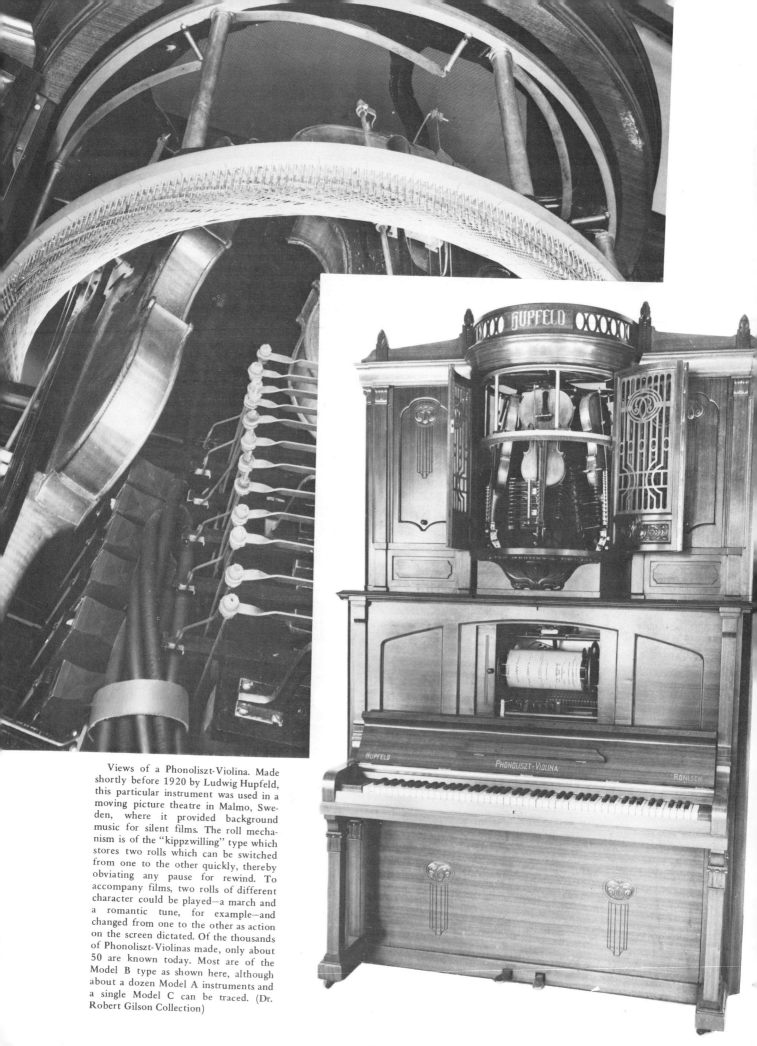

Views of a Phonoliszt-Violina. Made shortly before 1920 by Ludwig Hupfeld, this particular instrument was used in a moving picture theatre in Malmo, Sweden, where it provided background music for silent films. The roll mechanism is of the "kippzwilling" type which stores two rolls which can be switched from one to the other quickly, thereby obviating any pause for rewind. To accompany films, two rolls of different character could be played—a march and a romantic tune, for example—and changed from one to the other as action on the screen dictated. Of the thousands of Phonoliszt-Violinas made, only about 50 are known today. Most are of the Model B type as shown here, although about a dozen Model A instruments and a single Model C can be traced. (Dr. Robert Gilson Collection)

The violins are normally loud when the bow travels 27 r.p.m.; the piano is normally loud when it has 520 mm. of vacuum level (measured on a water manometer).

The piano treble coupler (hole 51) and separator (hole 52) control the upper 12 piano note holes in the tracker bar (34, 36, 38, 40, 42, and 44-50).

37+39+41 = Shutoff
37+39+41+43 = Rewind

VIOLIN EXPRESSION: Hole 71 rapidly slows the bow speed to 7 r.p.m. Holes 71+72 together slow the rate of decrescendo. 71+70 make the decrescendo even slower. Hole 73 reduces bow speed to MF (14 r.p.m.) if it is turning faster, and limits speed to MF if it is turning slower.

The rate at which hole 73 controls bow speed is also affected by holes 70 and 72. Hole 75 bypasses the motor governor and moves the violin stop cams to a position allowing maximum bow pressure. Hole 74 bypasses a constriction in the vacuum line feeding the violin play pneumatics, allowing the violins to be moved to the bow with maximum speed. Holes 74 and 75 are often used together for accents or rapid staccato.

The tremolo hole (76) is single stroke, with more "off" space or paper between holes than "on" hole perforation space. Because of the unequal on/off spacing, the tremolo sounds good only if the roll is moving at a speed sufficient to imitate the tremolo of a human violinist, which is rarely slower than about 7 beats per second. If the roll tempo is adjusted too slowly, the wonderfully human effect of the Phonoliszt-Violina is overshadowed by the uneven tremolo.

Historical Note: Several variations of Hupfeld violin players were made. In the early days the Dea-Violina, the Violina (no piano), and the Clavitist-Violina were made. Later, a Violina Orchestra (violin with orchestrion effects) was made. These each used different types of rolls. No specimens of these instruments are known to the authors today.

HUPFELD VIOLINA ORCHESTRA ROLL
Believed to be 11¼" wide; spaced 9 holes per inch

The following scale is listed in reverse order to make comparison with the Phonoliszt-Violina tracker bar scale easier. It was formulated by Art Reblitz after examining a copy of an original Hupfeld scale stick furnished by Frank Holland of the British Piano Museum. It is not verified, for the authors know of no surviving instrument of this type.

98 Hammer rail
97 Accompaniment expression MF-P
96 Melody expression MF-F
95 Sustaining pedal
94 Bass theme (solodant)
93 D switch over
92 D swell crescendo
91 D octave coupler
90 D swell decrescendo
89 Tympani
88 D tremolo
87 Tympani
86 Cymbal
85 D violin note switch
84 "Rosteller"?
83 Open D string
82 D#; with switch - C
81 E; with switch - B
80 F; with switch - A#
79 F#; with switch - A
78 G; with switch - G#
77 to 40, piano notes C# to D (keys 17 to 54 on keyboard)
39 Piano treble coupler (highest 12 piano note holes, 51 to 40 on the tracker bar, play unison or 8' pitch, keys 43 to 54 on the keyboard)
38 Piano treble separator (tracker bar holes 51 to 40 play an octave higher, or 4' pitch, piano key numbers 55 to 66)
37 A violin note switch

36 Open A string
35 A#; with switch - G
34 B; with switch - F#
33 C; with switch - F
32 C#; with switch - E
31 D; with switch - D#
30 E violin note switch
29 Open E string
28 F; with switch - G#
27 F#; with switch - G
26 G; with switch - F#
25 G#; with switch - F
24 A; with switch - E
23 A#; with switch - D#
22 B; with switch - D
21 C; with switch - C#
20 Violin slow crescendo
19 Violin soft
18 Violin fast crescendo
17 Violin MF
16 Violin on strongly
15 Violin accent
14 E tremolo
13 Violin mute
12 E switch over
11 A swell crescendo
10 A octave coupler
9 A swell decrescendo
8 A switch over
7 Snare drum roll
6 Flute tremolo
5 Treble theme (solodant)
4 Accompaniment expression accelerator
3 Melody MF-P
2 Melody expression accelerator
1 Accompaniment MF-F

The violin functions and expression in the Violina Orchestra are similar to the Phonoliszt-Violina, while the piano expression is similar to the Pan and Triphonola expression. The piano note range and couplers operate as in the Phonoliszt-Violina.

The clarinet apparently has a 28-note range, A to C. The lower octave of notes, which includes D through C, plays from the D violin note holes and note switch hole (85) whenever the D switch over hole (93) is perforated. The upper octave, including notes D-C, plays from the same holes when the D octave coupler hole (91) is perforated. The C# which is missing between the two octaves is activated by 83 and 85 together. (Hole 83, open D string, and 85, D note switch, would never otherwise be punched simultaneously because the switch does not affect the open string.) The low clarinet notes A to C# are turned on by holes 90 and 92, and off by holes 9 and 11, but the musical note holes to which they are coupled are not clearly indicated on the scale stick; they might be the violin D note holes, or they might be piano note holes 69-65.

The flute plays from the A violin notes and note switch, and possibly also from the E notes. The missing lower G# in the flute note scale is activated by holes 36 and 37 together, and the higher missing G# is activated by 36, 37, and 10.

Additional multiplexing indicated on the scale stick includes the following combinations of holes: mandolin, 90+92; harmonium, 18+20; piano off, 18+20+11; xylophone, 9+11. Judging from the sophistication of the Pan Orchestra "in person," as compared to an original Pan Orchestra scale stick, the authors believe that a Violina Orchestra, if one could be actually examined, would reveal many more multiplexing functions in addition to those listed here.

Detail view of the roll mechanism of a Hupfeld Phonoliszt-Violina. The top row of holes is used when the instrument plays Phonoliszt-Violina rolls (which are programmed to play the violins and the piano). The bottom row of holes is used for Phonoliszt (piano only) expression rolls. The shift from one to the other is made by a manually-operated lever. (Collection of Jerry and Sylvia Cohen)

Above: Although most Phonoliszt-Violinas had long since
disappeared from commercial service by the early 1970s, the
instrument shown above was a remarkable exception. It still
entertained European and other visitors to the Hotel de la Cignogne
in Munster, France. The instrument is a very early model, probably
dating from before 1914, and has the transposed name
"Violina-Phonoliszt" on the fallboard. The designation "Violina"
appears on the top crest. To the right can be seen a cabinet full of
rolls. (Robert Herzog photograph)

Right: This faded photograph, taken at the Hupfeld factory in
1925, shows a now-rare example of the Violina Orchestra. The
authors have been able to locate a number of photographs of the
Violina Orchestra from the days of long ago, giving rise to the
thought that these devices may have enjoyed a fairly wide sale.
However, so far as is known, no specimens have survived the years.
The photograph shows Max Deffner, who worked for Hupfeld.

Phonoliszt = Violina Mod. B

This early Phonoliszt-Violina illustration was made from a heavily retouched photograph and has many errors, including the wrong number of tuning pegs on each violin, absent doors at the upper front, and a roll of incorrect width (unless a wider roll was used in the very early times).

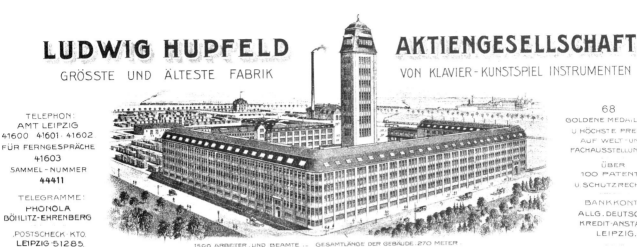

Above: Letterhead, circa 1922, of Ludwig Hupfeld, the world's largest manufacturer of automatic musical instruments. The factory still stands today and is used for the making of pianos, but not of the automatic kind. The above letterhead notes that Hupfeld won 68 gold medals and first prizes, held over 100 patents and trademarks, and had factories and agencies in many different areas.

Below: Musical program given to restaurant patrons at the Hotel Eisenbahn in Sursee, Switzerland. Listed are rolls available for listening on the Hupfeld Phonoliszt-Violina. Selections from 1 through 73 are violin and piano arrangements. Selections from 201 through 215 are piano only (without the violins).

1. Königl. Sven lifgardes		Marsch	Körner
2. Die lustigen Weiber v. Windsor		Ouvertüre	Nicolai
3. Klänge der aus Heimat		Oberländler	Gungl
4. Les Million d'arléquin		Polka	
5. Romanze		Operette	Beethoven
6. Mimi d'Amour		Valse	J. Vercolier
7. Romanze			Beethoven
8. Rigoletto		Fantasie	G. Verdi
9. Kol. Niderei		Operette	Max Bruch
10. Souvenier de Haydn		Fantasie	Leonard
11. Grossmütterchen		Ländler	Langer
12. Electric Girl		Shimmy-Fox	Helmburgh-Holmes
13. Home, sweet home		Lied	Bishop
14. Deutschmeister Regiments-Marsch			Jürek
15. Bayrischer Ländler		Tanzrolle	Benatzky
16. Morphium			
17. Tannhäuser		Lied	R. Wagner
18. Mignon		Lied	Thomas
19. Mignon		Ouverture	Thomas
20. Salome		Fox-Trot	R. Stolz
21. Gern hab' ich die Frauen gek.		Operette	Lehar
22. Alessandro Stradella		Ouverture	Flotow
23. Wienerwalzer			Benatzky
24. Szárdásfürstin		Walzer	Kálmán
25. Dreimäderlhaus		Walzer	Schubert
26. Susie		Fox-Trot	Sylve
27. Weinwalzer			Gross
28. Valantine		Onestep	Christiné
29. Hab' ein blaues Himmelsbett		Lied	Lehár
30. Elsässische Bauerntänze		Ländler	Merklin
31. Ave Maria			Schubert
32. Auf nach Valencia		Marsch	Eisengräber
33. Le Pas de fleurs		Walzer	Leo Delibes
34. Valencia			Josi Padilla
35. Cavalleria rusticana			Pietro Mascagni
36. Zwei verlassene Italiener		Walzer	Jul. Jehring
37. Sirenenzauber		Op.-Walzer	Waldteufel
38. Rigoletto		Fantasie	Verdi
39. Und zum Schluss		Shimmy	Hugo Hirsch
40. Der Zigeuerbaron		Lied	Johann Strauss
41. Sonate nach der Serenade		k. Nachten	W. A. Mozart
42. Die Zauberflöte			W. A. Mozart
43. a) Polnische Wirtschaft		Lunapark	J. Gilbert
b) Wer kann dafür		Walzer	J. Gilbert
c) Parade der Zinnsoldaten		Rheinländer	Jessel
d) Juanita		Mazurka	C. Morena
44. An der schönen blauen Donau		Walzer	J. Strauss
45. Parade der Zinnsoldaten		Charakterstück	Jessel

46. Kubelik Serenade			Drdla
47. Seemanns Los		Lied	A. Martell
48. Deutsche Volkslieder:			
a) Aennchen von Tharau			
b) Ach, wie ist's möglich dann			
49. Fledermaus, Quadrille		Tanzrolle	J. Strauss, Sohn
50. Martha		Ouverture	Fr. Flotow
51. Barcelona		Onestep	Polchard Evans
52. Dichter und Bauer		Ouverture	Fr. v. Suppe
53. Das haben die Mädchen so gerne		Marschlied	Jean Gilbert
54. Die Försterchristl		Christlwalzer	G. Jarno
55. Tango-Prinzessin, „Wenn das der Petrus wüsste"		Marsch	J. Gilbert
56. Ich hab' mein Herz in Heidelberg verloren		Marschlied	Frdy Reymond
57. Fehrbelliner Reitermarsch		Lied	Richard Henrion
58. Grüsse an die Heimat			K. Kramer
59. La Bohème		Fantasie	Puccini
60. Hochzeit der Winde		Walzer	John T. Hall
61. Parsifal		Fantasie	Rich. Wagner
62. Margarethe (Faust) grosse Balletmusik, I. Rolle			Ch. Fr. Gounod
63. Dito II. Rolle			Ch. Fr. Gounod
64. Zigeunerliebe		Walzer	Fr. Lehar
65. Bayerischer Ländler, I. Rolle			
66. Dito II. Rolle			
67. Frohsinn auf den Bergen			Oskar Fetras
68. Alte Kameraden		Marsch	Carl Teike
69. La Traviata		Fantasie	Verdi
70. Elefant und Mücke			H. Kling
71. Scardasfürstin		Twostep	Em. Kálmán
72. Der Bajazzo		Prolog	Ruggiero Leoncavallo
73. Zigeunerprimas		Walzer	Em. Kálmán
KLAVIER:			
201. Heroisch-Marsch			Liszt
202. Wilhelm Tell		Ouverture	G. Rossini
203. Ungarische Rhapsodie			Liszt
204. Menuett-Walzer			P. Hertel
205. Heinzelmännch. Wachtparade			Kurt Noak
206. Gruss an Bern		Marsch	C. Friedemann
207. Wer zuletzt lacht		Walzer	L. Jessel
208. Stammbuchverse		Foxtrot	Harry Waldau
209. Die Regimentstochter		Potpourri	G. Donizetti
210. Filmzauber			W. Rollo
211. Zigeunerliebe		Walzer	F. Lehár
212. Lucie de Lammermoor			L. Ascher
213. La Traviata		Potpourri	G. Verdi
214. Donauwellen		Walzer	J. Jvanovici
215. Hoch Habsburg		Marsch	J. N. Král

Konzert=
Programm

PHONOLISZT

VIOLINA

HOTEL EISENBAHN

SURSEE

Two different deluxe models of the Model A Hupfeld Phonoliszt-Violina. The above instrument, in the collection of the Netherlands Film Museum (Amsterdam, Holland), has two single-roll mechanisms arranged in duplex style side by side. The Model A pictured to the right, from the David Wilkinson Collection, is one of two examples known with a duplex automatic roll changing mechanism. The device incorporates two 6-roll automatic changers, giving the instrument a repertoire of 12 tunes. One roll mechanism uses Phonoliszt-Violina rolls and the other uses Phonoliszt expression piano rolls. In 1979 the Play-Rite Music Roll Company recut over 100 different Phonoliszt-Violina rolls for a group of 19 interested collectors and museums from around the world.

Following page: Close-up view of a Model A Phonoliszt-Violina similar to the Wilkinson Collection example. So far as the authors know, only two examples of the Phonoliszt-Violina with duplex 6-roll automatic changers exist today.

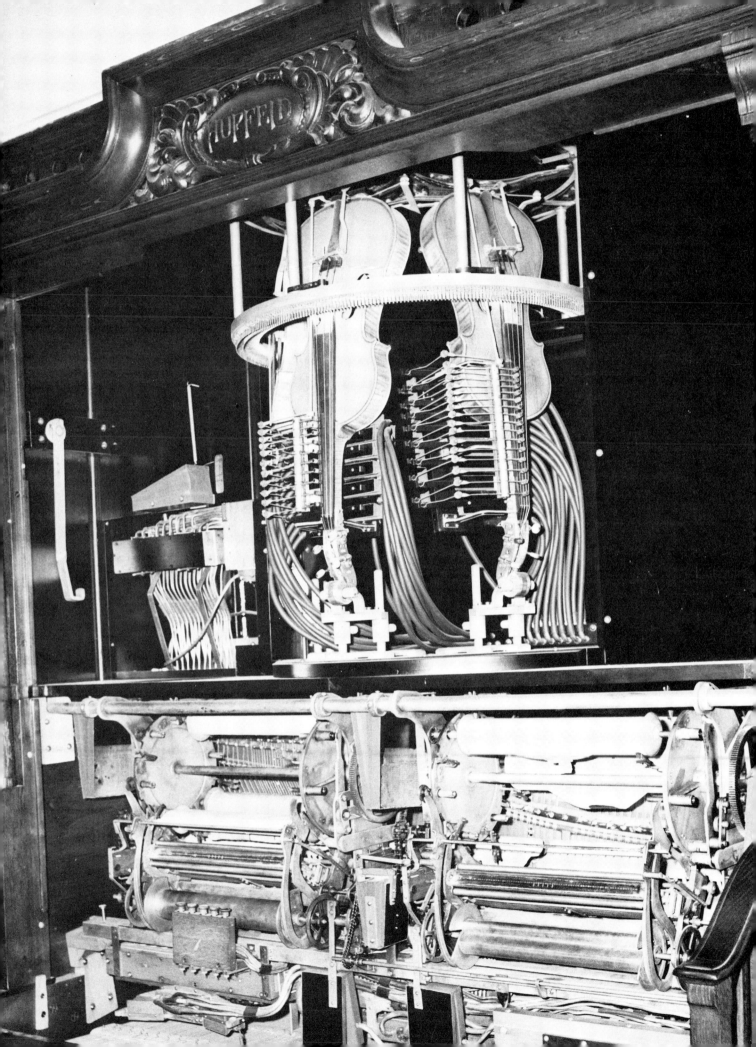

Hupfeld Violina Orchestra, Model II, as shown in the salesrooms of Charriere & Co., Bulle, Switzerland, in 1926. Although no specimens are known to the authors today, in the late 1920s the Violina Orchestra, made in two main case styles (with keyboard and without), was extensively advertised and featured in Hupfeld price lists. (Photograph courtesy of the late Otto Weber)

IMHOF & MUKLE
Coin Pianos
Orchestrions

Founded in Vohrenbach, Germany in the 1840s, the firm of Imhof & Mukle at first produced tall-case clocks with musical mechanisms consisting of flute pipes played by pinned cylinders. By the end of the 19th century the company was making large classic orchestrions, barrel-operated pianos (many of which were in richly figured wood cases), barrel organs, and other instruments, mostly actuated by pinned cylinders.

Sometime around the turn of the century the "Music Leaf System" was introduced. Basically, the system consisted of a long roll of music cut on tough cardboard-like manila paper. The rolls were "read" by a key frame, similar to that used in certain band organs and dance organs. Tiny spring-loaded "fingers" would pop up whenever a hole occurred in the roll, thus actuating a valve. Most of the rolls enumerated in the following listings are of the heavy manila paper type used on the Music Leaf System.

In later years, in the 'teens and 1920s, Imhof & Mukle converted to the standard thin-paper roll format used by other makers, so later products—the Ramona violin pipe piano, for example—use thin paper rolls.

The finest days of Imhof & Mukle were in the first decade of the 20th century. During this time many large and magnificent orchestrions such as the Admiral, Valkyrie, Commandant, Lucretia, Dinorah, Lohengrin, Tell, and Lord were made. Many of these were sold in the United States by agent Ernst Boecker. At one time the Hudson Day Line steamers which plied the river from New York to Albany entertained its passengers with Imhof & Mukle orchestrion music.

After World War I, the firm's prominence faded. By the 1920s Imhof & Mukle was a minor factor in the business.

The firm's pianos and orchestrions were finely constructed. And, no doubt some of the large orchestrions from the early 20th century represent some of the most ornate case designs ever produced. Several dozen large Imhof & Mukle orchestrions survive today in collections and museums around the world.

19 F
20 D#
21 E
22 D
23 D#
24 C#
25 D
26 C
27 C#
28 B
29 Middle C
30 A#
31 B
32 A
33 A#
34 G#
35 A
36 G
37 G#
38 F#
39 G
40 F
41 F#
42 E
43 F
44 D#
45 E
46 D
47 D#
48 C#
49 D
50 C
51 C
52 B
53 A#
54 A#
55 A
56 A
57 G
58 G#
59 F (Low)
60 Rewind
61 Mandolin on
62 Harp on
63 Violin pipes on

The note scale, from lowest to highest, is played by holes 59, 57, 55, and remaining odd numbers in descending order to 15; then 58, 56, 54, and remaining even numbers to 16.

IMHOF & MUKLE
LORD I AND DINORAH ROLL
45 playing notes

1 Melody flute on
2 Piano on
3 Piano, flute, violin pipes off
4 Clarinet on
5 Mandolin and clarinet off
6 Shutoff
7 Bass drum
8 Sustaining pedal off
9 Snare drum
10 Sustaining pedal on
11 Bells and harp (mandolin effect) off
12 Bells on
13 Crescendo off
14 Crescendo on
15 G
16 High F
17 F#
18 E

IMHOF & MUKLE
LORD I ROLL (variation)

An unknown type of Imhof & Mukle orchestrion uses the following abbreviated version of the Lord I scale:
1 Xylophone on
2 Xylophone and mandolin off
3 Shutoff
4 Bass drum and cymbal
5 Sustaining pedal off
6 Snare drum
7 Sustaining pedal on
8 Bells off
9 Bells on
10 Violin pipes crescendo off
11 Violin pipes crescendo on
12 to 58 (same as 15 to 61 on Lord I scale)

Imhof & Mukle Valkyrie orchestrion.

IMHOF & MUKLE
TRIBUT (or TRIBUTE) ROLL
GALANT ROLL
BADENIA ROLL
RECLAME ROLL
(As Lord I and Dinorah, but with the following differences)

1 Not used
2 Contra bass off
3 Contra bass on
4 Xylophone on
5 Mandolin and xylophone off
11 Bells off
12 Bells on
62 Hauptwerk off
63 Hauptwerk on

IMHOF & MUKLE
ADMIRAL ORCHESTRION ROLL
(51 playing notes)

1 Trumpet on
2 Trumpet off
3 Trumpet crescendo on
4 Trumpet crescendo off
5 Clarinet on
6 Clarinet off
7 Xylophone on
8 Xylophone off
9 Baritone, cello on
10 Baritone, cello off
11 Shutoff
12 G
13 G#
14 F#
15 A
16 F
17 A#
18 E
19 B
20 D#
21 C
22 D
23 C#
24 C#
25 D
26 Middle C
27 D#
28 B
29 E
30 A#
31 F
32 A
33 F#
34 G#
35 G
36 G
37 G#
38 F#
39 A
40 F
41 A#
42 E
43 B
44 D#
45 C
46 D
47 C#
48 C#
49 D
50 C
51 D#
52 B

53 E
54 A#
55 F
56 A
57 F#
58 G#
59 G
60 Low G
61 G#
62 Mandolin on
63 High A
64 Rewind
65 Violin pipes crescendo on
66 Violin pipes crescendo off
67 Tympani
68 Tympani
69 Bells on
70 Bells off
71 Bass drum
72 Snare drum
73 Sustaining pedal on
74 Sustaining pedal and mandolin off
75 Viennese flute on
76 Viennese flute off
77 Anschlag on
78 Anschlag off
79 Octave on
80 Octave off
81 Tenor bass on
82 Contra bass on
83 Contra bass off?
84 ?

The note scale, from lowest to highest, plays from holes 60, 58, 56 and the remaining even numbered holes in descending order to 12, and then 13, 15, 17, and remaining odd numbered holes in ascending order to 63.

IMHOF & MUKLE
WALKURE (in English, VALKYRIE) ROLL
LUCRETIA ROLL
VENUS ROLL
LORD II ROLL
TELL ROLL
The roll for the preceding instruments is similar to that of the Admiral, but it has fewer marginal functions and has the following differences:

1 to 6 Blank
7 Solo violin pipes on
8 Solo violin pipes off
9 Violin pipes crescendo on
10 Violin pipes crescendo off
75 Hauptwerk on
76 Hauptwerk off
77 Clarinet on
78 Clarinet off
79 to 84 Blank

IMHOF & MUKLE
LUCIA ROLL
The Lucia uses a roll similar to the Admiral but with just 64 holes, omitting Admiral holes 1 to 10 and 75 to 84.

Above is shown the Imhof & Mukle factory, circa 1910, with firemen climbing on the roof. Was it a practice drill? Albert Imhof, who furnished the picture, didn't know. Below is a sketch, dated 1907, of the Imhof & Mukle orchestrion custom made for the Jockey Club in New York City.

IMHOF & MUKLE
CORRECTOR ROLL
(Early style; "Music Leaf System")
(61 playing notes)

1 Violin pipes on
2 Violin pipes off
3 Piano on
4 Piano off
5 Mandolin on
6 Xylophone on
7 Mandolin and xylophone off
8 Violin pipes crescendo loud
9 Contra bass on
10 Contra bass off
11 Shutoff
12 Low C
13 G
14 C#
15 G#
16 D
17 A
18 D#
19 A#
20 E
21 B
22 F
23 C
24 F#
25 C#
26 G
27 D
28 G#
29 D#
30 A
31 E
32 A#
33 F
34 B
35 F#
36 C
37 G
38 C
39 G#
40 D
41 A
42 D#
43 A#
44 E
45 B
46 F
47 C
48 F#
49 C#
50 G
51 D
52 G#
53 D#
54 A
55 E
56 A#
57 F
58 B
59 F#
60 Middle C
61 G
62 C#
63 G#
64 D
65 A
66 D#
67 A#
68 E
69 B
70 F
71 High C
72 F#
73 Rewind
74 Sustaining pedal on

75 Sustaining pedal off?
76 Soft pedal on
77 Soft pedal off
78 Anschlag loud (or on?)
79 Anschlag soft (or off?)
80 Tremolo on
81 Tremolo off
82 Violin pipes crescendo soft

The note scale, from the lowest to the highest, plays from holes 12, 14, 16, and remaining even numbered holes in ascending order to 72, then 13, 15, and remaining odd numbered holes to 71.

IMHOF & MUKLE
CORRECTOR ROLL
11¼" wide; 9 holes per inch
(Later style; thin paper rolls)

1 Mezzoforte
2 Hammer rail slow, xylophone on/off
3 Mandolin on/off
4 Sustaining pedal
5 and 6, Bass accent
7 to 15, Blank
16 to 88, Note scale, G to G
89 to 91 Blank
92 Rewind
93 Shutoff
94 Treble accent
95 Treble accent
96 Blank
97 Fortissimo
98 Forte
99 Melody soft
Holes 2 and 3: short perforation = off; longer perforation = on.

IMHOF & MUKLE
RAMONA; COMMANDANT II AND III ROLL
11¼" wide; 9 holes per inch
(later style; thin paper roll)

1 Mezzoforte
2 Hammer rail up slowly
3 Bass soft + mandolin on/off
4 Sustaining pedal
5 Bass accent
6 to 20, Violin pipe note scale, middle C through D
21 to 78, Piano note scale, C to A
79 to 85, Continuation of violin scale, D# to A
86 Tremolo on
87 Violin pipes on
88 Blank
89 Blank
90 Tremolo off
91 Crescendo, soft violin pipes
92 Rewind
93 Shutoff
94 Treble accent
95 Blank
96 Hammer rail, melody violin pipes loud
97 Piano treble on (fortissimo)
98 Forte
99 Piano treble off
Hole 3: long perforation = functions on; short perforation = functions off.

IMHOF & MUKLE
ORCHESTRION ROLL; UNKNOWN STYLE
11¼" wide; 9 holes per inch
(Late style; thin paper roll)
Late style Admiral?

1 Sustaining pedal
2 Blank?
3 Tremolo on, melody off
4 Mandolin on
5 Crescendo soft (swell shutters?)
6 Xylophone on
7 Crescendo loud (swell shutters?)
8 Piano off
9 Bells and mandolin on
10 Triangle
11 Tremolo off, melody on
12 Piccolo on
13 Bells and mandolin off
14 Soft snare drum
15 Cymbal
16 Loud bass drum
17 Soft bass drum
18 Loud snare drum
19 to 76, 58 playing notes, C to A
77 Tympani
78 Tympani
79 Bassoon on
80 Trumpet on
81 Clarinet on
82 Bass gedeckt on
83 Cello on
84 Soft violin pipes on
85 Loud violin pipes on
86 Piccolo on
87 Flute on
88 General cancel
89 Mandolin off
90 Rewind
91 Blank?
92 Piano on

29 F
30 Triangle
31 D#
32 G
33 Bass drum
34 F#
35 C#
36 E
37 G
38 C
39 D
40 F#
41 D
42 C
43 E
44 E
45 A#
46 D
47 F#
48 G#
49 C
50 Snare drum
51 G#
52 A#
53 C
54 A#
55 G#
56 F
57 C
58 G#
59 D
60 A#
61 E
62 C#
63 F#
64 E

IMHOF & MUKLE
64-KEY ORCHESTRION ROLL

1 Octave coupler
2 F#
3 Trombone on
4 D#
5 Trumpet on
6 B
7 G
8 A
9 G
10 F
11 G
12 General cancel
13 D#
14 A
15 D
16 C#
17 A
18 B
19 B
20 B
21 C#
22 A
23 C#
24 D#
25 G
26 D#
27 F
28 F

IMHOF & MUKLE
ROLL FOR ORCHESTRION NO. 3327
Heavy cardboard Music Leaf system

1 Sustaining pedal off
2 Sustaining pedal on
3 Hammer rail down
4 Hammer rail up
5 Blank
6 Bells off
7 Bells on
8 Snare drum
9 Bass drum
10 Clarinet on
11 Violin pipes on
12 Piccolo on
13 General cancel for holes 10-12
14 to 23, Playing notes chromatically down from F# to A
24 Rewind
25 G
26 G
27 G#
28 F#
29 A
30 F
31 A#
32 E
33 B
34 D#
35 C
36 D
37 C#
38 C#
39 D

40 C
41 D#
42 B
43 E
44 A#
45 F
46 A
47 F#
48 G#
49 G
50 G
51 G#
52 F#
53 A
54 F
55 A#
56 F
57 B
58 D#
59 C
60 D
61 C#
62 C#
63 D
64 C
65 D#
66 B
67 E
68 A#
69 F
70 A
71 F#
72 G#
73 G
74 Blank

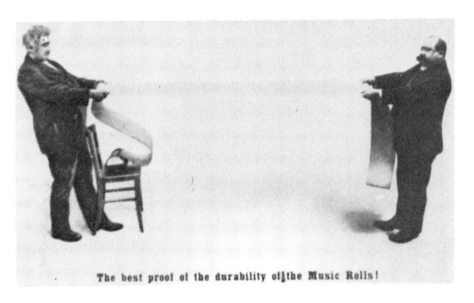

The best proof of the durability of the Music Rolls!

Looking like Trade and Mark of Smith Brothers' Cough Drop fame, two turn-of-the-century gentlemen demonstrate the desirability of the heavy manila Imhof & Mukle rolls by having a tug-of-war!

Next Three Pages: These pictures of an Imhof & Mukle keyboard style orchestrion were taken in the street outside of the factory, probably around 1908-1914. The instrument uses the heavy manila Music Leaf System type of roll. At the back of the instrument, in a special expression chamber with louvered glass swell shutters (a very unusual arrangement), seem to be one or several ranks of pipes, probably violins. (Courtesy of the late Albert Imhof)

KUHL & KLATT
Coin Pianos and
Orchestrions

Kuhl & Klatt, of Berlin, sold a wide variety of roll-operated pneumatic instruments, particularly during the first decade or so of the 20th century. Some incorporated Hupfeld mechanisms, and others were similar, if not identical, to contemporary Dienst models. During the 1920s the Kuhl & Klatt Accordeon (or Accordian or Accordion) pianos were popular, especially in Belgium, where they were sold in large quantities.

KUHL & KLATT ACCORDEON ROLL
"KK ACCORDEON" ROLL
34 cm. wide; approx. 21 holes per 10 cm.

1 Saxophone off, accordion on
2 Triangle
3 Shutoff
4 Bass drum
5 Crescendo
6 Wood block
7 Wood block
8 to 63, Playing notes, D to A
64 Forte
65 Pianissimo
66 Snare drum
67 Snare drum
68 Cymbal
69 Rewind
70 Saxophone on, accordion off
    Note: some rolls may use hole 64 for charleston cymbal.

KUHL & KLATT ROLL
(Unknown style)
As preceding, but with the following variations:

1 Blank
8 to 61, Playing notes in order
62 Snare drum brush
63 Maracca
70 Blank

KUHL & KLATT ROLL
(Unknown style)
As the Kuhl & Klatt Accordeon, but with the following variations:

1 Blank
2 Play
3 Shutoff
4 Mandolin off
5 Sustaining pedal
6 Xylophone on
7 C#
66 Xylophone off
67 Hammer rail
68 Mandolin on
69 Rewind
70 Blank

KUHL & KLATT "PNEUMA" ROLL

1 Shutoff
2 Mandolin off
3 Sustaining pedal
4 Xylophone on
5 to 63, Playing notes in order
64 Xylophone off
65 Hammer rail
66 Mandolin on
67 Rewind

KUHL & KLATT VIOLIN PIANO ROLL

1 Piano bass soft
2 Piano bass mezzoforte
3 Piano bass hammer rail
4 Piano bass forte
5 Piano bass fortissimo
6 Play
7 Rewind
8 Shutoff
9 Violin pipes mezzoforte
10 Violin pipes crescendo
11 Violin pipes decrescendo
12 Sustaining pedal
13 Blank
14 to 98, 85 piano notes, A to A
14 to 29, 37 violin pipe notes, A below middle C through A
99 Tremolo
100 Blank
101 Violin pipes off
102 Blank
103 Blank
104 Slow tremolo (used with hole 99)
105 Violin pipes on
106 Blank
107 Blank
108 Blank
109 Piano treble fortissimo
110 Piano treble forte
111 Piano treble hammer rail
112 Piano treble mezzoforte
113 Piano treble soft

    Hole 105 switches holes 14 to 29 and holes 78 to 98 from piano playing notes to violin pipe playing notes. Hole 101 switches these holes back to their piano functions.

Two trade paper advertisements by Kuhl & Klatt. The one at the left appeared in August 1928 when the firm's business was waning. By that time the company, founded in 1899, had been in business for nearly 30 years. At the right is an early advertisement from the turn of the century. It notes that the "Pneuma" self-playing apparatus was adaptable "for all [upright] pianos and grand pianos."

This illustration, indistinctly reproduced in a newsprint advertisement of the 1920s, is from Belgium and shows a Kuhl & Klatt basic piano with mandolin and xylophone to which two side cabinets and an accordion have been added. Eugene DeRoy, proprietor of the Symphonia Music Roll Company and builder and seller of many coin pianos and orchestrions, told one of the authors that these instruments, which were generally known as "KK Accordeons," were sold by the hundreds in Belgium during the 1920s. New rolls for them were being cut by Mr. DeRoy as late as the 1960s.

LINK PIANO COMPANY
Pianos and Orchestrions

The Link Piano Company, successor to the Automatic Musical Company, produced several hundred coin pianos each year in its Binghamton, New York factory. Most early pianos and orchestrions are of the keyboard style. Fashions changed, and in the 1920s cabinet-style instruments without keyboard) predominated. Many of the pianos were acquired from the Haddorff Piano Co. of Rockford, Illinois, a firm which also supplied Seeburg, Western Electric, and others (and thereby accounting for certain similarities among these makes). Link built the pneumatic mechanisms and added them to the basic piano cases. Correspondence with the Krakauer Piano Co. (successors to Haddorff) in the 1970s revealed that no manufacturing records, parts, or other relevant data is in Krakauer's possession.

Without exception, all Link coin pianos and orchestrions use endless-type rolls. The "roll" consists of one long continuous loop, often of 15-tune length. This system was standard in the coin piano industry in the early (circa 1898-1905) years, but, with the exception of Link, the other makers dropped it in favor of the easier-to-change rewind type of roll. However, as Link's instruments were mostly cared for by experienced route operators, the endless roll was no objection. In fact, the operators considered it to be an asset as the music would play continuously without a pause for rewinding. To the novice the endless Link roll appears to be hopelessly snarled, but in practice the loops remain untangled and the system works very well.

Link music rolls were made in three basic styles: RX and C rolls for coin pianos with mandolin or with mandolin and one extra instrument (very few piano-mandolin units were made; nearly all had a xylophone or a rank of pipes added); A rolls (not to be confused with Seeburg A rolls which are not related) with percussion effects for orchestrions; and organ rolls for Link theatre pipe organs. Most piano and orchestrion rolls were arranged by Ray Deyo (who continued making rolls under the "Deo" [sic] label after Link went out of business in the 1920s), and most organ rolls were arranged by Bill Sabin (who was formerly the first clarinetist with Sousa's band).

Most RX and A rolls of the 1920s are of 15-tune length. Earlier, rolls were made of varying length, from one tune per roll upward. Collectors today consider the xylophone arrangements in particular on the RX rolls to be among the finest coin piano rolls made during the "Roaring Twenties" era.

Exterior and interior views of a Link Style 2E piano.

LINK A ROLL

12" wide; 6 holes per inch
1 Hammer rail down
2 Hammer rail up
3 Blank
4 Sustaining pedal
5 Tambourine shaker
6 Left snare drum beater
7 Middle snare drum beater
8 Right snare drum beater
9 Triangle
10 Tom-tom (tambourine beater)
11 Right wood block beater
12 Left wood block beater
13 Front pipes or xylophone on
14 Cancel pipes, xylophone, and mandolin
15 Rear pipes on
16 Bass drum
17 to 65, 49 notes in order, G to G
66 Shutoff
67 Mandolin on
68 to 70 Blank

This type of roll was used on keyboard orchestrion styles A and AX and the Style 2-B cabinet orchestrion. The lowest 12 bass notes are octave-coupled, two notes per hole. One Style AX examined had a 12-note treble octave coupler turned on and off by a lock and cancel. It was surmised that it might logically be turned on by hole 15 and off by 14, since the Style AX has no pipes.

If a Link orchestrion using Style A rolls has a pneumatic expression device mounted on the pump, it is connected to holes 1 and 2 as in the RX roll (see following description of RX roll).

Anyone restoring a Link A-roll piano having some or all of its original tubing intact should take note of the tubing connections, as other variations may well exist. For example, hole 68 may be used to turn the mandolin off in some rolls or instruments.

LINK RX AND C ROLLS

12" wide; 6 holes per inch
RX rolls made for coin pianos
C rolls with classic arrangements

1 Expression loud (see text)
2 Expression soft (see text)
3 Soft pedal on (or xylophone or pipes on, see text)
4 Sustaining pedal
5 to 65, 61 notes in order G to G
66 Shutoff
67 Xylophone or pipes on (teed to hole 3 in some instruments)
68 Mandolin on
69 Cancel mandolin, pipes, xylophone (see text)
70 Blank

The expression controls and mechanisms varied over the years. According to Ed Link, the people who constructed the instruments in the factory sometimes tried new ideas or were otherwise innovative, which explains some of the variations. The following text covers several instruments examined; undoubtedly there are other variations as well.

Early Style C Piano

The scale is the same as the regular listed above, except for:
1 Full vacuum (quick release for 2)
2 Low vacuum (end of perforation: gradual crescendo back to full, unless 1 appears)
3 Hammer rail up
67 Pipes on
68 Mandolin on
69 Cancel pipes, hammer rail, mandolin

Early Style 2E Piano

1 Full vacuum (quick release for 2)
2 Low vacuum (gradual crescendo back to full, unless 1 appears)
3 Teed to 67, xylophone on
68 Mandolin on
69 Cancel mandolin and xylophone

The preceding 2E has no hammer rail movement. Another 2E has no vacuum control, but a hammer rail pneumatic which is raised by hole 2 gradually returns to normal unless hole 1 releases it quickly.

Late Style 2E (or 2EX)

1 Accent (full pump vacuum to stack); quick release for 2
2 Hammer rail up, low vacuum (gradual crescendo when released, unless 1 appears)

In this late system, hole 1 not only acts as a quick release for 2, but it also controls a bypass which applies full pump vacuum to the stack.

AUTOMATIC MUSICAL CO. EARLY COIN PIANO ROLL
12" wide; spaced 6 holes per inch; endless

1 Expression loud
2 Expression soft
3 Shutoff
4 Sustaining pedal
5 to 65, 61 playing notes G to G
66 Shutoff

This scale is based on the examination of United States roll no. 80525.

Link Style C piano with mandolin and flute pipes from the 1920 period. Although art glass designs varied greatly, this general case design was one of the Link Piano Company's most popular. (Lewis Graham Collection)

OUTSIDE VIEW
Style A, AX, B, C, D, E

Height, 6 ft. 4 in.; width, 5 ft. 6 in.; depth, 2 ft. 8 in.
Case design subject to change.
Art Glass Front, (design subject to change.)
Case, Oak, Mission Finish, or Two Tone Walnut.

Above: Link Style R coin piano with mandolin attachment and flute pipes. The loops of the endless Link RX roll can be seen at the top of the case. The main feature of the endless roll was an uninterrupted program; there was no "annoying pause for rewind," as one early copy writer put it. While endless rolls were cumbersome to change, many Link instruments were owned by experienced route operators who could do it quickly. (Jerry and Sylvia Cohen Collection)

Left: An original sales brochure, circa 1920, for the Style C, a somewhat similar instrument. The C case is taller than that of the Style R.

PAUL LÖSCHE
Coin Pianos and
Orchestrions

Paul Lösche, who began business in 1902, produced a wide variety of coin pianos, orchestrions, expression pianos, and other instruments until the late 1920s. Many of these were sold under the labels of various musical instrument merchandisers, so today it is not unusual to find a Lösche instrument under a different name. The firm's products were, for the most part, quite well made. The surviving models are highly valued by collectors.

73 General cancel
74 Bass drum
75 Snare drum
76 Tambourine?
77 Blank
78 Cancel pedal
79 Blank

LÖSCHE ANGELUS ROLL
LÖSCHE REPRODUCTA ROLL
35 cm. wide; spaced 2 holes per cm.

1 Tremolo
2 C
3 Flute on
4 to 58, Playing notes, D to G#
59 Piano treble off
60 Mandolin on
61 Rewind
62 Shutoff
63 Violin pipes on
64 General cancel
65 Xylophone on (clarinet in some instruments)
66 Sustaining pedal
67 Bass drum
68 Snare drum
69 Hammer rail up, low vacuum, swell closed

Some rolls and instruments use hole 3 for low C# and 65 for flute on.

LÖSCHE ORCHESTRION ROLL
Great Lösche in the DeRoy scale notation
Approx. 43 cm. wide; spaced 2 holes per cm.

1 to 12, Bass notes C to B
13 to 24, Accompaniment notes C to B
25 to 61, Notes C to C
62 Clarinet (and sustaining pedal?)
63 Xylophone on
64 Rewind
65 Cymbal?
66 Mandolin on
67 "Arc" (shutoff?)
68 Hammer rail
69 Grelot (jingle bells)
70 Violin pipes on
71 Cello and bass on
72 Flute on

LÖSCHE ORCHESTRION ROLL
11¼" wide; spaced 9 holes per inch

1 ?
2 Loud
3 Soft
4 Blank
5 Shutoff
6 Rewind
7 Blank
8 to 14 (see below)
15 Bass drum
16 Cymbal
17 Loud snare drum
18 Soft snare drum
19 Xylophone on
20 Soft violin pipes on
21 Cello on
22 Violin melody-tremolo register
23 Flute on
24 4' violin pipes on
25 8' clarinet pipes on
26 General cancel
27 Switch for holes 28 to 33
28 C or F#
29 C# or G
30 D or G#
31 D# or A
32 E or A#
33 F or B
34 G (should it be C?)
35 ? (an unknown sharp note)
36 D
37 D#
38 to 55, Cello notes E to A
56 to 91, xylophone, soft violin, melody violin, flute notes A# to A
92 Piano off
93 Piano on
94 Bells on
95 ?
96 Blank
97 Melody loud
98 Melody soft(?)
99 Blank
100 ?

The functions of holes 8 to 14 are unknown, but they are numbered from 1 to 7 on a scale stick from the DeRoy archives.

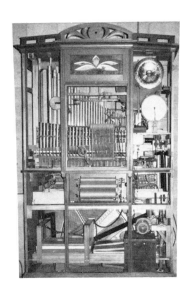

Above: This very large cabinet-style Lösche orchestrion was probably made before World War I. It contains several ranks of pipes, a xylophone, percussion devices, and many other effects, including a backlighted moving picture effect on the front. (Collection of Roy Haning and Neal White)

Above left: This large Lösche Titania orchestrion was used continually in a German restaurant from the time of manufacture, around 1905-1910, until about 1970. The case is of richly grained walnut, a wood used by few other European orchestrion manufacturers. (Jerry Doring Collection)

Left: This large Lösche orchestrion was photographed in its original location in the Gambrinus Cafe in Brasschaat, Belgium in 1972. The instrument had been converted years earlier to use Popper rolls. At the time the picture was taken the cafe had closed its doors, and the fate of the silent and no longer playing orchestrion was unknown. (Photograph courtesy of Arthur Prinsen)

LÖSCHE MODEL 1, TITANIA II ROLL
(From an orchestrion built in 1905)

1 to 61, Piano notes
   (25 to 54, 30 pipe notes)
   (37 to 55, 19 glockenspiel or bell notes)
62 Sustaining pedal and lighting effects on
63 Piano damper on
64 Rewind
65 Mandolin on
66 Mandolin off
67 Shutoff
68 Bells on
69 Swell shutters open
70 Violin pipes on
71 Cello pipes on
72 Flute pipes on
73 Cancel all registers
74 Kettle drum or tympani
75 Snare drum (short hole = single stroke; long hole = snare drum roll)
76 Castanets
77 Swell shutters and piano damper off
78 Sustaining pedal off
79 Blank

   The preceding scale was furnished to Claes O. Friberg by Schwelmer Orgelbau and was derived from the examination of a surviving example of the Titania orchestrion.

LÖSCHE VIOLIN PIANO

   This scale is the same as the Angelus scale (page 218) except for the following differences:
3 C#
58 Blank
66 Hammer rail down (and sustaining pedal on?)
67 Blank
68 Blank
69 Swell shutters

Lyon & Healy, leading Chicago-area musical instrument dealers, sold a number of coin-operated pianos under the Empress and Majestic labels. In most instances the Empress instruments, coin pianos and orchestrions, consisted of pneumatic mechanisms made by the Operators Piano Company and installed in various makes of pianos (Leland and Washburn, for example). Generally, Empress instruments use the same types of rolls used on contemporary Coinola (made by the Operators Piano Co.) styles. Refer to the A-roll section of this book for information on Empress instruments using this type of roll; to the Operators Piano Co. section for information on Empress instruments using type C or O rolls.

Around 1923 the Solo Expression Twin Tracker Empress piano was introduced. A brochure noted that "the roll plays in both directions, forward and reverse, one tracker for the downward and the other for the upward movement. This means no waste of time or energy for rewinding, no rolls torn from high-speed rewinding..." It was further noted that "seven degrees of expression are considered the extent obtainable in hand playing. The Solo Expression Empress has nine degrees of intensity." A competing instrument, the Nelson-Wiggen Selector Duplex organ, was constructed with the same double-width roll idea in mind.

EMPRESS STYLE L ROLL
SOLO EXPRESSION TWIN TRACKER
15¼" wide; 9 holes per inch

1 Bass hammer rail
2 Sustaining pedal
3 Forward
4 to 62, 59 notes in order C to A#
63 Accent
64 Treble hammer rail
65 2nd intensity
66 1st intensity
67 Shutoff

---

68 Bass hammer rail
69 Sustaining pedal
70 Reverse
71 to 129, 59 notes in order C to A#
130 Accent
131 Treble hammer rail
132 2nd intensity
133 1st intensity
134 Shutoff

The first five tunes on each roll are perforated in one direction using holes 1 to 67. After the fifth tune, the roll reverses itself, and the last five tunes play from the opposite half of the tracker bar in the opposite direction. There is no rewind or fast forward. The expression mechanisms consist of an accent pneumatic and a two-stage additive accordion pneumatic connected to the vacuum regulator.

Although 20,000 promotional leaflets for the Empress Style L were made in February 1923, sales were limited, with the result that instruments and rolls of this type are very rare today.

SOLO EXPRESSION
TWINTRACKER
EMPRESS
L-117

1 **Say It While Dancing.** Fox Trot
2 **Dancing Fool.** Fox Trot
3 **My Cradle Melodie.** Fox Trot
4 **Georgette.** Fox Trot
5 **Deedle Deedle Dum.** Fox Trot
6 **Down Old Virginia Way.** Waltz
7 **I Wish I Knew.** Fox Trot
8 **'Neath the South Sea Moon.** Fox Trot
9 **Rose of Bombay.** Fox Trot
10 **Kitten On the Keys.** Fox Trot

——

LYON AND HEALY
CHICAGO, ILL.

Illustration, circa 1923, from a faded brochure describing the Solo Expression Twin Tracker Empress coin piano.

MARQUETTE PIANO COMPANY
Coin Pianos, Orchestrions, and Photoplayers

The Marquette Piano Company, founded in Chicago in 1905, sold a wide variety of coin pianos, orchestrions, and photoplayers under the Cremona trademark until about 1920.

Basic coin-operated Cremona pianos with mandolin or with mandolin and one added instrument (such as a rank of flute or violin pipes) use regular type A rolls of the style also used by Seeburg and others. Cremona coin pianos equipped with the Cremona Tune Selector and Cremona orchestrions use special type M rolls. Certain large Cremona photoplayers use the large 134-note Cremona S rolls.

MARQUETTE (CREMONA) M ROLL
11¼" wide; 9 holes per inch

A Counter for selector (chain perforation in middle of each tune)
B Blank
C Play
D Selector play
1 Shutoff
2 Blank
3 Hammer rail up
4 Hammer rail down
5 Triangle
6 Low vacuum for piano and drums
7 Normal vacuum for piano and drums
8 Snare drum
9 Piccolo or xylophone on
10 Piccolo or xylophone off
11 Tympani
12 Bass drum and cymbal
13 Tympani
14 Violin on
15 Violin off
16 Flutes on
17 Flutes off
18 Piano treble off
19 Piano treble on
20 Mandolin on
21 Mandolin off
22 Sustaining pedal
23 Tambourine
24 Castanets
25 to 88, 64 notes in order A to C
E Fast forward or rewind (for selector)
F Rewind
G Blank?
H Shutoff

Holes C, 1, and F are the same as the play, shutoff, and rewind holes in an ordinary instrument and are used by Cremona instruments having no automatic tune selector, and by selector-equipped instruments when the knob is turned to "R" (rotation).

Operation of the Cremona Tune Selector

(The following is from p. 504 of *The Encyclopedia of Automatic Musical Instruments,* and earlier was in the Musical Box Society's "Bulletin")

The tune selector barrel has two main sections, both of which are channeled. Tubing from holes D and E is connected to one section, and tubing from the play, rewind, and fast-forward pneumatics is connected to the other section.

The front section of the selector barrel is turned in steps by the knob on the front of the cabinet. It has positions 1 through 10 and R (rotation). The rear section of the selector barrel is turned by the roll. It is normally locked into position, but whenever hole A comes up, a pneumatic releases the lock, and the barrel is allowed to turn one step in the direction the roll is moving. This counter has eleven positions. When a roll is first put on the machine, the counter is in position 1. As each tune plays, the counter is moved one notch, so position 2 is before tune 2, 10 is before tune 10, and 11 is after tune 10.

The knob may be positioned in various relations to the counter: knob in R or rotation position; knob as the same number as the counter; knob at any number higher than the counter; knob at any number lower than the counter.

Condition one: (knob at R, counter in any position): holes D and E are blocked; machine responds only to non-selective perforations C, 1, F, H. The counter continues to work from hole A, so the counter barrel remains in step with the roll.

Condition two: (knob at same number as the counter): channels in the counter barrel connect hole D with the play pneumatic; machine shifts to play.

Condition three: (knob at any number higher than the counter): channels connect hole E with the fast-forward pneumatic. When a coin is inserted, the machine shifts to fast forward and continues to do so until the counter catches up with the knob. At that time the channels are restored to Condition Two, and the roll shifts to play.

Condition four: (knob at any number lower than the counter): channels in the barrel connect hole E with the rewind pneumatic. When a coin is inserted, the machine shifts to rewind and rewinds until the barrel counts down to the same number at which the knob is set. This restores the channels to Condition Two, and the machine shifts to play.

In simpler terms, the roll automatically follows the counter to wherever the knob is set and then plays that tune. This is made possible and foolproof only by having three separate slots in the roll (A, D, and E) to operate the selector.

If the knob is left at a certain tune, the Cremona will repeat that tune as often as a coin is deposited. It is assumed that the customer who deposits money in the piano will either set the knob for the desired tune or turn it to R. However, if the selector always worked like this, patrons using a remotely located wallbox would always get the same tune unless the knob were set at "R". For this reason, tubes D and E go through a cut-out block which is normally open. When a coin is dropped in a wallbox, a magnet in the piano opens a channel to a valve which blocks the two selector tubes and makes the piano play in rotation regardless of where the knob is set. When the piano shuts off, it automatically reconnects the tubes so the selector device will work when a patron drops the next coin into the piano itself.

Everything is now accounted for except hole H, the shut-off after tune 10. Regular (non-selective) M roll pianos rewind the roll after 10 and then shut off. If the knob on a selector is set at 10, however, the piano will rewind after 10, get to the beginning of 10, shift back to "play" and repeat the tune over and over for one nickel. For this reason, the first shut-off hole (before tune 1) is taped off. The machine shuts off after 10, and another nickel is required to rewind the roll and play the first song, either with the selector or on rotation. A non-selective machine does not have the shut-off tubed to hole H, so that hole is ignored. So ends a description of the Cremona Tune Selector...

Cremona Notes

The connection of the piano treble mute to holes 18 and 19 was deduced by studying an original test roll and various music rolls. Large Cremona orchestrions contain three extra instruments: flute pipes, violin pipes, and piccolo pipes in the Orchestral K, and flute pipes, violin pipes, and xylophone (or, occasionally, orchestra bells with resonators, called "unafon bells") in the Orchestral J. If one of these orchestrions contains a piano treble mute, there presumably will always be one of the three extra instruments turned on when the piano treble is off. The cabinet model Cremona orchestrion (which has a piano treble mute) contains only two extra instruments—violin pipes and flute pipes—and some musical passages requiring the piccolo or xylophone might turn the piano treble off when neither flute nor violin are on. If this occurs, teeing "flutes on" to 16 and 9, and "flutes off" to 17 and 10 will prevent occasional silent sections in the music.

The cabinet model Cremona orchestrion has 58 piano notes, C to A. The lowest 11 bass notes are tuned an octave below their normal pitch to give the illusion of a larger piano. The correct tubing of the 58 notes to the 64 notes of the M roll is uncertain. If an instrument is located with the original tubing, care should be taken in noting the correct connections and tuning of the bass.

Note: Some Reproduco piano/organ rolls using the OS/NOS tracker scale are labeled with the letter M instead of OS. indicating mortuary music. They are not likely to be confused with Marquette/Cremona M rolls because the mortuary rolls are wound on single-tune player piano roll spools, and the two tracker scales are completely different.

MARQUETTE (CREMONA) STYLE "S" SOLO ROLL

(For Cremona photoplayers)
15¼" wide; spaced 9 holes per inch

1 Play
2 Bass swell open, 4-step ratchet
3 Normal vacuum for piano and drums
4 Low vacuum for piano and drums
5 Snare drum
6 Tympani
7 Bass drum and cymbal
8 Tympani
9 Castanets
10 Tambourine
11 Triangle
12 Bass swell closed, 4-step ratchet
13 Hammer rail down
14 Hammer rail up
15 Piano bass off
16 Piano bass on
17 to 77, 61 playing notes for piano, pipes, xylophone, and chimes, C to C
78 to 109, 32 note optional solo section for treble pipes, F to C
110 Treble pipes coupled to piano treble (holes 46-77)
111 Treble pipes coupled to solo section of tracker bar (holes 78-109)
112 Bass vox humana off
113 Bass vox humana on
114 Vox humana off
115 Vox humana on
116 Diapason (bass flute) off
117 Diapason on
118 Flute off
119 Flute on
120 Cello off
121 Cello on
122 Violin pipes off
123 Violin pipes on
124 Piano treble off
125 Piano treble on
126 Tremolo off
127 Tremolo on
128 Chimes off
129 Chimes on
130 Xylophone off
131 Xylophone on
132 Treble swell closed, 4-step ratchet
133 Treble swell open, 4-step ratchet
134 Rewind

The 134-note S rolls were used on Cremona Theatre Orchestras such as Solo styles O and M3. For added versatility some photoplayers were equipped with an 88-note home player piano tracker bar as well. The instruments, marketed in limited numbers in the 'teens, are very rare today.

An original test roll uses holes 2 and 12 for the bass swell shades; but one original music roll examined used 12 for sustaining pedal and does not use 2.

The normal/low vacuum device was called a "modulator" by Marquette. There are separate modulators for the piano and drums, both controlled by holes 3 and 4.

During fully scored passages, the pipes are usually coupled to the piano treble by hole 110. When it is necessary to play two different musical parts on the piano treble and pipes, hole 111 couples the pipes to holes 78-109, separating them from the piano treble. This eliminates redundant perforating during loud passages. Holes 110 and 111 cancel each other so no chain perforations are necessary.

MILLS NOVELTY COMPANY
Coin-Operated Instruments

The Mills Novelty Company, founded in 1890, rose to become America's foremost manufacturer of gambling machines and arcade devices. During the early 1900s Mills sold (but did not manufacture) pianos and other musical instruments made by others such as Pianova, Regina, and the Automatic Musical Co. In 1904 Henry K. Sandell joined Mills and began experimenting with an automatic violin player. The result was the Automatic Virtuosa, first marketed circa 1905, a device which contained a real violin which played four strings by means of rotating rosined celluloid discs which acted as bows. Tiny metal "fingers" stopped each string at the appropriate length called for by the music roll.

While the Automatic Virtuosa achieved some success in penny arcades and similar locations, sales must have been modest, for no specimens are known to exist today.

In late 1908 or early 1909, an Automatic Virtuosa was mated to a 44-note piano made by the Pianova Company, and was dubbed the Pianova-Virtuosa. Soon the name was changed to the Violano-Virtuoso, the nomenclature used from that time until the 1930s.

In 1911 Sandell filed a patent for a symmetrical piano with the longer strings at the center and shorter strings to each side. Despite the fact that this was hardly a new idea (Polyphon, for one, used a similar device a decade earlier on certain automatic pianos), a patent was granted. From the 1911-1912 era onward all Mills Violano-Virtuosos had a piano of the symmetrical configuration.

The United States Patent Office, seeking unusual items with a high "human interest" value for its exhibit at the 1909 Alaska-Yukon-Pacific Exposition in Seattle, learned of the interesting Mills violin player and invited the firm to exhibit a specimen. This was duly accomplished. Mills made promotional hay out of the affair, and thousands of later Violano-Virtuosos were sold with a large plaque which proclaimed to the world: "VIOLANO-VIRTUOSO. Designated by the U.S. government as one of the eight greatest inventions of the decade."

In the 'teens, 'twenties, and first year or so of the 'thirties (the 1931 Mills catalogue offered these for sale) saw nearly 5000 Violano-Virtuosos distributed. Most Violano-Virtuosos were of the standard design with a real violin (on which four strings were played) in combination with a 44-note piano. The units, like other Mills-made automatic musical instruments, were electromagnetically (rather than pneumatically) operated. Several hundred instruments designated as DeLuxe Violano-Virtuosos featured two violins. These used the same type of roll and played each violin with the same notes at the same time; the only difference being a slightly increased volume of sound and the reinforced tone which occurs when two instruments play in concert. Except for the early Automatic Virtuosa and the very early models of the Violano-Virtuoso, all Violano-Virtuosos used the same standard roll (described in the following text). A related instrument, the Violano-Virtuoso with the Violano Orchestra attachment, used a special roll of its own which featured provision for percussion instruments in addition to the violin and piano.

Several other "Viol-" type instruments were experimented with, including the Viol-Cello and the Viol-Xylophone. None of these is known today, nor is information concerning the rolls for these known.

In the 1920s the Mills Magnetic Expression Piano and its variation (with a diorama of racing horses), the Mills Race Horse Piano, achieved a modest degree of popularity. These use a special Mills Magnetic Expression Piano roll.

Most often seen today are specimens of the Violano-Virtuoso. Several hundred or more have survived, with the result that these interesting violin players are widely represented in collections. Hundreds of different rolls were made over the years, with the result that a wide variety of music is available. Most rolls of the 1920s were arranged to contain five tunes, set up with two fox trots, a waltz in the middle, and then two more fox trots. Classical numbers, including violin concertos, ethnic and special-interest music, and other categories were also made. Most tunes are longer than the approximate two-minute standard of other manufacturers. It is not at all unusual for a Violano-Virtuoso tune to play three or four minutes, and some classical numbers are even longer.

MILLS MAGNETIC EXPRESSION PIANO ROLL
(Mills Race Horse Piano)
8¾" wide; holes spaced .11428"

Note: This spacing and other irregular spacings listed in this book, spacings which are carried out to several decimal places, were derived by dividing the distance from the first to the last hole by the number of holes.

1 Blank
2 Hammer rail half down
3 Hammer rail up
4 Hammer rail down
5 Highest playing note C# chromatically down through:
69 Lowest playing note, A
70 Rewind
71 Sustaining pedal off
72 Shutoff
73 Sustaining pedal on
74 Hammer rail half up
75 Blank

In one instrument examined, hole 73 operates the sustaining pedal solenoid, which is turned off by a spring. Expression is provided by a four-stage hammer rail solenoid controlled by holes 2, 3, 4, and 74.

MILLS VIOLANO-VIRTUOSO ROLL
14¼" wide; holes spaced .11428"
(Listed left to right, as viewed from back of feeder)

1 Vanish (bow motor very slow)
2 Bow action (bow motor very fast)
3 Staccato (bows leave strings while fingers remain engaged)
4 Early rolls: tremolo; later rolls: rosin relay off
5 Loud (bow motor fast)
6 D bow & finger no. 12 - D
7 D bow & finger no. 7 - A
8 D bow & finger no. 2 - E
9 D bow & finger no. 9 - B

10 D bow & finger no. 4 - F#
11 D bow & finger no. 11 - C#
12 D bow & finger no. 6 - G#
13 D bow & finger no. 1 — D#
14 D bow & finger no. 8 - A#
15 D bow & finger no. 3 - F
16 D bow & finger no. 10 - C
17 D bow & finger no. 5 - G
18 Open D string, bow only
19 Rewind
20 Soft (bow motor slow)
21 Open E string, bow only
22 E bow & finger no. 7 - B
23 E bow & finger no. 2 - F#
24 E bow & finger no. 9 - C#
25 E bow & finger no. 4 - G#
26 E bow & finger no. 11 - D#
27 E bow & finger no. 6 - A#
28 E bow & finger no. 1 - F
29 E bow & finger no. 8 - C
30 E bow & finger no. 3 - G
31 E bow & finger no. 10 - D
32 E bow & finger no. 5 - A
33 E bow & finger no. 12 - E
34 E bow & finger no. 19 - B
35 E bow & finger no. 14 - F#
36 E bow & finger no. 21 - C#
37 E bow & finger no. 16 - G#
38 E bow & finger 22 - D
39 E bow & finger 18 - A#
40 E bow & finger 13 - F
41 E bow & finger 20 - C
42 E bow & finger 15 - G
43 E bow & finger 17 - A
44 Piano hammer rail up (soft)
45 Open G string, bow only
46 G bow & finger 7 - D
47 G bow & finger 2 - A
48 G bow & finger 9 - E
49 G bow & finger 4 - B
50 G bow & finger 11 - F#
51 G bow & finger 6 - C#
52 G bow & finger 1 - G#
53 G bow & finger 8 - D#
54 G bow & finger 3 - A#
55 G bow & finger 10 - F
56 G bow & finger 5 - C
57 G bow & finger 12 - G
58 Hammer rail down (loud)
59 A bow & finger 12 - A
60 A bow & finger 7 - E
61 A bow & finger 2 - B
62 A bow & finger 9 - F#
63 A bow & finger 4 - C#
64 A bow & finger 11 - G#
65 A bow & finger 6 - D#
66 A bow & finger 1 - A#
67 A bow & finger 8 - F
68 A bow & finger 3 - C
69 A bow & finger 10 - G
70 A bow & finger 5 - D
71 A bow & finger 13 - A#
72 Open A string, bow only
73 A bow & finger 14 - B
74 Tremolo (except early rolls which use 4)
75 Shutoff (if rosin device is controlled by relay, relay on)
76 to 119, piano note scale F to C, 44 notes
120 Piano extra loud
121 Sustaining pedal on (dampers lifted)
122 Piano very soft (resistor) or hammer rail very soft, violin mute
123 Sustaining pedal off (early machines), dampers against strings

MILLS VIOLANO-VIRTUOSO ROLLS
(Listed in order of function; cross-reference to preceding)

VIOLIN
Bow motor very soft (vanish) - hole 1
Bow motor soft - 20
Bow motor loud - 5
Bow motor very loud (bow action) - 2
Tremolo - 4 or 74
Staccato - 3
Bridge mute - 122 (with piano very soft)
Open G string - 45
G string finger 1 - G# - hole 52
G string finger 2 - A - 47
G string finger 3 - A# - 54
G string finger 4 - B - 49
G string finger 5 - C - 56
G string finger 6 - C# - 51
G string finger 7 - D - 46
G string finger 8 - D# - 53
G string finger 9 - E - 48
G string finger 10 - F - 55
G string finger 11 - F# - 50
G string finger 12 - G - 57
Open D string - 18
D string finger 1 - D# - 13
D string finger 2 - E - 8
D string finger 3 - F - 15
D string finger 4 - F# - 10
D string finger 5 - G - 17
D string finger 6 - G# - 12
D string finger 7 - A - 7
D string finger 8 - A# - 14
D string finger 9 - B - 9
D string finger 10 - C - 16
D string finger 11 - C# - 11
D string finger 12 - D - 6
Open A string - 72
A string finger 1 - A# - 66
A string finger 2 - B - 61
A string finger 3 - C - 68
A string finger 4 - C# - 63
A string finger 5 - D - 70
A string finger 6 - D# - 65
A string finger 7 - E - 60
A string finger 8 - F - 67
A string finger 9 - F# - 62
A string finger 10 - G - 69
A string finger 11 - G# - 64
A string finger 12 - A - 59
A string finger 13 - A# - 71
A string finger 14 - B - 73
Open E string - 21
E string finger 1 - F - 28
E string finger 2 - F# - 23
E string finger 3 - G - 30
E string finger 4 - G# - 25
E string finger 5 - A - 32
E string finger 6 - A# - 27
E string finger 7 - B - 22
E string finger 8 - C - 29
E string finger 9 - C# - 24
E string finger 10 - D - 31
E string finger 11 - D# - 26
E string finger 12 - E - 33
E string finger 13 - F - 40
E string finger 14 - F# - 35
E string finger 15 - G - 42
E string finger 16 - G# - 37
E string finger 17 - A - 43
E string finger 18 - A# - 39
E string finger 19 - B - 34
E string finger 20 - C - 41
E string finger 21 - C# - 36
E string finger 22 - D - 38

PIANO
Lowest note - F - 76
Highest note - C - 119

Hammer rail up (soft) - 44
Hammer rail down (loud) - 58
Very soft - 122 (with violin mute)
Very loud - 120
Dampers lifted - 121
Dampers released (against strings) - 123

MISCELLANEOUS FUNCTIONS
Shutoff - 75
Rewind - 19
Play - roller rides on lower spool (mechanical function)

If the violin notes were in consecutive order on the roll, the resulting hole patterns would seriously weaken the paper. Therefore, the violin notes are scrambled to strengthen the paper.

This tracker scale and descriptive notes include all musical features and devices encountered by the authors in numerous Violanos. Some of the features are found only in early machines, while others are found only in later ones. As Mills made minor changes constantly over the years, it is doubtful if any one instrument will be found which contains all of the expression devices.

Hole 3, staccato: Each violin bow magnet is in series with all of the finger magnets for that violin string. When a finger is activated, the bow is also engaged without using a separate hole. The bow magnets are of lower resistance than the finger magnets. Current going to the bow and finger magnets first passes through a series-parallel resistance circuit in the staccato resistor, which is adjusted so there is just adequate voltage to cause the bow and finger to operate. When hole 3 appears, it increases the current through the resistance in the circuit by grounding part of the staccato resistor. The corresponding decrease in voltage across the circuit renders the bow magnet too weak to overcome the bow return spring, which lifts the bow off the string. The finger magnet is small enough that it continues to hold the finger against the string. Some Violano-Virtuosos have a relay in this circuit, reducing the current, and consequent arcing between tracker bar brush and contact roller. In other instruments the staccato relay shorts across the bow magnets.

Without the staccato circuit, whenever the bow lifts from the string, the finger simultaneously releases the string, causing the pitch to change slightly as the tone fades away. The staccato device eliminates this undesirable effect by holding the pitch constant with the finger until the tone dies away a split second later. Unfortunately, if the roll accidentally gets stuck with the staccato hole open, the finger magnet may overheat and burn out. For this reason, many Violano-Virtuosos in commercial service have had the staccato wire disconnected.

Hole 4: Early rolls use this hole to operate a tremolo without breaker points. In later rolls, hole 4 turns the rosin relay off. In Violano-Virtuosos having a rosin relay, the relay is flipped on by the shutoff hole. When the next coin is deposited, starting the instrument, the rosin magnet is held on by the relay points until hole 4 comes along a few seconds later, flipping the relay off again. In this style of Violano-Virtuoso, a little rosin is applied to the bows at the beginning of each tune.

In most Violano-Virtuosos, the rosin magnet is controlled by an adjustable snap switch connected to the roller which rides the paper on the lower spool. The snap switch should be adjusted so the rosin magnet applies rosin to the bows for about 20 seconds during rewind, according to one Mills service manual, although it might be found that plenty of rosin will be applied in half this time.

Hole 19, rewind: In early machines this hole activates a large plunger relay which reverses the polarity of the feeder motor field. In later machines without the plunger relay the feeder motor has two opposing fields, one for forward and another for rewind. The rewind field may be turned on and off, but the forward field is always connected to the DC circuit (provided by a converter in the bottom of the cabinet), in series with the feeder resistor and governor. Because of the feeder resistor, the forward field is weaker than the rewind field. The rewind hole (19) closes a circuit through the rewind brush to the rewind field, overpowering the forward field and causing the motor to reverse. When the motor has run backwards for a few moments, the spoolbox gears automatically swing the tracker bar brush assembly away from the roll, and reverse the direction of the paper. Just as the rewind brush leaves the contact roller, breaking

the circuit to the rewind field of the motor, a new parallel circuit is made through a switch mounted on the spoolbox frame, holding the motor in its reverse mode. This switch is in series with a snap switch connected to the roller which rides on the lower spool. When most of the paper has been rewound, and the diameter of the lower spool gets small enough, the switch snaps open, breaking the rewind circuit and allowing the motor to resume its forward direction. After running forward for a few moments, the motor again shifts gears, latching the tracker bar brush assembly against the contact roller and turning the takeup spool in the "play" direction.

Hole 74, tremolo (replaces hole 4 tremolo used on early rolls): As long as the hole is punched, the tremolo mechanism in all but except very early Violano-Virtuosos continues to oscillate the violin tailpiece by means of a weighted pendulum, an electromagnet, and a set of breaker points. Because the Violano-Virtuoso usually sounds better with tremolo than without, the tremolo hole is perforated almost continuously from one end of the roll to the other, with just enough paper between one hole and the next to prevent the roll from tearing in half lengthwise. The inertia of the tremolo mechanism keeps it going between the holes. To prevent the tracker bar brush from tearing the rolls at a particularly vulnerable spot, many machines in commercial use have had the wire which originally ran to the tracker bar connected instead to the "P" post on the terminal board, with the tracker bar brush backed away from the roll. The tremolo then operates continuously, just like it does when operated by most rolls.

Hole 120, piano loud: If present, this activates a relay which shunts across a resistor, decreasing resistance in the piano magnet circuit and causing the piano to play extra loudly.

Hole 121, sustaining pedal on: In early machines this turns the sustaining pedal on until it is turned off by hole 123. In later machines the pedal stays on only as long as 121 is punched, and it is turned off by a spring.

Hole 122. Early instruments with piano relay and resistor: this shunts part of the piano current through a resistor, making the piano play extremely softly. This function of hole 122 is used in conjunction with hole 120 (piano extra loud).

Later instruments: this actuates a third stage of the hammer rail solenoid, putting the hammer rail in an extra soft position, or in other instruments, it lifts a hammer rail stop bumper out of the way, allowing the hammer rail to go into the extra soft position when hole 44 is open. When in the very soft position the hammer rail linkage closes a switch, energizing the violin bridge mute magnet (not to be confused with the aftertone damper).

Hole 123, sustaining pedal off: Used only in early machines which have one magnet to turn the pedal on and another to turn it off.

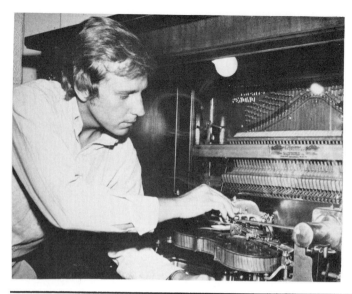

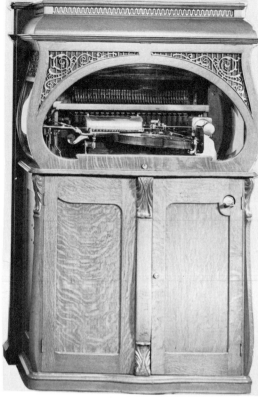

MILLS
Violano-Virtuoso

Violano-Virtuoso views. At the upper left Claes O. Friberg regulates an instrument. At the upper right is an early Commercial Model. At the lower right is a view of instruments being regulated at the Mills factory in Chicago. At the lower left is a Home Model. To the left is a price and description notice from the 1925 period. The Violano-Virtuoso was one of the most successful of all American coin-operated instruments. Approximately 5,000 were made.

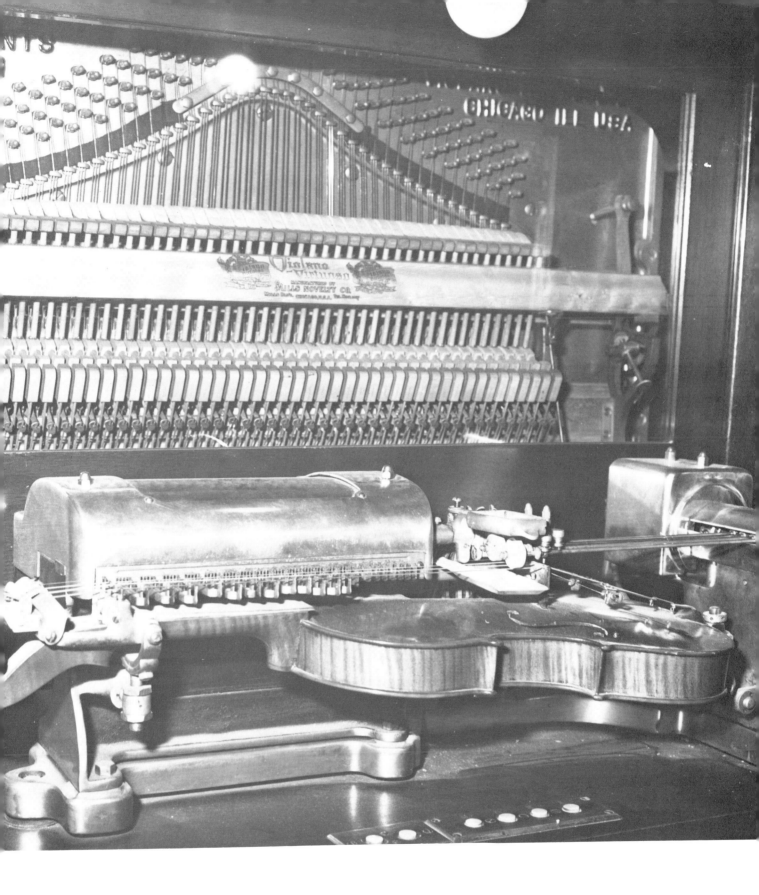

View of the violin in a Home Model Violano-Virtuoso.

Interior view of the DeLuxe or "Double Mills" Violano-Virtuoso violin player. To the left is a close-up view of some of the wire brushes which electrically "read" the holes in the instrument's roll. (Dr. Robert Gilson Collection)

Program card for the Mills Violano-Virtuoso. The center part of the card, a white insert listing five (usually) tunes, could be changed easily. Such signs were often posted at various strategic locations around a restaurant.

Electrical schematic diagram for a Mills Violano-Virtuoso (by Mel Locher)

A rare Violano Orchestra cabinet in combination with a DeLuxe (two violins) Violano-Virtuoso. Only a few of these were made. This instrument saw service for many years in a Chicago tavern.

Mills Violano Orchestra

The Violano Orchestra roll, usually (but not always) having a green label, is the same as the Violano-Virtuoso roll, with the following exceptions:

VIOLANO ORCHESTRA ROLL
(Dimensions same as the Violano-Virtuoso roll)

3 Hammer rail down (Staccato on the V-V roll)
5 Tom-tom (Bow motor loud on V-V roll)
20 Snare drum single tap (Bow motor soft on V-V roll)
44 Snare drum roll (Hammer rail up on V-V roll)
58 Bass drum (Hammer rail down on V-V roll)
74 Cymbal (Tremolo on V-V roll)
120 Wood block (Piano very loud on V-V roll)
122 Hammer rail up (piano very soft; violin mute on VV roll)

The tremolo is wired to operate continuously. Bow motor loud (5), soft (20), staccato (3), piano very loud (120), piano very soft and violin mute (122) are not used. Violin expression is provided by vanish (1) and bow action (2), while piano expression is provided by hammer rail down (3) and up (122).

The Violano Orchestra was made as an attachment for a regular Violano-Virtuoso, but with special wiring as indicated. Violano-Virtuosos originally equipped with the Violano Orchestra cabinet attachment had an X suffix to the serial number, 2178X being an example.

The Violano Orchestra rolls feature many snappily-arranged melodies displaying excellent arranging technique. Only a few Violano Orchestras are known to exist today.

NATIONAL AUTOMATIC MUSIC COMPANY
Coin Pianos

The National Automatic Music Company (also known as the National Piano Manufacturing Co.) of Grand Rapids, Michigan produced a keyboard-style coin piano equipped with an 8-roll automatic changer.

For the National, rolls of one-tune length were made. Most often encountered today are rolls featuring popular tunes of the 1920s.

NATIONAL COIN PIANO ROLL
12" wide; 6 holes per inch

1 Chest vacuum vent
2 Hammer rail down
3 Hammer rail up
4 to 68, 65 notes in order A to C#
69 Sustaining pedal
70 Low vacuum
71 Normal vacuum

Each roll has its own takeup spool in the magazine, and each spool assembly contains a rewind spring which becomes wound during play. Rewind is accomplished by means of a pallet valve which rides along the surface of the paper. At the end of the tune a large rectangular hole appears in the paper, allowing the pallet valve to fall open, activating the rewind mechanism which merely lifts the tracker bar and drive gear off the roll. The rewind spring, now fully wound, rewinds the roll until just before it comes off the takeup spool, at which time brakes in each spool bring the roll to a stop. The roll is now ready for replay. The piano shuts off at the same time the tracker bar is lifted off the roll unless another nickel has been deposited, causing it to select another roll.

The function of hole 1 is unclear. Holes 70 and 71 control a pair of opposing pneumatics which cover and uncover a small vent hole in the stack for loud and soft playing. A larger pneumatic and cam assembly apparently pumps air into or out of one of the small opposing pneumatics during the shutoff/rewind cycle in order to allow air to be vented into the piano stack, but the reason for the connection to tracker bar hole 1 is not known. Further information is invited from readers.

A National coin piano.

NELSON-WIGGEN PIANO COMPANY
Coin Pianos, Orchestrions,
and Organs

The Nelson-Wiggen Piano Company, located in Chicago, was a latecomer to the field of coin operated pianos and orchestrions. Activities were mainly confined to the 1920-1930 decade, with most sales being in the early 1920s.

Nelson-Wiggen coin pianos containing piano and mandolin, or piano, mandolin, and one extra instrument (such as a xylophone), used standard type A rolls (refer to the A-roll section in this book). Nelson-Wiggen orchestrions, most of which were built in the cabinet format, used 4X rolls (same scale as G rolls; refer to the G-roll section in this book). The 4X rolls, named after the Nelson-Wiggen Style 4X orchestrion, featured xylophone arrangements. An unusual Nelson-Wiggen coin piano was the Style 8, a cabinet instrument with piano, mandolin, xylophone, and orchestra bells. Some of these were made to use type A rolls (with an alternator switch so that the xylophone would play alternately with the bells), and others were made to use type 4X (or G) rolls.

Made for the mortuary trade (mainly) was the Nelson-Wiggen Selector Duplex Organ, although a specimen in the Jim Knudtson Collection was originally installed in a theatre and contains pushbutton-controlled solenoids for remote operation (and the spoolbox is equipped for fast forward and rewind; with this instrument were theatre-music type rolls). As is the case with the Empress Solo Expression Twin Tracker Piano, the Nelson-Wiggen Selector Duplex Organ roll plays five songs in one direction on one half of the tracker bar, reverses direction, and switches to the other half of the tracker bar to play the remaining five songs. This eliminates the silence which other single-roll instruments have during the rewinding period.

The Selector Duplex Organ was extremely well made using high quality components. An example which one of the authors located in a funeral parlor in Pittsfield, Maine in the 1960s was still playing 40 years after it was originally built.

NELSON-WIGGEN "NW" ROLL
(for Selector Duplex Organ)
15¼" wide; spaced 9 holes per inch

1 Piano?
2 Tremolo?
3 Forward
4 to 61, 58 playing notes, C to A
62 Organ bass?
63 Flute?
64 Quintadena?
65 Loud?
66 Soft?
67 Shutoff
----
68 Piano?
69 Tremolo?
70 Reverse
71 to 128, 58 playing notes
129 Organ bass?
130 Flute?
131 Quintadena?
132 Loud?
133 Soft?
134 Shutoff
  Note: Functions listed with question marks are not verified and are included only for the clues they might provide. Functions without question marks were verified by examination of roll NW-133. All control function holes are chain perforations; there are no lock and cancel mechanisms.

WHERE "THE BETTER AUTOMATIC" IS MADE

NELSON-WIGGEN PIANO CO.

BUILDERS OF
"THE BETTER AUTOMATIC"
AUTOMATIC PIANOS, ORCHESTRAS AND ORGANS
GRAND, UPRIGHT AND PLAYER PIANOS
REPRODUCING AND EXPRESSION PIANOS

1731-1745 BELMONT AVENUE

CHICAGO, ILL. FEBRUARY
26
1929

Sanders-Dreyer Piano Company,
3294 Gravois Avenue,
St. Louis, Mo.

Gentlemen:

Your letter of February 23rd at hand and we
note that you are interested in the RADIO PIANO.

It looks like this should be a pretty good
proposition and if we install a very good radio in this
instrument--something that will get long distance, I
think it will be a good seller because you can imagine
how much more productive this proposition would be than
the talking machine--looking at it from an operators
standpoint. There are no records to buy, no needles to
change and besides this you can pick anything that is on
the air. If you want base ball reports, just turn to that
station and get them and furthermore it would be a very
good revenue for the proprietor of the establishment.

The price on this instrument will be $1150.00
and it will wholesale at about $550.00.

By the way, can you use any of those old pianos
that we showed you at the time you were here at the factory?
We have a few of these on the floor and we made you some very
attractive prices on same.

Hoping we will hear from you on this proposition
we remain

Yours very truly,

NELSON-WIGGEN PIANO COMPANY

ON:ES.

This letter, signed by Oscar Nelson just before the advent of the Depression, mentions an attempt at
diversification. It is not known if any Radio Pianos were ever built. (Courtesy of Donald MacDonald, Jr.)

NORTH TONAWANDA MUSICAL INSTRUMENT WORKS
CAPITOL PIANO & ORGAN COMPANY
Coin Pianos, Orchestrions,
and Photoplayers

The North Tonawanda Musical Instrument Works was founded in North Tonawanda, N.Y. around 1906 by former employees of Eugene DeKleist of the same city. From then until about 1929 the firm produced a wide array of interesting instruments, some which were sold under different names (including Capitol, Rand, Fox, and Electrotone).

The main period of activity seems to have been circa 1908-1914, during which time the firm's Pianolin cabinet-style coin piano with pipes and the firm's military band organs furnished strong competition to DeKleist/-Wurlitzer and other manufacturers.

North Tonawanda Musical Instrument Works products use their own distinctive types of rolls. Exceptions are several styles of coin pianos made during the late 'teens and the 1920s which use standard 10-tune type A coin piano rolls (of the same type used by Seeburg, Western Electric, Nelson-Wiggen, et al).

PIANOLIN ROLL
6 5/8" wide; 8 holes per inch

1 Shutoff
2 Mandolin
3 Soft pedal
4 Sustaining pedal
5 to 48, 44 notes in order F to C
49 Pipes off (chain perforation)

The lowest 13 notes are connected to flute pipes; the upper 31 notes to violin pipes.

SEXTROLA ROLL
7 1/8" wide; 8 holes per inch

1 Shutoff
2 Mandolin
3 Soft pedal
4 Sustaining pedal
5 to 48, 44 notes in order F to C
49 pipes off (chain perforation)
50 Blank
51 Blank
52 Swell shutter open (chain perforation)
53 Bells

The lowest 13 notes are connected to the flute pipes and the upper 31 notes to the violin pipes, as in the Pianolin. The Sextrola has 12 bar-type orchestra bells which are connected to holes 31 through 42.

In its heyday, the 1908-1912 period, the Pianolin was one of the best selling coin pianos in America. One distributor, Peter Bacigalupi & Sons of San Francisco, reported that these sold as fast as they could be brought in. In contrast, the Sextrola had a small market, and only a few were sold.

STYLE L ROLL
11" wide; 8 holes per inch

1 Shutoff
2 Play
3 Soft pedal?
4 Sustaining pedal?
5 ?
6 to 78, 73 playing notes
79 to 81?
82 Mandolin?
83-84 ?
85 Rewind

The Style L, a keyboard-style piano in an especially heavy and ruggedly-built case, was a popular seller during the 'teens. Interestingly enough, the rolls for the Style L were usually of 14-tune length. Later, perhaps due to the declining market and the effort of providing up-to-date music, this general style was made to use standard type A rolls (as used by Seeburg, et al). An unusual feature is a swell shutter in the back of the case. Style L pianos were equipped with one rank of pipes (violin or flute) or, occasionally, a xylophone.

IDEAL MOVING PICTURE ORCHESTRA ROLL
11" wide; 8 holes per inch

1 to 3 Percussion?
4 to 6 Percussion?
7 to 10 Chain perforations
11 to 68, 58 playing notes
69 to 80 Chain perforations
81 Rewind
82 Play
83 Bass drum?
84 Chain perforations
85 Shutoff

The information for this tracker scale is based on assumptions made from the study of an original unmarked roll designated for "tuning and testing." The tests for holes 1 to 3 consist of series of rhythmically-spaced single punches, indicating the possibility of some type of percussion. The tests for holes 4 to 6 consist of single punches alternating among the three holes, possibly indicating three beaters on one percussion instrument. Hole 83 is tested by itself with a series of double punched holes in a rhythmic pattern, which may indicate a bass drum.

There appear to be no lock and cancel perforations; all the controls seem to be operated by chain perforations as in the Pianolin. As the Ideal Moving Picture Orchestra is a photoplayer and was equipped with two rolls (on two separate tracker bars), chain perforations would be better than lock and cancel perforations if a roll were to be started suddenly in the midst of a musical passage (otherwise the roll would have to advance silently or with piano only until control perforations were encountered). In such photoplayers it was customary to switch back and forth from one roll to another to fit the music—perhaps march or snappy music on one roll and slow or romantic music on the other—to the action on the screen.

As further speculation, hole 84 may turn the entire piano off. Holes 69 and 73 seem to control the bass and treble of one rank of pipes, respectively. Holes 70 and 72 seem to control the bass of another rank or ranks, with 71, 74, and 75 controlling the treble. Other chain perforations come on and off for short intervals during various tests, indicating some type of expression or other controls. Further information is solicited from any reader possessing same.

NORTH TONAWANDA MANDO-ORCHESTRA ROLL
CAPITOL JAZZ CONCERT ORCHESTRA ROLL
11" wide; spaced 8 per inch

1 Play
2 Shutoff
3 Wood block
4 Bass drum and cymbal
5 Snare drum
6 Crash cymbal
7 Bass drum
8 Castanets
9 Gong (door bell type)
10 Orchestra bells on
11 Lower piano notes off
12 Upper piano notes off
13 Lower pipe notes off
14 Upper pipe notes off
15 Snare release
16 Sustaining pedal
17 Hammer rail"
18 to 61, 44 piano notes, F to C
62 to 86, 25 mandolin notes, E to E
87 Rewind

Hole 15 controls a pneumatic which removes the snares from the snare drum to make it sound like a tom-tom when the beater plays from hole 5. Holes 10 through 17 are all chain perforations. Tracker bar holes 1-9, 18-61, and 87 are of normal size. Holes 10-17 are longer than normal, and holes 62-86 are shorter than normal.

The Mando-Orchestra, made by the North Tonawanda Musical Instrument Works (also sold as the Capitol Jazz Concert Orchestra), was described as having: "80 cremona-toned pipes; representing one first violin, one second violin, one viola, cello, and stringed bass; 44-note piano, with loud and soft pedal; 25-note mandolin playing first and second parts; set of drummers' traps consisting of bass and snare drums with loud and soft stroke; cymbal, crash cymbal, Chinese wood drum, castanets, tom-tom, and set of orchestra bells with resonators. Apparently only a few of these instruments were made.

The "gong" is a tubular chime which measures approximately 3' long by 1¼" in diameter. The mandolin mechanism is single stroke, and the reiteration is cut into the roll.

Pianolin 44-note piano with pipes, a best seller circa 1908 to 1912 for the North Tonawanda Musical Instrument Works. The Pianolin uses an endless roll. The above illustration, from a salesman's book of photographs used by Peter Bacigalupi & Sons, San Francisco distributor, probably dates from about 1912. Models with art glass at the top were made in limited numbers in comparison to regular plain-glass models. The white painted case is quite unusual as well. Most were of stained quartered oak. Joseph Bacigalupi, son of Peter, told one of the authors that the Pianolin was the hottest selling automatic musical instrument the company ever sold on the West Coast. Hundreds of them were in use around San Francisco.

JOHN BIRNIE, President
HENRY TUSSING, Vice-President

INCORPORATED 1906

GEO. H. MILLIMAN, Secretary
S. C. WOODRUFF, Treasurer

North Tonawanda Musical Instrument Works

MANUFACTURERS OF

MECHANICAL AND AUTOMATIC
MUSICAL INSTRUMENTS

Payne Avenue, Junction Niagara Falls
and Lockport Trolley Lines

Bell Phone 192

North Tonawanda, N. Y. Dc. 31ᴴ 1914

P. Bacigalupi & Sons.
908 Market St
San Franciso Cal.

Gentlemen:-

Enclosed please find a cut of our new "IDEAL MOVING
PICTURE ORCHESTRA" with a description of it's instrumentation,
size etc. shown on the back of it, with the exception that we
omitted to say that the number of pipes in it was 137.

The perfect balancing of the instrumentation and
the especially arranged music places the "IDEAL" MOVING PICTURE
ORCHESTRA" in advance of any other instrument of the kind on
the market today.

The tremolo, and the slurring of the violins, together with the exquisite shading of expression in the whole instrument is marvelous, the traps being played exactly as a trap
drummer would play them.

There are stops, or buttons directly before the operator
to be used in shutting off any part of the instrument, so that
if he desires musical effects to correspond with any phase of
the pictures, he can get just what is needed, whether it be a
church Organ, stringed quartette, country fiddler, straight piano,
drum corps, cello solo, violin solo, flute solo, all with piano
accompaniment, steamboat whistle, locomotive whistle, door bell
telephone and various other imitations of different noises.

The music roll is directly in front of the operator and
can be controlled so that any of the selections may be played at
will, by re-winding to any place on the roll and starting just
where the operator wants to, by using the re-wind and starting
buttons just below the tracker frame.

Good music cannot possibly be gotten out of an instrument of this kind by using ordinary 88 note player piano music,
for the simple reason that no provision is made in that kind of
music for anything but a piano, therefore in order to obtain the
very best musical effects, it is imperative that the music should
be specially arranged for an automatic orchestra of this character.

While we are on the subject of music, will say that we
are making up plenty of it, so that there will never be a dearth
of it, and besides that, every care is taken so as to have the
selections on each roll suitable for Moving Picture use, and at a
reasonable price for extra rolls.

The "IDEAL" is very simple to install, as there is no blower to be attached, because the big powerful four way pump furnishes
ample wind capacity, both vacuum and compressed air, and the cabinets
at each end of the piano are mounted on casters, so that they can
be easily rolled into place, and the connections between them and
the piano are clamped together in a very simple manner, after that
is done, all that is needed is to insert the electric connections

put on a roll of music, turn on the current, and the instrument will play charmingly.

There are no leather belts in the "IDEAL MOVING PICTURE ORCHESTRA" to slip and make awkward slumps in the music, as the motor is connected with four way pump by a silent running chain and the music roll is operated with gears and shafting.

The price of the IDEAL MOVING PICTURE ORCHESTRA including two rolls of finely arranged music and electric motor is $2500.00 less 10% for cash f. o. b. North Tonawanda.

We are also inclosing a cut of our keyboard Piano, style "L" which also has the description on the back, showing size and instrumentation, and also explaining about the new expressson device which makes the music play like that of a human artist.

This instrument also has starting and rewind buttons below the tracker frame which the operator can use when playing the piano automatically to select any of the pieces on the music roll to make the music match the pictures, and the music can be stopped suddenly and the instrument played manually, which is a very good point when there is need of something special for some peculiar part of the pictures.

There are 14 selections on each music roll, and two of those rolls are included in the price of the instrument, which is $800.00 including the electric motor also.

This piano has the same kind of a drive as the "IDEAL MOVING PICTURE ORCHESTRA" therefore is just the same dependable sort of an instrument, and with the specially arranged music and wonderful expression, it is a splendid and versatile instrument for Moving Picture Theatres of medium size, and the price is within the reach of Managers and Proprietors of those theatres.

The prices of the extra music rolls for each of these instruments is $6.00 per roll 7 to 10 selections for the "IDEAL MOVING PICTURE ORCHESTRA" and 14 selections for each roll for Keyboard piano style "L".

Now, friend, these instruments are both new and far above the ordinary ones you have heard about in the past, and are as near trouble proof as anything of the kind can be built, besides having the music that cannot be equalled by any of our competitors.

The reasons why we are able to accomplish better musical results in instruments of this kind is because we really have the greatest experts in this line in this country, nearly all of them having had many years experience in the oldest factory in America, and some of them having been at the heads of the oldest and best European factories in Europe.

We solicit your closest investigation and hope that you will be interested to the extent of either calling at the factory, or ordering one of them at an early date for a tryout and assuring you that you would be delighted with one of them upon hearing it play, and hoping that we may have the pleasure of hearing from you by an early mail, we beg to remain,

Respectfully yours,
NORTH TONAWANDA MUSICAL INSTRUMENT WORKS

GHM-L

Salesmanship, 1914 style, by the North Tonawanda Musical Instrument Works. At the time the market for photoplayers was at its height. Despite its stated advantages, the Ideal Moving Picture Orchestra was not one of the better sellers.

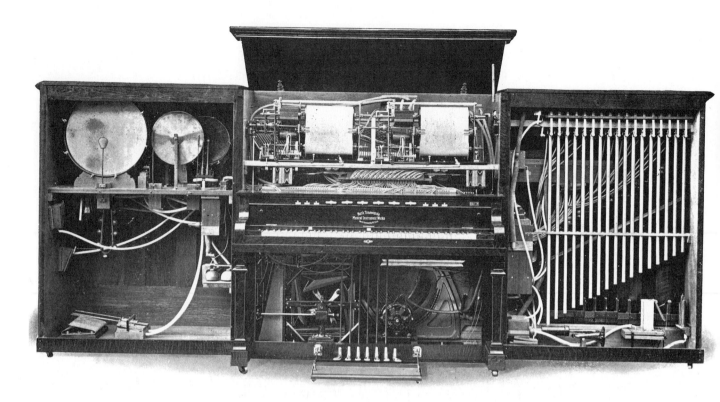

Interior of the "Ideal" Moving Picture Orchestra Style "G"

Above: The Style G Ideal Moving Picture Orchestra, a photoplayer made by the North Tonawanda Musical Instrument Works in the 1914 era, was sold in limited numbers. Note the duplex roll arrangement. It was the practice to put a lively roll, perhaps a march or ragtime number, on one side, and to put a slower roll, perhaps a classical number, on the other. As action on the screen progressed, the photoplayer operator could instantaneously switch from one roll to the other to provide appropriate accompaniment and background music. Although many different firms produced photoplayers, the "big three" makers were the Rudolph Wurlitzer Company, the American Photo Player Company, and the J.P. Seeburg Piano Company.

Below: A circular of Peter Bacigalupi, circa 1920, offers bargains on instruments and rolls. The main market in San Francisco for coin pianos and orchestrions consisted of taverns and bordellos. The taverns shut their doors, at least officially, after the advent of Prohibition.

Above: Interior view of a North Tonawanda Musical Instrument Works Style L coin piano with mandolin and a rank of violin pipes. The inscription on the piano plate, partially visible to the right of the pipes, probably reads CAPITOL PIANO AND ORGAN CO. Capitol, a sales organization, marketed many North Tonawanda Musical Instrument Works products during the early 1920s. The Style L piano was made in two formats: using special 14-tune Style L rolls, and using standard 10-tune Style A coin piano rolls (of the type used by Seeburg, Marquette, et al).

Left: A Pianolin 44-note piano with pipes is shown circa 1908-1910 in a photograph captioned "Crawford's Cafe, Jenison Park."

OPERATORS PIANO COMPANY
Coin Pianos, Orchestrions
Reproduco Organs

The Operators Piano Company, established in Chicago in 1904, was a major force in the coin piano and photoplayer field until the late 1920s, with the main period of activity coming during the 1915-1925 decade. Instruments were marketed under the Coinola (coin pianos and orchestrions) and Reproduco (piano and pipe organ combinations for theatres and mortuaries) trademarks. In addition, many coin pianos and orchestrions were sold to Lyon & Healy, Chicago musical instrument dealers, who distributed them under the Empress Electric name.

Most smaller Coinola instruments containing piano with mandolin attachment used regular type A rolls such as used by Seeburg, Nelson-Wiggen, and others in the industry. A limited number of pianos were made to use special type C rolls which provided expression effects; these are rare today. Pianos with mandolin attachment and one or two extra instruments (one or two ranks of pipes or a xylophone) usually (but not always) used a special type O roll. The O roll has the advantage of having the note section for the extra instrument (pipes or xylophone) scored separately on the roll, thus permitting it to play "solo" while, at the same time, the piano notes in the same section of the roll are silenced by a heavy felt damper. Thus the main section of the piano can play one part of a melody while the xylophone or pipes play different notes. The Seeburg type H roll (to which refer) accomplishes the same thing in a slightly different manner. The interested reader may wish to refer to a discussion of the solo arrangements and possibilities of the Coinola O scale and the Seeburg H scale, as evaluated by David L. Junchen, which appears on pages 716 and 717 of *The Encyclopedia of Automatic Musical Instruments*.

The Operators Piano Company had as a subsidiary the Columbia Music Roll Co. (name changed in 1924 to the Capitol Roll & Record Co.). Some very gifted music roll arrangers were employed who produced some really excellent music on O rolls for pianos and orchestrions and NOS (later called OS) rolls for Reproduco piano pipe organ combinations.

STYLE C EXPRESSION ROLL
11¼" wide; 9 holes per inch

As of the time this was written no single instrument was found which contained all of the mechanisms to utilize all of the possibilities of the C roll. Several Coinola C instruments, an Empress Cabinet Player, and an original roll were studied, with the results enumerated separately below:

COMPLETE C ROLL EXPRESSION
(As interpreted from examining a roll)
A Play
1 Soft (low vacuum)
2 Sustaining pedal
3 Loud (high vacuum)
4 to 84, 81 notes in order, C to G#
85 Bass hammer rail
86 Mandolin
87 Treble hammer rail
88 Shutoff
B Rewind

COINOLA STYLE C PIANO
(How several specimens were tubed)
A Play
1 Full hammer rail
2 Sustaining pedal
3 Blank
4 to 84, 81 notes in order, C to G#
85 Blank
86 Mandolin
87 Blank
88 Shutoff
B Rewind

EMPRESS ELECTRIC CABINET PLAYER
(How one specimen was tubed)
A Play
1 Low vacuum
2 Blank
3 High vacuum
4 4 to 84, 81 notes in order, C to G#
85 Blank
86 Blank
87 Blank
88 Shutoff
89 Rewind

The Coinola C instruments studied have had only one pneumatic for the entire hammer rail, a sustaining pedal pneumatic, and a mandolin attachment. The Empress Cabinet Player (sold by Lyon & Healy; containing Operators-built mechanisms) had only a softener pneumatic which constricts the vacuum from the pump to the stack, and a loudener pneumatic which closes the reservoir spill valve.

Apparently the C roll was designed to give a wider musical scale and to provide expression. To all but the most discerning ear (and how many discerning ears were there in taverns and speakeasies?) there was no great advantage of the C roll over the popular (and with a much, much wider selection of music) A roll, so only a few instruments were sold.

STYLE O ORCHESTRION ROLL
11¼" wide; 9 holes per inch

A Play
1 Tympani
2 Bass drum and cymbal
3 Tympani
4 Wood block, reiterating
5 Snare drum, single tap
6 Snare drum, roll
7 Triangle
8 Sustaining pedal
9 Hammer rail down
10 Hammer rail up
11 Mandolin off
12 Mandolin on
13 Flute on, swell shutter open
14 Bells or xylophone on
15 Low vacuum, piano and drums
16 Normal vacuum, piano and drums
17 Bells or xylophone off
18 Shutoff
19 Flute off, swell shutter closed
20 to 31, notes E to D#, octave coupled
32 to 85, continuation of note scale, E to A
86 Tambourine, reiterating
87 High vacuum
88 Crash cymbal
B Rewind

In Coinolas having two ranks of pipes with separate locks and cancels, the flute pipe rank is controlled by holes 13 and 19, and the violin pipe rank is controlled by 14 and 17. In the Coinola Style SO (introduced in March 1920 and sold only in limited numbers) both ranks of pipes turn on and off together from holes 13 and 19, and the xylophone is controlled by 14 and 17. Some early Coinolas have a set of metal organ or harmonium reeds which are controlled by 13 and 19.

Original Coinola orchestrions have a snare drum expression lock and cancel controlled by 15 and 16 but do not have a vacuum regulator controlled by a lock and cancel for the piano. Many O rolls, however, have these expression holes punched throughout, even when the drums are not playing (like the expression holes in a G, H, or M roll). The roll arranging department evidently thought holes 15 and 16 had an effect on the piano. Hole 87, found only in late O rolls, controls a pneumatic which closes the spill valve on the vacuum reservoir in large Coinola orchestrions, increasing the overall vacuum level to the entire instrument.

Keyboard style Coinola orchestrions and the Style SO (cabinet style) have the lowest 12 notes on the roll octave coupled in the piano, with a total of 78 playing notes on the piano for 66 notes in the roll. Cabinet style Coinola orchestrions do not have the lowest 12 notes, so holes 20 through 31 play one note each. Holes 86 to 88 are used only in late O rolls and late instruments.

Most collectors agree that O rolls sound their best on pianos and orchestrions featuring a 24-note xylophone or set of orchestra bells as the solo instrument. While the music for violin and flute pipes is satisfactory, the percussion instruments seem to use the roll to better advantage. For this reason many makers of modern orchestrions (often using an old player piano as a foundation) will use the O-roll system. Due to the effort and expense involved, few such units have pipes (which require a separate pressure system); most have a xylophone or a set of bells.

Most O rolls are of 10-tune length, with each tune lasting about two minutes.

When the pipes or xylophone are turned on, they play notes A# to A from holes 62 to 85. A thick felt muffler drops between the piano hammers and strings to mute the piano notes in this range.

OPERATORS STYLE M ORGAN ROLL
Some OS/NOS single-tune rolls for mortuary use have the M prefix. See the OS tracker scale.

OPERATORS NOS AND OS ROLL
(New Organ Series and Organ Series)
11¼" wide; spaced 9 holes per inch

A Vox humana on, flute off
AA Play
B Viola on, quintadena off
1 Hammer rail
2 Sustaining pedal
3 Swell shades closed
4 Swell shades open
5 Piano on (muffler off)
6 Diapason on
7 Flute on
8 Flute off
9 Diapason off
10 Piano off (muffler on)
11 Treble hammer rail up
12 Treble hammer rail down
13 to 82, 70 playing notes, A to F#
83 Quintadena (or violin pipes) off
84 Quintadena (or violin pipes) on
85 Tremolo
86 Mandolin
87 ?
88 Shutoff
C Xylophone on
CC Rewind
D Vox humana, viola, and xylophone off

The OS and NOS rolls were made by the Columbia Music Roll Co. and its successor, the Capitol Roll & Record Co., for use on the Reproduco piano-pipe organ made by the Operators Piano Co. (manufacturer of Coinola coin pianos and orchestrions).

If a Reproduco is tubed to the preceding original tracker bar scale, the piano is rarely used. In the few cases where holes 5 and 12 are punched, the hammer rail and sustaining pedal (1 and 2) are also used.

The Reproduco uses holes AA, 1 to 88, and CC; the Super Junior Reproduco uses AA, B, 1 to 88, CC, and D; and the Super Reproduco uses all of the functions listed.

The original factory tracker scale labels holes A and B "Vox on and off for flute," and "Viola on and off for quint." The meaning of this wording is unclear, but the functions listed in the preceding tracker scale for these two holes are probably correct. Additional information is welcomed from readers.

Some NOS rolls are perforated to play at an extremely slow paper speed, thus allowing about twice as much playing time on each roll.

One remaining example of an Operators Style O Midget Auto Organ was designed to play NOS and OS rolls and incorporates a piano and 49 flute pipes—the same as the flute/diapason rank in a Reproduco organ but without the 12 bass pipes. Little or no modification would have had to have been made to NOS rolls to play on this instrument.

OPERATORS UNIFIED REPRODUCO ORGAN ROLL
15¼" wide; spaced 9 holes per inch

The Unified Reproduco, a pipe organ without a piano, was popular for mortuary use. Most were made with a horseshoe-shaped console, often with a separate rack for chimes.

1 Blank
2 Play
3 Flute swell shades slightly open
4 Flute swell shades half open
5 Flute swell shades fully open
6 2' flute on
7 4' flute on
8 8' flute on
9 16' flute on
10 Blank
11 Blank
12 All flutes off
13 to 73, 61 lower manual notes, C to C
74 to 110, 37 upper manual notes, middle C to high C
111 Chimes on
112 Blank
113 Violin pipes on
114 4' tibia on
115 16' tibia on
116 Tibia and violin pipes off
117 Chimes off
118 Blank
119 Blank
120 Tibia and violin pipes swell shades slightly open
121 Tibia and violin pipes swell shades half open
122 Tibia and violin pipes swell shades fully open
123 Blank
124 Blank
125 Blank
126 Blank
127 Blank
128 Blank
129 Blank
130 Rewind
131 Blank
132 Shutoff

Note: If this roll actually has 134 holes (like the Marquette S and Nelson-Wiggen Selector Duplex Organ rolls of comparable width and hole spacing), the positions of the extra two holes are not known.

INTERIOR MIDGET
PIANO STYLE A

INTERIOR MIDGET
ORCHESTRION STYLE X

Coinola Midget Orchestrion has proven to be the most successful keyless instrument ever manufactured. It is equipped with the same "trouble proof" rewind mechanism and twenty coin magazines as the keyboard styles, and is a large "money getter." A handsome case design—quarter sawed oak veneered in rich mission finish. Beautiful art glass panel as show on cut.

EXTERIOR COINOLA MIDGET
HEIGHT 5 FT. 4" WIDTH 3 FT. 10½" DEPTH 2 FT. 2½"

Midget A plays piano and mandolin using regular 65 standardized music.

Midget Orchestrion X plays piano, mandolin and two octaves of solo Xylophones with vibrating pneumatics, using solo O music roll.

Midget Orchestrion F. plays piano, mandolin and two octaves of rich mellow solo flute pipes, using solo O music roll.

Midget Orchestrion V. plays piano, mandolin and two octaves of solo violin pipes, using solo O music roll.

Midget Orchestrion K. plays piano, mandolin and two octaves of solo flute and violin pipes, using solo O music roll.

INTERIOR MIDGET
ORCHESTRION'S STYLE'S K—F AND V

A selection of instruments as shown in an Operators Piano Company catalogue of the 1920s. Coinola instruments, made by Operators, were mainly distributed in the Midwest.

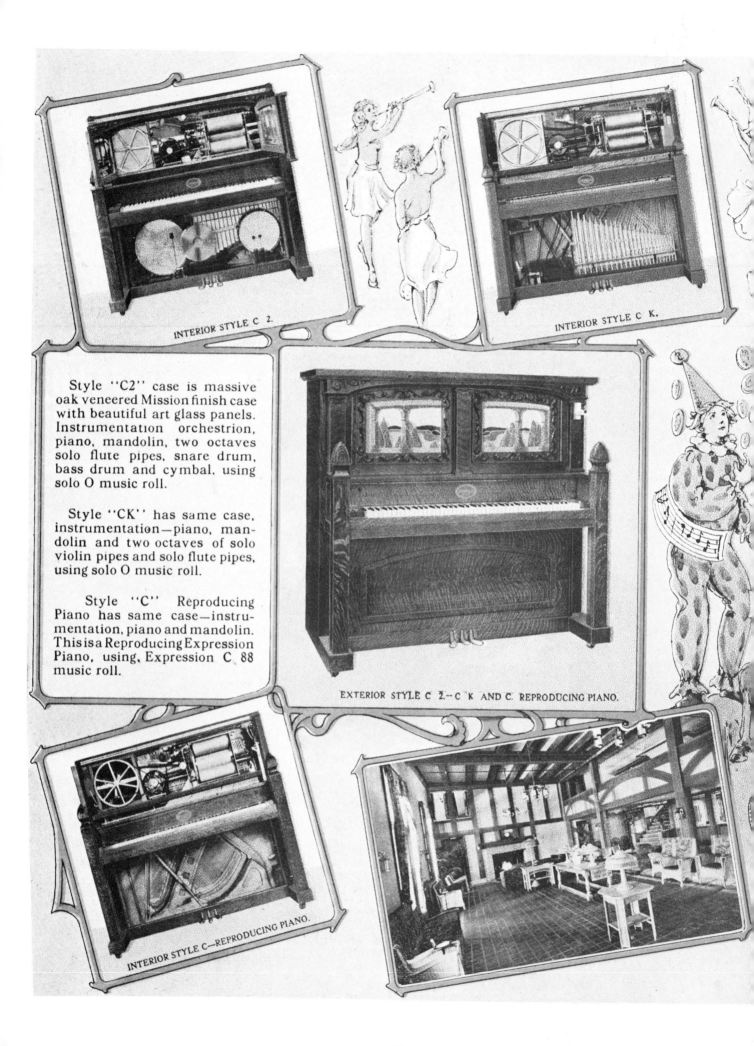

INTERIOR STYLE C 2.

INTERIOR STYLE C K.

Style "C2" case is massive oak veneered Mission finish case with beautiful art glass panels. Instrumentation orchestrion, piano, mandolin, two octaves solo flute pipes, snare drum, bass drum and cymbal, using solo O music roll.

Style "CK" has same case, instrumentation—piano, mandolin and two octaves of solo violin pipes and solo flute pipes, using solo O music roll.

Style "C" Reproducing Piano has same case—instrumentation, piano and mandolin. This is a Reproducing Expression Piano, using, Expression C 88 music roll.

EXTERIOR STYLE C 2.—C K AND C. REPRODUCING PIANO.

INTERIOR STYLE C—REPRODUCING PIANO.

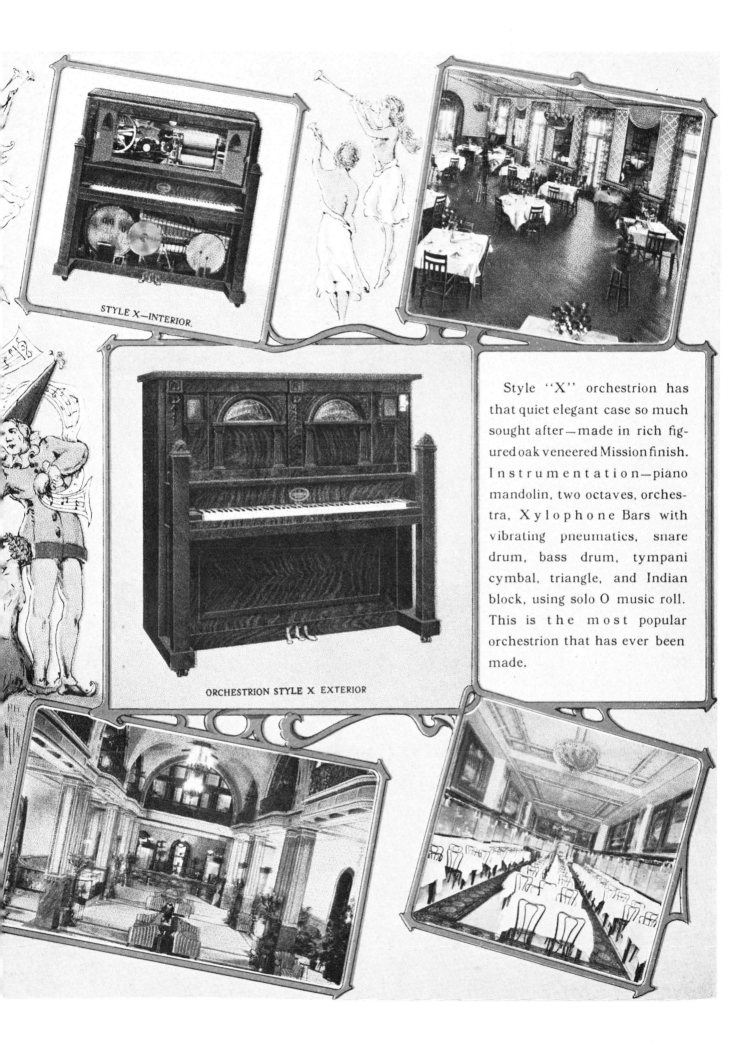

STYLE X—INTERIOR.

ORCHESTRION STYLE X EXTERIOR

Style "X" orchestrion has that quiet elegant case so much sought after—made in rich figured oak veneered Mission finish. Instrumentation—piano mandolin, two octaves, orchestra, Xylophone Bars with vibrating pneumatics, snare drum, bass drum, tympani cymbal, triangle, and Indian block, using solo O music roll. This is the most popular orchestrion that has ever been made.

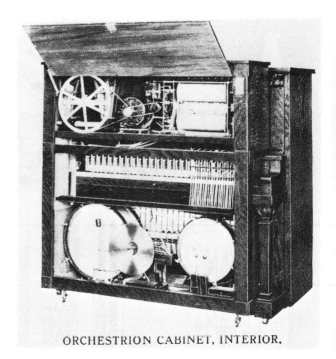

ORCHESTRION CABINET, INTERIOR.

The Coinola orchestrion cabinet was a curious device which pushed up to the keyboard of a regular upright piano. The object was to provide a full orchestrion at low cost by using a piano already owned by the restaurant or tavern. The unit used a type O orchestrion roll and had many of the same components found in the Coinola X and O orchestrions. Apparently, only a few such devices were ever made. Some were sold by Lyon & Healy under the Empress trademark.

STYLE "A F." SOLO FLUTE, INTERIOR.

STYLE "K" INTERIOR.

The Style AF and Style K Coinola pianos used type O orchestrion rolls, although some instruments of similar format were occasionally made to use standard type A rolls. The Operators Piano Company, maker of the instruments shown on this page, was especially active during the 1915-1925 decade.

Q. David Bowers with a Coinola Style O Midget Orchestrion made during the early 1920s. This instrument uses a 10-tune type O roll. The interior components include a piano, mandolin effect, set of 24 orchestra bells (glockenspiel), and numerous percussion effects. To the right is shown a somewhat similar instrument in its original location in Wiest's Pavilion, Indian Lake, Dowagiac, Michigan.

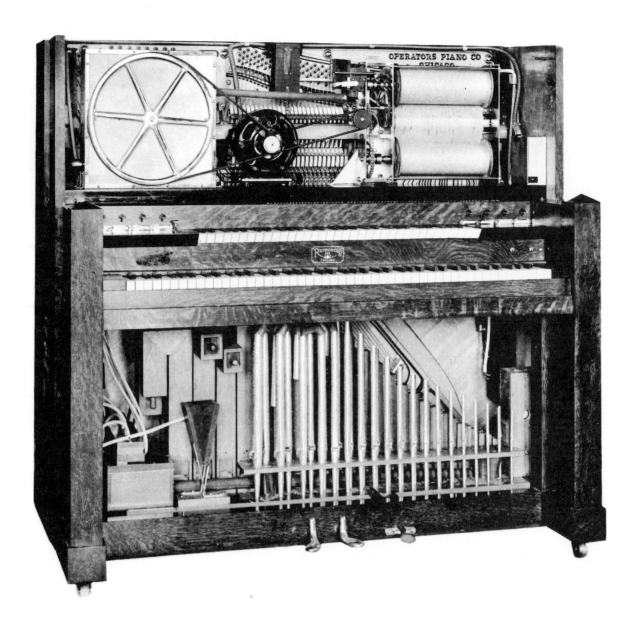

The Reproduco
The Giant In Musical Production
The Price within the reach of all

The Operators' Piano Company
Chicago, Illinois

The Reproduco, made by the Operators Piano Company (maker of Coinola pianos and orchestrions), was the most popular type of piano-pipe organ combination ever produced. Over a dozen different models and variations were manufactured. Most saw use in theatres, but numerous examples, particularly of the larger styles without piano (unlike this illustration), were purchased by mortuaries.

The Operators Piano Company owned the Columbia Music Roll Co., later known as the Capitol Roll & Record Co. From these firms came some of the finest arrangements to be heard on automatic instruments of the 'teens and 'twenties.

Don't Take the Word of a Solicitor

Partial List of Theatres

◄◄►

Imp. Benton, Ark.
Queen, Brownwood, Texas
Crystal, Center, Texas
Olympic, Canyon, Texas
Queen, Ft Stockton, Texas
Ideal, Ft Worth, Texas
Star, Goose Creek, Texas
Wright, Gurdon, Ark.
Victory, Henderson, Texas
New, Harlingen, Texas
Gem, Kenedy, Texas
Dixie, Kerrville, Texas
New, Loraine, Texas
Gem, Mineral Wells, Texas
New McCamey, Texas
Palace, Nacogdoches, Texas
Gem, Norphlet, Ark.
Strand, Paris, Ark.
Pharr, Pharr, Texas
Majestic, Rotan, Texas
Dixie, Rockdale, Texas
Star, Rogers, Texas
Cozy, Strawn, Texas
Sonora, Sonora, Texas
Theatre, Waldron, Ark.
Rialto, Wellington, Texas
Princess, Whitesboro, Texas
Palace, Yorktown, Texas
Queen, Crosbyton, Texas
Shuler Auditorium, Raton, N. M.
Blackstone, Detroit, Mich.
Bijou, Detroit, Mich.
Courtesy, Detroit, Mich.
Cozy, Detroit, Mich.
Dunbar, Detroit, Mich.
Dequindre, Detroit, Mich.
Embassy, Detroit, Mich.
Ferndal, Detroit, Mich.
Norwood, Detroit, Mich.
Picadilly, Detroit, Mich.
Republic, Detroit, Mich.
Willis, Detroit, Mich.
Wolverine, Detroit, Mich.
Woodward No. 1, Detroit, Mich.
Woodward No. 2, Detroit, Mich.
Universal, Detroit, Mich.
Campeau, Detroit, Mich.
Eagle, Monroe, Mich.
Strand, Port Huron, Mich
Park, Highland Park, Mich
Auditorium St. Croix Falls, Wis.
Star, Stanley, Wis.
Orpheum, Menominee, Wis.
Cozy, Medford, Wis.
Empire, Two Rivers, Wis.
Door, Sturgeon Bay, Wis.

Comet, Milwaukee, Wis.
Rudalt, Columbus, Wis.
Orpheum, Lancaster, Wis.
Idle Hour, Jefferson, Wis.
Majestic, Lake Mills, Wis.
Pastime, Kiel, Wis.
Cosmo, Winner, S. D.
State, Elk Point, S. D.
Cozy, Tyndall, S. D.
Cozy, Wagner, S. D.
Liberty, Sioux Falls, S. D.
Maryland, Omaha, Neb.
Victoria, Omaha, Neb.
Ideal, Des Moines, Ia.
Strand, Maringo, Ia
Muzu, Fonda, Ia.
Strand, Boone, Ia.
Lake View, Lake View, Ia.
Lyric, Rolf, Ia.
Empress, Cherokee, Ia.
King, Ida Grove, Ia.
New, Eldon, Ia
Star, Sioux City, Ia.
Strand, Sioux City, Ia.
Comfort, Sharpsburg, Pa.
Monarch, Wilson, Pa.
Amherst, Amherstdale, W. Va.
Amherst, Branholm, W. Va.
Paramount, Latrobe, Pa.
Ritz, Irwin, Pa.
Arcade, Morgantown, W. Va.
Regent, Linesville, Pa.
Blue Bird, Mill Hall, Pa.
Strand, Farrell, Pa.
Orpheum, Clarksburg, W. Va.
Seven Stars, Phillipsburg, Pa.
Lincoln, Hollidays Cove, W. Va.
Wampum, Wampum, Pa.
Nelson, Fairmont, W. Va.
Monaca, Monaca, Pa.
White Eagle, So. Bend, Ind.
Indiana, So. Bend, Ind.
Honeymoon, So. Bend, Ind
Chas. Wolf, Winnamac, Ind.
Fairy, Napanee, Ind
John Sanders, Kentland, Ind.
H. A. Giles, Garrett, Ind
S. Kartacek, Cleveland, Ohio
Michael Hudack, Cleveland, Ohio
Joe Leavitt, Cleveland, Ohio
Dreamland, Akron, Ohio.
K. E. Bradley, Cleveland, Ohio
Geo Barlow, Powhatan Point, Ohio
Odeon, Canton, Ohio
Regent, Akron, Ohio
Bijou, Toledo, Ohio

Victory, Rule, Texas
Crown, Houston, Texas
Grand, Electra, Texas
Pastime, Warren, Ark.
Sidney M. Nutt, Hot Springs, Ark.
Adams, Decatur, Ind
Apollo, Grand Rapids, Mich.
Minor, Dayton, Ohio
Bolton & Jones, Santa Barbara, Cal.
Capitol, California, Pa.
Chicago Home Co., Chicago, Ill.
Ideal, Hobart, Ind.
Dixie, Russellville, Ky.
Dreamland, Roodhouse, Ill.
Dreamland, Guthrie, Ky.
Cimaro, Pittsburgh, Pa.
Masonic, Guthrie, Ky.
Family, Braddock, Pa.
Fox, Minneapolis, Minn.
Eagle, Monroe, Mich.
Eastwood, Dayton, Ohio
Palace, Richmond, Ind.
The Imp, Pikeville, Ky.
Kaypee, Mt. Gilead, Ohio.
Strand, Kenosha, Wis.
Laurel, London, Ky.
Dixie, Paris, Ill.
Liberty, Franklin, Ky.
Imperial, Gadsden, Ala.
Palace, Athens, Tenn.
Princess, Morristown, Tenn.
Fred L. Freemand, Live Oak, Fla.
Rivoli, LaGrange, Ga.
Liberty, Malden, Mo.
Dixie, Miami, Ariz.
C. A. Lopeman, Tipton, Ia.
J. B. Mills, Dayton, Ohio
M. T. Mitchell, Petersburg Ind.
Strand Co., Reed City, Utah
Old Mill, Minneapolis, Minn.
Opera House, Tell City, Ind
Palace, Malta, Mont.
Peoples, Dayton, Ohio.
Playhouse, Justell, Ky
Poppy, Calipatria, Cal.
Rex, Minnecapolis, Minn.
Rivoli, Winchester, Minn.
Wabash, Clinton, Ind.
Strand, Pitcairn, Pa.
Subway, Elkhart, Ind.
Taylor, Big Stone, Va.
Victoria, Chicago, Ill
Victory, Shippensburg, Pa.
Western States, Miami, Ariz.
Tokyo, Veedersburg, Ind.
Hattie Mizelle, Dothan, Ala.

Marshall County Enterprises,
  Albertsville, Ala.
A. G. McCarty, Barnsville, Ga.
W. P. Riggins, Jesup, Ga.
S. G. Rogers, Marion, S. C.
Electric, Dardanella, Ark.
Woodies, Apollo, Pa.
Morfield, Detroit, Mich.
Coniff, Detroit, Mich.
The Fun, Detroit, Mich
The Pastime, Detroit, Mich.
White Star, Detroit, Mich.
F. R. Mellinger, Bement, Ill.
Sam Warick, Sheldon, Ill.
C. Armintrout, Pittsfield, Ill.
Columbia Amusement Co, Paducah, Ky
Iris, Belmont, N. C.
Bell, Tarrent City, Ala.
Star, Arcadia, Fla.
Strand, Alexander City, Ala.
H. D. Duering, Garnett, Kans.
Mrs. W. T. Brooks, Broken Arrow, Okla.
J. H. Thomas, Winfield, Kans.
Bijou, Indianapolis, Ind.
Gem, Hobart, Ind.
Columbia, Hammond, Ind.
Smith, Indiana Harbor, Ind.
Glen Ellyn, Gary, Ind.
Bradley, Buchanan, Mich
Owen, Cassinopolis, Mich.
Reeves, Paw Paw, Mich
Adams, Chicago, Ill.
Babitz, Chicago, Ill.
Cameo, Chicago, Ill.
Cornell Square, Chicago, Ill
Crystal, Chicago, Ill.
Crystal, Chicago, Ill.
Edwards, Chicago, Ill.
Empire, Chicago, Ill.
Garden, Chicago, Ill.
Gem, Chicago, Ill.
Harding, Chicago, Ill.
Harmony, Chicago, Ill.
Home, Chicago, Ill.
Hoyne, Chicago, Ill.
Irving, Chicago, Ill.
Cozy, Chicago, Ill.
Lawn, Chicago, Ill.
Lawndale, Chicago, Ill.
Liberty, Chicago, Ill.
Lynn, Chicago, Ill.
Marion, Chicago, Ill.
Newberry, Chicago, Ill.
Peerless, Chicago, Ill.
State, Chicago, Ill.
Chas. T. Rock, Watonga, Okla.

◄◄►

Walton, Selma, Ala.
Liberty, Roanoke, Ala
Wells, Anniston, Ala
Ingram, Ashland, Ala
First National, Sylacauga, Ala.
Pastime, Leeds, Ala.
Bijou, Mobile, Ala.
Empire, Mobile, Ala.
W. D. Patrick, Dothan, Ala
Woodlawn, Woodlawn, Ala.
Strand, Alexander City, Ala.
Princess, Albertsville, Ala
American, Sylacauga, Ala.
Bell, Tarrent City, Ala.
Imperial, Gadsden, Ala.
Hattie Mizelle, Dothan, Ala.
Royal, Opp, Ala.
Lyric Theatre, Townly, Ala.
Opera House, Talladega, Ala.
Grand, Wylam, Ala.
Meadows, Marked Tree, Ark.
Princess, N. Little Rock, Ark.
Highland, Little Rock, Ark.
Best, England, Ark.
J. F. Norman, England, Ark.
Garfield, Hollywood, Fla
Hollywood, Hollywood, Fla
Flamingo, West Palm Beach, Fla.
Capitol, Miami, Fla.
Dixie, Appalachicola, Fla.
Royal, Tarpon Springs, Fla.
Biggers, Winter Garden, Fla.
Grand, Lake City, Fla.
Biltmore, Buena Vista, Fla.
Princess, Lakeland, Florida
Rialto, Orlando, Fla.
Crescent, Dade City, Florida
Eustis, Eustis, Fla.
Delray, Delray, Fla.
Star Theatre Co., Arcadia, Fla.
American, Orlando, Fla.
Bender, Largo, Fla
Seminole, Homestead, Fla.
Fred L. Freeman, Live Oak, Fla.
Larkin, Larkin, Fla.
J. R. Minneham, Okeechobee, Fla.
S. M. Perkins, Jasper, Fla.
Frank C. Thompson, Frostproof, Fla.
Famous, Cocoa, Fla.
Dania, Dania, Fla.
H. Pettman, Clearwater, Fla.
10th St. Atlanta, Ga.
Cameo, Atlanta, Ga.
Tudor, Atlanta, Ga.
Ponce de Leon Theatre, Atlanta, Ga.

Paramount, Atlanta, Ga.
Toyland, Atlanta, Ga.
Victory, Atlanta, Ga.
J. A. Rebb, Atlanta, Ga.
Cameo, Atlanta, Ga.
Alamo, Atlanta, Ga.
Palace, Atlanta, Ga.
Austin Dillon, Atlanta, Ga.
Eighty-One, Atlanta, Ga.
West End, Atlanta, Ga.
Robert's new colored house, Atlanta
T. E. Thompson, Cedartown, Ga.
Palace, Cedartown, Ga.
Star, Savanah, Ga.
J. H. Wheeler, Decatur, Georgia
Criterion, Macon, Ga.
Strand, Athens, Ga.
Logan, Augusta, Ga.
Potare, Athens, Ga.
Palace, Athens, Ga.
Star, Covington, Ga.
Lyric, Columbus, Ga.
American, Columbus, Ga.
Lyric, Columbus, Ga.
Dream, Columbus, Ga.
Lenox, Augusta, Ga.
Wise, Winder, Ga.
Palace, Dawson, Ga.
Lee, Cuthbert, Ga.
New Theatre, Montezuma, Ga.
Fairfax, East Point, Ga
Capitol, Cordele, Ga.
Kidd (Colored) Gainesville, Ga.
Alamo, West Point, Ga.
Randall's, Lavonia, Ga.
Golden, LaGrange, Ga.
Colonial, Milledgeville, Ga.
Pastime, Sandersville, Ga.
Franklin, Ft. Valley, Ga.
Burton, Toccoa, Ga.

Palace	Colorado, Tex.
Best	Colorado, Tex.
Palace	Denton, Tex.
Olympic	Wichita Falls, Tex.
Connellee	Eastland, Tex.
Fair	Amarillo, Tex.
Grandi	Amarillo, Tex.
National	Breckenridge, Tex.
Lamb	Ranger, Tex.
Queen	Tyler, Tex.
Unique	El Paso, Tex.
Queen	Big Springs, Tex.
Broadway	Cisco, Tex.
Aldine	Corpus Christi, Tex.
Amusu	Corpus Christi, Tex.

American	McKinney, Tex.	Albany	Albany, Tex.
Gem	Palestine, Tex.	Liberty	Beaumont, Tex.
Star	Palestine, Tex.	Brittonian	Britton, Tex.
Adline	Robstown, Tex.	Simon	Brenham, Tex.
Queen	Sweetwater, Tex.	Rialto	Brownfield, Tex.
Odeon	Whitewright, Tex.	Queen	Brownsville, Tex.
Key	Galveston, Tex.	Gem	Brownwood, Tex.
Dixie No. 2	Galveston, Tex.	Royal	Arkadelphia, Ark
Dixie No. 3	Galveston, Tex.	Dunlap	Clarksville, Ark
Pastime	Canadian, Tex.	Majestic	Ft. Smith, Ark.
Queen	Pecos, Tex.	Hudson	Hot Springs, Ark.
Crown	Houston, Tex.	Lyric	Harrison, Ark.
Rembert	Longview, Tex.	Liberty	Nashville, Ark.
Elk's	Longview, Tex.	Grand	Searcy, Ark.
Victoria	Victoria, Tenn.	Palace	Hico, Tex.
Dreamland	Cuero, Tex.	New Theatre	Weatherford, Tex
Queen	Cuero, Tex.	Royal	Hamilton, Tex.
Queen	Winters, Tex.	Rialto	Harlingen, Tex.
Alcove	Stamford, Tex.	Star	Humble, Tex.
Dixie	Bryan, Tex.	Peoples	Munday, Tex.
Palace	Childress, Tex.	Holton	Port Arthur, Tex.
Majestic	Chillicothe, Tex.	Majestic	Santa Anna, Tex.
Mission	Clarksville, Tex.	Castle	Havana, Ill.
Queen	Clifton, Tex.	Coliseum	Marseilles, Ill.
Dixie	Coleman, Tex.	Orpheum	Savanna, Ill.
Majestic	Comanche, Tex	Colonial	Urbana, Ill.
Mission	Dalhart, Tex.	Princess	Galva, Ill.
Ronile	Dallas, Tenn.	Morrows	Decatur, Ill.
Strand	Dallas, Tex.	Central	Fairbury, Ill.
Liberty	DeLeon, Tex.	Royal	Minonk, Ill.
Majestic	Del Rio, Tex.	New Palace	Nekomis, Ill.
Majestic	Dublin, Tex.	Odd Fellows	Mount Olive, Ill.
Aztec	Eagle Pass, Tex.	New Grand	Mount Olive, Ill.
Lyric	Gainesville, Tex.	Liberty	Delevan, Ill.
Crescent	Garland, Tex.	Kozy	Eureka, Ill.
Regal	Gatesville, Tex.	Capitol	Springfield, Ill.
Crystal	Gilmer, Tex.	Strand	Rockford, Ill.
Colonial	Greenville, Tex.	Columbia	Rockford, Ill.
Yale	Groesbeck, Tex.	Victor	Davenport, Ia.
Haskell	Haskell, Tex.	Zenith	Davenport, Ia.
Queen	Hearne, Tex.	Ashton	New Orleans, La.
Pastime	Itasca, Tex.	Arcade	Brookhaven, Miss.
Opera House	Jacksboro, Tex.	Amite	Amite, La.
Palace	Kirbyville, Tex.	Blackman	St. Joseph, La.
Majestic	Lamesa, Tex.	Grand	Baton Rouge, La.
Rialto	Midland, Tex.	Home	Alexandria, La.
Long's	Navasota, Tex.	Majestic	McLain, Miss.
Olympic	Plainview, Tex.	Melz	Ferriday, La.
Liberty	Mason City, Ill.	Opera House	Rayne, La.
Majestic	Jacksonville, Ill.	Princess	Winnsboro, La.
Gem	Rosebud, Tex.	Richelieu	Tallulah, La.
Jewell	Rusk, Tex.	Scout	Minden, La.
Arcade	Weslaco, Tex.	Temple	Baton Rouge, La.
Palace	Wortham, Tex.		

How to pay for the cost of this book: Check out any of the preceding theatres in the circa 1925 list shown above. You might find a surviving instrument! If you do, let us know about it!

The duplex roll mechanism in this Reproduco piano and pipe organ combination permitted the instrument to play two rolls of different musical character. As one advertisement for an early photoplayer (of a different make) noted, "you can put jazz music on one side and good music on the other!" (The exclamation point is ours.) This particular instrument was found in a Kansas theatre in the 1960s. Around the same time Harvey and Marion Roehl, owners of the Vestal Press, found a virtually identical Reproduco in a theatre in Derry, Pennsylvania.

PEERLESS PIANO PLAYER COMPANY
(and related firms)
Coin Pianos and Orchestrions

From 1898 until shortly after 1920 the Peerless Piano Player Company of St. Johnsville, New York, and its various affiliates and reorganizations (including such names as Roth & Engelhardt, Engelhardt Piano Co., National Piano Player Co., and National Electric Piano Co.), produced a wide variety of coin pianos, orchestrions, and related instruments.

While some very late (circa 1916 through the 1920s) units used regular type A coin piano rolls (of the type used by Seeburg and others) and, rarely, type O (Operators Piano Co.) orchestrion rolls, most Peerless instruments used distinctive rolls not utilized by any other maker.

Peerless flourished during the 1905-1914 years. During the early part of this period it was one of the most prominent firms in America, rivalling Wurlitzer for a market share. As the 1912-1914 years passed on the calendar, Peerless did not effectively compete with Seeburg, Marquette, Operators, Wurlitzer, and others, and saw its share of the coin piano pie diminish. By the late 'teens a slump in the coin piano market plus some personal speculation in the stock market by the principals of the firm placed the company into receivership. In reorganized form the enterprise continued in business in the 1920s. The later Peerless and National pianos were a wide variety of styles, some of which were made by taking used instruments of other manufacturers and converting them to utilize Peerless-made mechanisms and/or rolls.

Peerless rolls were made with many designations, including 10,000, 20,000, 30,000, 40,000, and 50,000 series rolls, RR, DXM, Elite, Trio, etc. Sometimes numerical designations (such as "10,000 series rolls") were used; other times a name such as RR, DXM, etc. would be used. Many large Peerless orchestrions used a special Peerless type O roll of larger width and format than the similarly-named Operators Piano Co. O roll. Confusing the situation is the fact that Operators' O rolls were used on some very late Peerless orchestrions; and further confusing is the fact that certain Peerless rolls departed from the standard 10,000, 20,000, etc. series and used a non-related numbering system!

Peerless instruments, especially from the 1910 era, are often distinguished by especially rich and colorful art glass and cabinets with prominent quartered oak grain patterns. Such pianos and orchestrions are highly prized today.

Much remains to be learned about Peerless rolls and their arrangements. Information is solicited from interested readers possessing such knowledge.

Peerless Perplexities

The August-September 1925 roll bulletin issued by Peerless gives the following roll-numbering scheme which was in effect at that time:

Old Style Peerless 44-note (6,000 Series)	5 tune roll $2.75
D, DX, DM, DF, and A (7,000 Series)	5 tune roll 2.75
RR, Cabaret, F, V, and Seybold SA (10,000 series)	10 tune roll 4.50
O, DeLuxe Orchestrion, Arcadian, Wisteria and 2-unit Photo Orchestra (20,000 series)	10 tune roll 7.25
Elite (88-note) (30,000 Series)	10 tune roll 7.00
Trio (40,000 Series)	10 tune roll 4.50
Any other make (50,000 Series)	10 tune roll 3.35

"Any other make" refers to regular type A rolls (of the type used by Seeburg et al). Peerless made these available, sometimes under their own National Music Roll Co. label, with the same tunes as their other 10-tune rolls. Some of these were perforated by Columbia/Capitol (a subsidiary of the Operators Piano Co.). With the exception of A rolls and Operators' O rolls, the rolls used on Peerless instruments are believed to have been perforated in the Peerless factories.

Generalizations about which style of Peerless roll works on which model of instrument are impossible to make, because Peerless made different pianos using different rolls but designated these pianos with the same style letters! For example, some Cabaret and some Elite pianos used the 88-note Elite roll, while others used the Peerless O orchestrion roll. Earlier rolls appear in other numbering series than those given above. After the World War I era Peerless adapted many other manufacturers' pianos to play Peerless rolls of various kinds, while at the same time certain other firms altered old Peerless pianos to take other types of rolls (alterations from specialized Peerless rolls to standard A rolls were particularly popular). To determine which style of roll a piano or orchestrion marked "Peerless" plays, analyze the roll width, tracker bar hole spacing, and functions in the instrument.

PEERLESS 44-NOTE ROLL (6,000 SERIES)
8¼" wide; 6 holes per inch, endless

1 to 5, notes F to A
6 Shutoff
7 A#
8 B
9 Sustaining pedal
10 to 42, notes C to G#
43 Hammer rail down
44 Hammer rail up
45 to 48, notes A to C

The above tuning scale for the piano, F to C, is only assumed. Previously published tracker scales call for tuning the piano a half step lower, from E to B, but since other 44-note pianos (such as the Wurlitzer Pianino) are tuned from F to C, there is a good possibility that the E to B tuning was taken from a piano in which the pitch had dropped a half step. Since neither tuning is verified, use caution when tuning or restringing one of these instruments. Additional information is welcome from readers.

The continuous chromatic note scale is provided by holes 1-5, 7, 8, 10-42, and 45-48 in that order. The 44-note cabinet-style Peerless coin piano was a popular fixture in saloons, restaurants, and similar public places around the turn of the century.

PEERLESS RR, CABARET, F, V ROLL (10,000 SERIES)

11¾" wide; 6½ holes per inch

1 Instrument A on
2 Rewind
3 Sustaining pedal
4 Cancel instruments A and B
5 Instrument B on
6 to 71, 66 playing notes in order
72 Play
73 Shutoff

PEERLESS STYLE O ROLL (20,000 SERIES)

14½" wide; 7 holes per inch

1 Blank
2 Blank
3 Cymbal
4 Tympani, reiterating
5 Bass drum
6 Left snare drum beater
7 Middle snare drum beater
8 Right snare drum beater
9 Note C (displaced by sustaining pedal)
10 Hammer rail down
11 Hammer rail up (cancelled by 10); low vacuum (cancelled by 17)
12 to 16, notes from low G to B
17 Sustaining pedal
18 to 77, notes from C# to C
78 Shutoff
79 Rewind (except 95 is used for this on some rolls)
80 Violin pipes off
81 Violin pipes on
82 Flute pipes off
83 Flute pipes on
84 Castanets
85 Mandolin off
86 Play
87 Castanets
88 Triangle
89 Mandolin on
90 to 97 Blank (except 95 is rewind on some rolls)

Some Peerless O roll orchestrions have a 66-note piano stack, from G to C, playing from holes 12-16, 9, and 18-77 in that order. Other Peerless orchestrions have a full 88-note stack with the bass and treble octave coupled as follows: piano keys 1 to 10 are coupled to keys 13 to 22 respectively; keys 11 and 12 are not coupled; and keys 77 to 88 are coupled to keys 65 to 76 respectively.

The largest instruments to use the Peerless Style O rolls (not to be confused with Operators' Style O rolls) were the DeLuxe Orchestrion (Style O with coin slot; Style M with push-button operation for theatre use) and the Peerless Photo Orchestra. Little is known about the Peerless Photo Orchestra, a photoplayer for theatre use. Perhaps some of the "reserved space" on holes 90 to 97 was for contemplated use on such an instrument (which may have had many more effects than the Style O or Style M orchestrions).

PEERLESS PIANO ROLL (UNKNOWN STYLE)

11¾" wide; spaced 6½ holes per inch

1 Multiplex hole for hammer rail?
2 Rewind
3 Playing note C (displaced by sustaining pedal)
4 Hammer rail down
5 Hammer rail up
6 to 10, Playing notes G to B
11 Sustaining pedal
12 to 71, Playing notes C# to C
72 Play
73 Shutoff
    This scale is based on examination of roll 10293.

PEERLESS ELITE ROLL (30,000 SERIES)

14½" wide; 7 holes per inch

1 Blank
2 to 11, notes A to F#
12 Note C displaced by sustaining pedal (hole 20)
13 Hammer rail down
14 Hammer rail up
15 to 19, notes G to B
20 Sustaining pedal
21 to 92, notes C# to C
93 Shutoff
94 Play
95 Rewind
96 Mandolin off
97 Mandolin on

Holes 2-11, 15-19, 12, and 21-92 form the complete chromatic scale for all 88 notes on the piano. (In practice, most manufacturers found that the uppermost and lowest notes on the piano scale were rarely used, so to save expense 88-note scales were rarely used; the Peerless Elite scale being an exception.)

PEERLESS TRIO ROLL (40,000 SERIES)

11¾" wide; 6½ holes per inch

1 Blank
2 to 5 Automatic register controls
6 Blank
7 Register control
8 to 12, notes in order, F to A
13 Shutoff
14 A#
15 B
16 Sustaining pedal
17 to 49, notes in order, C to G#
50 Hammer rail down
51 Hammer rail up
52 to 55, notes in order, A to C
56 Rewind
57 Play

This scale was formulated by viewing an unmarked original Trio roll. Holes 1 and 6 are not used on that roll, while 2 to 5 and 7 turn various things on and off. The Trio contains a 44-note piano, 25 violin pipes, and 25 flute pipes; the roll is an expanded version of the 44-note Peerless roll, whose functions are the same as holes 8 through 55 of the Trio roll. Note, however, that the Trio is perforated at the spacing of 6½ holes per inch, while the 44-note roll is 6 holes per inch.

PEERLESS STYLE D ROLL

11¾" wide; spaced 6 holes per inch; endless

1 Playing note C (displaced by sustaining pedal)
2 Hammer rail down
3 Hammer rail up
4 to 8, Playing notes G to B
9 Sustaining pedal
10 to 69, Playing notes C# to C

4+6 = Shutoff

PEERLESS STYLE DX OR A ROLL

11¾" wide; spaced 6½ holes per inch; endless

1 Bass drum
2 Playing note C (displaced by sustaining pedal)
3 Hammer rail down
4 Hammer rail up
5 to 9, Playing notes G to B
10 Sustaining pedal
11 to 70, Playing notes C# to C
71 Snare drum
    5+7=Shutoff. In styles D and DX two of the low playing-note pneumatics are connected by a T-shaped lever. This lever allows each note to be played separately, but when both pneumatics are activated simultaneously, the "T" transfers their motion to the shutoff valve.

PEERLESS PIANO PLAYER CO.

F. ENGELHARDT & SONS, PROPS.

MAKERS OF

Peerless

AND **Harmonist**

Automatic

AND

Player Pianos

FACTORIES - ST JOHNSVILLE, N.Y.

HIGHEST AWARDS — GOLD MEDALS

BUFFALO, 1901   ST. LOUIS, 1904   PORTLAND, 1906   JAMESTOWN, 1907.
SEATTLE, 1909.

NEW YORK:

14-16 EAST 33RD STREET

(NEAR FIFTH AVENUE)

CHICAGO:

339 SO. WABASH AVENUE

TELEPHONE HARRISON 7413.

General Offices:

St. Johnsville, N.Y. _____ *191*

The 44-note cabinet style Peerless piano shown to the right was an early entry in the coin piano field in America. Many hundreds, if not thousands, were sold around the turn of the 20th century.

Interior view of an early 44-note coin piano made by the Peerless Piano Player Company of St. Johnsville, New York. Some of these instruments were converted to use Pianolin rolls (made by the North Tonawanda Musical Instrument Works) after Peerless rolls were no longer generally available.

This large and impressive Peerless orchestrion dates from the 1908-1910 period. The symmetrical rank of pipes at the center is an unusual feature. (From the Vince Aveni Collection; photograph taken by Dan Adams earlier when the instrument was in the Roy Arrington Collection)

One of the mysteries surrounding Philipps instruments involves the Pianella Orchestra. This elegant orchestrion, which stood 12' high, was listed in the 1909 catalogue for $3,000. The same catalogue listed Pianella (PM) rolls for $6 each and Cecilia (PC) rolls for $7 apiece. The Pianella Orchestra apparently took a different type of roll, designation unknown today, which sold for $7.50.

J.D. PHILIPPS & SONS
Coin Pianos and Orchestrions

In 1877 the firm of Philipps and Ketterer was founded. Earlier, Johann Daniel Philipps at the age of 23 entered the business by building a barrel-operated orchestrion for a dance hall. The year 1886 saw the firm change its name to the Frankfurt Orchestrion and Piano Factory—J.D. Philipps. Later, in 1911, the name evolved to J.D. Philipps & Sons.

Early instruments were of the barrel type. By the first years of the 20th century, a series of pneumatic orchestrions and pianos was being sold under the Pianella trademark. Most such instruments used PM (for Pianella Mandoline) rolls, although some very large orchestrions utilized PC (for Pianella Caecilia) rolls.

In 1902 Howard and Farny Wurlitzer, of the Rudolph Wurlitzer Co. in America, visited the Leipzig Trade Fair and were enchanted by the large Hupfeld orchestrions exhibited there. Seeking to establish a relationship with the gigantic Hupfeld firm, Wurlitzer was unsuccessful, for the amount of business proposed amounted only to several instruments, and Wurlitzer wanted to buy them on credit. Hupfeld referred Wurlitzer to J.D. Philipps, and thus the Wurlitzer-Philipps relationship was born. From 1903 until about 1914, over 1000 large Philipps orchestrions were purchased by Wurlitzer and sold in America under the PianOrchestra trademark.

The Philipps orchestrions which used PM rolls were sold as Mandolin PianOrchestras, and the orchestrions which used PC rolls were sold under the Concert PianOrchestra label. At the outset, rolls were imported from Philipps, but as the business grew, Wurlitzer perforated its own PM- and PC-style rolls in its North Tonawanda, New York factories.

In the early years Wurlitzer imported a number of Philipps orchestrions which featured an exposed bell lyre or glockenspiel mounted vertically on the front of the case. Some of these were sold as Style 17 PianOrchestras and used a special Style 17 PianOrchestra roll which differed from the PM and PC styles. Other roll variations in the early years included the Philipps PMX rolls (same basic size as the PM rolls but without percussion effects; with a special solo section for the xylophone) and PE rolls (special rolls with piano, mandolin, and xylophone for use on smaller keyboard pianos). It it doubtful if Wurlitzer ever imported instruments which used the PMX or PE roll types.

The PM rolls were used on the majority of Philipps orchestrions and were used on most of the PianOrchestras sold by Wurlitzer. Case designs of these instruments were wonderfully varied and often included rotating jeweled "wonder lights," back-lighted motion picture scenes, carvings, mirrors, and lamps. It was an era of elegance, and Philipps made the most of it!

Philipps advertised that the narrow PM and PC rolls, each of 23 cm. width in the metric scale, minimized tracking problems. In practice, a narrow roll with closely-spaced small perforations tracked neither better or worse than a wider roll with more generous spacing; it was all proportional. "Being about 23 cm. wide, which means only about half the normal size employed by other makes, our small music rolls include nevertheless the largest scale of notes. As dampness very easily makes the paper swell, thereby putting the instrument out of order, it is clear that this inconvenience increases in proportion to the size of the rolls..." noted a Philipps advertisement.

In 1910 Philipps introduced the Paganini, a large orchestrion with an expanded musical scale. With a name taken from Paganini, the famous violinist, the instrument featured one to several ranks of violin-toned pipes in combination with a piano and, in some larger instruments, other styles of pipes and percussion effects. Although Paganini instruments were made into the 1920s, the height of popularity seems to have been circa 1910-1914. A number of these were imported into the United States by Wurlitzer, where they were also sold under the Paganini name. Paganini rolls were made by Philipps as well as by Wurlitzer. The scales are the same.

The Duca reproducing piano, introduced around 1910, formed the basis for the piano part of the Paganini. Apparently, a few Duca pianos were sold in America by Wurlitzer (per information in the Wurlitzer archives).

The advent of World War I in 1914 cut off Philipps shipments to America. In the 1920s Philipps produced many new instrument case designs, most of which used PM rolls. The later styles were never marketed in America.

One of the most important Philipps innovations was the "Revolver System," an automatic roll-changing device developed in 1903-1904; the precursor of the automatic roll changers later made by Popper, Hupfeld, and others. In America, this device was known as the Wurlitzer Automatic Roll Changer. Philipps noted:

"By means of this most clever invention 6 paper rolls can be inserted at a time in our instrument, just like the cartridges of a revolver, and will change automatically."

While most roll changers accommodated 6 multiple-tune rolls, varieties were made to use 3, 5, 10, 12, or more rolls. Paper rolls which were made to be used on the changer had a metal (usually) or wood rod across the front of the leader, instead of the normal tapered leader with a tab at the end.

Today in various collections around the world there are dozens of Philipps instruments, most of which use PM rolls. Interestingly enough, of the about two dozen large keyboardless orchestrions which exist, nearly all were imported years ago by Wurlitzer. Apparently few Philipps orchestrions of large scale survived in Europe and elsewhere.

As Philipps and Wurlitzer had a very close relationship, refer to the Wurlitzer coin piano and orchestrion section of this book for additional information. Detailed histories of both firms can be found in *The Encyclopedia of Automatic Musical Instruments*.

PHILIPPS PIANELLA MANDOLINE (PM) ROLL
same as
WURLITZER MANDOLIN PIANORCHESTRA ROLL
8 7/8" wide; spaced 4 holes per centimeter

1 Bassoon (or clarinet) on
2 Clarinet (or viola) on
3 Shutoff
4 Snare drum
5 Sustaining pedal off
6 General cancel
7 Tympani
8 Tympani
9 Triangle
10 Bells on
11 Blank
12 Mandolin on
13 Sustaining pedal on
14 to 27, Notes C to C#
28 Rewind
29 to 50, Notes D to B
51 Blank (Shutoff on very early rolls)
52 to 76, Notes C to C
77 Swell shutters open
78 Swell shutters closed
79 Cello on
80 Violin pipes on
81 Flute on
82 Piano hammer rail down
83 Bass drum and snare drum expression loud
84 Tambourine
85 Bass drum and cymbal
86 Castanets
87 Piccolo on
88 Xylophone on

In many Mandolin PianOrchestras (Wurlitzer), the hammer rail operates with the swell shutters; many rolls have no holes punched in position number 82.

Philipps produced Pianella rolls, usually marked "PM," from the turn of the 20th century until around 1930. Wurlitzer imported Pianella rolls in the early years, but after about 1910 the American firm perforated its own rolls, labeled Mandolin PianOrchestra, at its North Tonawanda, New York factory.

Although there are exceptions, in general Wurlitzer Mandolin PianOrchestra rolls inclined toward popular tastes. Many ragtime, march, and other snappy tunes were arranged. On the other hand, after about 1915 most of the Wurlitzer Concert PianOrchestra (Philipps Caecilia scale) rolls found their use on theatre photoplayers; and, consequently, emphasis is on "mood music" type of arrangements.

In the 1920s a new type of theatre instrument, the Organette, was introduced by Wurlitzer. Rolls used on some Organettes are of the same width and hole spacing (but with a different note arrangement) and utilized the same roll perforators used to make Mandolin PianOrchestra and Concert PianOrchestra rolls in North Tonawanda.

Refer to the Wurlitzer section of this book for additional information concerning Wurlitzer's business and its use of certain Philipps instruments.

PHILIPPS ORCHESTRION ROLL
(Philipps designation unknown)
same as
WURLITZER STYLE 17 PIANORCHESTRA ROLL
same as
WURLITZER R.P.O. ("Regular PianOrchestra") ROLL
8 7/8" wide; spaced 4 holes per centimeter

1 Hammer rail down
2 Violin pipes off
3 Cello off
4 Snare drum
5 Sustaining pedal off
6 Shutoff
7 to 10, Bell notes C to D#
11 ?
12 Bell note E
13 Sustaining pedal on
14 to 27, Main note scale, C to C#
28 Cello on
29 to 50, Continuation of main note scale, D to B
51 Rewind
52 to 76, Continuation of main note scale, C to C
77 to 84, Bell notes F to C
85 Bass drum
86 Castanets
87 Violin pipes on
88 Hammer rail up

The foregoing is from an original Wurlitzer scale stick. This was used on the Style 17 PianOrchestra, a popular early (circa 1903-1910) style which featured a set of glockenspiel bells (bar-type bells) mounted on an exposed bell lyre on the front of the instrument. The bells played from a solo section in the roll. The only specimen known to the authors is in the Frank Rayle Collection and was formerly in the Forney Collection (Colorado). The Style 17 PianOrchestra models were among the first styles imported by Wurlitzer from Philipps.

The main note scale is played from holes 14-27, 29-50, and 52-76, for a total of 61 playing notes, plus 13 solo bell notes played from 7-10, 12, and 77-84. It is interesting to note that the later Wurlitzer Mandolin PianOrchestra (Philipps PM) and Concert PianOrchestra (Philipps PC) instruments also had 13 bells, but they did not play from a solo section in the roll. The Hupfeld Helios orchestrion rolls (to which refer) have a solo bell section of somewhat similar concept to the Style 17.

WURLITZER STYLE 17 PIANORCHESTRA ROLL
same as
WURLITZER R.P.O. ("Regular PianOrchestra") ROLL
(Variation)
Same as preceding scale, but with the following differences:

1 Flutes 2 off
2 Flutes 1 off
3 Loud pedal on (pipes)
4 Loud pedal off (piano)
11 Band leader (mechanical figure on front)
13 Loud pedal on (piano)
28 Loud pedal off (pipes)
87 Flute 1 on
88 Flute 2 on

The preceding is from a scale stick from the files of the Western Automatic Music Company of San Antonio, Texas. "Loud pedal (pipes)" is probably a control for swell shutters; the term "loud pedal" was used loosely on Wurlitzer scale sticks. The term "flutes" might be a general term meaning "organ pipes."

ANOTHER VARIATION: Another scale stick variation of the preceding has hole functions 3 and 28 reversed.

PHILIPPS PIANELLA CAECILIA (or CECILIA) ROLL (PC ROLL)
same as
WURLITZER CONCERT PIANORCHESTRA ROLL
8 7/8" wide; spaced 4 holes per centimeter

1 Bass violin pipes on
2 French horn (gedeckt pipes) on
3 Saxophone (bassoon) on
4 Snare drum
5 Sustaining pedal off
6 General cancel
7 Tympani
8 Tympani
9 Triangle
10 Bells on
11 Blank (Bandleader or mechanical figure?)
12 Crash cymbal
13 Sustaining pedal on
14 Quintadena on
15 Violin-gamba and gamba bass on
16 Oboe or clarinet on
17 Piccolo on
18 Tremolo on
19 to 27, Notes F to C#
28 Rewind
29 to 50, Notes D to B
51 Shutoff
52 to 76, Notes C to C
77 Swell open
78 Swell closed
79 Cello on
80 2nd violin on
81 Flute on
82 Piano hammer rail down
83 Drum expression loud
84 Tambourine
85 Bass drum and cymbal
86 Castanets
87 Piano on
88 Xylophone on

Holes 1 to 3 control ranks of bass pipes which are independent of the main pipe chest. Hole 15 controls violin pipes on both bass and melody pipe chests. The division between bass and treble pipe chests occurs between holes 45 and 46. The hammer rail is normally up, unless it is lowered by hole 82,

PHILIPPS CAECILIA ROLL
(Variation)
As preceding, but with these differences:

1 Viola
2 Cello
3 Saxophone
14 Clarinet
15 Violin pipes
16 Oboe
79 Bassoon
80 Viola

The preceding is from an original Wurlitzer Concert PianOrchestra scale stick.

Rolls for the Philipps Caecilia were often labelled "PC." In the early days (prior to about 1910) all rolls for these instruments were made by Philipps in Frankfurt-am-Main. Later, Wurlitzer, sensing the need for melodies more appropriate to American tastes and desiring to be more timely with current popular tunes, perforated Concert PianOrchestra rolls in North Tonawanda, New York. When Wurlitzer theatre photoplayers were introduced in the 'teens, many of the larger styles used Concert PianOrchestra rolls.

Wurlitzer had a vivid imagination and often gave fanciful names such as "French horn" to a pipe rank which would be otherwise identified as a wooden bass flute. Sometimes the pipe listings found in original Wurlitzer catalogues can be quite confusing, both as to the actual pipe within the instrument and to the quantity of pipes (some pipes were counted twice!).

PHILIPPS PAGANINI ROLL
same as
WURLITZER PAGANINI ROLL
13 5/8" wide, 4 holes per centimeter

1 Cello pipes on "O"
2 Soft violin pipes on "O"
3 Clarinet on "O"
4 Flute on "O"
5 Flageolet on "O"
6 Cancel "O" registers
7 Hammer rail down
8 Hammer rail up
9 Bass violin pipes on "X"
10 Bass cello pipes on "X"
11 Bass bassoon on "X"
12 Violin pipes on "X"
13 Baritone on "X"
14 Viola or quintadena pipes on "X"
15 Piccolo on "X"
16 Piano accent on
17 Piano accent off
18 Crescendo
19 Decrescendo
20 Snare drum
21 Piano on "X"
22 Cancel "X" registers
23 Tympani
24 Tympani
25 Triangle
26 Bells on "X"
27 Bass drum
28 Cymbal
29 Sustaining pedal
30 Tambourine
31 Castanets
32 Xylophone on "O"
33 Piano treble coupler on "X"
34 Tremolo
35 to 43, Bass notes F to C#
44 Swell fully open (release half-open stop)
45 to 47, Bass notes D to E
48 to 66, Continuation of note scale, accompaniment F to B
67 Accompaniment swell half open
68 to 80, Continuation of note scale, C to C

81 to 119, Solo note scale, G to A
120 Melody swell half open
121 Shutoff
122 Sforzando
123 Rewind
124 Mezzoforte on
125 Mezzoforte off
126 Harmonium on "X"
127 Swell fast (accent swell)
128 Loud violin pipes on "O"
129 Violin pipes high octave switch
130 Flageolet high octave switch

The registers in the "O" family and the registers in the "X" family are cancelled by different holes, so as permit greater musical versatility.

The violin pipes and the flageolet pipes each have an extra octave of notes in the treble, playing from note holes 108 to 119 whenever hole 129 or 130 appears.

Instrument ranges: Piano: F to C, holes 35 to 80, and when coupler (hole 33) is punched, CX to A, holes 99 to 119.

Violin pipes, cello pipes, harmonium (reed organ), clarinet pipes, piccolo: holes 81 to 119.

Flute pipes, flageolet pipes: holes 93 to 119

Highest octave for the violin pipes and flageolets: holes 108 to 119, in combination with 129 or 130.

Holes 9, 10, and 11 control loud harmonium, soft harmonium, and 16'-pitch harmonium, respectively, in some instruments.

Hole 32 is marked "O" on the scale stick from the DeRoy archives and on some Wurlitzer scale sticks; however, one Wurlitzer scale stick has it marked with the "X" notation.

The Wurlitzer Solo Violin Piano scale uses a condensed version of the Paganini scale and is included in the Wurlitzer piano and orchestrion section of this book.

Philipps Style PC-7 ("PC" represents Pianella Corona) piano with mandolin and xylophone. The instrument uses a Philipps PM roll (equivalent to Wurlitzer Mandolin PianOrchestra roll). The motion picture scene at the top features a zeppelin flying over a snowy landscape. The same motif was used on the front panel of the Style 28-B Wurlitzer Mandolin PianOrchestra. Although the above photograph probably dates from around 1915-1920, the PC-7 was continued in production for at least several years after that time. The Cesar Costers name at the top right of the photograph refers to Philipps' agent in Belgium. Costers also handled Imhof & Mukle products.

Above and above right: In 1910 the Style 9 Paganini earned a grand prize at the Brussels World's Fair.

Below: A Philipps Violine, Style PC-10, is shown on location in a Belgian restaurant in the late 1960s. The other photographs show the interior of a similar instrument. Due to the availability of current rolls from Eugene DeRoy's Symphonia Company, Belgium was the world's last holdout for the active use of coin pianos and orchestrions in commercial locations. As of 1960 nearly 100 were being used. Now, most of these are in the hands of appreciative collectors.

This Philipps coin piano with mandolin and xylophone was manufactured circa 1910 and used a Pianella (PM) roll. The roll leaders of Philipps rolls are usually marked "PM" (for "Pianella Mandoline" or "Philipps Mandoline") or "PC" (for "Pianella Cecilia" or "Philipps Cecilia"). Those with wire rods on the leader for use on the roll changer ("revolver mechanism") are marked "Rev." So, a Pianella Mandoline roll for use on an instrument with the changer would have the leader marked, for example, "PM Rev." Before Wurlitzer began making PM and PC rolls in its North Tonawanda facility the firm imported Philipps rolls. Probably the "Mandolin" and "Concert" PianOrchestra designations were derived so that the roll leader initials PM and PC provided by Philipps would bear some logical relationship to the names Wurlitzer used in the United States.

Interior view of a beautiful Style 3 Paganini violin piano which incorporates a piano with several ranks of violin pipes and a harmonium. (Collection of Dr. George and Susie Coade)

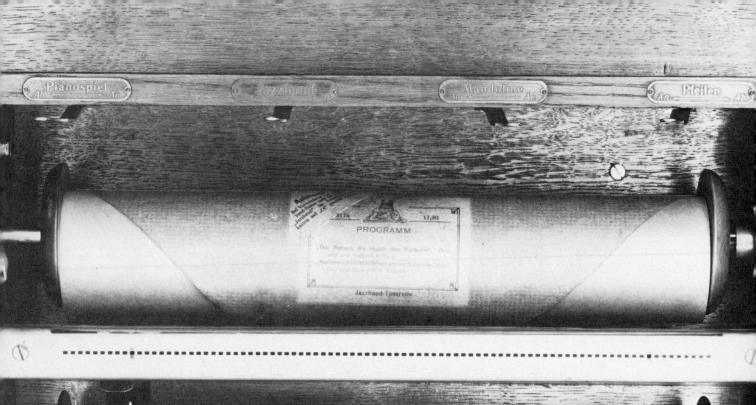

Above: The tracker bar, with a roll above it, of a Popper & Co. "Roland" orchestrion made in the 1920s and originally sold for use in a Belgian restaurant. The two-tune program is marked "Jazzband-Dance Roll" in German.

Left: Interior view of the "Roland." Instrumentation consists of piano, mandolin effect, 12 cello-toned pipes, 27 violin-toned pipes, triangle, cymbal, bass drum, snare drum, wood block, and Swanee whistle. The last-named attachment consists of a slide whistle (visible mounted on a board at the center of the photograph) which has a movable stopper to vary its tone. By means of a series of pneumatics, the Swanee whistle "follows" the highest notes in the music roll.

The Swanee whistle was used on Popper's "Roland," "Protos," and "Ohio" (variation) models. The devices were hard to keep adjusted and operating properly, so they saw limited use. (Dr. Robert Gilson Collection)

POPPER & CO.
Coin Pianos and
Orchestrions

In the 1890s Popper & Co., headed by Hugo Popper, rose into prominence as a major wholesaler and retailer of music boxes and other automatic musical instruments. By the late 1890s his Leipzig, Germany firm was the leading outlet for Polyphon disc-type music boxes. In the first decade of the 20th century Popper held the franchise in Germany for the orchestrions and other products of M. Welte & Sons. It was Hugo Popper who made it possible for the Welte-Mignon reproducing piano to achieve success. He arranged contacts with famous pianists who at first were reluctant to record for the device. And, when problems arose he helped to solve them. For example, when Teresa Carreno, the well-known pianist, heard her performances on Welte rolls she was appalled and demanded the Welte stop using her name in connection with the instrument. To soothe her feelings, she was given a new luxury automobile! All worked out well in the end, and Mme. Carreno continued as a featured artist in Welte advertisements.

By the early 20th century Popper & Company was manufacturing its own automatic pianos and orchestrions. Among the latter were many large and ornate styles, many rivalling the products of the gigantic Hupfeld firm.

An extensive line of barrel-operated pianos and orchestrions included such models as the Phadra II, Piccolo, Aida Luxus No. 2, Othello, Triumph, Lola, and others. These were produced in large numbers concurrently with roll-operated styles. Most barrel pianos were powered by a heavy weight which, when wound up or lifted to the top of the instrument at the back, would actuate a series of gears during its downward descent. Such instruments were ideal for the many locations which were not equipped with electricity.

Roll-operated pianos and orchestrions were made in many different styles. The violin piano intrigued the developers at Popper & Co., and a series of over a dozen different models which featured keyboard-style pianos with violin pipes reached the market. In 1930 and 1931, at the very end of the automatic musical instrument market, the Popper Violinovo, which featured a real violin in combination with a piano and other effects, was extensively advertised.

Reproducing pianos, some of which were sold under the Stella name, were aggressively marketed. Many of these were sold to commercial locations which equipped them with coin-controlled wallboxes. The Eroica pipe organ, which was extensively advertised during the first decade of the 20th century, used a roll which controlled the various stops and registers. A cousin to the Eroica was the Mystikon, a roll-operated harmonium in a Gothic case.

Literally dozens of different coin pianos were made for commercial use, including many simple keyboard styles sold under the Popper's Welt Piano label. Larger were the Superba pianos, some of which had mechanical mandolin devices or xylophones which played solo arrangements.

Popper was prominent in the field of large keyboardless "classic" orchestrions as well. Such products as the Bianca, Ohio, Oberon, Carmina, Matador, Con Amore, Diva, Clarabella, Extra, Iduna, Luna, Rex, Salon Orchestra, Simson, and the breathtakingly large Gladiator and Goliath models each achieved sales.

Among larger orchestrions, rolls seem to have been quite interchangeable. Thus a huge Gladiator orchestrion could use the same roll as an orchestrion with only a few orchestral effects. There may have been exceptions.

The musical arrangements on most Popper & Co. rolls are quite good. Today the various Popper instruments are favorites with collectors.

POPPER CON AMORE ORCHESTRION ROLL
13¾" wide; approx. 26 holes per 10 cm.
(Large cabinet-style orchestrion)

1 ?
2 ?
3 ?
4 Sustaining pedal
5 Shutoff
6 ?
7 to 25, Notes A to D#
26 ?
27 ?
28 ?
29 Rewind
30 to 83, Notes E to A
84 ?
85 ?
86 Swell closed
87 Swell open
88 ?

The Con Amore (literal translation: "With Love") orchestrion was sold circa 1907-1914. It contained a piano, mandolin effect, several ranks of pipes, and percussion effects.

POPPER REGINA ORCHESTRION ROLL

1 to 61, Playing notes
62 Sustaining pedal on
63 Hammer rail up
64 Rewind
65 Mandolin on
66 Mandolin off
67 Shutoff
68 Bells on
69 Accent on
70 Violin pipes on
71 Cello on
72 Flute on
73 General cancel
74 Bass drum
75 Snare drum
76 Castanets
77 Hammer rail down
78 Sustaining pedal off?
79 Blank

The Popper Regina, no kin to the Regina Music Box Co. products of the U.S.A., was a large keyboardless orchestrion sold during the early years of the 20th century.

This large Popper & Co. Salon Orchestra was probably made around 1920. It is one of four such instruments which were discovered by collectors in Belgium during the 1960s. The interior of a similar (but not the same one) orchestrion is shown on the next page.

POPPER SALON ORCHESTRA ROLL
13¾" wide

1 Soft bass drum
2 Loud bass drum
3 Viola on
4 Tympani
5 Tympani
6 Triangle
7 Piano soft register; dampers for bass drum, cymbal
  and bells
8 Piano loud register; swell shutters open
9 Mandolin on
10 Mandolin off
11 to 39, Notes C to E
40 Snare drum
41 Piano treble accent on
42 Piano treble accent and bass accent off
43 Xylophone on
44 Cymbal
45 Shutoff
46 Rewind
47 Harmonium treble
48 Harmonium bass
49 Snare drum, cymbal, and wood block soft
50 to 78, Continuation of note scale, F to A
79 Sustaining pedal
80 Blank
81 Wood block
82 Harmonium bass; swell shutters closed
83 Violin pipes on
84 Violin pipes (or flutes) on
85 Blank
86 Bells on
87 Bells off; piano bass accent on
88 General cancel for pipes, xylophone, and harmonium

The Popper Salon Orchestra was marketed from the early years of the 20th century through the 1920s. It was one of the best selling large keyboardless orchestrions.

POPPER JAZZBAND ORCHESTRION ROLL
13¾" wide
(Scale taken from instrument no. 6771)

1 Soft bass drum
2 Loud bass drum
3 Saxophone on
4 Tympani
5 Tympani
6 Triangle
7 Piano soft register; dampers for bass drum,
  cymbal, and bells
8 Piano loud register; swell shutters open
9 Mandolin on
10 Mandolin off (chain perforation);
   tremolo for violin and saxophone
11 to 39, Notes C to E
40 Loud snare drum
41 Piano on
42 Piano and accent off
43 Blank
44 Cymbal
45 Shutoff
46 Rewind
47 Blank
48 Cello on
49 Soft snare drum
50 to 78, Continuation of note scale, F to A
79 Sustaining pedal
80 Lotus flute (chain perforation)
81 Wood block
82 Damper (felt dampers for percussions); cello
   and violin pipes on
83 Violin pipes on
84 Flute on
85 Blank
86 Bells on
87 Bells off; swell shutters open
88 Cancel for saxophone, cello, violin pipes, and flute

POPPER SUPERBA ROLL
POPPER VIOL-SUPERBA ROLL
Approx. 345 mm. wide; approx. 37 holes per 100 mm.

1 Violin pipes off
2 Mandolin on
3 Violin pipes on, mandolin off, (and xylophone on?)
4 Crescendo
5 Decrescendo
6 Bass loud
7 Bass soft
8 to 72, Piano notes F to A
73 Sustaining pedal
74 Crescendo
75 Decrescendo
76 Melody loud
77 Melody soft
78 Hammer rail up
79 Hammer rail down
80 Shutoff
81 Rewind
82 to 114, Violin pipe, mandolin, and xylophone
   notes, separate solo section, E to C
115 Swell open
116 Swell closed
117 Tremolo

The scale stick examined has 6 blanks in the left margin and one in the right margin, for a possible total of 124 holes in the roll. The crescendo-decrescendo may operate in steps using consecutive perforations. The "Viol-Superba" nomenclature is from a Eugene DeRoy scale stick.

POPPER SALON ORCHESTRA ROLL
13¾" wide
(Variation; from a Eugene DeRoy scale stick)

1 Soft bass drum
2 Loud bass drum
3 Clarinet on (melody harmonium register)
4 Tympani
5 Tympani
6 Triangle
7 Piano soft register; dampers for bass drum,
    cymbal, and bells
8 Piano loud register; swell shutters open
9 Mandolin on
10 Mandolin off
11 to 39, Notes C to E
40 Snare drum
41 Piano off?
42 Piano on?
43 Xylophone on
44 Cymbal
45 Shutoff
46 Rewind
47 Bass gedeckt on (bass harmonium register)
48 Cello on
49 Snare drum, cymbal, and wood block soft
50 to 78, Continuation of playing notes, F to A
79 Sustaining pedal
80 Trumpet (or lotus flute)
81 Bassoon on (or wood block)
82 Soft violin pipes on
83 Loud violin pipes on
84 Flute on
85 Piccolo on

Another DeRoy variation is as preceding, but with hole 47 as
"bass off."

POPPER "LOUIS" ORCHESTRION ROLL
Similar to the Salon Orchestra roll but with the following
differences:

1 Bass drum and cymbal
2 Bass drum
3 Saxophone on
6 Maracca
41 Piano off
42 Piano on
44 Hi-hat cymbal
47 Bass on
48 Cello on
49 Snare drum brush
80 Trumpet on
82 Accordion
84 Flute on
85 Piccolo on
86 Tom tom

POPPER GLADIATOR ORCHESTRION ROLL
13¾" wide

A Popper Gladiator scale in the possession of the authors is
somewhat vague and may not be complete. It is essentially the
same as the Salon Orchestra scale but with the differences noted
below.

3 Clarinette
7 Swell shutters open
8 Swell shutters closed
41 Piano expression
42 Piano expression
47 Bass gedeckt (stopped flute)
48 Cello
80 Trumpet
81 Bassoon
82 Soft violin pipes
83 Violin pipes
84 Harmonic flute
85 Piccolo
86 Soft pedal
87 Blank

POPPER KONZERTIST COIN PIANO ROLL
A Popper Konzertist scale has the following functions, with all
of the holes which are not listed being blank or unused:

7 Soft pedal on
8 Soft pedal off
9 Mandolin on
10 Mandolin off
11 to 39, Playing notes
42 Accent?
45 Shutoff
46 Rewind
50 to 78, Playing notes
79 Sustaining pedal on
88 Sustaining pedal off

Popper & Co. apparently made rolls having the same basic
musical notes and the same percussion layouts but with different
register and expression controls for various models of orchestrions.
This would account for the interchangeability among large orchestrion rolls mentioned earlier.

Popper, Popper, where is the Popper? Not immediately recognizable to one of the authors when he visited the New Batavia Restaurant in Belgium in 1965 was the huge Popper Gladiator orchestrion painted white and standing against the back wall, laden with billiard trophies, vases, and a scoreboard! After due negotiation, the orchestrion, which originally had been discovered by Emil Baude, a Belgian showman, was dismantled, packed, and shipped to the United States. It now has been restored and is an attraction at J.B. Nethercutt's San Sylmar museum.

REGINA MUSIC BOX COMPANY
Coin Pianos

The Regina Music Box Company of Rahway, New Jersey was the dominant firm in the American music box industry from about 1894 to 1920. Nearly 100,000 music boxes were sold.

Around the turn of the century Regina imported from its parent firm, the Polyphon Musikwerke (of Leipzig, Germany), a number of mechanical pianos. Not pneumatic, these instruments were powered by springs or electric motors and were popular in places of public entertainment. Sometime after November 1904 Regina began the manufacture of mechanical pianos in its Rahway plant. Various names were assigned to these, including Regina Sublima Piano, Regina Sublima Junior, and Regina Sublima Piano & Mandolin Orchestra.

Pneumatic-type pianos, sold under the Reginapiano name, were purchased from the Peerless Piano Player Company (of St. Johnsville, N.Y.) and the Marquette Piano Company (Chicago maker of Cremona brand instruments). One extant Reginapiano is identical, except for the labeling, to a Cremona Style 3 coin piano. Presumably all Peerless-Regina pianos used Peerless rolls. The aforementioned Regina-labeled Cremona Style 3 uses regular type A coin piano rolls of the format used by Seeburg, et al.

REGINA SUBLIMA PIANO ROLL
REGINA SUBLIMA PIANO & MANDOLIN ORCHESTRA ROLL
19 5/8" wide

1 Shutoff
2 Blank
3 Expression loud
4 Expression soft
5 to 77, 73 playing notes, A to A
78 Mandolin off
79 Mandolin on

The Regina Sublima, patterned after mechanical (non-pneumatic) pianos made in Germany, uses a very thick and tough manila paper roll. The Regina Sublima Piano, made in several different case styles, was popular during the first decade of the 20th century.

The two expression keys, 3 and 4, provide crescendo and decrescendo via an oscillating gear and ratchet assembly. Rewind and play are accomplished by mechanisms in the spoolbox.

This Regina instrument bears the pretentious name "Sublima Piano & Mandolin Orchestra" and has a tune card titled "Mandolin Orchestrion." The program tunes are: "My Clarabella Waltz," "Underneath the Stars," "Babes in the Woods," "Hula-Hula," and "Garden of Roses." (Dan Adams photograph)

J.P. SEEBURG PIANO COMPANY
Coin Pianos, Orchestrions, Photoplayers
and Related Instruments

The firm was founded in 1907 when J.P. Seeburg left the Marquette Piano Co. factory in Chicago to form a special sales outlet for Marquette (Cremona brand) products. Within a short time the J.P. Seeburg Piano Co. was manufacturing a line of keyboard-style pianos which used type A rolls. By 1911 large orchestrion styles G and H were introduced.

From the outset, Seeburg pianos and orchestrions were sturdily built and were housed in very attractive cases, often ornamented with colorful art glass. Within a few years Seeburg caught up with the gigantic Rudolph Wurlitzer Company, and by the early 1920s the firm surpassed Wurlitzer in the coin piano marketplace.

Seeburg was ever-innovative. As the market changed, Seeburg changed with it. When photoplayers became popular in the 'teens, Seeburg produced a wide variety of Seeburg Pipe Organ Orchestras to fill the need. When in the 1920s large orchestrions (such as the tall and impressive styles G, L, J, and H) became passe, Seeburg featured the compact cabinet-style L, KT, KT Special and related instruments for use in speakeasies and similar locations. Seeburg prospered from the inception of the business in 1907 until its end in 1927-1928.

Seeburg instruments use a wide variety of rolls, including the type A and the type G (or 4X). Produced for exclusive use on Seeburg pianos and orchestrions and not used by any other manufacturer were the H and related MSR rolls as well as several styles of pipe organ rolls, and a modified A roll of six-tune length used on the Style Z Selective Roll Piano, an instrument about which little is known today. Seeburg XP expression rolls are similar to Apollo X and QRS Red X rolls which were used on other types of pianos.

The Seeburg H roll is considered by many (refer to David L. Junchen's comments on pages 716 and 717 of *The Encyclopedia of Automatic Musical Instruments,* for example) to have the most potential of any native American orchestrion roll. While actual musical arrangements varied from "so-so" to superb, there is no doubt that among extant H rolls can be found some really outstanding musical performances.

Most rolls for Seeburg instruments were cut by the coin-operated music department of QRS and, later, by the Clark Orchestra Roll Company. The Capitol Roll & Record Company produced G rolls. Several different firms made A rolls suitable for use on Seeburg coin pianos. The Automatic Music Roll Company, a division of Seeburg, marketed many rolls made by QRS and Clark.

The three main rolls used on coin-operated Seeburg instruments are the A, G, and H, which, in the early years were known as S, SS, and SSS respectively.

SEEBURG "A" COIN PIANO ROLL
(Refer to page 145)

SEEBURG "G" ORCHESTRION ROLL
(Same scale as 4X)
(Refer to page 171)

SEEBURG H ROLL
15¼" wide; 6 holes per inch
Early designation: SSS
(Refer also the the related MSR roll)

A Blank
1 Soft pedal
2 Sustaining pedal
3 to 14, notes in order E to D#. (See bass coupler information below)
15 to 34, continuation of note scale, E to B
35 Flute pipes off
36 Flute pipes on
37 Rewind
38 Violin pipes off
39 Violin pipes on
40 Piano treble off (C above middle C to highest A; the "solo" section of the roll)
41 Piano treble on
42 Play
43 Xylophone off
44 Shutoff
45 Xylophone on
46 Castanets
47 Low vacuum, piano and drums
48 Full vacuum, piano and drums
49 Snare drum
50 Bass drum and cymbal
51 Tympani
52 Tympani
53 to 86 Treble note scale C to A ("solo" section)
87 Mandolin (very early rolls only)
88 Triangle
B Blank

The H piano accompaniment section runs from low G up through B above middle C. The piano solo section runs from C above middle C to high A. Refer to the text below for the coupling of the bass.

The pipes play from the 34-note treble piano solo range, with the violin pipes always playing an octave below the piano, from middle C up. Some H orchestrions have flute pipes of the same pitch as the violin pipes, but most H units have the flutes an octave higher than the violin pipes, or at the same pitch as the piano. The 22-note xylophone is the same pitch as the piano and runs from C (two octaves below middle C) to high A.

The mandolin was never used except on very early rolls. This might have been because H rolls were frequently sold to the owners of photoplayers which use hole 87 for the control of swell shutters. Terry Borne, who has studied H rolls extensively, has observed that far more original H rolls are found on narrow-diameter (3") photoplayer spool cores than are found on larger (3½") orchestrion cores, indicating that most were probably used on photoplayers. In a separate article in this book, early music roll arranger P.M. Keast notes that during the 'teens there was a Seeburg "organ" (possibly a photoplayer) available for the roll manufacturers at QRS to check the rolls on. This would indicate that there was a preference for organ-type (i.e., photo-player) arrangements rather than the snappier orchestrion-type music.

Bass Octave Coupling: The piano notes, in order from the lowest upward, are coupled to the following holes: Note G (hole 6), G# (7), A (8), A# (9), B (10), C (11), C# (12), D (13), D# (14), E (3), F (4), F# (5), G (6), G# (7), A (8), A# (9), B (10), C (11), C# (12), D (13), D# (14), E (15), and so on.

The lowest three notes on the roll, E to F#, are not coupled. The next 9 notes, G to D# (holes 6 to 14), are coupled in the bass to play two octaves per hole. Some MSR instruments (refer to MSR organ scale in this book), however, have low F and F# coupled, and other variations may also exist.

The Seeburg J Solo Orchestrion, actively marketed circa 1912-1916, and the Seeburg H Solo Orchestrion, actively marketed circa 1911-1918, were the main users of the H roll. Instrumentation of the Style H orchestrion consisted of: piano, mandolin attachment, "68 pipes giving violin, piccolo, flute, and clarinet effects" (simply stated: 34 violin pipes and 34 flute pipes), bass drum, snare drum, tympani effect, cymbal, triangle, castanets, and xylophone. The Seeburg H, with two carved statues, four large art glass panels, and three art glass lamps on the front, was the most ornate keyboard-style orchestrion to be made in America. The Style J, usually made in a richly-finished walnut case with stunningly beautiful art glass panels illuminated from within, as similar instrumentation to the H except for the bass and snare drums and cymbal, which are omitted.

Most H rolls are of 10-tune length, with the average tune lasting for 2½ minutes. In addition to recuts of early rolls, new composite rolls have been made in recent years by Terry Borne, with some musical arrangements provided by David L. Junchen and Arthur A. Reblitz.

SEEBURG XP ROLL
11¼" wide; 9 holes per inch

1 Full vacuum to stack
2 Sustaining pedal
3 Expression soft, 4-step ratchet
4 Expression loud, 4-step ratchet
5 Rewind
6 Shutoff
7 to 92, 86 notes in order, B to C
93 Bass hammer rail
94 Treble hammer rail
95 Accent
96 Play

The Seeburg XP roll was made for use on the Seeburg Style X piano, an attempt to provide expressive musical arrangements on an instrument designed for restaurants and other public places. As was the case with its competition (the Wurlitzer Autograph Piano and Coinola pianos using C rolls, for example), the effort was not very successful, and only a few were sold. XP rolls were also used on the later (circa 1919-1920) Seeburg Phono-Grand and could be used on certain types of Seeburg pipe organs.

One Seeburg Style X piano examined has holes 1 and 95 teed together, both admitting full pump vacuum to the stack. The same piano has no hole in the tracker bar for 96. This tracker scale is the same as the Apollo X scale and the QRS Autograph Automatic scale.

SEEBURG STYLE HO PIPE ORGAN ROLL
11¼" wide; spaced 9 holes per inch
Spooled on regular home player piano spools

1 Blank
2 Blank
3 Swell closed, 4-step ratchet
4 Swell open, 4-step ratchet
5 Rewind
6 to 19, Blank
20 to 43, Notes from low C chromatically up through B below middle C; bass and accompaniment diapason pipes which are always on
44 to 80, Notes from middle C through high C; treble dolce, open flute and violin ranks controlled by lock and cancel holes 87-92
81 to 84, Blank
85 Tremolo off
86 Tremolo on
87 Dolce (soft) off
88 Dolce on
89 Open flute off
90 Open flute on
91 Violin pipes off
92 Violin pipes on
93 to 95, Blank
96 Play

This style of organ was designated for home, church, and mortuary use. The usual style of the console was in the form of a horseshoe, with a fringe of colored stop tabs to control the various functions when the organ was played by hand. Several extant Seeburg HO organs have a roll selector switch which enables the instrument to play either HO, CR, XP, or 88-note piano rolls.

SEEBURG MSR ROLL
ORCHESTRATED MSR ROLL
ORCHESTRION MSR ROLL
ORGAN MSR ROLL (early)
SEEBURG MO ROLL
15¼" wide; spaced 6 holes per inch

A Bass pipes on; piano off
1 Soft pedal
2 Sustaining pedal (R: vox humana)
3 to 14, Notes E to D# (see H octave coupler chart)
15 to 34, Continuation of note scale, E to B
35 Flute off
36 Flute on
37 Rewind
38 Violin or quintadena pipes off
39 Violin or quintadena pipes on
40 Piano treble off (see H orchestrion scale)
41 Piano treble on
42 Play
43 Xylophone off
44 Swell closed, 3 steps
45 Xylophone on
46 Castanets
47 Low vacuum for piano and drums
48 Normal vacuum for piano and drums
49 Snare drum
50 Bass drum and cymbal
51 Tympani
52 Tympani
53 to 86, Treble note scale, C to A
87 Swell open, 3 steps
88 Triangle
B Bass pipes off; piano on

The J.P. Seeburg Piano Company, famed makers of coin-operated pianos and orchestrions, made a variety of theatre photoplayers (called Pipe Organ Orchestras) and mortuary organs which used a variety of MSR rolls, including MSR, Orchestrated MSR, Orchestrion MSR, Organ MSR, and possibly others. Instruments were redesigned periodically, so no steadfast rules apply to all rolls and all instruments. In fact, nearly every MSR-roll instrument examined showed some minor variations.

SEEBURG ORGAN MSR ROLL (late)
SEEBURG MO ROLL
15¼" wide; spaced 6 holes per inch

A Bass pipes on
1 Soft pedal
2 Sustaining pedal
3 to 10, Blank
11 to 34, Notes from C to B (lowest note is 2nd C in piano bass)
35 Flute off
36 Flute on
37 Rewind
38 Quintadena or violin pipes off
39 Quintadena or violin pipes on
40 Entire piano off
41 Entire piano on
42 Play
43 Xylophone off
44 Swell closed, 3 steps
45 Xylophone on
46 Shutoff
47 Low vacuum
48 Normal vacuum
49 Blank
50 Blank
51 Blank
52 Blank
53 to 86, Continuation of note scale, C to A
87 Swell open, 3 steps
88 Blank
B Bass pipes off

The basic Orchestrated MSR and Orchestrion MSR scale is the same as the H orchestrion roll, with the exception of holes A, 44, 87, and B. The functions of holes A and B for these rolls, and holes 40 and 41 on the Organ MSR rolls, are assumed. Most Orchestrated MSR rolls have percussion; most Orchestrion MSR rolls do not, but both use the complete 66-note range (75 playing notes with bass octave coupler), and both are used by photoplayers, Celestas, the H orchestrion, and certain other organs having a 75-note stack, the MO being an example. Some of these rolls might have been arranged for a 66-note stack with no octave coupler, because some bass passages are "muddy" when played on an H orchestrion. (Refer to the H tracker scale for octave coupler tubing.)

Celesta piano/organ instruments usually have quintadena pipes instead of violin pipes, and have no percussion instruments, but they have a full 75-note piano stack.

In the Style R photoplayer and in any other model having vox humana pipes, the vox humana pipes are turned on by a chain perforation at hole 2. Some MSR rolls were made especially for the Style R. It is presumed that "MSR" originates with the intended use of this type of roll on photoplayer styles M, S, and R (although the sequence MSR is not alphabetical).

Some H and MSR rolls are punched for reiterating castanets, but all instruments examined have single-stroke castanets. This is probably a case of the roll arrangers not being completely familiar with the instruments. P.M. Keast, early orchestrion roll arranger, has said that the coin-operated roll division of QRS, maker of many H and MSR rolls, tested these rolls on a Seeburg *organ* (not an orchestrion).

Early (pre-1920) Organ MSR rolls were arranged in the style of organ music, using 58 of the 61 organ notes, but with piano solos thrown in using the complete 66-note range.

The late Organ MSR roll was designed for a model of the Seeburg MO which has a 58-note automatically-played range for both the organ *and* the piano. To accommodate this abbreviated instrument, these rolls have holes 3 to 10 (E to B) blank, and

play the 58 notes (C to A) from holes 11 to 34 and 53 to 86. Because of the missing bass notes on the roll, and non-coupled piano bass starting with C2, the piano plays the roll an octave lower than the Celesta, photoplayer, or H orchestrion, with the highest note (hole 86) being the 2nd from the top rather than high A.

If an Orchestrated MSR or Orchestrion MSR roll is played on a 58-note MO, the notes punched at holes 3 to 10 will be missing, and everything else will be shifted down an octave, producing musically unacceptable results. Therefore, only late Organ MSR rolls (produced from the early 1920s onward) are suitable for this model of the MO. On the other hand, late Organ MSR rolls may be satisfactorily played on photoplayers, Celestas, and H orchestrions, although very few of these rolls had percussion holes. Other MO organs have 68-note stacks. The tubing arrangement of these latter organs is not known to the authors at the present time.

Some single-tune and a few multiple-tune rolls are labeled MO instead of MSR. To add to the confusion, the various MSR rolls were carelessly labeled as to their type, so each roll must be examined individually to ascertain exactly which style it is.

The authors thank Terry Borne for information relating to the MSR and H scales.

SEEBURG-SMITH BH ORGAN ROLL
15¼" wide; spaced 9 holes per inch

Little is known concerning Seeburg-Smith organ rolls. The following information was derived from the examination of one original music roll. It is included only for the clues it might provide.

1 Swell or crescendo on, in steps
2 Swell or crescendo off, in steps
3 Crescendo or swell on, in steps
4 Crescendo or swell off, in steps
5 to 17, Pedal notes, C to C
18 to 30, Probably the low end of the accomp. playing notes
31 to 61, Accompaniment notes C# to G
62 Register control
63 Register control
64 Rewind
65?
66 Play
67 Bass drum
68 Reiterating percussion
69 Probably snare drum
70 to 90, Probably registers
91 to 134, Solo playing notes, C to G

Appreciations by Letter

THE AUTOMATIC MUSICAL CO.

Cleveland, Ohio, December 23, 1913.

J. P. Seeburg Piano Company,
904 Republic Bldg.,
Chicago, Illinois.

Gentlemen:—

In my fourteen years of handling various makes of automatic musical instruments, will say that I have had no greater success with any make from all possible viewpoints than I have had with the Seeburg make of pianos since I am handling them which is about three years, also, from the purchasers point of view, they have given absolute satisfaction, musically, mechanically, etc. With the large variety of instruments, I have had no trouble in taking care of all possible business and have very easily pleased our customers with your Original Case designs. Have been able to meet any and all opposition of other makes of instruments with the Seeburg line. In my opinion, the Seeburg piano is to the Automatic World, what the Steinway is to the regular piano world; I certainly cannot recommend the Seeburg line to highly. Have always gotten the maximum results when operating the Seeburg pianos for the minimum amount of cost, I say this with reference to comparisons with other makes of instruments. Wishing you success, I remain.

Yours respectfully,

Harry S. Lavine.

JULIUS WELLNER

Philadelphia, Pa., December 24, 1913.

I must say that your line of goods is very satisfactory and pleasing. I have a number of letters from my patrons expressing their satisfaction in your goods. I am very anxiously awaiting your new style instrument for moving picture parlors. I am sure I can do a great business with it. I have a number of parties who are waiting for the arrival of the same. I can assure you that your goods are more than worth priceing.

Wishing you success for the coming year, I am.

Yours very truly, Julius Wellner

Gentlemen:—

It gives me great pleasure to inform you that the orchestrion which I purchased from you last November has proven, a great success, and that my business has increased 25 per cent, which I attribute wholly to the Seeburg orchestrion style "G".

I can not express too highly my approval of the musical qualities of the Seeburg orchestrion, as well as the way the instrument has been running without getting out of order, considering that in the past eleven months there has gone through this instrument over thirty thousand (30,000) nickles.

The receipts from the orchestrion has far surpassed my expectations. I now own this instrument, with only the expense to me of the initial payment down.

It gives me great pleasure to recommend your instrument to anybody, whether interested or not, and I certainly shall be a booster for you whenever an opportunity presents itself.

Wishing you success, and hoping to install one of your new style "H" solo-orchestrion in the near future, I beg to remain,

Very truly yours,

Frank Wasikowski.

KREIDLER PIANO COMPANY

Duluth Minn., December 30, 1913.

It gives us pleasure to state that we have handled the Seeburg Electric Pianos for the past two years and we have found them first class in every respect. In fact, they surpass any other electric piano that we know of and we have handled quite a number of different makes. Sincerely yours,

F. W. Kreidler, President.

HOEFFLER MFG. CO.

Milwaukee, Wis., January 2, 1914.

J. P. Seeburg Piano Company,
Chicago, Illinois.
Mr. J. P. Seeburg, President.
Dear Sir:—

Just a few lines at the beginning of the New Year to express our appreciation of the pleasant and satisfactory business relations with you during 1913.

We take this occasion also to compliment you upon the progress made, not only in improving your product generally, but by introducing new ideas and features never before attained which combined with the many other desirable qualities, places your line in the front rank for merit, the established reputation for simplicity and durability, combined with your progressive methods of originating novel and desirable improvements in your instruments, is ample proof that you have the ideal proposition to offer your dealers, and it is our sincere wish that you merit continued success in abundant quantities during 1914.

As you know, we have been in the Automatic Musical Instrument business, exclusively and continually for the past fifteen years, during which time we introduced the first Electric Pianos in Wisconsin and Michigan, and during these years our purchases from various leading manufacturers whom we represented exclusively in this territory would run up into seven figures you will concede that our judgment is somewhat matured, and that we should be able to judge a good thing when we see it, and that is how the Seeburg line appeals to us. With personal regards, we remain. Yours truly,

A. Hoeffler, President.

FORT SIDE INN

Whitemarsh, Mont. Co., Pa., November 21, 1913.

Mr. Julius Wellner,
923 Walnut Street,
Philadelphia, Pa.
My Dear Mr. Wellner:—

The Seeburg Orchestrion, Style "H" which you sold me for my Dining Room, is certainly giving great satisfaction. All the former instruments that I had gave me a great deal of trouble, but I must say that during the five months time which I had this instrument, it has been playing continuously without any trouble whatever. My patrons are delighted with it, and I am sure it is a very good investment for me. I will be very glad to recommend this instrument to all my friends. I think I have a sale for one of these instruments, if you will call at my place of buusiness sometime in the near future, we will talk this matter over. I am, Yours very truly,

William P. Green, Prop

THE OTTO GRAU PIANO CO.

Cincinnati, Ohio, December 24, 1913.

We take great pleasure in expressing our endorsement of your famous line of Orchestrions and Electric Coin Operated Pianos.

During the past three years, we have sold some of the most prominent lodges, cafes, summer resorts and moving picture houses in this city and vicinity, including the Elks Temple and Eagles Hall, Hamilton, Ohio and Eagles Aerie, Middletown, Ohio.

It has been our experience that Seeburg Electric Pianos are the most durable and mechanically perfect of any coin operated instruments that we have ever handled as outside of changing rolls for customers, we have been occasioned but little trouble in the matter of upkeep.

Trusting the year 1914 will bring with it a still greater recognition which your splendid line so richly deserves, we beg to remain, with kindest regards and best wishes,

Yours very truly,

J. R. Richards, General Manager.

Some early (1913-1914) testimonials for Seeburg coin pianos and orchestrions. One owner noted that his Style G orchestrion took in 30,000 nickels ($1500) in eleven months!

STYLE "H"
SOLO—ORCHESTRION

A MARVEL of case design and orchestration. Height, 7 ft. 3 in. Width, 6 ft. 4 in. Depth, 2 ft. 10 in. Contains 68 pipes giving effect of Violin, Piccolo, Flute and Clarinet; high grade piano, Mandolin, Bass and Snare drums, Cymbal, Triangle, Tympani, Castanets and Xylophone.

A strong feature is the soft drum effects patented by the company, enabling instrument to give wonderful solo effects. The case is of mission oak, with carved wood Caryatids at each side, representing "Beauty and Strength," holding up the top of the case. The double doors on front are of very high grade art-glass with brass pipes thereon in bas-relief. From the top hang three very artistic art-lamps and on the inside there are four lamps which illuminate the art-glass at the corners and side of top only.

Equipped with tempo-regulator, magazine slot registering from 1 to 20 coins. Roll contains 10 to 20 selections on famous Seeburg rewind system.

J. P. SEEBURG PIANO CO.   MANUFACTURERS, CHICAGO

The Style H, made by the J.P. Seeburg Piano Company from about 1911 until 1927 (although most were made circa 1912-1918), represents the most ornate keyboard-style orchestrion ever produced.

The Seeburg Style H Solo Orchestrion shown on this and the facing page was once located in a Butte, Montana tavern. Following that service, it was acquired by the Whitney family and was exhibited for years at San Francisco's famous Cliff House, one of three(!) such instruments possessed by that famous resort.

Built around 1915, the Style H was described as having "piano, xylophone, 68 pipes (giving violin, piccolo, flute, and clarinet effects), mandolin attachment, bass drum, snare drum, tympani, cymbal, tri angle, and castanets; a 'masked marvel' equal to a 7-man orchestra. Equipped with patented soft drum control, enabling the instrument to render wonderful solo effects... Adorned with two hand-carved wood caryatids, representing 'Strength' and 'Beauty,' typical of this combination of excellence in case design."

And, in the field of case designs the Butte tavern owner did indeed pick a winner. In fact, no matter how hard he might have tried, he could have found no American-built keyboard style orchestrion which was more ornate. "Beauty," one of the two statues, is shown to the left.

In recent years Terry Borne has collected tunes from several different Style H rolls and has arranged them on composite 10-tune rolls containing favorite melodies, a collectors' delight.

It has been estimated that several hundred or more Seeburg Style H orchestrions were originally built. Of that number, only about three dozen can be traced with certainty today. Also using the H roll was the Style J orchestrion, which contained the same instrumentation as the H but without the drums. The Style J is even rarer; fewer than a half dozen are known to exist. Styles J and H were the largest orchestrions in the Seeburg line.

Seeburg Pipe-Organ Orchestra, Style "M"

The tremendous and constantly growing development of the Moving Picture Theater business has produced a peculiar problem in economical production of music and characteristic accompaniments which will support and lend character and action to the pictures shown. This problem is perfectly solved in the "Seeburg Pipe-Organ Orchestra." This problem involved the production of an instrument which would not only supply perfect music of a high quality, but which would also make it possible to produce sound effects to emphasize and bring out the action of the picture, and at the same time to accomplish this by individual operation in order that economy might be achieved.

It is manifest that unless these effects can be so accurately controlled that they may be always brought in at the right time, that they would better be dispensed with entirely, while — if properly produced both as to time and accuracy of sound — they add tremendously to the effect of the entertainment. **Seeburg instruments achieve these results.**

The air is supplied by the latest patent blower which can be placed in any convenient location. Two manuals, Organ and Piano, for hand playing. Equipped with the Seeburg **SOLO**-effect features and hand arranged rolls containing ten selections.

Double veneered hardwood case finished in Mission Oak.

Height 5 feet 3 inches. Width 3 feet 3 inches. Length 13 feet.
Weight boxed for shipment about 2000 pounds.

INSTRUMENTATION, "M"	
Organ-Piano	Octave Coupler
Violin	Crash Cymbal
Flute	Tom Tom Effect
Bass 8'	Fire Gong
'Cello	Steamboat Whistle
Tremolo	Thunder Effect
Mandolin	Wind Siren
Xylophone	Baby Cry
Organ Swell	Telephone Bell
Piano 88 notes	Door Bell
Bass Drum	Horse Trot
Snare Drum	Triangle
Tympani Effect	Castanets
Cymbal	Bird Whistle

An almost unlimited variety of effects may be obtained from key-board, such as: Cuckoo, Scotch Bag-pipe Effect, etc.

*"Wondrous range of orchestration
makes the SEEBURG reputation"*

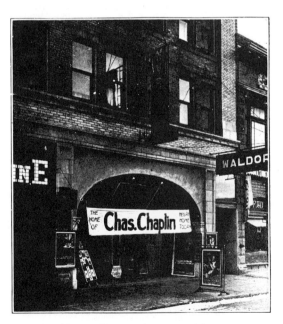

MYRTLE THEATRE, LEWISTOWN, MONT.

Some Seeburg-iana from the 1915 era. Many hundreds (at least) of Seeburg photoplayers were originally sold in all parts of the United States. About a dozen instruments are known to exist today.

The Myrtle Theatre

JOHN B. RITCH, MANAGER
Lewistown, Montana

December 8, 1915.

J. P. Seeburg Piano Co.
209 S. State Street, Chicago.

Gentlemen:—

I purchased one of your Style "M" Seeburg Pipe Organ a little more than one year ago, and have used it daily in the Myrtle Theatre ever since. The instrument has an exceptionally fine tone, has stood the work surprisingly well, and has not given me more than ordinary expense to keep it in condition to render the service required of it.

The tone of my Seeburg is more pleasing than that of other much higher priced instruments of other makes in use in this city.

Yours very truly,

John B Ritch

This theatre picture, circa 1915, shows the home of a Seeburg photoplayer and was originally part of the Seeburg factory records. (Courtesy of A. Valente) Below is shown a Style S photoplayer which uses 88-note home player piano rolls as well as type H rolls.

For SEEBURG Orchestrions Styles J and H, New Styles W and M, S, and R, and Pipe Organ-Orchestra, and Celesta DeLuxe Pipe Organ

Organ: Order these also for your Organs. They are popular.

NOTE: These rolls will play all Orchestrion effects, except Organ, on Styles M, S & R.

H-1132   NATURAL MELODY HITS
1. Highways Are Happy Ways, Fox Trot.
2. A Night In June, Fox Trot.
3. Roam On My Little Gypsy Sweetheart, Fox Trot.
4. Good News, Fox Trot.
5. Miss Annabelle Lee, Fox Trot.
6. Baby Feet Go Pitter Patter, Fox Trot.
7. The Calinda, Fox Trot.
8. Someday You'll Say "O. K.!" Fox Trot.
9. Oh! Ya! Ya! Fox Trot.
10. Who's That Pretty Baby? Fox Trot

H-1133   FLASHES FROM SONGLAND
1. Baby Your Mother, Fox Trot.
2. Swanee Shore, Fox Trot.
3. She Don't Wanna! Fox Trot.
4. Under the Moon, Fox Trot.
5. After I've Called You Sweetheart, Waltz.
6. Lucky In Love, Fox Trot.
7. Barbara, Fox Trot.
8. Love and Kisses, Fox Trot.
9. Sweet Someone, Fox Trot.
10. Vo-Do-Do-De-O Blues, Fox Trot.

H-1121   "A RIOT OF MUSIC HITS!"
1. You Don't Like It—Not Much, Fox Trot.
2. Wasn't It Nice? Fox Trot,
3. Ain't That a Grand and Glorious Feeling?
4. It's Too Late Now, Waltz.   Fox Trot.
5. Open Your Eyes, Fox Trot.
6. That Pretty Little So and So of Mine, Fox
7. The Kinkajou, Fox Trot.   Trot.
8. Watching the World Go By, Waltz.
9. Magnolia, Fox Trot.
10. Fifty Million Frenchmen Can't Be Wrong, Fox Trot.

H-1120   AN EAR FULL OF HARMONY
1. Chamberlin and Lindy, One-step.
2. You Should See My Tootsie, Fox Trot.
3. Nobody But My Baby, Fox Trot.
4. Hawaiian Mother O' Mine, Waltz.
5. Dear Eyes That Haunt Me, Fox Trot.
6. The Same Old Moon, Fox Trot.
7. My Connecticut Gal, Fox Trot.
8. Can't You Hear Me Say I Love You, Waltz.
9. Alibi-ing Papa, Fox Trot.
10. I'm Gonna Meet My Sweetie Now, Fox Trot.

H-1107   BEST YET
1. Hoosier Sweetheart, Fox Trot.
2. Hello Cutie, Fox Trot.
3. Somebody Else, Fox Trot.
4. Russian Lullaby, Waltz.
5. Pretty Little Thing, Fox Trot.
6. Since I Found You, Fox Trot.
7. Forgive Me, Fox Trot.
8. My Carolina Home, Waltz.
9. Where's That Rainbow, Fox Trot.
10. All I Want Is You. Fox Trot.

For SEEBURG Celesta De Luxe Pipe Organ and Styles S, M, R, T, V and A De Luxe, Pipe Organ Orchestras

HAND PLAYED ORGAN ROLLS

MSR-1134   ORGAN LIGHT COMEDY
1. Call Of the Sylphs.................Frascard
2. Moonlight Dreams ....Spry
3. Dancing Marionette ....Gahm
4. Before the Footlights ....Manney
5. The Dansant ....Moquin

MSR-1135   ORGAN HEAVY DRAMATIC
1. Anguish ....Vrionides
2. Evil Intentions ....Kempinski
3. Dramatic Suspense ....Vrionides
4. Ominous Moments ....Kempinski
5. Imprecations ....Baron

MSR-1136   ORGAN BALLADS
1. A Night Of Love.....................Spier
2. L'Amour-Toujours-L'Amour ....Friml
3. Neapolitan Nights ....Zamecnik
4. A Kiss Before the Dawn.......Ray Perkins
5. One Alone ....Romberg

MSR-1137   ORGAN POPULAR
1. Baby Feet Go Pitter Patter.
2. Just Once Again.
3. Baby Your Mother.
4. Under the Moon.
5. A Night in June.

MSR-1130   ORGAN—BALLADS
1. All For You...............Bertrand-Brown
2. If Tears Could Bring You Back to Me
         ....Johnson, Bibo & Ward
3. A Brown Bird Singing...............Wood
4. I Found You.....................Goodman
5. Just An Ivy Covered Shack...........Rupp

Above: Two pages from a roll catalogue offer new titles of H and MSR rolls. Note that the MSR titles are given designations of musical character, "Organ Light Comedy" and "Organ Heavy Dramatic," for example, for use in motion picture accompaniment.

Left: Seeburg piano and pipe organ combination in a rugged quartered oak case. This instrument will play H or MSR rolls, with the MSR rolls sounding better for they feature organ-type arrangements with extended perforations for sustaining pipe notes.

J. P. SEEBURG PIANO COMPANY

WORLD'S LARGEST MANUFACTURERS OF AUTOMATIC MUSICAL INSTRUMENTS

GENERAL OFFICES and FACTORY—1508-10-12-14-16-18 DAYTON STREET

Cable Address: "SEEBUR CHICAGO," ABC Code, 5th Edition

Telephone: Diversey 2551, All Depts.

Chicago   1926

Sanders & Dryer
3294 Gravois
St. Louis, Mo.

Gentlemen:

J. J. Reilly of the Princess Theatre, Alton, Ill. has been dickering with us for a "CELESTA DE LUXE PLAYER PIPE ORGAN". I saw him yesterday and was talking with him on the telephone today. We were unable to make a deal with him because of the fact that we do not agree to allow him more than $500 for the Style "M" pit instrument which they now have.

We had hoped to make the deal this way and turn it through you, giving you a nice profit and the Style "M" pit instrument besides.

Wurlitzer's have been trying to sell them and have offered them more money for the instrument than we had. However I discovered that they were charging them a long price for an organ and therefore could afford to do so.

If you think you would like to do this it might be well for you to make a trip to Alton and see Mr. Reilly and look this instrument over. By doing so, perhaps you could allow more for it than we offered them. If so, it might be possible for you to get to make a deal. However, should you decide to do this it must be done at once as Mr. Reilly is arranging with a man in St. Louis to over-haul the instrument he now has. You, no doubt know that the wholesale price on the "CELESTA" is $1085 and we have quoted them the price of $2250. I am enclosing a cut of this instrument for fear that you have none at hand so if you care to go to Alton and see this man it is barely possible that you can get him interested. He is a very fine gentleman to talk to and we would be pleased to have our instrument in his place. The writer was in St. Louis Monday morning and rang your office two or three times but was unable to get a response. No doubt you were out hustling business.

Ray has just asked me to advise you that he is waiting for either the carload order or the $25 as per the bet. When we were in St. Louis. You may rest assured that he doesn't forget anything and he will be after you as long as you live for that $25 unless you get busy and send in an order for the carload.

Yours sincerely

E. O. BALL

E.O.B*MB
OCT. 26TH

E. O. BALL
Salesman

ADDRESS ALL CORRESPONDENCE TO THE COMPANY, NOT TO INDIVIDUALS

An interesting piece of 1926 correspondence with a hint of Seeburg vs. Wurlitzer competition. (Courtesy of Donald MacDonald, Jr.)

STYLE "X"—"Expression"

Straight piano, reproducing expression, almost human in accomplishment.

MASTERFULLY exact. Designed for locations demanding a repro-ducing instrument—real artistic interpretation. Also constructed for home use when so desired.

Handsome in construction, finished in either oak, dull or bright mahog-any, or choice walnut, all double veneered.

Improved scale of seven and one-third octaves, over-strung copper bass, three unison throughout with full metal plate and bushed tuning pins.

Selected ivory keys.

Special tempo regulator with graded scale; tracker-bar adjuster; separate "on and off" control located in front of roll chamber; rewind control.

Uses specially arranged Style "XP" 4 to 6 selection reproducing roll. Also accommodates all standard 88-note rolls.

Height: 4 feet, 9½ inches; Width: 5 feet, 3 inches; Depth: 2 feet, 6½ inches. Weight, when boxed for shipment: 900 lbs.

Seeburg catalogue description of the Style X Expression piano. Few of these were sold, for proprietors of commercial locations preferred the more ornate A-roll instruments.

STYLE "Z"
SELECTIVE ROLL PIANO

THE newest Seeburg invention. Height, 4 ft. 10 in.; width, 5 ft. 3 in.; depth, 2 ft. 6 in. Plays a special cut 65-note electric rewind roll. The big feature of this marvelous instrument is that the person dropping the coin can select the particular number they wish to hear played. Pro-gram of music printed in plain view in special slot arrangement on piano, selection is made by simply turning indicator opposite name of piece desired.

Ornamental slot arrangement showing music program and full directions for selecting the number to be played.

Style Z may also be played same as other styles without using selector device.

Equipped with magazine slot registering 1 to 20 coins similar to other Seeburg styles.

For SEEBURG Style X, Xpression Pianos. These rolls will not play on any other Seeburg instru-ment excepting the Style X, also adapted for Apollo X

XP-420   SIX ROUNDS OF HITS
1. Under the Moon, Fox Trot.
2. Who-oo? You-oo! That's Who! Fox Trot.
3. After I've Called You Sweetheart, Waltz.
4. Roam On My Little Gypsy Sweetheart, Fox Trot.
5. Someday You'll Say "O. K." Fox Trot.
6. The Calinda, Fox Trot.

XP-421   PUSH 'EM ALONG
1. Vo-Do-Do-De-O Blues, Fox Trot.
2. Love and Kisses, Fox Trot.
3. Worryin' Waltz.
4. Baby Feet Go Pitter Patter, Fox Trot.
5. A Night In June, Fox Trot.
6. Highways Are Happy Ways, Fox Trot.

XP-422   FROM SOUP TO NUTS
1. Sweet Someone, Fox Trot.
2. Baby Your Mother, Fox Trot.
3. I've Lived All My Life Just For You, Waltz.
4. My Sweet Yvette, Fox Trot.
5. Barbara, Fox Trot.
6. She's Got "It," Fox Trot.

XP-394   "HITZ"
1. Thinking of You, Fox Trot.
2. How I Love You, Fox Trot.
3. Short an' Sweet, Fox Trot.
4. Fire! Fox Trot.
5. I'm Always Dreaming Sweet Dreams of You, Fox Trot.
6. Just One More Hour With You, Fox Trot.

XP-406   SWEET AND TENDER
1. Ain't She Sweet, Fox Trot.
2. Take Your Finger Out Of Your Mouth, Fox Trot.
3. I'll Take Care Of Your Cares, Waltz.
4. I Wonder How I Look When I'm Asleep, Fox Trot.
5. If I Didn't Know Your Husband, Fox Trot.
6. Following You Around, Fox Trot.

XP-411   HIGH FLYIN' TUNES
1. Where the Wild, Wild Flowers Grow, Fox Trot.
2. Sa-Lu-Ta, Fox Trot.
3. The Winding Trail, Waltz.
4. What Do I Care What Somebody Said, Fox Trot.
5. One Summer Night, Fox Trot.
6. I Can't Believe That You're In Love With Me, Fox Trot.

XP-413   "C'MON OVER, LISTEN"
1. One o'Clock Baby, Fox Trot.
2. Sweet Marie, Fox Trot.
3. I'm Looking For a Girl Named Mary, Waltz.
4. Ya Gonna Be Home To-Night? Fox Trot.
5. Rosy Cheeks, Fox Trot.
6. That's What I Think of You, Fox Trot.

Above: This page from a roll catalogue of the 1920s offers the latest selections cut for the Seeburg Style X piano.

Left: A mystery today is the Seeburg Style Z Selective Roll Piano. Apparently it used a modified type "A" coin piano roll with six selections (the program card on the front has spaces for six titles) and with some type of counting or registering perforations added to operate the selecting device. Apparently only a few of these were made, for no specimen of either an instrument or roll has been seen by the authors.

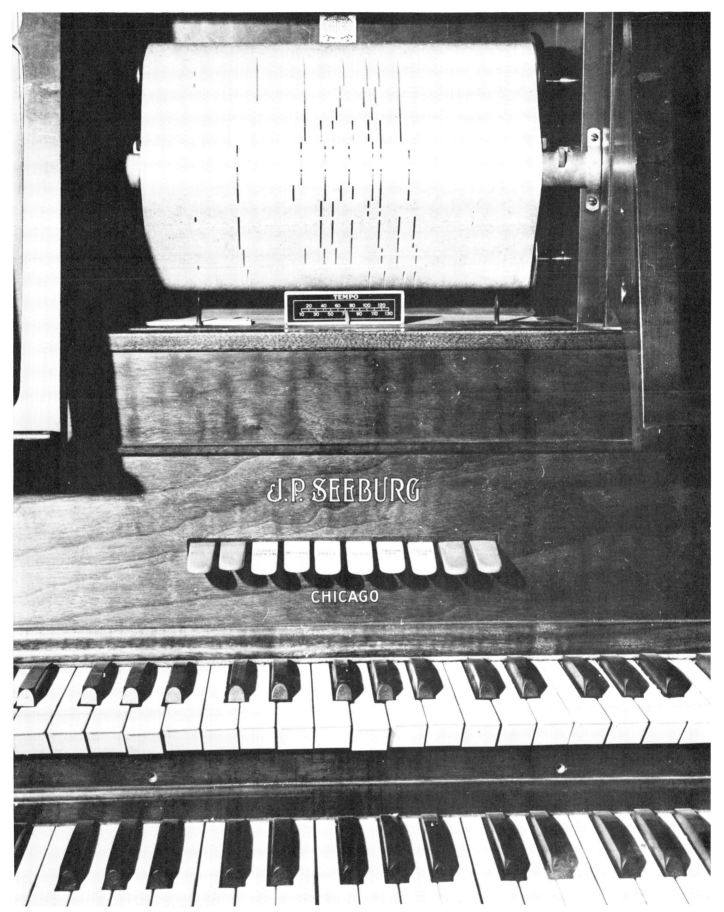

This Seeburg mortuary or residence organ uses several types of rolls, including special "HO" (for "Home Organ"?) rolls with long perforations for sustained pipe notes. (Instrument formerly owned by Larry Givens; now in the Vince Aveni Collection)

Weber's Maesto ⟨ *Neuheit* ⟩
⟨ *Nouveauté* ⟩

Konkurrenzloses Konzert=, Tanz= und Jazzband= Orchester

Orchestre de concert, danse et iazzband inégalable

Catalogue illustration, circa 1926, of the Weber Maesto orchestrion. "Beyond competition a concert, dance, and jazzband orchestra." The early (circa 1926) style had a richly mirrored center front panel as shown above. Later styles had pleated curtains in the center front. Just six examples of the Weber Maesto are known today.

GEBR. WEBER (WEBER BROTHERS)
Orchestrions

Founded in 1880, Gebr. Weber (Weber Brothers) produced in Waldkirch, in Germany's Black Forest, a number of different mechanical pianos, organs, and orchestrions. Early instruments were of the barrel type and used pinned wooden cylinders to actuate piano and pipe notes, percussion, and other effects. Around the turn of the century, Weber orchestrions and related instruments were made with key frames, a format similar to that used on band organs. Soon the key frame system was dropped, and a rewind-style roll format was adopted, with the rolls being read by pressure (rather than vacuum). This method was employed from the early 20th century until the end of the Weber business.

The Weber enterprise was known as the Waldkircher Orchestrionfabrik, or "Waldkirch Orchestrion Factory," which implies that only *orchestrions* were made. This seems to have been the case for the firm's 20th century output. All products were made with a piano and extra instruments; that is, no simple piano-only units were manufactured.

During the early 20th century a wide variety of interesting instruments left the Weber factory gates. Many of these were sold in America by Ernst Boecker, the New York City dealer who also handled Hupfeld and Imhof & Mukle products.

Weber was particularly proud of its violin-toned pipes, and instruments with this feature were highly acclaimed. In the early years, the Weber Violano and the Salon Piano with Violin were two styles, each made in a variety of case designs, which featured a piano with violin pipes. In the 'teens and 1920s the Weber Unika, a shorter (in height) keyboard-style piano with 28 violin pipes was very popular. Apparently hundreds were made. Several varieties of piano with xylophone were made at the time, culminating in the Grandezza, which was extensively marketed in the 1920s.

The Weber firm today has achieved a formidable reputation with collectors and historians, primarily because of the several extant Maesto orchestrions and their cousins, the Solea orchestrions. Harvey N. Roehl, in *Player Piano Treasury*, noted:

"There is little doubt that the Weber Maesto orchestrion is the most life-like of anything in its class of instrument ever perfected by man. This was, indeed, the aim of its German designers, and the fact that they succeeded in this effort can be attested by the many connoisseurs of automatic music machines who agree that there is simply nothing else that can equal it...

"The Weber Maesto is seldom found in private homes because of its size, and one should say seldom found, period—because of their extreme rarity today. This instrument is considered by many to be the outstanding example of the orchestrion builders of a bygone day, because it was built very late in the game, and every known device was incorporated to insure that it would resemble as closely as possible a human orchestra. To say that they succeeded well would be a gross understatement. Nothing can compare to the artistic renderings of the Maesto."

The Maesto traces its beginnings to the summer of 1913 when an event occurred that would indelibly imprint the name of Gebr. Weber on the roster of fame: young Gustav Bruder, born in 1890, joined the staff as a music composer and arranger. By the mid 1920s, Bruder's expertise and ability were recognized to the extent that he was invited to participate in the design of two new orchestrions, the Maesto and the redesigned Elite. Rather than directing Bruder's design toward the lowest production cost or the most efficient manufacturing methods, the green light was given to design instruments which would have incredible musical ability. "Make such instruments, and the market will develop by itself," it was reasoned.

In 1926 the first Maesto was ready. The instrumentation was impressive. Weber introduced the Maesto as an "unequalled concert orchestra, dance and jazz band. An incomparable electro-pneumatic artistic orchestrion comprising a piano of the first order (by Feurich), violin, violoncello, flute, clarinet, trumpet, saxophone, lotus flute, jazz trumpet, complete xylophone, and assorted percussion instruments, including bass drum, castanets, snare drum, tambourine, triangle, cymbal, and wood block."

A rich musical repertoire was made on rolls. An idea of their intricacy can be gained by Gustav Bruder's description, given in a letter to Art Reblitz, which noted: "In order to arrange and perfect a Maesto roll with four songs I spent an average of three weeks. When the notes were on paper, only half the work was done; then the entering of the complex register changes required an equal amount of time."

Several hundred different melodies in all were arranged for Maesto rolls. Classical numbers such as Bizet's *Pearl Fishers*, Rossini's immortal *William Tell Overture*, and Offenbach's lively *Orpheus in the Underworld* (with its lively "can-can" section) were made on single rolls with a playing time of 10 to 15 minutes. For use in restaurants and other places in the 1920s, the standard four-tune rolls filled the bill for musical entertainment. Typically, each of the four tunes at the time was a popular melody, although some have been forgotten since then.

Today, six specimens of the Maesto are known to exist: (1) Q. David Bowers Collection; (2) Dr. Robert Gilson Collection; (3) J.B. Nethercutt Collection, on display at San Sylmar; (4) Doyle Lane Collection, formerly in the Coade Collection; (5) Claes O. Friberg Collection, on display at the Mekanisk Musik Museum; and (6) Baud Freres Collection, l'Auberson, Switzerland.

Around the same time, Gustav Bruder designed a new version of the Elite orchestrion. Earlier, the Elite had been the largest orchestrion in the Weber line. In 1914 a group of large Elite instruments were shipped to Russia. Others were sold to various locations. Early in the 1920s a single specimen of a new-style Elite was made, then in 1927 and 1928 two more were built, the latter pieces incorporating many Bruder-designed innovations. In 1929 one of these was used to provide concerts on a weekly radio program in Germany. Alas, no specimens of the Elite have survived the ravages of time. Today we can only speculate what the redesigned Elite must have sounded like.

As noted earlier, Weber rolls of later years were used on a tracker bar which operates by air pressure rather than vacuum. The roll is pulled over the tracker bar by two rubber pinch rollers. A grooved brass roller rides heavily on the roll to keep it against the perforations in the tracker bar. As the following scales show, Weber layouts feature scrambled musical notes, perhaps a holdover from earlier days when barrel-operated instruments were made. This arrangement also helped to distribute the notes across the paper, which may have facilitated tracking (by reducing the paper's tendency to distort or stretch on one side or the other). In addition, Gustav Bruder and Eugene DeRoy noted that this arrangement, which is quite confusing when a music roll is viewed, helped prevent others from pirating the Bruder-Weber arrangements.

Weber made many different roll styles. Often these rolls could be used on more than one instrument type. For example, the Styria and Otero orchestrions used the same roll type, and the Maesto and Solea also share a common roll style.

WEBER ERATO ROLL
WEBER GRAZIELLA I ROLL
WEBER VENEZIA ROLL

1 Blank (or tremolo?)
2 Blank (or violin pipes on?)
3 Blank (or violin pipes off?)
4 D 2 (Bass)
5 F 43 (Melody, 3rd octave)
6 G 5 (Bass)
7 C# 40 (Melody, 3rd octave)
8 Piano accompaniment loud
9 A# 37 (Melody, 2nd octave)
10 Mandolin off
11 G 34 (Melody, 2nd octave)

12 G 10 (Piano accompaniment)
13 E 31 (Melody, 2nd octave)
14 A# 13 (Piano accompaniment)
15 C# 28 (Melody, 2nd octave)
16 C# 16 (Accompaniment)
17 A# 25 (Melody, 1st octave)
18 E 19 (Accompaniment)
19 G 22 (Melody, 1st octave)
20 D 17 (Accompaniment)
21 F 20 (Accompaniment)
22 B 14 (Piano accompaniment)
23 G# 23 (Melody, 1st octave)
24 G# 11 (Piano accompaniment)
25 B 26 (Melody, 1st octave)
26 F 8 (Piano accompaniment)
27 D 29 (Melody, 2nd octave)
28 Shutoff
29 F 32 (Melody, 2nd octave)
30 A 6 (Bass)
31 G# 35 (Melody, 2nd octave)
32 E 3 (Bass)
33 B 38 (Melody, 2nd octave)
34 Rewind
35 D 41 (Melody, 3rd octave)
36 Bass drum
37 Piano treble loud
38 Sustaining pedal
39 F# 21 (Melody, 1st octave)
40 D# 18 (Accompaniment)
41 A 24 (Melody, 1st octave)
42 C 15 (Accompaniment)
43 C 27 (Melody, 2nd octave)
44 A 12 (Piano accompaniment)
45 D# 30 (Melody, 2nd octave)
46 G# 9 (Piano accompaniment)
47 F# 33 (Melody, 3rd octave)
48 Blank
49 A 36 (Melody, 2nd octave)
50 B 7 (Bass)
51 C 39 (Melody, 3rd octave)
52 F 4 (Bass)
53 E 42 (Melody, 3rd octave)
54 C 1 (Bass)
55 Mandolin loud
56 Mandolin on
57 Piano and mandolin soft
58 Snare drum
59 Xylophone off
60 Xylophone on
61 Tympani
62 to 66, Blank

In the above listing, a notation such as "C 39" refers to the 39th piano note as found on the piano (not to hole 39), which, in this instance, is note C located in the 3rd octave of the melody section.

WEBER ERATO ROLL

(Variation)

Another Erato scale of 73 holes is the same as the foregoing so far as the musical notes. The other holes are as listed below. (All holes not listed are blank on this scale.)

2 Snare drum
9 Mandolin off
28 Shutoff
33 Rewind
35 Cymbal
46 Triangle
55 Mandolin on
58 Xylophone off
59 Xylophone on
60 Tympani

Weber Euterpe orchestrion, probably circa 1905. The large roll door indicates that this may have been a key-frame type of instrument. The late Gustav Bruder informed Q. David Bowers that Weber instruments from 1880 to about 1898 were of the barrel type, those during the seven-year period ending in 1905 were of the music book and key frame type, and those of 1905 and later were of the paper roll style, but undoubtedly there was some overlapping.

WEBER EUTERPE ROLL

1 Drums soft
2 Rewind
3 Blank?
4 F 6 (Piano note)
5 D# 28 (Pipe note)
6 G# 9 (Piano note)
7 C# 26 (Pipe note)
8 B 12 (Piano note)
9 B 24 (Pipe note)
10 D 15 (Piano note)
11 A 22 (Pipe note)
12 F 18 (Piano note)
13 G 20 (Pipe note)
14 G# 21 (Piano note)
15 F 18 (Pipe note)
16 B 24 (Piano note)
17 D# 16 (Pipe note)
18 D 27 (Piano note)
19 D 15 (Pipe note)
20 F 30 (Piano note)
21 Triangle
22 G# 33 (Piano note)
23 B 12 (Pipe note)
24 B 36 (Piano note)
25 A# 11 (Pipe note)
26 D 39 (Piano note)
27 Bass drum
28 F 42 (Piano note)
29 Piano on
30 F# 43 (Piano note)
31 Blank?
32 D# 40 (Piano note)
33 Cancel
34 C 37 (Piano note)
35 E 5 (Pipe note)
36 A 34 (Piano note)
37 D# 4 (Pipe note)
38 F# 31 (Piano note)
39 D 3 (Pipe note)
40 D# 28 (Piano note)
41 C# 2 (Pipe note)
42 C 25 (Piano note)
43 C 1 (Pipe note)
44 A 22 (Piano note)
45 Flute on
46 F# 19 (Piano note)
47 Gedeckt on
48 D# 16 (Piano note)
49 Violin pipes on
50 C 13 (Piano note)
51 F 6 (Pipe note)
52 A 10 (Piano note)
53 F# 7 (Pipe note)
54 F# 7 (Pipe note)
55 G 8 (Pipe note)
56 G 44 (Piano note)
57 G# 9 (Pipe note)
58 E 41 (Piano note)
59 A 10 (Pipe note)
60 C# 38 (Piano note)
61 Snare drum
62 AX 35 (Piano note)
63 C 13 (Pipe note)
64 G 32 (Piano note)
65 C# 14 (Pipe note)
66 E 29 (Piano note)
67 Shutoff
68 C# 26 (Piano note)
69 E 17 (Pipe note)
70 A# 23 (Piano note)
71 F# 19 (Pipe note)
72 A 20 (Piano note)
73 G# 21 (Piano note)
74 E 17 (Piano note)
75 A# 23 (Pipe note)
76 C# 14 (Piano note)
77 C 25 (Pipe note)

78 A# 11 (Piano note)
79 D 27 (Pipe note)
80 G 8 (Piano note)
81 E 29 (Pipe note)
82 D 3 (Piano note)
83 E 5 (Piano note)
84 D# 4 (Piano note)
85 C 1 (Piano note)
86 Blank?
87 Blank?
88 Blank?

The piano notes are numbered according to their position on the piano itself; 1 to 44 are notes C to G respectively, 2 (C#) is blank. The pipe notes are numbered in order from 1 (middle C) chromatically through 29 (high E). The function of hole 29, piano on, is unknown. If the piano treble has additional notes above G 44 (hole 56) coupled to the pipe note holes, it would be logical to turn the piano on and off in this solo range.

Violano
Salon=Piano mit Violinspiel
Piano=Violon artistique

WEBER VIOLANO ROLL
Approximately 17" wide; 5 holes per 2 cm.

1 Blank
2 Crescendo II
3 Shutoff
4 Decrescendo II
5 Decrescendo I
6 Crescendo I
7 Tremolo
8 Sustaining pedal
9 Piano soft?
10 Piano accompaniment pianissimo
11 Piano loud
12 Rewind
13 General cancel
14 ?
15 ?
16 to 29, violin pipe notes D to D#
30 to 57, Bass and accompaniment, C to D#
58 to 87, Melody E to A (76-87 high violin pipe notes A# to A)
88 to 93, Violin pipe notes, E to A
94 High violin pipes A# to A on
95 "Great octave on"
96 High piano notes A# to A on
97 C to F# on (or E to F# on)
98 G to B on
99 Coupler on
100 ?
101 ?
102 ?
103 Melody pianissimo

The Weber Violano, a piano with violin pipes, was a popular instrument during the years before 1920. After that time it was supplanted by the Unika, a violin-pipe piano of more compact construction.

The preceding scale information was taken from two incomplete scale sticks in the archives of Eugene DeRoy.

The violin playing notes, in order, are D to D# (16-29), E to A (88-93), and A# to A (76-87). The high violin and piano notes A# to A share the same holes in the tracker bar (76-87) and are controlled separately by hole 94 (high violin pipes on) and hole 96 (high piano notes on).

The tremolo and sustaining pedal holes are chain perforations. Some of the expression devices might be multiplexed. One of the scale sticks indicates that 11 is "hammer rail down," 10 is "hammer rail up," and a combination of 10+11 is "hammer rail mezzoforte," or half way up. The scale stick also indicates that hole 103, melody pianissimo, brings the hammer rail up, but it might also affect the vacuum level if the Violano is as sophisticated as some of the other Weber instruments. Crescendo I and Crescendo II may also be multiplexed.

The Weber Violano, aggressively advertised circa 1910 in the United States by Ernst Bocker (of New York), was highly esteemed for its musical qualities in its time. Today, only a few examples survive.

Unika
Elektrisches Piano mit Violine und Mandoline
Piano électrique avec violon et mandoline

WEBER UNIKA ROLL
27.1 cm. wide; 4 mm. per space on the tracker bar

1 Tremolo
2 Rewind
3 Mandolin off, bass octave coupler off
4 D 18
5 Violin pipes on
6 G 23 (11)
7 F 69
8 B 27 (15)
9 D 66
10 D 30
11 B 63
12 F 33
13 G# 60
14 G# 36 (24)
15 G 57
16 Swell open
17 D 54
18 Swell closed
19 B 51

20 Treble hammer rail down
21 G# 48
22 C 16
23 F 45
24 B 39
25 C# 41
26 D 42
27 E 44
28 F 21 (9)
29 G 47
30 A# 26 (14)
31 A# 50
32 C# 29 (17)
33 C# (53)
34 E 32
35 E 56
36 G 35
37 G 59
38 A# 38
39 A# 62
40 A 37
41 C# 65
42 G# 34 (22)
43 E 68
44 D# 31 (19)
45 G 71
46 C 28
47 C 40
48 A 25 (13)
49 D# 43
50 E 20
51 F# 46
52 Shutoff
53 A 49
54 Bass stack vacuum high (cancelled by 58), bass hammer rail down (cancelled by 65), sustaining pedal (chain perforation)
55 C 52
56 Piano treble on
57 D# 55
58 Bass stack vacuum low, treble hammer rail up, cancel violin pipes, cancel piano treble
59 F# 58
60 D# 67
61 A 61
62 F# 70
63 C 64
64 Mandolin on
65 Bass hammer rail up
66 Bass octave coupler on

Bass octave-coupled notes turned on and off by holes 66 and 3 are given in parentheses.

The Unika, a keyboard-style piano, features a piano, mandolin attachment (of the curtain type), and 28 violin-toned pipes. Included in the repertoire are many Gustav Bruder roll arrangements. Typically, the violin pipes will play solo and the piano will play accompaniment. Instruments of this type were especially popular in the 1920s, and large numbers were sold.

Weber=Otero

Grandezza

Elektrisches Piano mit Mandoline und nuancierendem Xylophon
Piano électrique avec mandoline et xylophone nuancé

WEBER GRANDEZZA ROLL

Weber Grandezza rolls are the same size as Otero, Styria, or Brabo rolls and have the same music note scale. Some original rolls (identifiable by having the Waldkircher Orchestrion-Fabrik Gebr. Weber name on the label) marked "Grandezza," when played on an Otero turn the pipes on when the xylophone should be turned on, but some other original Grandezza rolls play all functions on the Otero, including traps. Many of Eugene DeRoy's "Symphonia" rolls will play the Otero, Brabo, or Grandezza with all functions.

Brabo

Violinpiano mit Mandoline und Xylophon
Piano=Violon avec mandoline et xylophonie

Piano=Orchestrion Styria *modern*

Letzte Neuheit – Dernière nouveauté

WEBER OTERO ROLL
WEBER STYRIA ROLL
WEBER GRAZIELLA II ROLL
WEBER BRABO ROLL
32.4 cm. wide; 4 mm. per hole space

The scale for this type of roll is an expanded version of the Weber Unika roll (to which refer for note arrangement), with the following differences and additional holes:
3 Mandolin off
16 Bass drum
18 Triangle
56 Snare drum

58 Cancel pipes and piano treble; hammer rails up
65 Castanets
66 Cymbal
67 Piano treble on
68 Cancel xylophone
69 Flute on
70 Xylophone on
71 Blank
72 Tympani
73 Bass coupler on (blank in Otero)
74 Swell open
75 Blank
76 Swell closed
77 Bass coupler off (blank in Otero)
78 Drums soft
79 Piano bass vacuum low

The Otero has the same basic note scale as the Unika, but the keyboardless Otero piano has fewer notes than the full keyboard Unika piano. The first bass note in the Otero, C 1, is C 16 of the Unika keyboard. Thus, to figure the Otero note (or piano hammer) number, subtract 15 from each key number of the Unika tracker scale (to which refer). The Otero has no bass coupler.

The Styria and Brabo are keyboard style orchestrions, so their piano note numbers correspond to those of the Unika scale. The bass octave coupler is turned on by 73 and off by 74. If one of these instruments contains clarinet pipes, they are turned on by hole 71 and cancelled by 58.

Later rolls are seen with the "Otero-Styria" marking on the label. Some of these contain arrangements by Gustav Bruder (see introduction and general notes concerning Weber instruments).

WEBER MAESTO (and late Solea) ORCHESTRION ROLL

36 cm. wide; 4 mm. per space on the tracker bar

1 Blank
2 Rewind
3 Mandolin off; multiplex switch off
4 D 11
5 Violin pipes on
6 G 16 (4)
7 F 62
8 B 20 (8)
9 D 59
10 D 23
11 B 56
12 G 26
13 G# 53
14 G# 29 (17)
15 F 50
16 With switch off: bass drum and cymbal
   With switch on: blank
17 D 47
18 Triangle
19 B 44
20 Treble hammer rail down
21 G# 41
22 C 9
23 F 38
24 B 32
25 C# 34
26 D 35
27 E 37
28 F 14 (2)
29 G 40
30 A# 19 (7)
31 A# 43
32 C# 22 (10)
33 C# 46
34 E 25
35 E 49
36 G 28
37 G 52
38 A# 31
39 A# 55
40 A 30

41 C# 58
42 F# 27 (15)
43 E 61
44 D# 24 (12)
45 G 64
46 C 21
47 C 33 (middle C)
48 A 18 (6)
49 D# 36
50 E 13
51 F# 39
52 Shutoff
53 A 42
54 Bass stack vacuum high (cancelled by 58), bass hammer rail down (cancelled by 65), sustaining pedal (chain perforation)
55 C 45
56 Snare drum
57 D# 48
58 General cancel for trumpet, clarinet, flute, violin pipes, piano treble; hammer rails up
59 F# 51
60 D# 60
61 A 54
62 F# 63
63 C 57
64 Mandolin on
65 With switch off: castanets
   With switch on: wood block
66 Cymbal
67 Piano treble on
68 With switch off: xylophone off
   With switch on: xylophone off; main swell closed
69 Flute on
70 Xylophone on
71 With switch off: clarinet on
   With switch on: blank
72 With switch off: tympani, reiterating
   With switch on: blank
73 Clarinet swell shutters closed
74 Main swell shutters open
75 Clarinet swell accelerator (shutters open or close fast when used with hole 77 or 73)
76 With switch off: main swell closed
   With switch on: blank
77 Clarinet swell shutters open
78 Functions 16, 56, and 66 soft (chain perforation); 85 soft (lock, cancelled by 86)
79 Bass stack vacuum low (cancelled by 54)
80 With switch off: blank
   With switch on: clarinet on
81 With switch off: tremolo, medium speed
   With switch off and flute on: tremolo, fast
   With switch on: tremolo, slow
   With switch on and violin pipes on: tremolo, medium
82 Tambourine
83 Piano bass coupler on
84 Piano bass coupler off
85 Bass drum
86 Multiplex switch on, bass drum loud
87 Trumpet on
88 Blank

The preceding scale applies to all known Maesto orchestrions. Another tracker scale, probably for use on the early Solea orchestrion, indicates that hole 80 turns a saxophone rank on when the switch is off, and turns gedeckt pipes on when the switch is on.

The Maesto roll is an adaptation of the earlier Solea roll. The Solea, an orchestrion made from the early years of the 20th century onward, lacks some of the Maesto instrumentation but (at least in some models) has a rank of gedeckt pipes extending into the bass section. Early rolls marked "Solea" will not actuate the trumpet rank (found in the Maesto but not the Solea) and are not programmed to activate the multiplex switch functions.

Later style Solea orchestrions from the late 1920s were produced contemporaneously with the Maesto and feature redesigned mechanisms with faster-acting devices and with multiplexing. Two specimens of the late-style Solea are known to the authors: the one in the Lanick Collection and the one in Bellm's

Cars and Music of Yesterday Museum. One specimen of the early-style (with gedeckt pipes; without multiplexing) is known: that located for many years in the Cafe Fribourgoise in Bulle, Switzerland, where it was installed originally, circa 1908-1914.

Rolls from the late 1920s and early 1930s marked "Maesto" are largely the work of Gustav Bruder, whose talent is discussed in the introduction to this Weber section. The unique music of the Maesto has caused it to be the object of study by several scholars in the field, including Terry Hathaway and Dr. George Coade.

Rolls are of several characteristics. Most prevalent are "full orchestra" rolls which use singly and in concert the various orchestral components. Adding variety to the repertoire are "solo" rolls which typically feature a solo performance on one of the instruments, usually xylophone, violin pipes, or clarinet pipes, with the accompaniment of the piano.

The top of the Maesto contains a large set of swell shutters for expression effects. The Maesto orchestrions in the Q. David Bowers and Claes O. Friberg (Mekanisk Musik Museum) collections have ornate mirrors on the front. The examples in the Terry Hathaway, J.B. Nethercutt (San Sylmar), and Baud Freres collections also have swell shutters on the front, behind pleated cloth curtains. The specimen in the Doyle Lane Collection (formerly in the Coade Collection) has in addition sets of swell shutters at the sides, speaking into the roll storage area.

The clarinet pipes are housed in their own separate compartment within the main case. The clarinet rank has its own individual interior swell shutters which can open quickly or slowly and in full-open or intermediate positions. The expression of the clarinet is controlled separately from the main swell or crescendo shutters on the top of the case, giving the rank exceptional expression capabilities.

The repertoire on music rolls for the Maesto is quite varied and includes, in addition to classical melodies and overtures, such popular tunes as *Yes, Sir, That's My Baby, Charmaine, 12th Street Rag, Piccolo Pete, Singin' in the Rain, Bye, Bye Blackbird, Entry of the Gladiators, Cuckoo Waltz,* and others.

WEBER ELITE ORCHESTRION ROLL
43.2 cm. wide
(Late-style redesigned Elite)

1 Coupler or multiplex switch for holes 61 to 66?
2 to 22, Countermelody notes D to C, modified by couplers (holes 23-25)
23 Coupler III; transfers holes 16 to 22 to low notes G to C#
24 Coupler II; transfers holes 9 to 15 to high notes F# to C
25 Coupler I; transfers holes 2 to 8 to high notes B to F
26 Trumpet II
27 Flute II
28 Violin pipes II
29 Bells
30 Piccolo
31 Saxophone
32 Cancel holes 26 to 31
33 Triangle
33+40 Tambourine
33+42 Tambourine
34 Snare drum tap
34+40 Castanets
34+42 Wood block
35 Snare drum roll
36 Bass drum without cymbal
37 Cymbal
38 Tympani
39 Drums loud register on (affects holes 34 to 38)
   Sforzando for bass drum and cymbal (chain perforation)
40 Percussion multiplex switch (see holes 33 and 34)
41 Cancel for holes 39 and 40
42 Percussion "jazz" coupler (see holes 33 and 34)
43 Tremolo II
44 Tremolo I
45 Cancel for 43 and 44
46 Swell shutter fast operation
47 Swell shutter slow operation

48 Swell III
49 Swell II
50 Swell I
51 Main swell shutters? ("Ganzes Werk")
52 Cancel for swell shutters
53 Trumpet I
54 Clarinet
55 Flute I
56 Violin pipes I
57 Piano on (for partial note range)
58 "Hilfskoppel Trumpet and Clarinet" (?)
59 "Teiler" (divider or separator)
60 Cancel for holes 53 to 59.
61 Pedal/Cello
62 Melody pianissimo/Gedeckt II
63 Accompaniment pianissimo/Gedeckt I
64 Melody forte/accompaniment register
65 Accompaniment forte/Z bass
66 Cancel for holes 61 to 65
67 Trombone II
68 Trombone I
69 Gedeckt bass
70 Bass coupler II
71 Bass coupler I
72 Cancel for holes 67 to 71
73 to 140, Playing notes
73 to 133, Notes C to C
134 to 140, Multiplexed note scale D# to A
122 to 133, Continuation of multiplexed note scale A# to A
119 to 121, Continuation of multiplexed note scale A# to C
134 to 140, Continuation of multiplexed note scale C# to G

The treble end of the main note scale is multiplexed like the countermelody section so that the highest 15 notes of the main note scale and 29 additional solo notes are all available from the last 22 holes in the tracker bar. The multiplexing is possibly controlled by holes 58 and 59.

The preceding scale was formulated by Art Reblitz and is partially hypothetical, there being no extant Elite orchestrion available for examination. Information came from an original Elite tracker scale furnished to Q. David Bowers by the late Otto Weber, information furnished by the late Gustav Bruder, and the knowledge of the construction of other Weber orchestrions.

There were three variations of Elite orchestrions. The first and most popular was the regular style made in the early days, circa 1908-1914. A slightly redesigned Elite was made in the early 1920s, and then in the late 1920s two extensively redesigned Elite orchestrions were made. It is from the late 1920s style that the preceding information was taken.

Probably the redesigned Weber Elite orchestrion represented at one time the pinnacle of technological achievement and musical production in an orchestrion, if the somewhat smaller Weber Maesto, an instrument based upon the same principles, is any indication. Considering that only two Elite orchestrions were made with the preceding tracker scale, and considering that it took Gustav Bruder three weeks to arrange a single Maesto (and presumably would have taken him longer to arrange an Elite roll), it is probable that only a few late-style Elite rolls were ever produced. However, it is also probable that early-style Elite rolls would have been compatible with the new Elite as, for example, the Weber Maesto, a late-generation instrument, could also use early Solea rolls, although the full capabilities of the Maesto would not be utilized.

Gustav Bruder related that the Weber Elite had three or four separate interior expression chambers, each with its own set of swell shutters. The three holes 48-50 probably represented these. In addition, main swell shutters were on the top of the case.

Above: A Gebr. Weber letterhead used by Franz Breite, who represented Weber in the country of Austria. The Weber factory buildings are shown on the engraving. Some of these structures exist today. The large one in the foreground has been converted to apartments.

Right: Otto Weber is shown as a young man arranging rolls in the Weber factory. Shown is a composing drum and, above it, a rack for sheet music. In later years Otto Weber and Gustav Bruder designed the Weber Maesto orchestrion. (Courtesy of the late Otto Weber)

Below: A photograph of an old-style Weber Elite orchestrion, probably circa 1912-1917. For some reason, parts of the top crest have been lightened on the print. Perhaps it was intended to use the picture to redesign the top part. (Courtesy of the late Otto Weber)

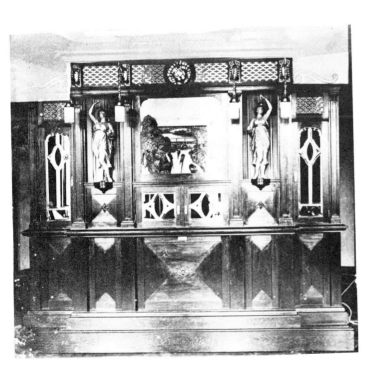

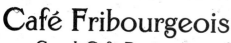

Café Fribourgeois
Grand Café-Restaurant

FÉLICIEN CHASSOT, Propr.

PROGRAMME

du célèbre

ORCHESTRION

Electro-Pneumatique Artistique

SOLÉA

le plus parfait des instruments automatiques
connus à ce jour.

RESTAURATION A TOUTE HEURE

Téléphone Nº 139

MUSIQUE CLASSIQUE ET POPULAIRE

Rouleaux

Nº		
1.	La Marseillaise	R. DE L'ISLE
	Le Régiment de Sambre et Meuse	PLANQUETTE
2.	La flotte aérienne, marche	TEIKE
	Clair de lune sur l'Alster	FÉTRAS
3.	Aisha, intermezzo indien	LINDSAY
	Les joyeux montagnards, tyrolienne	
4.	Amina, sérénade égyptienne	LINCKE
	Danse du Paraguay	
5.	Le chant du Moulin, Film enchanté	BREDSCHNEIDER
	Par monts et veaux, solo de xyloph.	KLING
6.	Danse des gnomes	MAYER
	Songe d'amour après le bal	CZIBULKA
7.	Le Trouvère, pot-pourri	VERDI
8.	Faust et Marguerite, pot-pourri	GOUNOD
9.	Le Rêve du Nègre, fantaisie	MIDDLETON
10.	Entrée triomphale, marche	PIEFKE
	Danse tyrolienne	LENGRIESSER
11.	Entrée des Gladiateurs, marche	FUCIK
	Les Jongleurs, galop	DIETRICH
12.	Sourire d'Avril, valse	DEPRET
13.	Le merle d'or, polka-marche	SCHWER
	Voilà notre tempérament, mazurka	ZIEHRER
	Heinerle n'a pas d'argent, schottisch	FALL
14.	Roses rouges, valse	LÉHAR
	Mon manchon est disparu, schottisch	LINCKE
	Eve moderne, valse	GILBERT
15.	Rulya, polka-marche	LINDENMANN
	Coppelia, mazurka	DELIBES
	Au rivage du Neckar, schottisch	
16.	Maxime, marche	LÉHAR
	Lambic, valse	FREMAUX
	Poupée, tu es ma lumière, marche	GILBERT
17.	Polonaise	OGINSKI
	Le Choclo, tango	VILLOLDO
	Amour joyeux, pas de deux	CHRISTINÉ
18.	Jeunes filles et nègres, pas de deux	SCOTT
19.	Etoile polaire, valse	WALDTEUFEL

☞ Pour chaque morceau, mettez 20 centimes dans l'un des appareils.

Rouleaux

Nº		
20.	Poète et Paysan, ouverture	FR. SUPPÉ
21.	Zigeunerbaron, fantaisie	JOH. STRAUSS
22.	Martha, ouverture	FLOTOW
23.	Mignon, ouverture	AMB. THOMAS
24.	Le Barbier de Séville, ouverture	ROSSINI
25.	La Cavalerie légère	
26.	Nibelung, marche	SONNTAG
	Oiseau du Paradis, valse	
	Barre fixe, galop	
27.	Sur les vagues, valse	ROSAS
	Les gaies, polka	
	C'est chez nous au sang, mazurka	
28.	Fantaisie pour violon	MULHING
	Les Huguenots, fantaisie	MEYERBEER
29.	L'Orange sans reproche, marche	
	Pigeon blanc, valse	
30.	Ballet, fantaisie pour violon	
	Non, je ne marche pas	
33.	Ouverture de « Joyeuses commères »	WINDSOR
34.	Zlata-Praha, Pot-pourri de chansons nationales bohémiennes	URBANK
35.	La Pie voleuse, ouverture	ROSSINI
36.	Ouverture de « Le Roi d'Yvetot »	ADAM
37.	Pot-pourri de « Chansons d'Etudiants »	KOHLMANN
	Rêve d'automne, valse	
38.	Chansons patriotiques, pot-pourri	
	Sous les Tilleuls, marche	KOLLO
39.	Kochanodschka, danse russe	KOLLO
	La lune luit, chanson russe	
40.	Aubade printanière	LACOMBE
	La Reine, Two-Step	SIEDE
41.	Fantaisie de « Onegin »	TCHARKOWSKY
	Sadosky, marche	
42.	Dorette, valse	HARIL
	A travers l'espace, marche d'aviateurs	SIEDE
43.	La Brabançonne, chant national belge	
	Les Cloches de Corneville, ouverture	PLANQUETTE
	Nuit tranquille, nuit sainte, chant de Noël	GRUBER
44.	Charme de la Danse, valse	
	Salut à la Patrie	
	Prière Néerlandaise	

☞ Pour chaque morceau, mettez 20 centimes dans l'un des appareils

---

Rouleaux

Nº		
45.	Mænne hak mir mal die Taille auf	
	Par le téléphone	
46.	Schumaritza, Hymne national bulgare	
	Marche des Chasseurs (Waidmannshiel)	
	La Nuit charmante	
48.	Les flots du Danube, valse	IVANOVICI
	Quand l'amour meurt, valse	
49.	Niki-Marche	
	Estudiantina, valse	WALDTEUFEL
	Carmen, marche	
50.	Hindoustan, fox-trott	
	Rêve de Valse, valse	O. STRAUSS
51.	Juxbaron, fox-trott	
	Verner Madel, valse	
52.	Salomé, fox-trott	
	Les Millions d'Arlequin, valse	DRIGO
	Halloh du Süsse Klingelfee, téléphonestep	
53.	Jes we have no bananas, one-step	SILVERᵍCOHN
	Quand Zézette zozotte, fox-trott	GAVEL
	La Violetera, shottisch espagñol	PADILLA
	Im hôtel zur grünen Wiese, fox-trott	BRINK
54.	Fernande, one-step	
	The Sheik, shimmy-fox	
	Affi,	
	Brigt eyes, fox-trott	
55.	Un peu, un tout petit peu	
	La Rose bleue, tango	
	Pasadena, fox-trott	
	Chili bom bom, marche	
56.	Und zum schluss, shimmy	
	Wenn ich dich, fox-trott	
	Eldgateln, fox-trott	
57.	Wilhelm Tell, ouverture	ROSSINI

☞ Pour chaque morceau, mettez 20 centimes dans l'un des appareils.

The Cafe Fribourgeois in Bulle, Switzerland ordered a Weber Solea from Gebr. Weber around 1912-1914. As of the 1970s the instrument was still in its original location. The program card reproduced here, probably printed in the 1920s, notes that tunes are 20 centimes each and that operation is via wall boxes (which were strategically scattered about the restaurant).

The instrument itself is described in rather exuberant terms as "The Celebrated Orchestrion, Electro-Pneumatic Artistic, SOLEA," and is noted as being the most perfect automatic instrument ever.

The orchestrion, of the old-style construction (lacking the sophisticated mechanisms designed by Gustav Bruder in the mid 1920s), uses Solea and Maesto rolls. As ceiling height was at a premium in the Cafe Fribourgeois, the Solea was constructed of a special design only about 8' high but quite wide. The front is decorated with mechanical "motion picture effect" scenes illuminated from behind.

Above: Left to right: Oscar Grymonprez, Mrs. Otto Weber (the only daughter of G.J. Gerard, Belgian distributor for Weber orchestrions), and Otto Weber. The photograph was taken in 1966 when the Webers visited the Grymonprez workshop in Ledeberg, near Gent (Ghent), Belgium. (Courtesy of Leonard Grymonprez)

Right: Carl Frei, Jr. stands in front of an early Weber Otero orchestrion in his band organ workshop in Waldkirch, Germany. This instrument was subsequently sold into the Jerry Doring Collection. (Photograph circa 1965, courtesy of Carl Frei, Jr.)

Below: Postcard view of the market square in Waldkirch, a few blocks from the Weber factory, as it appeared around 1970. Except for the automobiles the scene has not changed much from a half century earlier. High on the hill in the background is the ruin of an ancient castle, a famous Waldkirch landmark. Otto Weber related to one of the authors that he used to play around the castle when he was a child. Otto Weber died at the age of 74 in Heidelberg on April 26, 1973. (Postcard courtesy of Schoning & Co.)

This Weber Maesto was once used in the Transport Cafe in Ghent, Belgium. Built by Gebr. Weber, of Waldkirch, Germany, in 1926, it is one of about 60 to 70 such instruments originally made. Today, only six examples of the Maesto are known to exist: specimens in the collections of Q. David Bowers, Dr. Robert Gilson, J.B. Nethercutt, Doyle Lane, Claes O. Friberg, and Baud Freres. Many of the Maesto music rolls were the work of Gustav Bruder, one of the most gifted arrangers the world has ever known. The musical realism of a fine Gustav Bruder roll is unsurpassed.

Facing page: View of the Weber Maesto roll mechanism. When the roll is playing it is held against the tracker bar by a slotted brass roller similar to that used for certain types of keyless fairground organs. G.J. Gerard, mentioned on the plaques, was the Belgian outlet for Weber orchestrions.

Gérard G. J Bruxelles Rue des
GÉRARD G.I.
RUE DES FABRIQUES BRUXELLES

CAFÉ
TRANSPORT

134.73

Telefoon - ~~10834~~ - Téléphone

217, GASMETERLAAN, 217

- Boulevard du Gazomètre -

GENT - GAND

TARIEF - TARIF

Orchestrion " Webers Maesto „

||||||||||||||||| PICK-UP ||||||||||||||||||

Drukk. Wwe Fr. Petit. Spaarstr. 22. Gent

Built in 1926, Weber Maesto orchestrion 2543 (serial number) saw service in the Transport Cafe in Gent, Belgium. Located by Leonard Grymonprez in the early 1960s, it was subsequently sold to Q. David Bowers. The program reproduced on this and the following page was literally a musical menu given to patrons of the establishment. Operas, usually a full roll in length, cost one franc (equal to about 2c U.S. funds) to hear, operettas of shorter length cost 0.50 franc each, and "others" (popular tunes arranged four per roll) cost 0.25 franc. Payment was made by giving the required amount to a waiter who then operated the orchestrion.

Owners of large orchestrions were usually quite proud of their star attractions, with the result that many had programs specially printed for them. In America the Atlantic Garden (New York City) printed weekly announcements of the melodies to be played each day on its Welte orchestrion. In Europe, various owners of Hupfeld, Weber, and other large orchestrions did likewise.

The Weber Maesto program shown on the following page is a linguist's delight, or perhaps nightmare. Some tunes are listed in French, others in English, others in Flemish, and still others in German!

PROGRAMMA — PROGRAMME

1. Poète et Paysan.
2. La Bohême.
3. La Tosca.
4. La Mascotte.
5. Orphée aux Enfers.
6. Samson et Dalila.
7. Czardas Vorstin.
8. Aïda.
9. Guillaume Tell.
10. Martha.
11. Manon
12. Carmen.
13. Paillasse.
14. Madame Butterfly.
15. Cloches de Corneville.
16. La Traviata
17. Rigoletto.
18. Sambre et Meuse.
    Das Farmenmädchen.
19. Le Barbier de Séville.
    Rêve d'amour après le Bal.
20. Légère Cavallerie.
    Air varié.
21. Fantaisie Faust et Marguerite.
    Cavaleria Rusticana.
22. Mignon.
    Sérénade de Toscelli.
23. Entrée des Gladiateurs.
    Per Tandem.
24. Fantaisie de Bériot.
    Toreador et Andalouse.
25. Si j'étais Roi.
    Ständchen.
26. Die Bosniaken kommen.
    Hollandsch Wijfje
27. Le Trouvère (fantaisie)
    Ziegeuner Spiele
28. Carmen (marche)
    La Veuve Joyeuse.
29. Zampa (ouverture)
    Danse Autrichienne
30. Vaillance
    Les Dragons de Villars
31. Marche Loraine
    Polenbloed
32. Valse du Comte de Luxembourg
    Bleu Adria.

33. Sneidige Truppe - De Roos van Stamboel
34. Yes we have no bananas
    Quand Zézette zozotte
    La Violettera
    Im hôtel zum grünen Wieze
35. One Smile — Swane Smiles
    Yearning — Tango-Tango Maid
36. Elle n'est pas si mal que ca
    l'Eventail — C'est Paris — Les Bijoux.
37. Yes Sir that's my Baby — Loves Lottery.
    All alone — Bouquet
38. I wonder where my Baby is to night
    Araby - Love is just a gamble - Valencia
39. I want to be happy - Don 't wake me up.
    Let me linger longer in your arms.
    Toy drom major
40. I love my Baby — Haremsnacht
    One stolen kiss. — Show me to wary
41. Bye-Bye-Baby — Indian
    Rio Night — Tea for two
42. Colorado — Always
    Rosario — Li-Rah
43. Angora — Triglav
    Kom mit nach Vorasdin
44. Bye bye Blackbird
    High, high, high up in de hills
    So blue — Was macht der Maier
45 Charmaine
    Silver threads amoung the gold
    C'est vous — Hallelujah
46 Hören Sie zu : (Potpourri)
47. La Barcarolle
48. Trink Brüderlein trink - A blue serenade
    Leila — Constantinople
49. Sur un marché persan.
50. Les Pêcheurs de Perles
51. Petite aimée du Rhin
    Quant les lilas blancs fleurissent.
    Annekin, Annekin.
    That's my weakness now
52 Je moest je schamen Josefien
    Sleepy town.
    Just like a melody out the sky
    Piedad.

PRIJZEN — PRIX

Ouverture-Opéra 1 fr. — Opérettes 0.50 fr.

Andere - Autres 0.25 fr.

Elite

DIMENSIONS. — Hauteur : 3 m. 45.
Largeur : 5 m. 00.
Profondeur : 1 m. 35.

PRIX :　　　　　Francs.

RÉFÉRENCES :

Above: Original catalogue illustration of the late-style Weber Elite orchestrion of the 1928 era. "This most beautiful orchestrion plays grand concert symphony music and replaces an orchestra of 50 musicians. It is ideal for cafes, restaurants, cinemas, and dance halls. The cabinet is finished in white and or mirrored glass panels. The repertoire is most wonderful."

Left: Snapshot of a packing crate containing the last Weber Elite orchestrion made, being loaded for shipment to Amsterdam. (Courtesy of the late Otto Weber)

Below: A news article dated August 25, 1929 notes that the Freiburg radio station broadcast a program featuring a classical concert by the Weber Elite orchestrion.

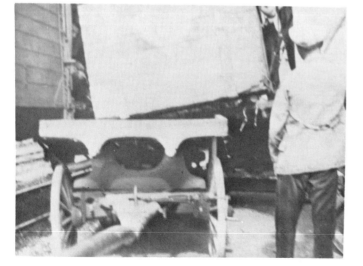

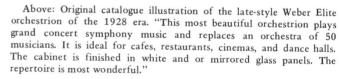

— **Orchestrionmusik im Rundfunk.** Die bekannte Fa. Gebr. Weber, Orchestrionfabrik in Waldkirch, übersandte uns einen Zeitungsbericht, dem wir entnehmen, daß der Freiburger Sender Anfang Mai ein meist klassischesKonzertprogramm auf dem „Weber Elite Orchestrion" aus dem Musiksaal der Fabrik seinen Hörern vermittelte.

Weber-Elite.

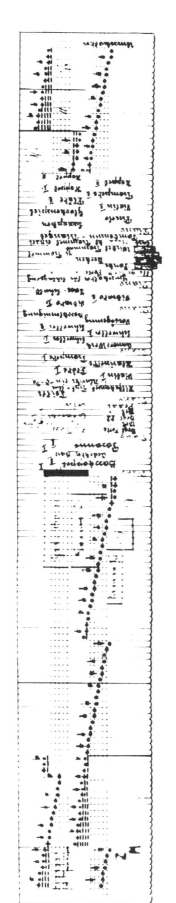

Original scale stick and notations, slightly reduced in size to permit reproduction here, for the late-style redesigned Weber Elite orchestrion of the 1920s. The scale is printed in an inverted position as it appeared originally on the sheet. Although no extant specimens of the Elite survive to prove the contention, many believe that the Weber Elite, featuring musical arrangements by Gustav Bruder, was probably the most musically sophisticated orchestrion ever built. (Courtesy of the late Otto Weber)

Artist's representation of two of the salesrooms (see also bottom illustration) of G.J. Gerard, Brussels, Belgium distributor for Weber, Philipps, and other automatic musical instruments. Otto Weber, a principal of Gebr. Weber, married a Gerard daughter, thus providing a strong bond between Weber and Gerard, which was Weber's largest-volume distributor. On a platform at the back of the room are, left to right, a Violano, Unika, another Violano, and a Brabo. To the right are several Grandezza and Unika models.

Another Gerard showroom, this one of non-Weber instruments, on the firm's premises at Rue des Fabriques 1a, Brussels, Belgium. The artist's drawings were probably made from photographs or are based upon heavily retouched photographs, for why else would one of the most prominent features be a steam radiator?

M. WELTE & SONS
Coin Pianos and
Orchestrions

The firm of M. Welte & Sons traces its origin to the mid 19th century when Michael Welte, a maker of flute-playing clocks, exhibited a mammoth orchestrion in Karlsruhe, Germany, in 1849. The acclaim for this impressive instrument was so great that additional orders and commissions were received. Within the space of 15 years the Welte enterprise grew to include a branch in New York City.

During the later decades of the 19th century Welte became famous for large barrel-operated orchestrions, many of which found homes in the mansions of the wealthy, in palaces (the Sultan of Turkey ordered a half dozen!), and other locations. Expensive in their day, these orchestrions were apt to cost from about $1000 to $5000 or more.

Around 1890 Welte shifted its emphasis to orchestrions with paper roll systems. Like the earlier models, the typical paper roll orchestrion of the 1890-1910 period contained many pipes plus percussion effects. These instruments, without pianos, often resembled large pipe organs, with rows of gleaming pipes visible through clear glass panels on the front.

Public places were users of Welte orchestrions as well. Robison Park in Indiana had a large model as did the Territorial House in Washington, D.C. The Atlantic Garden in New York City widely advertised its Welte orchestrion, a monster instrument which earlier won a prize at the 1893 World's Columbian Exposition in Chicago.

In the first decade of the 20th century emphasis shifted again, this time to piano-style orchestrions. Prominent were the Brisgovia series (Brisgovia being the ancient name for the section of Germany in which Freiburg, site of the main factory at the time, was located) which contained a piano, one or more ranks of pipes, and percussion effects. It is estimated that several hundred of these were sold in America, mainly circa 1908-1914. At the same time, certain models of the earlier configuration (without piano) were popular in skating rinks, dance halls, amusement parks, and other locales requiring a great volume of sound. Filling this bill were such styles as the Wotan Brass Band Orchestrion, the Wallhall, and the Donar.

Shortly after the turn of the 20th century, Welte, in combination with Hugo Popper (of Popper & Co.), introduced the world's first reproducing piano, the Welte-Mignon. This created a sensation, and after a few years the Welte sales emphasis was concentrated on instruments of this type. The Friburgia, an orchestrion with extra expression on the piano, was made in limited quantities circa 1912-1915. Certain mechanisms borrowed from the Welte-Mignon were employed.

By the 'teens Welte had a factory in Poughkeepsie, New York, and agents in most leading world cities. Welte Philharmonic Organs, made in a wide variety of sizes, were popular in churches, assembly halls, and private residences. The success of these organs marked the end of large orchestrion production.

Today several dozen Welte orchestrions, mainly of the roll-operated type without piano, and dating from about 1890 to 1910, survive. Most of these are of the so-called Cottage Orchestrion type, styles O through 3, although a few of the larger Concert Orchestrions exist as well.

WELTE 75-NOTE ORCHESTRION ROLL
(ORCHESTRION "F" SCALE)
12 57/64" wide; 6 holes per inch

1 Trumpet off
2 Triangle
3 Trumpet on
4 F
5 G#
6 G#
7 F#
8 A#
9 E
10 C
11 D
12 D
13 C
14 Trombone off
15 A#
16 Trombone on
17 G#
18 Gedeckt off
19 F#
20 Gedeckt on
21 E
22 Waldflute/gedeckt on(?)
23 D
24 Rewind
25 C
26 Tympani
27 A#
28 A#
29 G#
30 Snare drum
31 F#
32 G#
33 E
34 F#
35 D
36 E
37 Middle C
38 Crescendo loud
39 C#
40 Crescendo soft
41 D#
42 F
43 F
44 G
45 G
46 A
47 A
48 B
49 B
50 Tympani
51 C#
52 Clarinet off
53 D#
54 Clarinet on
55 F
56 Octave off
57 G
58 Octave on
59 A
60 Zinn (metal pipes) on / w. flute(?)
61 B
62 Zinn off
63 C#
64 D#
65 D#
66 C#
67 F

The music room in the Wade mansion, Cleveland, Ohio, around the turn of the 20th century. Against the back wall is a large roll-operated Welte orchestrion. To the left is shown an external view of the home.

Welte orchestrions were favorites of members of the Social Register. One of the Vanderbilts had a Welte orchestrion in his New York City home, another in his villa at the seaside in Newport, Rhode Island, and a third on board his yacht! P.T. Barnum, America's fabulous showman, listened to Welte music as did Adolph Sutro, Adelina Patti, and other personalities of the late 19th and early 20th centuries.

(Photographs courtesy of the Western Reserve Historical Society, Cleveland)

68 B
69 G
70 A
71 A
72 G
73 Bass drum
74 Bass drum
75 Shutoff

The following hole sequence plays the musical scale in ascending order: 4, 72, 6, 70, 8, 68, 10, 66, 12, 64, 36, 42, 34, 44, 32, 46, 28, 48, 37, 39, 35, 41, 33, 43, 31, 45, 29, 47, 27, 49, 25, 51, 23, 53, 21, 55, 19, 57, 17, 59, 15, 61, 13, 63, 11, 65, 9, 67, 7, 69, 5, 71.

Instruments examined often show slight differences from the preceding scale, not only in the registers but in the number of playing notes. Following are some of the actual tracker scales on instruments extant today:

WELTE STYLE 1 COTTAGE ORCHESTRION ROLL
(Variation of the Orchestrion F scale)

1, 3-6, 8, 14, 16, 18, 20, 22, 24, 26, 50, All blank
52 Trumpet off
54 Trumpet on
56 and 58, Blank
60 Zinn on
62 Zinn off
64, 66, 68, 71, 73, 74, All blank
Note: Rolls are rewound by hand cranking or by manual control.

WELTE STYLE 2 COTTAGE ORCHESTRION ROLL
(Variation of the Orchestrion F scale)
Circa 1880 cylinder-operated orchestrion converted to roll operation in 1897; attribution to Style 2 is tentative.

5, 6, 22, 24 Blank
60 Zinn on
62 Zinn off
71 Blank

WELTE STYLE 3 COTTAGE ORCHESTRION ROLL
(Variation of the Orchestrion F scale)

1, 3-6, 8, 18, 20 Blank
22 Viennese flute on
24 Viennese flute off
64, 66, 68, 71 Blank
73 Bass drum and cymbal
74 Blank

UNIDENTIFIED WELTE ORCHESTRION ROLL
(Variation of the Orchestrion F scale)

1 Shutoff
18 Trumpet off
20, 22, 24 Blank
52 Gedeckt off
54 Gedeckt on
74 Rewind
75 Bass drum

WELTE 100-HOLE ORCHESTRION ROLL
12 7/8" wide; 8 holes per inch

1 Blank
2 Sforzando off
3 Swell closed
4 Swell open
5 Sforzando on
6 Xylophone off
7 Xylophone on
8 Mandolin off
9 Mandolin on
10 Piano off
11 Piano on
12 Trumpet off
13 Trumpet on
14 Octave (piccolo) off
15 Octave (piccolo) on
16 Oboe (16' tonal length) off
17 Oboe on
18 Bassoon off
19 Bassoon on
20 Violin pipes A to A off
21 Violin pipes A to A on
22 Flute (or principal) off
23 Flute on
24 Violin pipes B to D off* (see footnote)
25 Violin pipes B to D on*
26 Viola da gamba pipes off
27 Viola da gamba pipes on
28 to 80, Note scale F to A; F#, hole 29, is blank
81 Bass bourdon off
82 Bass bourdon on
83 Soft bass drum
84 Loud bass drum
85 Tympani
86 Tympani
87 Snare drum
88 Triangle
89 Tremolo (on?)
90 Tremolo (off?)
91 Rewind
92 Shutoff
93 Pedal on
94 Pedal off
95 Sforzando (full organ) on
96 Sforzando (full organ) off
97 Crescendo on
98 Crescendo off
99 Blank
100 Blank

Although this "universal scale" Welte 100-hole orchestrion roll is ostensibly used for many different Welte orchestrion styles, including Concert Orchestrions nos. 5 to 10, Brisgovia IV to VII, Wallhall, Wotan, Philharmonic Organ I and II, and others, in actuality Welte manufactured special rolls using only those holes which would be appropriate to the registers and voicing of each model. Thus, while a roll made for a Wotan Brass Band Orchestrion will play on a much smaller Brisgovia orchestrion, the musical and expression results are not as satisfactory as if the correct roll is used on each instrument.

*Footnote: This "B" may be German for A#, with holes 24 and 25 controlling the upper part of the rank controlled by 20 and 21.

WELTE DIVINA COIN PIANO ROLL
12 7/8" wide; spaced 8 holes per inch

1 Bass mezzoforte off
2 Bass mezzoforte on
3 Bass crescendo off
4 Bass crescendo on
5 Bass sforzando off
6 Bass sforzando on
7 Hammer rail down
8 Hammer rail up
9 Motor resistance valve off (slower)
10 Motor resistance valve on (faster)
11 to 90, 80 playing notes C to G
91 Sustaining pedal on
92 Shutoff
93 Rewind
94 Sustaining pedal off
95 Treble sforzando on
96 Treble sforzando off
97 Treble crescendo on
98 Treble crescendo off
99 Treble mezzoforte on
100 Treble mezzoforte off

The Divina was essentially a reproducing piano equipped with a coin slot for commercial use. The preceding tracker scale is identical to the "red Welte" reproducing piano scale (to which refer), except that the functions for "sustaining pedal on" and "rewind" are reversed.

If the owner of a restaurant or other commercial extablishment (the usual customer for an instrument like the Divina) tried to play a "red Welte" reproducing piano roll on the Divina, the roll would rewind with the first "sustaining pedal on" perforation, probably within the first foot or so of the roll, thereby discouraging this practice and encouraging him to purchase more Divina rolls.

Sales of the Divina must have been very limited, for mention of this model appears only in a few scattered Welte catalogues. In practice, the few commercial locations that wanted Welte reproducing piano music used a regular Welte reproducing instrument, but with the addition of a coin slot or box. For example, near Welte's main factory town of Freiburg, the Guesthouse of the Sun ("Gasthaus Sonne") installed in 1910 a Welte Wotan Brass Band Orchestrion and, in the same room, a cabinet-style keyboardless Welte reproducing piano. On the wall of the ballroom in which the instruments were located were two separate wallboxes, one marked "Orchestrion" and the other marked "Piano." Thus, patrons had their choice of either.

WELTE FRIBURGIA ORCHESTRION ROLL
12 7/8" wide; spaced 8 holes per inch

1 Bass mezzoforte off
2 Bass mezzoforte on
3 Bass crescendo off
4 Bass crescendo on
5 Bass sforzando off
6 Bass sforzando on
7 Xylophone off
8 Xylophone on
9 Motor resistance valve off (slower)
10 Motor resistance valve on (faster)
11 Mandolin off
12 Mandolin on
13 Cymbal
14 Bass drum
15 Triangle
16 Tympani
17 Snare drum
18 Blank
19 Blank
20 to 90, 71 playing notes, A to G
91 Rewind
92 Shutoff
93 Sustaining pedal on
94 Sustaining pedal off
95 Treble sforzando on
96 Treble sforzando off
97 Treble crescendo on
98 Treble crescendo off
99 Treble mezzoforte on
100 Treble mezzoforte off

All functions except holes 7, 8, and 11-19 are the same as those on the "red Welte" reproducing piano roll. By deleting the soft pedal and the lowest 9 playing notes and adding orchestrion functions to these holes, Welte obtained orchestrion rolls with human expression.

Sales of the Friburgia (named after Freiburg, Germany, the site of the Welte factory) were modest and took place mainly in the half dozen years just before World War I. A number of these were sold in America, particularly in Upstate New York, where they may have been at least partially assembled by Welte's Poughkeepsie (N.Y.) factory.

No. 1
Cottage - Orchestrion

with Snare drum and Triangle.

Height 8 ft. 2 inches. — Width 4 ft. 10 inches. — Depth 2 ft. 10 inches.

Price, including 12 music rolls . . . $ **1200.**—
Extra music rolls, each . . . . . $ **10.**—

The owners of Welte orchestrions provided the firm with many testimonials, as the commentary from T.F. Roessle, proprietor of the Arlington House, illustrates. In the years from about 1890 to 1905, Welte had the American market for large orchestrions nearly all to itself. After 1905, the Wurlitzer PianOrchestras. Imhof & Mukle orchestrions, and other instruments which featured pianos in addition to pipes (most Welte instruments lacked pianos) captured most of the sales, and Welte orchestrions, with the exception of some few Brisgovia and related models, passed from the scene.

No. 3
Cottage-Orchestrion

With kettle drum effect, Snare and Bass-Drum, Triangle and Cymbal.

Height 8 ft. 11 inches. — Width 6 ft. —
Depth 3 ft. 4 inches.
Price including 12 music rolls . . . **$ 1800.—**
Extra music rolls, each . . . . . . **$ 10.—**

The No. 3 Cottage Orchestrion, shown here in a 1907 advertisement, was one of the most popular Welte models. In an era before roll-operated pipe organs were popular, such orchestrions were ornaments in the homes of the wealthy. Ballrooms, music rooms, and salons in several hundred private homes featured Welte instruments.

This Welte Style 4 Concert Orchestrion was originally sold by the Eilers Music Company of San Francisco.

No. 6
Concert-
Orchestrion

Contains all the striking devices.

Height 11 ft. — Width 7 ft. 9 inches. —
Depth 4 ft. 3 inches.
Price, including 12 music rolls . . . $ 3500.
Extra music rolls, each . . . . . . $ 10.

The No. 6 Concert Orchestrion must have been a limited production model, for the authors know of no examples which have survived to the present time. While Welte catalogues featured standard models, usually numbered from 0 through 10, in practice the case designs varied widely within the same model designation.

OPENING

Of the Summer Amusement Season,

Swift's
Park

Engagement extraordinary for one week only
Commencing

TO-DAY.

2-PERFORMANCES DAILY-2

AFTERNOON AND EVENING

THE WORLD'S FAMOUS

ZORELLA FAMILY of AERIALISTS

3 -BEAUTIFUL GIRLS—3

In their mid air flights. Apparatus illuminated
at night by electric lights. Don't miss the Big $10,000

ORCHESTRION.

Operated by electricity and playing all of the popular and classical music. None other like it in the
country.

Positively no charge for these attractions.

ADMISSION, FREE TO ALL.

Enjoy a cool ride on the river in the Steamer

CLEMENTINA.

2 Improved Naphtha Launches.
100 Row Boats.
The Italian Orchestra.
400 Acres of Beautiful Picnic Grounds with Rus-
tic Seats, Swings, Summer Houses, etc.
Just the place to take your family for a day's
outing.

The June 14, 1896 newspaper advertisement shown above heralded the opening of Swift's Park near Fort Wayne, Indiana. On June 29th of the same year the name of the attraction was changed to Robison Park, by which designation it was known until its closing in 1919. Owned by the Fort Wayne Consolidated Railway Company, a trolley-car line, the park was located seven miles north of the city at the end of a scenic route along the St. Joseph River. One dollar was the round trip fare. During the early 20th century "trolley parks" were often located on the outskirts of major cities and provided additional revenue for the streetcar lines which owned and operated them.

Robison Park's attractions included a large Welte orchestrion (shown in the old photograph above right) which was advertised: "Don't miss the Big $10,000 ORCHESTRION. Operated by electricity and playing all of the popular and classical music. None other like it in the country." A perusal of Welte catalogues of the period indicate that the price of the orchestrion was an exaggeration. (Information from "The Robison Park Photo Album," by Herb Harnish, published 1966 by the Allen County - Fort Wayne Historical Society)

The front of this Welte Wotan orchestrion shows Siegfried and Brunhilde, of opera fame, with a castle in the background. The scene, painted in oil, is illuminated from behind. (J.B. Nethercutt Collection)

William Kramer's Sons' Atlantic Garden, Bowery, N. Y. City
Largest Orchestrion ever built, taking the grand prize at the Chicago World's Fair

The Atlantic Garden, located in lower New York City, was one of the most famous beer halls of its time. From the Civil War era until it burned down in 1907, the Atlantic Garden featured Welte orchestrion music. The instrument pictured here is roll-operated and probably represents one of the largest styles ever built by Welte, if not THE largest (as the caption notes). Apparently the identical instrument was exhibited at the World's Columbian Exposition (Chicago, 1893), but the authors have not located a photograph of it in that earlier location. From the 1860s until the installation of the orchestrion shown above, the Atlantic Garden had another huge Welte, a cylinder-operated instrument the fate of which is unknown.

Grand Hotel, Trinidad, Colo.

Orchestrion in the Castle of Adelina Patti

Above: Welte Brisgovia B orchestrion shown in its original location in the Grand Hotel, Trinidad, Colorado, around 1910. The Brisgovia name was derived from the ancient designation for Breisgau, the section of Germany where the Welte factory was located. To the left in the same picture can be seen Mills Dewey and Cricket slot machines. To the right of the Brisgovia is a roll cabinet, two more slot machines, a Quartoscope peep show machine, and a Mills Owl slot machine. Colorado, in the heart of the "wild west," was the home of many orchestrions. They were a familiar part of the entertainment scene, especially in mining towns.

Left: A huge Welte orchestrion in Craig-y-nos Castle in Wales, the home of famous opera star Adelina Patti. "I have much pleasure in saying how greatly I appreciate the marvelous orchestrion you made for me, which has been the admiration of all the royal personages and celebrities who have listened to this perfection of mechanism and melody under my roof," she wrote to Welte.

A ROCKY MOUNTAIN ORCHESTRION. The following article appeared in the October 1916 issue of "Denver Field and Farm." It tells of what was probably a Welte or similar orchestrion. (Courtesy of Sanford A. Linscome)

FRONTIER SKETCHES: When Music, the heavenly maid, was young we did not hear much of her in Denver, and any old thing that could strike the high C in the treble clef was quite sufficient in its simple way to soothe the savage breast and to put the bawling babe to rest.

There was no brass band within a thousand miles and something had to be done to mix the muses and to enliven the tedium of our social order before going to sleep on ourselves. In the course of events a Moses appeared to lead the beknighted town folk out of the wilderness of their despair.

This noble philanthropist of enduring memories was Count Kohlenbach who had in 1873 succeeded Ed and John Chase at the Cricket on Blake Street. He more than made good by sending ten thousand dollars over to Germany for an orchestrion, the like of which had never been seen or heard in America.

Henry F. Fuerstein was the philharmonic mechanician who worked overtime for a week to put the musical wonder on its feet and pump the breath of attenuated life into its pulmonary compartment. Then the technical prodigy was ready for the grand music festival at the Cricket. Not only did the town turn out, but the miners came in from the hills until everything was full. No one had ever supposed there were so many Dutch [German] patriots on earth, and it was a marvel how the beer held out throughout the livelong night.

The great instrument looked more like a pipe organ than anything else, but it was something more for it had drums, a full set of tympanies, all kinds of horns and reeds, and a staff of tinkling accompaniments that sounded like an inspired xylophone trying to keep up with the swinettes and the bassoons.

When the crowd had assembled and was waiting in feverish expectancy, the count's son turned her loose and the first throw out of the box was "The Watch on the Rhine," followed by the "Rose Waltz," the "Lieberlungen," down through a long program so dear to the Teutonic heart. It was like a song that touched the heart accompanied by the breath of Bavaria or the classic etude of Leipzig to sit there and hear that grand contrivance playing everything from "Johnny Schmoker" to Beethoven's "Moonlight Sonata" or Schumann's "Traumerei."

It is a long leap from "Schubert's Serenade" to the Swiss yodel "Hi Le Hi Lo," but it was all there, and as the melodious night wore on and men began hugging strangers they had to get a fresh crew of shifters to change the cylinders and keep the concert going, for the guests could not get enough of such a good thing.

After three years of constant going, the Old Kohlenbacher, as the boys had come to call it, was taken up to Abe Corson's place at Black Hawk, and later it was removed to Seth G. Ernest's establishment in Georgetown, where the symphonic wonder awoke the echoes and made more music than Alexander's Ragtime Band. [Black Hawk and Georgetown are located immediately to the west of Denver, and during the late 19th century were important silver mining towns.]

Early in 1879 it returned to Denver and let out its dulcet strains from Mose's Home on Blake Street where with some new rolls it rendered the harmonies of "O Tannenbaum," "Silent Night," Handel's "Largo," and other melodies.

Then Herman Wortman got the orchestrion for the Concordia, and eventually Bill Gates fell heir to it for his Metropolitan Hall near the bridge on Blake Street, after which it reposed calmly for a time in cold storage and was again shipped off to the mining camps in the mountains. One memorable night in Aspen the clatter of the street was overshadowed by the sudden outburst of "Old Heidelburg," which rang out tumultuously from John Culter's thirst parlor. The rushing crowd soon learned that the automatic orchestra with its tinkling cymbals, sounding brass, squeally piccoloes, and resonant oboes had come to camp, and there was nothing more doing elsewhere that night.

The next stand was Joe Piquard's Tremont Saloon in Telluride in 1885 when the frolicking camp was at the height of its glory. Folks who had never heard the charming notes of the instrument were carried off their feet by the euphonies of it all.

The crescendoes of the merry machine however had passed, and the lilt of its passive allegro was waning, for it had become asthmatic in its tones, a wheezy phthisics attacked its bellows, and its joints became so

rickety rheumatic that it was finally laid away like the harp of a thousand strings in the cloister of hallowed time where all good orchestrions go when they run down . . .

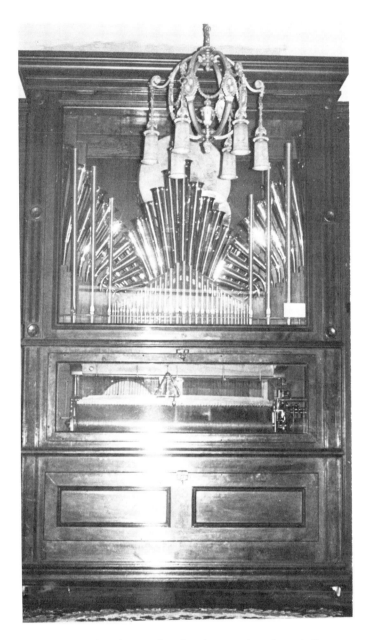

This large barrel-operated orchestrion may have been similar to the one described in the article on this page. Made by M. Welte & Sons in Germany in 1873, it was brought to the United States and installed on the staircase landing of the palatial Mellon family home in Pittsburgh. Later it became part of the collection of Larry Givens, and still later, one hundred years after it was made, it went back to Germany to become a featured attraction in Jan Brauer's musical museum in Baden-Baden, not many miles from where the Welte factory was originally located. (Photograph courtesy of Larry Givens)

RUDOLPH WURLITZER COMPANY
Coin Pianos and Orchestrions

The Rudolph Wurlitzer Company, founded in Cincinnati, Ohio in 1856, was a leading distributor of musical merchandise during the closing decades of the 19th century. In the 1890s Wurlitzer made an entry into the field of coin-operated automatic musical instruments by selling many Regina music boxes (made by the Regina Music Box Co. of Rahway, New Jersey). Believing that this commercial success could be extended to automatically-played pianos as well, Wurlitzer commissioned Eugene DeKleist, a North Tonawanda, New York manufacturer of barrel organs, to build a barrel-operated piano which would be activated via a coin slot. The result was the Tonophone, first marketed in 1899.

Within the span of a decade Wurlitzer broadened its line to include the Pianino 44-note coin piano, the 65-Note Automatic Player Piano, over a dozen different varieties of large PianOrchestra orchestrions, the Mandolin Quartette, and other instruments. Most of these used rolls which were not interchangeable with the products of other manufacturers.

In 1909 Wurlitzer acquired the DeKleist factory in North Tonawanda. From that point onward the firm made most of its own products there. In addition to coin-operated pianos, Wurlitzer produced thousands of player pianos, band organs, and theatre pipe organs.

From about 1900 until the World War I era Wurlitzer was the dominant firm in the coin piano industry in America. After that point, Wurlitzer's theatre pipe organ business flourished so greatly that it was more profitable to concentrate the North Tonawanda production facilities on these expensive (often $10,000 to $25,000 each or more) and large instruments. Innovation and development of coin pianos and orchestrions ground to a halt, with the result that when the 1920s came, Wurlitzer, save for its old-style Pianino 44-note piano, had no products to fill the market's need for compact cabinet-style pianos and orchestrions. The laurels of the industry leader were passed to the J.P. Seeburg Piano Company which, during the 1920s, sold thousands of Seeburg L, KT, KT Special, and similar cabaret-type pianos, while Wurlitzer production of coin pianos dwindled to a trickle.

Today the products of the Rudolph Wurlitzer Company are avidly sought by collectors. The wide variety of case styles, models, and musical capabilities of Wurlitzer instruments have made them favorites. The Wurlitzer Automatic Roll Changer, a device which stores six five-tune rolls on a ferris-wheel type of arrangement and plays them automatically in sequence, while not unique in its conception, was the only such mechanism actively marketed in the United States. The rotating "wonder light," a jeweled bulb which rotates against a petaled mirror background, an idea borrowed from European manufacturers, was likewise popular in its day and is intriguing to collectors of the present era.

Wurlitzer, in business today as a musical instrument manufacturer and retailer (but not of automatically-played units), is one of those fortunate few American firms whose name has a special aura for collectors—like Coca-Cola and Ford. In the minds of many, "Wurlitzer" and "nickelodeon" are synonymous, never minding the fact that the instrument might bear the name of Link, Berry-Wood, or whomever.

A line-up of roll perforators in Wurlitzer's North Tonawanda, N.Y. factory turned out a huge quantity of music. *The Encyclopedia of Automatic Musical Instruments* (cf. page 661 of that reference) notes: "With the possible exception of the style A roll (used by Seeburg, et al), the Wurlitzer 65-Note Automatic Player Piano Roll was made in larger quantities and with a wider selection of tunes than any other type of coin piano roll in America. A Wurlitzer roll catalogue issued about 1923 listed two thousand(!) different tunes that were carried in stock at that time. Of course, quantity doesn't necessarily equate to quality, and many of the musical arrangements were, as we would say today, just so-so."

Below we give information concerning various types of Wurlitzer rolls. With each roll type is an explanation of the instrument(s) using it. For additional Wurlitzer rolls refer to the sections on band organs and theatre pipe organs.

WURLITZER PIANINO ROLL
5½" wide; holes spaced 10 per inch

1 Shutoff
2 Hammer rail up; mandolin on
3 Rewind
4 Hammer rail down; mandolin off
5 Violin pipes on; flute pipes off
6 to 49, 44 playing notes in order, F to C
50 Snare drum
51 Sustaining pedal
52 Flute pipes on; violin pipes off

The Pianino, made in the early years by Eugene DeKleist, of North Tonawanda, N.Y., was marketed by Wurlitzer beginning 1902-1903. In the years that followed, until the late 1920s, many different styles and variations were made.

According to previously published tracker scales, very late rolls turn the xylophone on with holes 5+52, and off with holes 2+4. Dave Ramey reports that mid-1920s rolls never use the xylophone if tubed in this way—but they use it effectively if holes 2+4 turn it on and 4+51 turn it off. In rolls of this era, hole 51 is frequently punched together with 4 at the end of a chorus when no notes are playing, indicating a multiplex function.

Previously published tracker scales have the violin and flute controls reversed from the scale given here. However, in most rolls, hole 5 is punched before passages with the snare drum, and hole 52 precedes passages without drum parts, so it seems more logical to have the louder violin pipes play together with the drum. On the other hand, some collectors prefer to hear the Wurlitzer violin pipes when the drum isn't playing.

The Wurlitzer Bijou Orchestra, popular in the 'teens, uses a Pianino roll. While most were probably made with two ranks of pipes (violin and flute) and xylophone, an instrument restored by Terry Hathaway has no flute pipes and has the violin pipes on all of the time (not connected to a register). The xylophone on this instrument is turned on and off by holes 5 and 52 respectively. There is no multiplexing mechanism for the xylophone.

WURLITZER 65-NOTE AUTOMATIC PLAYER PIANO ROLL
WURLITZER AUTOMATIC PLAYER PIANO ROLL
9 5/8" wide; .1227" spacing (close to 8 holes per inch)

1 Shutoff
2 Hammer rail up, mandolin on
3 Hammer rail down, mandolin off
4 Sustaining pedal on
5 Sustaining pedal off
6 Snare drum
7 to 71, 65 notes in order, A to C#
72 Violin pipes on, flute pipes off
73 Flute pipes on, violin pipes off
74 Bass drum and triangle
75 Rewind

Replay is accomplished by a mechanical device in the spoolbox.
4+5 Bells on
2+3 Bells off
72+73 Xylophone on
2+3 Xylophone off

At the moment the xylophone or bells are turned on or off, one hole of the controlling pair is left open longer to set the mandolin, pedal, or pipes in the desired mode. The xylophone and bell holes were included only in late rolls made by Wurlitzer.

The Wurlitzer 65-Note Automatic Player Piano was first introduced in 1908. Early models featured piano with mandolin attachment or, in the case of Violin Piano—Style A, with a rank of violin pipes (occasionally flute pipes). Later, orchestrions were made to use this type of roll; instruments with piano, mandolin, ranks of violin and flute pipes (or just one rank), plus drum and trap effects—the Style B (with one rank of pipes) and Style C (with two ranks) orchestrions. During the 'teens and 'twenties many of these were equipped with the Wurlitzer Automatic Roll Changer device. Instruments with this feature were given an X suffix to the model designation. Hence, a Style B orchestrion with the Automatic Roll Changer was known as Style BX.

Generally, 65-Note Automatic Player Piano rolls made for the changer are of five-tune length, and ones made for instruments without the changer (or the "long roll frame") were of 10-tune length; although there were exceptions as far ranging as one tune per roll and 20 tunes per roll. In the 'teens and 'twenties the 65-Note Automatic Player Piano roll (the name was later shortened to the Wurlitzer Automatic Player Piano rolls; the "65-Note" designation was dropped) was used on several different styles of Wurlitzer theatre photoplayers, including the very popular Style O.

The word *standardization* was not a part of the Wurlitzer vocabulary, and over the years literally dozens of case style variations were made of instruments which used the Wurlitzer Automatic Player Piano roll. The *Encyclopedia of Automatic Musical Instruments* describes many of these.

Programs found on Wurlitzer Automatic Player Piano rolls are quite varied. Many consist of popular and show tunes of the time, while others are of a topical or ethnic interest (Christmas, Polish, Spanish, Irish music). Some are with fanciful titles as "Saxophone Solo Roll" or "Special Dance Roll With Drums," whereas no instruments using this type of roll had saxophone pipes and whereas, in the second instance, the drum arrangements were no different from those on a typical roll.

As is the case with nearly all other Wurlitzer roll types (Automatic Harp rolls being an exception), most Wurlitzer Automatic Player Piano rolls are on green paper, although early ones are apt to be on red (or occasionally white) paper. A few variants were made; some purple-paper rolls of the 1920s, for example.

As can be gathered from the roll layout, the Wurlitzer Automatic Player Piano roll began as a roll for a simple instrument. When later instruments with orchestra bells were made, it was necessary to multiplex (use holes in combinations) in order to provide the proper registration. A very few large orchestrions in the 1920s were made with an added xylophone (the only one known to the authors is a Style LX orchestrion in the J.B. Nethercutt Collection); this necessitated additional multiplexing as outlined above.

David L. Junchen, in a commentary on rolls which appeared in *The Encyclopedia of Automatic Musical Instruments* (cf. page 716 of that reference), made some observations which are relevant to the present text:

"In terms of controlling the auxiliary instrumentation, the Wurlitzer Automatic Player Piano roll is a real 'Rube Goldberg' situation! To wit:

"(1) Only two holes are available for percussion instruments, one for snare drum and the other for bass drum and triangle. Have you ever heard either a dance band or a symphony orchestra play the bass drum and triangle together?

"(2) The piano soft pedal and the mandolin cannot be operated independently. You must have both or neither. This removes an important expression capability for to soften the piano you must also turn on the mandolin attachment.

"(3) The pipe control mechanism was another innovation in the same vein. You can play either the flute pipes or the violin pipes, but not both. Nor can you play the piano alone, without pipes."

Apparently the planners at the Wurlitzer factory did not design the Automatic Player Piano with expression or elaborate tonal variations in mind. Many orchestrions of the Style B type (with just one rank of pipes; either violin or flute) were built with the pipes permanently in the "on" position and without the possibility of turning them off via the roll perforations. (However, they could be turned off manually.) The same was true of many Wurlitzer band organs; these were made without automatic registers. The result of this thinking is a "sameness" of sound when many Wurlitzer rolls are heard in succession. Some owners of Wurlitzer instruments have made modifications to the registers in order to permit more versatility in expression, especially with pipe ranks. And, it is probably the case that music roll arrangers of our own time will direct their attention to the Wurlitzer 65-Note Automatic Player Piano roll and will produce more imaginative and musically interesting arrangements than did those originally in the Wurlitzer roll department.

In the late 1920s Wurlitzer introduced a new type of band organ, the Caliola, which used Wurlitzer Automatic Player Piano rolls. These featured extended perforations for playing organ music and were labeled "Caliola."

The Wurlitzer Automatic Player Piano rolls recorded the American musical scene from the first decade of the 20th century until the 1930s. Virtually any well-known tune, and hundreds of long-forgotten ones, can be found among the titles.

WURLITZER STYLE 17 PIANORCHESTRA ROLL
WURLITZER MANDOLIN PIANORCHESTRA ROLL
WURLITZER CONCERT PIANORCHESTRA ROLL
WURLITZER PAGANINI ROLL

For a discussion of the preceding roll scales refer to the section in this book which covers Philipps rolls. In 1902 Howard and Farny Wurlitzer (two of Rudolph Wurlitzer's three sons) visited the Leipzig Trade Fair in Germany. While there they saw many marvelous orchestrions exhibited. They were particularly enchanted by the awesome products of Ludwig Hupfeld, the firm whose instruments dominated the exhibits. They sought to obtain license to distribute Hupfeld orchestrions in America, but the huge German firm was unimpressed with Wurlitzer's proposed credit terms and the smallness of the order (at first Wurlitzer wanted to buy just three or four units). Hupfeld referred Wurlitzer to J.D. Philipps & Sons, a smaller manufacturer from Frankfurt-am-Main. Wurlitzer visited Philipps and made arrangements to import several Philipps Pianella orchestrions to America. This was done, and the instruments were marketed under the PianOrchestra trademark.

Many different case styles and several roll-type variations were imported. Many early instruments with an exposed set of orchestra bells on the front (glockenspiel) used the Style 17 PianOrchestra rolls. Most used Mandolin PianOrchestra rolls (equivalent in scale to the popular Philipps PM rolls). Larger orchestrions utilized the Concert PianOrchestra rolls. Later, Wurlitzer adapted this roll for use on a large series of Wurlitzer One Man Orchestra photoplayers manufactured in North Tonawanda.

Around 1910 Philipps made a new type of orchestrion, the Paganini, which featured one to several ranks of violin-toned pipes in combination (on some models) with percussion effects. Wurlitzer imported a number of these, probably on the order of 50 to 100 or so, to America.

From 1903 until the advent of World War I in 1914 ended importations, Wurlitzer purchased from Philipps about 1,000 orchestrions. In addition, about 100 others were made in North Tonawanda by Wurlitzer, using certain Philipps components in combination with Wurlitzer-built exterior cabinets.

WURLITZER 88-NOTE AUTOMATIC PLAYER PIANO ROLL
10 7/16" wide; 10 holes per inch

1+2 Rewind (when opened simultaneously)
3 Cancel 2nd intensity
4 Cancel 1st intensity
5 Hammer rail down
6 Sustaining pedal
7 Shutoff
8 Hammer rail up
9 to 96, 88 notes in order
97 Cancel 3rd intensity
98 3rd intensity on
99 2nd intensity on
100 1st intensity on

The expression mechanism has three intensity pneumatics attached to a common lever, similar to an Ampico. The 1st intensity pneumatic is closest to the fulcrum and has the least effect.

The Wurlitzer 88-Note Automatic Player Piano, made in two styles (Style A for coin-operated use; Style B for home use), was mainly popular in the years 1906-1910. Many instruments were returned to the factory in later years and converted to the Wurlitzer 65-Note Automatic Player Piano roll system.

Today, only a few Wurlitzer 88-Note Automatic Player Pianos are known to exist.

WURLITZER AUTOGRAPH PIANO ROLL
12" wide; 9 holes per inch

1 Bass intensity 1
2 Bass intensity 2
3 Bass intensity 3
4 Cancel bass intensities
5 Bass diminuendo
6 Bass crescendo
7 Bass hammer rail
8 Sustaining pedal
9 Blank
10 Blank

11 Shutoff
12 to 94, 83 playing notes in order, B to A
95 Blank
96 Blank
97 Short perforation: cancel hammer rails and pianissimo; long perforation: rewind
98 Treble hammer rail
99 Pianissimo
100 Treble crescendo
101 Treble diminuendo
102 Cancel treble intensities
103 Treble intensity 3
104 Treble intensity 2
105 Treble intensity 1

This roll is an adaptation of the Apollo Art Echo roll for home reproducing pianos.

First produced in 1915, the Autograph Piano was made until 1926. Just 85 instruments were made. All were equipped with the Wurlitzer Automatic Roll Changer, so far as is known.

Despite Wurlitzer's suggestion that "this piano is to the public place of business what the reproducing player grand piano is to the private home," sales were disappointing. As Seeburg also learned with its contemporary Style X, also a piano with extended expression capabilities, the public was more interested in dropping nickels into a slot to hear ragtime, show tunes, and so on, than classical numbers.

WURLITZER SOLO VIOLIN PIANO ROLL
12" wide; spaced 9 holes per inch

This instrument uses a simplified version of the Paganini (see Philipps music rolls) roll. Paganini tracker scale hole numbers appear in parentheses after each function.

1 Soft violin pipes on O (2)
2 Cancel "O" registers (6)
3 Hammer rail up (7)
4 Hammer rail down (8)
5 Piano accent on (16)
6 Piano accent off (17)
7 Crescendo on (18)
8 Crescendo off (19)
9 Cancel "X" registers (22)
10 Rewind (123)
11 Piano treble coupler on X (33)
12 Tremolo (34)
13 to 56, piano note scale F to C (35-43, 45-66, 68-80)
57 to 95, violin pipe scale G to A (81-119)
96 Melody swell ½ open (120)
97 Shutoff (121)
98 Sforzando (122)
99 Sustaining pedal (29)
100 Mezzoforte on (124)
101 Mezzoforte off (125)
102 Accent swell (127)
103 Loud violin on O (128)
104 Violin high octave switch (129)
105 Swell fully open (release ½-open stop) (44)

The piano treble coupler and the violin high octave switch work the same as those on the Philipps/Wurlitzer Paganini.

The Solo Violin Piano, introduced in 1919, met with an indifferent market reception, and only 140 instruments were sold from then until discontinuation of the style in 1927. So far as is known, all were equipped with the Wurlitzer Automatic Roll Changer.

WURLITZER MANDOLIN QUARTETTE ROLL
WURLITZER MANDOLIN SEXTETTE ROLL
7 5/16" wide; 10 holes per inch

1 Shutoff
2 Hammer rail up
3 Hammer rail down
4 to 37, 34 piano notes in order, D to B
38 to 64, 27 mandolin notes in order, A to B
65 Sustaining pedal
66+67 Rewind (when opened simultaneously)

Developed by Eugene DeKleist at the behest of Wurlitzer, the Mandolin Quartette was billed as "one of the most desirable musical instruments ever produced. It is a combination of mandolin effects accompanied by a piano. The music is much louder than that of any piano . . . and the trilling of the mandolin, together with the piano accompaniment, produces a charming musical effect that cannot fail to delight the most fastidious music lover."

The mandolin section contains a ratchet-operated repeating mechanism similar to the "harp effect" mechanisms used in Germany by Hupfeld and others. Many, if not most or all, of the mandolin actions were imported by DeKleist/Wurlitzer from Germany.

Introduced in 1906, the Mandolin Quartette hit its peak in 1907, during which year 331 were shipped from the North Tonawanda factory. The last one was made in 1912, by which time the production total stood at 588.

The Mandolin Sextette, a variation of the Quartette, made its debut in 1908. From then until 1911, 137 were made. The Mandolin Sextette uses the same roll as the Quartette and has a rank of violin pipes in addition to the piano and mandolin.

The roll has no provision for turning the violin pipes on and off automatically, so the pipes were either on continuously or were off, as apparently they were controlled by hand-operated registers.

Note that the Mandolin Quartette/Sextette roll has two separate and distinct note scales; the mandolin notes are not an extension of the piano notes in order.

Most rolls were of five-tune length and were perforated on red paper. The arrangements are quite catchy and lively, particularly on those rolls featuring ragtime and patriotic tunes.

WURLITZER AUTOMATIC HARP ROLL
8½" wide; 8 holes per inch

1 Blank
2 Rewind
3 to 62, 60 playing notes in order, F to E
63 Shutoff
64 Nickel drop

When a nickel is deposited, it bridges two contact points, turning the motor on. At the end of the song, hole 64 is punched first, dropping the nickel and simultaneously closing a switch wired in parallel which keeps the motor running. Then hole 63 is punched, opening the switch and shutting off the motor. This overcomplicated mechanism replaced a simpler earlier design in which sparking would weld nickels to the contact points, preventing reliable shutoff. The tune indicator apparently is supposed to be teed to hole 63.

From 1905 until the World War I era about 1,500 Wurlitzer Automatic Harps, Style A (earlier and most popular style, with rectangular cabinet) and Style B (top curved in the profile of a harp), were made on contract by the J.W. Whitlock Company of Rising Sun, Indiana.

Factory records in the possession of the authors indicate that at least 239 different rolls, each of 6-tune length, were made. The rolls were produced in Rising Sun, using arrangements made by "recording" the masters from a piano keyboard. No attempt was made to produce arrangements in the style of a classical harp, so extant Automatic Harps all sound

as if they are playing piano rolls (which, in terms of musical arrangements, they are). The tonal quality is similar to a guitar playing, as noted, piano-type arrangements. Rolls are on white paper.

WURLITZER UNIDENTIFIED SCALE
FOR AN ORGAN OR ORCHESTRION

The following layout is taken from a Wurlitzer scale stick and seems to refer to a large orchestrion or elaborately orchestrated pipe organ.

1 Swell closed
2 Swell open
3 Sustaining pedal off
4 Sustaining pedal on
5 Piano off
6 Tambourine
7 Castanets
8 Xylophone on
9 Bells on
10 Mandolin on
11 Tympani
12 Tympani
13 Snare drum
14 Piano on
15 Blank?
16 Shutoff
17 to 72, 56 notes in order, F to C
73 Rewind
74 Triangle
75 Drums loud?
76 Bass drum
77 General cancel
78 Mixture 3+5th
79 Clarinet on
80 Saxophone on
81 Trumpet on
82 Bassoon on
83 Flageolet on
84 Violin on
85 Prestant on
86 Bourdon on
87 8v ("Octave" on?)

The usual Wurlitzer scale stick abbreviation for "sustaining pedal" is LP (Loud Pedal). "Drums loud" is labeled "Drum Loud Pedal" on some scale sticks. Holes 3, 4, and 75 in this scale are marked LP-(off), LPO-(on), and LPD respectively. Hole 78 is marked "3+5th," but the "+" looks like a "4," so it might be "3 4 5th."

Pipe rank ranges in the above scale are as follows: Bassoon (bass) 17 to 30, F to F#. Saxophone (accompaniment) 31 to 42, G to F#. Clarinet, Trumpet, Mixture (melody) 43 to 60, G to C. Flageolet 61 to 72, C# to C. Bourdon, prestant, violin 17 to 72, F to C.

If the preceding is an orchestrion it is a very large one, as evidenced from the extensive pipework. The prestant is a diapason rank of the type usually associated with classic pipe organs. Likewise, the mixture stop (hole 78) is usually associated with pipe organ (rather than orchestrion) terminology.

'Above: Wurlitzer's North Tonawanda, New York factory as it appeared in 1925. Because of record sales of expensive theatre organs Wurlitzer was riding a financial crest at the time and added the landscaped gardens shown in the foreground.

Right: Dave Bowers watches Farny Wurlitzer (1883-1972) look through a preliminary page layout copy of the book "Put Another Nickel In" prior to its publication in 1966. The book was based upon previously unpublished data which was made available from the Wurlitzer archives.

Below: Two 1966 photographs of older buildings in the Wurlitzer factory complex. A large plaque notes: "ERECTED 1892. EUG. DeKLEIST. ENLARGED 1902." Following Mr. Wurlitzer's 1972 death the factory buildings were sold. The manufacture of jukeboxes, which had been the prominent activity there since the 1930s, was discontinued.

**WURLITZER UNIDENTIFIED SCALE
FOR AN ORCHESTRION ROLL**
"J.W.T., Prog. Orches."
(From original Wurlitzer scale stick)

1 T (?)
2 Hammer rail up
3 Hammer rail down
4 Sustaining pedal
5 L.B.D. ("Loud bass drum"?)
6 S.B.D. ("Soft bass drum"?)
7 Snare drum
8 Castanets
9 to 52, 44 piano and violin pipe notes, F to C
53 to 72, 20 clarinet notes, C to G
73 to 85, 13 bell notes, E to E

**WURLITZER UNIDENTIFIED SCALE
FOR AN ORCHESTRION ROLL**
"Prog."
(From original Wurlitzer scale stick)

1 Bells on
2 General cancel
3 Castanets
4 W.D. ("Wood drum" or wood block?)
5 Snare drum
6 Cymbal
7 L.B.D. ("Loud bass drum"?)
8 S.B.D. ("Soft bass drum"?)
9 Tom tom
10 Bells on
11 Sustaining pedal
12 Hammer rail
13 to 70, 58 playing notes, C to A
71 2nd P. off
72 Bass 'off
73 Vox humana pipes off
74 Cello pipes off
75 1st P. off
76 1st V. ex (on?)
77 Flute off
78 3rd V. ex
79 2nd P. ex
80 2nd V. ex
81 1st P. ex
82 Tremolo
83 Rewind
84 Prep V (Play)
85 Chime
86 Trump off (?)
87 Shutoff

The preceding scale gives the original Wurlitzer abbreviations, many of which are unexplained, as listed. The roll may have been used on a theatre instrument.

**WURLITZER UNIDENTIFIED SCALE
FOR AN ORCHESTRION ROLL**
(Variation of preceding)

Another Wurlitzer scale stick is similar to the preceding but has holes numbered from 3 to 87 and shows the following instrument ranges (listed here with hole numbers from the preceding scale):

1st Piano C-F#, 13 to 43.
2nd Piano G to A, 44 to 70
Bells F to A, 42 to 58

Wurlitzer Style YU photoplayer. This unit uses 88-note home player piano rolls. A similar type of instrument, the Style CU, uses Wurlitzer Concert PianOrchestra rolls (equivalent to Philipps PC or Pianella Cecilia rolls).

This early Wurlitzer Pianino uses regular multi-tune Pianino rolls but winds them on a very small takeup spool, causing a rapid tempo increase as the paper builds up. To help compensate for this, a small roller riding on the front side of the takeup spool gradually decreases the speed of the spool by moving the friction-drive speed control wheel. A similar, but gear-driven, tempo compensation mechanism was used in some Cremona orchestrions. Most American coin piano and orchestrion builders solved the problem by using large-diameter takeup spools (which reduced paper buildup) and by perforating the music toward the end of the roll at a slower tempo. This eliminated the need for mechanical speed compensation devices. (Mike Kitner Collection; photograph by Dr. William Black)

Wurlitzer long-frame roll mechanism as used in a Style L orchestrion from the 1920s. The large spools permit the use of long-playing rolls, many of which are of 10-tune length. (Gary Sage Collection)

A rarity today is this Wurlitzer 88-Note Automatic Player Piano. Only a few examples are known to exist. (Curtis Lawyer Collection; photograph by Dr. William Black)

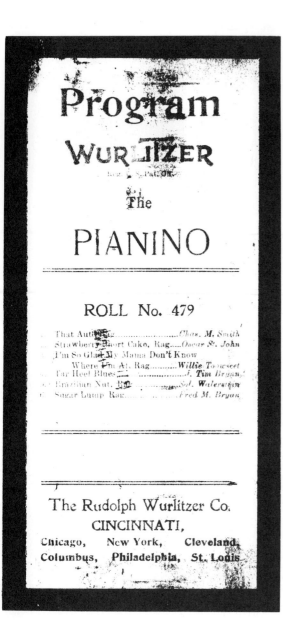

Program
WURLITZER
The
PIANINO

ROLL No. 479

That Auti...Rag.................*Chas. M. Smith*
Strawberry Short Cake, Rag.....*Oscar St. John*
I'm So Glad My Mama Don't Know
    Where I'm At, Rag........*Willie Toosweet*
Tar Heel Blues..................*J. Tim Bryan*
Brazilian Nut, Rag............*Sol. Walerstein*
Sugar Lump Rag...............*Fred M. Bryan*

The Rudolph Wurlitzer Co.
CINCINNATI,
Chicago, New York, Cleveland,
Columbus, Philadelphia, St. Louis

WURLITZER
PIANINO
ROLL No. 455
RAG ROLL

1. Broadway Blues............*Walsh & Sherman*
2. Possum and de Coon...,.....*Geo. P. Marshall*
3. Shoeboot's Serenade,..........*W. C. Handy*
4. Clover Leaf Rag...........*Geo. P. Marshall*
5. Domino Rag.................*C. E. Brandon*
6. Checkerboard Rag..........*E. W. Jimerson*

THE RUDOLPH WURLITZER CO.

WURLITZER
Reg. U S. Pat. Off.
PIANINO
ROLL No. 382

1. Everybody Snap Your Fingers With
  Me,...........................*Harry Puck*
2. San Francisco Bound,.............*I. Berlin*
3. That Lullaby Croon,.........*Tom E. Parker*
4. At the Yiddish Cabaret,.....*Lewis F. Muir*
5. My Man,.................*Conrad & Whidden*
6. Silver Star,....................*R. C. Phillips*

THE RUDOLPH WURLITZER CO.
CINCINNATI
Chicago   New York

Pianino Ephemera: The above tune card once saw service attached to or posted near a Wurlitzer Pianino. The three program cards show evidence of hard use and were taken from music roll leaders years ago.

WURLITZER
Reg. U. S. Pat. Off.
PIANINO
ROLL No. 437

1. By the Beautiful Sea,
  Two-Step...................*Harry Carroll*
2. My Skylark Love (Barcarolle)
  Waltz.......................*Lucien Denni*
3. On the Banks of Lovelight Bay,
  Waltz......................*W. R. Williams*
4. Along Came Ruth, Two-Step......*I. Berlin*
5. On Twilight Bay,...............*Jack Stanley*
6. The Violin My Great Grand-Daddy
  Made, Two-Step..........*Ernie Erdman*

THE RUDOLPH WURLITZER CO.
CINCINNATI
Chicago   New York

The Wurlitzer Pianino, a 44-note piano with mandolin attachment, was especially popular during the first decade of the 20th century. Interestingly, production continued through the 1920s, well into the time when the 44-note format was an anachronism.

CHAS. J. SANDOW'S

CAFE and RESTAURANT

11 ATLANTIC AVENUE

BROOKLYN, N. Y., _____September 20th_____ 191 3

The Rudolph Wurlitzer Company,

      32nd Street, bet. 5th & 6th Aves.

      New York City.

Dear Sirs :—

    I thought I would let you know just how much
receipts the Violin-Flute Piano I purchased from you about
a year ago is taking in. This instrument has taken in
every week since I have it from $20. to $40. per week.
You may think this unusual but it is a fact.

    The instrument is not only more than paying for
itself but it is a big attraction in my place and has
increased my business 50%. No cafe or restaurant should be
without one today.

        Yours very truly,

        Chas. J. Sandow

Wurlitzer often distributed testimonial letter copies such as the above to prospective customers. As the
Violin-Flute Pianino was probably equipped with a slot to take nickels, the letter indicates that it played
from 400 to 800 times each week.

Wurlitzer Violin Pianino

The regular Pianino (44 note Electric Piano with Mandolin attachment and without keyboard) combined with 21 Violin Pipes and 21 Flute Pipes.

The different case finishes are illustrated in natural colors on page **5**.

Height, 4 ft. 8 in.   Width, 3 ft.   Depth, 1 ft. 9 in.

Shipping weight, 625 lbs.

The Wurlitzer 65-Note Player Piano

Program

WURLITZER
Reg. U. S. Pat. Off.

Automatic Player Piano

ROLL NO. 20341

1. When A Blue Service Star Turns To Gold,
   Waltz .... Theodore Morse
2. In The Land Of Beginning Again,
   Fox Trot .... Geo. W. Meyer
3. An Irishman Was Made To Love And Fight,
   One step .... Joseph Santly
4. You'll Find Old Dixieland In France,
   Fox Trot .... Geo. W. Meyer
5. Follow The Flag, One step—from
   "Everything" .... Raymond Hubbell
6. When The Ships Come Home, Fox Trot .... Jerome Kern
7. Can It Be Love At Last? Waltz—
   from "Fiddlers Three" .... Alex. Johnstone
8. Who Do You Love? One Step Chorus .... James Hanley
9. Bagdad, Fox Trot—from "Sinbad" .... Al. Jolson
10. There's A Life In The Old Dog Yet, Fox Trot—
    from "The Girl Behind The Gun" .... Ivan Caryll

THE RUDOLPH WURLITZER CO.
CHICAGO   CINCINNATI   NEW YORK

Exterior view of a circa 1912 Wurlitzer 65-Note Automatic Player Piano. Below are shown 10-tune (for the long frame roll mechanism) and 5-tune (for the Wurlitzer Automatic Roll Changer) roll labels from the 1920 era.

WURLITZER
REG. U.S. PAT. OFF.

Price - $4.00

Automatic Player Piano

ROLL No. 0348

1. My Bicycle Girl, Waltz .... Chappell & Co.
2. Say It (Over and over Again),
   Fox Trot .... Famous Music Corp.
3. If You Love Me,
   Waltz .... Shapiro, Bernstein & Co.
4. Meet the Sun Half Way,
   Fox Trot .... Santley Joy Select, Inc.
5. Old Virginny, Waltz .... Mills Music, Inc.

THE RUDOLPH WURLITZER CO.
Please order from North Tonawanda, N. Y.
7840   Made in U. S. A.

Interior of Wurlitzer 65-Note Player Piano

The mechanisms of the 88-Note Player Piano, Pianino, Mandolin
Quartette and Mandolin Sextette, are practically the same.

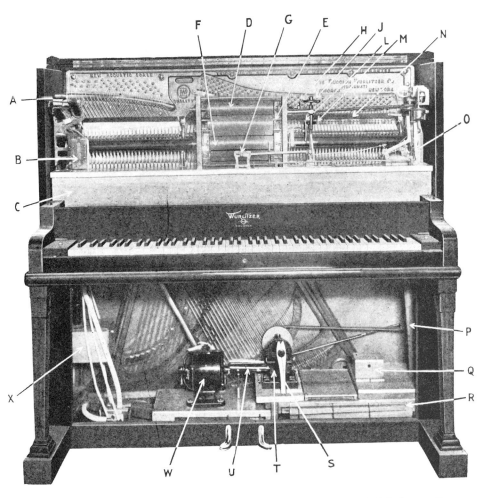

A—Slot approach.
B—Magazine for coins.
C—Action case.
D—Music roll.
E—Tracker bar.
F—Take-up roll.
G—Tempo Regulator.
H—Music roll friction disc.
J—Music roll friction pulley.
L—Take-up roll friction disc.

M—Take-up roll friction pulley.
N—Mandolin attachment.
O—Rewind device.
P—Suction tube to action case.
Q—Regulating valve.
R—Feeder bellows.
S—Pump sticks.
T—Standard for shaft gear.
U—Flexible shaft.
W—Motor.

X—Money drawer.

Interior view of the Wurlitzer 65-Note Automatic Player Piano as depicted in a
1912 catalogue. The various components are listed and identified. First shipped from
the factory in 1907, about 4000 examples of the basic 65-Note Automatic Player
Piano (including case design variations), were made from then until the 1930s.

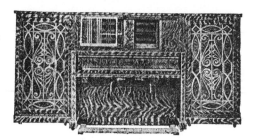
Excerpts from a Wurlitzer Player Piano (65-Note Automatic Player Piano) catalogue of the 1920s. Designed mostly for background and accompaniment music for motion picture theatres (although these rolls could be used on certain coin pianos and orchestrions as well), the long-tune tracker frame rolls featured music which, for want of a better term, was often rather monotonous. One of Wurlitzer's music roll arrangers at the time was paid on the basis of the footage of rolls he turned out, an incentive hardly calculated to produce intricate styling and techniques, according to a feature article which appeared in a Buffalo (N.Y.) newspaper. (Catalogue courtesy of Richard Howe)

La Crillita, Tango
La Hora de Te, Danza
Pepita, Ragtime....................................T. Romero S.
Por que bajas los ejos, Vals..............................L. Gallini
Por el Senderito, Danza...................................A. Wills

ROLL No. 20614
Not Taxable
Special Dance Roll

Slipova, Fox Trot.....................................Roy Bargy
Pianoflage, Fox Trot..................................Roy Bargy
Justin-Tyme, Fox Trot.................................Roy Bargy
Sunshine Capers, Fox Trot.............................Roy Bargy
Knice and Knifty, Fox Trot............................Roy Bargy
Jim Jams, Fox Trot....................................Roy Bargy

ROLL No. 20617
Not Taxable
March Roll

The Gallant Seventh, March.................John P. Sousa
Boy Scouts Parade, March.............Julius K. Johnson
From Sea To Sea, March.................Leon P. Thomas
King Of The Air, March................Julius K. Johnson
Yankee Tars, March.............................Boulton
Kadosh Commandery, March................L. P. Thomas
Aurora, March...........................H. L. Lincoln
Regimental Band, March................Chas. S. Sweeley

ROLL No. 20619
Length of Ten Piece Roll
SPECIAL MOTION PICTURE DRAMA ROLL
Not Taxable

Scherzo, Op. 31.............................F. Chopin
Soirees de Vienne, No. 6...................F. Schubert
Sonata Pathetique, 1st Movement............Beethoven
Sonata Pathequitue, 2nd Movement...........Beethoven
Consolation No. 6...............................Liszt

ROLL No. 20622
Not Taxable
Bohemian Music

Holka Jako Lusk, Pochod March...............E. Stolc
Vnasi Chaloupce, Valcik....................E. Stolc
Bily Satecek, Pochod.......................E. Stolc
Dvacetikoruna, Polka.......................A. Grill
Ty Ty Ty, Valcik...........................A. Grill
Co Se To Stalo, Pochod.....................E. Stolc
Otilie, Polka..............................E. Stolc
Cervena a Bila, Valcik.....................A. Grill
Prazska Krev, Pochod.......................E. Stolc
Nas Bobecek, Polka.........................E. Stolc

ROLL No. 20624
Not Taxable
Motion Picture Solo Roll

Sweet Genevieve................................H. Tucker
I Cannot Sing The Old Songs......................Claribel
Shadows On The Water....................August Lowney
Songs My Mother Taught Me.........................Dvorak
In The Shade Of The Palm,
   From "Floradora"..............................Stuart
Long, Long Ago..................................B...l
Nightengale Song.................................Zeller
All Through The Night...........................Boulton

ROLL No. 20627
Special Sentimental Motion Picture Roll

Old Pal (Why Don't You Answer Me), Ballad
                              M. K. Jerome
A Little Love, A Little Kiss, Ballad........Alfred Parker
Dear Old Pal Of Mine.....................Lieut. Gitz-Rice
Smilin' Through.........................Arthur A. Penn
When You Look In The Heart Of A Rose,
   Ballad...............................Florence Methven
Was There Ever A Pal Like You, Ballad..........I. Berlin
Can't Yo' Hear Me Callin' Caroline...........Caro Roma
Let The Rest Of The World Roll By, Ballad....E. R. Ball

ROLL No. 20630
Hand Played Roll

Three O'Clock In The Morning, Waltz..Terris & Robledo
Swanee River Moon, Waltz.....................H. P. Clarke
Peggy O'Neil, Waltz.................Pease, Nelson & Dodge
Why Should I Cry Over You, Waltz.......Miller & Cohn
Hawaiian Chimes, Waltz.................Bibo & Applefield
Dreaming, Valse Hesitation....................A. Joyce
Bluebird, Waltz...........................Clare Kummer
Destiny Waltz...................................Baynes
Waters of Venice, Waltz..............Albert von Tilzer

ROLL No. 20631
Hand Played Roll

Beautiful California, Waltz...................C. E. Storer
Call Me Back Pal O' Mine, Waltz...............H. Dixen
The Rose Of Memory, Waltz...............Lee S. Roberts
When You've Lost The Trail To Home Sweet Home,
   Waltz.......................................R. DeWitt
Manila Memories, Waltz.................L. F. Forbstein
Floreine, Waltz........................E. J. Schuster
Love in June, Waltzes...........................F. Arndt
Poinsetta, Waltz.............................C. H. Storer
Parisian Nights, Waltz.................Lee S. Roberts

Above: Wurlitzer LX orchestrion built in 1923 and originally sold for $2200. The instrument today is an attraction at Clark's Trading Post in North Woodstock, New Hampshire. (Photograph courtesy of Murray Clark)

Overleaf: Wurlitzer Style CX orchestrion in a California restaurant, circa 1916. The instrument was originally sold by the Leathurby Company of San Francisco.

Wurlitzer orchestrion, Style CX, from the 1916 period. The unit uses 5-tune Wurlitzer 65-Note Automatic Player Piano rolls and stores six of them on the Wurlitzer Automatic Roll Changer.

The Canyon Inn near Hayward, California was a good Wurlitzer customer. This area of the restaurant featured a Style F photoplayer, while the main dining room had a Style CX orchestrion. The sale may have been made by Peter Bacigalupi & Sons, an active Wurlitzer distributor in the 1916 era when this photograph was taken. The Style F uses the 65-Note Automatic Player Piano roll.

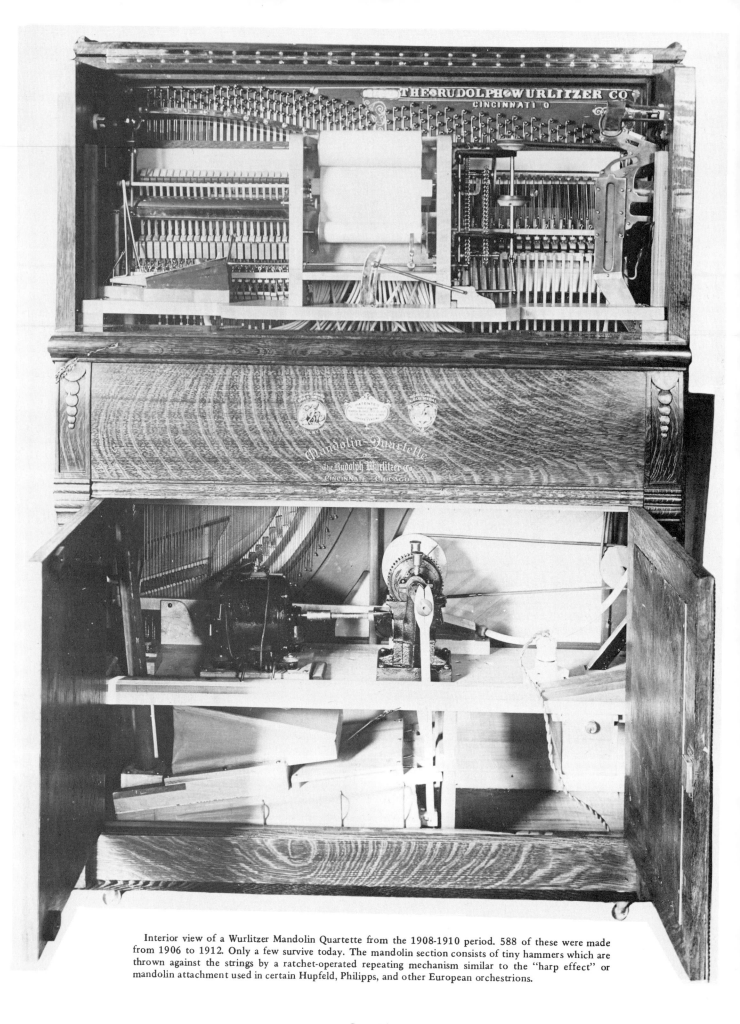

Interior view of a Wurlitzer Mandolin Quartette from the 1908-1910 period. 588 of these were made from 1906 to 1912. Only a few survive today. The mandolin section consists of tiny hammers which are thrown against the strings by a ratchet-operated repeating mechanism similar to the "harp effect" or mandolin attachment used in certain Hupfeld, Philipps, and other European orchestrions.

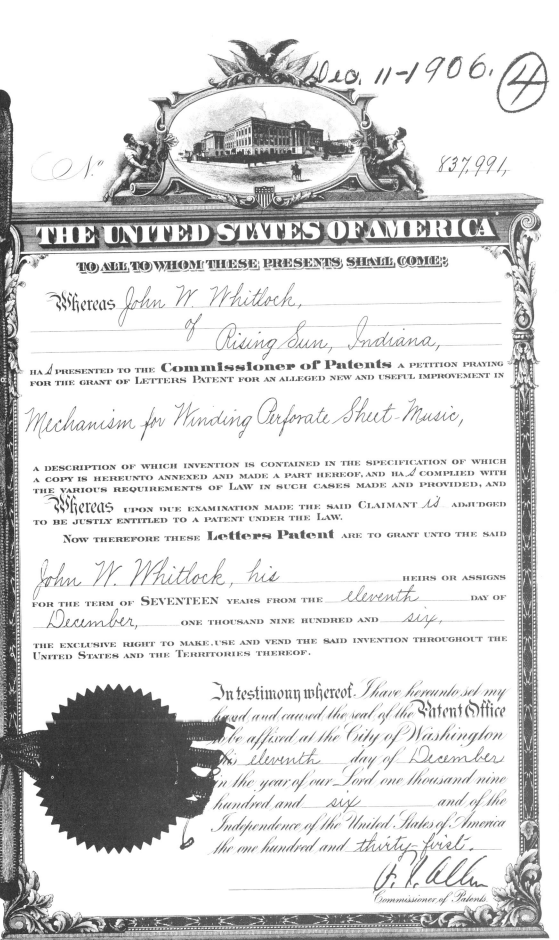

Dec. 11-1906. ④

N° 837,991,

THE UNITED STATES OF AMERICA

TO ALL TO WHOM THESE PRESENTS SHALL COME:

Whereas John W. Whitlock,

of Rising Sun, Indiana,

HAS PRESENTED TO THE **Commissioner of Patents** A PETITION PRAYING FOR THE GRANT OF LETTERS PATENT FOR AN ALLEGED NEW AND USEFUL IMPROVEMENT IN

Mechanism for Winding Perforate Sheet-Music,

A DESCRIPTION OF WHICH INVENTION IS CONTAINED IN THE SPECIFICATION OF WHICH A COPY IS HEREUNTO ANNEXED AND MADE A PART HEREOF, AND HAS COMPLIED WITH THE VARIOUS REQUIREMENTS OF LAW IN SUCH CASES MADE AND PROVIDED, AND *Whereas* UPON DUE EXAMINATION MADE THE SAID CLAIMANT IS ADJUDGED TO BE JUSTLY ENTITLED TO A PATENT UNDER THE LAW.

Now THEREFORE THESE **Letters Patent** ARE TO GRANT UNTO THE SAID

John W. Whitlock, his HEIRS OR ASSIGNS

FOR THE TERM OF SEVENTEEN YEARS FROM THE eleventh DAY OF December, ONE THOUSAND NINE HUNDRED AND six,

THE EXCLUSIVE RIGHT TO MAKE, USE AND VEND THE SAID INVENTION THROUGHOUT THE UNITED STATES AND THE TERRITORIES THEREOF.

In testimony whereof, I have hereunto set my hand and caused the seal of the Patent Office to be affixed at the City of Washington this eleventh day of December in the year of our Lord one thousand nine hundred and six and of the Independence of the United States of America the one hundred and thirty-first.

Commissioner of Patents.

Cover of the original patent issued to John W. Whitlock of Rising Sun, Indiana, who devised what later was known as the Wurlitzer Automatic Harp. The patent related to the roll mechanism in the instrument.

The anatomy of a Wurlitzer Style B Automatic Harp is revealed in this photograph taken at Wurlitzer's Cincinnati facility around 1908-1910. The photo retoucher forgot to excise the background which can be seen through the opening in the right side of the harp case!

No. 837,991   PATENTED DEC. 11, 1906

J. W. WHITLOCK.
MECHANISM FOR WINDING PERFORATE SHEET MUSIC.
APPLICATION FILED OCT. 5, 1905.

2 SHEETS—SHEET 1.

Right: J.W. Whitlock's patent drawing for the roll mechanism of what later became the Wurlitzer Automatic Harp. Whitlock, who lived in Rising Sun, Indiana, was apparently unaware of the state of the art in the coin piano business, so nearly every component of the Automatic Harp was built using Whitlock's original and innovative ideas.

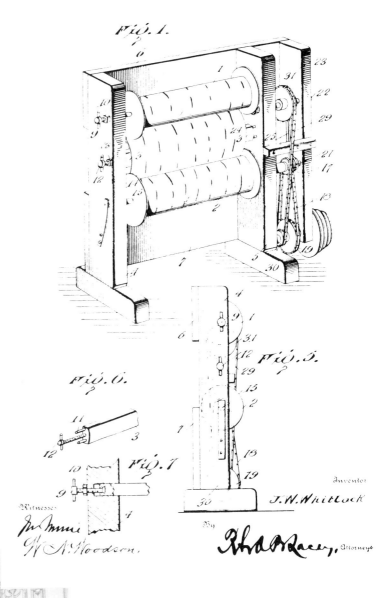

Left: This view of the collection of the late Otto Carlsen, taken in the 1960s, shows a Wurlitzer Style B Automatic Harp and several other instruments, including an Aeolian Hammond player electronic organ (extreme left, partially visible), a "double Mills" Violano-Virtuoso, and, to the right, a Multiphone phonograph.

Overleaf: A 1906 view of Eimer's Cafe, located at 532 Walnut Street in Cincinnati, Ohio, shows a Style A Wurlitzer Automatic Harp as a featured attraction.

Where the Wurlitzer Automatic Instruments are made

North Tonawanda, New York

Net Price List

of

Wurlitzer Automatic
Instruments

May 15th, 1920

The Rudolph Wurlitzer Co.
New York   Cincinnati   Chicago

WURLITZER

NET PRICE LIST OF

AUTOMATIC INSTRUMENTS

EFFFCTIVE MAY 15th, 1920.
This list cancels all former price lists.

Style	Catalogue Page No.	Price
Pianino 7		$ 600.00
Violin-Flute (Pianino) .. 8		800.00
S 9		950.00
I 11		1150.00
IX 12		1250.00
AX 14		1550.00
DX 15		1750.00
BX 16		2000.00
CX 17		2200.00
Solo Violin Piano..........		2100.00

F. O. B. Factory

WURLITZER

PIANORCHESTRAS

Style	Catalogue Page No.	Price
12 23		$ 2200.00
18 24		2950.00
29C 25		3500.00
33 26		4050.00
30A 27		3800.00
47 28		4050 00
34A 29		5250.00
32A 30		5750.00
3 Paganini 33		4250.00
2 "		3700.00
1 "		3500.00
Coin-Slot Boxes.. 31		15.00 each

F. O B. Factory

The Rudolph Wurlitzer Company periodically issued price lists of automatic musical instruments for sale. Separate lists, in the form of folding cards such as the May 15th, 1920 list shown here, were issued for pianos, band organs, and theatre organs.

The listing of styles 12, 18, 29C, 33, 30A, 47, 34A, 32A PianOrchestras and styles 1, 2, and 3 Paganini represent instruments manufactured circa 1910-1914 and still in stock.

WURLITZER

THE WURLITZER
PIANORCHESTRA

"Automatic Orchestra"

Shown on Pages Following.

THE PIANORCHESTRA is without question the most remarkable musical instrument ever built. It represents a combination of the different instruments used in a large orchestra, assembled in a single magnificent case and arranged to play in solo and concert just like a human orchestra.

It is a hopeless task to do the PianOrchestra justice in cold type. The many handsome cases must be seen and the music heard to obtain a fair conception of their appearance and musical possibilities.

Some idea of what the PianOrchestra does musically may be had from the lists of instruments they represent as printed in connection with each style in this catalog.

All the instruments listed are represented in the PianOrchestra and are perfectly regulated by automatic stops which control their playing in much the same manner as an orchestra leader directs his players by the wave of his baton.

In hotels, cafes, theatres, and the better class of public places, where the PianOrchestra is played as a substitute for a human orchestra, it never fails to prove a great drawing card, both because of the fine grade of music it furnishes and its novelty.

In places where a number of coin slot boxes can be distributed, connected with the instrument, so that it may be played from any part of the house by dropping a coin, the PianOrchestra will pay its own way besides increasing patronage.

The PianOrchestra is operated by electricity—a small electric motor being placed inside the case. It plays from paper music rolls which contain from one to six selections. The rolls can be changed in a few seconds.

The Wurlitzer Automatic Roll Changer

All PianOrchestras now come equipped with the Wurlitzer Automatic Roll Changer described on page 9 of this catalog.

This wonderful invention recently perfected by us carries six music rolls at a time and automatically rewinds and changes the music after each piece is played through.

A musical program of an hour and a half to three hours is thus provided without repetition or bother.

The mechanism is constructed with the care and precision of a fine watch, is practically trouble proof and will wear a life time.

The Case Designs

The PianOrchestra cases are magnificent, no finer combined example of the artist designer and master cabinet maker's art are to be found anywhere.

The woods are carefully chosen from the markets of the world—are beautifully carved with the most original designs and embellished with rich decorations of gold leaf and brass in combination with striking art glass panels, beveled French mirrors and showy inlaid wood effects.

The interiors light up while playing and show the artistic art glass effects.

Some of the Wurlitzer PianOrchestras have the most original motion picture effects in front. The center panels are in the shape of translucent oil paintings. When the interiors light up the arrangement is such that a vivid motion picture is produced.

Fountains ripple and overflow their basins; mountain streams flow and waterfalls tumble in the most picturesque cascades; aeroplanes race with steamboats, and so on.

To give all the variety possible and make each PianOrchestra exclusive, the case designs are constantly being changed and in this way only a few of any particular style are sent out exactly alike—slight variations are made in the cases that practically give every purchaser an exclusive, different style of case.

Wurlitzer Style 15 Mandolin PianOrchestra. This particular example saw many years of use in a New York City ice cream parlor. It was discovered in the 1950s by Mrs. Ruth Bornand, who sold it into the Haning and White Collection. Made in 1915, this was one of 19 similar instruments manufactured during the 1913-1915 years in Wurlitzer's North Tonawanda (N.Y.) facility. (William Wherry Collection)

Interior view of the Wurlitzer Style 15 Mandolin PianOrchestra. This particular unit features an unusual 12-roll automatic changer. The main chassis, changer mechanism, and certain other components were made by J.D. Philipps & Sons, and the drums, coin mechanism, piano, and cabinet were the work of Wurlitzer. Interestingly, the cabinets of Wurlitzer-built PianOrchestras are made in sections and are separate from the chassis; the chassis slides in and out.

The Edgemont Cafe

1936 BROADWAY

S. E. COR. 65TH STREET

BRANCH: S. E. COR 125TH ST. & PARK AVE.
TELEPHONE 977 HARLEM

New York September 23, *1913*

The Rudolph Wurlitzer Co.,
25–27 West 32d Street,
New York City.

Gentlemen:–

I have made such a success with your automatic musical instruments that it gives me pleasure to relate my experience.

The first instrument I purchased of you about four years ago, was one of your $700 Player Pianos, which earned a little over $2100 in about two years. I then traded this in for one of your Roll Changer Flute Pianos, receiving a fair allowance for my original piano. This new piano earned almost double the receipts of the first piano, because of the automatic roll changer, which gives a greater variety of music. Recently, I traded the second piano for a $2000 Pian-Orchestra. The Pian-Orchestra is earning still more money than either of the other instruments, and crowding my dining room nightly. It is not only the earnings I have received from these instruments, but they have been the means of doubling my business.

The fact that I have invested $3900.00 with you in three different instruments, getting a better one each time, in the last four years, is the best evidence of my success.

If you have any prospective customers who doubt the value of your instruments in the Cafe business, I will take pleasure in showing them the results I have received.

Wishing you the success you deserve, I remain

Yours very truly,

D. Niemeyer

A particularly good Wurlitzer customer was D. Niemeyer, proprietor of the Edgemont Cafe, who kept escalating his instrument purchasers until he was the owner of the ultimate orchestrion in the Wurlitzer line, the PianOrchestra. "The PianOrchestra is earning still more money than either of the other instruments, and crowding my dining room nightly."

Wurlitzer Mandolin PianOrchestra—Style 28 B

With Automatic Roll Changer

The finish illustrated above is silver gray oak.

Instrumentation:

Piano with Mandolin attachment

37 Violins	Bass Drum and Cymbals
18 Violoncellos	Snare Drum

Height, 9 ft. 2 in.   Depth, 2 ft. 8 in.   Width, 5 ft. 4 in.   Shipping weight, 1600 lbs.

The Wurlitzer Style 28-B was one of the most popular styles sold in the 1910-1915 era. An extant specimen has colorful art glass instead of a motion picture scene on the center front panel and was originally used in a pavilion in New Kensington, Pennsylvania. Over 1,000 Mandolin and Concert PianOrchestras were originally sold by Wurlitzer. Of that number, fewer than two dozen survive today.

Mandolin PianOrchestra—Style 29 C

The Wurlitzer Style 29-C Mandolin PianOrchestra was one of the most popular models in the 1910-1914 period. The photograph above shows one on location in the Louis Fashion Restaurant at 524 Market Street, San Francisco. Another was used in the Banner Theatre, a nickelodeon in Los Angeles. The latter instrument survives today and is on exhibit at Knott's Berry Farm in Buena Park, California.

The illustration shown to the left is from the 1912 Wurlitzer catalogue. Collectors today consider the arrangements on Mandolin PianOrchestra rolls to be among the very finest ever produced by Wurlitzer. Hundreds of different rolls, nearly all of five-tune length, were made from about 1909 until the late 1920s. Before 1909 Wurlitzer imported red-paper Philipps PM (Pianella Mandoline) rolls from J.D. Philipps & Sons in Germany.

Height, 10 ft.   Width, 6 ft. 8 in.   Depth, 3 ft. 4 in.

PRICE—Including Automatic Roll Changing Device, 6 Rolls of Music and 1 Slot Box..**$2,600.00**

This style may also be had without Roll Changing Device.   Price.......... 2,400.00

The Style 16 Wurlitzer Mandolin PianOrchestra, with its colorful art glass front and green art glass domes on top, was just the thing to bring life to a dance hall or restaurant. From 1913 to 1915 eight of these were shipped to various destinations from Wurlitzer's North Tonawanda (N.Y.) facility. The chassis was made by J.D. Philipps & Sons of Frankfurt-am-Main, Germany. The cabinet, drums, piano, and pipes were made by Wurlitzer.

Of the eight originally made, two were originally used in the Minneapolis, Minnesota area. One was junked in the mid 1920s by Oswald Wurdeman, who used part of the case wood to build a tool box! At the time large orchestrions were obsolete, and there was no commercial demand for them. If a buyer could be found for such a used instrument, the price was apt to be no more than a couple hundred dollars, if indeed that much. For this reason, most were destroyed.

Another Style 16 apparently was used in a large ballroom on a pier in Atlantic City, New Jersey during the 'teens and 1920s. According to several reports, it was located at the far end of the ballroom, distant from the front doors, and was on a small platform. The ballroom lights were dimmed when the orchestrion played, accenting its appearance.

A third Style 16 was originally used in the Shanghai Cafe in Minneapolis. This establishment, an expensive restaurant, featured two carved dragons at the front entrance. The interior was richly ornamented with Oriental decorations, including carved teakwood chairs and tables. Live birds flitted around the room. This orchestrion later was acquired by Osborne Klavestad, owner of the Stagecoach Inn, located in Shakopee, a suburb of Minneapolis. At the Stagecoach Inn it was in good company with a collection of other old-time automatic musical instruments, including Seeburg H and L orchestrions, a Wurlitzer 153 organ (which Mr. Klavestad obtained in its original factory crate), a Wurlitzer 150 organ with a natural (unpainted) oak facade, a Coinola X, a Violano-Virtuoso, and other attractions.

Wurlitzer PianOrchestra—Style 16
With Wurlitzer Automatic Roll Changer

Instrumentation:

Piano — Orchestration of 42 Violin and Violoncello Pipes
Chimes — Bass, Snare and Kettle Drums, Cymbals and Mandolin Attachment.
Xylophone — Tambourine — Castanets

Height over all, 8 ft. 8 in.   Height without Globes, 7 ft. 10 in.   Width, 5 ft. 10½ in.
Depth, 2 ft. 11 in.   Shipping weight, 1600 lbs.

Price, with Electric Motor and 6 Music Rolls..................**$2,200**

The Wurlitzer Style 32-A Concert PianOrchestra shown above and on the following page saw service for many years in the Crystal Palace Hotel in Leadville, Colorado. The proprietor, Johnny Bernat, bought it directly from Wurlitzer, probably in the 'teens. The chassis of the orchestrion was built by J.D. Philipps & Sons of Frankfurt-am-Main, Germany. The exterior case was crafted by Wurlitzer in North Tonawanda, New York, and measures 8'7" high by 7'9" wide by 6' deep. The chassis and case are completely separate; the chassis sits on the floor, and the free-standing case is assembled around it.

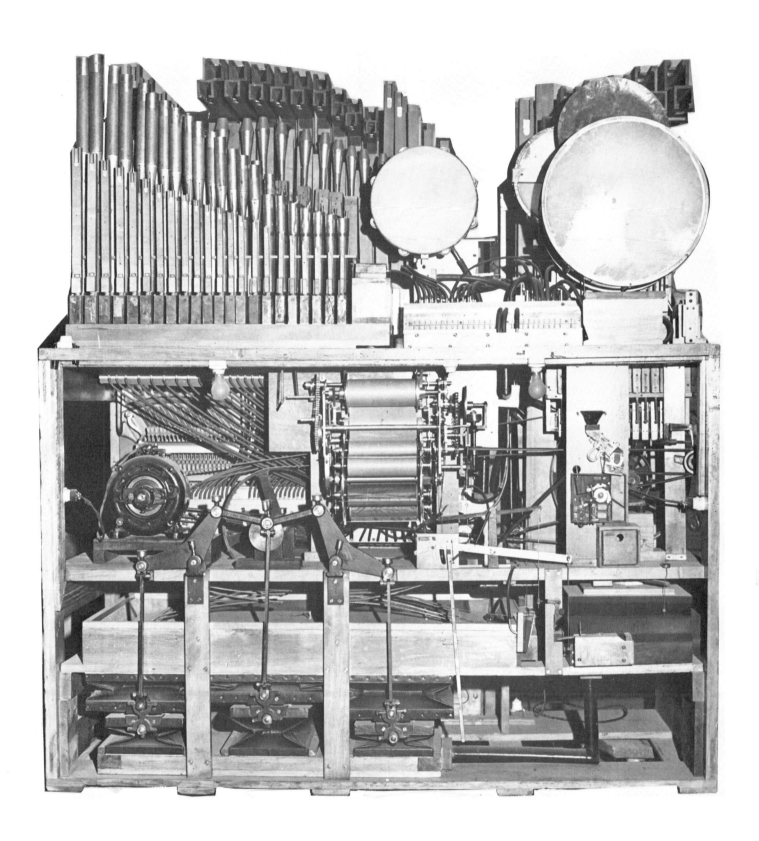

Interior view of the Wurlitzer Style 32-A Concert PianOrchestra. Just three Concert PianOrchestra orchestrions are known to exist today: the one illustrated here, in the collection of Jerry and Sylvia Cohen; a Style 32 at Disney World in Florida; and another case design of Style 32 in J.B. Nethercutt's San Sylmar museum in California. Wurlitzer Concert PianOrchestra rolls, originally known as Philipps Pianella Caecilia rolls, were made for these instruments as well as for several different styles of Wurlitzer photoplayers. As far more photoplayers using these rolls were sold than were PianOrchestras, most music rolls arranged after the early 'teens are of the accompaniment or mood music type.

The Automatic Roll Changing Device

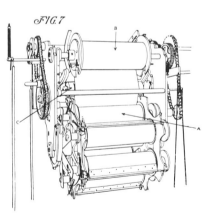

Above: Sketch of the Wurlitzer Style 32-A Concert PianOrchestra as it appeared in the back room of the Crystal Palace Hotel, Leadville, Colorado, in 1939. The drawing is one of many made of Colorado mining towns and memorabilia by Muriel S. Wolle, who later published "Stampede to Timberline," a collection of essays, observations, and illustrations. (Sketch courtesy of the late Muriel S. Wolle)

Right: Wurlitzer's 1912 description of the Automatic Roll Changer. The device, made in Germany by J.D. Philipps, was of machined steel and was of higher quality than the domestically-manufactured changers used on Wurlitzer keyboard orchestrions. The configuration of the Philipps device, used on the PianOrchestra and the Paganini, differs from the Wurlitzer-made changer. In the Philipps changer the rolls are stored below the tracker bar and are drawn upward to the takeup spool, just the opposite of the Wurlitzer arrangement. The Philipps changer was a very reliable device. Osborne Klavestad, who operated a Style 16 Mandolin PianOrchestra for several decades at the Stagecoach Inn (Shakopee, Minnesota), advised the authors that in countless thousands of operations the roll changer did not fail, tear a roll, or otherwise operate less than perfectly!

One of the most important improvements made in the PianOrchestra in late years, is the Automatic Roll Changing Device, which is patented, and cannot be found in any other instrument. By means of this wonderful device, six different music rolls are put on an instrument at one time, and are automatically changed from one to the other, as each roll is played through and automatically rewound on its spool.

Thus, from 30 to 40 selections may be placed on the instrument at one time, and played through one after the other, without any attention whatsoever.

The advantage of such a large and varied program of music, without the necessity of changing the rolls, is almost incalculable. It means that the owner of a PianOrchestra, equipped with this new device, can give his patrons an entertainment of an hour and a half to three hours' duration, with a continuous change of music, and without changing his music rolls or bothering with the instrument in any way whatever.

This wonderful device, whose mechanism is entirely of steel, is built on the same principle as the famous original Ferris Wheel, which was seen at the Chicago and St. Louis World's Fairs. The six music rolls in the wheel are carried around to their proper positions with regard to the Tracker Bar (C) in the same manner as the cars in the Ferris Wheel were operated. It works as smoothly as a fine watch movement.

For instance, the music roll (A) is shown in position to be played by passing over the Tracker Bar (C). After it is played through, it is automatically rewound by means of our Automatic Rewinding Device, and the Magazine Wheel revolves far enough to carry it out of the way and bring the succeeding roll into its place. This one is immediately taken up by the take-up roll (B), and the music continued. This operation is repeated at the end of each roll, and is continued without the slightest attention as long as the instrument is kept running.

The Automatic Roll Changing Device contains our special Tempo Regulator, described on page 10, and an Automatic Action Case Protector, which is incorporated in the Tracker Bar, and prevents dust and other foreign matters entering the action case.

Wurlitzer Orchestra Installed in
ELDORADO THEATRE,
1297 Wilkins Ave., New York City.

Wurlitzer Orchestra Installed in
THE BOULEVARD THEATRE,
1571-1573 Gratiot Ave., Detroit, Mich.

Mr. John J. Wittman, President, writes:

"The Wurlitzer Orchestra for my Eldorado Theatre certainly far exceeds my expectations, and more than meets the demands you claim in every way.

It is a great box office attraction, and I do not see why every exhibitor does not take advantage of the wonderful instruments the Wurlitzer Company has introduced."

John J Wittman

President of Cinema Motion Picture
Exhibitors of the Bronx.

J. C. Ritter, Secretary and Treasurer, writes:

"The Wurlitzer One-Man Orchestra is one of the best investments we have ever made.

We have had your instrument now during the worst two months for the show business in the year; we are doing a bigger business than ever. The Orchestra plays beautifully. The fact that after thirty days we gave you our check for the balance due, is evidence enough of what we think of it."

The Boulevard Theatre Co.,

Per *J. C. Ritter*

Secretary and Treasurer.

Wurlitzer's publicity for the styles H and K photoplayers (which used a Concert PianOrchestra roll) included illustrations of nickelodeon theatres in which they were used. Below right is the center piano section of a typical instrument with an explanation of the various stop tabs, buttons, and foot pedals. While basic orchestration (such as pipe ranks on and off and limited percussion) were programmed on the roll, the novelty effects (such as bird whistle, auto horn, etc.) were controlled by the operator.

The Numbered Arrows Give the Complete Orchestration and Effects

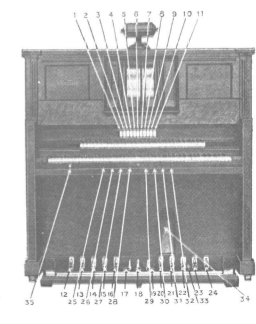

— Stopped Bass (Diapason)
— Cello
— Flute
— Violin
— Horns
— Vox Humana (Human Voice Effect)
7 — Piano
8 — Xylophone
9 — Orchestra Bells
10 — Cathedral Chimes
11 — Tremulant
12 — Horse Trot

13 — Tympani or Kettle Drum
14 — Triangle
15 — Crash Cymbal
16 — Bass Drum and Cymbal
17 — Piano Pedal
18 — Snare Drum, Bass Drum and Cymbal in one
19 — Piano Sustaining Pedal
20 — Snare Drum
21 — Tambourines
22 — Castanets
23 — Tom Tom

24 — Fire Gong
25 — Mandolin On
26 — Mandolin Off
27 — Train Effect
28 — Auto Horn
29 — Steamboat Whistle
30 — Coupler On
31 — Coupler Off
32 — Re-roll
33 — Bird Whistle
34 — Swell Pedal (Loud)
35 — Door and telephone bell

Paganini Violin Piano—Style 1

With Wurlitzer Automatic Roll Changer

Represents a Piano in combination with a Violin.

Height, 8 ft. 8½ in.   Width, 6 ft. 6 in.   Depth, 3 ft. 3 in.   Shipping weight, 1400 lbs.

WURLITZER
Solo Paganini Violin and Piano

Installed in The Famous

View of Interior of
Poodle Dog Restaurant and Hotel,
San Francisco

Poodle Dog Restaurant

San Francisco

The Poodle Dog Restaurant is a high class place, and caters to a fashionable money-spending trade.

Nothing can gain admittance to the exclusive "Poodle Dog" that is not superlatively fine.

The fact that Mr. A. B. Blanco, proprietor, after considering all other forms of musical attraction, selected the Wurlitzer Paganini, proves that the Paganini is the only instrument that meets the requirements of a high class Restaurant.

Mr. Blanco writes:

"I consider my Wurlitzer Paganini one of the wonders of the age." I cannot recommend it too highly. It is the most wonderful and pleasing musical instrument that money can purchase."

In 1914 San Francisco's Poodle Dog Restaurant had a Wurlitzer Style 1 Paganini Violin Piano. The interior components consisted of a fine piano in combination with one rank of violin-toned pipes. The instrument used Paganini rolls and was equipped with the automatic roll changing device. The interior parts were made by J.D. Philipps & Sons of Germany. The cabinet was made by Wurlitzer in North Tonawanda, New York.

According to the late Joseph Bacigalupi, who used to sell and service Wurlitzer and other instruments, the Poodle Dog Restaurant had an adjacent bordello which served a high class clientele. A special automobile entrance, equipped at the end with a platform-type turntable to turn the cars around for ease in parking, was provided so that customers could enter and leave the establishment discreetly. After a session in the bordello, a fine meal in the Poodle Dog, complete with Paganini music, was just the thing to cap an evening's entertainment.

Interior view of a Wurlitzer Solo Violin piano of the 1920s. With mechanisms inspired by the Wurlitzer-Philipps Paganini, the Solo Violin Piano imitated the stringed instrument by means of an extended rank of violin-toned pipes housed in a special compartment behind the piano sounding board. The above instrument is in a mahogany case and, like all of its kind, is equipped with the Wurlitzer Automatic Roll Changer, which permits six rolls to be stored on the instrument and played in succession. (Collection of Jerry and Sylvia Cohen)

COIN PIANOS AND ORCHESTRIONS
Various Manufacturers

In this section are listed tracker scales for coin pianos, orchestrions, and related instruments by various manufacturers not described elsewhere. Throughout the history of roll-operated instruments there have been many dozens of manufacturers which have made limited production models, items which did not do well in the marketplace, or instruments which for other reasons are not in the forefront of collector interest today, although they are historically and technically significant. The Resotone Grand, of which just one example is known to the authors, represents such an instance. Other scales in this section may represent models once made in quantity but which are rare today.

ACCORDEO-JAZZ

ACCORDEO-JAZZ ROLL
"ACCORDION BOY" ROLL
NIZA ACCORDEON JAZZ ROLL
11¼" wide; spaced 6 holes per inch

1 Wood block
2 to 13, bass notes, G to F#
14 to 25, accompaniment notes, G to F#
26 to 30, melody notes, G to B
31 Bass drum
32 Shutoff
33 Loud
34 Rewind
35 Soft
36 Cymbal
37 Snare drum
38 to 66, continuation of melody, C to E
67 Wood block

From an original Eugene DeRoy scale stick marked "Niza Accordeon Jazz." Devices of this general type, with the accordion (alternate spellings: accordian or, especially in Europe, accordeon) as the featured instrument, were made with varying amounts of extra percussion effects. Makers of this genre (but not necessarily of the specific instrument listed above) include Blessing, Seybold, and Hohner.

An original Wurlitzer scale stick for an instrument of this general type is similar to the preceding layout, except that holes 1 and 67 are for castanets and the total range of playing notes is C to A rather than G to E.

LEOPOLD DeVISSCHER

Leopold DeVisscher, of Antwerp, Belgium, apparently produced roll-operated pneumatic pianos for commercial locations in the early 20th century. Little is known of the firm, its operations, or its products.

LEOPOLD DeVISSCHER COIN PIANO ROLL
13 1/8" wide; spaced approx. 5½ holes per inch

1 Mandolin
2 Blank
3 Shutoff
4 Mandolin
5 Sustaining pedal
6 to 66, 61 playing notes, C to C
67 Soft
68 Blank
69 Rewind
70 Blank

E. DIENST & CO.

The firm of E. Dienst & Co., located in Leipzig, Germany, was an important maker of barrel pianos and orchestrions around the turn of the 20th century. Some roll-operated instruments were produced as well, including ones marketed under the Mezon name. Certain models were similar to those sold by Kuhl & Klatt (to which refer).

MEZON ROLL
Approx. 34 cm. wide; 21 holes per 10 cm.

1 Bass drum
2 Percussion switch
3 Shutoff
4 Mandolin off
5 Sustaining pedal
6 Xylophone on
7 to 65, Playing notes, C# to B
66 Xylophone off
67 Hammer rail
68 Mandolin on
69 Rewind
70 Snare drum?
71 Cymbal, triangle

Hole 2 switches the functions of holes 70 and 71.

MEZON ROLL
(Variation of the preceding, with the differences noted)

1 "P.E. mandoline"
2 "Avance" (Play?)
70 Blank
71 Blank

ELMAN

ELMAN ROLL
34 cm. wide; spaced 8 holes per 1½ inches

1 Rewind
2 "Loud bellows"
3 "Loud bellows"
4 to 65, 61 playing notes, C to C
66 "Soft bellows"
67 "Soft bellows"
68 Play

Little is known of the Elman automatic piano, presumably coin-operated, which was used in Europe during the early 20th century. The two holes marked "loud bellows" and the two marked "soft bellows" might be lock and cancels for the sustaining pedal and hammer rail respectively.

GABY

GABY ROLL
Approx. 16" wide; approx. 53 holes per 10 inches

1 to 5, Notes A to C#
6 Hammer rail
7 to 37, Notes D to G#
38 Snare drum
39 Pianissimo
40 Swell forte
41 Fortissimo
42 to 71, Notes A to D
72 Sustaining pedal
73 Bass drum
74 Shutoff
75 Mandolin on
76 Rewind
77 Xylophone on
78 General cancel

F.O. GLASS

F.O. Glass, of Klingenthal (Saxony, Germany), produced during the years after 1880 a large series of barrel-operated pianos and orchestrions. Trade names included Eldorado and Valsonora.

In the early 20th century years a series of roll-operated instruments made its appearance. Apparently these were mostly, if not entirely, of smaller format and contained a piano, mandolin, and an extra instrument such as a xylophone.

GLASS ROLL
Approx. 12 5/8" wide; approx. 8½ holes per inch

1 Snare drum
2 Bass drum
3 Snare drum
4 Blank
5 Shutoff
6 Hammer rail
7 Sustaining pedal
8 to 16, Xylophone notes C, D, E, F, F#, G, G#, A, A#
17 to 81, Note scale A to C#
82 to 90, Xylophone notes B, C, C#, D, E, E, F, G, A
91 Blank
92 Xylophone on
93 Expression I (soft)
94 Expression II (very soft)
95 Rewind
96 Mandolin on

Xylophone holes 82 to 90 are probably marked incorrectly on the scale from which the preceding was taken; they probably should be tubed to the xylophone in ascending note order.

GEORG HEINRICH & CO.

Georg Heinrich & Co., of North Berlin, Germany, produced barrel-operated and roll-operated instruments, mostly of smaller formats. A typical advertisement noted that the firm offered a piano with mandolin, xylophone, and imitative violin (violin pipes). Apparently, Heinrich produced only a relatively small number of instruments, for they are virtually unknown today.

HEINRICH ROLL
Approx. 255 mm. wide; approx. 10 holes per 30 mm.

1 Violin pipes
2 Flute
3 Pedal
4 Bass drum
5 Snare drum
6 Bells
7 Automat?
8 Mandolin
9 to 72, Note scale
73 Blank
74 Xylophone
75 Shutoff
76 Soft
77 Loud
78 Cymbal
79 Violin pipes
80 Cello pipes

76+77 = Rewind

The note scale for this instrument is unclear. The scale stick (from the late Eugene DeRoy) indicates the following: 9 to 31, F to D#; 32 C; 33 C#; 34 to 57 G to F#; 58 to 72, G to A. Instrument ranges are: Mandolin, xylophone, violin pipes, G to F#, 34 to 57 (24 notes). Bells, cello pipes, flute, G to A, 58 to 72, (15 notes).

PASQUALE

PASQUALE ROLL
11¼" wide; 9 holes per inch

1 Pianissimo
2 Mandolin
3 Sustaining pedal
4 Crescendo (bass accent?)
5 to 91, Playing notes
92 Rewind
93 Crescendo (treble accent?)
94 Shutoff
95 Pianissimo
96 Melody loud

RESOTONE GRAND CO.

The Resotone Grand Company of New York City marketed a roll-operated chrysoglott (metal bars with resonators, struck by felt-covered piano-like hammers) during the early 20th century. The hole spacing on the endless rolls varies from a more compact arrangement at the center to wider spacing at the edges of the tracker bar.

RESOTONE GRAND ROLL
9 11/16" wide; irregular hole spacing
Endless

1 Shutoff
2 to 5 Blank
6 to 51, 46 playing notes, D-B

RHEIMER

RHEIMER ORCHESTRION ROLL
35 cm. wide; spaced about 22 holes per 10 cm.

1 ? (DeRoy notation: "Fasten af")
2 Blank
3 Sustaining pedal on
4 Sustaining pedal off
5 to 17 Bass C, D-G, D
18 Swell shutters? (DeRoy: "Schellen")
19 to 32, Accompaniment E to F#
33 to 39, Melody G to C#
40 Xylophone on
41 Xylophone off
42 to 60, Melody D-G, A
61 Shutoff
62 Loud violin pipes on
63 Soft violin pipes on
64 Clarinet on
65 Mandolin on
66 General cancel
67 Rewind
68 Snare drum
69 Bass drum
70 Cymbal
71 Piano soft
72 (DeRoy: "Fasten Frei")

Some rolls may have the on and off holes reversed for the sustaining pedal and the xylophone.

SEYBOLD

In conjunction with Hohner, Seybold (a former Hohner employee) made a line of electric pianos and accordion players. These are not to be confused with the American piano of the same Seybold name. Some instruments consisted of a piano with a pneumatically-actuated accordion on the top; others used accordion-style harmonium reeds mounted in chests. Some instruments used a piano; others did not. Some were made with drums and other percussion devices. The era of greatest popularity was the 1920s.

SEYBOLD PIANO ACCORDEON-JAZZ ROLL
8" wide; spaced 9 holes per inch

1 Bass drum
2 Cymbal
3 Snare drum
4 Sustaining pedal
5 to 16, Bass notes, F to E
17 to 30, Accompaniment notes, F to F#
31 to 39, Expression (see footnotes)
40 to 65, Melody notes C to C, D
66 Bass off, without accordion register
67 Rewind
68 Shutoff
69 Melody off; cancel
70 Register off, with accordion register

Expression holes 31 through 39 control the loudness of the accordion by means of a 9-stage pneumatic attached to the spill valve spring. The original French notation for certain holes is as follows: 66 Basse arret, sans registre accordian; 69 Discant arret, trou/neant; 70 Register arret; avec registre accordian.

F. WEBER

The Erika, a coin-operated piano, was advertised as an "electric piano without keyboard, in the form of a cabinet, with the tone of the accordion and banjo." It used endless rolls which were stored in a bin to the left side on the interior, a similar arrangement to that used in the Pianolin (made by the North Tonawanda Musical Instrument Works). The case dimensions: 142 cm. high by 133 cm. wide by 49 cm. deep.

F. WEBER "ERIKA" COIN PIANO ROLL
Endless

1 Blank
2 Shutoff
3 Treble hammer rail up
4 Playing note
5 Bass hammer rail up
6 to 51, Playing notes
52 Sustaining pedal
53 Playing note
54 Coupler?
55 Playing note

PIANO MELODICO

Mechanical piano, Style 1 as illustrated in the center of page 361 of *The Encyclopedia of Automatic Musical Instruments.* Uses folding cardboard music books.

1 A
2 B
3 C#
4 D
5 E
6 F#
7 G
8 G#
9 A
10 B
11 C
12 C#
13 D
14 E
15 F#
16 G
17 G#
18 A
19 A#
20 B
21 C
22 C#
23 D
24 D#
25 E
26 F
27 F#
28 G
29 G#
30 A

UNIDENTIFIED SCALES
for
COIN PIANOS AND ORCHESTRIONS

The following scales, obtained from the B.A.B. Organ Company files and the Eugene DeRoy archives, have not been identified with certainty, although it is possible that some of the DeRoy scales are for Delta-brand instruments. Why list these scales when certain obscure scales which are known (barrel organ scales, for example) are not listed in this book? The answer: for diversity, and to show the raw information which intrigues researchers in the field.

UNIDENTIFIED PIANO ROLL (PEERLESS?)
11¼" wide; spaced 6 holes per inch; endless

1 Hammer rail down
2 Hammer rail up
3 Shutoff
4 to 63, 60 playing notes
64 Sustaining pedal on
65 Sustaining pedal off
  This scale is based on examination of rolls 75069 and 75324, possibly made by Peerless.

UNIDENTIFIED ORCHESTRION ROLL - 65 HOLES
(From a B.A.B. Organ Co. scale stick)

1 to 7, C, F, G, A, A#, B, C
8 to 13, D, D#, E, F, F#, G
14 to 45, A to D, E, F
46 to 59, G to G, A
60 Bass drum
61 Pipes on
62 Sustaining pedal (or loud?)
63 Snare drum
64 Bells on
65 Soft pedal (or soft?)

  The pipes and bells play from holes 46 to 59. During the early 20th century the B.A.B. Organ Co., of New York, made music for many types of band organs, especially those imported from Europe prior to 1914. Their business was especially active during the 1920s and 1930s. B.A.B. improvised its own scales for certain organs, and it may have also done this for orchestrions, as this scale would seem to indicate.

UNIDENTIFIED ORCHESTRION ROLL - 65 HOLES
11¼" wide; 6 holes per inch
(From a DeRoy scale stick)

1 Shutoff
2 Expression loud
3 Bass drum
4 Snare drum
5 Snare drum
6 Blank?
7 Wood block
8 Wood block
9 Play
10 Rewind
11 Cymbal
12 to 23, Bass notes, F to E
24 to 62, Playing notes, F to A
  The scale stick bears the wording "51 musical notes F-A." If this is correct, then the scale is not fully chromatic, for 51 notes starting on the scale at F will end on G.

UNIDENTIFIED ORCHESTRION ROLL - 67 HOLES
Approx. 13¾" wide; 2 holes per cm.
(From a DeRoy scale stick)

1 to 59, 59 playing notes, C to A#
60 ? ("Gebrayage")
61 Shutoff
62 Flute on
63 Register control?
64 Register control?
65 Xylophone
66 Bass drum
67 Snare drum

  Note: The flute pipes play from holes 32 to 64

UNIDENTIFIED ORCHESTRION ROLL
(From Eugene DeRoy scale stick)

  Left side:
1 Saxophone on
2 Violin pipes on
3 Triangle
4 Tremolo on
5 Cello on
6 Wood block
7 Clarinet on
8 General cancel
9 Bass drum
  Right side:
1 Sustaining pedal
2 "Piano" (piano on, or perhaps soft)
3 Oboe on
4 General cancel
5 Blank
6 Violin pipes on
7 Flute on

UNIDENTIFIED ORCHESTRION ROLL - 71 HOLES
Approx. 338 mm. wide; approx. 21 holes per 100 mm.
(From a DeRoy scale stick)

1 Bass drum
2 Percussion switch
3 Shutoff
4 Mandolin off
5 Sustaining pedal
6 Xylophone on
7 to 65, Notes C# to B
66 Xylophone off
67 Hammer rail
68 Mandolin on
69 Rewind
70 Snare drum; or 70+1, wood block
71 Cymbal; or 71+1, triangle

  The mandolin plays from holes 37 to 65, and the xylophone plays from holes 44 to 63.

  Note: Eugene DeRoy manufactured some distinctive orchestrion models in the 1920s and 1930s. Some of these were sold under the Delta name.

ROLLS FOR NEW INSTRUMENTS

During the 1940s and 1950s and to an extent during the 1960s a collector of automatic musical instruments could build a huge collection, filling a series of rooms with instruments and rolls for a modest sum of money. While the instruments were and still are rare in many instances, the diligent collector could acquire the classic orchestrions of Seeburg, Wurlitzer, Operators Piano Co. ("Coinola"), and, on a larger scale, Hupfeld, Welte, and Weber, for a relatively low cost. During the 1960s and 1970s interest and knowledge spread, and more and more collectors came into the field. Spearheaded by the publications of the Vestal Press, the hobby enjoyed a strong and steady growth rate. Whereas interest before 1970 was mainly confined to collectors in England, America, and Holland, during the 1970s collectors' organizations were formed in France, Germany, and elsewhere, with the result that by the end of the decade the field of automatic musical instruments commanded worldwide attention. America, England, Canada, Japan, Australia, France, Denmark, Italy, Germany, Sweden, and other countries were the sites of many fine collections. One enlightened government, that of Holland, expanded its national musical museum (in Utrecht) to become a showcase containing superb examples from all areas of automatic music. In America, the Smithsonian Institution exhibit, "Music Machines American Style," originally scheduled to be open for a year in the early 1970s, proved so popular that it was continued for several years. Interest grew and grew, and it continues to grow.

Years ago there was relatively little interest in making new instruments or recutting old music rolls or making copies of old music box discs, simply because originals could be obtained for the same price or less than the copies. Now, it is no longer possible in many instances to go into the marketplace and buy a Seeburg H orchestrion, or a large Ruth or Bruder band organ, or a Wurlitzer PianOrchestra, or a Weber Maesto, or a Coinola X orchestrion, even if you have a well-padded checkbook, simply because such instruments don't change hands often. And, when they do, the price usually represents a hefty increase from the last recorded sales figure! As a result, many collectors who wish to enjoy the music from "the good old days" have turned to the making of new instruments, some of which are innovative in concept and appearance and others of which are copies of older styles. Still another interest is from those who want instruments to use in restaurants or other commercial locations and who do not want to expose a valuable original instrument to hard use or abuse.

Most prevalent is the making of new orchestrions by using an old player piano as a basis. As the usual 88-note or 65-note player piano rolls are not orchestrated and will not play extra instruments, the question "What type of roll should I use?" arises. After reading this book you might decide that it would be really great to build a new orchestrion which uses Hupfeld Pan Orchestra, Weber Maesto, or, for that matter, North Tonawanda Mando-Orchestra rolls. But would one of these be a good choice?

There are several categories of roll rarity. It would pay the reader who contemplates a roll style to investigate the category into which a given roll falls. Also to be considered is the type of music desired. Some examples are given below.

1. Common rolls. This category includes orchestrion rolls which were originally made in large numbers, with the result that many original rolls are still available today. In addition, recut rolls have been made from time to time (or, in some instances, are made on a continuous basis). Among common rolls are the American A, G, O, and Wurlitzer 65-Note Automatic Player Piano styles. Generally, almost any tune, especially in the popular category, of the 1900-1930 era can be found on these rolls.

2. Scarce rolls. Rolls which are more elusive but which were originally made with a wide variety of tunes. Examples are Link RX, Marquette M, Mills Violano-Virtuoso, Operators NOS and OS (for the Reproduco), and Seeburg H. Some of these are available in recut form. Originals are hard to find in many instances. With the expanding circle of interest, chances are good that recuts will become more available in the future.

3. Rare, limited rolls. This category pertains to rolls which were originally made in very limited quantities and, more important, with a limited number of tunes available. Even if recuts were to become available, a really comprehensive "library" of music would not be a possibility. Examples include Empress L, Wurlitzer Mandolin Quartette, Hupfeld Pepita, Hupfeld Violina Orchestra, Weber Elite, many different types of Peerless rolls, North Tonawanda Mando-Orchestra and Orchestrina, and Mills Violano Orchestra. While an original instrument with a modest selection of rolls would be a superb addition to a collection, the modern orchestrion builder would undoubtedly do better to choose a type with a wider selection of music.

4. Large classic orchestrion rolls. This category includes rolls for very large classic orchestrions such as the Wurlitzer Mandolin PianOrchestra (Philipps PM), Hupfeld Helios and Pan, Weber Maesto, and others. Originals are very rare in most instances, simply because the instruments were exceedingly expensive and few were sold in comparison to the smaller, cheaper styles. However, a marvelous repertoire of superbly-arranged music is often available, including popular tunes as well as melodies not usually available for instruments in the preceding category 1; classical music being an example. However, there are problems with using these rolls on new orchestrions. First, recuts of most are not available. (This will probably change, as each year sees new types of rolls being recut.) Second, the mechanisms are complex as is the instrumentation, which would result in expensive duplication cost. And, third, the orchestrions are very large in size.

The American reader may find that the most practical alternative for a new orchestrion is to use A, G, or O rolls. Actually, A rolls are not *orchestrion* rolls but, rather, are for simpler instruments. Here are some guidelines which may be helpful.

Style A rolls play the piano with two levels of expression, operate a mandolin attachment, and have the capability of playing one extra instrument, usually a xylophone or set of bells (although a rank of pipes could be used as well, but this would entail building a pressure system or adapting the vacuum pump exhaust for this purpose, whereas the xylophone or bells operate from the same vacuum source used for the piano). The style A coin piano is the most economical of the three types to build. Converting a player piano to style A rolls involves adding a new roll frame, modifying the front to make it look like a "nickelodeon," and adding a coin slot and mechanism.

Style G rolls play the piano with multiple levels of expression, operate two extra instruments (such as two ranks of pipes or one rank of pipes and a xylophone), a mandolin attachment, and five percussion effects (with expression). These rolls are arranged to play full chords on the pipes, making much better use of them than O rolls do. 4X rolls, while similar to and compatible with G rolls, are arranged specifically for a single-stroke xylophone and sound best with this as an extra instrument. The percussion effects are lively and well-arranged on many early 4X rolls and on G rolls, but the bass drum and snare drum play almost constantly on the latest 4X rolls. Nevertheless, a good variety of tunes and musical arrangements are available on these rolls. If you want to make the best use of flute pipes, violin pipes, or perhaps an accordion or a single-stroke xylophone, choose the G roll.

Style O rolls have achieved a popularity with many collectors, probably because these rolls have more holes for percussion instruments (9 totally), more playing notes, a separate solo section for an extra instrument, and a little more expression than G rolls have. Some collectors feel that the solos add a great deal to the appeal of the music. However, the xylophone, bells, or pipes in an O-roll orchestrion play only one or two notes at a time and never play large chords. Many arrangements thus are quite "thin" in comparison to those on a G roll. The solo section is smaller, so there are fewer pipe notes than on a G roll. The solo sections are arranged for reiterating xylophone or orchestra bells and not for single-stroke instruments. While some may like it, music in the solo section played on pipes seems to many to be rather thin and weak. Unquestionably, the O roll hits its stride in instruments which have either a set of bells or a repeating xylophone. If you like the sound of catchy solos and duets played on the solo instrument, the most possible percussion effects, a musical scale which plays the most notes on the piano, and slightly more elaborate expression capabilities, choose the O roll.

While three different types of rolls are discussed above, there is the possibility that another type of roll will appeal to you; the Wurlitzer 65-note Automatic Player

This Peerless "Arcadian" orchestrion once was used in a Catskills (N.Y.) resort. Now restored, it plays melodies once again. Rewind-type Peerless Style O rolls (different from Coinola O rolls) provide the programming. While rolls of this type feature many excellent musical arrangements, their best use, due to their scarcity, is on original instruments such as this one. (Collection of Bellm's Cars & Music of Yesterday Museum, Sarasota, Florida)

Piano roll, for example. Or, perhaps the music arrangements on a type of rarer roll hold a special fascination for you. One collector informed us that he wanted to build an orchestrion to play the Peerless O roll, for this type contained certain ragtime arrangements not available elsewhere. Another collector, impressed with the Weber Maesto, expressed a desire to make one of these immense orchestrions. Still another plans to build a Wurlitzer Mandolin PianOrchestra.

The German collector may want to investigate building an instrument which uses either Hupfeld Helios or Philipps PM (Wurlitzer Mandolin PianOrchestra) rolls, for both of these roll types were originally made with a vast selection of music, international tunes as well as those with a native German flavor.

Before making a decision, listen to several different types of instruments, study their tracker scales, and observe the instruments "in action." Determine what types of rolls are available. The Vestal Press, publisher of this book, can supply names and addresses of roll manufacturers.

An entry into the field of modern orchestrions is this "Universal Nickelodeon" made by the Universal Piano Company of Los Angeles, California. The model shown is from a 1979 sales brochure. Instrumentation consists of a piano which is advertised as having a "full 88-note direct action on large rugged perimeter plate," xylophone or orchestra bells, wood block, tambourine, triangle, cymbal, mandolin, snare drum, and bass drum. It uses type "O" Coinola orchestrion rolls wound on small-diameter spools.

THE QUESTION
of
TUNING MUSICAL ANTIQUES

by Arthur W.J.G. Ord-Hume

The following article gives opinions and observations of Arthur W.J.G. Ord-Hume, prominent British author in the field of automatic musical instruments; a gentleman who for many years has been editor of "The Music Box," official journal of the Musical Box Society of Great Britain. The author's observations pertain mainly to very early instruments and not to American, British, and continental European instruments of the present century, for the most part. Owners of 19th century and earlier music boxes, chamber barrel organs, musical clocks, pipe organs, and related devices will find Mr. Ord-Hume's message to be especially important.

I was intrigued to receive an invitation to contribute to this valuable reference work some comments on the question of tuning. This book is concerned with tuning scales. I find it paradoxical that while many people think they understand what is meant by the expression "tuning," very few indeed really know what this means, let alone how to put it into practice. Most, I find, understand even less on the subject of "tuning scales" and, furthermore, have little appreciation of the significance of musical pitch. And yet this subject is the very heart of musical instrument restoration, preservation, and conservation.

Rare 19th century revolver cylinder box with a cluster of six 6-tune cylinders. In addition to two music combs the box has an organ section. The cylinders measure 17" long. There are 22 organ notes. The maker is unidentified but is undoubtedly Swiss. (Ruth Bornand photograph)

Now this word which so many of us use called "tuning" is really a pretty vague term to describe a vital and delicate operation. That we are able to "tune" a piano or pipe organ, banjo, or guitar is one thing; that we understand what tuning *means* in respect to an antique instrument is another.

Why, I hear you asking, is all this important? The answer is simple. Very many automatic musical instruments, in particular the early ones, were not "tuned" to the same pitch pattern as that which we use today, and any attempt to bring the pitch into line with, say, a piano or modern fixed-pitch instrument is certain to result in irreparable damage.

Tuning is another aspect of restoration, yet while many will spend hours over polishing rusted metal and cleaning woodwork, little thought is given to the very essence of restoration: *the restoration of the original sound.*

Before any handbook tells you about french polishing it tells you a little about wood and polish. Before any handbook tells you how to work in metal it tells you something about the properties of the metal and how to form it. By the same token, before we can talk about restoring the original sound we must consider for a few moments some of the basic factors which govern sound and make it what it is.

All of this comes under the general heading of *conservation.* Always remember that if you have a mechanical musical instrument in your collection you do not *own* it; you own the *right* to look after it, to preserve and to cherish it. Nobody can ever own the skill, the love, and the craft of a long-passed master who created a piece in the dim distant past.

From this you will understand that I am more concerned with the "tuning" of instruments other than the average modern-production player piano or pipe organ or reed organ. I am concerned here about the instruments built between the earliest days of self-acting musical instruments through the time of the musical box, the European dance organ, and to the fairground organ and similar machines which were "tuned" to a scheme not compatible with the pianoforte.

Where shall we start? Well, let's begin by analyzing what this business of "tuning" is all about. A musical scale is a set of divisions which separate the spectrum of sound from the lowest up to the highest note into a small number of perfectly equal steps which are called *octaves*. These are sounds which have the same fundamental but which are spaced at twice the number of vibrations as the preceding one. Our initial staircase of octave steps, though, is too coarse to be used for playing music since all the notes are basically similar in origin, just their vibrations are doubled. We have to build a

The face of an ornate musical watch from the early 19th century. (Lewis Graham Collection)

smaller staircase between each step in order to do that. This creates the notes between the octave jump.

To simplify this a little, sound is, as we know, a series of vibrations. The slower the vibrations, the lower the pitch of the sound. As the vibrations increase to more and more in number per second of time, so the pitch of the sound increases. When we reach approximately 440 vibrations per second we hear a sound which we define as A below middle C on the keyboard of the modern pianoforte or organ.

If we take that musical note A and we play the next A above it or below it, we find that we have the same type of sound, a harmonious sound, only the speed of the vibrations is halved (for the lower A) or doubled (for the higher A). Our musical scale, then, is the set of steps which leads upwards and downwards from one A to the next. Because we always delineate the musical scale from the note which is called C, it is more usual to work from this note than A, but the same system exists between any of the notes on the pianoforte; for example, we can measure an octave from G, from D sharp or from B flat—wherever we start there is always a staircase to the same harmonious note above or below.

These steps which form the staircase, however, differ from the steps we are accustomed to running up or down in one important way: they are not of equal height! This one fact is the big clue to the problem which faces the restorer of antique musical instruments—the steps in which the musical octave is divided cannot be relied upon to be of the same height or necessarily of the same height as those of similar steps on any other musical instrument. Imagine, if you will, trying to

match the wooden steps from a 17th century corn-grinding windmill against the staircase in your own house. The overall height of the staircase may be the same, but the length of the staircase is bound to be different, and the individual treads will not match either.

So here is our big, big problem. We know that musical instruments have a scale to which they are tuned, but we have to be certain in our own mind that the steps which we decide to divide the octave into are the same as those originally intended.

Does it really matter? There are three types of instruments which can be considered here: stringed instruments, pipe instruments, and comb instruments which, in typical examples, include early pianos, pipe organs, and musical boxes. There are very real musical reasons why the original tuning system should never be altered, but, before looking at those, there are some practical reasons which are equally important. Let's first consider stringed instruments; in particular, the harps in harp clocks and early piano-type instruments with wooden frames. To adjust the tuning of these instruments to bring them into line with today's standards invariably means tightening up the strings to a much greater amount than originally intended. The tension in a wire increases dramatically as you move higher up the scale for smaller and smaller increases in pitch. Wind these strings up to modern pitch and two things may well happen. First, the strings may break because of the extra tension and, second, the wooden frames will slowly distort and the tuning pins will pull out.

As for the pipe organ, to tune to modern pitch will mean shortening many of the pipes. In so doing the vital proportions of the pipes will be altered as you move further up the scale. An organ pipe is designed along very precise and accurate geometry; the speaking length and the height of the lip or languid are critical. Adjust one and the other is lost. Do not, therefore, attempt to alter the fundamental pitch of an early organ.

With the musical box comb, of course, things are much, much worse since any attempt to re-base the tuning scale will result in disproportionate amounts of metal being removed from individual teeth. The tone and timbre of sound produced by a musical box comb tooth is very dependent on its extremely accurate proportions and the relationship of one tooth to another is critical for the evenness of sound between individual teeth.

So now you see that attempting something which sounds like a simple operation can in fact be very, very destructive and destroy forever the original sound.

What about the music? Before looking at this we must consider carefully some more of the technicalities of the ways of tuning. You may be reassured to know that more hot air has been released over musical instrument tuning than over any other subject. To begin with there are at least two types of tuning which center on what is called "temperament," which means the adjustment in tuning which is needed to ameliorate or dispense with inaccuracies in the intervals between certain notes. This comes about because our staircase which makes up the octave has seven steps—from, say, middle C on the pianoforte to the next C above—to which are added five "half tones" or sharps, making a total of 13 divisions in the octave. If the octave is separated into seven main component parts (as it is by the notes C-D-E-F-G-A-B and then C again), each note produces a set of harmonics, the strongest of which are the *octave* and the *fifth.* This means that C will produce the harmonics of the C above and the G a fifth above that. From this we can deduce that the two most important musical intervals are the octave (which we know from experience) and the fifth. So our octave of notes ought to contain a total of seven culpable fifths but, owing to an unfortunate acoustic quirk which I won't bore you with, the actual figure is in excess of seven; in precise figures it turns out to be 7.019550008654.

The fifth is an important interval since it forms the basis of all common chords; i.e., C-E-G and its minor variant C-E flat-G, but if we tune a piano in perfect fifths we end up with a quarter of a semitone which just doesn't fit in. In a manner of speaking, we have stumbled across the "Pythagorean Comma," a sort of artistic quark discovered by Pythagoras and thereby no doubt qualifying as the first and only genuine quark! Whereas we may think of an ordinary comma as insignificant, this particular one is such a menace that it is probably standing point uppermost to pierce our boots as well as trip us up.

If we attempt to tune our piano in perfect—really perfect—fifths, from a low C and down in perfect fifths from a high one, the two processes at once prove how wild that comma is, for we find we move upwards from C to G, D, A, E, B, F sharp, C sharp, G sharp, D sharp, A sharp, E sharp, B sharp, and down C, F, B flat, A flat, D flat, G flat, C flat, F flat, B double-flat, E double-flat, A double-flat, D double-flat. At this point we throw our hands up in despair, burn the piano and take up fishing!

In the early days of music, namely the first two thousand years or so, the fifth was inviolate and the bit left over at the end was ignored. This was fine so long as you sang or played music in only a few keys. But as music became more venturesome and polyphony replaced plainsong and along with it inspiration which suggested that music should modulate from one key into another, the "mean-tone" system came into use. Here it was the major thirds which were considered fixed and all other intervals were adapted to suit. It became possible to perform music in about six major keys and three minor and, in truth, the slight dissonances which the acute ear today detects in some of these keys were really rather attractive, and certainly some keys were rendered especially bright. This characteristic of brightness was one which many composers and instrument makers sought to use to advantage. But outside these keys, though, things got out of hand, and excessive dissonance reared its ugly head. Not without cause did the malady take the soubriquet of "the wolf."

Well, there had to be an answer. Many people reckon that it was Johann Sebastian Bach who finally laid the "wolf" with his "well-tempered klavier." It wasn't, of course, for Bach's own words were just that: "well-tempered" and nothing more. But certainly he was a strong advocate of introducing a large number of small wolves into the octave in place of a few really big ones. Indeed, the success of his approach inspired the "48 Preludes and Fugues" which he wrote for his well-tempered klavier.

A barrel-operated piano made in Germany in the late 19th century displays automaton figures on the front. (Claes Friberg Collection, Mekanisk Musik Museum, Copenhagen)

The solution had to be some sort of *equal temperament* in which neither fifths nor thirds are *absolutely* perfect, Pythagoras' Comma being cut into small pieces and evenly distributed throughout the octave—and the little wolves become an acceptable fact of musical life.

Let me emphasize that equal temperament does not automatically mean that a musical performance must be better when performed to such tonal constraints and, as I said earlier, unequal and mean-tone temperament can actually enhance the beauty of music in certain keys.

So what did our early automatic musical instrument makers know about temperament when they came to tune their instruments or, as we say in musical instrument manufacture, to *lay the scale*. A good deal, it seems, although neither system was universal. Many of the outstanding Swiss musical boxes made up to the mid-1850s and, in some cases, even later, conform more nearly to mean-tone than to unequal or equal temperament. German disc-playing musical boxes came, of course, much later. These benefited from the later experiences in tuning built on the prognostications of Andreas Werckmeister in the seventeenth century, through Bach and to the high standards of mid-nineteenth century German organ building. It is interesting to compare these later German disc machines with the early Swiss ones and to note that in many instances the early Swiss machines were appreciably brighter in registration. This brightness was achieved at the expense of dissonance in the remote keys—back to the wolves again, but intentionally so.

Another consideration is the very foundation of pitch. I mentioned earlier that about 440 cycles per second represented the musical note A. But this has not always been so, nor has it remained constant throughout the world of musical instrument manufacture. Pitch has climbed steadily since the early days, particularly during the last century. At the time of Handel, the note A equalled 422.5 cycles per second. Mozart's A was 421.6, while during the life of Beethoven it varied between 415 and 430. During the 19th century, pitch rose by more than a semitone, particularly in Britain. In 1813 A was 423.7, later it was 433.2, and then the London Philharmonic Society increased it to 452.5. At the end of the nineteenth century the French introduced "diapason pitch," which was known in America as international or French pitch. This had a value for A of 435. Significantly, an examination of Swiss musical boxes in original condition suggests that A was about 420 in 1810, 410 by mid-century, and between 445 and 450 by 1880, although combs of similar periods show marked variations. Disc musical boxes also varied, with A ranging from 452 to an extraordinary 465 in some small Symphonions.

For the restorer today to try to tune an existing comb to modern standards is not just a formidable task involving the adjustment of every note in the octave, but it is a most destructive exercise which robs the instrument of its very character. Makers such as Lecoultre and Ducommon Girod knew all about temperament and the wolves. Ducommon Girod boxes feature dissonant trills in many arrangements; dissonances which are indeed pronounced but which are always resolved into the dominant in a manner which is so much more satisfactory than were the comb tuned to an equal-type of temperament.

German orchestrions of the early 19th century were almost all tuned to the higher pitch and to equal temperament. French barrel organs of the earliest period were tuned to Mozartian pitch and to unequal temperament, while those from around the middle of the 19th century were tuned to what today is called Old Philharmonic Pitch, with A approximating 452.5 cycles per second, and mean-tone. The popular European organs of the street and dance hall were generally tuned a whole tone and occasionally a minor third higher; i.e., C would sound D sharp. This is a feature of Gavioli, among many others.

Keyboard instruments (including early barrel and finger pianos, barrel and finger organs, and automatic reed organs) are generally tuned to modern temperament, but it is always necessary to check most carefully before attempting to adjust the tuning.

As a corollary to all this, then, you will appreciate that you cannot attempt to "tune" a musical box, early piano or organ, street organ or dance organ, or early reed instrument to a modern piano, harmonium, or pitch pipe. Those who advocate this (and there are many of them) have obviously never tried it. It reminds me of the story of the accompanist and the soprano who kept asking for the pianist to transpose down a shade, then up a shade, then down again, until in desperation he

This 19th century English barrel organ has two 10-tune pinned cylinders and was probably made for use in a small church or chapel. (Sunley Collection)

cried from the keyboard, "Madam, you may be a great singer, but you are singing in the cracks between my keys!"

Well, I can hear you saying, what about the electronic tuning devices on the market which allow a totally deaf person to tune a piano? Fine, I say. They are excellent for tuning your modern player piano or reproducing piano, but they are never to be used on a genuine antique instrument because their accurately-contrived octave divisions cannot in any way match the steps in the octave of your vintage mechanism.

There is another reason why electronic tuning aids are not to be used on very early instruments. This is because many of the early makers knew that they had one more trick up their sleeves to make the music sound even better. This was to stretch the tuning slightly in both directions. It is a technique widely used by professional piano tuners even today. It consists of making the treble octaves very slightly but progressively sharper the higher you go, and by making the lower octaves very slightly longer (flatter) the lower you go. The effect, when properly executed, is in no way detectable as dissonance, yet it strengthens the musical sound in a subtle way.

Gerry Planus was once puzzled to detect this characteristic in a musical box comb until I was able to explain it to him. He plotted the values of all the notes on a piece of paper together with their calculated pitches, only to find that the straight-line ideal pitch was crossed by the actual pitch line at a point equal to just below the midpoint C. The technician who had made that comb had stretched his octaves by ear. His great accuracy of hearing could now be demonstrated many years after his death by the calibration of his surviving work.

Now the finest aid to tuning is the ear. Unless you have a good ear, the presence of a piano or tuning fork or what-have-you can in no way help you. Even in this modern age if you visit a piano factory you will see that the tuners do not use electronic gadgets. The real skill comes only from the ear.

Having said that, if you must use electronics, use an infinitely variable frequency calibrator showing either a matching trace on a cathode ray tube or, much to be preferred, a digital read-out. This will help you to establish the octaves. Avoid instruments which have the musical intervals of modern-day pitch switch-selectable as these will only match the modern pianoforte.

[Ed. note (by Art Reblitz): My experience in the United States is that some of the finest piano makers are using electronic tuners. Further, I have found that the Hale Sight-O-Tuner or the Conn Strobotuner can be used to duplicate any temperament, old or new; neither has a digital or CRT readout.]

Now so far I have carefully avoided the use of the word "scale" because here is a word which needs very careful identifying indeed. This book contains plenty of scales; but what are scales? A complete scale is like a ladder: it reaches from the lowest note up to the top note either by all the available steps in each octave (the thirteen divisions we mentioned earlier), or by a selected few of them. It is, for example, quite often that the lower octaves of some instruments will be abbreviated into just those notes which are needed; observe, for

A German craftsman builds a barrel-operated orchestrion, circa 1905. Today, the tuning of such an instrument should only be done after much careful study.

example, the sparse bass register of a small dance or band organ. Now that ladder comprising the scale ideally should start from the ground level, but like any other ladder you could take it, for example, to the top of the garden wall before propping it against the side of the house. The ladder still has the same number of steps, and the second step is still the second step, only the bottom of the ladder is much higher off the ground. Conversely, you could stand the ladder in a hole in the ground in which case there are steps on the ladder which are still in the same position on the ladder, but which are below the level of the ground.

This is just what a musical scale is. If I tell you that I will sing the note C to you, you may assume that I shall sing it at modern concert pitch and produce a sound at about 512 cycles per second. But I could just as well have my scale (ladder) lower down (in a hole in the ground) and sing my C based on the pitch of Mozart's piano.

My scale of notes, then, is valueless unless I tell you clearly where the foot of the ladder is. Saying it is on the ground is just not sufficient since the ground can be very uneven. I must state the basic pitch on which I start my progression of steps through the octave.

In practical terms, then, how can we determine what pitch was originally used when an instrument was built? Are there any clues on the instrument which will tell us? The short answer is yes, there are plenty of clues, but you may need to look carefully before detecting them.

I think we can forget musical boxes in this discussion since, unless you are making a new comb with nothing to go by for a tonal pattern, the musical box always has some teeth which produce the clue sound. Just let me say that the lower in the scale the tooth plays, the less likely it is to have been affected in terms of musical pitch by wear and rusting. [An exception are certain bass teeth with lead weights, sometimes called "resonators," which tend to oxidize or corrode and undergo a change in pitch. —Ed.] You can thus gain important clues to the tuning of a new tooth in a musical box comb from the others around it. Don't tune them unless it is absolutely vital through, say, severe corrosion.

Let's look at a pipe organ. Almost always the scale of the pipes will be marked on the pipes in pencil or ink. Check for this very carefully before cleaning the pipes in case you erase the vital information. Now the higher up the scale the pipe sounds, the more critical is the speaking length of the pipe. An open pipe should not have altered at all over the years because there is nothing to modify its length and so its pitch. However, an open pipe which has a pipe-metal shade, or a stopped pipe with a leather-covered wooden stopper, may well have changed its pitch due to the shade or the stopper having been moved over the years.

As I said just now, the higher up the scale we go, the more precise has to be the position of the shade or stopper to give the right pitch. From this it becomes easy to see that lower down the scale a reasonable amount of movement of these parts can be tolerated without too much effect on pitch. This means that if you take a surviving pipe in good condition fairly near the lowest note of the organ and provided that it is in good condition, gently blow it, and it will give you a very good idea of the foundation pitch on which all the other pipes are tuned. I prefer to take perhaps half a dozen pipes from the lower register of the middle rank of an organ (for example, the four-foot stopped rank in a chamber barrel organ) and sound two or three octave C pipes, the matching E and G pipes, and then from this make my adjustments to bring these into approximate line. This I then use as the tuning foundation, at all times being careful to see that the shorter pipes do not require excessive adjustment to bring them into tune. If this is so, I will made fresh adjustment to the lower notes and then work over the scale again.

The important thing to remember here is that we use the divisions of the scale in their correct proportions only; do not concern yourself with their pitch, since the foundation pitch is unlikely to match modern standards.

Always remember that the essence of restoration should be the restoration of the original sound which should be of primary concern. Appearance and finish is of secondary importance to this.

Having said that, there are some occasions when a precise preservation of the sound is, for various reasons difficult or impossible to obtain. These should never affect the pitch of the sound (meaning the "scale" and the "tuning") but may affect the processes of attainment. Let me explain. Many early pianos, dulcimers, and harp-clocks, for example, were strung with a quality of music wire no longer available. German music wire, for instance, was of very high tensile strength for its gauge or thickness and frequently it is impossible to bring modern wires up to pitch. An excellent early reference is Pinet's *Harmonium & Piano Tuner,* which shows which gauge of wire produced a certain pitch of sound when stretched through a specific distance.

As a general rule, all wood-framed pianos (that is, pianos without iron frames or plates) I restring up to two gauges lighter. This has two primary effects. First, it reduces the overall strain on the frame while not upsetting the pitch. Second, it helps to brighten the sound and thereby compensate in some measure for deterioration of the hammers and the inevitable alteration in the down-bearing of the strings on the soundboard which has come about with age. (In instances in which the hammers have become hardened, the brightness is already increased.) Because such a process is reversible and errs on the side of preserving the instrument, lightening the stringing is a process which I do not condemn on the otherwise inviolate grounds of absolute originality.

In replacing organ pipes in an instrument, remember that the speaking length of the pipe only affects the pitch of the sound produced. There are other factors which govern the timbre of the sound, the tone of the pipe, and its harmonics. Besides the physical proportions of the obvious parts such as length, cross-section and shape of the cut-up for the mouth, there are the considerations of the proportions of the actual pieces of wood from which the pipes are glued together. Every single piece of wood in an organ pipe bears a precise dimensional relationship to the pipe. When you have to make up a new pipe, it is well worth very carefully examining the proportions of the pipe either side of the missing one so as to gauge these dimensions as accurately as possible.

I hope that my words have served to dissuade well-meaning enthusiasts from tackling jobs which can genuinely result in the destruction of a fine instrument. If you have any doubts whatsoever, then get advice before attempting to "tune."

By all means undertake tuning instruments manufactured in the United States and Britain after about 1900 or in continental Europe after about 1920. But for instruments prior to these dates, please think before you act.

No one will thank you for making a misguided attempt at modifying an instrument. Be warned! If and when you go to heaven, you can be certain that a long-dead instrument maker will be waiting to meet you—and he won't be in a very good mood! Also, just think what it would be like if all of the angels' harps were tuned by people who were amateurs.

When I hear someone say of a musical instrument, "it needs tuning," he probably thinks I know what he means. In truth, I don't. And I know he probably doesn't either.

The following table, abbreviated from my book *Barrel Organ,* shows the different nomenclature used to define the intervals of the octave:

English: C, D, E, F, G, A, B; German: C, D, E, F, G, A, H; French: ut or do, re, me, fa, sol, la, si; Italian: do, re, me, fa, sol, la, si. Note that B flat in English is B in German, and that B in English becomes H in German.

Chapter 7

REED, PIPE and ELECTRONIC ORGANS

MANUFACTORY AND GENERAL OFFICE

OF THE

Tournaphone Music Co.

No. 9 May Street,

WORCESTER, MASS., U. S. A.

Controllers of Seventy Patents upon Automatic
Musical Instruments,
embracing every Valuable Invention of
this class in THE WORLD.

—◊—

TOURNAPHONES,
AUREPHONES,
CABINETTOS.
AUTOMATIC ORGANS,
MUSICAL CABINETS.

1200 Pieces of Perforated Music
on Spools.

Send for Catalogues and Circulars.

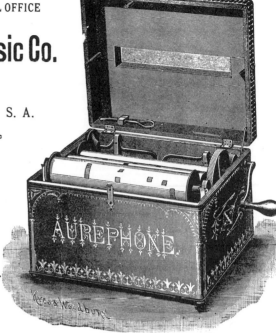

Worcester, May 21st 1885

Messr. Wolfe & Leiser;

Lewisburgh, Pa.,

Gentlemen;

We have an over due account of about
$33.00 against W. P. Thomas, pianos, Lewisburg.

If you will take & push this claim
for a per centage on such amount as you collect, please state for what per centage you will
undertake its collection without suit, & for what
per centage you will bring suit, if necessary,
plus such costs as you can obtain from Thomas.

Yours in confidence

Tournaphone Music Co..

AUTOMATICALLY-PLAYED
REED, PIPE, AND ELECTRONIC ORGANS
and Related Instruments

Beginning in the 1870s, small table-top reed organs played by means of paper or cardboard strips, discs of metal or cardboard, and pinned cylinders became very popular. These instruments, sold under such names as Ariston, Mechanical Orguinette, Gem Roller Organ, etc., usually were priced from about $3 to $15 and were distributed all over the world.

The two most successful organettes from the standpoint of quantities originally manufactured were the Ariston, a disc-operated instrument made in Germany, and the Gem Roller Organ, made in Ithaca, New York, which used pinned wooden cylinders or "cobs."

Although organettes are of limited musical scale, some very fine arrangements can be found on various discs, cylinders, rolls, and paper strips. Although some organettes were made by large firms which also produced keyboard-style player reed or pipe organs (Aeolian, for example), all of the organette scales in this book are listed at the beginning of the present chapter, to show their interrelationship and to permit comparison, rather than with the other larger products of the firms which produced them.

During the late 19th and early 20th century a number of automatically-operated reed organs, pipe organs, mortuary organs, and theatre photoplayers achieved commercial success. Earlier, many different types of player organs had been made, but most were either one-of-a-kind or were strictly limited in production. The Apollonicon barrel-operated organ exhibited in London during the first part of the 19th century and the marvelous Electromagnetic Orchestra, an orchestrion-organ made in America by the Schmoele Brothers of Philadelphia and shown at the 1876 Centennial Exhibition in Philadelphia are examples.

In the 1890s Wilcox & White, maker of the Symphonia and other organettes, introduced its Symphony roll-operated keyboard-style reed organ. At the same time the larger Aeolian Company, which had its inception with the sale of Mechanical Orguinettes (organettes), was beginning to sell keyboard roll-operated reed organs under the Aeolian Grand label and other names. Merritt Gally was another maker of roll-operated organs, but only a few were of the keyboard format. Still others each had a small share of the market.

By 1910 the Aeolian Company, which marketed a wide variety of case designs for its Grand, Orchestrelle, and Solo Orchestrelle reed organs and several varieties of player pipe organs, was dominant in the industry. Over 2000 roll-operated pipe organs were sold for installation in private residences during the next few decades, and many additional thousands of player reed organs were marketed.

The popularity of motion picture theatres spawned the photoplayer industry during the 1910-1920 decade. Built like orchestrions, but with the components in low cabinets or side chests to permit installation below a movie screen, these were made by Marquette, Seeburg, Hupfeld, Operators, Link, and others prominent in the coin piano field. While many of these used orchestrion rolls or regular 88-note home player piano rolls (in which instance the orchestra effects had to be turned on and off by hand), some used distinctive photoplayer-type

rolls, the Seeburg MSR being an example. Refer to the Marquette, Seeburg, Hupfeld, and Operators coin piano and orchestrion sections for information on photoplayers made by these firms. The products of other firms such as Link and Wurlitzer are listed in the present chapter.

The mortuary trade furnished additional opportunities for Wurlitzer, Operators, and others to sell roll-operated pipe organs of compact format.

Today, electronic technology has made possible the recording of pipe organ performances on magnetic discs and tapes, thus rendering obsolete such elaborate paper roll systems as the Austin Premier Quadruplex. However, the existing thousands of Estey, Wurlitzer, Austin, Aeolian, Welte, and other pipe organ rolls contain a rich legacy of actual recorded performances by famous keyboard artists of the early 20th century, so the present chapter will provide the modern organ builder or rebuilder with the necessary information to understand the rolls of yesteryear, the information they contain, and perhaps the motivation to translate some of these classic performances from rolls to modern electronic reproducing systems. And, of course, there are many collectors, organists, museums, and others who own original Welte, Wurlitzer, Aeolian, and other instruments who wish to keep them exactly as they were built.

The present chapter contains first a listing of organette scales, then a listing in order by maker or trademark of large reed, pipe, and electronic organ layouts. The most widely used scales are given—those of Aeolian, Welte, and Wurlitzer—as well as a selection of lesser-known scales such as Austin and Estey, and a representation of obscure scales such as that of the firm of Verlinden, Weickhardt & Dornoff.

ORGANETTE SCALES

AMERICAN ORGUINETTE, STYLE 2
*12 5/8" wide

1 G
2 A
3 C
4 D
5 E
6 F
7 F#
8 G
9 A
10 B
11 C
12 C#
13 D
14 E
15 F
16 F#
17 G
18 A
19 B
20 C
21 D
22 E
23 F

ARISTON
(also used on the Orpheus mechanical zither)
33 cm. diameter cardboard discs; holes 3 mm. wide, 3.9 mm. apart

1 A
2 B
3 D
4 E
5 A
6 B
7 C#
8 D
9 E
10 F#
11 G
12 A
13 B
14 C#
15 D
16 D#
17 F
18 F#
19 G
20 G#
21 A
22 B
23 C#
24 D

A German tuning scale stick indicates note 11 as G#.

AMORETTE
8 7/8" discs

1 E
2 F#
3 B
4 C#
5 D#
6 E
7 F#
8 G#
9 A#
10 B
11 C#
12 D#
13 E
14 F
15 F#
16 G#

AUREPHONE
HARMONIA
Tournaphone Music Co.

1 F#
2 G#
3 A#
4 C
5 C#
6 D
7 D#
8 E
9 F
10 F#
11 G
12 G#
13 A#
14 C
15 C#
16 D#
17 F

AUTOPHONE
H.B. Horton, Ithaca, N.Y.
13.65 cm. wide strips; 5.05 mm. per space

1 G#
2 A
3 A#
4 B
5 C#
6 D
7 D#
8 E
9 F#
10 G#
11 A
12 A#
13 B
14 C#
15 D
16 D#
17 E
18 F#
19 G#
20 A
21 B
22 C#

CELESTINA
Mechanical Orguinette Co.
14 cm. wide; holes 6.3 mm. per space

1 A#
2 D#
3 F
4 G#
5 A#
6 C
7 D
8 D#
9 E
10 F
11 F#
12 G
13 G#
14 A
15 A#
16 C
17 D
18 D#
19 F
20 G

Another Celestina uses this scale but is tuned one step lower and uses tune sheets 9.25 cm. wide with 4.2 mm. hole spacing.

Another scale is three half-steps lower, beginning on G. The same basic scale, in various keys, is used by Seraphone and Ariel organettes as well as the Mandolina (which is a variation of the Celestina). The Bijou Orchestrone also uses this scale, transposed a whole step lower. It plays a roll 3 5/8" wide.

COLUMBIAN ORGUINETTE
Bates Organ Manufacturing Co., Boston
(Scale is from right to left)

1 A#
2 C
3 D
4 D#
5 F
6 G
7 G#
8 A
9 A#
10 C
11 D
12 D#
13 F
14 G

A 14-note Melodia organette using a 7¾" paper roll uses the same scale, transposed one whole step down, from G# to F. The 14-note "Big Bonanza" organette also uses this scale, transposed down a half step, from A to F#.

GEM ROLLER ORGAN
HOME MUSIC BOX
CONCERT ROLLER ORGAN
NEW AMERICAN MUSICAL BOX
AMERICAN MUSICAL BOX
CHAUTAUQUA ROLLER ORGAN, etc.
Uses pinned wooden cylinders or "cobs"
Notes listed by the top row of reeds left to right, then the bottom row left to right.

1 D
2 G
3 A
4 B
5 C
6 C#
7 D
8 E
9 F#
10 G
11 G#
12 A
13 B
14 C
15 C#
16 D
17 E
18 F#
19 G
20 A

Gem Roller Organs, Concert Roller Organs, and the identical instruments marketed under different names were made in various keys. The actual playing pitches sometimes differ from those stamped on the reeds. To find the actual pitches of a given organ, find the actual pitch of one or more reeds and then transpose the rest of the scale from the one printed here. (Refer to "Transposing a Band Organ Scale" in the band organ section of this book.)

Gem Roller organs and their relatives were not tuned to any particular pitch standard, so some organs were sharper than others, and some organs were flatter. The tuners apparently tuned each set of reeds hastily to whatever pitch necessitated the least amount of tuning, so no two organs were necessarily tuned exactly the same.

JUBAL ORCHESTRONE
McTAMMANY MECHANICAL ORGUINETTE
REED PIPE CLARIONA
Approx. 20 cm. wide; 13.6 mm. per space

1 A
2 B
3 C#
4 D
5 E
6 F#
7 G
8 G#
9 A
10 B
11 C#
12 D
13 E
14 F#

The lowest two notes on the Jubal Orchestrone are in the octave below the rest of the scale. The Gately Automatic Organ and the Melodia also use this scale but are tuned a half step lower, and one Gately examined by the authors is tuned a full step lower. Other instruments probably exist which were tuned in other keys.

MUSETTE
IMPROVED MUSETTE
Mechanical Orguinette Co., New York
3 9/16" wide

1 F#
2 G#
3 A#
4 B
5 C
6 C#
7 D
8 D#
9 E
10 F
11 F#
12 G#
13 A#
14 B
15 C#
16 D#

The Organina manufactured by the American Automatic Organ Company uses the same note scale as the Musette and Improved Musette but plays punched cards 14.5 cm. wide with holes spaced 8.7 cm. apart, and tuned one fourth higher, starting on B.

ORGANINA

1 B
2 C#
3 D#
4 E
5 F
6 F#
7 G
8 G#
9 A
10 A#
11 B
12 C#
13 D#
14 E
15 F
16 F#

ORGANINA THIBOUVILLE
(Paris, France)
15.45 cm. wide; 6.25 mm. per space

1 A#
2 C
3 D#
4 F
5 A#
6 C
7 D
8 D#
9 E
10 F
11 G
12 G#
13 A
14 A#
15 C
16 D
17 D#
18 E
19 F
20 G
21 G#
22 A
23 A#
24 C

PHOENIX ORGANETTE
14 17/32" disc

1 C
2 F
3 G
4 A
5 A#
6 C
7 D
8 D#
9 E
10 F
11 F#
12 G
13 A
14 A#
15 B
16 C
17 C#
18 D
19 D#
20 E
21 F
22 G
23 A
24 A#

ROLMONICA
3¼" wide

1 E
2 F
3 G
4 B
5 C
6 D
7 E
8 F
9 G
10 A
11 C
12 B

Note 12 (B) falls between 10 and 11 in the musical scale. Music rolls for the 12-note model are numbered at least up to the 500s. Rolls for the 16-note size (see scale below) are in the 2000 series. Dr. Howard Fitch described the Rolmonica in the Spring 1972 issue of *The Bulletin of the Musical Box Society International.*

CHROMATIC ROLMONICA
3 11/16" wide roll

1 E
2 F#
3 G#
4 A
5 A#
6 B
7 C
8 C#
9 D
10 D#
11 E
12 F
13 F#
14 G
15 G#
16 A

TOURNAPHONE
CABINETTO
Tournaphone Music Co., Worcester, Mass.
13¾" wide

1 C
2 D
3 E
4 F
5 G
6 A
7 A#
8 B
9 C
10 C#
11 D
12 E
13 F
14 F#
15 G
16 G#
17 A
18 A#
19 B
20 C
21 D
22 E
23 F
24 G
25 A

For further information on organettes the reader may refer to an article, "Comparison of Roller Organ Scales," by Wesley B. Reed, in the Spring-Summer 1977 *Bulletin of the Musical Box Society,* the source for several scales in this section.

J. McTAMMANY.
AUTOMATIC MUSICAL INSTRUMENT.

No. 328,503.   Patented Oct. 20, 1885.

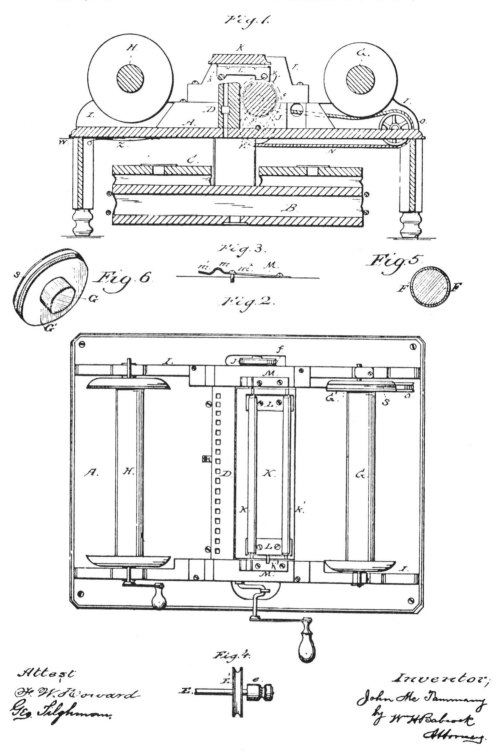

Fig. 1.

Fig. 3.

Fig. 6.   *Fig. 5.*

Fig. 2.

Fig. 4.

Attest   Inventor;
H. W. Howard   John Mc Tammany
Geo. Tilghman   by W. H. Babcock
                                Attorneys.

A John McTammany patent of 1885 showing a roll-operated organette. Despite a proliferation of patents, most organettes operated in one of three ways: (1) the paper-as-a-valve type which admitted air to the reed when the roll uncovered a hole in the tracker bar, (2) the pneumatic action system in which air is admitted to a pouch through a tracker bar hole, and in turn a valve is operated which admits air to the reed, and (3) the key system in which a metal key is depressed or lifted and a valve or flap opens to admit air to the reed.

A PERFECT MUSICAL INSTRUMENT.

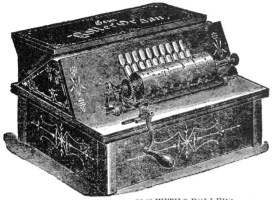

GEM ROLLER ORGAN, PRICE $6.00 WITH 3 ROLLERS. Weight, Boxed, 15 lbs., Length, 16 in., Width, 14 in., Heigth, 9 in.

CONCERT ROLLER ORGAN, PRICE $12 WITH 5 ROLLERS. Weight, Boxed 30 lbs., Length, 19 in., Width, 16 in., Height, 14.

The Gem Roller Organ does not belong to the large class of instruments, most of them mere toys, which depend upon a perforated sheet of paper, frail and easily torn, to produce their music.

This musical marvel EMPLOYS NO PAPER; but its music is obtained from a ROLLER, furnished with pins similar to those of a music box. These pins operate upon valve keys, made of hard steel, the roller being driven by suitable gearing, which also works the bellows. All the working parts of the instrument are easily accessible, and are made of solid metal, the rollers and keys being mounted on iron castings, and the whole as durable and well made as the best sewing machine. Nothing has been omitted to give this grand instrument its crowning qualities of EXTREME SIMPLICITY AND DUABILITY.

The reeds are of organ size, and their volume of tone, and full sustaining and carrying power, equal to that of a full organ. The case is handsomely made of imitation black walnut.

To remove the roller and replace it by another is but the work of an instant, and can be done by a child. By this means a result is attained that was NEVER REACHED BEFORE. The beauty and permanency of a music box Orchestra, combined with the endless variety of music, which makes this instrument ever new and pleasing no matter how long in use.

It has a fuller volume of tone, and far more sustaining and carrying power than any two pianos. It will fill any ordinary sized hall, and furnish acceptable music for any occasion; at the same time it is so fully under control, by means of a swell attachment, that the softest passages can be rendered with exquisite delicacy. For dances, &c., it is most admirable, and when otherwise musicians would have to be engaged, it will save its cost in one night; and is, upon the whole, the most perfect mechanical instrument in design, operation and effect, that has yet been produced.

The case is strongly made of solid black walnut, and is elegantly finished, forming a handsome parlor ornament.

We are glad also to announce that by means of new and automatic machinery, we are enabled to produce music rollers in large numbers so that we can offer them to the public at a price not exceeding the average cost of music paper; and a roller will give a very much better performance besides OUTLASTING A THOUSAND PAPER SHEETS.

There are ready, over 800 sacred and popular tunes which have been arranged for the Roller Organ.

Symphonia.

Length, 17 in.; Height, 14½ in.; Depth, 14 in.; Weight, boxed, 3? lbs.

SIZE OF MUSIC SPOOL.—Length, 6¼ in.; Diameter, 1½ in.

Order by Number.

Black-Walnut Case beautifully embellished in Gold-Leaf and Carving.

In power, sweetness and purity of tone; in design, finish and beauty of case; in simplicity, durability and superior workmanship; in all that goes to make a desirable musical instrument and beautiful parlor ornament, this instrument stands unrivalled.

THE WILCOX & WHITE ORGAN CO.,
Meriden, Conn.

POPULAR MUSIC.

Roll 261   **90 Cents**
Little Annie Rooney............*Nolan*
2 verses.

Roll 262   **95 Cents**
I whistle and wait for Katie..........

Roll 263   **$1.05**
Tommy, make Room for your Uncle.
        Lonsdale
Mary Ann, I'll tell your Ma.....*Thorn*
Champagne Charlie................*Lee*
Oh! George, tell them to stop....*Meen*
Over the Garden Wall..........*Fox*

Roll 264   **85 Cents**
Men of Harlech.....................
Minstrel Boy......................
Rule Britannia....................
God Bless the Prince of Wales*Richards*
God Save the Queen.................

Roll 265   **$1.15**
Killarney..................*Balfe*
Kate Kearney................*Morgan*
Come where my Love lies dreaming.
        Foster
Sally in our Alley...............*Levy*

Roll 266   **$1.00**
Blue Alsatian Mountains......*Adams*
Some Day....................*Welling*
Maggie's Secret.............*Claribel*
Four Jolly Smiths.............*Leslie*

Roll 267   **75 Cents**
The Meeting of the Waters...........
Oft in the Stilly Night......*Stevenson*
Believe me if all those endearing*Moore*
The Bloom on the Rye.........*Bishop*

Roll 268   **75 Cents**
John Anderson, my Jo..........*Burns*
Jock O'Hazeldean................*Scott*
Bonnie Prince Charlie............
Scotch Lassie Jean.................

Roll 269   **$1.15**
Operatic and Popular Medley.......

Roll 270   **95 Cents**
Finigan's Wake...............*Glover*
Mary Kelly's Beau......... *Braham*
John Riley's always dry...... "
Little Widow Dunn........ "

Roll 271   **80 Cents**
The Soldier Boy's Canteen ...*Braham*
School Days................. "

Roll 272   **$1.00**
Always take Mother's Advice.*Lindsay*
Poor Old Dad..................*Yorke*

Roll 273   **85 Cents**
Sailing.. .....3 verses........*Marks*

Roll 274   **75 Cents**
The Midshipmite............ .*Adams*
3 verses.

Roll 275   **$1.35**
We'd better bide a wee.......*Claridel*
Won't you tell me why, Robin? "
Little Maid of Arcadee......*Sullivan*
Kerry Dance.. ....*Molloy*

Roll 276   **$1.10**
Jack's Yarn ....*Diehl*
Our Jack's come Home. ....*Devers*

Roll 277   **$1.05**
U. S. Black Marines... ......*Braham*
Mulberry Springs............ "

Roll 278   **95 Cents**
The Toboggan Slide.... ....*Braham*
Ho, Molly Grogan. ... . "

Roll 279   **90 Cents**
The Light House by the Sea....*Davies*

Roll 280   **80 Cents**
Lay me on the Hillside.......*Mitchell*

Roll 281   **95 Cents**
Paddy's Wedding...............*West*

Roll 282   **90 Cents**
Massa's Wedding Night......*Braham*
The Old Barn Floor.... ... "

Roll 283   **75 Cents**
I am such a simple Young Man.*Jones*
4 verses.

Roll 284   **90 Cents**
The Cork Leg.......................

Roll 285   **75 Cents**
Tippecanoe and Morton too..*Rosenfeld*

Roll 286   **75 Cents**
The Red Bandanna.. ....*Rosenfeld*

The Symphonia organette, made by the Wilcox & White Organ Company, was popular during the 1890s. As the tune list above shows, rolls varied in price, the variance being due to the length. If a television show like Name That Tune ever runs out of ideas for obscure melodies, the above list should be of help!

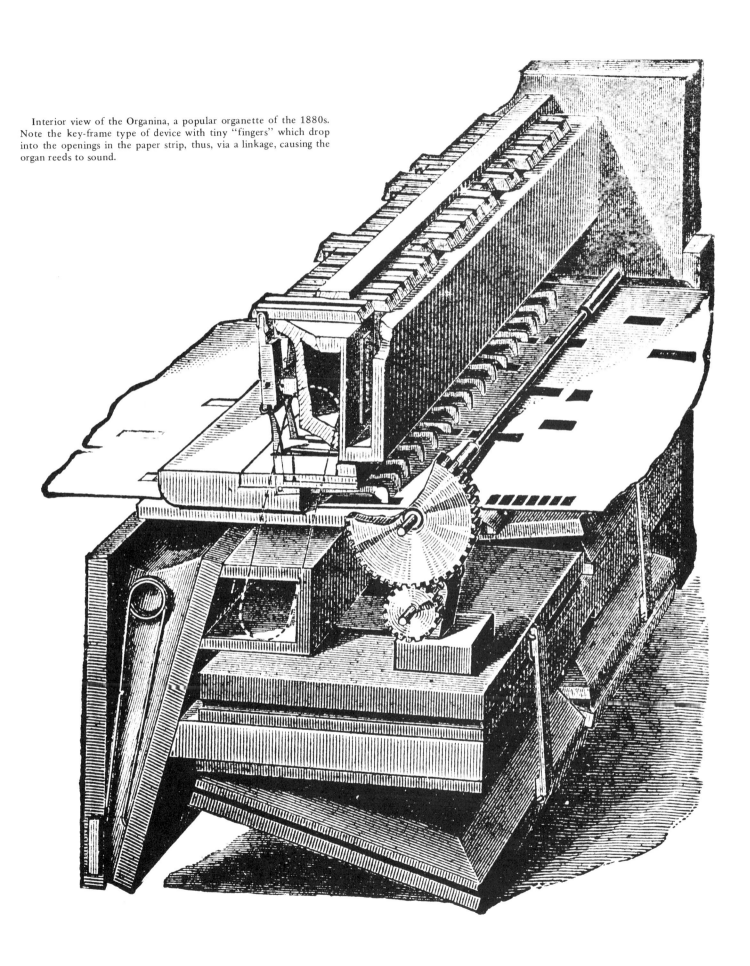

Interior view of the Organina, a popular organette of the 1880s. Note the key-frame type of device with tiny "fingers" which drop into the openings in the paper strip, thus, via a linkage, causing the organ reeds to sound.

The Ariston, made in Germany, was probably the most popular organette in terms of the quantities originally manufactured, with America's Gem and Concert Roller Organs (Autophone Company, Ithaca, N.Y.) coming in second. A cardboard disc with Strauss' "Roses of the South" is shown in the playing position. Such discs were inexpensive to make and were produced by the millions.

Many different types of disc-operated organettes were made in Germany. In addition to the Ariston, such trademarks as Diana, Amorette, Intona, and Phoenix were commercially successful. By contrast, most American organettes used paper strips or rolls (the Gem and Concert Roller Organs being notable exceptions).

The American organette industry had its beginnings in the 1870s. Elias P. Needham was granted a patent in 1877 for such a device, and by 1878 the Mechanical Orguinette Company (which evolved into the Aeolian Company) was located at 11 East 14th Street, New York City. In later years John McTammany, who styled himself (on the cover of his book, "The Technical History of the Player") as "the inventor of the player piano," claimed to have been first in the field, but as Dan Tillmanns, who has carefully researched organettes, wrote to the authors, "the McTammany claim to fame is based heavily on a book written by himself."

By the 1890s organettes were a worldwide novelty and millions had been sold.

The Aurephone, made during the late 19th century, uses a wide paper roll with large openings. As the holes cross the tracker bar, air is sucked into the organ reeds, thus causing the appropriate notes to sound. This type of organette was designed to be played with the lid closed. A shutter in the top could be opened or closed to give a degree of expression.

THE AUTOPHONE COMPANY, located in Ithaca, New York, was the most important American maker of organettes during the 19th century. The following article, from "Ithaca and its Resources," by D. Morris Kurtz, published in 1883, tells of the firm:

"The Autophone Company. Within the last few years public attention has largely been drawn to automatic musical instruments through the efforts of men of acknowledged genius and ability to perfect an instrument that, unlike the much execrated hand organ or more desirable music box even, would produce all the latest music of the day as well as possess the range to give the variety of the costly organ or piano, without requiring the skill and the ability requisite to the performance on those instruments. While almost every person is attracted and pleased, more or less, by music, there are comparatively few who can master the trained ear or facility of execution necessary to success—to render correctly the simpler melodies even, let alone the grand conceptions of the masters—and that there is a demand for such instruments has been conclusively proven by the avidity with which the public have purchased the results of every attempt in this direction, however crude.

"Various degrees of success have attended the efforts of those who have attempted to produce such an instrument, and the country has been literally flooded with their inventions, most of which are awkward and complicated, lacking in both simplicity and economy and giving very imperfect and unsatisfactory results. Among those who engaged in the attempt was Mr. H.B. Horton, of Ithaca, whose genius and ability are well known. After working several years on the problem, he was finally rewarded for his perseverance with its satisfactory solution, and produced as a result, the Autophone, which is now so widely and favorably known as the most perfect and desirable automatic musical instrument ever invented.

(Continued on following page)

The basic hand-operated Autophone which originally sold for $5.

"The Autophone possesses many points of advantage over all other automatic musical instruments in elegance, utility, simplicity of construction, economy, and execution, but chiefly in its music, the condensation of the music allowing a greater number of notes and consequently more harmony. Unlike the others, too, the feed of the music is intermittent, being controlled by a simple piece of mechanism forming one of the features of the patent, and the regularity and perfection with which the music is rendered is remarkable. The vast range of music it is capable of rendering embraces not only the sacred and instrumental music commonly known, and the popular songs of the day, but the more difficult and classical compositions which only the professional artists perform, as well as the operas. The instruments are manufactured of the very best materials and finished in styles both unique and handsome, making them a decided ornament in any household, while their durability is such that with reasonable care they will last a long time, and even if from any cause they become out of tune the reeds can be detached, returned to the factory and re-tuned at a very slight cost. They are not toys, but substantial musical instruments of remarkable power, sweetness, and purity of tone, capable of spreading delight and happiness into many homes which otherwise would be debarred from the pleasure and refining influence of music, as also affording novelty and pleasure to those even, whose circumstances permit them to indulge their taste in a costly organ or piano.

"The catalogue of music prepared for the Autophone now embraces nearly 1000 tunes—sacred and instrumental music, popular airs and the operas—and the more fully it is understood and introduced the more popular it must become. Letters patent were first granted Mr. Horton for the Autophone in October 1877 and again in December 1878, and he tried to interest capital in the formation of a company for its manufacture, but was then unsuccessful, owing to the fact that special music, differing materially from that used in other automatic musical instruments, was required, and there was a general incredulity as to his ability to construct a machine that would cut it. Having satisfactorily demonstrated this point, however, by the construction of a press, the Autophone Company was formed by F.M. Finch, H.F. Hibbard, and H.B. Horton, and in September 1879, incorporated. A room was secured—half of the second floor—in the west wing of the Ithaca Calendar Clock Company's building and the work of manufacturing the Autophone begun.

"When placed upon the market its novelty and decided merit won for it immediate popularity, and about 75 Autophones were produced monthly, until in the spring of 1880, when the whole of this floor was taken and the capacity of the factory about doubled. The demand for them steadily increasing, the capacity was again enlarged during the same year, and early in 1881 the entire west wing of this large building was occupied by the company. During 1882 they manufactured 15,000 of the small-sized instruments and 3,000 of the other sizes, and as the demand for the larger instruments is even greater this year, the aggregate amount of business for 1883, in dollars, will probably equal the large business of 1882, while the prospects for the future are even brighter.

"Having purchased Horton's patents, a new organization of the company was effected in April 1883, and the officers now are F.M. Finch, President; H.A. St. John, Vice President; and H.M. Hibbard, Treasurer. Mr. St. John and Mr. Hibbard have been actively connected with the company since February 1881, however, and the latter is especially well versed in the business. Four sizes of the Autophone are made, the smallest instrument (22 notes) selling for $5; the concert style, $12; concert style, with stand (32 notes) $16; and the cabinet Autophone, $35; and the company are also now manufacturing Prof. Cleaves' Patent Study Table, a most convenient and useful article for the student or writer. A working force of 45 people is employed, which number is nearly doubled in preparation for the holiday trade, and the facilities for producing the Autophone are of the most complete character. The machinery is principally that adapted and invented for the business, and includes five presses for cutting music. These presses are wonders of ingenious mechanism, and it might here be mentioned that the Autophone Company are the only manufacturers of automatic musical instruments who cut their own music. When it is considered what an immense amount of skilled labor is required to produce one of these little instruments it is surprising how they can be sold so cheaply. The reeds are carefully and accurately tuned as those of an organ, while the material is of the very best quality and the workmanship expended on the cases, on every part of the instrument, is fully equal to that expended on an organ. But the result justifies the expenditure of both time and money, for the popularity of the Autophone is steadily

(Continued on following page)

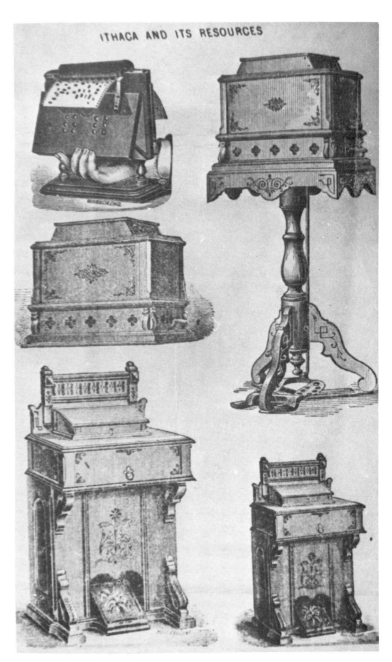

ITHACA AND ITS RESOURCES

Five different styles of organettes manufactured by the Autophone Company in 1883. Most instruments were of the basic hand-operated model as shown at the upper left. The authors know of no existing specimens of the foot-pumped styles, and it is presumed that only a few were made.

increasing and it is constantly making new friends and patrons where other automatic musical instruments are consigned to oblivion.

"The Autophone Company are just beginning to export their products and with the favorable reception the Autophone is meeting in other countries and the still greater demand here at home they have every reason to feel gratified at their past success as well as pleased with the prospects of the future. They have an abundance of capital, the enterprise is conducted by gentlemen of ability and there is every indication that the industry will not only continue to thrive and prosper, but add still more largely to the wealth, prosperity, and industrial reputation of Ithaca."

Today the Autophone, which uses a perforated paper strip propelled intermittently by means of a ratchet mechanism, is quite scarce, and only a few dozen examples are known to exist. Nearly all are of the basic model which sold for $5 originally.

By the early 1890s the Autophone organette was a thing of the past, and the Gem and Concert Roller Organs formed the main products of the Autophone Company. A contemporary article described the firm:

"The Autophone Company. Another concern which has gained a world-wide reputation is the Autophone Company, which was established 12 years ago with a capital stock of $50,000.00 for the manufacture of these instruments. They are made in two types, namely: the 'Gem Roller Organ' and 'Concert Roller Organ.' These musical marvels employ no paper but the music is obtained from a roller furnished with pins similar to those of a music box. All the working parts of the instrument are easily accessible and the whole as durable and well made as the best sewing machine.

"Nothing has been omitted to give this grand instrument its crowning qualities of extreme simplicity and durability. The reeds are of organ size and their volume of tone and full sustaining and carrying powers equal that of a full organ. By the aid of new and automatic machinery they are enabled to produce music rollers in large numbers, so as to furnish them to the public at a price not exceeding the average cost of sheet music. That the Roller Organ is a perfect musical instrument is attested by the fact that the last year's sales reached 14,000 organs and 200,000 music rollers. Nothing could be more desirable than one of these instruments which will produce all the latest music of the day, as well as the costly organ or piano without requiring the skill requisite to the performance on those instruments. They are of remarkable power, sweetness, and purity of tone and of substantial construction. The plant consists of three floors 120x200 feet and contains all the intricate machinery and appliances necessary in the construction of these instruments. Forty-five people are employed and the Roller Organ can be found throughout the United States and foreign countries. The officers are Messrs. H.A. St. John, president, and H.M. Hibbard, secretary and treasurer; both gentleman are pronounced business men and progressive in every sense of the word."

The Gem Roller Organ and Concert Roller Organ were sold well into the 20th century with a total production estimated at several hundred thousand units. Several hundred or more examples survive today.

Concert Roller Organ made by the Autophone Company in the 1890s. The Gem Roller Organ had a similar mechanism but was built in a smaller case and usually did not have a glass lid. The Gem and Concert Roller Organs were sold under a wide variety of trade names, including Chautauqua Roller Organ, New American Musical Box, Home Roller Organ, and The Roller Organ.

REED, PIPE, AND ELECTRONIC ORGAN SCALES

AEOLIAN 46-NOTE REED ORGAN ROLL
9 5/8" wide; spaced 5 holes per inch

1 G
2 A
3 C
4 D
5 to 46, Notes in order G to C

This roll was used on a very compact keyboard-style early Aeolian reed organ. The roll provided the notes. Changes in tonal volume were accomplished by manually- or knee-operated swell shuttters. Different banks of reeds, or registers, were controlled by manually-operated draw stops.

AEOLIAN GRAND ORGAN ROLL
10 1/8" wide; spaced 6 holes per inch

58 Playing notes in order, C to A

The Aeolian Grand rolls were made for use on the Aeolian Grand player reed organ and the regular (not Solo) Orchestrelle player reed organ. Rolls of this style were issued in very large quantities, and it was not uncommon for the owner of an instrument to collect several hundred or more.

The Aeolian Company aggressively marketed the Grand and Orchestrelle instruments in America, England, and elsewhere, with the result that many thousands were sold. Aeolian Grand organs mainly cost in the $500 to $1000 range, and smaller models of the Orchestrelle cost from about $1000 to $2500, a considerable sum of money in an era in which the average factory worker in America earned only about $6 to $15 per week.

The Aeolian Orchestrelle, housed in cabinets which were triumphs of the cabinetmaker's art, were offered in glowing advertisements. The following is typical:

"Leading an orchestra is quite different from personally playing any musical instrument except the AEOLIAN ORCHESTRELLE.

"The orchestral conductor experiences none of the wearying slavery of scales and exercises—and yet his temperamental control is just as pronounced. He throws himself into the spirit of the music in a far greater degree than does, for instance, the pianist, who is compelled to devote so large a proportion of his mental capacity to the mere sounding of the notes, This exacting technique is not necessary to the conductor of an orchestra. A wave of his baton introduces the different voices, swells or diminishes the tone or volume, produces the delicate pianissimo, the thunderous fortissimo.

"The player of an Aeolian Orchestrelle can be likened to no one so much as to the conductor of an orchestra. The notes are sounded for him. He controls the registration of the tones, the shadings of tempo, the phrasing, the tone-coloring, all the orchestral effects are at the command of the owner of an Aeolian Orchestrelle. It can easily be learned by anybody and yet allows the greatest possible scope for study and improvement.

"The Aeolian Orchestrelle is a home orchestra.

"We would be glad to have you come and hear it play your favorite music—Wagner, Beethoven, Bach, Handel, Schubert, a delicious waltz, a stirring march, a bright two-step. The wonderful versatility of the Aeolian Orchestrelle makes it the most universally interesting musical instrument for the home.

"We would be glad to have you come and try it yourself. You can learn to play it in ten minutes, master it in a month."

The Aeolian Grand roll contains 58 playing notes. Changes in the tonal character are accomplished by pulling draw knobs by hand, in accordance with an ever-changing set of instructions printed on the roll and visible as the roll is played. From time to time other controls such as tempo changes and swell shutter operation are indicated by printed instructions. This manual setting permitted "individual interpretation," according to Aeolian's advertisements. "To remove all difficulties from the way of the performer in producing the correct tonal effects the Aeolian Company has also devised a system of simple and easily understood registration marks, whereby the performer is directed at each stage of the music as to which stops and combinations are required."

AEOLIAN PIPE ORGAN ROLL
(Aeolian Double; 116 notes)
10 1/8" wide; spaced 12 holes per inch
(spacing in two staggered rows of 6 per inch)
Two sets of 58 playing notes for two manuals,
Note range C to A
No automatic registration

These rolls, based on a musically expanded version of the Aeolian Grand tracker scale, were made for use on large Aeolian Solo Orchestrelle player reed organs (the largest model of which, the Style F, sold for up to $5,000, an awesome price at the time!) and Aeolian player pipe organs.

In the pipe organs, the lowest octave of pedal notes plays from the lowest octave of Great holes when the pedal stops are drawn. Suggested stop changes are printed on the roll, as are tempo and crescendo (swell shutter) instructions. The notes for one manual are punched as elongated holes, while the notes for the other manual are punched as chain perforations, enabling a novice operator to tell the precise moment at which stops should be changed.

Handsomely bound books titled *The Aeolian Pipe Organ and Its Music* were given or sold to clients. "Over 300 Aeolian Pipe Organs have already been installed in homes throughout America and Europe," noted the 1910 edition. The 1919 edition indicated an improved state of affairs: "Over 1,000 Aeolian Pipe Organs have already been installed . . ."

The preface to the catalogue noted, in part:

"No time in the history of music has the organ received so much attention as at the present day, or won so much general appreciation on the part of all lovers of dignified and elevating music.

"Today the ideal organ for the home is an instrument furnished, on the one hand, with complete manual and pedal claviers, and all the requisite mechanical appliances for the use of the skilled organist, while on the other hand it is provided with an absolutely perfect automatic, or self-playing, device, commanding the entire musical resources of the instrument, and under easy control, by means of which musical compositions can be effectively rendered by those who are not skilled performers on the manuals, and who may have little or no knowledge of musical notation or of the meaning of the numerous signs associated therewith.

"This is provided for in the Aeolian Pipe Organ by the special construction of the Aeolian Solo System and by the use of its unique two-manual music rolls, which open up an entirely new world of organ effects—for they can, and do, render, without the slightest difficulty or uncertainty, complex musical compositions and transcriptions, utterly impossible of rendition by the organist who has only his two hands to command the manuals.

"Master arrangements of ancient and modern scores have been made for the Aeolian Pipe Organ by men representing the highest artistic standard in music, including: Felix Weingartner, Berlin; Felix Mottl, Munich; Arturo Vigna, Milan; Gustav F. Kogen,

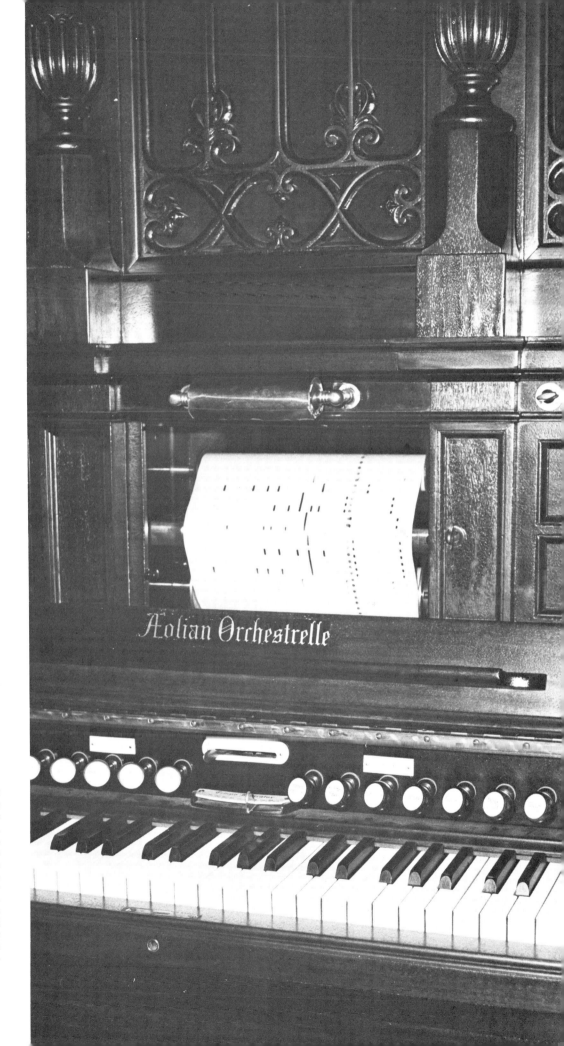

Views of a Style F Aeolian Solo
Orchestrelle. Made by the Aeolian
Company in 1908, the player reed
organ saw many years of service in a
fine Bangor, Maine home. At one
time the Style F, the largest regular
Orchestrelle in the Aeolian line,
carried a price tag of $5,000, a
fantastic sum in an era when a week's
wages for a factory worker were only
slightly more than one-thousandth of
that figure.

The Style F, like other Orches-
trelles in the "Solo" category, can
use two types of rolls: 58-note
Aeolian Grand rolls and 116-note
Aeolian Organ rolls. A switching lever
is provided for this purpose.

The draw stops control different
banks of reeds, each of which is
assigned a fanciful name such as
trumpet, oboe, orchestral flute,
French horn, violin, dolce violin,
piccolo, clarinet, melodia, eolian
harp, muted strings, bass clarinet,
flute, dolce viola, viola, trombone,
contra bass, and double bass. Expression is provided by two knee-
operated levers, one of which controls a bank of louvered swell
shutters on the front, and the other
of which, when fully pressed, puts on
all of the reed banks for a "crescendo" or "full organ" effect.

Frankfurt; Alfred Hertz, New York; Walter Damrosch, Harry Rowe Shelley, Wallace Goodrich, Archer Gibson, Samuel P. Warren, and others. In addition to these master arrangements, some of the most distinguished musicians are composing especially for the Aeolian Pipe Organ. Notable among these stand Engelbert Humperdinck, Moritz Moszkowski, Camille Saint-Saens, Victor Herbert, and Edwin H. Lemare..."

Rolls were presented in an enticing manner, often described with a mixture of melody, history, and charm. For example, to offer two rolls, no. 555 ("Old Folks at Home") and no. 791 ("Songs of the South"), more than a full page of catalogue space was devoted to the biography of Stephen C. Foster and the background of the tunes offered.

Or, who after reading the following description of roll no. 816, "Consolation," by Franz Liszt, could resist buying it?

"Those who have sought to explain the title 'Consolation' have come to the conclusion that this composition, as well as the several others that bear the same general title, were written to console the composer in his love griefs. It is also believed that they were written several years before they were published, and by this it is intimated that they sprang to life during the days that Liszt spent under Italian skies. One analyst finds them too tender for the German climate and declares that they remind him of palms and cypresses. This is probably especially applicable to the present Consolation, for it breathes nought else. The solo voice sings of sentiment and the mood of tenderness envelops all."

Lest the reader think that all is tender sentiment with Aeolian Organ rolls, we hasten to say that such is not the case. The repertoire contained many snappy pieces such as . . .

"No. 689. March — Stars and Stripes Forever. Sousa scarcely needs an introduction to the public for his name is a household word with lovers of popular music, and his marches have won for him the title of 'March King.' The son of a Spanish trombonist of the United States Marine Corps Band, John Philip Sousa was born in Washington, D.C., studied music, became a violinist and conductor, and was appointed bandmaster of the Marine Band, from which he resigned to organize his own band at the head of which he has toured all over the world. His compositions are many, but the public favor in which he basks is founded chiefly upon his numerous marches, the most patriotic of which is here presented, 'Stars and Stripes Forever.' It has that same engaging lilt which has made this composer of popular music so beloved, while in the second episode there is voiced appealing sentiment, and in the Trio Section a broad melody and its brilliant preparation imparts thrills to the patriotically inclined listeners."

Indeed, anyone in need of a broad musical education had but to read in detail the Aeolian Pipe Organ roll catalogue!

The large and impressive Aeolian Solo Orchestrelle organs and the built-in installations of the Aeolian Pipe Organ brought joy to their owners. While one had to maintain a degree of alertness to change the registers, the majesty of the organ music encoded on Aeolian rolls doubtless gave rest from the cares of the day to those who could afford the instruments.

AEOLIAN DUO-ART ORGAN ROLL

15¼" wide; spaced 12 holes per inch
(spacing in two staggered rows of 6 per inch;
with automatic registration)

ODD NUMBERS: Great and Pedal. Bottom row on tracker bar
1 Tremolo
3 Tonal (Great and Pedal sforzando)
5 Harp
7 Great ext. 61 note
9 Pedal 2nd octave
11 Pedal 3rd octave
13 Great shade 1
15 Great shade 2

17 Great shade 3
19 Great shade 4
21 Great shade 5
23 Great shade 6
25 Pedal bassoon 16'
27 Pedal string 16'
29 Pedal flute f 16'
31 Pedal flute p 16'
33 to 147, Pedal and Great, 58 playing notes, C to A
149 String pp
151 String p
153 String f
155 Flute p
157 Flute f
159 Flute 4'
161 Diapason f
163 Piccolo
165 Clarinet
167 Trumpet
169 Chimes
171 L.C.W. (Echo coupler)
173 L.C.W.
175 Ventil control

EVEN NUMBERS: Swell. Top row on tracker bar
2 Echo
4 Chimes
6 Tremolo
8 Harp
10 Trumpet
12 Oboe
14 Vox humana
16 Diapason mf
18 Flute 16'
20 Flute 4'
22 Flute p
24 String celeste f
26 String f
28 String mf
30 String p
32 String pp
34 to 148, Swell, 58 playing notes, C to A
150 Swell shade 1
152 Swell shade 2
154 Swell shade 3
156 Swell shade 4
158 Swell shade 5
160 Swell shade 6
162 Swell ext. 61 note
164 L.C.W.
166 L.C.W.
168 Soft chimes
170 Rewind
172 Ventil control
174 Normal
176 Pedal to upper holes

Duo-Art Pipe Organ rolls (no tracker layout relationship to Duo-Art piano rolls) are built around the earlier Aeolian Pipe Organ rolls, with stop changes, couplers, and expression added to the margins. Many Aeolian pipe organs play both Aeolian Pipe Organ rolls and Aeolian Duo-Art Pipe Organ rolls, using two separate spoolboxes. Previous to 1977, it was believed that all Aeolian Duo-Art Organs contained pipes; but a discovery of a large Aeolian Duo-Art Orchestrelle with reeds, an original instrument found by William Edgerton, indicates that some larger Orchestrelle models were equipped to play Duo-Art Organ rolls, rather than the usual Aeolian Pipe Organ rolls.

All stops on the Duo-Art roll are reversible; each registration hole turns its rank of pipes on, and then off the next time the hole is punched.

Holes 7 and 162, Great and Swell note extensions, switch their respective manual keys 47-49 up to keys 59-61.

The lowest octave of Great note holes normally controls the lowest octave of pedal notes if any pedal stops are turned on. Hole 176 switches these pedal notes from the Great to the lowest Swell notes in the top row of the tracker bar. The tracker bar plays the lowest octave of pedal notes unless hole 9

This particularly ornate console has a tracker bar which uses the 116-note Aeolian Pipe Organ roll. With elaborate carvings and mother-of-pearl inlay it must have been built on special order. (Dan Tillmanns Collection)

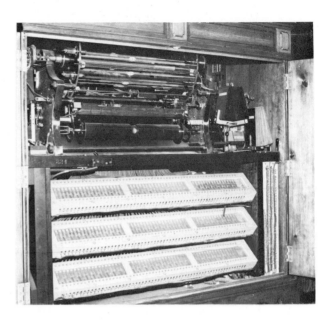

Above: Cabinet housing the "Concertola" roll-changing mechanism for Aeolian Duo-Art Organ rolls. Electrical contacts and relays are located in the bottom of the cabinet. A similar device, although of reduced proportions, was made for Duo-Art reproducing piano rolls.

Below: Aeolian pipe organ console with a roll mechanism to accommodate Duo-Art Organ rolls. Note the split tracker bar (visible in the bottom right photograph), a method of insuring proper tracking when rolls expanded or contracted due to humidity or dryness. (J.B. Nethercutt Collection)

The Aeolian-Hammond player electronic organ, circa 1938, was sold in limited numbers. The roll player, an outgrowth of the Skinner Pipe Organ roll of earlier years, was not self-registering. The operator had to read the dozens of printed notations on each roll and then manually operate the reverse-color keys to achieve the desired tonal effect. In addition, the drawbars had to be adjusted or pre-set to various positions.

or 11 is punched, switching over to the 2nd or 3rd octave of pedal notes.

Hole 172 turns on the vacuum to the player pouch contacts. It might also have been used to cancel all stops as a redundant safety feature at the beginning of each roll. Hole 174 was intended for reversing the stops available on the two manuals, connecting the Great stops to the Swell, and vice versa, but was rarely if ever used.

A different tracker scale is a variety which uses hole 172 for general cancel and 174 for ventil control.

The terms "Great" and "Swell" refer to the two manual keyboards of the organ (although in practice many instruments had just one manual; this made no difference, as the pipes or reeds were controlled directly, and, apart from hand playing, the number of keyboards was not important). "Pedal" refers to the pedal keyboard.

As noted, Aeolian Duo-Art Pipe Organ rolls are adaptations of the earlier Aeolian Pipe Organ rolls. Most Duo-Art Pipe Organ rolls have numbers in the 3,000 series. There seems to be no special number correlation between the two types of rolls.

Of the 2000+ home installations of Aeolian Pipe Organs mentioned under the preceding section, probably about 1,250 or so used Duo-Art rolls.

AEOLIAN-HAMMOND ORGAN ROLL
(Electronic organ)

1 Rewind
2 Blank
3 Blank
4 to 15, Pedal notes C to B
16 to 73, Swell notes C to A
74 to 120, Great notes B to A

This roll is a simplification of the E.M. Skinner semi-automatic pipe organ roll of the same dimensions and hole spacing.

The Aeolian-Hammond roll-operated electronic organ was introduced in 1938. About 210 instruments were produced totally. The roll used is not self-registering. The operator sets the draw bars and other tonal controls by watching printed instructions on the roll.

ARTISTOUCH CONSOLETTE SERIES ROLL
(Clark Organ Roll)
11¼" wide; spaced 9 holes per inch

1 Crescendo pedal on, 5-step ratchet
2 Crescendo pedal off, 5-step ratchet
3 Swell open, 6-step ratchet
4 Swell closed, 6-step ratchet
5 to 16, Pedal notes; may be extended upward another octave by perforation no. 65, giving a total range of 24 notes
17 to 28, Countermelody notes (choir). Stops used in this range play only when they have been drawn on by countermelody perforations 51+65 (see details following) and need not be from the third manual. Any suitable stop in the organ may be selected. Affected by 4' and 16' accompaniment couplers which, with unison off, provide a 36-note range. Plays an octave higher than the accompaniment range.
17 to 48, Accompaniment notes (Great). Stops used in this range are those most suitable for accompaniment purposes, and the proper balance with the solo stop should be carefully sought. The entire range is extended up and down by octave couplers with unison off, providing a 56-note range.
49, Cancel combinations: single perforation cancels all primary combinations. Holes 49+51 punched together cancel all secondary combinations.
50 Shutoff (mortuary rolls only)
51 Secondary combination switch. When used with any of the fifteen perforations controlling combinations (holes 52 to 66), this draws secondary combinations (see following description).
52 to 66, Primary combinations (see following description). Each perforation draws solo stop, suitable accompaniment, and pedal stops; and if perforations 51+65 are used, each perforation also draws a countermelody stop (see following description)
67 to 98, Solo notes (Swell). The stops used in this range are those most suited for solo purposes. The entire range is extended up or down an octave by couplers with unison off, providing a 56-note range.
1+2 Sforzando (chain perforation)
3+4 Swell closed instantly (chain perforation)
50+51 Rewind

This type of roll is available on 88-note player piano roll spools for residence and mortuary organs, and on 3½" diameter cardboard cores for theatre pipe organs.

Replay is accomplished by a mechanical device in the spoolbox.

The combinations in the following primary and secondary combination descriptions are those recommended by Clark in a 1929 blueprint accompanying an original factory tracker scale.

PRIMARY COMBINATIONS
for the Artistouch Consolette Series

The following descriptions show the function of each hole and the combinations it draws in the Swell section (Solo, holes 67 to 98), Great (Accompaniment, holes 17 to 48), Choir (Countermelody, holes 17 to 28, when drawn by 51+65), and Pedal.

52 SWELL: 8' medium flute (concert flute). Tremolo; GREAT: 8' soft string (dulciana); CHOIR 8' vox humana (soft reed); PEDAL: 16' soft flute
53 SWELL: 8' stopped flute (flute d'amour). Tremolo. GREAT: 8' softest string (aeoline); CHOIR: 8' vox humana (soft reed); PEDAL: 16' soft flute
54 SWELL: 8' strong flute (tibia). Tremolo. GREAT: 8' soft flute; CHOIR: 8' clarinet (medium reed); PEDAL: 16' bourdon
55 SWELL: 8' strong open flute (grosse flute). Tremolo; GREAT: 8' flute; CHOIR: 8' clarinet (medium reed); PEDAL: 16' bourdon
56 SWELL: 8' soft string; 8' string celeste. Tremolo. GREAT: soft string (dulciana); CHOIR: 4' soft flute; PEDAL: 16' string
57 SWELL: 8' medium string (viol da gamba). Tremolo; GREAT: 8' soft flute (dulciana); CHOIR: 4' tibia (strong flute); PEDAL: 16' bourdon
58 SWELL: 8' medium reed (orchestral oboe). Tremolo. GREAT: 8' soft flute; CHOIR: 8' tibia (strong flute); PEDAL: 16' bourdon

59 SWELL: 8' medium reed (clarinet). Tremolo; GREAT: 8' soft flute; CHOIR: 8' tibia (strong flute); PEDAL: 16' bourdon; 8' cello
60 SWELL: 8' heavy reed (tuba). Tremolo; GREAT: 8' string and flute; 8' string celeste; CHOIR: 8' and 4' tibia (strong flute); PEDAL: 16' diapason
61 SWELL: Solo to Solo 4' coupler
62 GREAT: Accompaniment to Accompaniment 4' coupler; CHOIR: Choir to Choir 4' coupler
63 SWELL: Solo unison off
64 GREAT: Chimes A to E, 20 notes
65 PEDAL: Pedal 8' (not coupled)
66 SWELL Harp T.C. to C, 49 notes

SECONDARY COMBINATIONS
for the Artistouch Consolette Series

51+52 SWELL: 2' medium flute (piccolo). Tremolo; GREAT: 8' soft string; CHOIR: 8' tuba (heavy reed); PEDAL: 16' lieblich gedeckt
51+53 SWELL: 4' stopped flute (flute d'amour). Tremolo; GREAT: 8' soft string (aeoline); CHOIR: 8' vox humana (soft reed); PEDAL: 16' bourdon
51+54 SWELL: 4' strong flute (tibia). Tremolo; GREAT: 8' soft flute; CHOIR: 8' clarinet (medium reed); PEDAL: 16' bourdon
51+55 SWELL: 16' strong flute (tibia). Tremolo; GREAT: 8' soft flute; CHOIR: 8' clarinet (medium reed); PEDAL: 16' bourdon
51+56 SWELL: 16' soft string; 16' string celeste. Tremolo; GREAT: 8' soft flute (dulciana); CHOIR: 4' soft flute; PEDAL: 16' string
51+57 SWELL: 4' medium string (viol da gamba). Tremolo; GREAT: 8' soft flute (dulciana); CHOIR: 4' tibia (strong flute); PEDAL: 16' bourdon
51+58 SWELL: 4' string; 4' string celeste. Tremolo; GREAT: 8' soft flute (dulciana); CHOIR: 8' tibia (strong flute); PEDAL: 16' bourdon
51+59 SWELL: 8' soft reed (vox humana). Tremolo; GREAT: 8' soft flute (dulciana); CHOIR: 8' tibia (strong flute); PEDAL: 16' lieblich gedeckt
51+60 SWELL: 16' bourdon. Tremolo; GREAT: 8' soft flute; CHOIR: 8' and 4' tibia (strong flute); PEDAL: 16' string
51+61 Solo to Solo 16', coupler
51+62 GREAT: Accompaniment to Accompaniment 16', coupler; CHOIR: Choir to Choir 16', coupler
51+63 GREAT: Accompaniment unison off; CHOIR: Choir unison off
61+64 SWELL: Tremolo off; GREAT: Tremolo off; CHOIR: Tremolo off
51+65 CHOIR: Countermelody (octave higher than Accompaniment)
51+66 GREAT: Harp T.C. to C, 49 notes

ARTISTOUCH CR ROLL
(Clark Organ Roll)
11¼" wide; spaced 9 holes per inch

1 Diapason off
2 Play
3 Diapason on (solo range; this perforation appears with other stop perforations and is not drawn alone)
4 Shutoff
5 Sustaining pedal
6 Soft pedal (hammer rail)
7 Swell shutters open, 4-step ratchet
8 Swell shutters closed, 4-step ratchet
9 Piano on (if organ has no piano, may be used for harp or some other stop not included in this list, such as 2' piccolo)
10 Piano off
11 Tremolo on
12 Tremolo off
13 Bass vox on (Pedal and Accompaniment range, 17 to 45)
14 Bass vox off
15 Treble vox on (Solo range, 46 to 77)
16 Treble vox off
17 to 45, Pedal and Accompaniment notes (17 to 28 are reserved for Pedal)
46 to 77, Solo notes (generally reserved for solo purposes)
78 Cello on (Pedal plus Accompaniment string)
79 Cello off
80 Bass flute on (Pedal and Accompaniment)
81 Bass flute off
82 Violin on (string for Solo range)
83 Violin off
84 Flute on (Solo range)
85 Flute off
86 Gedeckt on (Solo range)
87 Gedeckt off
88 Melody combination (8' oboe or other solo stop or combination of stops suitable for solo purposes. This perforation occurs only with single melody notes in the Solo range, never alone, but always plays with other stop perforations)
89 Rewind
90 Melody combination off

Additional perforations, if present:
0 Harp on (Accompaniment range only)
91 Harp off
5+10 Chimes on (drawn on by combination of holes 5+10, held on by 5 as a chain perforation until the end of the hole)

This type of roll is available on standard 88-note home player piano spools for use on home and mortuary organs, and on 3½" diameter cardboard cores for use on theatre organs.

The information given here was taken from original Clark specifications which accompanied a letter sent by Clark in 1929. Upon examination of roll CR-96 (*Stars and Stripes Forever*), several apparent differences were found. Hole 3 is used as a register during the music, but it is also perforated as a series of tiny dots at the end of the piece. Hole 90 is used as a cancel during the music, but it is also punched with hole 89 (rewind) after the end of the music. This particular roll was manufactured by Roesler-Hunholz, Inc., successors to the Clark Orchestra Roll Company, so these differences may represent additional multiplexing added to the basic roll scale after 1929, or they might represent special coding added for a particular organ. Both of these possibilities are only speculation.

Clark published the following chart recommending stops and combinations to be drawn by various perforations when the rolls were used on organs having fewer or more ranks than those listed in the basic tracker scale:
STOPS recommended for small, medium, and large organs:
SOLO STOPS
84 Small organ (3 stops): 8' flute; Medium organ (6 stops): 8' flute; Large organ (12 stops): 8' concert flute; 8' orchestral flute
3 Small organ: 8' flute; Medium organ: 8' flute; Large organ: 8' open diapason; 8' gemshorn
82 Small organ: 8' violin; Medium organ: 8' violin; Large organ: 8' vox celeste; 8' violin
15 Small organ: 8' vox humana (or 8' flute); Medium organ: 8' vox humana; Large organ: 8' vox humana; 8' dulciana

86 Small organ: 8' violin; Medium organ: 8' gedeckt (or 8' tibia); Large organ: 8' quintadena; 8' tibia

88 Small organ: 8' flute; Medium organ: Melody combination (16' oboe plus 4' flauto traverso); Large organ: 16' oboe or clarinet; 4' flute d'amour

9 Small organ: Piano (or 8' violin); Medium organ: Piano (or 2' piccolo); Large organ: 2' piccolo; 4' Tibia

5+10 Small organ: Chimes; Medium organ: Chimes; Large organ: Chimes

7 For a medium- or large-size organ Clark suggested that after all of the stops except the Melody combination were drawn, the swell pedal should be coupled to the crescendo pedal, each succeeding step of the swell adding to the stops drawn until, with the last step, full organ is drawn.

ACCOMPANIMENT AND PEDAL STOPS

(Accompaniment and pedal list divided by a diagonal: /)

80 Small organ: 8' flute/ 8' flute; Medium organ: 8' flute/ 8' or 16' flute; Large organ: 8' concert flute; 8' orchestral flute/ 16' bourdon

78 Small organ: 8' cello/ 8' cello; Medium organ: 8' cello/ 8' cello; Large organ: 8' violin; 8' salicional/ 16' string

13 Small organ: 8' vox humana (or 8' flute)/ 8' vox humana (or 8' flute); Medium organ: 8' vox humana/ 8' vox humana; Large organ: 8' vox humana; 8' dulciana/ 16' bourdon

0 Small organ: Harp (or 16' bourdon plus 2' flute); Medium organ: Harp (or 16' bourdon plus 2' flute); Large organ: Harp (or 16' bourdon plus 2' flute)

9 Small organ: Piano (or 8' cello); Medium organ: Piano (or 8' gedeckt); Large organ: 8' melodia; 4' tibia/ 8' flute

AUSTIN PREMIER QUADRUPLEX ROLL

21" wide; spaced 12 holes per inch
(spaced with 2 staggered rows of 6 per inch)

1 Blank (new rolls: percussion)
2 Blank (new rolls: percussion)
3 to 21, Pedal notes C to F#
22 Old rolls: Registration, wired to 27
   New rolls: Expanded registration
23 to 26, Tracker bar expansion control (continuous chain perforation
27 Registration
28 to 40, Continuation of pedal notes G to C
41 to 101, Choir notes C to C
102 Crescendo, step 4
103 Crescendo, step 2
104 Crescendo, step 1
105 to 117, Great notes C to C
118 Rewind
119 to 122, Automatic tracking device (continuous chain perforation
123 Rewind (wired to 118)
124 to 171, Continuation of Great notes C# to C
172 Great-Choir shades, step 4
173 Great-Choir shades, step 2
174 Great-Choir shades, step 1
175 to 235, Swell notes C to C
236 Swell shades, step 4
237 Swell shades, step 2
238 Swell shades, step 1
239 to 240, Player vacuum on, when covered by a roll; also replay if switch is set accordingly

Whenever registration holes 22 and 27 are punched, the registration mechanism in the organ momentarily changes the holes in the following list to their registration mode, sets all stops which are punched, cancels all previous registration, and then switches the holes back to their playing mode. This entire sequence takes about ¼th of a second.

Registration Functions
Austin Premier Quadruplex Rolls
29 16' Pedal bourdon I
30 16' Pedal bourdon II
31 16' Pedal violone
32 8' Pedal cello
33 8' Pedal flute
34 8' Choir gross flute
35 8' Choir cello
36 8' Choir concert flute
37 8' Choir dulciana
38 8' Choir unda maris
39 4' Choir harmonic flute
40 8' Choir trumpet
41 8' Choir clarinet
42 8' Choir piano
43 Choir harp
44 8' Great diapason
45 8' Great gross flute
46 8' Great cello
47 8' Great concert flute
48 8' Great dulciana
49 4' Great harmonic flute
50 8' Great trumpet
51 Great chimes
52 Old rolls: Great soft chimes
   New rolls: Pedal 16' piano
90 16' Swell bourdon
91 8' Swell viola
92 8' Swell stopped flute
93 8' Swell viol d'orchestre
94 8' Swell viol celeste
95 8' Swell salicional
96 4' Swell flute
97 2' Swell piccolo
98 8' Swell oboe
99 8' Swell vox humana
100 Swell tremolo
101 Great tremolo

The automatic tracking device operates from four tracker bar holes: 23-24, 25-26, 119-120, and 121-122. Each of these holes is L-shaped and occupies the width of two regular tracker bar holes. One continuous chain perforation is punched down the length of the roll between 120 and 121, controlling an automatic tracking device which keeps the paper centered on the center section of the tracker bar. The bar is divided into five sections which telescope proportionally to paper expansion and contraction caused by humidity changes; this telescoping action is controlled by another continuous chain perforation riding between 24 and 25. A somewhat similar type of device is used on Aeolian Duo-Art Organ tracker bars.

The crescendo and shutter perforations (102-104, 172-174, and 236-238) control binary mechanisms, giving 8 steps for each set of three holes.

The Austin Company did not include the two holes at each side in their numbering system, so their original tracker scale was considered to have 236 holes. Functions which are marked "new rolls" are for rolls manufactured in recent times. An expanded registration system is being planned which will add 24 more stops, activated by hole 22. (Old rolls have holes 22 and 27 punched together as a safety measure; for the same reason there are two rewind holes, 118 and 123.) Allen Miller, 5 Sutton Place, Bloomfield, Connecticut 06002, did much work with Austin players in the 1970s.

CLARK STANDARD PIPE ORGAN RECORDING ROLL
XR ROLL
11¼" wide; spaced 9 holes per inch

1 Pedal key release: switches pedal note holes to registration functions
2 Great to Pedal coupler
3 Shades open
4 General cancel for couplers; also, pedal note sustain
5 Combine Great and Pedal; extends Pedal to full compass
6 Great to Swell coupler
7 Swell to Great coupler
8 Echo to Swell coupler
9 to 28, Pedal notes C to G
29 to 51, Great notes G# to F#
52 to 90, Swell notes G to A
91 Rewind
92 Swell sforzando (92+7 = Great sforzando)
93 Shades closed
94 Great note sustain
95 Swell note sustain
96 Great key release: switches Great note holes to registration functions
97 Swell piston
98 Swell key release: switches Swell note holes to registration functions

Registration

Each division of the organ has a registration hole (1, 96, and 98 for Pedal, Great, and Swell respectively) which disconnects the playing notes for that division from the tracker bar, allowing that portion of the tracker bar to be used for registration. While the registration hole is open, most of the holes in that section of the bar control stops. One additional hole turns any stops which are punched "on" and another hole turns them "off." When the registration hole passes, the holes under its control revert to their note-playing functions. There are also three note-sustain holes — 4 (Pedal), 94 (Great), and 95 (Swell). Any notes which are playing may be captured and held on by the appropriate note sustain hole, as long as the sustain hole is kept open. Notes are sustained in this manner to prevent silent gaps in the music during registration changes. First, the appropriate sustain hole or holes capture the notes being played, then the appropriate key release holes are punched, stops are turned on and others are turned off, the key release holes end, and the sustain holes end, with the organ now ready to play on the newly-selected ranks.

Pedal Stops
1 Pedal registration switch
9 Pedal stops on
10 Pedal stops off
11 Pedal multiplex switch (see below)
12 16' diapason
13 16' bourdon
14 16' gedeckt
15 16' string
16 16' tuba
17 16' bassoon
18 8' flute
19 8' diapason
20 8' string
21 Chimes
22 Bass drum
23 Cymbal
28 Major tremolo

Holes 1+11 punched simultaneously shift the Pedal holes to the following:
12 to 23, D# to G
24 Chinese gong
25 Siren
26 Bird whistle
27 Crash cymbal

With hole 1 punched, holes 22 and 23 control the playing of the bass drum and cymbal from the Pedal notes; when turned on, these instruments will play each time a Pedal note is played. When holes 1+11 are punched, the effects played by holes 24-27 operate whenever one of these holes is punched, as when a toe piston is pressed at the console.

Great Stops
96 Great registration switch
29 Great stops on

30 Great stops off
33 8' diapason
34 4' octave
35 16' flute
36 8' flute
37 4' flute
38 2' piccolo
39 8' string
40 4' string
41 2 2/3' string
42 8' vox humana
43 8' oboe
44 8' clarinet
45 8' tibia
46 4' tibia
47 8' dulciana
48 4' dulciana
49 8' trumpet
50 4' clarion
51 Chimes
52 Bells
53 Tom-tom
54 Tambourine
55 Snare drum
56 Castanets

Swell Stops

98 Swell registration switch
81 Swell stops on
82 Swell stops off
57 8' diapason
58 16' bourdon
59 8' flute
60 4' flute
61 2 2/3' twelfth
62 2' piccolo
63 8' string
64 4' string
65 2 2/3' string
66 8' celeste
67 4' celeste
68 16' vox humana
69 8' vox humana
70 4' vox humana
71 8' oboe
72 8' clarinet
73 8' tibia
74 4' tibia
75 8' aeoline
76 4' aeoline
77 2 2/3' aeoline
78 Chimes
79 Bells
80 Xylophone
85 French horn
86 Trumpet
87 Clarion
88 16' Pedal piano
89 8' Great piano
90 4' Swell piano

Additional Registration Holes

Using the holes listed above, Swell stops are controlled by the Swell note holes in the tracker bar, and Great stops are controlled by the Great note holes. Additionally, Swell stops may be controlled by the Great note holes and vice-versa, to enable one division of the organ to keep playing while its own stops are being changed, without use of the note sustain hole. This is accomplished by use of the following holes:
96 Great key release
31 Swell stops on
32 Swell stops off
33 to 56 Swell stops in same order as holes 57-80 above

98 Swell key release
83 Great stops on
84 Great stops off
57 to 80 Great stops in same order as holes 33-56 above

Control of Echo Organ

The Echo division is played by coupling it to the Swell with hole 8. Echo stops are controlled as follows:
96 Great key release
90 Echo stops on
45 Echo stops off
33 Pedal Echo chimes
34 Pedal Echo bourdon
35 8' flute
36 4' flute
37 2' piccolo
38 8' string
39 4' string
40 8' dulciana
41 4' dulciana
42 8' vox humana
43 Harp
44 Chimes
Holes 33 and 34 are Pedal stops changed from the Echo section.

Control of Shades

The shades are opened or closed in seven steps by a series of short holes at 3 or 93 respectively. They are opened or closed slowly by a long hole at 3 or 93. Holes 3 and 93 punched simultaneously open the shades quickly; hole 93 first, then joined by 3, closes them quickly.

Couplers

6 Extends Great to 29-80, G# to B
7 Extends Swell to 33-90, C to A
8 Plays Echo organ from Swell holes
4 Cancels 6-8

Comments

The Clark Standard Pipe Organ Recording seems to be versatile and sophisticated, but, unfortunately, only one roll player, a test roll (XR-100), and one music roll (XR-104, *Indian Love Call*) were known to exist in 1980 when the preceding was compiled. These were acquired by Mel Luchetti from the estate of Cecil Nixon, inventor of the famous android "Isis." Nixon's colorful personality, interesting mansion, and the android and other artifacts are described by Howard Fitch in *The Bulletin of the Musical Box Society,* Vol. 23, Nos. 1 and 3. The preceding tracker scale information was taken from the original test roll and was provided by Mel Luchetti and Craig Williams.

ESTEY PIPE ORGAN ROLLS

The Estey Organ Company, founded in 1846, was located in Brattleboro, Vermont, from its inception until its stock was dispersed in the early 1960s. During the 19th century Estey was a principal maker of parlor reed organs (non-player type) and church organs. Estey's 20th century business was mainly with large pipe organs for churches and homes. Estey player pipe organs were made in several different styles. Most players were installed in private residences. While the majority were of the single-roll type, apparently an automatic changing device, similar to that used on certain models of the Welte Philharmonic Organ, was available. One of the authors obtained an Estey roll changer at the factory in the 1960s, but it is not known if it was a prototype or whether the mechanism was produced in commercial quantities.

ESTEY ORGAN CO.
EARLY NON-REGISTERING ROLL
10 1/8" wide; same as the Aeolian double pipe organ roll

ESTEY ORGAN CO.
SELF-REGISTERING PIPE ORGAN ROLL
10¾" wide; spaced 12 holes per inch (2 staggered rows of 6 holes per inch)
(Registration holes were added to the margin of early rolls without the registration feature)

Top Row
1 Combination 1 and 1+
2 Combination 3 and 3+
3 Combination 5 and 5+
4 to 61, 58 Swell playing notes
62 Shutters closed (in three steps)
63 Combination 6 and 6+

Bottom Row
1 Combination 2 and 2+
2 Combination 4 and 4+
3 to 14, 12 Pedal and Great notes
15 to 60, 46 remaining Great notes
61 General cancel/rewind
62 Shutters open (in three steps)

When a combination hole is opened the first time, the basic combination is drawn. When it is opened the second time, the "plus" combination is drawn, each combination cancelling the others.

Combinations
Solo
1 8' string
1+ 8' string
2 8' flute
2+ 8' flute, 4' flute
3 Vox humana
3+ Vox humana, stopped diapason
4 8' flute F
4+ 8' flute, tuba
5 Woodwind
5+ Woodwind, chimes
6 Mezzo forte
6+ Fortissimo

Combinations
Accompaniment
1 8' flute
1+ 8' flute, harp
2 8' string
2+ 8' string
3 String
3+ String, harp
4 String, flute
4+ String, flute; add suitable accompaniment
5 Suitable accompaniment
5+ Suitable accompaniment
6 Mezzo forte
6+ Fortissimo

ESTEY ORGAN CO.
"NEW MUSIC" (late 1920s to 1933)

Estey "new music" rolls use an elaboration of the earlier combination system, using the same tracker bar. When a combination hole is opened for the first time, the basic combination is set; when opened the second time, the "plus" combination is set, as in the earlier rolls. When the combination hole, "swell shutters open" and "swell shutters closed" are opened simultaneously, the "A" combination is set, and then these three holes are opened simultaneously the second time, the "A+" combination is set. Thus, four combinations are available for each combination hole in the tracker bar: the basic combination, the +, the A and the A+ combinations. With this system, the six combination holes provide 24 combinations.

Automatic Combinations for "New Music" rolls
(Swell/Great/Pedal/Tremolo divided by diagonal marks)
1 String / Flute / Bourdon / Yes
1+ Not used / Flute or harp / Not used / Yes
1A String / String / No Pedal / Yes
1A+ Not used / Flute / Not used / Yes
2 8' flute / String / String / Yes
2+ Doppelflute, piccolo / String, flute / Bourdon / Yes
2A 4' flute / String / String / Yes
2A+ Mixed Solo, heavy / Diapason / Bourdon / No
3 Vox humana / String / String / Yes
3+ Vox humana, flute / Harp, string / String / Yes
3A Clarinet / String / String / Yes
3A+ Reed / String, flute / Bourdon / Yes
4 Flute F / String / Bourdon / Yes
4+ Flute F, reed / String / Bourdon / Yes
4A Diapason / String, flute / Bourdon / Yes
4A+ Diapason, oboe / String, flute / Bourdon / Yes
5 Oboe / String / Bourdon / Yes
5+ Flute or chimes / Soft string / Not used / Not used
5A Saxophone / Flute / Bourdon / Yes
5A+ 8' String, 16' string / Not used / Not used / Yes
6 F unison / F unison / Bourdon, string / No
6+ FF unison / FF unison / Bourdon, string / No
6A FF unison / FF unison / Bourdon, string / No
6A+ 8' flute, 4' flute / Not used / Not used / Yes

The combination holes are drawn by a system of cams and pins. Blanks in the above combination chart (marked "Not used") represent positions in the combination setting having no cams. All 32 Pedal notes are playable by means of multiplexing controlled by the highest two Great note holes.

THE ESTEY RESIDENCE ORGAN

Do not dismiss the idea of a pipe organ in your home on the ground of cost, difficulty of installing, or the thought that maybe you would not care for organ music. Once really hear an Estey Pipe Organ and you will know that you like organ music, just as you like orchestra music. Once you want an organ, all the rest becomes easy—even the paying for it. A good organ can be bought for the price of a good motor car, and its addition becomes an architectural feature in your home. And you can play it yourself by means of the Estey Organist, a self-interpreting device.

THE ESTEY ORGAN COMPANY, *Brattleboro, Vermont.*

KIMBALL ORGAN ROLLS

The W.W. Kimball Company, established in 1857, shipped thousands of organs from its Chicago headquarters. Upright and grand pianos (players as well as non-players) were also marketed.

A 1913 trade notice observed: "Kimball pipe organs are now an established feature for lodges and private residences. They are especially so on account of the Kimball Soloist. This feature is a remarkable achievement in self-playing devices. Every imaginable combination of the grandest music is adapted to its possibilities. The catalogue of its library embraces practically the entire literature of music, from a Bach fugue to a Sousa march, a Beethoven sonata, or a Strauss waltz. The Soloist may be built in any organ and in no way interferes with the instrument manually."

Kimball produced player organs through the 1920s and early 1930s. In 1932 Kimball bought the Welte-Tripp Organ Corporation, together with its patents and other assets. By that time the market for large residential and other pipe organs was approaching zero due to the Depression. In later years Kimball produced the 1200 Series Electronic Organ, which used rolls similar in size to a home player piano roll.

KIMBALL ELECTRONIC ORGAN ROLL
1200 SERIES
11¼" wide; spaced 9 holes per inch

0 Reset speed control
1 Rewind
2 Constant vacuum
3 Mute switch
4, 6, 8, 10, Speed controls
5, 7, 9, Volume controls
11-15 Blank
16 to 27, Pedal notes C to B
28 to 44, Accompaniment manual notes C to E
45 to 76, Solo manual notes F to C
77-78 Blank

Holes 4, 6, 8, and 10 set the roll speed periodically throughout long play rolls to compensate for paper buildup on the takeup spool. Hole 0 resets the speed control. Hole 2 is connected to constant suction in the valve chest; it pulls the paper to the tracker bar to prevent false rewind impulses caused by paper buckling.

For information concerning Kimball-Welte organ rolls refer to the Welte organ section of this book.

LINK PIANO AND ORGAN CO.
OLD SCALE ROLL (rolls under serial no. 118 approx.)
12" wide; spaced 6 holes per inch
Endless type

1 Tremolo off
2 Shades closed
3 Shades open
4 Blank
5 Blank
6 Blank
7 Blank
8 Blank
9 Blank
10 to 21, Pedal playing notes, C to B
22 to 58, Solo manual playing notes
59 8' open diapason on
60 8' open diapason off
61 4' flute on
62 4' flute off
63 8' violin on
64 8' violin off
65 8' stopped diapason on
66 8' stopped diapason off
67 Blank
68 Blank
69 Tremolo on

LINK PIANO AND ORGAN CO.
NEW SCALE ROLL
12" wide; spaced 6 holes per inch
Endless type

1 Tremolo off
2 Shades closed
3 Shades open
4 Register shift 1
5 Register shift 2
6 Register shift 3
7 Register shift 4
8 Register shift 5
9 Blank
10 to 22, 16' Pedal, 8' Pedal and Accompaniment
22 to 29, Overlapping Accompaniment
30 to 58, Solo manual playing notes
59 to 66 (See Registration Shift Chart following)
67 8' tuba on
68 8' tuba off
69 Tremolo on

Registration Shift Chart for New Scale
(Shifts 1, 2, 3, 4, and 5 divided by diagonal marks)
59 Harp celeste on / Bells on / Xylophone on / 8' tuba great on / Chimes on
60 Harp celeste off / Bells off / Xylophone off / 8' tuba great off / Chimes off
61 8' quintadena on / Bass drum on / Snare drum on / 8' melodia on / 4' flute on
62 8' quintadena off / Bass drum off / Snare drum off / 8' melodia off / 4' flute off
63 8' viol celeste on / 4' violin on / 2' twelfth on / 16' viola on / 8' flute on
64 8' viol celeste off / 4' violin off / 2' twelfth off / 16' viola off / 8' flute off
65 8' dulciana on / 2' violin on / 8' vox humana on / 16' bourdon(?) on / 8' string on
66 8' dulciana off / 2' violin off / 8' vox humana off / 16' bourdon(?) off / 8' string off
67 1 3/5' tierce on / 4' octave diapason on / 8' oboe on / 4' trumpet on / ? on
68 1 3/5th tierce off / 4' octave diapason off / 8' oboe off / 4' trumpet off / ? off

2+3 = Vox humana on - entire range
1+69 = Vox humana off
2+3+69 = 4' coupler on
1+3+69 = 4' coupler off

The Link Selective Roll Reproducing Player

The Theatre's Musical Insurance Policy

Selective control box, operating player from any distance. Touch of button instantly changes rolls to follow picture.

In Constant Control of Every Note and Expression

THE LINK REPRODUCING PLAYER is the most marvelous musical invention of today, because it does that which is beyond the scope of any other player. It not only is self playing, but it plays without mechanical effect, reproducing the "human appeal" characteristic of music when rendered by master musicians.

It plays with exact interpretation anything from the simplest musical composition to the most difficult classic, and it does not require the aid of the human hand in order to bring out the best there is in the music. Our player is the only mechanical player that dominates the whole instrument constantly, obviating the necessity of any hand manipulation during the rendition of any selection.

The LINK Reproducing Player is distinctly a delight to all accomplished musicians. We challenge any organist to play a pipe organ any better than our mechanical player. One reason why our player will easily win any such contest is because we have through it constant control of every note on the instrument all of the time, and are not obliged to relinquish any part of that control to manipulate stops and swell shades. The organist, at best, has but twelve points of contact with the instrument and must frequently surrender, momentarily at least, some of them in order to manipulate the stops or expression controls. Through our player we have instant control of every function of the instrument, and are, therefore, able to shade expression perfectly and with human deftness, while at the same time we can secure as many additional effects as may be desired, because we are not like the individual, limited to ten fingers and two feet.

Link theatre organs, marketed in the 1920s under the C. Sharpe Minor Unit Organ name, achieved popularity with theatre owners. The roll mechanism featured a cabinet which stored four endless rolls. The operator could, via pushbuttons, shift from one roll to another instantly to fit the mood of the music to the theme on the screen.

Wide Range - No Rewind Annoyance

The LINK Player is particularly adapted to the needs of the theatre, because it has such a wide range in the character of its music. There are four compartments for endless rolls. Each roll has an equivalent to fifteen selections and runs approximately thirty minutes before repeating, so that with the four rolls you have enough music to play a two hour show and not play the same piece twice.

The rolls are like an endless belt so that you do not have to rewind, thereby eliminating all rewind annoyances. The music on each roll is all of the same character— for instance, one roll may be all dramatic music, another roll love scenes, still another hurry, and another popular songs, dances or marches. If so desired, the same type of music can be put in all four compartments.

Positive Control of Various Types of Music, from a Distance

The control of this wide variety of music is through a master control box. One control box is usually placed in the operator's booth, and as many additional control boxes can be placed throughout the theatre as desired. Instantly by the pressing of a button in one of these control boxes, the the music can be changed from one selection to another, even to the stopping of any selection at any note and the beginning of another of entirely different tempo the next second.

Instantaneous Changes in Music to Co-ordinate with Pictures

The **right music** at the **right time** with **instantaneous changes** from one selection to another, with changing tempo at the instant the scenes are shifted on the screen is a most important factor for the successful display of a film, without which the proper effect of the picture is nullified. This is one main reason why even the owners of larger theatres, who, in the past, would not consider a player on their organs, immediately see where the LINK Player can take the place of the relief organist, save them money, and still not lower one iota the high standard of music they want to maintain. In the great majority of cases the LINK Player, through our rolls, made by master musicians, produces even a higher standard of music than before. Managers have confided to us that patrons, not knowing the relief was a LINK Player, have complimented them on their relief organist and have suggested his promotion to regular organist.

Link Players Never Go Out on Strike

We have also had exhibitors tell us that they consider their LINK Player a musical insurance policy. As they say, they insure their building and everything else, why not insure against a performance without music? Their LINK Players never go out on strike.

Perhaps, in print, some of these statements sound exaggerated. We have, however, been very conservative in our claim. Our Player has been proved by the test of time, a thoroughly practical feature in many theatres. Simple and rugged in construction, it is built to withstand hard usage, and to render music which it is impossible to describe through mere words. The LINK REPRODUCING PLAYER actually must be heard to be appreciated fully. Certainly you will agree with us that this Player is an additional feature to our organs which cannot be discounted, and is a gold bond investment for any theatre.

Exuberant advertising was characteristic of theatre organ builders in the 1920s, and Link was no exception, as the above indicates. "Managers have confided to us that patrons, not knowing the relief was a LINK player, have complimented them on their relief organist and have suggested his promotion to regular organist."

MÖLLER ARTISTE ORGAN ROLL

The Möller player normally uses the tracker bar holes for controls and to play notes on various divisions of the organ, according to this scale:

Row 1 (bottom row)

1 to 59, Playing notes
60 Separator
61 Tremolo cancel
62 Combination (kicker): general cancel, mute for playing notes, allows registration to be set
63 Rewind
64 Shade 1 (p)
65 Shade 2 (mf)
66 Shade 3 (f)
67 Shade 4 (ff)

Row 2 (top row)

1 to 12, Bass notes
13 to 32, Tenor notes
33 to 61, Treble notes
62 Crescendo
63 Shade 1 (p)
64 Shade 2 (mf)
65 Shade 3 (f)
66 Shade 5 (ff)

When a registration change is desired, the combination hole is punched. This disconnects row 1 from its playing notes, cancels previous registration, and allows new registration to be set according to this scale:

1-12 Fundamentals
13-17 Pedal stop combinations
18-28 Swell stop combinations
29-39 Great stop combinations
40-50 Choir stop combinations
51-59 Solo stop combinations

The fundamentals (1-12) couple the various divisions of the organ to various sections of playing note holes on the tracker bar. The stop combinations turn stops on in each division. The fundamentals and combinations for a 3-manual organ are listed here; the Artiste player was probably only rarely applied to a 4-manual instrument. The fundamental number, 1 to 12, is listed to the left. The four functions: Row 1, Row 2 Treble, Row 2 Tenor, and Row 2 Bass, are separated by diagonals.

1 Swell, Choir / Great / Great / Pedal
2 Great, Choir / Swell / Swell / Pedal
3 Swell, Choir / Great / Pedal / Pedal
4 Great, Choir / Swell / Pedal / Pedal
5 Great, Choir / Swell 16' / Swell 16' / Pedal
6 Great, Choir / Swell 16' / Pedal / Pedal
7 Swell / Choir / Great / Pedal
8 Swell / Great / Choir / Pedal
9 Great / Swell / Choir / Pedal
10 Great / Choir / Swell / Pedal
11 Choir / Swell / Great / Pedal
12 Choir / Great / Swell / Pedal

Swell Stop Combinations

18 Vox humana and tremolo
19 Salicional, celeste, tremolo
20 Viol d'orchestre, tremolo
21 8' gedeckt, tremolo
22 Salicional, tremolo
23 Diapason, tremolo
24 Oboe, tremolo
25 Orchestral oboe, tremolo
26 4' string, tremolo
27 4' flute, tremolo
28 16' bourdon, tremolo

Great Stop Combinations

29 Dulciana, tremolo
30 Gemshorn, tremolo
31 Minor flute, tremolo
32 Major flute, tremolo
33 Viol d'orchestre, tremolo
34 4' octave, tremolo
35 4' flute, tremolo
36 Diapason, tremolo
37 Trumpet
38 Harp
39 Chimes

Choir Stop Combinations

40 Dulciana, tremolo
41 Gemshorn, tremolo
42 String, tremolo
43 String, celeste, tremolo
44 Concert flute, tremolo
45 French horn
46 ?
47 Diapason, tremolo
48 2 2/3' twelfth, tremolo
49 Quintadena, tremolo
50 Clarinet, tremolo

Pedal Stop Combinations

13 Soft 16'
14 Medium 16'
15 Softer 8'
16 Louder 8'
17 All pedal stops not already drawn by combinations 13-16

The crescendo hole (hole 62, row 2) switches holes 33-61, row 2, to their crescendo functions; the following list shows a typical crescendo:

33 Swell to 1, Choir to 1, Great to 1, Pedal bass, Pedal tenor, Great dulciana, Pedal 16' gedeckt
34 Swell salicional, Pedal dolce viol
35 Swell celeste
36 Great concert flute 8'
37 Pedal 16' bourdon
38 Swell flute 8'
39 Pedal flute 8'
40 Swell flute 4'
41 Great gross flute
42 Pedal bass flute 8'
43 Great 4' flute
44 Great 4' gross flute
45 Great viol d'orchestre
46 Great diapason
47 Great celeste
48 Pedal cello 8'
49 Great octave 4'
50 Choir clarinet
51 Swell viol d'orchestre
52 Swell diapason
53 Swell 4' to row 1
54 Choir 4' to row 1
55 Swell 4' string
56 Great trumpet
57 Pedal 16' diaphone
58 Swell 16' to row 1
59 Choir 16' to row 1
60 Great 16' to row 1
61 Great 4' to row 1

The crescendo relays are additive, with the highest crescendo hole punched adding all functions below it. When the crescendo is in use, music is playable only from row 1, and also holes 1-32 of row 2.

The stop combinations and crescendo were individually wired to suit each organ to which the players were attached.

The separator hole is a multiplexing device for controlling additional sets of swell shades.

The tremolo cancel hole cancels tremolo from any combination which is set.

ROBERT-MORTON CHAPEL ORGAN ROLL
STYLE 350
11¼" wide; spaced 9 holes per inch

1 Blank
2 Blank
3 Blank
4 Blank
5 Treble flute off
6 Play
7 Treble flute on
8 Blank
9 Blank
10 Blank
11 Swell closed, 3 steps
12 Swell open, 3 steps
13 Treble dulciana on
14 Treble dulciana off
15 Tremolo on
16 Tremolo off
17 Bass quintadena on
18 Bass quintadena off
19 Treble vox humana on
20 Treble vox humana off
21 to 81, 61 playing notes, C to C
82 Bass dulciana on
83 Bass dulciana off
84 Bass flute on
85 Bass flute off
86 Teed to hole 13
87 Teed to hole 14
88 Teed to hole 7
89 Teed to hole 5
90 Treble quintadena on
91 Treble quintadena off
92 Teed to hole 90
93 Rewind
94 Reed to hole 91
95 Blank
96 Blank
97 Blank
98 Blank

The Robert Morton notation omits holes 1 to 4 and 95 to 98, for a total of 90 holes in actual use.

ROESLER-HUNHOLZ CONCERT ORGAN ROLL
11¼" wide; spaced 9 holes per inch

The Concert model roll uses an elaboration of the Artistouch Consolette tracker scale, with four levels of registration multiplexing instead of two, and additional swell shade and sforzando (crescendo) multiplexing. This roll has 100 holes, with one hole added to each side of the Consolette tracker scale. To compare the two systems, subtract 1 from the Concert tracker bar hole number, or add 1 to the Consolette hole number, to arrive at the same function.

1 ?
2 Great shades open one increment (Choir shades are coupled to Great shades)
3 Great shades closed one increment
4 Swell shades open one increment (Echo shades are coupled to Swell shades)
5 Swell shades closed one increment
6 to 17, Pedal notes
18 to 49, Great or Choir notes
50 Cancel primary combinations
50+52 Cancel secondary combinations
50+100 Cancel tertiary combinations
50+52+100 Cancel quaternary combinations
50+51 Rewind
52 (with 53-67) Secondary combination multiplex switch
52+100 (with 53-67) Quaternary combination multiplex switch
53 to 67, Combinations
68 to 99, Swell or Echo notes
100 (with 53-67) Tertiary combination multiplex switch

2+3 Sforzando (crescendo) level 1
4+5 Level 2
3+4 Level 3
2+5 Level 4

Hole 51 is also used in some other way; in the test roll, it appears in a "Pedal 8' by cancel 51" test. This might have something to do with cancelling the 8' pedal which is set by hole 66.

The three sections of note holes (6-17, 18-49, and 68-99) may be combined to allow access to all 61 notes of one manual, by certain tertiary combinations labeled "61 note." (See tertiary combinations listed below)

Primary Combinations

See Artistouch Consolette Primary Combinations. Additionally, hole 62 controls Echo to Echo 4', and hole 64 controls Echo unison off.

Secondary Combinations

See Artistouch Consolette Secondary Combinations. Additionally, holes 52+62 control Echo to Echo 16', and holes 52+65 turn Echo tremolo off. (All Consolette functions are one tracker bar hole number less than Concert tracker bar hole numbers.)

Tertiary Combinations
100+54 Great to 61 note; Choir to 61 note
100+55 Swell to 61 note; Echo to 61 note
100+57 Pedal: Swell to Pedal
100+59 Swell: Silent
100+61 Swell: Silent
100+62 Swell: Silent
100+63 Swell: Silent; Great: Silent; Pedal: Violone
100+64 Swell: Silent; Pedal: Fagatto
100+65 Pedal: Cello
100+66 Pedal: Pedal 4'
100+67 Pedal: Great to Pedal

Quaternary Combinations
100+52+53 or 54, 55, 56, 57, 58, or 59 Swell: Silent; Pedal: Silent
100+52+60 Swell: Silent; Great: Silent
100+52+61 Swell: Silent; Pedal: Silent
100+52+62 Great: Swell to Great 4'
100+52+63 Swell: Silent
100+52+64 Pedal: Pedal tone off (16')
100+52+65 Great: Great tremolo off
100+52+67 Swell: Swell off; Echo on Swell

The preceding information for the Roesler-Hunholz Concert model organ player was taken from a Kilgen organ player and test rolls at an installation in Woodside, California, by Craig Williams.

SKINNER ORGAN ROLL
Semi-automatic type

1 Rewind
2 Pedal pilot 1
3 Pedal pilot 2
4 to 15, Pedal notes, C to B
16 to 73, Swell notes, C to A
74 to 120, Great notes, B to A

Pedal pilot 1 switches the Pedal notes to the lowest octave. Pilot 2 switches them to the next higher octave. Each pilot hole cancels the other. The semi-automatic Skinner roll was later adapted, without the Pedal pilot holes, to play the Hammond electronic player organ, the so-called Aeolian Hammond Duo-Art.

SKINNER ORGAN ROLL
Fully automatic type

This roll is an elaboration of the above semi-automatic roll. Additional pilot controls serve to multiplex many of the Pedal, Swell, and Great playing notes for registration purposes. The following scale shows the multiplex functions.

1 Spare
2 Pedal pilot 1
3 Pedal pilot 2
4 Pedal pilot 3
5 Left to Pedal (coupler)
6 Still gedeckt
7 Trombone 16'
8 Spare
9 Spare
10 Spare
11 Gedeckt 8'
12 Echo lieblich gedeckt 16'
13 Spare
14 Bourdon 16'
15 Spare
16 Piano 16'
17 Spare (or harp)
18 Swell pilot 1
19 Swell pilot 2
20 Swell pilot 3
21 Spare
22 Diapason
23 Voix celeste
24 Sp. flute
25 Swell tremolo
26 Great tremolo
27 Spare
28 Flute celeste
29 Gedeckt
30 Unda maris 4'
31 Spare
32 Cornopean
33 Harp
34 Celesta (chrysoglott)
35 Piano
36 Spare
37 Echo vox humana
38 Echo flute celeste
39 Echo chimney flute
40 Chimes
41 Spare
42 Spare
43 Diapason
44 Chimney flute
45 Flute 4'
46 Spare
47 Voix celeste-cello
48 English horn
49 Clarinet
50 Flugelhorn
51 Spare
52 French horn
53 Tuba
54 Vox humana
55 Rewind
56 General cancel
57 Spare
58 Great pilot 1
59 Great pilot 2
60 Great pilot 3
61 Diapason
62 Chimney flute
63 Flute 4'
64 Spare
65 Voix celeste-cello
66 English horn
67 Clarinet
68 Flugelhorn
69 Spare
70 French horn
71 Tuba
72 Vox humana
73 Chimes
74 Harp
75 Celesta (chrysoglott)
76 Echo vox humana
77 Echo flute celeste
78 Echo chimney flute
79 Spare
80 Spare
81 Spare
82 Spare
83 Diapason
84 Voix celeste
85 Sp. flute
86 Spare
87 Spare
88 Spare
89 Flute celeste
90 Gedeckt
91 Unda maris 4'
92 Spare
93 Cornopean
94 Piano
95 Right to piano (coupler)
96 Right tremolo
97 Spare
98 Swell shutters 0
99 Swell shutters 1
100 Swell shutters 2
101 Swell shutters 3
102 Swell shutters 4
103 Spare
104 Great shutters 0
105 Great shutters 1
106 Great shutters 2
107 Great shutters 3
108 Great shutters 4
109 L. tuba
110 Sforzando
111 Spare
112 Decrescendo
113 Crescendo on, R.L. on
114 Crescendo off, R.L. off
115 Spare
116 Spare
117 Spare
118 Spare
119 R. tuba
120 Spare

This Skinner pipe organ roll player unit probably dates from the 1930s. With the device shown here were nearly 150 different rolls, including performances by Marcel Dupre, Albert Snow, Lynwood Farnum, George Faxon, and Chandler Goldthwaite. (Photograph courtesy of F. Lee Eiseman, Teradyne, Inc.)

Rear view of the Skinner roll player unit plus pneumatic-to-electric and electromagnetic relay devices associated with it. (Photograph courtesy of F. Lee Eiseman, Teradyne, Inc.)

STANDARD PIPE ORGAN PLAYER ROLL
(Made by the Clark Orchestra Roll Co.?)
11¼" wide; spaced 9 holes per inch

1 to 12, Pedal notes, overlaps with Great
13 to 42, Continuation of Great
43 Cancel
44 Rewind
45 Great flute 8'
46 Great flute 4'
47 Great salicional 8'
48 Great viol 4'
49 Great dulciana 8'
50 Chimes
51 Tremolo
52 Swell bourdon 16'
53 Swell flute 8'
54 Swell flute 4'
55 Swell naz.
56 Swell salicional 8'
57 Swell viol 4'
58 Swell dulciana 8'
59 Vox humana
60 Shutter 4
61 Shutter 3
62 Shutter 2
63 Shutter 1
64 to 100, Swell notes

VERLINDEN, WEICKHARDT & DORNOFF ORGAN ROLL
11¼" wide; spaced 9 holes per inch

1 Register
2 Register
3 Register
4 Register
5 Register
6 Register
7 Unknown
8 Unknown
9 Unknown
10 Unknown
11 Unknown
12 Unknown
13 Unknown
14 Unknown
15 Unknown
16 Unknown
17 Unknown
18 Unknown
19 Unknown
20 to 80, 61 playing notes, C to C
81 Unknown
82 Unknown
83 Unknown
84 Unknown
85 Unknown
86 Unknown
87 Unknown
88 Unknown
89 Unknown
90 Unknown
91 Play
92 Rewind
93 Swell?
94 Swell?
95 Swell?

The preceding information was obtained by studying two hymn rolls. The swell shutter control holes seem to operate reversible swell shades or some type of ratchet controls. Each registration hole might operate a combination, as there is no obvious general cancel hole. Holes 5 to 92 correspond to holes 1 to 88 of an ordinary home player piano roll. The box labels are printed, with the titles typed on the labels. The title only is typed on the end tab. The rolls examined have no numbers. Each half of the box, and the beginning of the roll, is rubber stamped "Player Action and Automatic Roll Control by Edmund Verlinden."

WANGERIN ORGAN ROLL
11¼" wide; spaced 9 holes per inch

1 Blank
2 Chimes
3 Register?
4 Register?
5 Register?
6 to 11, Combinations 1 through 6
12 Blank?
13 Blank?
14 Blank?
15 Blank?
16 to 76, 61 playing notes, C to C
77 Swell closed
78 to 86, Swell shades open
87 Blank
88 Rewind

WELTE PHILHARMONIC ORGAN ROLL
STYLES III and IV

1 Blank
2 Blank
3 Violin Dolce 8' on
4 Violin Dolce 8' off
5 Diapason 8' on
6 Diapason 8' off
7 Flote Dolce 8' on
8 Flote Dolce 8' off
9 Flote 4' on
10 Flote 4' off
11 Bassoon on
12 Bassoon off
13 Piccolo(?) on
14 Piccolo(?) off
15 Tympani
16 to 73, Manual I playing notes C to A
74 Crescendo on
75 Crescendo off
76 Forzando on
77 Forzando off
78 to 107, Manual II playing notes G to C
108 "Rewind stop"(?)
109 Tremolo on
110 Tremolo off
111 Horn on
112 Horn off
113 Oboe on
114 Oboe off
115 Clarinet on
116 Clarinet off
117 Pedal bourdon on
118 Pedal bourdon off
119 Blank
120 Blank

The pedal is played by the lowest Manual I notes.

STANDARD WELTE PIPE ORGAN ROLL

1 Transpose cancel
2 Solo transpose
3 General cancel
4 Rewind
5 Pedal control
6 Pedal on
7 Manual with pedal
8 Accompaniment shades open
9 Accompaniment shades closed
10 Accompaniment expression accent
11 Solo shades open
12 Solo shades closed
13 Solo expression accent
14 to 74, Accompaniment notes 1 to 61
75 Automatic tracking device
76 Automatic tracking device
77 to 113, Solo notes 1 to 37
114 to 125, Countermelody notes 1 to 12
126 Countermelody shades open
127 Countermelody shades closed
128 Countermelody expression accent
129 to 149, Combinations 1 to 21
150 General cancel

WELTE PHILHARMONIC ORGAN ROLL
STYLES III, IV, V, and VI
15¼" wide; spaced 4 holes per cm.

1 Pedal on
2 Manual off
3 Swell diapason 8'
4 Pedal violin bass 16'
5 Pedal bourdon 16'
6 Pedal flute 8'
7 Great harp
8 Great viol d'orchestre 8'
9 Great solo string
10 Great bassoon 8'
11 Great harmonic flute 4'
12 Great diapason 8'
13 Great voix celeste 8'
14 Great flauto traverso 8'
15 to 72, 58 Great notes
73 Shades open, slowly
74 Shades closed, slowly
75 Automatic tracking device
76 Automatic tracking device
77 Sforzando on (shades open fast)
78 Sforzando off (shades close fast)
79 to 134, 56 Swell notes, C to G
135 Swell dolce flute 8'
136 Swell viola da gamba 8'
137 Swell aeoline 8'
138 Swell bourdon 8'
139 Swell cor anglais 8'
140 Blank
141 Swell philomela horn 8'
142 Swell oboe 8'
143 Swell clarinet 16'
144 Great chimes
145 Swell tremolo
146 Swell vox humana 8'
147 Echo organ
148 Rewind
149 Tutti
150 Blank

The Pedal shares the lowest 30 Great notes, holes 15 to 44. The Pedal is turned on by hole 1, and the lowest 30 Great notes are turned off, if desired, by hole 2. Later rolls can play all 32 Pedal notes, apparently by using Great hole notes 15 to 46.

All stops are reversible, as in the Aeolian Duo-Art Organ player. Each hole turns its rank "on" the first time it is punched, and "off" the next time.

WELTE-MIGNON PIPE ORGAN ROLL
150 SCALE

The Welte-Mignon 150 Scale pipe organ rolls have the same functions as the Welte Philharmonic III-VI scale, except that hole 150 controls a 16' pedal trombone, and rewind is accomplished by first punching 146 and then 148.

KIMBALL-WELTE PIPE ORGAN ROLL

Kimball-Welte pipe organ rolls, made after 1932 when Kimball acquired Welte-Tripp, have the same functions as the Welte Philharmonic III-VI scale, with the following exceptions:
6 Pedal cello flute 8'
73 Shades open in 12 steps
74 Shades close in 12 steps
77 Expression accent - all 12 shades open
78 Rewind
148 Bass drum
150 General cancel

In the Kimball-Welte system, each registration hole locks its rank on until cancelled by the general cancel hole 150. (In the Philharmonic III-VI roll, the stop holes are reversible.) Pedal trombone 16' comes on with tutti.

WELTE-PHILHARMONIE-ORGEL IM HEIM DES HERRN K...., FLORENZ.

Above: This Welte catalogue page of the 1920s omits the customer's name and notes that the view is of a "Welte Philharmonic Organ in the home of Mr. ....., Florence." The late Richard C. Simonton, who was a close friend of the Welte family, told the authors: "This is a view of the Welte organ in the villa of Mr. Kraft, a Swiss who owned the two largest hotels in Florence, Italy. We carried an introduction [from Edwin Welte] to Mr. Kraft and were guests in his beautiful Grand Hotel. He had, however, sold the villa and the organ had been removed and was installed in a church in Rome. Mr. Kraft also had two Steinway-Welte grand pianos."

Right: Welte Philharmonic Organs as offered by Welte circa 1912-1914. Although the notation "the greatest invention for increasing picture house receipts" is given, only a few Welte Philharmonic Organs were ever installed in theatres. Most were installed in private residences.

An Orchestra and Organ in ONE

THE GREATEST INVENTION FOR
INCREASING PICTURE HOUSE RECEIPTS

*Playing Automatically, by Means of Paper Rolls, Reproducing all Orchestral
Effects, or can be Played by Hand with Keyboard,
so as to Accompany a Singer*

ELIMINATE EXPERIMENTS

WHEN you purchase a Welte instrument you eliminate experiments. Your value is represented in every detail. Built to endure severe tests. Built to satisfy a discriminating public, and conceded by artists as being musically correct; as is attested by being in the homes of the wealthiest and most representative people in the world.

EIGHTY YEARS OF SUCCESS

A Welte instrument represents eighty years of successful building of Automatic Musical Instruments, backed up by a concern whose product has been sold in practically every nation on the globe; a house whose integrity is beyond question, and whose product has captured first and grand prizes at all world's exhibitions for over fifty years.

MUSIC ROLLS FOR WELTE INSTRUMENTS

The House of Welte cuts the largest repertoire of music rolls of any manufacturer of automatic musical instruments in the world, and their collection of higher grade music, such as the classics, overtures and sacred music is unparalleled. The latest popular Broadway hits are constantly being made.

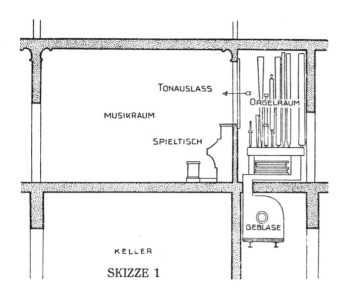

SKIZZE 1

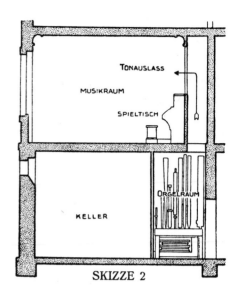

SKIZZE 2

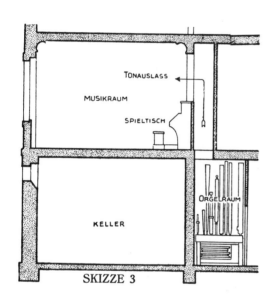

SKIZZE 3

There's more than one way to install a Welte Philharmonic Organ, as these five sketches from a Welte catalogue of the 1920s indicate. The German-English equivalents are: "Keller" = cellar; "Geblase" = organ blower; "Orgelraum" = organ pipe chamber; "Tonauslass" = sound opening or swell shutters; "Musikraum" = music room; and "Spieltisch" = organ console or keydesk. Sketch 1 shows the pipe chamber and music room on the same level. Sketches 2 and 3 show the pipe chamber installed in the cellar or in a lower level. Sketch 4 shows the pipe chamber in the attic. Sketch 5 shows still another idea.

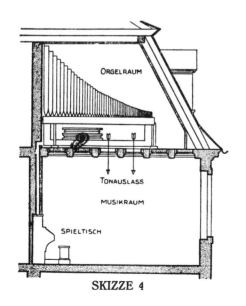

SKIZZE 4

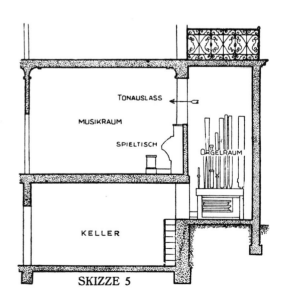

SKIZZE 5

WICKS ORGAN ROLL
11¼" wide; spaced 9 holes per inch

A Blank
B Play
1 Violine on
2 Violine off
3 Blank
4 Swell open
5 Swell closed
6 Salicional on
7 Dulciana on
8 Dulciana off
9 Salicional off
10 Blank
11 Blank
12 Blank
13 Blank
14 Blank
15 Blank
16 to 76, 61 playing notes, C to C
77 Blank
78 Blank
79 Blank
80 Blank
81 Chimes off
82 Chimes on
83 Flute off
84 Flute on
85 Blank
86 Blank
87 Blank
88 Blank
C Rewind
D Blank

WILCOX & WHITE ORGAN ROLLS

Wilcox & White, located in Meriden, Connecticut, was a leading maker of organettes and player reed organs around the turn of the century. The Symphony player reed organ featured a keyboard, was foot-pumped, and used the roll described below. Many different attractive case designs were made.

WILCOX & WHITE
SYMPHONY REED ORGAN ROLL
9¼" wide; spaced 5 holes per inch

1 C
2 D
3 to 44, Notes G to C

WURLITZER MORTUARY ORGAN ROLL
STYLE MO
11¼" wide; spaced 9 holes per inch

1 Blank (if present)
2 Bass hammer rail on
3 Mandolin
4 Sustaining pedal
5 Blank
6 Rewind
7 General cancel X
8 Swell open - 2nd stage
9 Swell shut
10 Swell open - 1st stage
11 Piano on
12 Diapason on
13 Flute on
14 Flute off
15 Diapason off
16 Piano off
17 Open bass on X
18 Salicional bass on X
19 to 88, 70 playing notes, A to F#
89 Quintadena off
90 Quintadena on
91 Tremolo
92 Swell open - 3rd stage
93 Open treble on X
94 Salicional treble on X
95 4th intensity
96 3rd intensity
97 2nd intensity
98 1st intensity
99 Treble hammer rail on
100 Blank (if present)

Mortuary organs using this style of roll were made in various sizes. Some Wurlitzer scale sticks include all of the above functions, while others omit some register controls. One scale stick indicates that only large organs include functions marked "X," and it includes only holes 4 to 94. The preceding scale is arranged with the playing notes in the center so that 88-note home player piano rolls can also be utilized, but without expression capability.

The Wurlitzer Mortuary Organ has the following note ranges: Piano, holes 19 to 88, A to F#; quintadena pipes, holes 46 to 82, C to C; flute pipes, holes 51 to 88, F to C; and bourdon pipes (diapason), holes 22 to 50, C to E.

Some Style W organs were made with a tracker bar with holes spaced 9 per inch, indicating that they might use MO rolls instead of Style W (Organette) rolls.

WURLITZER ORGANETTE ROLL
WURLITZER STYLE W ORCHESTRA ROLL
WURLITZER STYLE W ORGAN ROLL
8 7/8" wide; spaced 4 holes per cm.
(Width and spacing similar to PianOrchestra rolls)

Several varieties of Organette or Style W organ rolls were made, all with the same width and hole spacing. The style which was probably used by most standard Style W Organettes has the following scale:

1 Blank
2 Piano bass octave coupler on
3 Shutoff
4 Blank
5 Sustaining pedal off
6 General cancel
7 Blank
8 Blank
9 Blank
10 Blank
11 Tremolo on

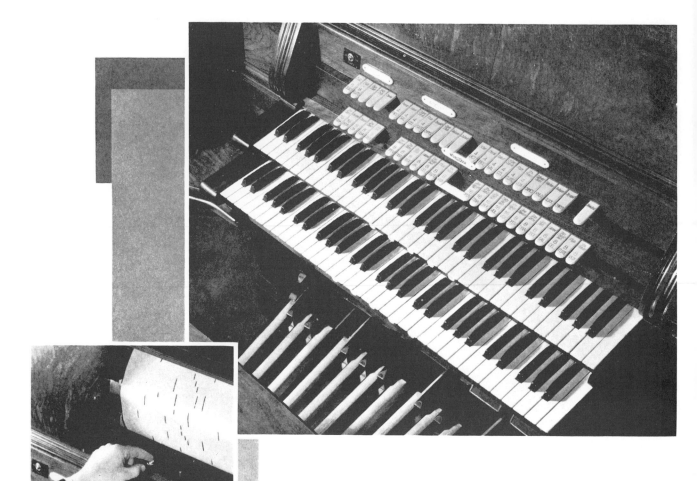

‹ ‹ and the Organist is YOU!

YOU can play the Wurlitzer Residence Pipe Organ . . . and without any technical knowledge of music. To the fascinating interpretations of famous organists you may add — at the touch of a button — your own variations, all that your favorite music means to you.

And should you desire it, this pipe organ will play your chosen selections continuously . . . a soft background of melody during dinner, perhaps.

Your family and your friends will delight in the richness of tone and the responsiveness of this superb instrument when used for informal recitals.

The Wurlitzer Residence Organ has been created to fit your home. Its console is not as large as a grand piano. For the first time it is possible to possess a really distinguished pipe organ by making only a moderate investment.

You will enjoy hearing, and playing, this instrument at your most convenient Wurlitzer Studio . . . New York, Buffalo, Chicago, Cincinnati, Cleveland, Detroit, Los Angeles, or Pittsburgh.

The price —
$6500 and upward

WURLITZER
Reproducing
Residence Pipe Organ

A beautiful brochure, with photographs of installations, may be obtained from any Wurlitzer store.

12 Mandolin on
13 Sustaining pedal on
14 to 27, Playing notes, C to C#
28 Rewind
29 to 50, Continuation of playing notes, D to B
51 Quintadena off
52 to 76, Continuation of playing notes, C to C
77 Swell shades open, hammer rail down
78 Swell shades closed, hammer rail up
79 Bourdon on
80 Quintadena on
81 Flute on
82 Piano bass on
83 Piano treble on
84 Sforzando (piano accent - chain perforation)
85 Blank
86 Piano forte on
87 Blank
88 Blank

The original Wurlitzer test roll for the preceding scale includes the following expression test:
Hammer rail up PP
Hammer rail down P
Rail up and sforzando MF
Rail down and piano forte F
Sustaining on FF
5, 6, 51, 78, then 82 and 83, then chord: PP
77 and 86, then 13, then chord: FF

Another Organette or Style W scale indicates the following differences:
1 Salicional
11 Blank
51 X
80 VQ
87 Salicional
88 SW

Another Wurlitzer scale stick marked "Style W" has all of the functions the same as the standard Organette scale, except for the following functions which are the same as the Wurlitzer Mandolin PianOrchestra (Philipps PM) scale: 4, 7 to 10, 84 to 88. Refer to the Philipps Pianella scale.

Still another Wurlitzer scale stick marked "Style W" is a Concert PianOrchestra (Philipps Pianella Caecilia) scale stick blueprint with the following functions added in ink:
1 to 3, Bass*
11 Mandolin off
14 Clarinet O
15 Violin X
16 Oboe X
17 Piccolo O
77 Swell open
78 Swell closed
79 Bassoon*
80 Violin X
81 Flute O
82 Mandolin on

Bass F to F#, 19 to 45
Flute G to C, 46 to 76
Violin pipes, C to C, 39 to 76

This would seem to indicate that Wurlitzer contemplated or built one or more Style W organs which were tubed to play Wurlitzer Concert PianOrchestra rolls, with the bass, flute, and violin pipes controlled by holes marked *, O, and X respectively, and with the mandolin control holes added at holes 11 and 82 (Concert PianOrchestras have no mandolin).

Adding to the confusion is the indication that Wurlitzer apparently made some Style W Organs (Organettes) which had 9-to-the-inch hole spacing and which were tubed to play Wurlitzer MO (Mortuary Organ) rolls.

WURLITZER 98-NOTE CONCERT ORGAN ROLL
WURLITZER RS ORGAN ROLL
(also known as 97-NOTE CONCERT ORGAN ROLL)
Spaced 9 holes per inch

1 Sforzando (swell quick)
2 Hammer rail
3 Sustaining pedal
4 16' tibia clausa on (bourdon)
5 16' diaphone on (bass)
6 16' tuba on
7 8' open diapason on
8 8' tuba on
9 8' viola on (salicional)
10 8' flute on
11 4' Flute on
12 Snare drum
13 Tympani
14 Bass drum
15 Castanets
16 Tambourine
17 Drum expression loud
18 Triangle
19 Cymbal
20 Rewind
21 to 81, 61 playing notes, C to C
82 Swell open, 10 steps
83 Swell closed, 10 steps
84 General cancel
85 Piano on (piano and accent)
86 8' tuba on
87 16' cello on (salicional)
88 16' clarinet on
89 Bells on
90 Chimes on
91 Xylophone on
92 4' violine on (salicet)
93 8' oboe on
94 8' violine on (salicional)
95 8' flute on
96 4' flute on (piccolo)
97 8' vox humana on
98 Tremolo on

Registration in parentheses was taken from an original Wurlitzer blueprint marked "98-note tracker bar." All other information was taken from an original scale stick marked "R.S. -98 Note Organ." Holes 4 (bourdon) and 87 (salicional) are marked "player only" on the blueprint. The 97-note scale omits hole 1 (sforzando).

Note ranges for the Wurlitzer 98-Note Concert Organ rolls are as follows: holes 4 to 6, 12 notes, range CCC to BB; hole 7, 61 notes, CC to C; holes 8 to 11, 31 notes, CC to F#; holes 86 to 96, 30 notes, G to C; hole 97, 61 notes, CC to C.

WURLITZER RJ ORGAN ROLL
Spaced 9 holes per inch

1 Pedal octave coupler
2 Pilot 3
3 Pilot 2
4 Pilot 1
5 to 16, Pedal notes, C to B
17 to 30, 14 stops, 1 to 14 (when fired by pilots)
17 to 58, 42 Accompaniment notes, C to F
59 to 100, 42 Solo (Great) notes, G to C
101 Swell pilot
102 to 104, three stages of swell shutters (when fired by 101)
105 Second touch traps

The lowest 12 accompaniment holes are used for registration when one of the pilots (holes 2 to 4) is punched. The following registration chart is taken from a Wurlitzer blueprint labeled "105-Note Tracker Bar for Home Organ RJ-4," which apparently was for a small four-rank organ. At the left side of the column are the stop numbers 1 through 14. Pilot 1, Pilot 2, and Pilot 3 are separated by diagonals.

1 Solo 8' flute / Blank / Solo 4' flute
2 Solo 8' flute / Accompaniment 8' flute / Solo 4' octave (open)
3 Solo 8' flute / Accompaniment 4' flute / Solo 8' salicional
4 Solo 4' flute / Accompaniment 4' salicet / Solo 8' flute
5 Solo 4' salicet / Accompaniment 4' salicet / Solo 8' salicional
6 Solo 4' salicet / Accompaniment 4' flute / Solo 8' salicional
7 Tremolo / Accompaniment 8' salicional / Solo 8' oboe horn
8 Blank / Accompaniment 8' flute / Solo 8' oboe horn
9 Blank / Accompaniment 8' salicional / Solo 8' open diapason
10 Pedal 8' flute / Accomp. 8' salicional / Solo 16' contre viol
11 Pedal 8' cello / Accompaniment 8' flute / Solo 16' oboe horn
12 Pedal 8' open diapason / Accompaniment 8' oboe horn / Solo 16' oboe horn
13 Pedal 16' bourdon / Accompaniment 8' open / Solo 16' open diapason TC
14 Pedal 16' bourdon / Blank / Solo 8' flute

The above layout was originally made for a larger organ; "RJ-4" is written over another number, and many of the before-listed stops are written over other stops which are scratched out. The following chart includes the legible stops for the larger organ.
1 Solo chimes / Accompaniment snare drum / Solo 4' ?
2 Solo xylophone / Accompaniment chrysoglott / Solo 4' ?
3 Solo chrysoglott / Accompaniment 4' flute / Solo 8' vox humana?
4 Solo 4' flute / Accompaniment 4' octave celeste / Solo 8' flute
5 Solo 4' viol? celeste / Accompaniment 4' salicet / Solo 8' celeste
6 Solo 4' salicet / Accompaniment 4' piccolo? (tibia) / Solo 8' salicional
7 Tremolo / Accompaniment 8' vox humana? / Solo 8' tibia clausa?
8 Pedal cymbal / Accompaniment 8' flute / Solo 8' oboe horn
9 Pedal bass drum / Accompaniment 8' celeste / Solo 8' open diapason
10 Pedal 8' flute / Accompaniment 8' salicional / Solo 16' contre viol
11 Pedal 8' cello / Accompaniment 8' tibia clausa? / Solo 16' tibia clausa?
12 Pedal 8' open diapason / Accompaniment 8' oboe horn / Solo 16' oboe horn
13 Pedal 16' bourdon / Accompaniment 8' open / Solo 16' open diapason TC
14 Pedal 16' (tibia clausa?) / Blank / Solo orchestra bells

WURLITZER 140-NOTE ORGAN ROLL
(140-Note Denver Organ)

1 Quick sforzando swell
2 Swell closed
3 Swell open
4 Bass drum
4+6 = Crash cymbal
5 Cymbal
6 Triangle
7 Castanets
8 Tambourine
9 Tympani
10 Snare drum
11 Blank
12 to 35, 24 bass notes, C to B
36 to 59, 24 Accompaniment notes, C to B
60 Stop roll control
61 to 97, 37 orchestral section notes, C to C
98 to 134, 37 solo notes, C to C
135 Piano accent, tom-tom, bird whistles
136 Blank
137 Blank
138 Swell 1; main and brass
139 Sustaining pedal and Swell 2 foundation + Solo
140 Hammer rail and Swell 3 Echo + percussion

Percussion Ranges
Harp C to C, 36-59, 61-85
Sleigh and electric bells C to C, 73-97
Sleigh and electric bells C to C, 110-134
Echo chimes G to G, 68 to 92
Large chimes D to D, 100-124
Inside xylophone C to C, 61-97
Inside xylophone and glockenspiel C to C, 98-134
Outside xylophone C to C, 98-134
Marimba C to C, 98-134

One original Wurlitzer scale stick for the preceding scale is drawn with a hole spacing of 4 per cm.; two other scale sticks are drawn at 9 holes per inch.

Two further scale sticks, both drawn 9 holes per inch, labeled "Register Scale for 140-Note Denver Organ, have the following scale:
1 to 23, Bass section
24 Stop roll control
25 to 58, Accompaniment section
59 Rewind
60 Last Accompaniment section hole
61 to 110, Orchestral section
111 to 140, Solo section

This 140-Note Denver Organ scale is a duplex system, with two separate rolls; one with the notes, expression, and percussion, and the second roll with the registration. The first roll passes over the tracker bar at a constant speed. The second, or registration, roll remains still until a new registration is called for; then it advances slightly; then it stops again. Hole 60 in the first roll ("stop roll control") and hole 24 in the registration roll control the movement of the registration roll and the momentary connection of the organ registration relays to it.

Wurlitzer Theatre Orchestra and Pipe Organ

With Human Voice

For

Vaudeville and Motion Picture Theatres

Style L

WURLITZER

The Style L Wurlitzer Theatre Orchestra and Pipe Organ (also related to the Style J, which sold for $7500 circa 1916) was in one model equipped to play Concert PianOrchestra rolls, although apparently certain models used special Wurlitzer theatre organ rolls. This general type of instrument was popular during the 1914-1918 era, and apparently sales were all that Wurlitzer hoped for. At one point the factory was six months behind in filling orders.

There are two keyboards and (pedal board) to which the entire instrumentation of both organ and orchestra may be coupled.

The whole organ and orchestra may be unified into a grandeur of tone equal in magnitude to the majestic rolling tone of the greatest Cathedral organs.

The Vox Humana pipes, designed to imitate the human voice in solo and choir effect, make a forceful appeal to the heart. The Cathedral Chimes are dignified and add great church color.

Distinctly different from any other instrument, the Style L possesses a great range of expression. Furthermore, the quick changes so important to the proper playing of a film through all its many phases are for the first time made possible because of the one musician operating both organ and orchestra with all effects under complete instant control.

The Key Desk or Console is detached and movable, and may be placed any distance from the organ where most convenient. The touch is as light as that of a piano, the pipes responding instantly. There are a number of toe pistons placed for the convenience of the organist from which many of the effects are controlled.

ORCHESTRA DEPARTMENT:

Contains many of the actual orchestral instrumentations. Prominent among these will be found Violins, Violas, Violoncellos, Flutes, Piccolos, *Piano*, Oboes, Chimes, Tubas, Clarinets, Xylophone, Castanets, Triangle, Crash, Tambourine, Cymbals, Bass Drum, Snare Drums, Glockenspiel, Autohorn, Steamboat Whistle, Horse Trot, Electric Bell, etc.

PIPE ORGAN DEPARTMENT:

1. Tuba Bass, 16 foot.	7. Violin Bass, 8 foot.
2. Tuba Bass, 8 "	8. Flute Bass, 8 "
3. Tuba Bass, 8 "	9. Piccolo Treble, 4 "
4. Clarinet, 16 "	10. Violin Treble, 8 "
5. Oboe Horn, 8 "	11. Flute Treble, 8 "
6. Violin, 8 "	12. *Cathedral Chimes.*

13. Vox Humana (Human Voice).

Price List

WURLITZER
O R G A N S

F. O. B. Factory

In Effect September 1, 1927

Style 115 Straight Console		$5,500.00
120 Piano Console		6,000.00
125 " "		6,450.00
130 " "		6,850.00
140 Curved Console		9,000.00
150 " "		10,000.00
165 " "		12,750.00
175 " "		13,750.00
190 " "		16,250.00
200 " "		18,000.00
205 " "		20,500.00
220 " "		22,500.00
225 " "		25,000.00
230 " "		26,500.00
240 " "		28,500.00
250 " "		36,000.00
260 " "		40,000.00
270 " "		50,000.00
280 " "		62,500.00

Any WURLITZER ORGAN can be equipped with a music roll attachment and the music roll attachment can be furnished in two styles.

An additional charge of 10% will be made if any of the instruments up to and including Style 175 have to be divided. The larger organ from Style 190 up are divided instruments.

The style "B" music roll attachment consists of the Duplex 88-note roll and the style "C" attachment plays the Concert Organ roll, so arranged that on the same tracker bar any ordinary 88-note roll can be used.

Either of these two systems can be had at the following prices:

Styles 115 to 130 (incl.)	$1,000.00	extra
" 140 to 190 (incl.)	1,600.00	"
" 200	1,750.00	"
" 205	1,850.00	"

In the style 115, the Duplex roll attachment is installed in the straight console. In the styles 120 to 130, inclusive, it is installed in the piano console. In the styles 140 to 205, inclusive, it is installed in a piano equipped with stop keys for drawing the stops.

The Rudolph Wurlitzer Co.

These Wurlitzer price lists of March 1, 1920, November 15, 1923, and September 1, 1927 offer roll mechanisms as an optional extra for any theatre organ. Many theatre photoplayers and organs were equipped with mechanisms which used ordinary 88-note home player pianos. This format would allow the organ operator to have the notes played for him, a distinct advantage if he wasn't a musician. His function would be to manually operate the stops to bring various ranks of pipes and effects in and out of play and via toe pistons to operate the percussion and novelty sound effects. The 88-note roll system had the advantage that thousands of tunes, including the latest numbers, were readily available at low cost. In practice, many smaller organs were equipped with roll mechanisms, whereas most larger ones were not. Any theatre which could afford the $20,000 to $62,500 cost of styles 205 through 280, for example, could afford to have a full-time skilled organist.

WURLITZER STYLE R ORGAN ROLL
WURLITZER REPRODUCING ORGAN ROLL
16 7/8" wide; spaced 4 holes per cm.

1 Main shutters pilot
2 Solo pilot
3 to 8, Six stages of Main or Solo shutters when fired by 1 or 2
9 Pedal stops pilot
10 Accompaniment pilot
11 Great pilot
12 Solo pilot
13 Second touch traps
14 to 18, Stops 1 through 5
19 to 30, 12 Pedal notes
31 to 85, 55 Accompaniment notes
86 to 143, 53 Great notes
144 to 146, 3 top Accompaniment notes
147 Pedal unison off, octave on
148 Rewind
149 to 163, Stops 6 through 20
164 Transposer on
165 Transposer off

The transposer switches the note ranges to the following:
31-37, 7 Solo notes, tenor F-B
38-67, 30 Accompaniment notes, G to C
68 to 85, 18 Solo notes, 2' C-F
86 to 134, 49 Great notes, 2' C-C
135-141, 7 Solo notes, 2' F#-C
142-146, 5 Solo notes, tenor C-E

Holes 14 to 18 and 149 to 163 control the stops listed as follows. The stop number is given to the left, and the Pedal, Accompaniment, Great, and Solo functions are divided by diagonals.

1 Ophicleide 16' / Tuba 8' / Ophicleide 16' / Trumpet 8'
2 Diaphone 16' / Diaphonic diapason 8' / Diaphone 16' / Tuba 8'
3 Tibia 16' / Tibia 8' / Tibia 16' / Diaphonic diapason 8'
4 Bourdon 16' / Clarinet 8' / Clarinet TC 16' / Tibia 8'
5 Clarinet 8' / Viol d'orchestre 8' / French horn TC 16' / Orchestral oboe 8'
6 Flute 8' / Viol celeste 8' / Contra viol TC 16' / String 8'
7 String 8' / Oboe horn 8' / Bourdon 16' / Oboe horn 8'
8 Cello 8' / Flute 8' / Tuba 8' / Quintadena 8'
9 Bass drum 2nd / Vox humana 8' / Diaphonic diapason 8' / Piccolo 4'
10 Kettle drum 2nd / Viol 4' / Tibia 8' / Xylophone
11 Crash cymbal 2nd / Octave celeste 4' / Orchestral oboe 8' / Glockenspiel
12 Cymbal 2nd / Flute 4' / Clarinet 8' / Chimes
13 Triangle 2nd / Vox humana 4' / French horn 8' / Solo tremolo
14 Main tremolo / Harp / String 8' / Vox humana tremolo
15 Great harp / Chrysoglott / Viol d'orchestre 8' / Great 2 2/3' twelfth
16 Great celeste 4' / Snare drum / Viol celeste 8' / Great piccolo 2'
17 Great flute 4' / Tambourine / Flute 8' / Great chrysoglott
18 Great xylophone / Castanets / Vox humana 8' / Great aeoline 8'
19 Great glockenspiel / Tom-tom / Piccolo 4' / Great aeoline 4'
20 Great chimes / Chinese block / Viol 4' / Spare

Hole 13 sends an impulse to the group of Pedal 2nd touch stops, causing whichever stops are registered to play. The Accompaniment traps automatically receive an impulse to play whenever any Accompaniment note is played, just like playing the organ manually.

WURLITZER ORGAN ROLL
UNKNOWN STYLE

1 Harp on (G-C, 30 notes)
2 Sleigh bells on (C-C, 15 notes)
3 Snare drum accented beat
4 Tibia 16', 26 notes
5 Diaphone 16', 26 notes
6 Clarinet 8', 26 notes
7 Piccolo 2', 26 notes
8 Flute 4', 26 notes
9 Tuba 16', 30 notes
10 Tuba 16', 26 notes
11 Swell accelerator
12 Celeste 8', 30 notes
13 Celeste 8', 26 notes
14 Violin 4', 26 notes
15 Violin 8', 26 notes
16 Flute 8', 26 notes
17 Tuba 8', 26 notes
18 Snare drum
19 Sustaining pedal off
20 General cancel
21 Tympani
22 Tympani
23 Triangle
24 Bells on
25 Blank
26 Cymbal
27 Sustaining pedal on
28 Clarinet 16', 30 notes
29 Violin 8', 56 notes
30 Oboe 8', 30 notes
31 Piccolo 4', 30 notes
32 Tremolo
33 to 41, Playing notes F to C#
42 Rewind
43 to 64, Playing notes D to B
65 Shutoff
66 to 90, Playing notes C to C
91 Swell open
92 Swell closed
93 Cello 16', 30 notes
94 Violin 8', 30 notes
95 Flute 8', 30 notes
96 Hammer rail up
97 Drums loud register
98 Tambourine
99 Bass drum
100 Castanets
101 Piano on
102 Xylophone on

There are 46 control holes in the preceding layout and only 56 playing notes!

Holes 18 to 102 of this roll are the same as holes 4 to 88 of the Wurlitzer Concert PianOrchestra (Philipps Pianella Caecilia) roll. The preceding roll may have been used on a Wurlitzer Style J Motion Picture Orchestra (or a similar model such as Style L); a theatre organ style which was variously equipped with roll players for Concert PianOrchestra, 88-note home player piano, and perhaps the foregoing rolls. This genre of organ featured a console in the form of an upright piano with a roll mechanism (or two, in the case of 88-note roll players) in the center. The pipes and percussion devices were situated in a separate cabinet, faced with ornate golden display pipes, which was connected electrically and which could be located at any distance from the console. This general format was popular circa 1914-1920.

WURLITZER ORGAN ROLL
UNKNOWN STYLE
11¼" wide; spaced 9 holes per inch

This scale features playing notes without any automatic registration or expression. The relay couples the tracker bar to the organ in four arrangements, listed here with Pedal/Great/Swell divided by diagonals:

1 1-12 / 13-41 / 42-73
2 1-24 / 25-41 / 42-73
3 1-18 / 19-36 / 37-73
4 1-24 / 25-48 / 49-73

The tracker bar has 73 holes. Numbers 1 through 4 of the preceding are not tracker bar holes but are four different ways in which the organ divisions can be coupled to the tracker bar holes.

WURLITZER ORGAN ROLL
UNKNOWN STYLE

1 to 13, Blank
14 Cancel A
15 Cancel B
16 Cancel C
17 to 47, Scale A, 31 notes, C to F#
48 to 77, Scale B, 30 notes, G to C
78 to 96, Scale C, 19 notes, C# to G
97 ?
98 ?
99 to 105, Blank

The preceding scale is from a Wurlitzer scale stick. An orange line is marked over hole 97, and a blue line is marked over hole 98, indicating "on" and "off," respectively, for an unknown function.

WURLITZER ORGAN ROLL
DESIGNATED "CONCERTINOLA"

The following is from an original Wurlitzer scale stick marked "6/27/21 L.M. Folmsbee." The playing note scale is divided between holes 30 and 31.

1 Accent 1
2 Accent 2
3 Accent 3
4 Cancel
5 Crescendo
6 Diminuendo
7 16' reed
8 Reed cancel
9 Blank (or play)
10 Blank
11 Blank
12 Blank
13 Rewind
14 to 30, notes G to B
31 to 55, notes C to C
56 Shutoff
57 Blank
58 Blank
59 Blank
60 Blank
61 8' reed
62 Diminuendo
63 Crescendo
64 Cancel
65 Accent 3
66 Accent 2
67 Accent 1

Perfecting the Organette for the small theatre is one of the outstanding accomplishments of Wurlitzer, the world's foremost musical organization, a national institution of tremendous financial resources, with retail branches and dealers extending from coast to coast, and throughout the civilized world.

The Organette is singularly opportune, because it not only fulfills the musical requirements of the moderate sized theatre, but its attractive appearance and remarkable tonal quality enhances the enjoyment of your patrons. Its versatility adds more realism to motion pictures than any other instrument of this character.

THE WURLITZER ORGANETTE

An Organette, or Style W Organ, from a Wurlitzer catalogue of the 1920s, and the label from a Style W test roll. From 1924 to 1930 Wurlitzer shipped 249 of these instruments, first called the Style W Orchestra and later called the Organette.

The Orpheum Theatre in Cincinnati featured a Wurlitzer organ with a two-manual piano-type console as shown to the left. The upper 61-note manual plays the organ, and the lower full keyboard plays the piano. Many consoles of this style were equipped with roll players.

Wurlitzer Hope-Jones Unit Orchestra Installed in Orpheum Theatre, Cincinnati, Ohio

SEATS 2,500. A wonderful building six stories high, costing $300,000. Plays a double performance, in the theatre proper and on the roof.

One of the largest and finest theatres in the United States devoted exclusively to motion pictures. Located in a thickly populated residential district. The building is the last word in theatre architecture. Decorative scheme—ivory, green and gold. Proscenium surmounted by beautiful mural painting. Concrete and steel construction throughout. Two balconies of cantilever construction, eliminating supporting posts. Two elevators in constant operation, taking patrons to the balconies and roof garden.

Special Note — The Orpheum Theatre has purchased two Wurlitzer Orchestras, both of which are played simultaneously in the theatre and on the roof.

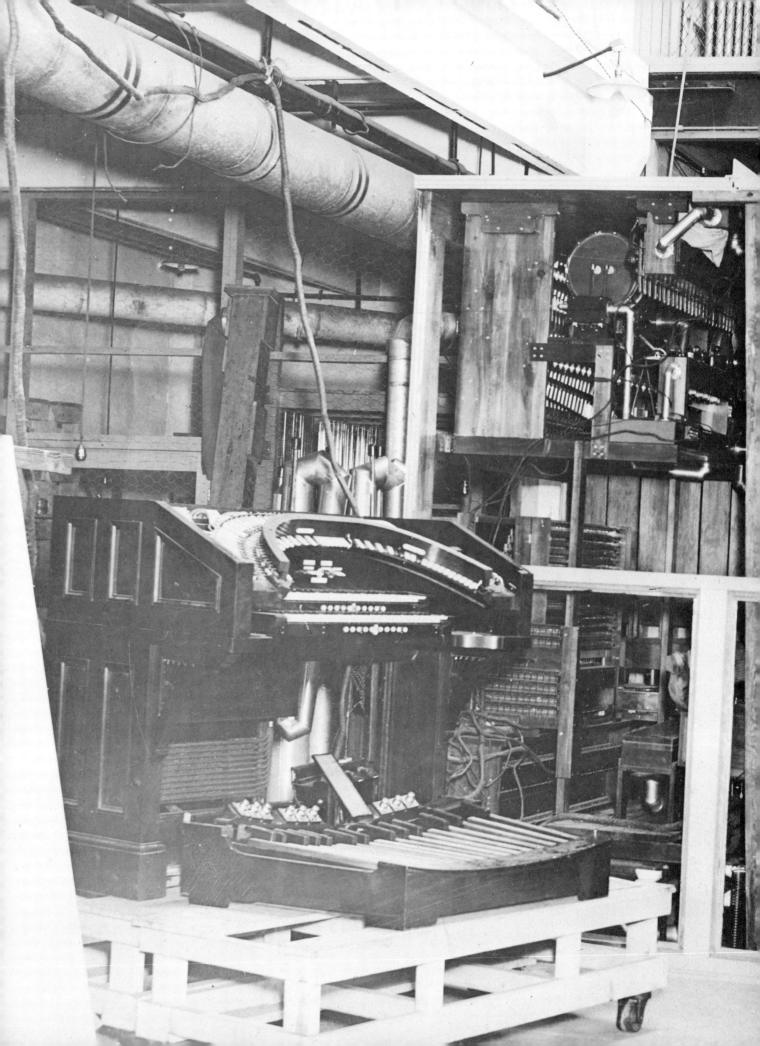

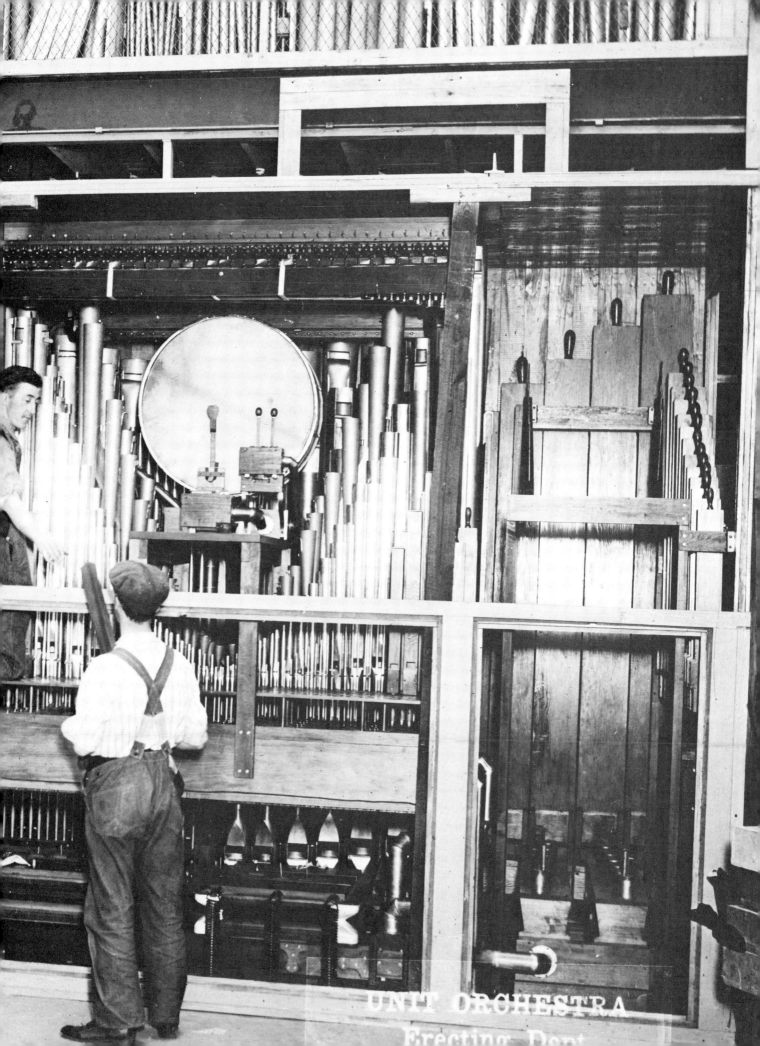

UNIT ORCHESTRA
Erecting Dept.

Chapter 8
BARREL ORGANS

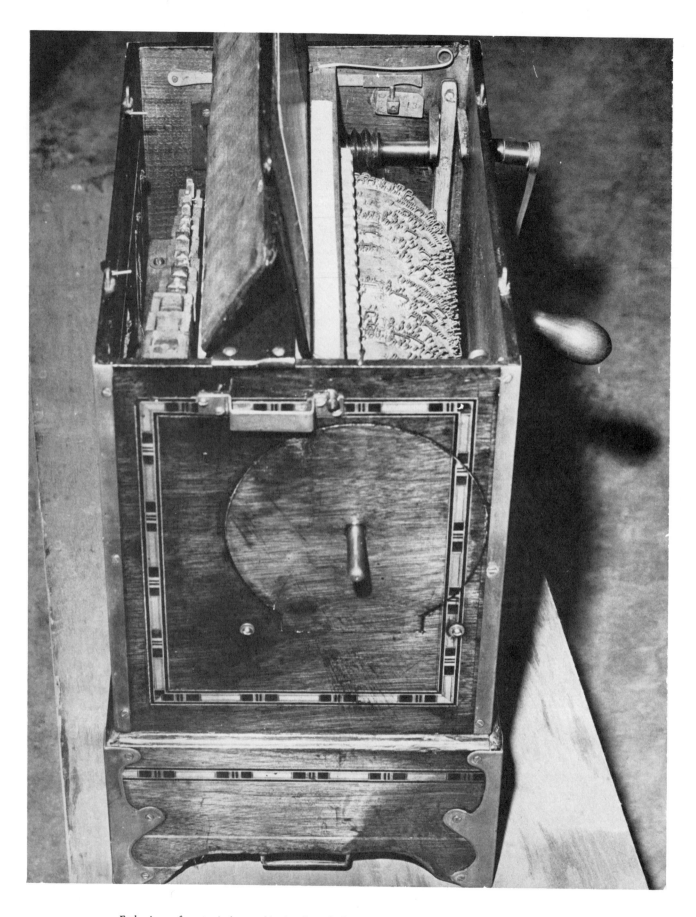

End view of a typical portable hand-cranked barrel organ. Although Bruder, Molinari, Frati, Bacigalupo, Gavioli, and many others made this type of instrument, the basic construction of the different models was quite similar.

BARREL ORGAN SCALES

Only a few representative barrel organ scales are included in this book because there are nearly as many different scales as there are individual organs. Most early Gavioli, North Tonawanda Barrel Organ Factory (Wurlitzer), Bruder, Ruth, and other pinned cylinder organs which were made at the turn of the century or earlier and which remained in use after about the 1910-1915 period were converted to play cardboard or paper music. During the transition period, especially around 1905-1910, certain manufacturers such as Niagara, Wurlitzer, and the North Tonawanda Musical Instrument Works offered the same basic type of organ in two formats: with the cylinder music system or with the paper roll system. For example, a certain North Tonawanda Musical Instrument Works organ was sold as Style 92 with the pinned cylinder system or Style 192 with the paper roll system.

The key layout in a pinned cylinder organ corresponds to the pipes and other functions as they are laid out on the wind chest from one side to the other. Small portable instruments, often called monkey organs today, made for outdoor use by organ grinders were designed for compactness rather than symmetry of pipes, although they sometimes featured a symmetrical rank of little brass trumpets or piccolos on the front. In these tiny organs the bass notes are usually on both ends, the high musical scale is in order of size from one side to the other, and the accompaniment is placed wherever the pipes fit. Trumpet keys are usually spread across the width of the wind chest, in musical order if the pipes are in order of size, or scrambled if the pipes are arranged symmetrically.

When manufacturers of larger organs began using cardboard music in place of pinned cylinders, Bruder, Ruth, and a few others arranged their cardboard music scales in the same order as the barrel keys. In other words, the cardboard music scale, like the earlier barrel key frame, was simply a list of the valves in the wind chest from one side of the organ to the other.

Most large barrel organs have one large main wind chest with a manifold to supply air to any bass and accompaniment pipes which may be mounted on the bottom of the instrument. The melody pipes are usually arranged symmetrically toward the center of the wind chest, flanked by symmetrically arranged countermelody or piccolo pipes on either side. The trumpet and sometimes the trombone pipes are often spread across the chest, with the accompaniment and bass pipes usually mixed together toward each end. The reader who is interested in the way large outdoor barrel organ scales were arranged may learn this by examining some of the many scrambled Bruder and Ruth cardboard music scales in this book.

Indoor barrel organs such as church and chamber barrel organs often had the pipes in order of size on the wind chest, with some of the bass pipes located at each end. The scales for small instruments are sometimes similar to table top organette scales. In larger instruments such as Welte and Imhof & Mukle barrel orchestrions, the melody and trumpet pipes are arranged symmetrically. The Welte 75-hole orchestrion scale listed in this book is representative of this type of barrel organ. For a detailed study of many different types of barrel organs the reader may want to refer to *The Barrel Organ*, by Arthur W.J.G. Ord-Hume.

We give some representative barrel organ scales, together with a "translation" of the scales in musical order.

20-KEY MOLINARI BARREL ORGAN SCALE

1 C, note 1
2 E, note 6
3 A, note 8
4 D, note 5
5 B, note 9
6 B, note 3
7 C, note 10
8 C, note 4
9 D, note 11
10 G, note 7
11 E, note 12
12 F, note 13
13 F#, note 14
14 G, note 15
15 A, note 16
16 B, note 17
17 C, note 18
18 D, note 19
19 E, note 20
20 G, note 2

(20-KEY MOLINARI BARREL ORGAN SCALE)
Translation with notes in musical order

1 C, key 1
2 G, key 20
3 B, key 6
4 C, key 8
5 D, key 4
6 E, key 2
7 G, key 10
8 A, key 3
9 B, key 5
10 C, key 7
11 D, key 9
12 E, key 11
13 F, key 12
14 F#, key 13
15 G, key 14
16 A, key 15
17 B, key 16
18 C, key 17
19 D, key 18
20 E, key 19

Notes 1 and 2 are bass notes, 3 through 8 are accompaniment notes, and the rest are melody notes.

20-KEY B.A.B. BARREL ORGAN SCALE
(Made in 1932)

1 C, note 2
2 D, note 3
3 E, note 4
4 F, note 5
5 F#, note 6
6 G, note 7
7 A, note 8
8 D, note 11
9 E, note 12
10 E, note 20
11 C, note 18
12 A, note 16
13 F#, note 14
14 F, note 13
15 G, note 15
16 B, note 17
17 D, note 19
18 C, note 10
19 B, note 9
20 G, note 1

Cocchi, Bacigalupo & Graffigna

BERLIN N.

78. Schönhauser Allee 78.

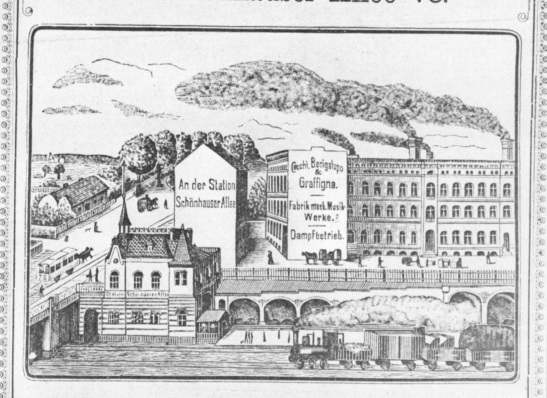

Manufacturers of Mechanical Musical Instruments

✦ Steam Works ✦

Speciality: Orchestrions, Military-Concert-Organs,
Concertinos, Barrel-Organs, Piano-Organs, Hand- and
Handle-Pianofortes.

Cable Address: Cobagra, Berlin.

Catalogue No. 2.

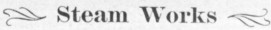

☞ In giving Orders we beg our Customers please to state the
◆ No. of Catalogue. ◆

Around the turn of the 20th century the firm of Cocchi, Bacigalupo & Graffigna, located in Berlin, was a major producer of barrel-operated pianos, organs, and orchestrions. Many of these were sold in America.

(20-KEY B.A.B. BARREL ORGAN SCALE)
Translation with notes in musical order

1 G, key 20
2 C, key 1
3 D, key 2
4 E, key 3
5 F, key 4
6 F#, key 5
7 G, key 6
8 A, key 7
9 B, key 19
10 C, key 18
11 D, key 8
12 E, key 9
13 F, key 14
14 F#, key 13
15 G, key 15
16 A, key 12
17 B, key 16
18 C, key 11
19 D, key 17
20 E, key 10

23-KEY MOLINARI BARREL ORGAN SCALE

1 G, note 1
2 E, note 23
3 B, note 4
4 D, note 22
5 C, note 5
6 C, note 21
7 B, note 20
8 D, note 6
9 A, note 19
10 E, note 7
11 G, note 18
12 F, note 8
13 F#, note 17
14 F#, note 9
15 F, note 16
16 G, note 10
17 E, note 15
18 A, note 11
19 D, note 14
20 D, note 3
21 C, note 13
22 C, note 2
23 B, note 12

(23 KEY MOLINARI BARREL ORGAN SCALE)
Translation with notes in musical order

1 G, key 1
2 C, key 22
3 D, key 20
4 B, key 3
5 C, key 5
6 D, key 8
7 E, key 10
8 F, key 12
9 F#, key 14
10 G, key 16
11 A, key 18
12 B, key 23
13 C, key 21
14 D, key 19
15 E, key 17
16 F, key 15
17 F#, key 13
18 G, key 11
19 A, key 9
20 B, key 7
21 C, key 6
22 D, key 4
23 E, key 2

26-KEY GAVIOLI MELOTON BARREL ORGAN SCALE
Right to left:

1 G
2 C
3 D
4 G
5 A
6 B
7 C
8 D
9 E
10 F
11 F#
12 G
13 A
14 B
15 C
16 C#
17 D
18 E
19 F
20 F#
21 G
22 A
23 B
24 C
25 D
26 E

This pinned cylinder organ has harmonium reeds instead of pipes. Organ pipes must be placed in scrambled musical order to fit the most pipes in the least amount of space. By comparison, reeds take up no more width than their wind chest pallet valves, so they can be arranged in ascending musical order, making it easier for the music arranger to mark the cylinder.

31-KEY BACIGALUPO BARREL ORGAN SCALE

1 G, note 4
2 C, note 7
3 A, note 5
4 G, note 12
5 B, note 6
6 A, note 13
7 B, note 14
8 C, note 15
9 D, note 16
10 E, note 17
11 F, note 18
12 F#, note 19
13 G, note 20
14 A, note 21
15 B, note 22
16 C, note 23
17 D, note 24
18 E, note 25
19 F, note 26
20 F#, note 27
21 G, note 28
22 A, note 29
23 B, note 30
24 C, note 31
25 F#, note 11
26 F, note 10
27 E, note 9
28 D, note 8
29 D, note 3
30 C, note 2
31 G, note 1

(31-KEY BACIGALUPO BARREL ORGAN SCALE)
Translation with notes in musical order

1 G, key 31
2 C, key 30

SEASON 1895-1896.
AUGUST POLLMANN,
SOLE AGENT for the United States and Canada for the Celebrated
FRATI & CO.
MANUFACTURE OF
Organs, Orchestrions, Mechanical Pianos, Etc.

FOR

Streets,
Shows,
Circus,
Saloons,
Panoramas,
Razzle-Dazzle,
Merry-Go-Rounds,
Coasters,
Picnics,
Swings,
Seaside Resorts,
Steamboats,
etc., etc.

FOR

Dining Rooms,
Concert Halls,
Club Houses,
Lodge Rooms,
Summer Resorts,
Winter Gardens,
Dancing Rooms,
Skating Rinks,
Bicycle Schools,
Restaurants,
Ice Cream Parlors,
Fairs,
Shows,
Entertainments,
etc., etc.

The Pollmann Marble Buildings,
just West of Broadway.

Address your correspondence and orders to
AUGUST POLLMANN,
Importer and Manufacturer of Musical Instruments.

1895-1896 catalogue cover of a catalogue issued by August Pollmann. Most instruments offered in the listing were of the pinned cylinder type.

3 D, key 29
4 G, key 1
5 A, key 3
6 B, key 5
7 C, key 2
8 D, key 28
9 E, key 27
10 F, key 26
11 F#, key 25
12 G, key 4
13 A, key 6
14 B, key 7
15 C, key 8
16 D, key 9
17 E, key 10
18 F, key 11
19 F#, key 12
20 G, key 13
21 A, key 14
22 B, key 15
23 C, key 16
24 D, key 17
25 E, key 18
26 F, key 19
27 F#, key 20
28 G, key 21
29 A, key 22
30 B, key 23
31 C, key 24

42-KEY BACIGALUPO TRUMPET BARREL ORGAN SCALE

1 G, note 4
2 A, note 5
3 B, note 6
4 D trumpet
5 C, note 7
6 E trumpet
7 D, note 8
8 E, note 9
9 F trumpet
10 F, note 10
11 F#, note 11
12 G, note 12
13 F# trumpet
14 A, note 13
15 C, note 14
16 D, note 15
17 G trumpet
18 E, note 16
19 F, note 17
20 F#, note 18
21 A trumpet
22 G, note 19
23 A, note 20
24 B, note 21
25 B trumpet
26 C, note 22
27 C#, note 23
28 C trumpet
29 D, note 24
30 E, note 25
31 F, note 26
32 F# trumpet
33 F#, note 27
34 G, note 28
35 A, note 29
36 D trumpet
37 B, note 30
38 C, note 31
39 E trumpet
40 C, note 2
41 G, note 1
42 D, note 3

(42-KEY BACIGALUPO TRUMPET BARREL ORGAN SCALE)
Translation with notes in musical order

1 G, key 41
2 C, key 40
3 D, key 42
4 G, key 1
5 A, key 2
6 B, key 3
7 C, key 5
8 D, key 7
9 E, key 8
10 F, key 10
11 F#, key 11
12 G, key 12
13 A, key 14
14 C, key 15
15 D, key 16
16 E, key 18
17 F, key 19
18 F#, key 20
19 G, key 22
20 A, key 23
21 B, key 24
22 C, key 26
23 C#, key 27
24 D, key 29
25 E, key 30
26 F, key 31
27 F#, key 33
28 G, key 34
29 A, key 35
30 B, key 37
31 C, key 38
(The order of the trumpets is unknown.)

NORTH TONAWANDA MUSICAL INSTRUMENT WORKS
52-KEY BARREL ORGAN SCALE, STYLE 92

1 Bass drum and cymbal
2 G accompaniment
3 A accompaniment
4 B accompaniment
5 C accompaniment
6 A trumpet
7 C# accompaniment
8 C trombone
9 D accompaniment
10 E trumpet
11 E accompaniment
12 F accompaniment
13 B trumpet
14 E high melody
15 C# high melody
16 F# trumpet
17 B high melody
18 D trumpet
19 G high melody
20 E trombone
21 F melody
22 D melody
23 F trumpet
24 C melody
25 A melody
26 C trumpet
27 G melody
28 G trombone
29 F high trumpet
30 B melody
31 C# melody
32 C# high trumpet
33 E melody
34 F# melody
35 A high melody
36 F# high trumpet
37 C high melody
38 D high melody

39 F trombone
40 D high trumpet
41 F# accompaniment
42 G high trumpet
43 F bass
44 E bass
45 C high trumpet
46 D bass
47 C bass
48 E high trumpet
49 G bass
50 D trombone
51 G trumpet
52 Snare drum

organ was available in a format using paper rolls and was known as Style 192, with an F# added to the top end of the accompaniment. It used the same style of rolls as the B.A.B. 57 (61) and Artizan Style D instruments.

(NORTH TONAWANDA STYLE 92 BARREL ORGAN SCALE)
Translation with notes in musical order

Trombone
G, key 28
C, key 8
D, key 50
E, key 20
F, key 39

Bass
G, key 49
C, key 47
D, key 46
E, key 44
F, key 43

Accompaniment
G, key 2
A, key 3
B, key 4
C, key 5
C#, key 7
D, key 9
E, key 11
F, key 12

Melody
G, key 27
A, key 25
B, key 30
C, key 24
C#, key 31
D, key 22
E, key 33
F, key 21
F#, key 34
G, key 19
A, key 35
B, key 17
C, key 37
C#, key 15
D, key 38
E, key 14

Trumpet
C, key 26
D, key 18
E, key 10
F, key 23
F#, key 16
G, key 51
A, key 6
B, key 13
C, key 45
C#, key 32
D, key 40
E, key 48
F, key 29
F#, key 36
G, key 42

Trombones 8 and 50 as well as 20 and 39 may be reversed. The same

FLUTE and PICCOLO HAND ORGANS.

NOS. 4, 5 AND 6.

No. 4—32 Keys, 8 tunes, fancy front, inlaid work, black walnut case, weight 32 lbs......Price $ 120.00
Extra Cylinder.......................... 35.00

No. 5—35 Keys, 9 tunes, fancy front, inlaid work, black walnut case, weight 40 lbs......Price 140.00
Extra Cylinder.......................... 35.00

No. 6—42 Keys, 10 tunes, fancy front, inlaid work, black walnut case, weight 47 lbs......Price 175.00
Extra Cylinder.......................... 50.00

Above is shown a listing from a Molinari price list of the 'teens. The same illustration, a "stock cut," was used to illustrate organs of other makers in other catalogues. Below is a Molinari business card of the 1920s.

A North Tonawanda Barrel Organ Factory portfolio . . .

consisting of numerous cylinder-operated band organs, nearly all previously unpublished in a collectors' publication, made around the turn of the century by Eugene DeKleist's firm, which in 1909 was acquired by the Rudolph Wurlitzer Company. The North Tonawanda Musical Instrument Works, founded in 1906, had a somewhat similar name but was not related.

This large and ornate organ features five mechanical figures on the front. Such figures, common on European organs, were rarely used on instruments of American manufacture, the instruments pictured in this portfolio being remarkable exceptions.

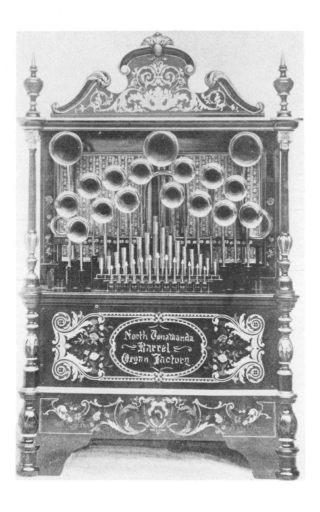

Four cylinder-operated organs from the turn of the century, each with brass horns on the front. The style shown below was later made in a paper-roll format and became known as the Wurlitzer 150. The cylinder-operated style of this organ was known as the Wurlitzer 20-A or, alternately, as the Style 2537.

(Photographs of North Tonawanda Barrel Organ Factory instruments are courtesy of Barbara Charles of Staples & Charles)

Four different cylinder-operated organs of various sizes made by the North Tonawanda Barrel Organ Factory under the ownership of Eugene DeKleist, who earlier worked with Limonaire Freres in Paris. The crude lettering on the portable "monkey organ" below suggests that the factory name was probably added to the photographs and was not on certain instruments originally. DeKleist was a contract manufacturer for several musical outlets (including Wurlitzer after 1898) which put their own trade names on the facades.

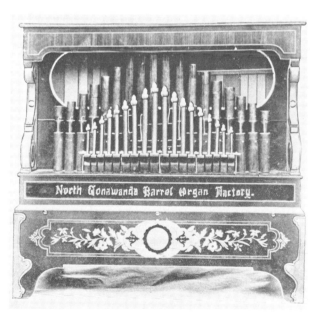

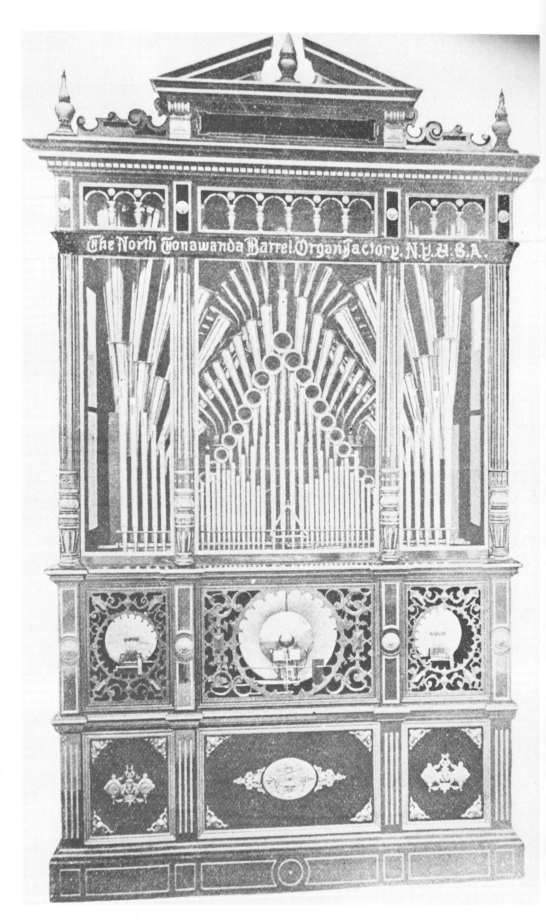

The North Tonawanda Barrel Organ Factory. N.Y. U.S.A.

A large barrel-operated orchestrion made by the North Tonawanda Barrel Organ Factory around the turn of the 20th century. Although similar instruments were made by Schoenstein, Frick, Dufner, and others, very few barrel-operated orchestrions made in America still survive today.

ARRANGING MUSIC FOR BARREL ORGANS
and
HOW TO PIN THE BARRELS

by Claes O. Friberg

Claes O. Friberg, who operates the Mekanisk Musik Museum at Vesterbrogade 150, Copenhagen, Denmark, has collected instruments for many years. Among his favorite interests are hand-cranked barrel organs. The following article, which is technical in nature and which is designed for the collector with a knowledge of music theory, will do one of two things for you: (1) It will enable you, with perseverance, to arrange and pin new music for a barrel organ in the style of the grand masters of the past, or (2) it will help you appreciate the great amount of skill, effort, and time which went into the pinning of barrels years ago. Either way, the article provides much valuable information on what has almost become a lost art.

If you decide one day to take a walk down the street and interview a hundred people about their knowledge of portable hand-cranked barrel organs (if you call them monkey organs or hurdy-gurdies they will surely know what you mean), then probably 95% of them will tell you that these instruments make loud, horrible, jarring noises that don't have much to do with music. It is a pity that this sentiment has been affixed to the barrel organ, for all of these instruments were originally built to make music which is pleasant to hear.

Why, then, did the organs sound awful in their day? Well, actually many of them sounded quite fine, but it is a typical human characteristic that pleasant music will go in one ear and out the other, while grating and irritating sounds will be long remembered. Most barrel organ grinders rented their instruments from a local company whose business was to buy the organs from the manufacturers and hire them out. While barrel organs are long gone from the American scene, in my native Denmark they were a common sight in the streets a few decades ago, and even now scattered instruments are used to provide music for fund raising, weddings, anniversaries, and other occasions. Those who hired the organs usually cared very little about their upkeep. The firms which owned them often had the same attitude; as long as they could be rented and as long as the rent was paid each week, little attention was paid to doing anything more than keeping them playing, even if barely. In contrast were persons who owned their own barrel organs and who had justifiable pride in their ownership. They did not look like beggars; they were well dressed, called themselves musicians, and they knew if the organ played well their earnings would be better. Here in Europe only a very few of these are still playing professionally in the streets. Most have been destroyed, but some organs still survive in private collections.

During the 20 years I have been collecting automatic musical instruments I have seen many fine barrel organs that have been restored. The cabinets are beautiful. The bellows have been recovered properly and professionally. The pipes have been repaired and tuned. But, there's a problem: the instruments often sound poor simply because the most important parts of the organ were neglected—the barrel and the key frame. It does not suffice just to clean and brush up these parts. What should be done? This article will give you some of my thoughts.

Originally barrel organs were often supplied with two barrels. When the organ was out playing, the company which owned the instrument could arrange new popular tunes of the day on the other barrel left in the shop. This was often part of the hiring contract. After many years, the replacement of the original tunes by new melodies was often so complete that none of the original program remained. Unfortunately, many organ owners were not as talented or careful as were the original manufacturers, with the result that many organs played at a level far below what the original manufacturers intended.

This article should help owners of barrel organs to understand how music was arranged years ago and how barrels were pinned. With this information every owner of such an instrument will have the possibility of restoring a barrel and regulating the organ properly. Also, I will describe a useful and easily understandable way to pin a barrel so as to achieve good results. The adjustment of pins and the key frame will be discussed as well. I will be the first to admit that making a new barrel with 8 to 10 tunes is time consuming, but with the very high value of barrel organs on today's market I am sure that you will agree that it is worthwhile to make your instrument sound as fine as possible—just as fine as it did when it originally came from the factory of Cocchi, Bacigalupo & Graffigna, or Gavioli, or Frati, or whomever.

Barrel organs come in sizes from small 10-note serinettes (or "bird organs") up to huge barrel orchestrions with 100 or more keys. Of course, there is a different method needed to arrange for a small organ than is used to arrange for a large one, but the basic ideas are the same. I have chosen to explain the procedures for the typical hand-cranked street barrel organs made circa 1880 to 1930 by Bacigalupo, Frati, Bruder, Molinari, Gavioli, Limonaire, and others. I have put down on paper two typical arrangements for barrel organs; 38-key and 44-key. The musical style is similar to that used at the turn of the 20th century by these leading manufacturers.

The barrel is made up by using a center spindle or axis of beech wood. On this, two studs are mounted, one of which has tracks for the various tunes. Over the spindle the surface of the barrel is built up by 6 to 8 pieces of wood that are glued together. The best wood to use is well-seasoned poplar or alder, for these woods permit the insertion of pins by pliers and have a consistency or texture which "grabs and holds" the pins nicely. Some organ builders originally used pear wood, which has the same characteristics. Still other barrels were originally made of lime wood, but lime is harder, and a hammer is necessary to drive the pins into the surface.

Before pinning begins the barrel must be turned on a lathe to insure that its dimensions are perfectly true. Otherwise it may be uneven or "wobble" during playing. Even if you are using an old barrel it is a good idea to turn and trim it on a lathe to be sure it is true. If a barrel has rested in the same position—usually where the tunes start—for, say, 80 years it may sag in the middle. It is not important that the diameter

A Danish entertainer: This Bacigalupo portable hand-cranked barrel organ, made in Germany during the early 20th century, is shown with its owner, Claes O. Friberg, who has used it to play for many 25th wedding anniversaries in Copenhagen. Playing a barrel organ early on the morning of a silver wedding anniversary is a Danish tradition. (The same instrument and person, both ten years younger, are shown on page 811 of "The Encyclopedia of Automatic Musical Instruments.")

may be reduced slightly by lathe turning, for the key frame can always be regulated correspondingly.

In order to prevent the barrel from becoming distorted in the future it is a good idea not to have the barrel stay in the same position or orientation for years and years. Play the organ at least once a month, and once you've enjoyed the music then choose a different place on the barrel to stop. It is a bad habit for a barrel organ player to stop in the middle of a tune, but if you do it when no one is listening or if you just silence the organ by lifting the key frame there should be no problem. It may be desirable for you to divide the barrel into 12 sections and make a mark on the surface for each month of the year. In this manner, January can equal position 1, February position 2, and so on. As it is not desirable to change from one tune to another except in the "start" position on the barrel, each time you want to play the organ, continue with the tune in which you've stopped part way until it reaches the end, and then shift to another tune.

Whether you are using an old or a new barrel white paper must be pasted on to the surface. This covers the old pin holes. The paper can then be marked with a pencil and with the key frame pins. If you want to pin only one, two, or several new tunes while at the same time you want to keep some of the old tunes, then narrow strips of paper can be pasted on the tracks from which old pins have been removed. Removing just one tune is a difficult task. In the old days the firms normally removed at least two adjacent compositions, making it possible to use wider strips of paper and making it easier to glue the strips in their proper positions.

Most of the portable barrel organs you are likely to encounter will have 8, 9, or occasionally 10 tunes pinned on the barrel. The tunes are changed by moving the protruding stud on the right side of the organ, which is being held in position by means of a "knife." A spring keeps the knife down in one of the grooves or tracks by means of a locking mechanism. When this device is lifted up, the key frame pins are moved away from the barrel pins and the barrel can slide freely. Also, the knife is unlocked and the barrel can be shifted to the left or right to a new track. When the desired track has been found, the knife is placed back in its groove, and the barrel is locked into its new position.

A typical early 20th century barrel-operated orchestrion has 6 to 8 tunes, while English chamber barrel organs often have from 10 to 12 tunes pinned on the barrels. Most of the large classic barrel orchestrions from the 19th century have the pins arranged in a continuous spiral, rather than in specific tracks, so that a complete overture of many minutes in length can be played automatically. This system is also found in a very few portable hand-cranked barrel organs of the period.

Before we start arranging the music we must take a look at the scale of the organ and learn how it is divided. An accompanying illustration shows a typical 38-key barrel organ scale as it is printed on the keyboard. You will see that the melody is on the top line with the lowest note in the center, and the higher notes in this particular organ are divided on both sides of the lowest melody note—changing from left to right respectively as the pitch increases. This pyramidal arrangement is typical for a barrel organ with piccolos symmetrically set up at the front of the instrument. In between are the trumpets spread out from one far end to the other. They are shown on the second line. Key 35 is the lowest trumpet, and then comes key 32. After that the higher trumpets start from key 1 and jump to keys 4, 7, 10, 15, 19,

23, and finally key 27, which is the highest trumpet. Due to the size of the trumpets they can be located at many various places in an organ, so it is therefore important to check the exact order of the scale and to note where they are located on the key frame. Also, the accompaniment found on the third line has its two lowest notes on the right side and the rest on the left side of the key frame. In this instrument all the bass notes are to the right, but often some are found to the left. You will also discover that these four notes are "spread out" in an illogical way from a musical viewpoint. From the lowest to the highest they are: F (key 38), G (key 36), C (key 34), D (key 37). Bass notes are normally found on the line with the accompaniment, and like the other notes they have been stamped (or, rarely, written) on the key frame. To distinguish them from the accompaniment they are circled.

In order to learn quickly what is what on the scale it is a very good idea to mount a strip of paper with your notations on the top of the key frame. Since the notes that are stamped into the vertical side of the key frame are often quite indistinct it is a good idea to transfer them on to the strip of paper that you place horizontally on top of the key frame. Make three lines and put the melody on the first line in small letters, the trumpets on the second line with capital letters with red ink, the accompaniment on the third line with black capital letters, and, also on the third line, the bass in capital letters with a circle around each. Then above or below each note you can mark how high or low the notes are in relation to each other.

This helping strip is also very useful when you want to arrange a tune which is in a different key from that which the organ normally plays. Instead of rewriting a whole musical score, it is much easier to transpose an organ scale to the key you want—something which can be done in a few minutes. You put the new scale strip on top of the keyboard covering the original scale and—voila!—you are ready to start. Remember that the relationship between high and low notes is still the same, so your original personal notes are as valid as they were before.

Now let's discuss the musical arrangements for the barrel organ. I will state right now that musical knowledge—the ability to read music and an understanding of musical theory—is necessary in order to arrange the tunes. It is important to understand counterpoint. If you play an instrument—a piano or organ, for example—this will be helpful, but it is not absolutely necessary. Artistic imagination and skill combined with fantasy are important ingredients for the success of the barrel organ arranger.

Theoretically, every tune ever written can be transferred to a barrel organ, but the results are apt to differ. Let us therefore at this point say that there is music which is "impossible"—music which you can put on a barrel, but it would never do justice to either the music or the instrument itself. So, choose your music carefully. The best results are achieved if you use music which was composed around the time that the organ was new: waltzes, polkas, marches, fox trots, two-steps, hymns, and so on. Most music of this general character will work well.

It has been claimed that the intention or feeling of the composers should be transferred as accurately as possible from their musical scores to the barrel organ, but I disagree. A few classic composers such as Beethoven, Mozart, and Haydn wrote music for specific barrel organs and orchestrions, but I doubt if the composers from the turn of the 20th century—the

The author of the accompanying article marks a new tune on a barrel using the system described in the text.

main era of the barrel organs being considered here—would be very happy to hear their music played on these instruments, although one could claim that this would be additional evidence of the music's popularity. So, for the barrel organ arranger the important thing is to use the capability of the organ as much as possible so that the music will play loudly and clearly in the street when you are ready to demonstrate the instrument.

A major problem is that barrel organs are rarely chromatic. If you want to use a tune with sharps and flats you must slightly rewrite the score. With some exercise and musical experience it is not difficult to find another note that will substitute for the original. Often it is best to alter one or two other notes at the same time so that the "new" melody will be better accepted by the listeners. Running through such critical passages by hand on the keyboard of an organ or piano is often helpful and leads to creative ideas.

Professional barrel organ music arrangers could take a sheet of music published for the piano, put some of their own notations on the sheet within a short time, divide the bars so as to be suitable for a particular organ, and then start marking the barrel using their barrel-divider device (which will be explained later in the present article). However, in order to achieve the best results it is recommended that from a sheet of music—for example, a piano score—the complete score for the barrel organ should be notated on a separate music sheet which you will use when marking the barrel. This seems to be a tedious thing to do, but if you consider the value of the organ and the satisfaction of listening to a well-arranged tune on it, you will have a lot of fun if you take the time to write your own separate score.

Before you start writing down the music you must know how much music can be put on the barrel. There are three main types of barrels: (1) 48-bar waltz (= 36/40-bar march) plays approximately 42 seconds; (2) 64-bar waltz (= 46/52-bar march) plays approximately 55 seconds; and (3) 80-bar waltz (= 64/68-bar march) plays approximately 68 seconds.

The waltz rhythm is considered basic, for one turn of the crank is normally one waltz bar. Mathematically, one turn of the handle takes 0.86 of a second. All the above should enable you to decide how many bars of music you can use on one turn of the barrel of a specific instrument.

Two musical scores are shown on the accompanying illustrations. The waltz was arranged for the 38-key trumpet organ with 10 trumpets. The march is for a related 44-key trumpet organ but which has 13 trumpets. The music has been divided into four sections: (1) Melody, (2) Trumpet, (3) Countermelody, and (4) Accompaniment and Bass. With such a score in your hands the marking on the barrel will be a joy (and, remember how much fun it was to make up the score!).

When you make up the score you should start with the Melody. This will normally follow the original sheet music closely, except for transcriptions to provide alternatives for certain sharps and flats. In addition, it will contain various embellishments in the form of triplets and trills. Before the turn of the century and in the first few years after 1900 trills were very popular. This was before trumpet organs achieved their height of popularity. Trills were used to have Violino-Pan and similar barrel organs play as loudly as possible. Some of the arrangements had so many embellishments and trills that they were distasteful, but the technique worked to increase the overall loudness of the music. With the rising popularity of trumpet organs this style of arranging faded out, but I believe

that a few trills at the proper places can still do much to improve an arrangement. Trills are a part of the soul of a barrel organ. You will see them on the examples pictured in this article.

The musical theme should always be heard in the Melody, even if the Trumpets take over the Melody for some bars. This is because it could be necessary to turn the Trumpet register off when the organ is played under conditions which do not require a full volume of sound. Also, Trumpets are apt to get out of tune easily, and then it is convenient to discontinue the Trumpet register until tuning is possible.

Trumpets have their best effect if they do not play all of the time. Some arrangers have them play constantly and follow the Melody, but this is completely wrong. They should play from about half the bars in the tune up to a maximum of two-thirds of the bars. They can start with, for example, four inspiring bars, then remain silent for eight bars or so, and then come back again... and thus come and go. But if the Trumpets are to be "shown off" or featured, they should be on for at least 12 continuous bars.

It is true to say that the Trumpets are the most independent register in the barrel organ. They have their own personality, so to speak. If you are a talented arranger, then the Trumpets provide many interesting opportunities. They can play the Melody like the violins and piccolos, make interesting countermelodies which will surpass the normal Countermelody and make fanfares, syncopation, and afterbeat.

The Countermelody has its own tune to "whistle" all through the playing. It is an understanding of counterpoint which makes the Countermelody do its best. For the new arranger it means a lot of exercise to use the Countermelody, but when this art is mastered it becomes an increasingly fascinating challenge. Excellent results can be obtained by practicing this special feature of the barrel organ. The main problem is that you will have to steal the notes from the Accompaniment notes of the organ, but with some flexibility it can be mastered. Therefore, on larger organs it is a dream to work with the Countermelody because there are more Accompaniment notes available.

The normal Accompaniment and Bass should not present any problems since they are arranged similar to the method used when playing a piano or organ.

Finally, you will have to number all the bars of your score just as it is shown in the accompanying illustration. Before you think you are finished it would be a good idea to try the music on your piano or organ. The late Giovanni Bacigalupo once demonstrated to me how he could play on his piano the Melody with his right hand, the Countermelody, Accompaniment, and Bass with his left hand, while singing the Trumpet part of a score! I admit this is very difficult, but if you play the piano you could record on tape the Melody and Accompaniment, and then you could play the tape while experimenting with adding Trumpet and Countermelody.

Let's look at the key frame now. This can be regulated by means of various screws that are all of equal importance. The lateral adjustment is made by the two screws on each side of the barrel organ's cabinet. Put the barrel in position for the first tune (the "knife" will run in the first groove) and measure how far the last right key pin is from the end of the barrel. Then proceed to the last tune and measure how far the last left pin is from the barrel end. Then adjust the key frame so that there is equal space from these pins to the barrel's edges in both of the mentioned positions. Normally there should be from two to four millimeters. When regulated properly, both lateral adjustment screws should rest against the sides of the key frame in a position so that the key frame can move up and down smoothly.

The height is adjusted by two screws on the top of the key frame. Turn the screws until the pins are 0.5 mm. from the surface of the barrel. Do this slowly, and be sure that both screws are resting properly without any separation of one of them from the bearings. You will probably notice now that not all key pins have the same distance from the barrel surface. This can be compensated for through the turning of the individual adjuster rail along the backside edge of the key frame. When finally all pins are 0.5 mm. from the barrel you have the right adjustment for playing the music properly. If you desire the music to be more staccato you can adjust the keyframe in a higher position, and if you want it to be more legato you can lower the key frame slightly. When you start marking tunes on the barrel you should always lower the key frame so that it nearly touches the surface of the barrel (about 0.1 mm. distant from it).

The key pins should all be the same distance from each other, and the front of the pins must be at right angles to the surface of the highest point of the barrel. This can only be corrected by careful use of pliers. Take your time—it is a very important regulation.

The backs of the key pins are shaped in an angle of approximately 22.5 degrees. This means that the key pins (usually made of steel or iron) will more smoothly attack the soft brass pins of the barrel. Also, this makes the music sound more beautiful. Small organs like serinettes used to have an angle of only 10 degrees, while large barrel orchestrions had angles of up to 30 degrees.

At this point we must also make sure that the driving cog of the barrel and the worm gear on the crankshaft are close together. If there is some space between them the barrel will turn irregularly. The worm gear can be moved close to the driving cog if you loosen the two or three screws on the right side of the cabinet holding the bearings for the crankshaft, press the worm gear firmly toward the driving cog, and tighten the screws again.

Now you are ready to put start-marks on to the barrel. Lower the key frame so it nearly touches the barrel and press the key pins towards the barrel surface one by one. This is your zero point from where the markings will start. To distinguish these marks from the marks which you put for the pins to be inserted you should circle them with red ink. If you are pinning a barrel and if you have left some of the old tunes on the barrel, you must be sure to follow the original zero points marked by the former pinner and adjust the key frame completely according to these marks. Hopefully, such marks were made when the key frame was adjusted perfectly (just like you have just learned to do). If not, this is really a problem, and it may be necessary to remove all of the old tunes and make the barrel completely over with new arrangements. Of course, tunes that are of special historical or musical importance should never be removed. In this case it is better to make new arrangements on a second barrel.

Your musical score can now be marked on the barrel. However, first we must find a method to spread the music out over the entire barrel. Several systems have been used over the years, the best known being the one described by Engramelle in his book *La Tonotechnie ou L'Art de Noter les Cylindres*, published in Paris in 1775. This method uses a dial placed around the axis of the barrel drive shaft. It is divided up according to the music bars, and through various combinations of dials nearly all types of music can be spread out on the barrel. The system requires quite a bit of breadth of view. To help out with the marking you will usually have to put down the numbers of the bars on the barrel. The system is thoroughly described in Arthur W.J.G. Ord-Hume's book, *Barrel Organ*.

Before Engramelle published his ideas it was common to draw the music as lines on a piece of paper which was then glued on to the barrel surface. However, this method required such a high degree of accuracy that the results were often imperfect. Already in the beginning of the 19th century machines were constructed which by means of interchangeable gear wheels could divide all musical rhythms on the barrel. Normally the barrel and the key frame were taken out of the organ and mounted on an arranging bench and coupled to the dividing device. A variation of this system was the Micrometer invented by Flight & Robson in England around 1830. This enabled the machine to be mounted directly on the instrument and the music could be marked directly on the barrel while it was remaining in the organ. This gave very excellent and precise results.

In practice it is my own preference to mark the barrel while it is in the organ, and thus Engramelles method would be of interest, but I have decided to use a system with a dial mounted directly on the axis of the barrel. I have found this to be useful. It avoids the inaccuracy that can arise in the gearing of the driving cog and the worm gear, and it is easy to use since you have an overall view all the time of what you are doing.

The dial is made of wood, is 6 mm. thick, and has a diameter of 65 cm. In the middle a metal center is mounted with a hole of 3 cm. diameter. Through the side of this center are placed four screws which enable the dial to be mounted on any barrel stud (below 3 cm. diameter). We want the dial to tell us how we spread the music over the barrel so that it will be rhythmically possible to play a tune several times without missing a bar or part of a bar. Therefore, the next thing is to draw tracks on the dial which correspond exactly to the normal musical divisions into bars. This is a matter of mathematics and geometry. In order to make your own dial you should seek advice from an engineer or mechanic. All collectors of barrel organs should have one in their circle of friends! Surely, he will be able to easily make the dial for you.

I had the great luck of obtaining a dial from an old barrel organ music arranger. The dial had the following divisions:

Waltz bars: 80, 78, 64, 50, 48, 44, 40, 32, 30 (3/4 notations)

March bars: 68, 64, 56, 52, 48, 42, 40, 38, 32 (4/4 notations)

Plus a strange 39-bar 4/4 division probably used for a hymn or similar style of melody.

The divisions with the many bars should be tracked at the edge of the dial, while the small ones (the short tunes) should be placed nearer to the center. Keep a distance of about 6 to 7 cm. between the tracks, and never get any closer than 20 cm. from the center with a track. When all bars are mathematically outlined on the dial, each bar is divided into 3/4 marks (for waltz or 6/8 marches) or 4/4 marks. I suggest that the above divisions for waltz and march are used since these are the most common. You might want to keep some tracks clear for your own experimental divisions of other rhythms or for hymns.

Views of the dial (above) and the dial and pointer (right) in use, as described in the accompanying article.

"Fest und Treu" as arranged for the barrel organ. (Courtesy of Bernt W. Moller)

"Koster Waltz" as arranged for the barrel organ. (Courtesy of Bernt W. Moller)

This photograph shows how the 38 keys on a particular barrel organ are located on the key frame and how this corresponds to the notes on the sheet music.

The dial can now be mounted on the left axis stud of the barrel, and a pointer should be fastened on the organ cabinet with its top pointing exactly at the zero point of the desired division. Also, the barrel must be precisely at its zero point.

The marking is started by first lowering the key frame until it nearly touches the barrel. Then wind the handle until the pointer comes to the first 1/3 or 1/4 in the bar, and tip the key pins down on the surface of the barrel according to the notes in your score which you have in front of you on the organ's lid or similar convenient place. This will make visible marks on the paper so you know where to put the pins afterward. Of course, there are also notes to be marked in between the 1/3 or 1/4 marks in your bars. Experienced arrangers can divide this by eye, but if you wish to be sure you are doing it exactly, the crochets can on the dial be divided into quavers and semiquavers, and even demisemiquavers (crochets, quavers, semiquavers, and demisemiquavers are quarter-, eighth-, sixteenth-, and thirty-second-notes respectively).

A special type of shorthand is necessary in order to show with pencil marks what sort of pins and bridges are to be put into the barrel. If you have observed the method described earlier in this article concerning the size of the barrel compared to how many bars you can fill in on the barrel, and if you follow these rules, the marking is simple. Let us take the march tempo. A 1/4 note is just marked without any further pencil markings. We know this mark is a 1/4 note (the same applies for the waltzes: a 1/3 note is just the pin mark. The method for the march is the same as for the waltz). A 1/8 note mark is accompanied by a small pencil mark at the right side of the mark. A 1/16 note gets two similar pencil marks, and a 1/32 note gets three such pencil marks. Notes longer than 1/4 are marked with the start of the note and the end of it. Both marks are then linked together with a pencil line, thus indicating that a bridge will be used on the barrel at this point. A very important thing when marking the long notes is that they should not be given their full values on the barrel. To achieve distinct music (and not muddy chords) these notes should start at the normal point but should be finished 1/4 note before actually shown on the score. Only if a legato is wanted or if a certain note should be emphasized such notes could be shortened by only 1/8 value. On the other hand, all bass notes should be kept longer in order to give them the chance to speak out. Basically, there are to be used bridges 1.5 mm. thick for marches and 2.0 mm. thick for waltzes. This should be done always, in spite of a music sheet which shows just 1/4 or 1/3 notes. If the score shows longer bass notes (which only rarely should happen) they can be given up to their complete value length on the marking of the barrel, but not more value than other long notes marked simultaneously.

When you have trills that are obviously linked together, as the barrel is being marked you need not put the three pencil marks beside the marks in the barrel, as it is obvious that here the pins for 1/32-notes are required. Also, it is important that you start a trill with the upper tone and end with the lower—which can be pinned as a 1/16 or 1/8 note in order to give this more importance since the lowest note in a trill is always the basic dominant.

Hopefully, it will not be too confusing for you to make all of the voices—Melody, Trumpet, Countermelody, Accompaniment, and Bass—at one time. But, as mentioned earlier, it gives more accuracy to do the whole score at one time. I should also mention that if some scores start with an upbeat you should

still start the barrel on the zero point, but the dial must start the relevant 1/4s or 1/3s (normally one or two) earlier. This implies that the dial finishes before its normal end, and thus everything is again back the usual way. It is a tradition that the zero point is always kept free of pins, so all tunes should start at the same no. 1 point—also in the case of upbeats.

Tipping the key pins down on the barrel is normally described as being done with a small hammer. However, this method is a little difficult when you work with the barrel in the organ. It is much easier to use your fingers—just as if you were playing an instrument. Use both hands—mainly the left hand because your right hand will have to turn the organ's winding handle as the arrangement progresses. The forefinger and the middle finger are the most suitable for this work. Your fingers might hurt more or less after a day's work of marking, but after a while your body will get used to it and you will not have any more pain. As a curiosity I can tell you that many years ago I met a man who had spent 30 years of his life marking barrels for barrel pianos. Four of his fingertips were rectangular!

It is advisable to pin all the tunes on the barrel when you have set it up for arranging and pinning. Of course, errors might slip in—but these can be corrected when all of the pins are put into the barrel. Wrong pins can be taken out, and right ones can be inserted. Therefore, keep the score on hand until the final test.

The pins that you will use are made of flat brass wire 1.2 mm. wide. The thickness of the wire for bridges and 1/3 and 1/4 note pins is 0.7 mm., for 1/6 and 1/8 pins it is 0.6 mm., and for smaller values of notes it is 0.5 mm. The pins should all stick 8 to 9 mm. into the wood of the barrel. The protruding part of the pins above the surface of the barrel should measure: (1) Bridges and 1/3 and 1/4 value pins: 3.2 mm. Flat head; (2) 1/6 and 1/8 value pins: 3.2 mm. Sharp head; (3) From 1/9 to 1/16 value pins: 2.6 mm. Sharp head; (4) From 1/17 to 1/32 value pins and all trills: 2.0 mm. Sharp head.

In order to drive the pins into the barrel you will need some sets of flat-nosed pliers with grooves drilled into their noses. For the pinning you will use the following four pliers with the sizes of the grooves as measured here (the numbers correspond to the numbers of the above-mentioned types of pins): (1) Length 3.2 mm, width 1.3 mm., depth 0.7 mm.; (2) Length 3.2 mm., width 1.3 mm., depth 0.6 mm.; (3) Length 2.6 mm., width 1.3 mm., depth 0.5 mm.; (4) Length 2.0 mm., width 1.3 mm., depth 0.5 mm.

The soft brass wire can in most instances be bought locally. With some persuasion it is often possible to have a small workshop make up the various sizes of pins for you. Of course, the part of the pins going into the wood must be sharpened to a point. The single pins for 1/3 and 1/4 notes should be flat on the top, while all other single pins should be sharp on the top. If 3/4 or 4/4 notes are marked for staccato you should use a pin like you would normally do (3.2 mm. high and 0.7 mm. deep) but with its top sharpened.

The bridges were normally made on a special machine which in Germany was called a Klammermaschine (although in the 19th century they were made by means of pliers of different sizes—a slow job). This machine had 40 to 50 dies of various lengths which could be put into the machine, and then bridges up to the size of 25 mm. could be punched. If longer bridges are needed on the barrel you can combine various lengths of bridges as you wish. An advanced example of a Klammer-

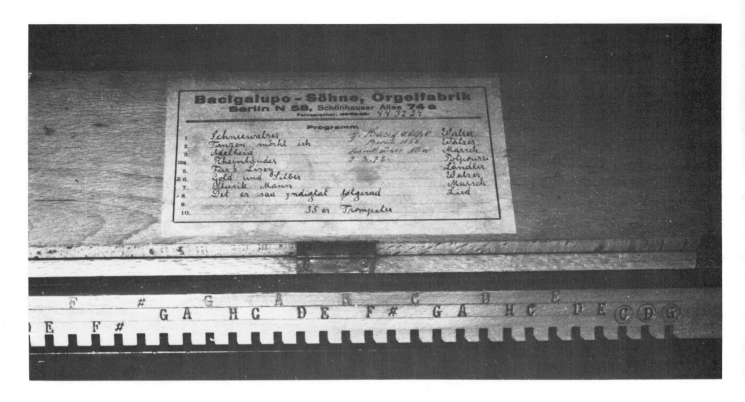

A typical key frame layout on a Bacigalupo hand-cranked organ. The program lists tunes pinned by the late Giovanni Bacigalupo in March 1972, one of the last barrels he ever arranged.

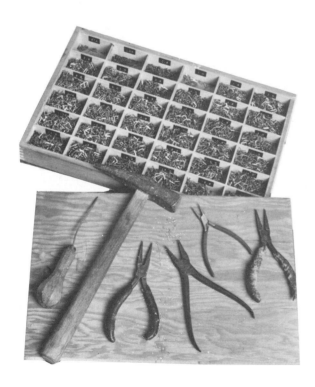

Tools and boxes of pins used to pin an organ barrel.

Giovanni Bacigalupo's "Klammermaschine."

maschine (given to the author by Giovanni Bacigalupo because, as Bacigalupo said, "You know how to use it") is on exhibit at the Mekanisk Musik Museum in Copenhagen. If you visit the museum and bring with you some flat brass wire, arrangements can be made to make for you the required bridges.

In order to keep track of pins and bridges it is useful to have a box divided into compartments where you can put the various sizes. Do not write the note values on the compartments, but, rather, mark the sizes (length and depth) of the pins and bridges. After you get used to marking the barrel and putting the pins into it, you will be able to select the right size right away—even with your eyes closed, if you will.

It is easiest to pin the barrel when you take it out of the organ and place it on a table with the two axis studs supported by a pair of blocks in a way that the barrel is slightly above the surface of the table and can be turned easily. With the pliers it is easy to drive the pins into the wood of the barrel. Start with the smallest and lowest pins, 1/32s, 1/16s, and so on. When you have finished putting the flat-headed pins into the barrel, the bridges are next to be done. These must be hammered into the wood while being supported by pliers. When all the bridges are in the barrel you can carefully go over the whole barrel with your hammer and ascertain that the bridges are punched down to the same height as the 1/4 note pins; that is, 3.2 mm. above the surface. All pins shall protrude at right angles to the surface of the barrel. Some pinners of years ago placed the pins in a slanted position in order to strengthen them, but I do not recommend this as it is difficult to place them evenly in this manner.

All that remains to do is to line up the pins, for surely some are not at a true right angle to the surface of the barrel. Take 8 tracks at a time when you look at the surface, hold your eyes at the same height at the top of the barrel, and turn it slowly. Any oblique pins will immediately be discovered and can be corrected. After this is over take a rest, and then go to one side of the barrel and look at the pins as the barrel is turned slowly. When this is done, go to the other side of the barrel and repeat the procedure. When all of this is over, it is time to listen to the music. If you have followed my instructions you should be able to listen to a concert of rich and beautiful sounds that you would never expect from a barrel organ. Oops! I nearly forgot to mention that there will probably be some wrong notes—if you've been careful, perhaps just one or two—and these can now be removed and replaced by the right pins.

Arranging music for barrel organs and pinning barrels was a highly respected art centuries ago. In this article I have tried to give you an idea and provide examples of how you can start your own artistry in this field. Modern techology can never make great barrel organ music. Only people with musical understanding, artistic imagination, skill, and fantasy can make it. If the foregoing explanation of the art of making music for the barrel organ has enabled you to make an instrument come to life again, I can assure you that my purpose has been fulfilled.

———Claes O. Friberg

Chapter 9

BAND, DANCEHALL, and FAIRGROUND ORGANS

WRITE FOR SPECIAL CATALOGUE DEVOTED TO
THE WURLITZER MILITARY BANDS
ESPECIALLY BUILT FOR
SUMMER PARKS-CAROUSELS-SKATING RINKS-FAIRS & CARNIVALS

Style 150

Style 165

Style 125

Style 18

Several Wurlitzer military band organ styles as shown in a circa 1914 catalogue. Styles 150, 165, and 125 are roll-operated. Style 18 is a cylinder instrument.

BAND ORGAN AND DANCE ORGAN SCALES

Band Organ Scales

Whenever possible, each band organ scale has the notes for each section printed on one line, like this:

WURLITZER 150
7 to 9, Trombone G, C, D
10 to 12, Bass G, C, D
13 to 21, Accompaniment G, A, B, C, D, E, F, F#, G
etc.

This format was found to be the most efficient way of presenting the most information in a relatively compact space. In any scale with non-chromatic note sections, such as the Wurlitzer 150 scale, all of the notes are printed. Any note scale which is fully chromatic is printed like this:

WURLITZER 155
60 to 77, Piccolo D to G

Whenever part of a note scale is fully chromatic and the rest of the scale is not, a combination of the two above systems is used:

WURLITZER 155
78 to 98, Trumpet G, A, A#, B, C, D, E-D, E-G

Each hyphen or equivalent word "to" represents the fully chromatic scale between the two printed notes, so if the above example were listed in its entirety, it would look like this:

WURLITZER 155
78 to 98, Trumpet G, A, A#, B, C, D, E, F, F#, G, G#, A, A#, B, C, C#, D, E, F, F#, G

In some scales, such as the 84-key Mortier, register names are followed by the letter (M) or (CM) to indicate whether that rank or section is in the melody or countermelody section of the organ.

Scrambled Organ Scales

In the scrambled scales, each note is identified by having in parentheses the section of the organ in which that note appears, as A (bass). To simplify retubing a band organ having a scrambled scale, convert the scale from this book into a chart by the following method. First, write the tracker bar or key frame numbers in a vertical column down the left side of a sheet of paper, and write the sections of the organ (such as bass, trombone, accompaniment, low violin, melody low octave, melody high octave, and trumpet) as column headings across the top. Then distribute the notes into their appropriate columns on the chart. This will make it easy to find all the notes in each section and to make sure the organ is tubed correctly.

Finding the Correct Scale for an Organ

Many band organs have several more keys than actual functions (notes, registers, percussions, etc.) in the organ, with the result that the traditional number-name for the scale often includes several blank keys. An example is a 101-key Mortier scale which has 97 functions, 3 blank keys, and a key frame key, for a total of 101. Each scale in this book is labeled by the number of keys. Some scales, such as the aforementioned 101-key Mortier scale, are labeled with their traditional name, which includes blank keys. Many others, such as the 55-key Frati scale, were taken from original music arrangers' scale sticks which indicate only the actual working functions and do not show the position of the key frame key or the presence of blank marginal keys. Some of these will be found to be labeled with the correct number, while others are for organs with a few more keys.

When attempting to match a scale in this book with an existing organ for which the scale is unknown, first count the number of keys in the key frame (or holes in the tracker bar or keyless frame) to get close to the right number in the book. Then count the number of functions in the organ—the number of notes in each section (bass, accompaniment, melody, etc.), registers, percussions, etc.—to try to find the exact scale which matches these functions. The brand name of the organ and scale will sometimes help. For example, a Decap dance organ with numerous percussions generally uses a Decap scale, and a Gavioli band organ with a supply of original old music books probably uses a Gavioli scale. However, due to frequent remodelling, the brand does not provide conclusive evidence as to which scale will always be used. In America, many cardboard book organs were converted to play standardized, mass-produced Wurlitzer or B.A.B. music rolls, while in Europe many older fair and dance organs were cut down in size and made into Dutch street organs. Many large fairground (band) organs were cut down in order to make the acquisition of new music more economical or to fit a music style more readily available. Numerous 110-key Gavioli organs were converted to the 89-key Gavioli scale for this reason. Some organ companies such as Wurlitzer, Bursens, Gavioli, and Decap standardized their scales so that one style of music roll or book would fit many organs. Other companies, notably Mortier, purposely designed many musically identical organs with minor variations in the key frame layouts so the organ owners could not exchange music with each other. Thus, some scales fit numerous organs perfectly, while others fit only one specific organ and are included for the clues they might provide for tubing similar organs.

In America the Rudolph Wurlitzer Company "modernized" many organs made by the North Tonawanda Musical Instrument Works, Artizan, Niagara, Bruder, Gavioli, and others when music for the other makes was not readily available. A catalogue of Wurlitzer band organs noted:

Arthur Prinsen adjusts cardboard leaves in his Brasschaat (a suburb of Antwerp, Belgium) workshop. A professional musician, he has spent most of the past two decades arranging music and making books for band organs and dance organs. In addition, he has produced numerous paper rolls for Arburo (by Arthur Bursens) dance organs. During the 1960s much if not most of his business was with collectors in England, including members of the Fairground Organ Preservation Society. In the 1970s interest in preserving Mortier, Bursens, Gavioli, and other book-operated organs spread to the United States, Germany, and other countries, and now he has customers in all parts of the world.

REMODEL THAT OLD BAND ORGAN. During its long years of service, that old organ has more than paid its way for you. Send it in when you can spare it, and we will give you an estimate for modernizing it . . .

Thus, many organs which use Wurlitzer 125, 150, or 165 rolls are not Wurlitzer organs at all, but are other makes which have been converted. There are numerous other examples.

Deducing an Unknown Dance Organ Style

The following information should enable anyone with experience repairing band organs and with a basic knowledge of music theory to deduce the scale of most unknown music books. Lacking either of these, the reader trying to decipher a scale should enlist the help of a musician friend. Dance organ books were chosen here to describe the basic process of deducing unknown scales because they contain lots of registers and percussion devices.

After making a list of everything observed in the organ, make a cardboard strip about two inches wide and as long as the music book (or roll) is wide. This will be the scale stick. Mark the position of all of the key frame or tracker bar holes on it.

Determine which is the top and bottom, the beginning and the end, of the book. The top of a well-used book has faint lines down its length *between* the keys, made by the key guide roller, while the bottom has faint lines corresponding to *the middle of the holes* made by the keys (or tracker bar holes in a keyless organ). The beginning of the piece can be determined by studying hole patterns, in the absence of an obvious indication such as a printed trademark, hand-written song title, an arrow, or a word (in various languages) equivalent to "start" or "commence." The end has a solitary cancel or shutoff hole, while the beginning usually has several register holes punched at once.

After identifying the top and beginning of the book, find the shutoff hole (if used) at the end, and mark it on the scale stick. Verify by checking through the entire melody; the shutoff hole will appear nowhere else.

Find and mark the general cancel. Most melodies end with this hole just before the shutoff. Verify by looking through the book; a cancel hole usually appears every few feet, simultaneously with one or more register holes.

Study several books; find and mark all of the register holes. They are usually from 1" to 1¾" long, longer than the usual bass and accompaniment holes but shorter than sustained melody holes. They are usually all the same length in a given book, usually (but not always) accompanied by a shorter general cancel hole, and seldom in alignment with note holes. In many dance organ scales, one or more registers are located between the accompaniment and melody, and melody and countermelody note sections, simplifying the process of identifying these sections.

Find and mark the bass note section. Only one bass note is punched at a time; there are as many bass holes as there are bass notes in the organ.

Find and mark the accompaniment section, which usually has several short holes punched simultaneously in rhythmic patterns, forming the accompaniment chords.

By the process of elimination, the melody and counter-melody sections are usually obvious, each section having the same number of holes as there are notes in that section of the organ.

Locate the percussion holes. In a small organ there are usually three: the bass drum hole, approximately coinciding with a bass note at the first beat of the measure; and two snare drum holes which occasionally alternate rapidly with each other. The percussion holes are consistently shorter than the average length of all other holes. In many small organs there are three percussion holes for six beaters. During soft passages the triangle plays from the bass drum hole, and two castanets or wood block beaters play from the snare drum holes. When the trombone or forte register is punched, it operates a pneumatic switching device which routes the signals to the bass drum and cymbal and to the snare drum beaters. In other small organs the bass drum plays during soft passages, and the cymbal is mechanically coupled to it by the trombone or forte register. If one of these arrangements is used, it will be obvious by the percussion mechanisms in the organ.

In a dance organ with a large battery of percussion instruments, their holes in the key frame layout can usually be deduced by studying the beater mechanisms and the use of each hole in the book.

There are three basic arrangements of beater pneumatics. In the "normally inflated; deflate to play" type, the pneumatic is normally filled with air which holds the spring-loaded beater away from the instrument. When the hole is punched, a valve opens the pneumatic to outside atmospheric pressure, and large springs force the pneumatic shut, hitting the beater against the instrument. This type of mechanism is nearly always used for the bass drum. The hole in the book, usually a little longer than other percussion holes, is punched so the leading edge slightly precedes the playing notes, allowing time for the air to be exhausted from the pneumatic by the large springs.

In the "inflate and deflate to play" type, the pneumatic and beater are normally closed and held against the instrument by springs. The hole in the book inflates the pneumatic in advance of the playing notes, and the *trailing* edge shuts the air off, allowing the springs to force the beater quickly against the instrument. These holes are easily identified because the *end* of each hole slightly precedes or coincides with the appropriate playing notes. This type of mechanism is nearly always used for the snare drum, temple blocks, tom-toms (or tympani), and, in some organs, the tap cymbal.

In the "inflate to play" type, the pneumatic is normally deflated, and the hole causes it to inflate, playing the instrument. It is often used for maraccas and other shaking-type instruments, and, in some organs, the tap cymbal. These holes are punched with the leading edge either slightly preceding or coinciding with the playing notes, but they are usually shorter than the bass drum holes.

Further clues to the function of each percussion hole are furnished by their rhythmic patterns. A tap cymbal often plays all four beats of the measure in a fox trot for eight or more measures at a time. Maraccas are used in Latin music, like rhumbas, sometimes playing all four

With the sheet music for "Wheels" in front of him, and with a key frame scale for ready reference, Arthur Prinsen arranges music on a composing drum. The series of holes at the left (below his hand) are arranged in several different spacings and aid with the tempo. The musical notes and control notations are marked on paper. The paper is overlaid on a music book, and the holes are cut out on a foot-actuated punching machine. The paper is saved for future use as a stencil for additional copies of the book.

beats, and at other times adding Latin-style punctuation to the rhythm. Tom-toms or tympani sometimes play in alternating patterns but are not always spaced as closely together as the alternating snare drum holes. If the triangle has a reiterating mechanism, its holes might be punched in different lengths, depending on whether the music arranger desired a single tap or a roll. Multiple temple block holes are obvious, as they are usually adjacent in the book and often appear as triplet patterns alternating between the blocks.

Now that the locations of each note section, the registers and cancel, percussions, and shutoff holes are located, mark any unused keys on the scale stick. Key frame organs have some means of turning off the air supply to the keys so that the organ won't "roar" when the key frame is opened. If this function is controlled by a key, that key might be mounted so it slightly precedes the alignment of the other keys, and it will never have a hole punched in the books. If the music should run out of the key frame, the key frame key will pop up before the rest, turning the organ off. Many organs do not have a key frame key but have a lever or pin mounted so it is released when the frame is opened.

The next part of decoding a book consists of figuring out the actual notes. In a straightforward scale such as the 92-key Decap everything will fall into place, with the lowest pipe in each section of the organ connected to the lowest hole in that section of the book. In this case it is unnecessary to figure out the playing notes. Some organs, however (notably Mortier instruments), have the bass arranged in a different way, with the longest pipe playing a bass note toward the middle of the bass note section in the book. In these organs, if the bass pipes are connected in the usual way, they will play the wrong bass notes. The following procedure is for figuring out such an organ or for deducing a book for which no organ is present.

Go to the end of the melody. The last chord is almost always the tonic chord in the key of the piece, usually a simple major chord, sometimes with an added sixth. The last bass note is the key note of the piece, and the chord notes in each section form a major chord in the root position or an inversion. For simplicity's sake, call the last bass note C. In any organ having no more than 12 accompaniment notes, the accompaniment chord is frequently C-E-G, E-G-C, or G-C-E. By examining the hole spacing, the inversion of the chord will be evident. The same chord is usually punched in the melody, probably in a different inversion, and the countermelody will also have one or more notes of the same chord punched. Mark them on the scale stick,

Back up to the previous chord: there is a high probability that this is a dominant chord (G or G7). By careful examination and by comparing against the tonic chord already tentatively marked, enough notes can usually be found that the rest can be filled in by the process of elimination. If the organ is fully chromatic, everything will fall into place. If any of the sharps or flats are missing, careful examination of the book by a musician will enable the notes to be marked; or, if the organ is available, the pipes will be arranged in the same order in the organ as the note holes are in the book, simply omitting the missing notes.

If a Mortier or other organ has the bass pipes made with the lowest note playing one of the middle notes of the bass section in the book, after one or two bass notes have been correctly identified on the tentative scale stick, the rest will fall into place. In many Mortiers, the trombones play from the bass holes when the trombone register is on, but the longest bass bourdon and violin pipes play G while the longest trombone plays C. When tubing the organ, if the pipes are coupled by size, they will obviously play the wrong notes, so they must be coupled by note name, with some trombones playing an octave apart from the bourdons.

Deducing the correct register holes can be the most difficult part of deciphering a large organ scale. Every possible clue must be observed carefully: marks on the outside or inside of the key frame, register control box, or wind chests; remnants of original tubing; or clues provided by a test book (if it is the correct one for the organ). If a correct test book is present but has two or three sets of markings which were written on it by several people over the life of the organ, study it carefully and compare each set of markings to the actual pipes in the organ. Pursue every possibility of finding the person who make the cardboard music books (in the case of modern organs), and send him photos of the organ along with a list of all functions. The music arranger will usually provide information if he has it, for a reasonable fee. If none of the above lead to the correct scale, then the registers must be deduced.

Typically, the end of each tune is loud, with multiple ranks of violin pipes in the melody section; cello, baritone, or saxophone in the countermelody; the trombone turned on in the bass section; and no tremolo. When long frequent glissandos occur during a melody or countermelody section, a flute or vibratone is usually on, often with tremolo.

When a vibratone or jazz flute plays solos with glissandos, and the countermelody plays sustained chords, the chords are often played on a 4' rank or ranks such as vox celeste, unda maris, or another vibratone or flute. Deeper countermelody ranks often play long sustained single countermelody notes against more active melody parts and are not usually used for large chords. In dance hall organs the trumpet is used sparingly, sometimes in staccato chords. If the organ has facade saxophones, the countermelody will play only one note at a time when the saxophone is on. The accordions typically play from all sections of notes and often have string celeste ranks on at the same time. These clues might help identify some of the registers, reducing the guesswork by the process of elimination. As a last resort, it might be possible to find a similar but correctly-tubed organ ("live" or on a recording) which plays one or more of the same songs made by the same arranger as the books for the organ in question. By listening carefully to the register changes it might be possible to deduce the correct tubing connections.

Deducing Other Organ Scales

In small fairground organs there are usually only two register keys, piano and forte. These terms have been changed to "soft" and "loud" in this book, to eliminate

Above: A cardboard music book is being cut out on a foot-actuated Bossmann punching press. Producing cardboard books is a laborious process, for they usually have to be cut out individually. Some savings can be effected in the earlier music arranging process, however, by using "stock arrangements" and adding or deleting notes or controls to fit a particular organ.

Left: This multiple-punch press in the Prinsen workshop makes it possible to quickly cut out long perforations for sustained notes.

Arthur Prinsen has cut music for all of the organs on this page, an indication of the diversity of his business. Above is shown a 78-key "Orchestre Moderne" dance organ by E. Fasano & Company. To the right is a 78-keyless Wellershaus band organ. At the lower right is a 98-key Gavioli organ, the "Troubadour." Directly below is a large 114-key Gaudin & Co. organ, Arthur Prinsen's personal instrument. While new book music for organs is not inexpensive, the owners of organs have the advantage that they can order a program of old or new tunes specifically filling their interests. In the early 1970s Arthur Prinsen arranged a large "library" of music for the 101-key Mortier "Taj Mahal" organ. Included were such old and new melodies as "At a Georgia Camp Meeting," "Stars and Stripes Forever," "Diana," "Green, Green Grass of Home," "The House of the Rising Sun," "Entry of the Gladiators," "Tennessee Waltz," "Way Down Yonder in New Orleans," and many others.

any possibility of confusion in scales which also have controls for a piano (the stringed instrument). Once the soft and loud register holes are located; in the book, it is easy to decide which hole controls which function, because most pieces begin and end loudly. Larger fairground organs have fewer stops and percussions and more notes than do dance organs of comparable key size. One note section frequently overlaps with another, such as the melody and piccolo sections in large Gavioli organs. A study of the fair organ scales contained in this book, along with a reading of *The Fairground Organ*, by Eric Cockayne, will provide insight into their tonal design.

If a fairground organ has separate holes for bass and snare drums and bell ringers or a band leader, the bell ringer or band leader holes will resemble the bass drum holes, but they are more easily identified because the bass drum almost always plays during passages in which the snare drum is playing, but the bell ringer or band leader holes appear during other passages as well. Some fairground organ scales have a percussion or other hole in the middle of some of the note sections. The odd holes are easily identified, but they tend to make it more difficult to tell the exact locations of the note sections. A study of the fairground organ scales in this book will help in deciphering such scales.

Many fairground organ books have a separate note section for the trombone pipes, which consequently do not need an automatic register. Sometimes, as in the Wurlitzer 150 and smaller B.A.B. rolls, the bass and trombone note sections are adjacent in the roll. In other cases, such as the 89-keyless Frei street organ scale used by "De Gouden Engel," the two sections are separated by other note sections. When deciphering an organ book with separate trombone and bass note sections, the bass section will be seen to play all through the music, while the trombone section only has notes punched during louder passages, making it easy to identify which section is which.

Some street organs economize on register control holes by turning the melody bourdon celeste ranks on with the general cancel and off with the melody violin register. Register holes which turn some ranks on and others off are also used in some fairground organs. These functions can usually be deduced by studying the connections on the register control box.

Transposing a Tuning Scale

Many band organs play in a key other than that indicated by the pitches marked on the pipes. Also, music book and roll arrangers frequently made several scale sticks for the same organ, with each stick in a different key according to the key of the sheet music they were using. For these reasons many of the scales in this book will be found to be in a different key than organs which use them. After finding a scale in this book, or making one from scratch according to the above procedure, it will be necessary to transpose it into the actual key of the organ.

Find a pipe in the organ which is probably tuned near the correct pitch; violin pipe tuning slides usually show tarnish or corrosion on the parts exposed to the atmosphere for many years, so if there is no "fresh" or bright section of metal, you can assume that the slide is

in its original position of years ago. Blow on the pipe, if possible using the same pressure that the organ originally used, and compare it to a well-tuned piano or other instrument to find the true concert pitch. If the organ pumps and reservoir have been restored, then the original pressure can be closely approximated. If not, then learn the pressure in a comparable style of instrument.

Note: Many organs were tuned "in the cracks" between the notes, as compared to a modern piano, because of different tuning systems in use earlier or because of the desire of an organ builder to make the instrument "brighter" in sound. Thus, caution should be used when actually tuning the organ. Metal or wood should not be physically removed from any pipe. If you are in doubt, enlist the assistance of a professional when tuning.

Once the pitch of a pipe has been determined, then learn which key in the key frame or hole in the tracker bar is connected to that pipe; then mark that position on the scale stick with the correct pitch. Make two rulers marked as follows with the letters of the musical scale:

CONCERT PITCH

C C# D D# E F F# G G# A A# B C C# D D# E F F# G G# A A#

G G# A A# B C C# D D# E F F# G
TENTATIVE SCALE STICK

By sliding the two rulers in relation to each other, all notes can be transposed from one key into any other key. If a hole marked C on the tentative scale stick plays a pipe which actually sounds F, align C on the lower ruler with F on the upper one, and then mark the rest of the notes on the scale stick with the corresponding pitches on the upper ruler. The scale stick can now be used as an actual tuning scale for the organ.

ARTIZAN FACTORIES, INC.
B.A.B. ORGAN COMPANY
NORTH TONAWANDA MUSICAL INSTRUMENT WORKS
Band Organs

Formed around 1906 by former employees of Eugene DeKleist, the North Tonawanda Musical Instrument Works was a leading manufacturer of coin pianos, organs, and related automatic musical instruments from that point until the 1920s.

Early organs were mainly of the pinned cylinder type. The facades were very similiar, indeed virtually identical, to contemporary DeKleist (sold by Wurlitzer) styles. Later instruments used paper rolls of the endless types. Many different organ styles were made, most of which were used in skating rinks (particularly those with brass horns) and on carousels.

Shortly before 1920, the firm was acquired by the Rand Company, Inc. By that time the organ business had declined sharply, and only a few models were being made. In 1922 certain principals of the North Tonawanda Musical Instrument Works, disenchanted with the Rand policies, left to form the Artizan Factories, Inc.

During the 1920s many North Tonawanda Musical Instrument Works organs were converted to play Wurlitzer rolls. Later, many were changed to use B.A.B. music.

North Tonawanda Musical Instrument Works ideas, concepts, and scale designs were incorporated into certain Artizan products. Later, many Artizan assets were acquired by the B.A.B. Organ Co. This interrelationship accounts for the similarity among scales of the three firms.

As noted earlier, The Artizan Factories, Inc. enterprise was established in 1922 by a number of the original principals of the North Tonawanda Musical Instrument Works after the Rand interests gained control.

From this time until the late 1920s the firm manufactured a line of band organs, each of which used a compressed air system on the tracker bar. In 1927 and 1928 the Air-Calio, a calliope, was marketed.

After the late 1920s many of the Artizan scales, patterns, and other items apparently passed to the B.A.B. Organ Company. Today, when an Artizan organ is encountered it is often converted to play either B.A.B. or Wurlitzer music. However, it is interesting to note that at one time Wurlitzer did perforate and sell Artizan and North Tonawanda Musical Instrument Works rolls, possibly using equipment salvaged from Artizan after it closed down.

The B.A.B. Organ Company, named for its founders, Messrs. Borna, Antoniazzi, and Brugnolotti, was located in Brooklyn, New York from the 1920s until 1957. The firm repaired and maintained band organs and manufactured folding cardboard music books and paper music rolls. Much of the B.A.B. equipment was acquired by Charles Bovey and moved to his restored Montana mining town, Virginia City.

Earlier, B.A.B. had acquired the assets of Molinari, another New York area firm which specialized in organs, mainly of small sizes.

B.A.B. manufactured a number of standardized 8-holes-per-inch music rolls for use on European organs which had been converted from the original book music system. Some styles of B.A.B. rolls were compatible with organs manufactured by the North Tonawanda Musical Instrument Works and by the Artizan Factories. Today it is sometimes difficult to separate the music systems and formats of the B.A.B., North Tonawanda, and Artizan firms. Remodelling and conversion of many Artizan and North Tonawanda organs to the related B.A.B. system has made identification even more of a problem in many instances.

Generally, Artizan Factories organs operate entirely on air pressure, using pressure-operated unit valves and a pressure roller which holds the paper against the tracker bar. North Tonawanda Musical Instrument Works organs use vacuum-operated valves and need no roller; the original music rolls in nearly all (but there are exceptions) instances are endless. B.A.B. organs which bear the B.A.B. name on the front or which use B.A.B. roll systems are generally organs manufactured by someone else; these use either cardboard music or were converted to B.A.B. roll music using Artizan-style valves and spoolboxes manufactured by B.A.B. The B.A.B. Organ Company possessed certain patterns for casting Artizan components, spoolboxes included.

The B.A.B. Organ Company, as the leading repairer of band organs on the East Coast, acquired much technical data. Many of the Gavioli, Limonaire, Ruth, Gebr. Bruder, and Wilhelm Bruder scales in this book were taken from original scale sticks in the B.A.B. files, which were preserved by the late Charles Bovey and loaned to Art Reblitz.

B.A.B. rolls were apparently identified by the number of holes in the tracker bar of the original organ from which each scale was derived. As time progressed, more functions were added to the margins, but the rolls retained the same number-names for ease of identification. Thus, the B.A.B. 46 roll has 49 holes, the 48 roll has 53 holes, the 66 roll has 67 holes, and so on.

Early B.A.B. rolls were arranged by various individuals. From the 1930s onward most of the B.A.B. popular-tune rolls were the work of J. Lawrence Cook, the noted piano roll arranger. These rolls are characterized by more solos and countermelodies than Wurlitzer rolls of the same era (which were made in North Tonawanda by T.R. Tussing, who acquired the Wurlitzer band organ roll business), with the result that a number of Wurlitzer organs were converted to B.A.B. music. Unfortunately, the B.A.B. music rolls are often characterized by sloppy rhythmic connections between repeated choruses and by note errors. Many collectors today, however, are willing to put up with this sloppiness to get the variety of arranging which is lacking in many Wurlitzer rolls.

The late Charles Bovey compiled some statistics pertaining to B.A.B. rolls, which Art Reblitz has further studied. Results are given herewith.

The Style 46 roll, width 6 5/8", was discontinued in 1957. Roll numbers, with the year of manufacture in parentheses, for the Style 46 roll are given: 2 (1928), 6 (1932), 7 (1933) 8 (1934), 9 (1935), 10 (1936), 12 (1938), 14 (1939), 15 and 16 (1940), 17 (1941), 18 (1942), 19 (1943), 21 (1944), 22 (1945), 23 (1946), 24 (1947), 25 (1948), 26 (1949), 27 (1950), 28 (1951), 29 (1952), 30 (1953), 31 (1954), 32 (1955), 33 and 34 (1956), and 35 (1957).

The Style 48 roll, width 7 1/8", was discontinued in 1957. Roll numbers and dates of manufacture, where known, are: 7 (1936), 8 (1937), 9 (1938), 11 and 12 (1940), 14 (1941), 16 (1943), 17 (1944), 18 (1945), 19 (1946), 20 and 21 (1947), 22 (1948), 24 (1949), 25 (1950), 26 (1951), 27 (1952), 28 (1953), 29 (1954), 30 (1955), 32 (1956), and 33 (1957).

The Style 52 roll, width 7 1/8", was discontinued in 1936 and was replaced by Style 48.

The Style 57 roll, width 8 1/8", was also discontinued in 1936 and was replaced by Style 48.

The Style 61 roll, width 8 1/8", was likewise discontinued in 1936 and replaced by Style 48. Roll numbers and dates of manufacture, where known, are: 8 (1932), 11 (1933), 12 (1934), and 14 (1935).

The Style 65 roll, width 9", was apparently discontinued in 1945.

The Style 66 roll, width 9", was apparently discontinued in 1957. Roll numbers and manufacturing dates, where known, are: 8 (1932), 13 (1933), 14 (1935), 15 and 16 (1936), 17 (1937), 18 (1938), 19 (1939), 20 (1940), 21 and 22 (1941), 23 (1942), 24 (1943), 25 and 26 (1944), 27 and 28 (1945), 29 (1946), 30 (1947), 31 and 32 (1948), 33 and 34 (1949), 35 (1950), 36 and 37 (1951), 38 (1952), 39 (1953), 40 (1954), 41 (1955), 43 (1956), and 44 (1957).

The Style 82 roll, width 11 1/8", was discontinued in 1936 and was replaced by Style 87.

The Style 87 roll, width 11 1/8", was discontinued in 1951. Roll numbers and dates of manufacture, where known, are: 5 (1932), 10 (1933), 11 (1934), 12 (1935), 13 (1936), 14 (1937), 15 (1938), 17 (1940), 18 and 19 (1941), 20 (1942), 21 (1943), 22 and 23 (1944), 24 (1945), 25 (1946), 26 (1947), 27 (1948), 28 (1949), and 29 (1951).

When a roll style was discontinued, an organ using these rolls could be modified to use a replacement or substitute roll of the same width by rearranging the tracker bar tubing. In later years, Oswald Wurdeman, who worked with Charles Bovey, recut many B.A.B. rolls.

B.A.B. 28-HOLE BAND ORGAN ROLL; UNKNOWN STYLE

1 Play
2 ?
3 ?
4 ?
5 E
6 F
7 F#
8 G
9 A
10 B
11 C
12 C#
_____
13 d
14 e
15 f
16 f#
17 g?
18 a?
19 b?
20 c
21 c#
22 d
23 e
24 f
25 f#?
26 g?
27 a?
28 Rewind

B.A.B. 48-HOLE BAND ORGAN ROLL: UNKNOWN STYLE

5 Trombone notes
5 Bass notes
9 Accompaniment notes
14 Melody notes
13 Trumpet notes

1 Bass drum
2 Snare drum
3 to 7, Trombone G, C, D, E, F
8 to 12, Bass G, C, D, E, F
13 to 21, Accompaniment G, A, B, C, C#, D, E, F, F#
22 to 35, Melody G, A, A#, B, C, C#, D, E, F, F#, G, A, B, C
36 to 48, Trumpet E, F, F#, G, A, B, C, C#, D, E, F, F#, G

Style "C-2" Military Band—57 Keys
COMPRESSED AIR SYSTEM
PATENTED

*Only ORGAN With Compressed Air System Playing Perforated Paper
Music Rolls Spooled and Endless*

**This Organ is of new and modern design.   Decorations are attractive and made to
meet present day demands**

INSTRUMENTATION:

Basses, open, octave and contra; Wood Trombones; Wood Trumpets; Violin,
Open and Stopped Pipes in accompaniment and melody; 20" Bass Drum; 14"
Snare Drum and Cymbal.   In all 136 sounding instruments.

STOPS:

1 for Trombones, 1 for Trumpets, 1 for Violin Pipes.

DIMENSIONS:

Height 7 feet 4½ inches, Width 9 feet 3½ inches, Depth 3 feet ½ inch including 2" shaft projection.

MUSIC:

2 ten piece spooled rolls or 18 numbers in single or grouped in 3 piece endless
rolls and tester-tuning roll with each instrument.   The endless system we recommend for skating rink work as it permits the same piece of music to be played
indefinitely, thus giving the same time, for an unlimited time for special occasions such as prize competitions, grand march work and exhibition skating.
This instrument can be equipped with 2 Rewind Tracker Frame system to play
continuous music and with 16 bells.

The Artizan Factories, in business during the 1920s, produced several different models of band organs,
one of which is described above. Note that two types of roll systems were offered: the endless style and
the rewind format.

B.A.B. 46 BAND ORGAN ROLL
ARTIZAN STYLE A ROLLS
NORTH TONAWANDA STYLES 137, 138, 146, 155, 156, 158, 159
6 5/8" wide, spaced 8 holes per inch

    3 Trombone notes
    5 Bass notes
    9 Accompaniment notes
    14 Melody notes
    13 Trumpet notes

1 Shutoff
2 Bass drum
3 Snare drum
4 to 6, Trombone G, C, D
7 to 11, Bass G, C, D, E, F
12 to 20, Accompaniment G, A, B, C, C#, D, E, F, F#
21 to 34, Melody G, A, A#, B, C, C#, D, E, F, F#, G, A, B, C
35 to 47, Trumpet E, F, F#, G, A, B, C, C#, D, E, F, F#, G
48 Rewind
49 Play

B.A.B. 48 (52) BAND ORGAN ROLL
NORTH TONAWANDA STYLES 164, 173, 182, 184
7 1/8" wide; spaced 8 holes per inch

    3 Trombone notes
    3 Bass notes
    8 or 9 Accompaniment notes
    16 Melody notes
    15 Trumpet notes

1 Shutoff
2 Bass drum
3 Snare drum
4 to 6, Trombone G, C, D,
7 to 9, Bass G, C, D
10 to 18, Accompaniment G, A, B, C, D, E, F, F#, G
19 to 34, Melody G, A, B, C, C#, D, E, F, F#, G, A, B, C, C#, D, E
35 to 49, Trumpet C, D, E, F, F#, G, A, B, C, C#, D, E, F, F#, G
50 Bells on
51 Play
52 Bells off
53 Rewind

Some rolls and organs do not use hole 18, accompaniment high G. The Style 48 roll has holes 1-49; the Style 52 roll has all 53 holes.

B.A.B. (57) 61 BAND ORGAN ROLL
ARTIZAN STYLE D
NORTH TONAWANDA STYLES 186, 188, 191, 192, 194, 198

    5 Trombone notes
    5 Bass notes
    9 Accompaniment notes
    16 Melody notes
    15 Trumpet notes

1 Blank (if present)
2 Shutoff
3 Bass drum
4 Snare drum
5 to 9, Trombone G, C, D, E, F
10 to 14, Bass G, C, D, E, F
15 to 23, Accompaniment G, A, B, C, C#, D, E, F, F#
24 to 39, Melody G, A, B, C, C#, D, E, F, F#, G, A, B, C, C#, D, E
40 to 54, Trumpet C, D, E, F, F#, G, A, B, C, C#, D, E, F, G
55 Rewind
56 Play

57 Bells on
58 Bass on
59 Trumpet on
60 Violin pipes on
61 General cancel
62 Cymbal
63 and 64, Blank (if present)

An original Wurlitzer Company (sic) scale stick indicates that the 61-key Artizan uses holes 2 to 63 of the above scale, and that a 52-key Artizan organ uses holes 1 to 55, with hole 1 being "play."

B.A.B. 66 BAND ORGAN ROLL
9" wide; spaced 8 holes per inch

    6 Bass notes
    10 Accompaniment notes
    21 Melody notes
    14 Countermelody notes

0 Shutoff
1 Bass drum
2 Snare drum
3 Snare drum
4 to 9, Bass C, D, E, F, G, A
10 to 19, Accompaniment G, A, A#, B, C, C#, D, E, F, F#
20 to 40, Melody G-D, E
41 to 54, Countermelody F-D, E-G (baritone, clarinet)
55 Band leader
56 General cancel
57 Trombone on
58 Play
59 Rewind
60 Bells on (M)
61 Celeste on (M)
62 Violin pipes on (M)
63 Flute on (M)
64 Piccolo on (M)
65 Trumpet or baritone on (CM)
66 Swell shades open

B.A.B. 66-HOLE BAND ORGAN ROLL; UNKNOWN STYLE

1 to 48, Holes the same as "B.A.B. 48" roll
49 "Picla"(?)
50 "X"
51 Loud
52 "X"
53 Bells
54 Band leader
55 General cancel
56 Trombone on
57 Play
58 Rewind
59 Bells on?
60 Celeste on?
61 Violin pipes on
62 Flute on
63 Piccolo on
64 B C (?)
65 Swell shades open
66 ?

This seems to be a hybrid composed of parts of the style 48 and 66 B.A.B. rolls.

B.A.B. 82 BAND ORGAN ROLL
ARTIZAN STYLE E
NORTH TONAWANDA STYLES E, 1100, 1110
11 1/8" wide; spaced 8 holes per inch

       8 Trombone notes
       8 Bass notes
     11 Accompaniment notes
     18 Melody notes
     13 Piccolo notes
     21 Trumpet notes

1 Play
2 Shutoff
3 Bass drum
4 Snare drum
5 to 12, Trombone G, A, A#, B, C, D, E, F
13 to 20, Bass G, A, A#, B, C, D, E, F
21 to 31, Accompaniment G, A, A#, B, C, C#, D, E, F, F#, G
32 to 49, Melody G, A, A#, B, C, C#, D, E, F, F#, G, A, A#,
   B, C, C#, D, E
50 to 62, Piccolo F, F#, G, A, A#, B, C, C#, D, E, F, F#, G
63 to 83, Trumpet G, A, A#, B, C, C#, D, E, F, F#, G, A,
   A#, B, C, C#, D, E, F, F#, G
84 Band leader
85 Bell ringer
86 Bells (chain perforation)
87 Rewind

B.A.B. 87 BAND ORGAN ROLL
11 1/8" wide; spaced 8 holes per inch

       8 Bass notes
     10 Accompaniment notes
     17 Melody notes
     17 Piccolo notes
     18 Countermelody notes

1 Rewind
2 Play
3 Bass drum
4 Snare drum
5 Snare drum
6 Tambourine
7 to 14, Bass F, G, A, A#, B, C, D, E
15 Trombone on
16 General cancel
17 to 26, Accompaniment G, A, A#, B, C, C#, D, E, F, F#
27 Clarinet on (M)
28 Violin on (M)
29 Piccolo and flute on (M)
30 to 46, Melody G to B
47 to 63, Piccolo C-D, E, F
64 Viola on (CM)
65 Cello on (CM)
66 Saxophone on (CM)
67 Trumpet on (CM)
68 Swell shades open
69 to 86, Countermelody C-D, E, F, F#
87 Bells on (M)

   The melody and piccolo sections overlap. This roll layout was
modified from an original Gavioli cardboard layout and was used
on Gaviolis converted by B.A.B. to play rolls. With the right
musical arrangements this style of roll comes closer to the
original "Gavioli sound" than any other American-made roll.

Style 100 and 1100 band organ, circa 1912, made by the North
Tonawanda Musical Instrument Works.

View of the North Tonawanda Musical Instrument Works factory.
In later years this structure was used to make Victor office
machines.

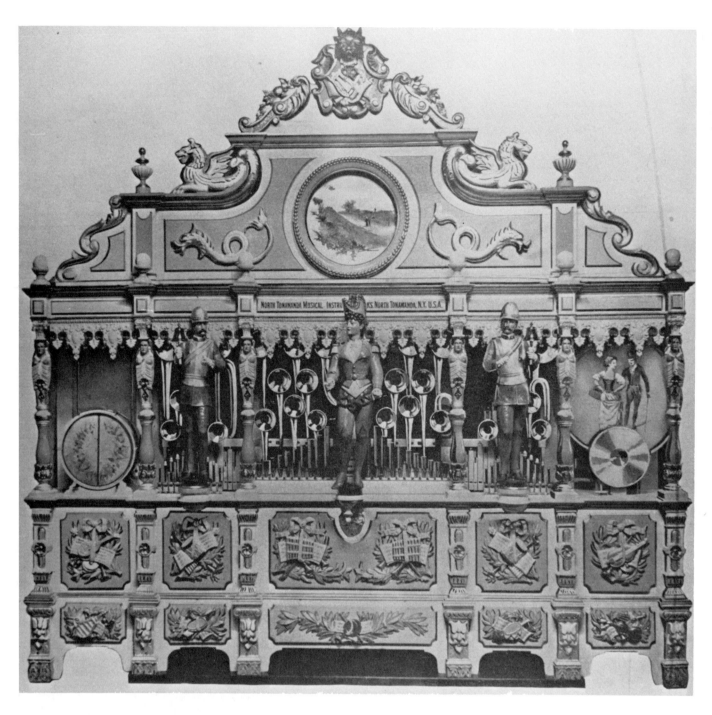

Above: The North Tonawanda Musical Instrument Works (not to be confused with the North Tonawanda Barrel Organ Factory of somewhat similar name), founded in 1906, produced many different styles of band organs, including the Grand Military Band Organ No. 316 shown here. Operated by a pinned cylinder, the instrument had 100 keys which operated many pipes and percussion effects.

Left: A North Tonawanda Style 56 (cylinder operated) or 156 (roll operated) band organ is shown at the center of a No. 1 Riding Gallery made by the Herschell-Spillman Co., also of North Tonawanda, and featuring 24 horses, 4 chariots, and many folding chairs mounted on a 40' diameter platform. Herschell-Spillman featured North Tonawanda Musical Instrument Works and Wurlitzer organs in its catalogues. (Photographs courtesy of Staples & Charles)

North Tonawanda Musical Instrument Works Style 92 (with cylinder operation) or Style 192 (with paper rolls) band organ. 52-keys. 8'9'' wide by 7'9'' high by 2'9'' deep. With four registers for piccolos, clarionettes, trumpets, and trombones. This style was mostly used in roller skating rinks. Indeed, skating rinks seem to have been the main area for sales of the North Tonawanda Musical Instrument Works at the time (circa 1908-1914), for much of the sales literature of the firm is oriented in this direction. Merry-go-rounds were also a good market, but more for instruments with wooden trumpets. Note the rich quartered oak grain in the facade of the above-illustrated organ. A similar instrument is in the Roehl Collection.

BRUDER (GEBR. BRUDER, WILHELM BRUDER'S SONS, ET AL)
Band Organs

Waldkirch, deep in Germany's Black Forest area, was once the world's leading center for band organ manufacturing. The products of the Bruder family and A. Ruth & Son, manufactured there, became famous. In time, the French organ builders, Gavioli and Limonaire, established branches there (which were short-lived). Gebr. Weber, the orchestrion builder, was likewise located in Waldkirch, and the firms of M. Welte & Sons and Imhof & Mukle were in towns a short distance away.

Of all Waldkirch organ makers the foremost family was Bruder. In the 19th century, the Bruder family operated three firms: Gebruder Bruder (Bruder Brothers), Ignaz Bruder's Sons, and Wilhelm Bruder's Sons. The genealogy of the Bruder family is traced in *The Encyclopedia of Automatic Musical Instruments,* to which refer.

Particularly prominent was the firm of Gebr. Bruder. Included in this firm's product line were some of the most ornate instruments made by any firm during the early 20th century; such products as the "Symphony Orchestra Organ," "Elite Orchestra Apollo," and the "Military Symphony Orchestra, Selection." Bruder organs were favorites for use on American carousels, and many were sold in the United States. Some of these bore the name "Columbia" on the facade. A particularly ornate organ, the 94-key "Military Symphony Orchestra, Selection," with over a dozen moving figures on the front was purchased circa 1912 for Feltman's carousel at Coney Island. The cost was reputed to be well over $10,000, an immense figure at the time.

Bruder organs of the 19th century were mostly of the pinned cylinder type. 20th century products were of the keyless type (using folding cardboard music books which were pressed against a tracker bar, of the piano type without protruding metal keys, by rubber rollers) or used paper rolls. The Rudolph Wurlitzer Company imported a number of Gebr. Bruder organs prior to 1914 and sold them under the Wurlitzer Style 165 name (these organs were equipped with Wurlitzer roll frames) as well as other designations. The products of A. Ruth & Son, which were often made by the same facade carvers, are quite similar in external appearance to certain Bruder styles.

41-KEYLESS BRUDER ORGAN SCALE

5 Bass notes
15 Accompaniment notes
17 Melody notes

1 Bass F
2 Key frame key
3 to 6, Bass G, A, C, D
7 Bass drum
8 to 11, Accompaniment (baritone) g, a, a#, b
12 Snare drum
13 Snare drum
14 to 24, Accompaniment (baritone) c, c#, d, e, f, f#, g, g#, a, a#, b
25 to 41, Melody c, c#, d, e, f, f#, g, a, a#, b, c, c#, d, e, f, f#, g

41-KEYLESS WILHELM BRUDER STYLE 78 SCALE
180 mm. wide

4 Bass notes
4 Trombone notes
7 Accompaniment notes
22 Melody notes

1 G (trombone)
2 Bass drum
3 D (trombone)
4 d (2nd octave melody)
5 d (accompaniment)
6 g (2nd octave melody)
7 c (accompaniment)
8 c (1st octave melody)
9 a# (1st octave melody)
10 f (1st octave melody)
11 e (1st octave melody; lowest note)
12 a (1st octave melody)
13 b (1st octave melody)
14 b (accompaniment)
15 f# (2nd octave melody)
16 c# (accompaniment)
17 c# (2nd octave melody)
18 C (trombone)
19 Snare drum
20 F (trombone)
21 Registers loud
22 F (bass)
23 G (bass)
24 e (3rd octave melody)
25 b (2nd octave melody)
26 a (2nd octave melody)
27 e (2nd octave melody; lowest note)
28 c# (1st octave melody)
29 a (accompaniment)
30 f# (1st octave melody)
31 g (accompaniment; lowest note)
32 g (1st octave melody)
33 a# (accompaniment)
34 d (1st octave melody)
35 f (2nd octave melody)
36 a# (2nd octave melody)
37 c (2nd octave melody)
38 f (3rd octave melody)
39 D (bass)
40 C (bass)
41 Registers soft

42-KEYLESS GEBR. BRUDER ORGAN SCALE
7¾" wide

     6 Bass notes
    10 Accompaniment notes
    21 Melody notes
    14 Trumpet notes

1 Snare drum
2 D (bass)
3 F (bass)
4 G (bass)
5 Trumpet on (another scale: trumpet off)
6 Registers soft
7 e (2nd octave melody)
8 c# (2nd octave melody)
9 b (2nd octave melody)
10 a (2nd octave melody; trumpet "x")
11 g (2nd octave melody; lowest note; trumpet "x")
12 f (1st octave melody; trumpet "x")
13 d (1st octave melody; trumpet "x")
14 c (1st octave melody; trumpet "x")
15 a# (1st octave melody; trumpet "x")
16 g# (1st octave melody; trumpet "x")
17 f (accompaniment)
18 d (accompaniment)
19 c (accompaniment)
20 a# (accompaniment)
21 g (accompaniment; lowest note)
22 a (accompaniment)
23 b (accompaniment)
24 c# (accompaniment)
25 e (accompaniment)
26 f# (accompaniment)
27 g (1st octave melody; lowest note; trumpet "x")
28 a (1st octave melody; trumpet "x")
29 b (1st octave melody; trumpet "x")
30 c# (1st octave melody; trumpet "x")
31 e (1st octave melody; trumpet "x")
32 f# (1st octave melody; trumpet "x")
33 g# (2nd octave melody; trumpet "x")
34 a# (2nd octave melody)
35 c (2nd octave melody)
36 d (2nd octave melody)
37 f (2nd octave melody)
38 Registers loud (piccolo, trombone)
39 A (bass)
40 E (bass)
41 C (bass)
42 Bass drum and cymbal

  Hole 5 couples trumpet notes (marked trumpet "x") to melody.

  Another 42-keyless Gebr. Bruder scale indicates the following differences: 2 G, 3 C, 4 D, 17 f#, 18 e, 25 d, 26 f, 39 E, 40 A, and 41 C. All other functions are the same.

43-KEYLESS GEBR. BRUDER ORGAN SCALE
43-KEYLESS WILHELM BRUDER'S SONS ORGAN SCALE
43-KEYLESS CARL FREI ORGAN SCALE

198 mm. (7 7/8") wide; paper rolls

     5 Bass notes
    10 Accompaniment notes
    20 Melody notes
    13 Trumpet notes

1 Melody C# (which falls between C and D, holes 30 and 31)
2 Trumpets off
3 Triangle
4 Bass drum and cymbal
5 to 14, Accompaniment G, A, A#, B, C, C#, D, E, F, F#
15 to 33, Melody G, A, A#, B, C, C#, D, E, F, F#, G, G#, A, A#, B, C, D, E, F
34 Registers soft
35 to 39, Bass D, C, A, G, F
40 Rewind
41 Snare drum
42 Wood block
43 Violin pipes off
  Thirteen trumpets, G to A, are coupled to melody holes 15 to 27 when hole 2 is not punched. Some organs only have trombones in the bass. Carl Frei, of Waldkirch, has built many organs using this scale.

VARIATION OF PRECEDING
2 Saxophone
34 Registers loud

ANOTHER VARIATION OF PRECEDING
2 Saxophone on
3 Bass drum and cymbal
4 Cancel 2 and 34
34 Registers loud
41 Snare drum
43 Snare drum

45-KEYLESS BRUDER ORGAN SCALE
Paper rolls 6 9/16" wide

     8 Bass notes
    34 Accompaniment-melody notes

1 Bass drum
2 to 9, Bass C, D, E, F, G, A, A#, B
10 to 13, Accompaniment and melody f, g, a-d, e, f
44 Snare drum
45 Snare drum

PREIS-LISTE

FABRIK-ANSICHT

Preismedaille vom Jahre 1854.

Preismedaille vom Jahre 1856.

der

Orgelfabrik

von

Gebrüder Bruder

WALDKIRCH

BADEN

Lith. & Druck v. Aug. Faller, Waldkirch i/B.

48-KEYLESS WILHELM BRUDER ORGAN SCALE

      7 Bass notes
      5 Trombone notes
   21 Accompaniment, melody, and trumpet notes

1 Registers soft
2 B (bass)
3 f (1st octave trumpet/melody)
4 g (1st octave trumpet/melody)
5 C (bass)
6 D (bass)
7 c (1st octave trumpet/melody)
8 d (1st octave trumpet/melody)
9 e (3rd octave trumpet/melody)
10 c# (2nd octave trumpet/melody)
11 f# (2nd octave trumpet/melody)
12 g# (2nd octave trumpet/melody)
13 a (2nd octave trumpet/melody)
14 g (2nd octave trumpet/melody)
15 c (2nd octave trumpet/melody)
16 d (2nd octave trumpet/melody)
17 d# (1st octave trumpet/melody)
18 c# (1st octave trumpet/melody)
19 G (bass)
20 C (trombone)
21 a (1st octave trumpet/melody)
22 f# (1st octave trumpet/melody)
23 F (bass)
24 G (trombone)
25 g (accompaniment; lowest note)
26 Registers loud
27 e (1st octave trumpet/melody; lowest note)
28 a# (accompaniment)
29 Snare drum
30 Snare drum
31 b (1st octave trumpet/melody)
32 c (accompaniment)
33 A (bass)
34 F (3rd octave trumpet/melody)
35 f (2nd octave trumpet/melody)
36 d (accompaniment)
37 c# (accompaniment)
38 a# (2nd octave trumpet/melody)
39 b (2nd octave trumpet/melody)
40 D (trombone)
41 b (accompaniment)
42 e (2nd octave trumpet/melody; lowest note)
43 E (bass)
44 A (trombone)
45 a (accompaniment)
46 a# (1st octave trumpet/melody)
47 Bass drum
48 F (trombone)

The scale stick indicates that trumpets play from octave 1 e through octave 2 f, and violins play from octave 2 f# through octave 3 f. The melody might actually run from octave 1 e through octave 3 f, with the trumpets playing from the melody section when their register is turned on by the "registers loud" key.

Note: Some of the scale sticks examined during the preparation of this book, especially the scrambled scales of Ruth, Bruder, and others, were made be experienced arrangers who knew every detail of the organs by memory and did not mark each note as to its section of pipes in the organ. In particular, the divisions between accompaniment, low violin (cello), and melody sections, and the notes to which trumpets were sometimes coupled in these sections, were not indicated on some scales. In this book, such scales are printed with the notes arranged into octaves, with "1st octave" referring to the lowest octave of notes. Examination of an actual organ will show exactly which notes belong to which group of pipes and which trumpet notes are coupled.

52-KEYLESS GEBR. BRUDER MODEL 107 ORGAN SCALE
(Right to left)
238 mm. wide paper roll

     5 Bass notes
   10 Accompaniment notes
   15 Melody notes
   14 Trumpet notes (7 of which are coupled to cello)

1 Snare drum, single stroke. First beater
2 Triangle
3 Snare drum, single stroke. Second beater
4 G (bass)
5 G (trumpet; lowest trumpet note)
6 A (bass)
7 Registers soft
8 D (bass)
9 A (trumpet)
10 E (accompaniment; lowest note)
11 F (accompaniment)
12 A# (trumpet)
13 F# (accompaniment)
14 G (accompaniment)
15 A (accompaniment)
16 B (trumpet)
17 A# (accompaniment)
18 B (accompaniment)
19 C (accompaniment)
20 C# (accompaniment)
21 D (accompaniment; highest note)
22 C (trumpet)
23 F (2nd octave melody; highest note)
24 D (2nd octave melody)
25 C (2nd octave melody; lowest note)
26 C# (trumpet)
27 A# (1st octave melody; highest note)
28 G (1st octave melody)
29 F (1st octave melody)
30 D (1st octave melody)
31 C (1st octave melody)
32 C# (1st octave melody)
33 E (1st octave melody)
34 F# (1st octave melody)
35 D (trumpet)
36 A (1st octave melody)
37 B (1st octave melody)
38 C# (2nd octave melody)
39 E (2nd octave melody)
40 B (cello; highest note)
41 A# (cello)
42 A (cello)
43 G (cello)
44 F# (cello)
45 F (cello)
46 E (cello; lowest note)
47 Trumpets off (chain perforation)
48 C (bass)
49 Registers loud
50 F (bass)
51 Bass drum
52 Rewind (variation: band leader)

The preceding scale, with hole 52 used as rewind, is for an instrument which uses paper rolls. Holes 40 through 46 inclusive are also for 7 trumpets, with hole 40 (note B) being the highest trumpet. When hole 47, a chain perforation, appears the trumpets are shut off, thus permitting the 7 cellos to play a countermelody.

Symphonie-Orchester-Orgel „Terpsichore"

Made by Gebr. Bruder around 1912, the Symphony Orchestra Organ "Terpsichore" was one of the firm's best-selling models. Many of these were imported into the United States where they were used on carousels and other public attractions. These were made in 67, 80, and 94-key formats. Certain Bruder organs were sold in the United States under the Columbia name. The catalogue described it as follows: "Pompous facade, baroque style with artistic paintings, very rich gilding. Two dancing groups in sculpture plus three artistic paintings. Rich instrumentation; wonderful tonal shading. Suitable for shows as well as for large dancing and concert locations."

54-KEYLESS WILHELM BRUDER ORGAN SCALE

      4 Bass notes
    11 Accompaniment notes
    20 Melody notes
    13 Trumpet notes

1 E (1st octave melody)
2 Band leader
3 A (2nd octave melody)
4 C (trumpet; lowest note)
5 B (2nd octave melody)
6 Registers loud
7 G# (trumpet)
8 D# (trumpet)
9 F# (2nd octave melody)
10 G (accompaniment)
11 C# (1st octave melody)
12 F (trumpet)
13 A (1st octave melody; lowest note)
14 B (accompaniment)
15 F# (accompaniment)
16 G (trumpet)
17 E (accompaniment)
18 A# (1st octave melody)
19 D (trumpet)
20 A (trumpet)
21 F (2nd octave melody)
22 Snare drum
23 Snare drum
24 D (2nd octave melody)
25 F (bass)
26 A# (2nd octave melody)
27 G (2nd octave melody; lowest note)
28 D (1st octave melody)
29 C# (trumpet)
30 F (1st octave melody)
31 C (bass)
32 C (trumpet)
33 D (accompaniment)
34 C (2nd octave melody)
35 F (accompaniment)
36 B (trumpet)
37 G (high 2nd octave melody)
38 C (1st octave melody)
39 E (trumpet)
40 G (high accompaniment)
41 B (1st octave melody)
42 C (accompaniment)
43 F# (trumpet)
44 A# (accompaniment)
45 E (2nd octave melody)
46 A (accompaniment)
47 C# (2nd octave melody)
48 F (accompaniment; lowest note)
49 A# (trumpet)
50 D (bass)
51 F# (1st octave melody)
52 Bass drum
53 Registers soft
54 G (bass)

56-KEYLESS BRUDER ORGAN SCALE
Paper rolls
(Right to left)

      5 Trombone notes
      6 Bass notes
    11 Accompaniment notes
    20 Melody notes
    11 Trumpet notes

1 See below
2 to 6, Trombone F, G, A, C, D
7 Snare drum
8 See below
9 to 14, Bass G, A, C, D, E, F
15 Registers soft (chain perforation)
16 to 26, Accompaniment G, A, A#, B, C, C#, D, E, F, F#, G
27 Rewind
28 to 32, Melody G#, A, A#, B, C (coupled to high trumpets)
33 Coupled trumpets off
34 to 48, Continuation of Melody C#, D, E, F, F#, G, G#, A, A#, B, C, C#, D, E, F
49 Bass octave coupler (chain perforation)
50 to 55, Low trumpets C, D, E, F, F#, G
56 Bass drum

Hole 1 is punched as a short hole on the first beat of each measure, almost constantly throughout the music, possibly for the control of a bell ringer figure or a band leader. Hole 8 is punched the length of the bass notes, almost constantly throughout the music, possibly for a band leader. Hole 15 turns off a loud quintadena mixture in the accompaniment and melody sections.

59-KEYLESS GEBR. BRUDER ORGAN SCALE
Paper roll

      4 Trombone notes
      6 Bass notes
    12 Accompaniment notes
    18 Melody notes
    11 Trumpet notes

1 ?
2 ?
3 Bass drum
4 ? (percussion?)
5 to 10, Bass G, A, C, D, E, F
11 to 22, Accompaniment G to F#
23 ? (register?)
24 to 41, Melody G to C
42 ? (chain perforation)
43 to 46, Trombone C, D, F, G
47 ? (register?)
48 to 58, Trumpet G to F
59 Snare drum

Holes 23 and 47 might operate a lock and cancel mechanism.

61-KEYLESS WILHELM BRUDER'S SONS ORGAN SCALE
MODEL 61B
261 mm. wide

8 Bass notes
8 Trombone notes
11 Accompaniment notes
28 Melody notes

1 G (bass or trombone)
2 Bass drum and cymbal
3 A# (bass or trombone)
4 Band leader
5 C (bass or trombone)
6 F# (melody 3rd octave)
7 E (bass or trombone)
8 C (melody 2nd octave)
9 A# (melody 2nd octave)
10 C# (accompaniment)
11 E (melody 1st octave)
12 D (melody 1st octave)
13 A (accompaniment)
14 G# (melody 1st octave)
15 F# (melody 1st octave)
16 Registers loud
17 Registers soft
18 G (melody 1st octave)
19 A (melody 1st octave)
20 A# (accompaniment)
21 D# (melody 1st octave)
22 C (accompaniment)
23 A (melody 2nd octave)
24 B (melody 2nd octave)
25 D (bass or trombone)
26 F (melody 3rd octave; lowest note)
27 B (bass or trombone)
28 Snare drum
29 Snare drum
30 A (bass or trombone)
31 F (bass or trombone)
32 F (trombone or bass)
33 A (trombone or bass)
34 B (trombone or bass)
35 D (trombone or bass)
36 G (melody 3rd octave)
37 D# (melody 2nd octave)
38 C# (melody 2nd octave)
39 D (accompaniment)
40 G (melody 2nd octave)
41 F (melody 2nd octave; lowest note)
42 C# (melody 1st octave)
43 B (melody 1st octave)
44 G (accompaniment)
45 F (melody 1st octave; lowest note)
46 F (accompaniment; lowest note)
47 E (accompaniment)
48 F# (accompaniment)
49 A# (melody 1st octave)
50 C (melody 1st octave)
51 B (accompaniment)
52 F# (melody 2nd octave)
53 G# (melody 2nd octave)
54 D# (accompaniment)
55 D (melody 2nd octave)
56 E (melody 2nd octave)
57 A (melody 3rd octave)
58 E (trombone or bass)
59 C (trombone or bass)
60 A# (trombone or bass)
61 G (trombone or bass)

62-KEYLESS WILHELM BRUDER ORGAN SCALE

5 Trombone notes
8 Bass notes
11 Accompaniment notes
19 Melody notes
12 Trumpet notes

1 G (trombone)
2 F (bass)
3 G (bass)
4 A (bass)
5 D# (trumpet)
6 C (accompaniment)
7 C# (accompaniment)
8 G (accompaniment)
9 B (accompaniment)
10 G (high melody)
11 D (high melody)
12 C (high melody)
13 G# (low melody)
14 B (trumpet)
15 C# (low melody)
16 Registers loud
17 Band leader
18 F (low melody)
19 A (low melody)
20 B (low melody)
21 E (high melody)
22 A (high melody)
23 C (low melody)
24 G# (accompaniment)
25 F (accompaniment)
26 E (accompaniment)
27 E (bass)
28 D (bass)
29 Snare drum
30 Snare drum
31 D (trumpet)
32 F (trombone)
33 C (bass)
34 A (trombone)
35 E (trumpet)
36 D (trombone)
37 F# (trumpet)
38 F# (accompaniment)
39 A# (accompaniment)
40 G# (trumpet)
41 F# (high melody)
42 C# (high melody)
43 A# (trumpet)
44 G (low melody)
45 D (low melody)
46 High C (trumpet)
47 Registers soft
48 E (low melody)
49 F# (low melody)
50 A# (low melody)
51 A (trumpet)
52 F (high melody)
53 G (trumpet)
54 A (accompaniment)
55 D (accompaniment)
56 F (trumpet)
57 B (bass)
58 A (bass)
59 C (trombone)
60 C (trumpet)
61 Bass drum, bell ringer, and cymbal
62 Key frame key

Gebr. Bruder Military Symphony Orchestra built in the style of a domed mosque. A number of these were imported into the United States by C.W. Parker (Abilene, Kansas amusement outfitter) and others. "Musical effect of about 25 musicians. Extraordinarily strong military music. Instrumentation consists of trumpets, clarinets, etc., and, if desired, also brass trombones. Rich gilded facade in the Oriental style." 59-keys in size.

Symphonie-Orchester-Orgel „Sirene"

Prachtfassade in Weiß und Glanzvergoldung mit 4 künstlerischen Figuren.

Reiche Orchesterinstrumentierung mit feiner Nuancierung der Toneffekte.

---

59 Tonstufen.　Musikeffekt von annähernd 22 Mann.

67 Tonstufen.　Musikeffekt von annähernd 30 Mann.

80 Tonstufen.　Musikeffekt von annähernd 40 Mann.

80 Tonstufen, mit Glockenspiel (Xylophon).

Musikeffekt von annähernd 42 Mann.

Gebr. Bruder Symphony Orchestra Organ "Sirene," circa 1912. This style was available in 59, 67, and 80-key models representing about 22, 30, and 40 musicians respectively. A contemporary English catalogue of the firm noted that the instrument had a "pompous facade, painted white with bright gilt trim. 4 artistic figures. Instrumentation like a big orchestra with most wonderful tone effects."

Elite-Orchester „Apollo"

Gebr. Bruder Elite Orchestra "Apollo," as shown in a catalogue from the 1912 era. Like most contemporary Gebr. Bruder organs of large size, this facade style was available with chassis of varying size and musical strength: 65 keys, representing an orchestra of 38 musicians; 69 keys, representing 40 men; and 80 keys, representing 56 men.

Dozens of the 69-key size were imported into the United States and were adapted by Wurlitzer to play Wurlitzer Style 165 rolls and were sold as Style 165 Duplex Orchestral Organs. The identical illustration shown above, with a cherub at the top and with two statues on pedestals to the left and right of the center of the facade, was used by Wurlitzer in its early catalogues. Later, when Wurlitzer copied the facades in its North Tonawanda facility, the statues and cherubs were deleted.

In 1912 the Elite Orchestra "Apollo" sold in Germany for 7,200 marks (65-key model), 9,000 marks (69-key model), and 12,000 marks (80-key model). Music books cost 5.7 marks per meter, 6.4 marks, and 8 marks for the three sizes. At the time a German mark was equal to about 20c United States funds.

65-KEYLESS GEBR. BRUDER ORGAN SCALE
"ELITE ORCHESTRA APOLLO"

    6 Bass notes
    10 Accompaniment notes
    22 Melody notes
    14 Trumpet notes

1 Xylophone (or shutoff?)
2 D (bass)
3 F (bass)
4 A (bass)
5 Castanets; snare drum
6 F (trumpet; lowest note)
7 F (accompaniment)
8 G (trumpet)
9 D (accompaniment)
10 A (trumpet)
11 C (accompaniment)
12 B (trumpet)
13 A# (accompaniment)
14 C# (trumpet)
15 G (accompaniment; lowest note)
16 E (trumpet)
17 F# (trumpet)
18 Swell shades open
19 Baritone on
20 Flute on
21 General cancel
22 F (2nd octave melody)
23 D (2nd octave melody)
24 C (2nd octave melody)
25 A# (2nd octave melody)
26 G# (2nd octave melody)
27 F# (1st octave melody)
28 E (1st octave melody)
29 D (1st octave melody)
30 C (1st octave melody)
31 A# (1st octave melody)
32 G# (1st octave melody)
33 G (1st octave melody; lowest note)
34 A (1st octave melody)
35 B (1st octave melody)
36 C# (1st octave melody)
37 D# (1st octave melody)
38 F (1st octave melody)
39 G (2nd octave melody; lowest note)
40 A (2nd octave melody)
41 B (2nd octave melody)
42 C# (2nd octave melody)
43 E (2nd octave melody)
44 Violin pipes on
45 Piccolo on
46 Vox celeste on
47 Forte (trombone) on
48 G (high trumpet)
49 F (high trumpet)
50 A (accompaniment)
51 D (trumpet)
52 B (accompaniment)
53 C (trumpet)
54 C# (accompaniment)
55 A# (trumpet)
56 E (accompaniment)
57 G# (trumpet)
58 F# (accompaniment)
59 F# (trumpet)
60 Triangle; bass drum
61 G (bass)
62 E (bass)
63 C (bass)
64 Band leader
65 Bells on

The melody section contains violin pipes, vox celeste, flute, and bells. The trumpet (or countermelody) section contains saxophone (baritone) and cornet.

In the early years before World War I cut off imports from Germany (in 1914), the Rudolph Wurlitzer Co. imported a number of Gebr. Bruder Elite Orchestra Apollo organs into the United States. Regular models were designated as Wurlitzer 165 organs; slightly larger versions were designated as Wurlitzer 166 organs. It is believed that Wurlitzer purchased the chassis (without key frame mechanisms) and facades from Bruder. At North Tonawanda, N.Y., the Wurlitzer 165 roll mechanisms, percussion instruments, and (in some instances) pipes were added. A somewhat similar procedure was followed with the importation from J.D. Philipps of orchestrion chassis which Wurlitzer built cases for, added percussion and pipes, and sold under the Mandolin PianOrchestra name (specifically the instruments listed on pages 681 and 682 of *The Encyclopedia of Automatic Musical Instruments*).

Although the Bruder Elite Orchestra Apollo layout is in different order from the Wurlitzer 165 layout, the note functions are the same. Refer to the Wurlitzer section in this book for more information.

C.W. Parker, carousel manufacturer and amusement park outfitter of Leavenworth and Abilene, Kansas, was a prolific importer of Bruder band organs, including at least several of the Elite Orchestra Apollo models. These, unlike those sold by Wurlitzer under the Style 165 label, used Bruder music systems.

Elite-Orchester „Apollo".

Diese Werke vereinigen in ihrer Zusammensetzung sämtliche Instrumente eines großen, modernen Künstlerorchesters nebst vollständigem Schlagzeug, als Pauke, große Trommel, Becken, Kastagnetten, sowie Roulier-Trommel, Glockenspiel (Xylophon), oder Mandoline bezw. Harfe. Zur Erhöhung des Musikeffektes ist das Werk mit automatisch funktionierenden Schwelljalousien versehen, wodurch der seelische Eindruck der Musik ungemein erhöht wird.

Die Fassade ist in Weiß und Gold gehalten, mit hervorragender Bildhauerarbeit und 6 Kunstfiguren, wovon bei dem Modell 106 Tonstufen 3 überlebensgroß.

---

69 Tonstufen.   Musikeffekt von annähernd 45 Mann.

80 Tonstufen.   Musikeffekt von annähernd 60 Mann.

106 Tonstufen.   Musikeffekt von annähernd 80 Mann.

Gebr. Bruder Elite Orchestra "Apollo," one of several styles bearing this name. Made in 69, 80, and 106-key sizes. "On the 106-key model three of the statues are life-size."

67-KEYLESS GEBR. BRUDER ORGAN SCALE "No. 103"

7 Trombone notes
6 Bass notes
34 Accompaniment-melody notes
13 Trumpet notes

1 Band leader
2 Bass drum
3 C (trombone)
4 F (trombone)
5 A (trombone)
6 C (bass)
7 D (bass)
8 G (first octave trumpet; lowest note)
9 E (bass)
10 F (1st octave accompaniment-melody; lowest note)
11 A# (1st octave trumpet)
12 F# (1st octave accompaniment-melody)
13 G (1st octave accompaniment-melody)
14 G# (1st octave accompaniment-melody)
15 C (1st octave trumpet)
16 A (1st octave accompaniment-melody)
17 A# (1st octave accompaniment-melody)
18 B (1st octave accompaniment-melody)
19 C# (1st octave trumpet)
20 C (1st octave accompaniment-melody)
21 C# (1st octave accompaniment-melody)
22 D (1st octave accompaniment-melody)
23 D (1st octave trumpet)
24 E (3rd octave accompaniment-melody)
25 C# (3rd octave accompaniment-melody)
26 B (3rd octave accompaniment-melody)
27 E (1st octave trumpet)
28 A (3rd octave accompaniment-melody)
29 G (3rd octave accompaniment-melody)
30 F (3rd octave accompaniment-melody; lowest note)
31 F (1st octave trumpet)
32 D (2nd octave accompaniment-melody)
33 C (2nd octave accompaniment-melody)
34 C# (2nd octave accompaniment-melody)
35 E (2nd octave accompaniment-melody)
36 F# (1st octave trumpet)
37 F# (3rd octave accompaniment-melody)
38 G# (3rd octave accompaniment-melody)
39 A# (3rd octave accompaniment-melody)
40 G (1st octave trumpet)
41 C (3rd octave accompaniment-melody)
42 D (3rd octave accompaniment-melody)
43 A (2nd octave trumpet)
44 B (2nd octave accompaniment-melody)
45 A# (2nd octave accompaniment-melody)
46 A (2nd octave accompaniment-melody)
47 B (2nd octave trumpet)
48 G# (2nd octave accompaniment-melody)
49 G (2nd octave accompaniment-melody)
50 F# (2nd octave accompaniment-melody)
51 B (1st octave trumpet)
52 F (2nd octave accompaniment-melody; lowest note)
53 E (1st octave accompaniment-melody)
54 D# (1st octave accompaniment-melody)
55 A (1st octave trumpet)
56 A (bass)
57 G (bass)
58 Registers soft
59 F (bass)
60 G (trombone)
61 F# (trombone)
62 Registers loud
63 E (trombone)
64 Trombone
65 D (trombone)
66 Snare drum
67 Bell ringers?

70-KEYLESS WILHELM BRUDER ORGAN SCALE

8 Trombone notes
9 Bass notes
33 Accompaniment and melody notes
13 Trumpet notes

1 G (trombone)
2 C (trumpet; lowest note)
3 A# (trombone)
4 C# (trumpet)
5 C (trombone)
6 F (trumpet)
7 E (trombone)
8 Triangle
9 C# (1st octave accompaniment-melody)
10 G (1st octave accompaniment-melody)
11 B (1st octave accompaniment-melody)
12 A (trumpet)
13 F (3rd octave accompaniment-melody)
14 B (trumpet)
15 B (2nd octave accompaniment-melody)
16 G (2nd octave accompaniment-melody)
17 F (2nd octave accompaniment-melody)
18 Registers loud
19 Registers soft
20 F# (2nd octave accompaniment-melody)
21 G# (2nd octave accompaniment-melody)
22 C (3rd octave accompaniment-melody; lowest note)
23 E (3rd octave accompaniment-melody)
24 A (3rd octave accompaniment-melody)
25 D (2nd octave accompaniment-melody)
26 A# (1st octave accompaniment-melody)
27 F# (1st octave accompaniment-melody)
28 F (1st octave accompaniment-melody)
29 D# (1st octave accompaniment-melody)
30 D (1st octave accompaniment-melody)
31 Snare drum
32 Snare drum
33 E (bass)
34 D (bass)
35 C (bass)
36 F (trombone)
37 D (trumpet)
38 A (trombone)
39 E (trumpet)
40 B (trombone)
41 F# (trumpet)
42 D (trombone)
43 E (1st octave accompaniment-melody)
44 G# (trumpet)
45 G# (1st octave accompaniment-melody)
46 C (2nd octave accompaniment-melody; lowest note)
47 A# (trumpet)
48 F# (3rd octave accompaniment-melody)
49 D (3rd octave accompaniment-melody)
50 A# (2nd octave accompaniment-melody)
51 C (high) (trumpet)
52 E (2nd octave accompaniment-melody)
53 Band leader
54 D# (2nd octave accompaniment-melody)
55 D (high) (trumpet)
56 A (2nd octave accompaniment-melody)
57 C# (3rd octave accompaniment-melody)
58 D# (3rd octave accompaniment-melody)
59 G (3rd octave accompaniment-melody)
60 C# (2nd octave accompaniment-melody)
61 A (1st octave accompaniment-melody)
62 G (trumpet)
63 C (1st octave accompaniment-melody; lowest note)
64 B (bass)
65 A# (bass)
66 A (bass)
67 G (bass)
68 F# (bass)
69 F (bass)
70 Bass drum

76-KEYLESS GEBR. BRUDER ORGAN SCALE

The 76-keyless Gebr. Bruder scale is the same as the 80-keyless Gebr. Bruder scale (to which refer), except that holes 1, 2, 79, and 80 are omitted.

80-KEYLESS GEBR. BRUDER ORGAN SCALE

      7 Trombone notes
    11 Bass notes
    18 Accompaniment and low violin notes
    19 Melody notes
    14 Trumpet notes

1 Xylophone off
2 Band leader
3 Bass drum
4 C (trombone)
5 F (trombone)
6 G (trombone)
7 A (trombone)
8 A (bass)
9 A# (bass)
10 A (trumpet)
11 B (bass)
12 C (bass)
13 C# (bass)
14 B (trumpet)
15 D (bass)
16 D# (bass)
17 E (accompaniment; lowest note)
18 C# (trumpet)
19 F (accompaniment)
20 F# (accompaniment)
21 G (accompaniment)
22 E (trumpet)
23 G# (accompaniment)
24 A (accompaniment)
25 A# (accompaniment)
26 B (accompaniment)
27 F (trumpet)
28 Flute on
29 F (high melody)
30 D (high melody)
31 F# (trumpet)
32 C (high melody)
33 A# (high melody)
34 G# (melody)
35 G (high trumpet)
36 F# (melody)
37 E (melody)
38 D (melody)
39 C (melody)
40 G# (high trumpet)
41 A# (melody; lowest note)
42 B (melody)
43 C# (melody)
44 D# (melody)
45 A (high trumpet)
46 F (melody)
47 G (melody)
48 A (high melody)
49 B (high melody)
50 A# (high trumpet)
51 C# (high melody)
52 E (high melody)
53 Violin pipes on
54 D (trumpet)
55 A (low violin)
56 G# (low violin)
57 G (low violin)
58 F# (low violin)
59 C (trumpet)

60 F (low violin)
61 E (low violin)
62 D# (low violin)
63 D (low violin)
64 A# (trumpet)
65 C# (low violin)
66 C (low violin; lowest note)
67 G# (bass)
68 G (trumpet; lowest note)
69 Registers soft
70 G (bass)
71 F (bass)
72 Registers loud
73 F# (trombone)
74 D (trombone)
75 Snare drum
76 E (bass)
77 E (trombone)
78 Snare drum
79 Bell ringers
80 Xylophone on

80-KEYLESS GEBR. BRUDER ORGAN SCALE
No. 2

10 Bass notes
14 Accompaniment notes
23 Melody notes
20 Trumpet notes

1 D (bass)
2 F (bass)
3 G (bass)
4 A (bass)
5 B (bass)
6 Snare drum
7 Castanets
8 Swell shades open
9 C (1st octave trumpet; lowest note)
10 F (high accompaniment)
11 D (1st octave trumpet)
12 D# (accompaniment)
13 E (1st octave trumpet)
14 C# (accompaniment)
15 F# (1st octave trumpet)
16 B (accompaniment)
17 G# (1st octave trumpet)
18 A (accompaniment)
19 A# (1st octave trumpet)
20 G (accompaniment)
21 C (2nd octave trumpet; lowest note)
22 D (2nd octave trumpet)
23 F (accompaniment; lowest note)
24 E (2nd octave trumpet)
25 F# (2nd octave trumpet)
26 Piston on
27 Trompette on
28 Flute on
29 General cancel
30 F (2nd octave melody)
31 D# (2nd octave melody)
32 C# (2nd octave melody)
33 B (2nd octave melody)
34 A (2nd octave melody)
35 G (2nd octave melody; lowest note)
36 F (1st octave melody)
37 D# (1st octave melody)
38 C# (1st octave melody)
39 B (1st octave melody)
40 A (1st octave melody)
41 G (1st octave melody; lowest note)
42 G# (1st octave melody)
43 A# (1st octave melody)
44 C (1st octave melody)
45 D (1st octave melody)
46 E (1st octave melody)
47 F# (1st octave melody)
48 G# (2nd octave melody)
49 A# (2nd octave melody)
50 C (2nd octave melody)
51 D (2nd octave melody)
52 E (2nd octave melody)
53 Violin pipes on
54 Piccolo on
55 Clarinet and cello on
56 Bombardon or. (trombone)
57 G (2nd octave trumpet)
58 F (2nd octave trumpet)
59 F# (accompaniment)
60 D# (2nd octave trumpet)
61 C# (2nd octave trumpet)
62 G# (accompaniment)
63 B (1st octave trumpet)
64 A# (accompaniment)
65 A (1st octave trumpet)
66 C (accompaniment)
67 G (1st octave trumpet)
68 D (accompaniment)
69 F (1st octave trumpet)
70 E (accompaniment)
71 D# (1st octave trumpet)
72 F# (high accompaniment)
73 C# (1st octave trumpet)
74 Triangle
75 Bass drum
76 A# (bass)
77 G# (bass)
78 F# (bass)
79 E (bass)
80 C (bass)

Gebr. Bruder Military Symphony Orchestra "Selection" organ, circa 1912. "Automatic instrument with 94 keys. Extraordinary effect. This instrument represents a complete military band of 15 men. These figures are dressed in real cloth coats and handle their instruments in the most natural manner with the music so that people think they see a living band, the more so as the musicians move their heads and eyes. The organ is supplied with all of the orchestra instruments and plays from the very soft piano to the most powerful fortissimo the most difficult compositions. Baroque facade, painted white and gold, with rich sculptures and four statues. Musical effect of about 80 musicians."

One of these was shipped to Coney Island, New York and was used on Feltman's carousel for many years. The above illustration, from a Gebr. Bruder catalogue, shows that identical instrument. The cartouche below the bandmaster has been photographically retouched to show a spray of flowers. On the original instrument the carved incised inscription "Gebr. Bruder, Waldkirch i/B Germany" appears (see unretouched photograph of the same instrument on the next two pages). "i/B" in the signature means "in Breisgau." Breisgau is the Black Forest district in which Waldkirch is located.

With a price of 38,880 German marks, this model was the most expensive in the Gebr. Bruder catalogue. Music books cost 8 marks per meter.

94-KEYLESS GEBR. BRUDER ORGAN SCALE
MILITARY SYMPHONY ORCHESTRA "SELECTION"

9 Trombone notes
10 Bass notes
12 Accompaniment notes
32 Melody notes
20 Trumpet notes

1 Xylophone off (or bells on)
2 Band leader (or animated figures on)
3 Bass drum
4 C (trombone)
5 F (trombone)
6 A (trombone)
7 G (trombone)
8 B (trombone)
9 D (bass)
10 D (1st octave trumpet)
11 F (bass)
12 G (bass)
13 F (1st octave trumpet)
14 A (bass)
15 A# (bass)
16 B (bass)
17 G (1st octave trumpet)
18 C (accompaniment; lowest note)
19 C# (accompaniment)
20 D (accompaniment)
21 A (1st octave trumpet)
22 D# (accompaniment)
23 E (accompaniment)
24 F (accompaniment)
25 B (1st octave trumpet)
26 F# (accompaniment)
27 G (accompaniment)
28 G# (accompaniment)
29 C# (2nd octave trumpet)
30 A (accompaniment)
31 A# (accompaniment)
32 B (accompaniment)
33 D# (2nd octave trumpet)
34 Flutes on; violins off
35 F# (3rd octave melody)
36 F (2nd octave trumpet)
37 E (3rd octave melody)
38 D (3rd octave melody)
39 G (2nd octave trumpet)
40 C (3rd octave melody; lowest note)
41 A# (2nd octave melody)
42 G# (2nd octave melody)
43 A (2nd octave trumpet)
44 F# (2nd octave melody)
45 E (2nd octave melody)
46 D (2nd octave melody)
47 G# (2nd octave trumpet)
48 C (2nd octave melody; lowest note)
49 A# (1st octave melody)
50 B (1st octave melody)
51 F# (2nd octave trumpet)
52 C# (2nd octave melody)
53 D# (2nd octave melody)
54 F (2nd octave melody)
55 E (2nd octave trumpet)
56 G (2nd octave melody)
57 A (2nd octave melody)
58 B (2nd octave melody)
59 D (2nd octave trumpet)
60 C# (3rd octave melody)
61 D# (3rd octave melody)
62 C (2nd octave trumpet; lowest note)
63 F (3rd octave melody)
64 G (3rd octave melody)
65 Flutes off; violins on
66 A# (1st octave trumpet)
67 A (1st octave melody)
68 G# (1st octave melody)
69 G (1st octave melody)
70 G# (1st octave trumpet)

71 F# (1st octave melody)
72 F (1st octave melody)
73 E (1st octave melody)
74 D# (1st octave melody)
75 F# (1st octave trumpet)
76 D (1st octave melody)
77 C# (1st octave melody)
78 C (1st octave melody; lowest note)
79 E (1st octave trumpet)
80 G# (bass)
81 F# (bass)
82 E (bass)
83 C (1st octave trumpet; lowest note)
84 C (bass)
85 Registers soft (trumpet off)
86 A# (trombone)
87 F# (trombone)
88 Snare drum I
89 Registers loud (trumpet on)
90 D (trombone)
91 E (trombone)
92 Snare drum II
93 Triangle (or animated figures off)
94 Xylophone on (or bells off)

A Gebr. Bruder Military Symphony Orchestra "Selection" being restored for Q. David Bowers by Ron Cappel has holes 2 and 93 control the 15 animated musician figures on the front. The figures themselves are operated by a complex series of rods and cranks. As it is important that the eyes, arms, etc, of the musicians move only when music is actually playing, hole 2 is punched as the music begins, and hole 93 is punched as it ends; thus the musician figures do not move when blank areas of the book (such as before the beginning and after the end of a melody) are passing through the keyless frame. Apparently 94-key Bruder organs of at least one other style were made; presumably, these did not have animated figures and used holes 2 and 93 (as well as certain others) for different purposes.

Analysis of the 94-keyless Military Symphony Orchestra "Selection"

MELODY	BASS
8' Stopped Flute	8' Stopped flute
	4' Cello
Flute register:	4' Stopped flute
2' Piccolo	
4' Open flute	
4' Harmonic flute	TRUMPET
Violin register:	8' Stopped flute
8' Violin celeste	8' Wooden trumpet
8' Violin unison	
8' Trumpet	Forte register:
	8' Brass trumpet
Forte register:	
2' Open flute	TROMBONE
2 2/3' Open flute	
4' Open flute	8' Wooden trombone

ACCOMPANIMENT

8' Stopped flute
8' Cello

REGISTER KEY NUMBERS
Bells: 1 on / 94 off
Flute: 34 on / 65 off
Forte register:
Violin: 34 off / 65 on
1 3/5' Open flute
Piano: 85
2' Open flute
Forte: 89
2 2/3' Open flute
4' Open flute

The organ contains a total of 426 pipes.

ARTHUR BURSENS
Dance Organs

From a workshop and warehouse in Hoboken, a suburb of Antwerp, Belgium, Arthur Bursens and his partner, Frans de Groof, produced hundreds of dance organs, fairground organs, and street organs. Most famous today are the roll-operated Arburo (from ARthur BURsens) dance organs and the book-operated Ideal dance organs. Most of these display brightly painted Art Deco or other modern styling and are often decorated with an accordion, saxophone (particularly Ideal organs), and percussion instruments displayed where they can be seen as they play.

38-KEY BURSENS ORGAN SCALE
14 cm. wide

8 Bass notes
12 Accompaniment notes
15 Melody notes

1 Bass drum and cymbal
2 to 9, Bass G, A, A#, B, C, D, E, F
10 Snare drum
11 to 22, Accompaniment G to F#
23 Snare drum
24 to 38, Melody G to A

52-KEY BURSENS ORGAN SCALE
19.5 cm. wide

8 Bass notes
12 Accompaniment notes
22 Melody notes

1 General cancel
2 Registers loud
3 Violin pipes on (M)
4 to 11, Bass C, D, E, F, G, A, A# B
12 Flute on (or trumpet) (M)
13 to 24, Accompaniment G to F#
25 Bourdon on (M)
26 to 47, Melody G to E
48 Snare drum
49 Bass drum and cymbal
50 Snare drum
51 Key frame key?
52 Band leader

64-KEY BURSENS ORGAN SCALE

8 Bass notes
9 Accompaniment notes
16 Countermelody notes
19 Melody notes

1 General register
2 Register?
3 Register?
4 to 11, Bass
12 to 20, Accompaniment
21 to 36, Countermelody
37 Tremolo on
38 to 56, Melody
57 Violin pipes on (M)?
58 Cello on (CM)?
59 Violin celeste on (CM)?
60 Bass drum
61 Snare drum
62 Jazz flute on (M)
63 Snare drum
64 Shutoff?

68-KEY BURSENS ORGAN SCALE
24.5 cm. wide

8 Bass notes
10 Accompaniment notes
16 Countermelody notes
19 Melody notes

1 General cancel
2 Registers loud
3 Clarinet on (M)
4 to 11, Bass G, A, A#, B, C, D, E, F
12 to 21, Accompaniment G-D, E, F
22 to 37, Countermelody C, D, E, F-F
38 Melody tremolo on
39 to 57, Melody G, A, G, C-C, C#, D, E
58 Violin pipes on (M)
59 Cello on (CM)
60 Vox celeste on (CM)
61 Bass drum
62 Wood block; or, if 2 is punched, snare drum
63 Jazz flute on (M)
64 Wood block; or, if 2 is punched, snare drum
65 Shutoff
66 Jazz flute tremolo
67 Accordion on
68 Saxophone on (CM)

68-KEY BURSENS STREET ORGAN SCALE
24.5 cm. wide

       8 Bass notes
      10 Accompaniment notes
      22 Melody notes
      17 Countermelody notes

1 Bass drum
2 General cancel
3 Violin pipes on
4 to 11, Bass C, D, E, F, G, A, A#, B
12 to 21, Accompaniment G, A, A#, B, C, C#, D, E, F, F#
22 Vox celeste on
23 Registers loud
24 Bourdon on
25 to 46, Melody G to E
47 Trumpet on
48 Cello on
49 to 65, Countermelody C to E
66 Snare drum
67 Tremolo on
68 Snare drum

69-KEY BURSENS ORGAN SCALE
25 cm. wide

      8 Bass notes
      10 Accompaniment notes
      22 Melody notes
      18 Countermelody notes

1 General cancel
2 Forte register
3 Violin pipes on
4 to 11, Bass C, D, E, F, G, A, A#, B
12 to 21, Accompaniment G, A, A#, B, C, C#, D, E, F, F#
22 Bourdon on
23 to 44, Melody G to E
45 Flute on
46 Cello on
47 to 64, Countermelody C to F
65 Violin celeste on
66 Snare drum
67 Melody tremolo
68 Snare drum
69 Bass drum and cymbal

88-KEYLESS "ARBURO" DANCE ORGAN SCALE
Paper roll 13¾" wide; 26 holes per 10 cm.

1 Temple block 1
2 Temple block 2
3 Temple block 3
4 Tenor drum
5 Tenor drum
6 to 8, Blank
9 Saxophone on (CM)
10 Bass drum
11 Hi-hat cymbal
12 Snare drum (reiterating)
13 Snare drum (brush)
14 Wood block
15 Wood block
16 Crash cymbal
17 to 24, Bass G, A, A#, B, C, D, E, F
25 to 33, Accompaniment G, A-D, E, F
34 to 43, Countermelody C, D, E, F-B

44 Violin pipes on (M)
45 Clarinet on (M)
46 Shutoff
47 Rewind
48 Jazz flute on (M)
49 to 54, Countermelody continued, C to F
55 to 73, Melody G, A, B-D, E
74 Voix celeste on (CM)
75 Cello on
76 General tremolo on
77 Swell shutters open
78 General cancel
79 Blank (or bourdon on)
80 Blank (or unda maris on)
81 Jazz tremolo
82 Accordion off
83 Accordion on (bass, accompaniment, M, CM)
84 Blank
85 Blank (or saxophone on)
86 Blank (or vibratone or piano on)
87 Blank
88 Maracca

   When "accordion on" is punched, other stops are also punched. In small organs having no accordion, these other stops are turned on. In organs with accordion, "accordion on" automatically turns all other stops off.

97-KEY BURSENS ORGAN SCALE
34.5 cm. wide

      12 Bass notes
      12 Accompaniment notes
      18 Countermelody notes
      23 Melody notes

1 General cancel
2 Registers loud or swell shutters open
3 Vibratone on (Melody)
4 Bourdon or trumpet on (M)
5 Jazz flute on (M)
6 Violin pipes on (M)
7 Unda maris on (M)
8 to 19, Bass G to F#
20 Jazz tremolo on
21 Accordion on
22 Tremolo on (M)
23 Clarinet on (M)
24 to 35, Accompaniment G to F#
36 Temple block 1
37 Bourdon or vibratone on (CM)
38 Temple block 2
39 Vox celeste on (CM)
40 Temple block 3
41 Cello on (CM)
42 Temple block 4
43 to 61, Countermelody C to F#
62 to 84, Melody G to F
85 Prestant on (CM)
86 Bass drum
87 Saxophone on (CM)
88 Snare drum brush
89 Hi-hat cymbal
90 Maracca
91 Snare drum
92 Triangle
93 Wood block 1
94 Shutoff
95 Wood block 2
96 Tenor drum (or tympani)
97 Key frame key(?)

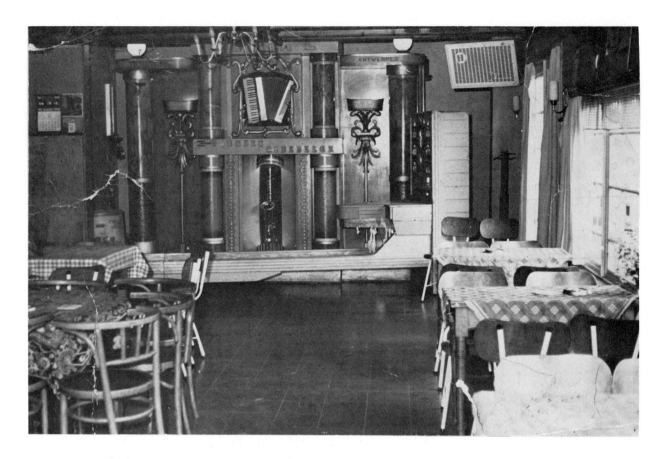

This large Bursens Ideal book-operated dance organ was entertaining patrons in a Belgian cafe in the 1950s as this photograph shows. Today in Belgium dance organs are still to be found in various locations, although many are of the modern electronic style made by Decap.

Interior and exterior views of another Ideal dance organ made by Arthur Bursens. Hundreds of Arburo and Ideal organs, no two of which were precisely alike in configuration or external appearance, were once in service, primarily in Belgium.

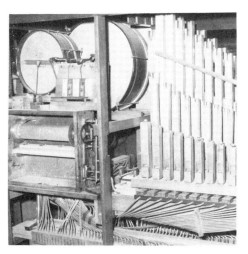

Above: A large Arburo dance organ features an extensive display of visible instruments on the front. Claes O. Friberg is shown standing in front. Left and right: interior views of another Arburo organ. In the late 1960s the firm of Hathaway & Bowers purchased 49 Arburo and Ideal dance organs from Arthur Bursens, who earlier had operated them in various commercial locations. A detailed brochure was prepared to offer these to collectors, but before it could be published word had spread and most were sold!

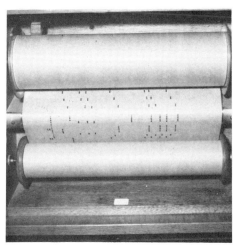

DECAP BROTHERS
Dance Organs

From a factory in Antwerp, Belgium, the Decap Brothers have produced a large variety of dance hall organs. During the 1920s and 1930s a number of loudly-voiced fairground organs were produced, but the main emphasis was on instruments of softer voicing for use in restaurants, dance halls, cafes, and similar locations.

During the 1940s, 1950s, and 1960s Decap produced many dance organs with modern fronts, usually ornamented with exposed functional instruments and changing multi-colored lights. Several of these were very large in size and used 121-key music. Others were quite compact and were of more modest conception. Electronic organ units were featured in many instruments. Today the Decap firm builds key-frame-operated organs which are mostly electronic in nature.

72-KEY DECAP ORGAN SCALE
26 cm. wide

        8 Bass notes
        9 Accompaniment notes
        16 Melody notes
        16 Countermelody notes

1 to 8, Bass C, D, E, F, G, A, A#, B
9 to 17, Accompaniment F, G, A, A#, B, C, C#, D, E
18 to 33, Countermelody E to G
34 to 49, Melody C-D, E
50 General cancel
51 Violin pipes on (M)
52 Jazz flute on (M)
53 Vibratone on (M)
54 Vox celeste on (CM)
55 Saxophone on (CM)
56 Accordion on
57 Bass drum
58 Hi-hat cymbal
59 Snare drum
60 Maracca
61 Snare drum
62 Temple block
63 Temple block
64 Temple block
65 Temple block
66 Cymbal
67 Tom tom
68 Jazz tremolo on
69 Tom tom
70 Alto vibratone (CM)
71 Wood block
72 Shutoff

78-KEY DECAP ORGAN SCALE
28 cm. wide

        10 Bass notes
        12 Accompaniment notes
        22 Melody notes
        16 Countermelody notes

1 Triangle
2 Violin celeste on
3 General cancel
4 to 13, Bass D to G and A to C
14 Baritone on
15 to 26, Accompaniment G to F#
27 Trumpet on
28 to 49, A to F#
50 Violin pipes on
51 to 66, Countermelody F to G#
67 Flute on
68 Xylophone on
69 Bass drum and cymbal
70 Snare drum
71 Tremolo on
72 Snare drum
73 Wood block
74 Trombone on
75 Wood block
76 Cornet on
77 Bassoon on
78 Key frame key

87-KEY DECAP ORGAN SCALE

        12 Bass notes
        12 Accompaniment notes
        22 Melody notes
        16 Countermelody notes

1 General cancel
2 Vox humana
3 Violin celeste on
4 to 15, Bass C to B
16 to 27, Accompaniment A to G#
28 Unda maris on
29 Trumpet on
30 Jazz flute on
31 Vibratone on (M)
32 to 53, Melody A to F#
54 Accordion on
55 Cello on (CM)
56 Vibratone on (CM)
57 Jazz tremolo on
58 to 73, Countermelody F to G#
74 Saxophone on
75 Shutoff
76 Bass drum
77 Cymbal
78 Snare drum
79 Tremolo on
80 Snare drum
81 Maracca
82 to 85, Temple blocks
86 Wood block
87 Key frame key

Note the similarity between this scale and the "standard" 92-key Decap scale.

During the 1920s Decap built a number of piano-type orchestrions in tall upright cases with keyboards, one of which is shown here. The Decap Brothers name appears in many different styles on the instruments. Decap is sometimes spelled as DeCap. "Brothers" appears as "Freres" (the French style, as shown on the front of the instrument pictured above) or as "Gebroeders" (the Belgian or Flemish style). When one of the authors visited the Decap premises at 22 and 24 Esschenstraat, Antwerp, in the 1970s, the original location also used by Decap decades earlier, he saw several large dance organs being built. Typically such units were a combination of traditional pipes and percussion with electronic organs added. Despite sale prices the equivalent of tens of thousands of dollars in United States funds, the firm had a substantial backlog of orders.

88-KEY DECAP ORCHESTRION-ORGAN SCALE
Paper rolls 13¾" wide; .15187" per space

1 Bass drum
2 Cymbal
3 Snare drum
4 Triangle?
5 Blank
6 Wood block
7 Wood block
8 to 14, Blank
15 to 26, Bass C to B
27 to 45, Accompaniment C to F#
46 Register?
47 Register?
48 to 74, Melody G to A
75 Register?
76 Chain perforation
77 Blank
78 4' violin pipes on
79 Register
80 Blank
81 8' violin celeste on (2 ranks)
82 4' violin celeste on
83 Register?
84 Jazz flute on
85 Blank
86 Rewind
87 Shutoff
88 General cancel

The instrument examined has a rank of cello pipes which serve as accompaniment and countermelody, playing from holes 27 to 45. The 27-note melody chest is divided into 12 lower notes and 15 upper notes. The 4' and 8' violin and celeste ranks all have 27 notes, while the jazz flute has only the upper 15 notes. Whenever the jazz flute is turned on, the upper 15 notes of all other melody ranks are automatically turned off, leaving the lower 12 notes of whatever is turned on in play. The tremolo comes on automatically with the jazz flute.

Hole 79 in the instrument examined turns the air on for a two-rank pipe chest located behind the other melody ranks. The chest has a set of valves but has no pipes and is capped with a wooden top.

An unusual feature is a lock and cancel mechanism which controls the air pressure in the melody chest for loud and soft, a very unusual arrangement which also affects the tuning if adjusted for any significant contrast. Its correct tracker bar control holes are unknown.

Another instrument, restored by Ron Cappel, has the following registers: 75 Swell shutter, 76 Tremolo, 77-80 Blank, 81 Celeste I on, 82 Flute on, 83 Celeste II on, 84 Jazz flute on, 85 Xylophone on.

92-KEY DECAP ORGAN SCALE

1 General cancel
2 Violin pipes on (M)
3 Voix celeste on (CM)
4 to 15, Bass C to B
16 to 27, Accompaniment A to G#
28 Unda maris on (M)
29 Trumpet on (M)
30 Jazz flute on (M)
31 Vibratone on (M)
32 to 53, Melody A to F#
54 Accordion on
55 Cello on (CM)
56 Vibratone on (CM)
57 Jazz tremolo
58 to 73, Countermelody F to G#
74 Cello grave on (CM)
75 Blank (or xylophone on)
76 Bass drum
77 Hi-hat cymbal
78 Snare drum brush

12 Bass notes
12 Accompaniment notes
22 Melody notes
16 Countermelody notes

79 Blank
80 Snare drum
81 Rhumba (rattle)
82 to 85, Temple blocks
86 Maracca
87 Tom-tom
88 Saxophone on (CM)
89 Tom-tom
90 Alto vibratone on (CM)
91 Shutoff
92 Cymbal

The Decap organ in the Al Svoboda Collection has the following differences:
2 Blank
28 Violin pipes on
56 Vibratone celeste (CM)
74 Bassoon on
75 Xylophone on
77 Tap cymbal
78 Snare drum
79 General tremolo on
81 Maracca
86 Snare drum brush
87 Tympani
89 Tympani
90 Blank
92 Blank

121-KEY DECAP "PIGALLE" ORGAN SCALE

12 Bass notes
12 Accompaniment notes
25 Melody notes
20 Countermelody notes
16 2nd countermelody notes

1 General cancel
2 Bells on
3 2nd countermelody tremolo on
4 to 19, Second countermelody G to A#
20 Alto flute (2CM)
21 Saxophone on (2CM)
22 to 33, Bass A to G#
34 Trombone
35 to 46, Accompaniment
47 Accordion on (earlier, "loud violin on")
48 Soft violin on (M)
49 to 73, Melody A to A
74 Unda maris on (M)
75 Trumpet on (M)
76 Jazz flute on (M)
77 Vibratone on (M)
78 to 97, Countermelody D to A
98 Baritone on (CM)
99 Vibratone on (CM)
100 Krumhorn on (CM)
101 Saxophone on
102 Celeste on (CM)
103 Bassoon on (CM)
104 Accordion on
105 Bass drum
106 Cornet on
107 Cymbal
108 Jazz tremolo on
109 Snare drum
110 Maracca
111 Snare drum
112 to 115, Temple blocks
116 Hi-hat cymbal
117 Tom-tom
118 Wood block
119 Tom-tom
120 General tremolo
121 Key frame key(?)

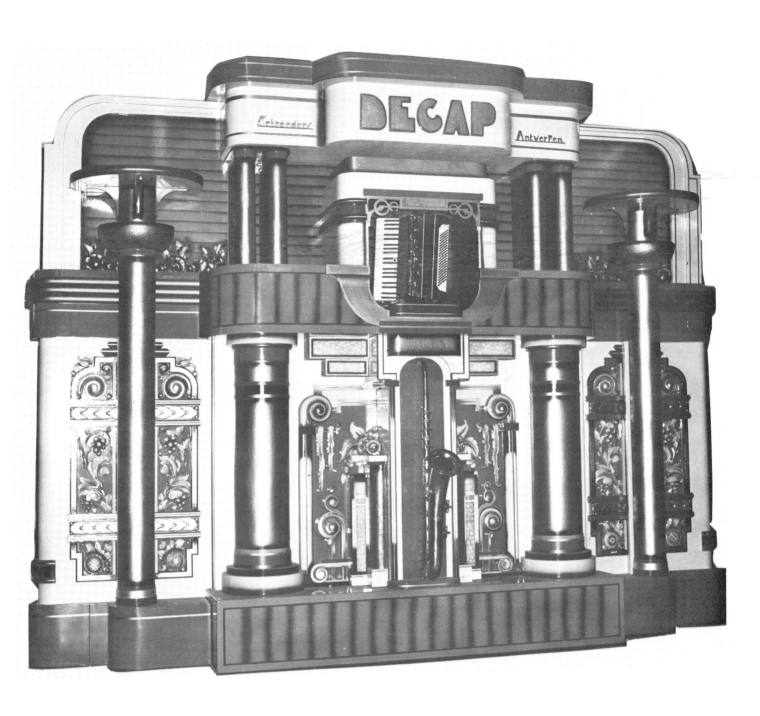

This large Decap dance organ in its modern Art Deco style case was once a great attraction in a Belgian dance hall. It was brought to America in the late 1960s and restored to its original condition. (Roy Haning and Neal White Collection)

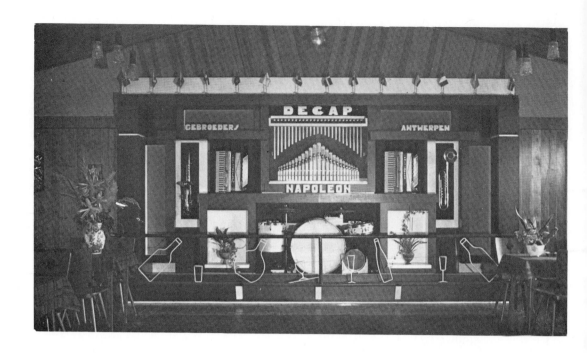

Above: This postcard from the 1960s shows a modern Decap dance organ in use at the Napoleon Restaurant in Rijsbergen, Belgium, on the road from Antwerp to the Dutch town of Breda.

Left: The Cafe Blauwe Donau ("Blue Danube Cafe") in Brasschaat, near Antwerp, notes on the front of this menu cover that a featured attraction is the "Latest New Electronic Organ by Decap Brothers." So popular is the dance organ that busloads of visitors come to see it and dance to its music. The cafe sells several different stereo records of the Decap.

Below: Leonard Grymonprez watches a music book go through the key frame of a 121-key Decap dance organ in this 1965 photograph. The instrument was later sold to Charles Hart of St. Albans, England.

REMOND DUWYN
Dance Organs

Remond Duwyn (or Duwijn) left the factory of Th. Mortier and founded his own organ business in Wilrijk, Belgium. Several dance organs per year were produced, mainly for use in the country of their origin. A Duwyn dance organ in the Haning and White Collection is extremely well constructed and plays with a very mellow and "warm" sound. It originally saw service in a restaurant on the main street of Tubize, Belgium and was obtained from that source by Roy Haning in 1965.

53-KEY DUWYN ORGAN SCALE

      6 Bass notes
      9 Accompaniment notes
      14 Melody notes
      14 Countermelody notes

1 Blank
2 Snare drum
3 to 8, Bass C, D, E, G, A, B
9 to 12, Accompaniment G, A, B, C
13 General cancel
14 to 18, Accompaniment C#, D, E, F, F#
19 Snare drum
20 to 33, Melody G, A, B-A, B
34 Bass drum
35 to 48, Countermelody E, F, F#, G, G#, A, B, C, C#, D, D#, E, F, G
49 Melody tremolo
50 Vox celeste on (CM)
51 Blank
52 Cello on (CM)
53 Carillon (pipe ranks) on (M)

The melody section includes violin, harmonic flute, and carillon pipes. The countermelody includes cello and vox celeste.

74-KEY DUWYN "SATURNUS" ORGAN SCALE

      6 Bass notes
      9 Accompaniment notes
      20 Melody notes
      16 Countermelody notes

1 Snare drum
2 Tremolo (M)
3 Snare drum
4 to 9, Bass G, A, B, C, D, E
10 to 13, Accompaniment G, A, B, C
14 General cancel
15 to 19, Accompaniment C#, D, E, F, F#
20 to 39, Melody G, G#, A, B-A, B, C, C#, D, D#, E
40 Swell shutters open
41 Violin pipes on (M)
42 Flute 4' on (M); or hi-hat cymbal
43 Harmonic flute on (M)
44 Unda maris on (M); or clarinet on
45 Bourdon on (M)
46 Bass drum
47 to 62, Countermelody E, F, F#, G, G#, A, B, C, C#, D, D#, E, F, F#, G, A
63 Trombone on
64 Baritone on (CM)
65 Cello on (CM)
66 Celeste on (CM)
67 Baxophone on (M)
68 Xylophone on (M)
69 Cello grave on (CM)
70 Flute 8' on (CM)
71 Blank (or hi-hat cymbal)
72 Trumpet on (M)
73 Key frame key?
74 Blank

FRATI & CO.
Band Organs

Frati & Co., located in Berlin, Germany, was a leading maker of organs, particularly during the 1880s, 1890s, and early 1900s. Most of the Frati products were barrel-operated, although a number of key-frame instruments which used folding cardboard books were made. In the United States such firms as August Pollmann, the North Tonawanda Musical Instrument Works, Muzzio, and Molinari imported Frati organs, often putting their own names on the facade.

Frati ceased being an important function in the organ business a few years prior to the onset of World War I. In 1923 the firm's assets were acquired by J.D. Philipps & Sons.

55-KEY FRATI ORGAN SCALE

    3 Trombone notes
    3 Bass notes
    8 Accompaniment notes
    15 Melody notes
    9 Trumpet notes
    15 Piccolo notes

1 to 3, Trombone G, C, D
4 to 6, Bass G, C, D
7 to 14, Accompaniment G, A, B, C, D, E, F, F#
15 to 29, Melody G, A, B, C, C#, D, E, F, F#, G, A, B, C, D, E
30 to 38, Trumpet C, D, E, F, F#, G, A, B, C
39 to 53, Piccolo G, A, B, C, C#, D, E, F, F#, G, A, B, C, D, E
54 Bass drum
55 Snare drum

65-KEY FRATI ORGAN SCALE

    6 Trombone notes
    18 Bass and accompaniment notes
    23 Melody notes
    13 Countermelody notes

1 to 6, Trombone C, D, E, F, G, A
7 to 12, Bass F, G, A, B, C, D
13 to 24, Accompaniment E, F, F#, G, A, A#, B, C, C#, D, D#, E
25 to 47, Melody F-C#, D, E
48 Shutoff
49 to 61, Countermelody A, B, C, C#, D, E, F, F#, G, A, A#, B, C
62 Bass drum
63 Snare drum
64 Registers loud
65 Registers soft

This scale is from a B.A.B. scale stick. The dividing points between bass, accompaniment, and melody are unclearly marked and would more logically occur between 13-14 and 23-24.

66-KEY FRATI No. 1 ORGAN SCALE

1 G
2 C
3 D
4 E
5 F
6 F#
7 G
8 A
9 A#
10 B
11 C
12 C#
13 D
14 E
15 F
16 F#
17 G
18 G#
19 to 43, A to A
44 B
45 C
46 to 58, D to D
59 E
60 Bass drum
61 "V" on (violin pipes on?)
62 "V" off
63 Snare drum
64 "X" on (Bells or xylophone on?)
65 "X" off
66 "A" (probably a register)

The dividing points between sections are unknown.

66-KEY FRATI ORGAN SCALE

1 Snare drum
2 Shutoff
3 Snare drum
4 to 8, Trombone F, G, A, C, D
9 Trombone (or bass?) E
10 to 12, Bass G, C, D
13 to 30, Accompaniment E, F, G, A, A#, B, C, C# D to B
31 to 49, Melody C to D, E, F, F#, G
50 to 65, Trumpet C, D, E, F, F#, G, A, A#, B, C, C#, D, E, F, F#, G
66 Bass Drum

The dividing points between trombone, bass, accompaniment, and melody are uncertain.

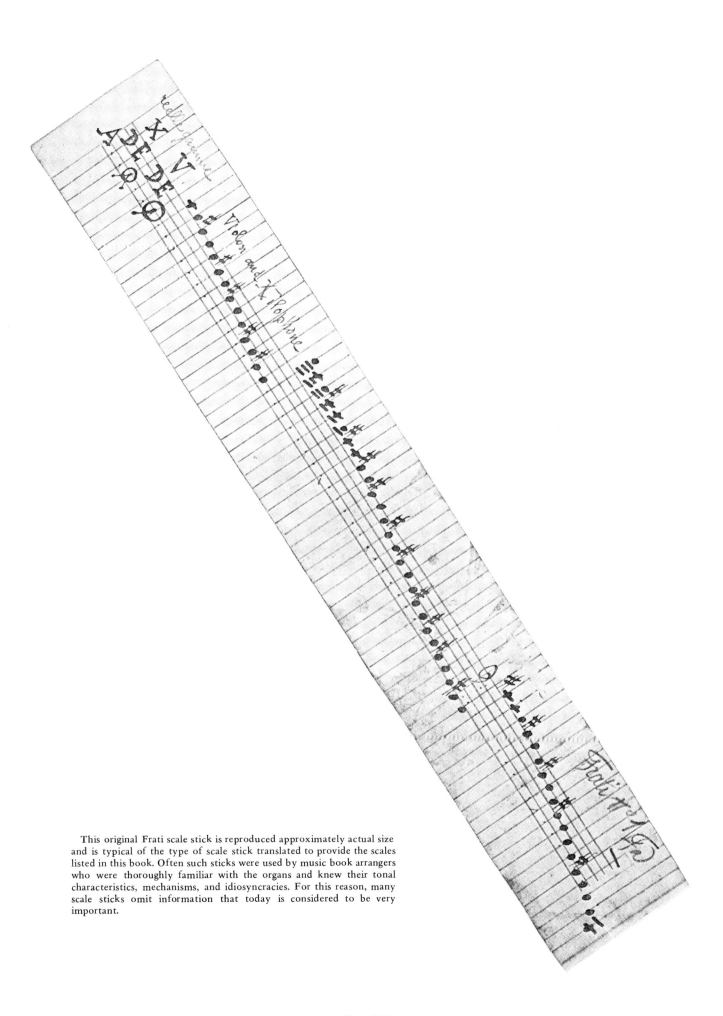

This original Frati scale stick is reproduced approximately actual size and is typical of the type of scale stick translated to provide the scales listed in this book. Often such sticks were used by music book arrangers who were thoroughly familiar with the organs and knew their tonal characteristics, mechanisms, and idiosyncracies. For this reason, many scale sticks omit information that today is considered to be very important.

CARL FREI
Band Organs

In Waldkirch, Germany the firm of Carl Frei continues today as a rebuilder of old organs and as a maker of new ones, including small roll-operated portable instruments.

The company was founded by Carl Frei, Sr., who served his apprenticeship with Wilhelm Bruder and Sons in Waldkirch around 1890. In 1892, his training completed, he went to Gavioli & Cie. in Paris, where he improved his skills in arranging, composing, and other areas. Later, Frei moved to Belgium and joined Th. Mortier, the celebrated maker of dance organs. Soon thereafter he set up his own organ business in Antwerp (Belgium), where he made organs and also sold instruments imported from Marenghi in Paris. The Frei works were closed in 1914 at the onset of World War I. In 1921 the company started anew in Breda, Holland. 52-, 67-, 72-, and 90-key street organs, among other instruments, were made. The Breda enterprise continued until the beginning of World War II.

After the war, Carl Frei and his son, Carl Frei, Jr., founded the Carl Frei & Sohn Orgelfabrik in Waldkirch. Carl Frei, Sr. died in 1967, since which time the business has been continued by his son.

The relatively modern Frei organs, including some of the 112-keyless size, are highly regarded for their appearance and tonal quality.

20-KEYLESS CARL FREI ORGAN SCALE
Paper rolls 110 mm. wide

1 to 3, Bass G, C, D
4 to 20, Accompaniment and melody E, F, F#, G, A, B, C, D, E, F, F#, G, A, B, C, D, E

35-KEYLESS CARL FREI ORGAN SCALE
Cardboard books 140 mm. wide

5 Bass notes
10 Accompaniment notes
20 Melody notes

1 to 5, Bass G, C, D, E, F
6 to 15, G, A, A#, B, C, C#, D, E, F, F#
16 to 35, Melody G-C, D, E

44-KEYLESS CARL FREI ORGAN SCALE
Cardboard books 180 mm. wide

This scale is the same as the 35-keyless Carl Frei organ scale but with the following additions:
36 Snare drum
37 Snare drum
38 Bass drum and cymbal
39 Band leader
40 to 42, Bass A, A#, B
43 Violin pipes
44 Bourdon

65-KEYLESS CARL FREI ORGAN SCALE
(Converted from Bruder)

           8 Bass notes
           8 Accompaniment notes
          27 Melody notes

65 Key frame key?
64 to 56, Blank
55 Bourdon on (Melody 1 and 2)
54 Trombone on
53 Harmonic flute on (Melody 2)
52 ?
51 Violin pipes on (Melody 1 and 2)
50 General cancel
49 Cello on (Melody 1)
48 Snare drum or castanets
47 Celeste on (Melody 2)
46 Snare drum or castanets
45 Celeste on (Melody 1)
44 to 37, Bass G, A, A#, B, C, D, E, F
36 to 29, Accompaniment G, A, A#, B, C, C#, D, D#
28 to 15, Melody 1: E to F
14 to 4, Melody 2: F#D, E, F
3 Bass drum
2 Melody 2: High F#
1 Melody 2: High G

    The violin and bourdon ranks play from the entire melody section, holes 28 to 4. The celeste is broken into two sections: melody 1, low notes 28-15, and melody 2, high notes 14-3, 2, and 1. The cello plays only melody 1 notes, and the harmonic flute plays only melody 2 notes.

72-KEY CARL FREI ORGAN SCALE
26.4 cm.

           8 Bass notes
          11 Accompaniment notes
          22 Melody notes
          13 Countermelody notes

72 Flute on (CM)
71 Countermelody tremolo on
70 to 68, 3 lower countermelody notes A, G# G
67 to 58, 10 upper countermelody notes, G chromatically down
    through A#
57 Biphone II on (CM)
56 Wood block
55 Biphone I on (M)
54 Bourdon on (M)
53 Trombone on
52 Unda maris on (CM)
51 Wood block
50 Violin pipes on (M)
49 General cancel
48 Cymbal
47 Snare drum
46 Violin celeste on (M)
45 Snare drum
44 Melody tremolo on
43 to 36, Bass G, A, A#, B, C, D, E, F
35 to 25, Accompaniment G, A to F#
24 to 3, Melody G to D, E, F
2 Bass drum
1 Blank

    The preceding scale is based on the 56-key Limonaire street organ scale.

Another 72-key Carl Frei scale has the following differences:
72 Biphone on (M)
71 Countermelody biphone tremolo on
57 Biphone on (CM)
55 Band leader
48 Accompaniment note G#
1 Melody note: high G

78-KEY RICHTER/FREI ORGAN SCALE

           8 Bass notes
          23 Accompaniment notes
          25 Melody notes
          17 Trumpet notes

1 Bass drum
2 to 9, Bass C, D, E, F, F#, G, A, B
10 to 32, Accompaniment F, G-E
33 to 57, Melody F to F
58 Registers loud
59 Registers soft
60 to 76, Trumpet G, A-C
77 Snare drum
78 Not used (or key frame key)

78-KEYLESS CARL FREI ORGAN SCALE

    The 78-keyless Carl Frei scale is the same as the 90-keyless Carl Frei scale (to which refer) except that holes 79 to 90 are omitted, and the following differences occur:
2 Violin pipes on
4 Biphone II on (CM)
5 Countermelody tremolo on
7 Unda maris on
19 Melody tremolo on
21 Bourdon celeste on (M)
57 Blank
61 Biphone I on (M)

79-KEY CARL FREI ORGAN SCALE

    Similar to the 72-key Carl Frei scale, but with the following additions:
79 Blank
78 Blank
77 to 73, High countermelody notes C, B, A#, A, G#

89-KEYLESS CARL FREI ORGAN SCALE
325 mm. wide

8 Bass notes
8 Trombone notes
16 Accompaniment notes
23 Melody notes
18 Countermelody notes

1 to 8, Bass F, G, A, A#, B, C, D, E
9 to 24, Accompaniment D# to F#
25 to 47, Melody G to F
48 Bass drum and cymbal
49 to 55, Trombone F, G, A, A#, B, C, D
56 Snare drum
57 Trombone E
58 General cancel
59 Violin pipes on (M)
60 Violin celeste on (M)
61 Carillon pipes on (M)
62 Melody tremolo on
63 Trompete on
64 Unda maris on (CM)
65 Biphone on (CM)
66 Bourdon celeste on (M)
67 Countermelody tremolo on
68 Countermelody G
69 Snare drum
70 to 86, Countermelody G# to C
87 Band leader
88 Blank
89 Blank

In the organ "de Gouden Engel" the "general cancel" turns the principal melody violin pipe ranks in the main pipe chest on. "Bourdon celeste on" turns the melody violin pipes off. Hole 59 (violin pipes on) controls an extra rank in the side chests.

90-KEYLESS CARL FREI ORGAN SCALE

8 Bass notes
18 Accompaniment notes
23 Melody notes
18 Countermelody notes

1 Celeste on (M); or, on another scale, accordion on
2 Cymbal
3 Bass drum
4 Triangle
5 Castanets (another scale: tremolo countermelody)
6 Snare drum
7 Castanets (another scale: unda maris on, CM)
8 Snare drum
9 Trombone on
10 to 17, Bass G, A, A#, B, C, D, E, F
18 to 24, Low accompaniment C, C#, D, D#, E, F (another scale: hole 19, unda maris on)
25 to 36 Accompaniment G to F#
37 to 59, Melody G to F
60 to 77, Countermelody G to C
78 General cancel
79 Violin pipes on (M)
80 Biphone I on (M)
81 8' flute on (M)
82 Bourdon on (M)
83 Melody tremolo on
84 Flute 4' on (CM) (another scale: biphone II on, CM)
85 Unda maris on (CM)
86 Baritone on (CM)
87 Cello on (CM)
88 Cello grave on (CM)
89 Blank
90 Blank

102-KEYLESS CARL FREI ORGAN SCALE
385 mm. wide

1 to 87, Same as 89-keyless Carl Frei scale
88 Bass drum and cymbal II
89 Castanets(?)
90 Wood block (?)
91 to 97, Notes C to F# (Low countermelody?)
98 Forte
99 to 101, Low accompaniment C, C#, D
102 Blank

105-KEYLESS CARL FREI ORGAN SCALE
(Converted from 112-key Marenghi)

12 Trombone notes
12 Bass notes
14 Accompaniment notes
23 Melody notes
18 Countermelody notes

1 to 12, Trombone C to B
13 to 16, Bass G#, C#, D#, F#
17 Celeste on
18 Cymbal
19 Bass drum
20 Triangle
21 Castanets
22 Snare drum
23 Castanets
24 Snare drum
25 Accompaniment and melody forte
26 to 33, Bass G, A, A#, B, C, D, E, F
34 to 40, Low accompaniment C to F#
41 to 52, Accompaniment G to F#
53 to 75, Melody G to F
76 to 90, Countermelody G to A
91 to 93, Countermelody E, F, F# (probably low notes)
94 General cancel
95 Violin pipes on (M)
96 Baxophone on (M)
97 Harmonic flute on (M)
98 Bourdon celeste on (M)
99 Melody tremolo on
100 Flute 8' on (CM)
101 Unda maris on (CM)
102 Baritone on (CM)
103 Cello on (CM)
104 Cello grave on (CM)
105 Trumpet on (CM)

112-KEYLESS CARL FREI ORGAN SCALE
400 mm. wide

1 to 101, Same as 102-keyless Carl Frei scale
102 to 106, Tubular chimes A, F, C, D, G
107 Piston on
108 Cello grave on
109 Bells on
110 Flute on
111 Blank
112 Blank

GASPARINI & CO.
Band Organs

52-KEY GASPARINI ORGAN SCALE

      7 Trombone notes
    10 Accompaniment notes
    20 Melody notes
    11 Countermelody notes

1 to 7, Trombone G, A, A#, C, D, E, F
8 Band leader
9 to 18, Accompaniment G, A, A#, B, C, C#, D, E, F, F#
19 to 38, Melody G, A-D, E
39 to 49, Countermelody F-D, E
50 Snare drum
51 Bass drum
52 Snare drum

  Melody: violin and piccolo pipes; countermelody: violin, flageolet (or clarinet). The organ is tuned one fifth higher than the
scale.

  Another 52-key Gasparini scale uses the countermelody section
for piccolos, having three pipes per note: Viennese flute, harmonic piccolo, and gedeckt flageolet.

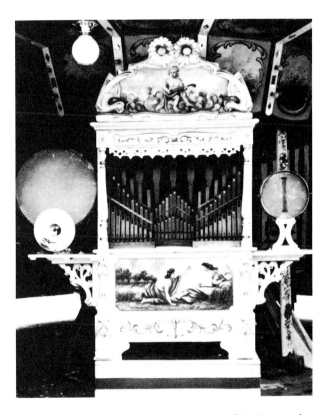

52-key Gasparini organ in the collection of D. Hinzen of
Roermond, Holland. (Photograph by Jan van Dinteren)

52-key Gasparini organ in the From Music Boxes to Street
Organs Museum in Utrecht, Holland. (Photograph by J.
Brink)

GAUDIN & CO.
Band Organs and
Dance Organs

During the 'teens and 1920s the firm of Gaudin & Cie., located in Paris, France, manufactured band organs and dance organs. During the earlier years production was mainly of band organs, many of which were shipped to England. During the later years of the firm's activities many dance organs were made, a number of which were shipped to Belgium, where sales outlets were established in Lokeren and Antwerp.

97-KEY GAUDIN ORGAN SCALE
34 cm. wide

> 12 Bass notes
> 12 Accompaniment notes
> 23 Melody notes
> 20 Countermelody notes

1 General cancel
2 Carillon pipes on
3 ?
4 to 15, Bass G to F#
16 Violin pipes on
17 Violin pipes on
18 Harmonic flute on
19 Baxophone on
20 Unda maris on
21 to 32, Accompaniment G to F#
33 Xylophone on
34 Trumpet on
35 Clarinet on
36 Jazz flute on
37 Jazz tremolo on
38 to 60, Melody G to F
61 Piffaro on
62 Vox celeste on
63 to 82, Countermelody C to G
83 Triangle
84 Cello on
85 Baritone on
86 Snare drum
87 Tremolo on
88 Snare drum
89 Cello grave on
90 8' flute on
91 Bass drum
92 Trombone on
93 Tom tom
94 Bassoon on
95 Tom tom
96 Blank
97 Blank

114-KEY GAUDIN ORGAN SCALE
405 mm. wide

> 12 Bass notes
> 12 Accompaniment notes
> 32 Melody notes
> 25 Countermelody notes

1 Blank
2 Blank
3 Bourdon on (CM)
4 to 6, Accompaniment notes E, D# D
7 Baxophone on (M)
8 Carillon pipes on (M)
9 Blank
10 Xylophone on (M)
11 Blank
12 Tremolo on(?)
13 Cello grave on (CM)
14 Harmonic flute on (M)
15 Tubaphone on
16 Vox celeste on (CM)
17 Unda maris on (M)
18 Swell shutters open
19 Hautbois (oboe) on (M)
20 Wood block
21 Tympani (or tom tom) register
22 8' flute on (CM)
23 Loud violin pipes on (M)
24 Trombone on
25 Baritone on (CM)
26 to 29, Bass F, F#, G, G#
30 Trompette on (M)
31 Cello on (CM)
32 to 35, Bass A, A#, B, C
36 Piston (trumpet) on (M)
37 Bassoon on (CM)
38 to 41, Bass C#, D, D#, E
42 to 49, Accompaniment F to C
50 Soft violin pipes on (M)
51 Snare drum/tympani
52 Accompaniment C#
53 General cancel
54 to 78, Countermelody C to C
79 Snare drum/tympani
80 to 111, Melody C to G
112 Triangle
113 Bass drum
114 "T" (?)

GAVIOLI & CO.
Band Organs

The firm of Gavioli & Cie., with headquarters in Paris, was probably the leading European maker of fairground organs during the 19th and 20th century. Certainly it was the leading French maker in the field.

The firm, which had origins dating back to 1806 in Italy, was relocated in Paris in 1845, when Ludovic Gavioli I moved there from Modena, Italy. In 1863, Anselme Gavioli became manager of the firm. During the late 19th century many different styles of pinned cylinder organs were made, ranging in size from small portable hand-cranked models to large organs of 100 keys or more.

By around 1905 most larger models were of the folding cardboard "book" type. The firm had prospered to the point at which over 300 workers were employed, mainly in Paris, but some in branches in New York City and Waldkirch (Germany). In addition, sales agencies were operated in London, Manchester (England), Antwerp, Barcelona, Milan, and other localities.

Miss Andree Gavioli, a family member, related that in 1901 Charles Marenghi, one of the firm's prized technicians, left Gavioli and founded his own firm. Sometime after that date, Marenghi, Gavioli, Gasparini, and Limonaire discussed the standardization of organ scales, registers, and key sizes, so that such a wide array of instruments would not have to be built. The group, with Limonaire abstaining, evidently carried out this plan for a limited time.

The most famous style of the Gavioliphone (as Gavioli styled its organs) among the larger models was the 110-key size. Apparently, these were made in fairly large numbers, perhaps to the extent of several dozen in all. There were no "standard" models; each had its own distinctive front. Some had particularly elaborate scenic or show fronts, were designed to be the front part of a tent or gallery, and had doors for the entry and exit of the public.

A 112-key Gavioliphone which used paper rolls (instead of cardboard books) was made for a short time, but it was not a success due to tracking difficulties (caused by changes in the climate). The six 112-key organs sold in England were all converted to smaller key formats.

By World War I Gavioli was out of business. As original music was no longer available, most Gaviolis in America were converted to other music systems. A fortunate exception was the compact 110-key organ used by the Humphrey Co. at Euclid Beach Park in Cleveland, Ohio. In the 1960s this organ, still with its original 110-key music system, went into the collection of Dr. Robert Miller.

35-KEY GAVIOLI ORGAN SCALE
(Right to left)

5 Bass notes
9 Accompaniment notes
20 Melody notes

1 Blank
2 to 6, Bass G, A, C, D, E
7 to 15, Accompaniment C, A, B, C, C#, D, E, F, F#
16 to 35, Melody G-A, B, C, C#, D, E

A variation of this scale adds snare drum before hole 1 and bass drum after hole 35. Still another variation, with 10 accompaniment notes, uses holes 1 to 5 for the bass notes, 6 to 8 for the accompaniment notes G, A, A#; the rest of the scale is the same as the preceding.

45-KEY GAVIOLI ORGAN SCALE
(Expanded from the 35-key scale)

8 Bass notes
10 Accompaniment notes
21 Melody notes

1 to 5, Bass G, C, D, E, F
6 to 15, Accompaniment G, A, A# B, C, C#, D, E, F, F#
16 to 35, Melody G-C, D, E
36 Snare drum
37 Snare drum
38 Bass drum and cymbal
39 Melody high F
40 to 42, Bass A, A#, B
43 Violin pipes on (chain perforation)
44 Bourdon on (chain perforation)
45 Blank

46-KEY GAVIOLI ORGAN SCALE
(Right to left)

8 Bass notes
11 Accompaniment notes
23 Melody notes

1 Snare drum
2 Shutoff
3 Snare drum
4 to 11, Bass F, G, A, A#, B, C, D, E
12 to 22, Accompaniment F, G, A, A#, B, C, C#, D, D#, E, F
23 to 45, Melody F#D, E, F
46 Bass drum and cymbal

48-KEY GAVIOLI ORGAN SCALE

A 48-key scale uses the above format but with "registers soft" preceding hole 1 and "registers loud" following hole 46.

49-KEY GAVIOLI ORGAN SCALE

       4 Bass notes
      28 Accompaniment and melody notes
      13 Countermelody notes (trumpet or piccolo)

1 Bass drum
2 to 5, Bass F, G, C, D
6 to 18, Accompaniment-melody F, G, A, A#, B, C, D, E, F,
  F#, G, A, A#
19 Snare drum
20 to 34, Accompaniment-melody, continued B, C, C#, D, E, F,
  F#, G, A, A#, B, C, D, E, F
35 to 47, Countermelody D, E, F, F#, G, A, A# B, C, C#, D,
  E, F
48 Snare drum
49 Key frame key (or shutoff?)

50-KEY GAVIOLI ORGAN SCALE
8 5/16" wide

      6 Bass notes
     10 Accompaniment notes
     17 Melody notes
     11 Piccolo notes

1 Shutoff
2 Snare drum
3 Registers soft
4 Registers loud
5 Snare drum
6 to 11, Bass C, D, E, F, G, A
12 to 21, Accompaniment G, A, A#, B, C, C#, D, E, F, F#
22 to 38, Clarinet, violin G to B
39 to 49, Piccolo C, C#, D, E, F, F#, G, A, A#, B, C
50 Bass drum

    Trumpets, if present, are coupled to holes 19-34, E-G.

57-KEY GAVIOLI ORGAN SCALE

      6 Bass notes
     10 Accompaniment notes
     16 Melody notes
     18 Piccolo notes

1 Shutoff (or key frame key)
2 Snare drum
3 to 8, Bass G, A, B, C, D, E
9 Bass drum
10 to 12, Accompaniment D, E, F
13 Band leader
14 to 18, Accompaniment F#, G, A, B, C
19 Registers loud
20 and 21, Accompaniment C#, D
22 to 24, Melody D#, E, F
25 Registers soft
26 to 38, Melody F#, G, G#, A, B, C, C#, D, E, F, F#, G, A
39 to 56, Piccolo G, A, B, C, C#, D, D#, E, F, F#, G, G#, A,
  B, C, C#, D, E
57 Snare drum

57-KEY GAVIOLI ORGAN SCALE

    Another 57-key Gavioli scale is a variation of the preceding and is transposed up a fourth, with the bass beginning on C, and has the following differences:
13 Trombones on
20 Highest accompaniment note
21 Lowest melody note
25 General cancel

57-KEY GAVIOLI No. 2 ORGAN SCALE

      6 Bass notes
     12 Accompaniment notes
     17 Melody notes
     18 Countermelody notes

1 Snare drum
2 Shutoff (or key frame key)
3 Snare drum
4 to 9, Bass C, D, E, G, A, B
10 to 21, Accompaniment E, F, F#, G, G#, A, B, C, C#, D,
  D#, E
22 to 38, Melody C, D, E, F, F#, G, G#, A, B, C, C#, D, D#, E, F, F#,
  G
39 to 56, Countermelody G, A, B, C, C#, D, D#, E, F, F#, G, G#, A, B,
  C, C#, D, E
57 Bass drum

65-KEY GAVIOLI No. 2 (Waldkirch) ORGAN SCALE

      6 Bass notes
     10 Accompaniment notes
     21 Melody and piccolo notes
     17 Countermelody notes

65 Shutoff (or key frame key)
64 Snare drum; castanets
63 Trombone on (and percussion shifter)
62 to 57, Bass C, D, E, G, A, B
56 Snare drum; castanets
55 to 51, Accompaniment F#, G, A, B, C
50 Band leader (or trumpet on)
49 to 45, Accompaniment C#, D, D#, E, F
44 to 24, Melody F#-A, B, C, C#, D, E
23 Clarinet on
22 Violin on
21 Piccolo on
20 Bass drum
19 to 3, Countermelody D-D, E, F, F#, G
2 Saxophone on
1 General cancel

    The preceding scale is from a stick used in America by the B.A.B. Organ Co. A different test book is marked the same except for the following differences:

23 Piccolo on
22 Clarinet on
21 Violin pipes on

    Note: An unusual 65-key Gavioli band organ in the Herbert Brabandt Collection (earlier in the Bellm Collection) has a keyboardless upright piano mounted directly behind the facade, with several ranks of pipes located behind it.

CARD BOARD GAVIOLIPHONE

Powerful symphonic instrument, representing an orchestra of 50 musicians.

MODEL No. 724

No. 724

Front Louis XV, 6 metal Figures
with electric lamps,
Battery on consols.

Xylophone.

Front lighted
by 200 electric lamps.

Length .. .. .. 6 yd. 2 ft. 8 in.
Height .. .. .. 5 yd. 0 ft. 10 in.

NET PRICE :

No. 685

Front *Art nouveau*,
8 Figures in 3 Groups.

Xylophone.

Length :
7 yd. 0 ft. 4 in.

Height :
5 yd. 2 ft. 8 in.

NET PRICE :

MODEL No. 685

Two different Gavioli organs from a catalogue issued during the first decade of the 20th century. The
Gavioli line ranged from portable hand-cranked models to large instruments which measured 35 feet or
more wide. Many Gavioli organs were originally distributed in America.

A scale listed under "65-KEY UNKNOWN (Frati?)" may be for a similar but smaller instrument with separate keys for the piano and pipes. The same scale has four keys for the snare drum. Providing four such keys is unusual, but so is including a piano in a band organ. Band organ and orchestrion builders tried all sorts of ideas. Most non-standard variations were short-lived. Often subsequent owners and rebuilders would add their own inventions. Such gadgets as pipe organs with a row of tuned bottles, a pipe organ with a Mills Violano-Virtuoso attachment, etc. are occasionally seen. Study can usually enable the owner of such contraptions to determine whether they came from the factory as original equipment or whether they are from a rebuilder's shop.

68-KEY GAVIOLI ORGAN SCALE

      6 Bass notes
      10 Accompaniment notes
      21 Melody notes
      17 Countermelody notes

1 Bass drum
2 and 3, Bass G, A
4 to 12, Countermelody D, E, F#, G#, A#, C, D, F, G
13 to 16, Accompaniment F, E, D#, D
17 to 37, Melody D, C, A, G, F, D#, C#, B, A, G, F#, G#, A#, C, D, E, F#, G#, B, C#, E
38 Violin pipes on (M)
39 General cancel
40 Piccolo on (M)
41 to 46, Accompaniment C#, C, B, A, G, F#
47 Triangle
48 Clarinet on (CM)
49 to 56, Countermelody F#, E, C#, B, A, G, F, D#
57 Saxophone on (CM)
58 Trombone on
59 to 62, Bass F, D, C, B
63 Castanets
64 Snare drum
65 Castanets
66 Snare drum
67 Bells on (M)
68 Shutters open

80-KEY GAVIOLI ORGAN SCALE
12 5/8" wide

      8 Bass notes
      10 Accompaniment notes
      17 Melody notes
      17 Piccolo notes
      20 Countermelody notes

1 General cancel
2 Trombone on
3 Baritone (or large clarinet) on (CM)
4 Swell open
5 Violin on (CM)
6 Bass drum
7 to 14, Bass F, G, A, A#, B, C, D, E
15 to 24, Accompaniment G, A, A#, B, C, C#, D, E, F, F#
25 to 41, Melody G to B
42 to 58, Piccolo C-D, E, F
59 to 78, Countermelody A-D, E, F
79 Snare drum
80 Snare drum

A B.A.B. test book for this organ is marked "89-key Gavioli changed to 80-keyless."

84-KEY GAVIOLI ORGAN SCALE

      7 Trombone notes
      9 Bass notes
      16 Accompaniment and baritone notes
      23 Melody notes
      17 Piccolo notes

1 Band leader
2 Snare drum
3 General cancel
4 Snare drum
5 Registers loud
6 to 12, Trombone C, D, E, F, G, A, B
13 to 21, Bass C, D, E, F, G, G#, A, A#, B
22 to 37, Baritone and accompaniment C to D#
38 to 65, Melody E to G
66 to 82, Piccolo G, A-C
83 Bass drum
84 Registers soft

87-KEY GAVIOLI ORGAN SCALE

      8 Bass notes
      8 Trombone notes
      10 Accompaniment notes
      33 Melody notes
      20 Countermelody notes

1 Bell ringers
2 to 9, Bass F, G, A, A#, B, C, D, E
10 Band leader
11 to 20, Accompaniment G, A, A#, B, C, C#, D, E, F, F#
21 to 53, Melody G-D, E
54 Bass drum
55 to 62, Trombone F, G, A, A#, B, C, D, E
63 Melody: high F
64 Snare drum
65 Band leader
66 to 85, Countermelody A-D, E, F
86 Snare drum
87 Key frame key

The pipe ranges are: clarinet 21-37, violin 21-42, and flageolet 38-53. This is the original 87-key Gavioli scale from which the 89 G4, 89 VB, and 98-key scales evolved. Gavioli, Limonaire, Marenghi, Hooghuys, and Chiappa all built organs to this scale or to variations of it. One 86-key scale omits hole 1 but is otherwise the same. An 89-key Limonaire scale has the following exceptions to the preceding layout: 1 "V" register (violin pipes on?), 2 General cancel, 3 to 88 are the same as 2 to 87 above, 89 "F" register (flute on?). (This information provided by Ken Smith)

"The Reliance"---89 Key

With bass and snare drums and cymbal set on detachable wings.
The most perfect, powerful and melodious organ ever built; made to execute
any selection or overture, accomplishing the exact effect of a
Symphony Orchestra.

Extremely rich facade of artistic sculpture with life-size statues. Most
luxurious decorations in gold and silver leaf.

DESCRIPTION

Dimensions: 22 feet long, 18 feet high, 4 feet wide.

Page from a Berni Organ Company (New York) catalogue offering an 89-key Gavioli organ.

87/89-KEY GAVIOLI No. 1 ORGAN SCALE

8 Bass notes
8 Trombone notes
10 Accompaniment notes
34 Melody and piccolo notes
20 Countermelody notes

1 Blank
2 Blank
3 to 10, Bass G, G, A, A#, B, C, D, E
11 Band leader
12 to 21, Accompaniment G, A, A#, B, C, C#, D, E, F, F#
22 to 38 Clarinet G-B
39-55 Piccolo C-D, E, F
56 to 63, Trombone F, G, A, A#, B, C, D, E
64 Bass drum
65 Snare drum
66 Snare drum
67 to 86, Countermelody A-D, E, F
87 Key frame key
88 Blank
89 Blank

89-KEY GAVIOLI No. 2 ORGAN SCALE

1 Violin pipes on (CM)
2 General cancel
3 to 10, Bass F, G, A, A#, B, C, D, E
11 Blank
12 to 21, Accompaniment G, A, A#, B, C, C#, D, E, F, F#
22 to 38, Clarinet G to B
39 to 54, Piccolo C-D, E
55 Bass drum
56 to 63, Trombone F, G, A, A#, B, C, D, E
64 Highest piccolo: F
65 Snare drum
66 Saxophone on (CM)
67 to 86, Countermelody A-D, E, F
87 Snare drum
88 Key frame key
89 Blank

Note: The Marenghi VB (violin-baritone) scale is similar. See Marenghi section for details.

89-KEY GAVIOLI Nos. 3 and 4 ORGAN SCALE

8 Bass notes
8 Trombone notes
10 Accompaniment notes
34 Melody and piccolo notes
20 Countermelody notes

1 Violin pipes on
2 General cancel
3 to 10, Bass F, G, A, A#, B, C, D, E
11 Band leader
12 to 21, Accompaniment G, A, A#, B, C, C#, D, E, F, F#
22 to 38, Melody G to B
39 to 54, Piccolo C-D, E
55 Bass drum and cymbal
56 to 63, Trombone F, G, A, A#, B, C, D, E
64 Highest piccolo: F
65 Snare drum
66 Clarinet on (M)
67 to 86, Countermelody A-D, E, F
87 Snare drum
88 Key frame key
89 Registers loud (forte)

The melody section includes 17 clarinets and 22 violins. The countermelody section in the No. 3 scale includes cello (and saxophone, when the forte register is on); and in the No. 4 scale includes saxophone (and trumpet, when the forte register is on). In both scales, "forte" adds saxophone (reed) pipes to bass and accompaniment.

The general cancel silences the melody voices such as violin, clarinet, and forte. In large organs with additional countermelody ranks, a better designation for the general cancel hole is "registers soft," because additional foundation ranks remain in play.

An 87-key scale omits holes 1 and 89 and uses hole 2 for bell ringers.

A variation on the G4 scale from a B.A.B. scale stick has one extra accompaniment note and no clarinet register, shifting functions 22-65 in the preceding scale one number higher in each instance.

89-KEY GAVIOLI ORGAN SCALE
(Variation of preceding)

Another variation, also from the B.A.B. Organ Co. files, has the following differences:

11 Swell shutters open
12 to 21, Accompaniment notes
22 to 43, Melody G to E
44 to 59, Piccolo C-D, E
60 Bass drum
61 Piccolo: high F
62 Snare drum
63 to 82, Countermelody notes
83 Snare drum
84 ?
85 Trombone on
86 Saxophone on
87 Flute on
88 Flageolet on
89 Trumpet or oboe on

This organ, which has been variously attributed as an 89-key Gavioli or a 98-key Marenghi, is shown in use with a British show.

This large 110-key Gavioli organ served as the front for a biograph (motion picture) show and has doors for the entry and exit of the public. Certain Gavioli organs also had built-in ticket booths!

View of an organ attributed as an 87-key Gavioli on the stage of Anderton's Empire Palace, which the facade describes as "up to date."

94-KEY GAVIOLI ORGAN SCALE

      12 Bass notes
      16 Accompaniment notes
      24 Melody and piccolo notes
      21 Countermelody notes

1 Diapason on
2 Key frame key
3 and 4, Bass C, F
5 Accompaniment G
6 Triangle (or bells on?)
7 "Niche" (?)
8 Castanets
9 Violin celeste on (M)
10 Shutoff
11 Registers fortissimo
12 Registers forte
13 2nd violin pipes on
14 Castanets
15 Snare drum
16 Saxophone on (CM)
17 to 26, Bass A, A#, B, C#, D, D#, E, F#, G, G#
27 Snare drum
28 to 37, Accompaniment F#, G#-E
38 Bass drum
39 to 43, Accompaniment F to A
44 to 67, Melody and piccolo A# to A
68 Violin pipes on (M)
69 Flageolet (or piccolo) on (M)
70 Oboe on
71 to 91, Countermelody C#-A
92 Cello on (CM)
93 Flute on (CM)
94 General cancel

98-KEY GAVIOLI ORGAN SCALE

      8 Bass notes
      8 Trombone notes
      10 Accompaniment notes
      17 Melody notes
      17 Piccolo notes
      20 Countermelody notes

1 1st violin on
2 2nd violin on
3 Bells on
4 to 11, Bass F, G, A, A#, B, C, D, E
12 Baritone on
13 to 22, Accompaniment G, A, A#, B, C, C#, D, E, F, F#
23 to 39, Melody G to B
40 to 55, Piccolo C-D, E
56 Bass drum
57 to 64, Trombone F, G, A, A#, B, C, D, E
65 Highest piccolo: F
66 Snare drum
67 Saxophone on
68 to 87, Countermelody A-D, E, F
88 Snare drum
89 Trumpet on
90 Trombone chant on
91 Blank
92 General cancel
93 Blank
94 Castanets
95 Blank
96 Key frame key
97 Baritone on
98 Voix celeste on

    The 98-key Gavioli scale is an expanded version of the 89-key Marenghi VB (violin-baritone) scale, to which refer.

110-KEY GAVIOLI ORGAN SCALE

      24 Bass and trombone notes
      13 Accompaniment notes
      18 Countermelody notes
      42 Melody and piccolo notes

1 General cancel
2 Registers loud
3 to 14, Bass C to B
15 Trombone C
16 Violin pipes on
17 to 22, Trombone C#-F#
23 Clarinet on
24 to 28, Trombone G to B
29 Melody registers loud (or baritone on)
30 to 42, Countermelody C to C
43 Castanets
44 to 48, Countermelody C# to F
49 Snare drum
50 to 62, Melody G to C
63 Castanets
64 to 72, Melody G# to E
73 Bass drum
74 to 80, Piccolo F to B
81 Snare drum
82 to 94, Piccolo C to C
95 Registers medium loud
96 to 108, Trumpet C to C
109 Trumpet on
110 Key frame key

    In the preceding scale the melody and piccolo sections overlap.

    Another 110-key Gavioli scale has the following differences:

50-63 Melody G to G#
64 Castanets
65 to 73, Melody A to F
74 Bass drum
75 to 81, Piccolo F# to C
82 Snare drum
83 to 94, Piccolo C# to C

112-KEY GAVIOLI ORGAN SCALE

      21 Bass notes
      16 Accompaniment notes
      21 Countermelody notes
      38 Melody and piccolo notes

1 Blank
2 General cancel
3 Registers loud
4 to 16, Bass C to C
17 Violin pipes on
18 to 23, Bass C# to F#
24 Clarinet I on
25 Bass G
26 Bass G#
27 to 29, Countermelody A to B
30 Saxophone on
31 to 43, Countermelody C to C
44 Castanets
45 to 49, Countermelody C# to F
50 Snare drum
51 to 67, Melody E to G#
68 Castanets
69 to 77, Melody A to F
78 Bass drum
79 to 90, Piccolo F# to F
91 Cello on
92 Snare drum
93 to 100, Accompaniment E to B
101 Bass reed on
102 to 109, Accompaniment C to G
110 Trumpet on
111 Band leader
112 Key frame key

OSCAR GRYMONPREZ & ZOON
Dance Organs

Oscar Grymonprez and his son Leonard, of Ledeberg (near Ghent), Belgium, have been in the organ business for many years. The firm has remodeled many Decap, Mortier, and other organs and has modernized the facades with the addition of lights, accordions, etc.

In the 1960s Leonard Grymonprez developed an extensive correspondence with various collectors in America and England and was responsible for the sale of many large organs to those countries. In addition, he was the leading exporter of coin pianos and orchestrions which were sold by agents for Weber, Hupfeld, and others years earlier and which remained in use in Belgium long after they were obsolete in other areas of the world.

101-KEY GRYMONPREZ ORGAN SCALE

        12 Bass notes
        12 Accompaniment notes
        22 Melody notes
        16 Countermelody notes

1 General cancel
2 Unda maris on (M)
3 Violin celeste on (CM)
4 to 15, Bass C to B
16 to 27, Accompaniment A to G#
28 Violin pipes on (M)
29 Trumpet on (M)
30 Jazz flute on (M)
31 Vibratone on (M)
32 to 53, Melody A to F#
54 Accordion(s) on
55 Cello on (CM)
56 Vibratone on (CM)
57 Jazz tremolo on
58 to 73, Countermelody F to G#
74 Bassoon on (CM)
75 Blank
76 Bass drum
77 Cymbal
78 Snare drum
79 Carillon (pipes) on (M)
80 Snare drum
81 Maracca
82 to 85, Temple blocks
86 Triangle
87 Tom-tom
88 Alto vibratone on (CM)
89 Saxophone on (CM)
90 Wood block
91 Piffaro on
92 Crash cymbal
93 Castanets
94 Xylophone on (M)
95 Blank
96 Tambourine
97 Shutoff
98 Cello grave on (CM)

This photograph, taken in 1966, shows Oscar Grymonprez with his son Leonard standing to his right (viewer's left). In the background is a dance organ which has been constructed using Mortier facade parts and other components. (Photograph provided by Leonard Grymonprez)

This organ, remodelled by Oscar Grymonprez & Son during the early 1970s, uses a scale which closely resembles the 92-key Decap layout.

LOUIS HOOGHUYS
Band Organs

In 1880 Louis Hooghuys founded his business of manufacturing fairground organs. Later, the firm was continued by his son and grandson in Grammont, Belgium. Many Hooghuys organs in existence today are distinguished by their extremely loud voicing, much louder than the contemporary instruments of Gavioli, Bruder, Limonaire, et al. An especially large Hooghuys organ is on view at the From Music Boxes to Street Organs Museum (Utrecht, Holland), under the curatorship of Dr. Jan Haspels.

An interesting feature of certain large Hooghuys instruments was a mandolin/piano attachment which used tuned piano strings.

Hooghuys organs were originally distributed mainly in Belgium and Holland.

60-KEY HOOGHUYS ORGAN SCALE

6 Bass notes
10 Accompaniment notes
25 Melody notes

60 Key frame key
59 Swell open
58 Swell closed
57 Register
56 Register
55 Register
54 Register (vox humana or trumpet?)
53 Register
52 Register (celeste?)
51 Register (harmonic flute?)
50 Register (violin?)
49 Trombones on
48 Saxophone on (or baritone?)
47 Bass drum and cymbal
46 to 41, Bass F, G, A, C, D, E
40 to 31, Accompaniment G, A, A#, B, C, C#, D, E, F, F#
30 to 12, Melody G, A, A#, B, C, C#, D, E, F, F#, G, A, A#, B, C, C#, D, E, F
11 Wood block
10 to 5, Melody F#, G, A, A#, B, C
4 General cancel
3 Snare drum
2 Wood block
1 Snare drum

57-KEY HOOGHUYS ORGAN SCALE
21.7 cm. wide

8 Bass notes
11 Accompaniment notes
30 Melody notes

57 Snare drum
56 Key frame key
55 General cancel
54 Bass drum and cymbal
53 to 46, Bass F, G, A, A#, B, C, D, E
45 to 35, Accompaniment G, A to F#
34 to 5, Melody G to C
4 Forte
3 Triangle
2 Trombones on
1 Snare drum

66-KEY HOOGHUYS ORGAN SCALE
25 cm. wide

8 Bass notes
11 Accompaniment notes
22 Melody notes
19 Countermelody notes

66 Bass drum
65 to 58, Bass F, G, A, A#, B, C, D, E
57 to 47, Accompaniment G, A to F#
46 to 28, Countermelody C to F#
27 Band leader
26 to 5, Melody G to D, E, F
4 Forte
3 Snare drum
2 General cancel
1 Snare drum

69-KEY HOOGHUYS ORGAN SCALE
26.1 cm. wide

        8 Bass notes
       11 Accompaniment notes
       31 Melody notes
       13 Countermelody notes

69 Register
68 Bass drum and cymbal
67 to 62, Bass G, A, C, D, E, F
61 to 51, Accompaniment G, A to F#
50 to 20, Melody G to C, D
19 to 7, Countermelody C to C
6 Forte
5 Unknown (triangle?)
4 Trombone on
3 Snare drum
2 General cancel
1 Snare drum

70-KEY HOOGHUYS ORGAN SCALE

        6 Bass notes
       10 Accompaniment notes
       16 Countermelody notes
       19 Melody notes

1 Key frame key
2 English horn on
3 Tremolo on
4 Harmonic flute on
5 Vox humana on
6 Xylophone on
7 Accordion on
8 Violin on
9 Baritone on
10 Bombardon on
11 Mandolin on
12 Swell open
13 Swell closed
14 Bass drum
15 to 20, Bass F, G, A, C, D, F
21 to 30, Accompaniment G, A, A#, B, C, C#, D, E, F, F#
31 to 46 Countermelody C, C#, D, E, F, F#, G, A, A#, B, C, C#, D, E, F, F#
47 Triangle
48 to 66, Melody G, A, A#, B, C, C#, D, E, F, F#, G, A, A#, B, C, C#, D, E, F
67 General cancel
68 Snare drum
69 Castanets
70 Snare drum

90-KEY HOOGHUYS ORGAN SCALE

        8 Bass notes
       12 Accompaniment notes
       19 Countermelody notes
       34 Melody and flageolet notes

90 "Klink of/Grondel-kl."?
89 Accompaniment G#
88 Cello on
87 to 84, Flageolets D, G#, A#, E
83 Melody D#
82 Melody F#
81 Flageolet A
80 Flageolet C#
79 Melody G
78 Flageolet C
77 Flageolet B
76 Vox humana on
75 Castanets
74 Flageolet F
73 Musette celeste on
72 Melody violin pipes on
71 Oboe on
70 Harmonic flute on
69 Cello bass on
68 Xylophone on
67 Cymbal
66 Bass drum
65 to 58, Bass F, G, A, A#, B, C, D, E
57 to 47, Accompaniment G, A-F#
46 to 28, Countermelody C to F#
27 Triangle
26 to 5, Melody G-D, E, F
4 Trombone on
3 Snare drum
2 General cancel
1 Snare drum

The high end of the melody section is missing D#. This D#, plus high F# and G, are located at holes 83, 82, and 79. The G# which is missing from the accompaniment section is located at hole 89.

"84-KEY" HOOGHUYS ORGAN SCALE

This "84-key" Hooghuys scale is similar to the 90-key Hooghuys scale, except that holes 90 through 86 are omitted, and the 84-key scale has the following differences:

85 Tympani?
84 Blank
83 "Klink klavier"
82 ?
81 Tremolo
80 Tympani?
79 Fugara on
78 Expression
77 General cancel
74 Wood block
73 Mandolin on
67 Cello on

Nᵒ 201 bis.
Orchestrophone 30 touches.

Nᵒ 255.
Orchestrophone 35 touches, ouvert.

262. — Orchestrophone 38 touches avec registres. — Façade sculptée.

Nᵒ 256. — Orchestrophone 49 touches, ouvert.

Nᵒ 252. Orchestrophone 57 touches, Registres automatiques.

Nᵒ 259. — Orchestrophone 52 touches, renforcé, façade riche.

Nᵒ 218. — Orchestrophone 49 touches, grand modèle renforcé à doubles niches.

More Limonaire band organs from the early part of the present century. The 49-key model notes that the firm won a gold medal at the 1900 Paris Exposition.

LIMONAIRE FRERES
Band Organs

Founded in 1840, the firm of Limonaire Freres, located in Paris, continued in business for nearly a century, until the 1920s. Early instruments were of the pinned cylinder style. Organs made from the late 1890s onward were mostly of the key-frame type and used folding cardboard music books. Instruments of the early 20th century ranged in size from 30 to 118 keys. Particularly popular were the 49-, 52-, and 60-key formats. Many of these organs were sold under the "Orchestrophone" trade name.

Particularly impressive were large 100-key organs with elaborate facades which included entry and exit doors for the public. These were used to face traveling tents and similar shows, including early moving picture exhibits. Certain "double case" models were built with standard components, but with two of each item—thus effecting an increased volume of sound. In the 1920s several models of the "Jazzbandophone" were marketed.

The peak years of the firm seem to have been from about 1900 to 1914.

35-KEY LIMONAIRE ORGAN SCALE

6 Bass notes
25 Melody and accompaniment notes

1 D?
2 Bass drum
3 Bass C
4 Accompaniment b
5 D
6 c
7 E
8 d
9 F
10 e
11 G
12 f
13 A
14 f#
15 Highest note f
16 Snare drum
17 e
18 g
19 d
20 a
21 c#
22 a#
23 c
24 Snare drum
25 b
26 b
27 a#
28 c
29 a
30 c#
31 g
32 d
33 f#
34 e
35 f

Bass section notes are capitalized. Accompaniment and melody notes from lowest to highest are 4, 6, 8, 10, 12, 14, 18, 20, 22, 26, 28, 30, 32, 34, 35, 33, 29, 27, 25, 23, 21, 19, 17, 15.

35-KEY LIMONAIRE ORGAN SCALE
(Limonaire/B.A.B.; from B.A.B. Organ Co. files)
5½" wide

6 Bass notes
25 Melody and accompaniment notes

1 Bass drum
2 to 7, Bass C, D, E, F, G, A
8 to 32, Accompaniment and melody b, c, d, e, f, f#, g, a, a#, b, c, c#, d, e, f, f#, g, a, a#, b, c, c#, d, e, f
33 Snare drum
34 ?
35 Snare drum

N° 227bis. — *Orchestrophone* **60** *touches.* **3** *statuettes.* **2** *groupes de valseurs.*

N° 226. — *Orchestrophone* **60** *touches.* **3** *statuettes.*

ORCHESTROPHONES
MODÈLES NOUVEAUX

N° 261. — *Orchestrophone* **38** *touches.* — *Registres automatiques.*

Several varieties of Limonaire band organs, trademarked "Orchestrophones," from a catalogue of the early 20th century. "Touches" is the French equivalent of "keys."

N° 215. — *Orchestrophone* **49** *touches. Art nouveau.*

N° 250 — *Orchestrophone* **67** *touches. Registres automatiques.*

48-KEY LIMONAIRE ORGAN SCALE

      8 Bass notes
    33 Total accompaniment and melody notes

1 Triangle
2 Band leader?
3 Blank
4 Snare drum
5 Key frame key (or shutoff?)
6 to 13, Bass G, A, A#, B, C, D, E, F
14 to 46, Accompaniment and melody g, a-d, e, f
47 Bass drum
48 Snare drum

    Note the similarity to the 56 key Limonaire scale. If the note scale is identical, then the dividing point between the accompaniment and melody is 24/25, for a total of 11 accompaniment and 22 melody.

50-KEY LIMONAIRE ORGAN SCALE

      4 Bass notes
      9 Accompaniment notes
    13 Clarinet notes
    10 Piccolo notes
    10 Trumpet notes

1 Shutoff
2 to 5, Bass G, C, D, F
6 Bass drum
7 to 15, Accompaniment G, A, B, C, D, E, F, F# G
16 and 17, Clarinet G, A
18 Snare drum
19 to 29, Clarinet B, C, C#, D, E, F, F#, G, A, B, C
30 Snare drum
31 to 40, Piccolo G, A, B, C, C#, D, E, F, F#, G
41 to 50, Trumpet G, A, B, C, C#, D, E, F, F#, G

Some organs might have flageolet instead of piccolo.

56-KEY LIMONAIRE "JAZZBANDOPHONE" ORGAN SCALE
235 mm. wide

      8 Bass notes
    11 Accompaniment notes
    22 Melody notes

1 Blank
2 Swell shades open
3 Swell shades closed
4 Vox humana on
5 Bassoon (trombone) on
6 Flute on
7 Clarinet on
8 Violin pipes on
9 General cancel
10 Blank?
11 Wood block; snare drum
12 Xylophone on
13 Wood block; snare drum
14 Key frame key?
15 to 22, Bass G, A, A#, B, C, D, E, F
23 to 33, Accompaniment G, A-F#
34 to 55, Melody G-D, E, F
56 Triangle; bass drum

Percussion is shifted by the "trombone on" register.

56-KEY LIMONAIRE ORGAN SCALE
(Standardized street organ scale)

      8 Bass notes
    11 Accompaniment notes
    22 Melody notes

56 Biphone II on (CM)
55 Wood block
54 Biphone I on (M)
53 Bourdon on (M)
52 Trombone on
51 Unda maris on (M)
50 Wood block
49 Violin pipes on (M)
48 General cancel
47 Cymbal
46 Snare drum
45 Violin celeste on (M)
44 Snare drum
43 Tremolo on (M)
43 to 35, Bass G, A, A#, B, C, D, E, F
34 to 24, Accompaniment G, A-F#
23 to 2, Melody G-D, E, F
1 Bass drum

    Smaller organs do not use 50, 51, or 54-56. A variation of this scale, reported by Romke deWaard in his book, *From Music Boxes to Street Organs,* has the following differences:

1 and 2, Blank
3 to 48, same as 1-46 in the preceding scale
49 General cancel
50 Violin pipes on
51 Blank
52 Trombone on
53 Bourdon on
54 to 56, Blank

    SPECIAL NOTE: In this book most non-scrambled band organ scales are laid out with the lowest notes closest to the key frame hinge. The musical scale of each section, in most cases, runs upward away from the hinge. A few scales, however, are laid out in the reverse order with the lowest notes the most distant from the hinge. In instances in which this is known to be the case, the scales are printed in the reverse order in this book, with the highest number first. In this order the notes run from low to high, making comparison with other scales easier.

    Scrambled scales and scales with one note section running in a direction contrary to the other note sections are printed with the functions as marked from left to right on the scale stick, unless otherwise indicated.

68-KEY LIMONAIRE ORGAN SCALE

("Scale No. 77")
9 3/8" wide

     5 Bass notes
     6 Trombone notes
     8 Accompaniment notes
     14 Melody notes (clarinet)
     10 Piccolo notes
     11 Countermelody notes (cello)

1 Shutoff (or key frame key)
2 to 6, Bass G, C, D, E, F
7 Bass drum
8 Snare drum
9 to 13, Accompaniment G, A, B, C, D
14 Snare drum
15 Band leader
16 to 18, Accompaniment E, F, F#
19 to 32, Clarinet G, A, B, C, C#, D, E, F, F#, G, A, A#, B, C
33 to 42, Piccolo (or flageolet) C#, D, E, F, F#, G, A, A#, B, C
43 Trumpet on?
44 to 49, Trombone G, A, C, D, E, F
50 to 60, Cello G, G#, A, A#, B, C, C#, D, E, F, F#

In a variation of this scale, hole 15 is not used, and hole 13 is used for the band leader.

68-KEY LIMONAIRE ORGAN SCALE

(also known as 66-key Limonaire organ scale)
24.5 cm. wide

     6 Bass notes
     9 Accompaniment notes
     21 Melody notes
     17 Countermelody notes

1 Blank
2 Blank
3 Snare drum
4 to 6, Bass G, A, C
7 Trombone on
8 to 10, Bass D, E, F
11 Bass drum
12 to 20, Accompaniment G, A, A#, B, C, D, E, F, F#
21 Band leader?
22 General cancel
23 Flute on
24 to 35, Melody G, A-G
36 Violin pipes on
37 to 45, Melody G# to D, E, F
46 Saxophone on
47 to 54, Countermelody C to G
55 Clarinet on
56 to 64, Countermelody G# to D, E, F
65 Snare drum
66 Xylophone
67 Trumpet on
68 Blank(?)

88-KEY LIMONAIRE ORGAN SCALE

     8 Bass notes
     8 Trombone notes
     11 Accompaniment notes
     22 Melody notes
     16 Piccolo notes
     16 Countermelody notes

1 General cancel
2 to 9, Bass E, F, G, A, A#, B, C, D
10 Snare drum
11 to 13, Accompaniment E, F, G
14 Snare drum
15 Accompaniment A
16 Register (bells on?)
17 Accompaniment A#
18 Register (trumpet on?)
19 and 20, Accompaniment B, C
21 Bass drum
22 Accompaniment D
23 Bell ringer (or bells on?)
24 to 26, Accompaniment E, F, F#
27 to 48, Melody G to E
49 to 64, Piccolo F to G, A
65 to 72, Trombone E, F, G, A, A#, B, C, D
73 to 88, Countermelody E to G

Nº 246. — *Orchestrophone* **100** *touches, chromatique, deux portes, vingt-trois statuettes.*

The two 100-key Limonaire models shown on this page, top and bottom, have particularly elaborate facades with doors for the entry and exit of the public. Such instruments were used as "show fronts" for tents and traveling amusement structures, especially magic lantern and biograph productions. Gavioli, Gebr. Bruder, and Marenghi made similar instruments with doors. So far as is known, these were never originally used in America. England seems to have provided the main market.

Nº 243. — *Orchestrophone* **92** *touches, avec registres automatiques.*

Nº 254. — *Orchestrophone* **100** *touches, chromatique, deux portes, deux contrôles-caisses.*

N° 217. — *Orchestrophone 49 touches, Art nouveau, renforce.*

N° 231. — *Orchestrophone 87 touches, genre art nouveau.*

N° 214. — *Orchestrophone 49 touches, Art nouveau.*

Limonaire band organs were made in a wide variety of styles, as these catalogue illustrations indicate. Of the French organ makers, Limonaire's production quantity was second only to Gavioli during the early 20th century. Most Limonaire instruments were originally distributed in Europe.

N° 225. — *Orchestrophone 60 touches, façade sculptée.*

N° 242. — *Orchestrophone 89 touches, avec registres automatiques.*

Made during the 1920s by Limonaire Freres of Paris, this 52-key "Jazzbandophone" organ was once used to furnish dance music in a large ballroom in a French mansion. The case and facade combined dimensions are: 10'5" high by 10' wide by 4'1" deep. The instrument was found in its original location by Alain Vian, a Paris collector. (Pete Levine Collection)

CHARLES MARENGHI & CIE.
Band Organs

Charles Marenghi, who was a foreman at the Gavioli works in Paris, founded his own firm shortly after 1900. Within a few years his company had achieved prominence in its own right. Under the name of "Ideal Orchestre," Marenghi instruments were made in 60-, 69-, 87-, 89-, 92-, 94-, 98-, 100-, 102-, and 104-key formats, among others. When the Gavioli factory closed, Marenghi hired many of the workmen and acquired many unfinished components. This, plus the earlier Gavioli relationship, accounts for the similarity between many Gavioli and Marenghi instruments seen today.

In the early days a number of large organs with "show fronts" were made for traveling carnivals, moving picture exhibits, and the like. A few of these had two key frames; one for the standard music books and the other to operate a special book containing programming for changing the lights on the facade.

Charles Marenghi died in 1919, after which his business was conducted by the Gaudin brothers.

47-KEY MARENGHI ORGAN SCALE
(Right to left)

        8 Bass notes
      11 Accompaniment notes
      22 Melody notes

1 Snare drum
2 Key frame key?
3 Snare drum
4 to 8, Bass F, G, C, D, E
9 g (treble note)
10 to 12, Bass A, A# B
13 to 23, Accompaniment c to a#
24 to 45, Melody b-g, a
46 Cymbal
47 Bass drum

49-KEY MARENGHI ORGAN SCALE
204 mm. wide

        8 Bass notes
      23 Accompaniment notes
      13 Piccolo notes

1 Bass drum
2 to 9, Bass C, D, E, F, G, A, A#, B
10 to 17, Accompaniment F, G, A, A#, B, C, C#, D
18 to 32, Melody D#, to F
33 to 46, Piccolo C to C, D
47 Snare drum
48 Castanets
49 Snare drum

The accompaniment and melody dividing point is uncertain.

This promotional picture of a 98-key Marenghi band organ proclaimed that "This Orchestra Has Just Arrived From PARIS" and "The Finest ORCHESTRA Ever Played on a Fair Ground." The instrument was used in England. (Photographs on this page courtesy of A.C. Upchurch)

This very large and ornate Marenghi organ with brass trumpets and trombones, several carved figures, and many panels of oil paintings was used by Anderton's, a traveling English show.

A large and ornate 98-key Marenghi organ. The instruments shown on this page were all originally used in England, where such instruments often accompanied traveling amusement and biograph shows.

78-KEY MARENGHI ORGAN SCALE

1 Snare drum
2 Bass C
3 Bass drum
4 to 5, Bass F, G
6 Flute on?
7 and 8, Bass A, A#
9 V3 (register?)
10 Bass B
11 Accompaniment C
12 V2 (register?)
13 and 14, Accompaniment D, D#
15 Triangle
16 and 17, Accompaniment E, F
18 Cello on?
19 and 20, Accompaniment F#, G
21 Piano on?
22 and 23, Accompaniment A, A#
24 General cancel?
25 to 30, Accompaniment B to E
31 to 54, Piano and flute notes F to D, E, F
55 to 76, Cello and violin notes C to A
77 Snare drum
78 M (?)

The dividing point between the bass and accompaniment is unclear.

89-KEY MARENGHI VB ORGAN SCALE

8 Bass notes
8 Trombone notes
10 Accompaniment notes
34 Melody and piccolo notes
20 Countermelody notes

The 89-key Marenghi VB (violin-baritone) scale is quite similar to the 89-key Gavioli No. 2 scale (to which refer), but with the following differences:

2 Bells on
11 Baritone on (M)
12 to 19, Accompaniment G, A, A#, B, C, C#, D, E
30 to 38, Melody F to B
89 General cancel

The 98-key Gavioli scale (to which refer) is an enlarged version of the Marenghi VB scale.

95-KEY MARENGHI ORGAN SCALE

12 Bass notes
9 Accompaniment notes
30 Melody notes
23 Countermelody notes

1 "Piano" (piano on, or registers soft)
2 Swell shutters open
3 Cello on (CM), or mandolin on
4 Xylophone on (M)
5 Trombone on
6 Baritone on
7 Saxophone on (CM)
8 Harmonic flute on (CM)
9 Clarinet on (CM)
10 Trumpet on (M)
11 Voix celeste on (M)
12 Violin on (M)
13 Piccolo on (M)
14 Tremolo on
15 General cancel
16 Bass drum
17 to 22, Bass F, G, A, B, C#, D#
23 to 27, Baritone F, G, A, B, C#
28 to 38, Countermelody D#, F, G, A, B, C#, D#, F, G, A, B
39 to 68, Melody E, D, C#, A#, G#, F#, E, D, C, A#, G#, F#, E, D, C, C#, D#, F, G, A, B, C#, D#, F, G, A, B, C#, D#, F
69 to 80, Countermelody C, A#, G#, F#, E, D, C, A#, G#, F#, E, D
81 to 84, Baritone C, A#, G#, F#
85 to 90, Bass E, D, C, A#, G#, F#
91 Snare drum
92 Tambourine (or cello on)
93 Snare drum
94 Triangle
95 Castanets

In another version of this scale, holes 1 and 94 control countermelody notes C# (next to D#, hole 28) and C# (next to D, hole 80). Baritone note holes 23 to 27 and 81 to 84 are evidently the accompaniment section.

Th. MORTIER

From the Belgian factories of Theofiel Mortier (pronounced MOR-TEER, not MOR-TEE-AY) came some of the most ornate and elaborate organs the world has ever known. *The Encyclopedia of Automatic Musical Instruments* features a large "portfolio" of Mortier designs (see pp. 892-905 of that reference). The "Taj Mahal," a particularly fancy 101-key instrument, survives today, as do a number of other interesting large styles. While there was some similarity among large Mortier organs, most were different from each other.

Th. Mortier, a cafe owner and the proprietor of an organ rental service, began business by importing organs from Gavioli. Problems soon developed, and Mortier started building his own organs. Litigation with Gavioli concerning patent rights was settled by Mortier's agreement to buy a number of Gavioli organ chassis (without fronts) over a period of time. This arrangement, plus a copying of Gavioli mechanisms, accounts for the strong similarity between many Mortier and Gavioli products. However, Mortier organs were generally more softly voiced than Gavioli instruments.

Certain "smaller" Mortier organs were designated as "orchestrions" and were made in standard models. Larger "classic" styles were made, as noted, on a one-of-a-kind basis. It is believed that well over 1,000 organs were produced by Mortier from the 'teens through the 1930s. The firm continued in business until the 1950s. Products of the 1930s onward were mainly of the cafe organ type with modern fronts, often decorated with a functional accordion, percussion, and other devices. Later, certain Mortier assets were acquired by Gebr. Decap.

66-KEY MORTIER ORGAN SCALE

        8 Bass notes
      18 Countermelody notes
      23 Melody notes

1 General cancel
2 8' flute on
3 Vibratone on
4 to 11, Bass notes
12 Maracca
13 Snare drum
14 Violin pipes on
15 to 32, 18 countermelody notes
33 Violin pipes II on
34 Snare drum
35 Blank
36 Blank
37 to 59, 23 melody notes
60 Jazz tremolo on
61 Bass drum
62 Wood block
63 Triangle
64 Castanets
65 Shutoff
66 Blank

    Part of the countermelody section probably serves as accompaniment.

67-KEY MORTIER ORGAN SCALE
24.7 cm. wide

        12 Bass notes
        12 Accompaniment notes
        22 Melody notes
        7 Countermelody notes

1 General cancel
2 Swell shutters open
3 Bass register loud
4 to 15, Bass G to F#
16 Harmonic flute or jazz flute on
17 Unda maris on
18 Snare drum
19 to 30, Accompaniment G to F#
31 Violin pipes on
32 Snare drum
33 Tremolo on
34 to 56, Melody G to F
57 Bass drum
58 Jazz tremolo on
59 Carillon (pipes) on
60 to 66, Countermelody C, C#, D, D#, E, F, F#
67 Shutoff

    This scale, from the archives of Eugene DeRoy, has a very unusual seven-note countermelody. Only very limited countermelodies could be played on seven notes, so the countermelody note section is an extension of the accompaniment section, with countermelody notes played in both sections.

67-KEY MORTIER ORGAN SCALE
24.7 cm. wide

1 General cancel
2 Swell shutters open
3 Registers loud
4 to 15, Bass G to F#
16 Harmonic flute on
17 Unda maris on
18 Snare drum/wood block
19 to 30, Accompaniment and trumpets C to B (or G to F#?)
31 Violin pipes on
32 Snare drum/wood block
33 Harmonic flute tremolo (jazz tremolo) on
34 to 56, Melody G to F
57 Bass drum
58 Carillon pipes on
59 Trumpet pipes on
60 to 66, Countermelody and trumpets C to F#
67 Shutoff

    This organ, presently in the collection of Dr. Robert Gilson, apparently underwent modification in the past, and a harmonic flute rank was added to the original organ. The organ contains registers for both general tremolo and jazz tremolo, but there is no obvious key used for the general tremolo. There are no swell shutters in the organ. Earlier the organ was in the collection of Jim Miller of Reed City and Manistee, Michigan.

72-KEY MORTIER ORGAN SCALE

      8 Bass notes
      9 Accompaniment notes
     16 Countermelody notes
     16 Melody notes

1 to 8, Bass C, D, E, F, G, A, A#, B
9 to 17, Accompaniment F, G, A, A#, B, C, C#, D, E
18 to 33, Countermelody E to G
34 to 49, Melody C to E
50 General cancel
51 Violin pipes on
52 Jazz flute on
53 Vibratone on
54 Violin celeste on (CM)
55 Saxophone on
56 Accordion on
57 Bass drum
58 Hi-hat cymbal
59 Snare drum brush
60 Maracca
61 Snare drum brush
62 to 65, 4 temple blocks
66 Crash cymbal
67 Tom-tom
68 Jazz tremolo on
69 Tom-tom
70 Alto vibratone (CM)
71 Wood block
72 Shutoff

73-KEY MORTIER ORGAN SCALE
26.6 cm. wide

      8 Bass notes
     11 Accompaniment notes
     22 Melody notes
     20 Countermelody notes

73 to 54, Countermelody C to G
53 Bourdon on
52 Trombone on
51 Baritone on
50 Violin pipes on
49 Unda maris on
48 General cancel
47 Unknown (cymbal?)
46 Snare drum
45 Register
44 Snare drum
43 Tremolo
42 to 35, Bass G, A, A#, B, C, D, E, F
34 to 24, Accompaniment G, A to F#
23 to 2, Melody G to D, E, F
1 Bass drum

80-KEY MORTIER ORGAN SCALE
11 3/8" wide

      8 Bass notes
     10 Accompaniment notes
     22 Melody notes
     18 Countermelody notes

1 Violin celeste on (CM)
2 General cancel
3 Carillon pipes/xylophone on
4 to 11, Bass G, A, A#, B, C, D, E, F
12 to 21, Accompaniment G, A, A#, B, C, C#, D, E, F, F#
22 to 43, Melody G to E
44 Violin pipes on (M) and percussion switch
45 to 62, Countermelody C to F
63 to 65, Temple blocks
66 Saxophone on (CM)
67 Accordion on
68 Jazz flute on (M)
69 Vibratone on (M)
70 Trumpet on (M)
71 Bass drum
72 Snare drum/wood block
73 Blank
74 Snare drum/wood block
75 Melody tremolo
76 Cymbal
77 Jazz tremolo
78 Flute on (CM)
79 Blank
80 Key frame key

    The carillon pipes and xylophone play alternately each time hole 3 is punched. These registers and the temple blocks and the countermelody flute were added to the organ and were not part of its original design.

80-KEY MORTIER ORGAN SCALE
11 3/8" wide

      8 Bass notes
     10 Accompaniment notes
     23 Melody notes
     18 Countermelody notes

1 Violin celeste on (CM)
2 General cancel
3 Swell shutters open
4 to 11, Bass G, A, A#, B, C, D, E, F
12 to 21, Accompaniment G, A, A#, B, C, C#, D, E, F, F#
22 to 44, Melody G to F
45 Violin pipes on (M)
46 Vibratone on (M)
47 to 64, Countermelody E to A
65 Trombone on
66 Saxophone on (CM)
67 Cello on (CM)
68 Vibratone on (CM)
69 Jazz flute on (M)
70 Jangles
71 Bass drum
72 Wood block or snare drum
73 Tremolo on
74 Wood block or snare drum
75 Xylophone on (M)
76 Unda maris on (M)
77 Baxophone on (M)
78 Cello grave on (CM)
79 Accordion on
80 Trumpet on (M)

    This scale was deduced by studying an instrument without tubing and by examining the music books for it. The trombone register shifts wood block to snare drum and couples the cymbal to the bass drum.

Style 36 Mortier orchestrion from a catalogue of the 1920 era. Small (in comparison to most of the company's products) organs with relatively compact facades were called "orchestrions" by Mortier, although the instruments, often of 67- or 84-key size, were simply smaller versions of the 97-, 101-, and other large-key dance organs made by the firm. Mortier orchestrions were made in over three dozen different styles. Most measured about 7' to 9' high and about as wide. By contrast, typical 101-key Mortier dance organs usually measured over 20' wide and over 16' high. The orchestrions found use in small cafes, restaurants, and other locations with limited space or ceiling height.

Another 80-key Mortier organ layout (for the organ "The Golden Heads") has the following differences:

22 to 43, Melody G to E
44 Violin pipes on
45 to 64, Countermelody C to G
66 Cello on
67 Saxophone on
68 Baxophone on
69 Harmonic flute on
70 Trumpet on
77 8' flute on
78 Triangle
79 ?
80 ?

82-KEY MORTIER ORGAN SCALE
(Scale stick marked 84-90 Key C)

8 Bass notes
10 Accompaniment notes
23 Melody notes
20 Countermelody notes

1 General cancel
2 Violin celeste on
3 Swell shutters open
4 to 11, Bass G, A, A#, B, C, D, E, F
12 to 21, Accompaniment G, A, A#, B, C, C#, D, E, F, F#
22 Trumpet on (M)
23 Carillon on (M)
24 to 46, Melody G to F
47 Loud violin on (M)
48 "Bouche Celeste" on (CM)
49 to 68, Countermelody C to G
69 Trombone on
70 Saxophone on
71 Cello on
72 Alto flute on
73 Harmonic flute on
74 Soft violin pipes on
75 Bass drum
76 Snare drum
77 Tremolo on
78 Snare drum
79 Xylophone on
80 Grand violin on
81 Baxophone on
82 Triangle

84-KEYLESS MORTIER PIANO ORCHESTRION ROLL
Paper rolls spaced 9 holes per inch

1 General cancel
2 Fortissimo off
3 Swell shades
4 Jazz tremolo
5 Bass coupler
6 Mute
7 Loud cello
8 Blank
9 Rewind
10 Sustaining pedal
11 Violin pipes on
12 Hammer rail
13 Clarinet (or vox celeste) on
14 to 25, Bass C to B
26 to 69, C to G
70 Bass drum
71 Shutoff
72 Snare drum
73 Piano on

74 Alto on
75 Blank
76 Snare drum
77 "Sweller" (expression)
78 Jazz flute on
79 Mandolin on
80 Triangle
81 Fortissimo on
82 Flageolet on
83 ?
84 Violin tremolo

The DeRoy scale stick labels hole 3 "jalousie" (swell shades) and hole 77 "sweller."

84-KEY MORTIER ORGAN SCALE
30.5 cm. wide

8 Bass notes
10 Accompaniment notes
23 Melody notes
20 Countermelody notes

1 General cancel
2 Violin celeste on (CM)
3 Bourdon on (M)
4 to 11, Bass G, A, A#, B, C, D, E, F
12 to 21, Accompaniment G, A, A#, B, C, C#, D, E, F, F#
22 Trumpet on (M)
23 Flageolet on (M)
24 to 46, Melody G to F
47 Loud violin on (M)
48 Clarinet on (CM)
49 to 68, Countermelody C to G
69 Trombone on; switches wood block to snare drum
70 Baritone on (CM)
71 Cello on (CM)
72 8' flute on (CM)
73 Strong flute on (M)
74 Soft violin pipes on (M)
75 Bass drum and cymbal
76 Wood block; with 69 on, snare drum
77 Tremolo (M)
78 Wood block; with 69 on, snare drum
79 Xylophone on (M)
80 Unda maris on (M)
81 Band leader
82 Shutoff
83 Triangle
84 Key frame key

84-KEY MORTIER ORGAN SCALE

12 Bass notes
12 Accompaniment notes
23 Melody notes
18 Countermelody notes

1 General cancel
2 Swell shutters open
3 Bass registers loud; percussion shifter
4 to 15, Bass G to F#
16 Jazz flute on (M)
17 Unda maris on (CM)
18 Wood block or snare drum
19 to 30, Accompaniment G to F#
31 Violin pipes on (M)
32 Wood block; snare drum
33 Tremolo on
34 to 56, Melody G to F
57 Vox celeste on (CM)

The woodcarving on Mortier organs was often of a very high quality, as the head of this Mortier statue indicates. The statue was one of two built for an organ whose facade was a copy of the entrance to the 1910 World's Fair in Brussels.

58 Cello on (CM)
59 8' flute on (M)
60 to 77, Countermelody C to F
78 Carillon (pipes) on, or trumpet on (M)
79 Triangle; bass drum
80 Xylophone on (M)
81 Jazz tremolo on
82 Blank
83 Shutoff
84 Key frame key

80/84-KEY MORTIER ORGAN SCALE
"VAN DER BOSCH"

A scale stick marked "80/84 Van der Bosch" in the DeRoy archives
has a total of 86 keys. Mr. Van der Bosch was apparently associated
with Mortier and built late-style organs with electronic components.
The scale is similar to the preceding 84-key Mortier scale but with the
following differences:

80 Tympani?
81 Tympani?
82 Xylophone on
83 "P" (?)
84 "CB" (?)
85 Jazz tremolo on
86 "S" (shutoff?)

A number of Mortier orchestrion-organs used a somewhat
standardized key frame layout based on the general 84-key scale.
One 80-key Mortier orchestrion examined has the following
differences:

33 Tremolo - chain perforation
80 Key frame key
81 to 84, Blank

84-KEY MORTIER ORGAN SCALE
"VAN DER BOSCH"

12 Bass notes
12 Accompaniment notes
14 Countermelody notes
22 Melody notes

1 General cancel
2 Accordion bass on
3 Saxophone on
4 to 15, Bass G to F#
16 Accordion on (M)
17 High octave on
18 Blank, or jazz flute on
19 to 30, Accompaniment G to F#
31 Univox or clavioline on (M)
32 Blank, or tremolo on
33 to 46, Countermelody F to F#
47 Low octave on
48 to 69, Melody G to E
70 Univox or clavioline F-PP
71 Accordion F-P
72 Cymbal
73 Bass drum
74 Hi-hat cymbals
75 Accordion on (CM)
76 Tom-tom
77 Univox or clavioline on (CM)
78 Tom-tom
79 Wood block (or claves)

80 Snare drum brush
81 Maracca
82 Snare drum brush
83 Shutoff
84 Key frame key

The univox and clavioline are simple electronic organs; one or the
other was used in dance organs with this scale. 36 notes are used; 22
melody and 14 countermelody.

86/90-KEY MORTIER ORGAN SCALE

12 Bass notes
12 Accompaniment notes
23 Melody notes
18 Countermelody notes

1 General cancel
2 Swell shutters open
3 Unda maris on (M)
4 to 15, Bass G to F#
16 Harmonic flute on (M)
17 Baxophone on (M)
18 Flute 8' on (CM)
19 to 30, Accompaniment G to F#
31 Soft violin pipes on (M)
32 Loud violin or trumpet on (M)
33 Tremolo on (M)
34 to 56, Melody G to F
57 Vox celeste on (CM)
58 Cello on (CM)
59 Saxophone on (CM)
60 Piffaro on (CM)
61 Cello grave on (CM)
62 to 79, Countermelody E to A
80 Bass drum and cymbal
81 Trombone on
82 Snare drum or wood block
83 Xylophone on (M)
84 Snare drum or wood block
85 Carillon (pipe ranks) on (M)
86 Key frame key
––––––––––––
The 90-key scale adds the following:
60 Blank
86 Piffaro on (CM)
87 Jazz flute on (M)
88 Blank
89 Blank
90 Key frame key

92/97-KEY MORTIER ORGAN SCALE

12 Bass notes
12 Accompaniment notes
19 Countermelody notes
23 Melody notes

1 General cancel
2 Unda maris on
3 Wood block
4 to 15, Bass G to F#
16 to 20, Accompaniment G, G#, A, A#, B
21 to 39, Countermelody C to F#
40 to 62, Melody G to F
63 Blank
64 Cymbal
65 Jazz flute on
66 Cymbal
67 Loud violin pipes on
68 Cello on
69 Wood block

Built in 1913, the above organ is reported to have been of 81-key size. It saw original service in Gent (Ghent in the English language), Belgium.

The citizens of Reed City, Michigan had a real treat in 1969 when the collection of Jim Miller of that city was exhibited in the municipal auditorium. The impressive lineup of automatic musical instruments includes, left to right, Style 41 Mortier orchestrion, Wurlitzer 125 band organ, Mortier dance organ with new front, Western Electric "A" roll piano, Style 30 Mortier orchestrion, and a 53-note National calliope. (Photograph courtesy of Jim Miller)

70 Bassoon on
71 Triangle
72 Bell
73 Vox celeste on
74 Wood block
75 Trombone on
76 Temple block
77 Bass drum
78 Snare drum
79 Bass drum
80 Temple block
81 Trumpet on
82 Temple block
83 Bells on
84 Gong
85 Melody tremolo on
86 Jazz tremolo on
87 Vibratone on
88 Baxophone on
89 Swell shutters open
90 "S"
91 "V"
92 Accompaniment forte
——————————
93 Blank
94 "Tam-tam"
95 Blank
96 "Tam-tam"
97 Blank (or key frame key)

This interesting scale borrows the five accompaniment notes and the seven highest countermelody notes to play the trombones when the trombone register is on. The trombones play C to B, holes 33-39 and 16-20.

92/97/101-KEY MORTIER ORGAN SCALE

12 Bass notes
12 Accompaniment notes
23 Melody notes
20 Countermelody notes

1 General cancel
2 Swell shutters open
3 Unda maris on (M)
4 to 15, Bass G to F#
16 Harmonic flute on (M)
17 Baxophone on (M)
18 Carillon (pipe ranks) on (M)
19 to 30, Accompaniment G to F#
31 Soft violin pipes on (M)
32 Loud violin pipes on (M)
33 Melody tremolo on
34 to 56, Melody G to F
57 Vox celeste on (CM)
58 Cello on (CM)
59 Saxophone on (CM)
60 to 79, Countermelody C to G
80 Bass drum
81 Trombone on
82 Snare drum or wood block
83 Xylophone on (M)
84 Snare drum or wood block
85 Flute 8' on (CM)
86 Cello grave on (CM)
87 Jazz flute on (M), or piffaro on (CM)
88 Trumpet on (M)
89 Blank
90 Blank
91 Blank
92 Key frame key
——————————
The 97-key scale continues as follows:
89 Triangle
90 Hi-hat cymbal

91 Bell G
92 Bell B
93 Bell C
94 Bell D
95 Cymbal
96 Bassoon on (CM)
97 Key frame key
——————————
The 101-key scale continues as follows
93 Jazz tremolo (no bell C)
97 Reiterating wood block
98 Vibratone on
99 Blank
100 Blank
101 Key frame key

97-KEY MORTIER ORGAN SCALE

12 Bass notes
12 Accompaniment notes
23 Melody notes
20 Countermelody notes

1 General cancel
2 Blank
3 Swell shutters open
4 Swell shutters closed
5 to 16, Bass G to F#
17 Unda maris on (M)
18 to 29, Accompaniment G to F#
30 Baxophone on (M)
31 Trumpet on (M)
32 to 51, Countermelody C to G
52 Wood block
53 Tremolo on
54 Wood block
55 Triangle
56 Soft violin pipes on (M)
57 Loud violin pipes on (M)
58 to 80, Melody G to F
81 Cello grave on (CM)
82 Cello on (CM)
83 8' flute on (CM)
84 Vibratone on (M)
85 Saxophone on (CM)
86 Castanets
87 Snare drum
88 Trombone on
89 Snare drum
90 Voix celeste on (CM)
91 Jazz flute on (M)
92 Jazz tremolo on
93 Xylophone on (M)
94 Bass drum
95 Cymbal
96 Key frame key
97 Blank

This angular view of the key frame of a 67-key Mortier dance organ shows the upper slotted roller and rubber-covered pinch roller in the raised position. The 67 tiny brass "fingers," or keys, are below the slotted roller at the right edge of the wood panel. (Dr. Robert Gilson Collection)

97/101-KEY MORTIER ORGAN SCALE

  12 Bass notes
  12 Accompaniment notes
  20 Countermelody notes
  23 Melody notes

1 Cymbal
2 Cymbal
3 to 14, Bass G to F#
15 Snare drum
16 to 27, Accompaniment G to F#
28 Snare drum
29 General cancel
30 Saxophone on
31 Cello on
32 Cello grave on
33 Celeste on
34 Bassoon on
35 Vibratone on
36 Prestant on
37 to 56, Countermelody C to G
57 Gong
58 Trombone on
59 Tambourine
60 Wood block
61 to 83, Melody G to F
84 Wood block
85 Jazz flute on
86 Violin I on
87 Violin II on
88 Baxophone on
89 Tremolo on
90 Xylophone on
91 Jazz tremolo on
92 Unda maris on
93 Trumpet on
94 Bell 1
95 Bell 2
96 Bell 3
97 Accordion on
——————————
 101-key scale adds the following
98 Vibratone on
99 Bombarde on
100 Vibratone on
101 Key frame key

101-KEY MORTIER ORGAN SCALE
35.5 cm. wide

  12 Bass notes
  12 Accompaniment notes
  23 Melody notes
  20 Countermelody notes

1 General cancel
2 Accordion on
3 Unda maris on
4 to 15, Bass G to F#
16 Vibratone on
17 Maracca
18 Bells on
19 to 30, Accompaniment G to F#
31 Soft violin pipes on
32 Loud violin pipes on
33 Tremolo on
34 to 56, Melody G to F
57 Vox celeste on
58 Cello on
59 Baritone on
60 to 79, Countermelody C to G
80 Bass drum
81 Trombone on
82 Snare drum

83 Blank
84 Snare drum
85 8' flute on
86 Cello grave on
87 Jazz flute on
88 Trumpet on
89 Blank
90 Cymbal
91 to 94, Temple blocks
95 Jazz tremolo on
96 Bassoon
97 Hi hat cymbal
98 Wood block
99 Blank
100 Wood block
101 Key frame key?

101-KEY MORTIER ORGAN SCALE

  12 Bass notes
  12 Accompaniment notes
  23 Melody notes
  20 Countermelody notes

1 Cymbal
2 Triangle
3 Bass drum
4 Accordion on (CM)
5 Baxophone on
6 Unda maris on
7 Trumpet on
8 Loud violin pipes on
9 Soft violin pipes on
10 Jazz flute on
11 Xylophone on
12 to 34, Melody, F chromatically down through G
35 Snare drum
36 to 47, Accompaniment, F# chromatically down through G
48 Snare drum
49 to 60, Bass, F chromatically up through E
61 Wood block
62 to 81, Countermelody, C chromatically up through G
82 Wood block
83 Vox celeste
84 Accordion on
85 Bassoon on
86 Cello grave on
87 Vibratone on (CM)
88 General cancel
89 Blank
90 Jazz tremolo on
91 Trombone on
92 Saxophone on
93 Blank
94 Cello on
95 Swell shutters open
96 Vibratone on
97 Tremolo on
98 Blank
99 Blank
100 Blank
101 Key frame key?

 The multiplicity of 101-key scales is explained by Mortier's desire that the owners of 101-key (and other large styles) organs not be able to exchange music with each other.

The "Spirit of Music" statue on the front of the very ornate 101-key "Taj Mahal" organ built by Mortier in 1924. The figure was hand-carved in Italy.

101-KEY MORTIER ORGAN SCALE
The "Taj Mahal"

    12 Bass notes
    12 Accompaniment notes
    20 Countermelody notes
    23 Melody notes

1 General cancel
2 Bass loud
3 Swell shutters open
4 Swell shutters closed
5 to 16, Bass A# to A
17 Unda maris on
18 to 29, Accompaniment A# to A
30 Baxophone on (M)
31 Trumpet on (M)
32 to 51, Countermelody D# to A#
52 Wood block
53 Tremolo on
54 Wood block
55 Triangle
56 Soft violin pipes on (M)
57 Loud violin pipes on (M)
58 to 80, Melody A# to G#
81 Cello grave on (CM)
82 Cello on (CM)
83 8' flute on (CM)
84 Bassoon on (CM)
85 Saxophone on (CM)
86 Castanets
87 Snare drum
88 Trombone on
89 Snare drum
90 Violin celeste on (CM)
91 Carillon pipes on (M)
92 Harmonic flute on (M)
93 Xylophone on (M)
94 Blank
95 Tubular chimes on (M)
96 Jazz flute on (M)
97 Bass drum
98 Cymbal
99 Large bell
100 Blank
101 Key frame key

The large bell played by hole 99 sounds like a ship's bell or gong and is used to signify the end of a tune or to indicate that dancing partners should be changed. It is not scored as part of the musical arrangements. Elaborate light-changing circuits are controlled by pipe registers.

The Taj Mahal 101-key Mortier organ, built in 1924, is one of the most ornate automatic musical instruments ever made. Music books have been made for it by many well-known arrangers, as the books from Pierre Verbeeck, Eugene Peersman, Abel Frans, L. Chassen, Arthur Prinsen, A. Schollaert-Ghysbrecht, Louis Callaert, and the Mortier factory ("Usines Th. Mortier") illustrate.

101-KEY MORTIER ORGAN SCALE

    12 Bass notes
    12 Accompaniment notes
    23 Melody notes
    20 Countermelody notes

1 General cancel
2 Swell shutters open
3 Unda maris on (M)
4 to 15, Bass G to F#
16 Baxophone on (M)
17 Harmonic flute on (M)
18 Stopped flute on (CM)
19 to 30, Accompaniment G to F#
31 Soft violin pipes on (M)
32 Loud violin pipes on (M)
33 General tremolo on
34 to 56, Melody G to F
57 Violin celeste on (CM)
58 Cello on (CM)
59 Saxophone on (CM)
60 to 79, Countermelody C to G
80 Bass drum
81 Trombone on
82 Snare drum
83 Xylophone on (M)
84 Snare drum
85 8' flute on (CM)
86 Cello grave on (CM)
87 Jazz flute on (M)
88 Trumpet on (M)
89 Triangle
90 Cymbal
91 Blank
92 Wood block
93 Jazz tremolo
94 Wood block
95 Tremolo on?
96 Bassoon on (CM)
97 Vibratone on (M)
98 Blank
99 Blank
100 Blank
101 Key frame key

101-KEY MORTIER ORGAN SCALE

    12 Bass notes
    12 Accompaniment notes
    20 Countermelody notes
    23 Melody notes

1 General cancel
2 Bell 1
3 Swell shutters open
4 Swell shutters closed
5 to 16, Bass G to F#
17 Unda maris on (M)
18 to 29, Accompaniment G to F#
30 Baxophone on (M)
31 Trumpet on (M)
32 to 51, Countermelody C to G
52 Wood block
53 Melody tremolo
54 Wood block
55 Triangle
56 Soft violin pipes on (M)
57 Loud violin pipes on (M)
58 to 80, Melody G to F
81 Cello grave on (CM)
82 Cello on (CM)
83 Flute 8' on (CM)
84 Piffaro on (CM)
85 Saxophone on (CM)
86 Castanets
87 Snare drum
88 Trombone on
89 Snare drum
90 Vox celeste on (CM)
91 Carillon on (M)
92 Harmonic flute on (M)
93 to 96, Blank
97 Bass drum
98 Hi-hat cymbal
99 Bell 2
100 Bell 3
101 Key frame key

    Another 101-key Mortier organ uses the above scale but with the following differences:

16 Vibratone on (M)
17 Baxophone on (M)
18 Bourdon II (piffaro) on (CM)
59 Baritone on (CM)
90 Wood block
91 Bell
92 Bell
94 Bell
95 Cymbal
96 Large wood block
97 Bassoon on (CM)
98 Wood block
100 Bourdon I on (M)

    The Bourdon I and II are added ranks which were not originally in the organ.

102-KEY MORTIER ORGAN SCALE

    12 Bass notes
    12 Accompaniment notes
    23 Melody notes
    20 Countermelody notes

1 Hi-hat cymbal
2 Triangle
3 Cymbal
4 Blank
5 Cymbal
6 Blank
7 Trumpet on (M)
8 Unda maris on (M)
9 Violin on (M)
10 Jazz flute on (M)
11 Maracca
12 to 34, Melody G to F
35 Snare drum
36 to 47, Accompaniment G to F#
48 Snare drum
49 to 60, Bass G to F#
61 Wood block or tam-tam
62 to 81, Countermelody C to G
82 Wood block or tam-tam
83 Celeste on
84 Accordion on
85 Temple block
86 Triangle

87 Vibratone on (CM)
88 General cancel
89 Temple block
90 Jazz tremolo on
91 Blank
92 Saxophone on (CM)
93 Temple block
94 Cello on (CM)
95 Temple block
96 Vibratone on
97 Melody tremolo on
98 Shutoff
99 to 101 Blank
102 Key frame key?

105-KEY MORTIER ORGAN SCALE
36 cm. wide

12 Bass notes
12 Accompaniment notes
23 Melody notes
20 Countermelody notes

1 General cancel
2 Accordion F on
3 Unda maris on
4 to 15, Bass G to F#
16 Jazz flute on
17 Jazz tremolo on
18 Vibratone on (M)
19 to 30, Accompaniment G to F#
31 Soft violin pipes on
32 Swell shutters open
33 Loud violin pipes on
34 to 56, Melody G to F
57 Vox celeste on
58 Cello on
59 Baritone on
60 to 79, Countermelody C to G
80 Bass drum
81 Cymbal
82 Gong
83 Snare drum
84 Tremolo on
85 Snare drum
86 Trombone on
87 Tom tom
88 Wood block
89 Tom tom
90 Bassoon
91 Maracca
92 Vibratone (CM)
93 Maracca
94 Musette accordion on
95 Triangle
96 Trumpet on
97 Tambourine
98 Xylophone on
99 Tambourine
100 Crumhorn on
101 Castanets
102 Tremolo on
103 Castanets
104 Shutoff
105 Key frame key?

112-KEY MORTIER ORGAN SCALE
40 cm. wide

12 Bass notes
12 Accompaniment notes
30 Melody notes
24 Countermelody notes

1 Cymbal
2 Bass drum
3 to 14, Bass G to F#
15 Snare drum
16 to 27, Accompaniment G to F#
28 Snare drum
29 General cancel
30 Baritone on
31 Cello on
32 Cello grave on
33 Vox celeste on
34 Bassoon on
35 Vibratone on (CM)
36 Quintadena on
37 Temple block
38 Blank
39 Temple block
40 Triangle
41 to 64, Countermelody C to B
65 Wood block
66 Trombone on
67 Jazz tremolo on
68 to 97, Melody C to F
98 Blank
99 Maracca
100 Jazz flute on
101 Wood block
102 Baxophone on
103 Violin pipes on
104 Tremolo on
105 Violin pipes on
106 Unda maris on
107 Trumpet on
108 Maracca
109 Xylophone on
110 Vibratone on (M)
111 Accordion on
112 Key frame key?

STYLE 75
Operated by Pinned Cylinder,
55 keys, 9 selections.

STYLE 76
Operated by Perforated Paper,
55 notes, 18 selections.

NIAGARA MUSICAL INSTRUMENT MANUFACTURING CO.

The Niagara Musical Instrument Manufacturing Company was in business in North Tonawanda, New York around 1909. Despite the issuance of several attractive catalogues and price lists, apparently sales were very small, for today Niagara instruments are virtually unknown. The authors were unable to locate any Niagara organs equipped with original Niagara music systems.

The organ illustrated on this page shows a practice used by Wurlitzer, the North Tonawanda Musical Instrument Works, and others of the era: the same instrument could be ordered with either a pinned cylinder mechanism or a perforated paper roll system. The pinned cylinder instruments were recommended for ice skating rinks, merry-go-rounds, and outdoor locations in which there might be trouble with music rolls (especially on account of dryness or excessive humidity). However, cylinders were very expensive in comparison to music rolls, and it was not practical to change musical programs, so within a few years cylinder-operated organs were anachronisms.

Style No. 75
55 Keys—With Drums and Cymbal.
Representing a Band of twenty-five pieces.
Operated by a Pinned Cylinder with nine selections.
One cylinder included with instrument.

INSTRUMENTS

Visible— 5 Brass Trombones, 16 Brass Trumpets, 17 Brass Clarionets, 17 Brass Piccoloes.
Inside— 5 Open Basses,17 Violin Pipes, 10 Violoncello Pipes, 27 Stopped Pipes.
Bottom— 5 Stopped Double Basses, 5 Stopped Basses.
Dimensions— Height 7 feet 1 inch,—width 8 feet 10 inches,—depth 2 feet 10 inches.
Case— Double Veneered, "inside and outside" with Hardwood Core.
Finish— Quarter-cut Oak, Mission Finish,—Quarter-cut Oak, Piano Polish,—Mahogany Stain, Piano Polish,—White Enamel with Gold inlaid Carvings.
    Net weight 700 pounds Boxed for shipment 1100 pounds.
    This instrument is provided with 5 outside Slide Stops to silence Piccoloes, Clarionets, Trumpets, Trombones, Drums and Cymbal. Also 2 inside Stops for (Cello, Bass and Violin) and (Melodian and Open Basses).

Style No. 76
55 Notes—With Drums and Cymbal.
Representing a Band of twenty-five pieces.
Operated by Perforated Paper Rolls.
Eighteen Selections included with instrument.

The two instruments above mentioned are of the very latest design and equipment. For a Roller Rink or Dancing Pavillion, nothing more exquisite could be desired. Its Drum actions are as perfect as the human touch. The instrumentation throughout is well balanced. Any amusement man may well be proud to own this wonderful Niagara Military Band.

RICHTER
Band Organs

78/79-KEY RICHTER ORGAN SCALE
334 mm. wide

    8 Trombone notes
   11 Bass notes
   11 Accompaniment notes
   24 Melody notes
   16 Trumpet notes

1 Xylophone and flute on
2 F (trombone)
3 G (bass)
4 D (trombone)
5 Snare drum
6 B (trombone)
7 Snare drum
8 A (bass)
9 Registers soft
10 Registers loud
11 A (trumpet)
12 B (bass)
13 C# (bass)
14 B (trumpet)
15 D# (bass)
16 F (bass)
17 C# (trumpet)
18 G (accompaniment)
19 A (accompaniment)
20 B (accompaniment)
21 D# (trumpet)
22 Xylophone and flute off
23 C# (accompaniment)
24 Violin pipes off
25 F (trumpet)
26 D# (accompaniment)
27 E (2nd octave melody)
28 High G (trumpet)
29 D (2nd octave melody)
30 C (2nd octave melody)
31 A# (2nd octave melody)
32 High A (trumpet)
33 G# (2nd octave melody)
34 F# (2nd octave melody)
35 E (1st octave melody)
36 D (1st octave melody)
37 C (1st octave melody)
38 High C (trumpet)
39 A# (1st octave melody)
40 G# (1st octave melody)
41 High B (trumpet)
42 F# (1st octave melody)
43 F (1st octave melody; lowest note)
44 G (1st octave melody)
45 A (1st octave melody)
46 High G# (trumpet)
47 B (1st octave melody)
48 C# (1st octave melody)
49 D# (1st octave melody)
50 F# (trumpet)
51 F (2nd octave melody)
52 G (2nd octave melody)
53 A (2nd octave melody)
54 B (2nd octave melody)
55 E (trumpet)
56 C# (2nd octave melody)
57 D# (2nd octave melody)
58 D (trumpet)
59 E (accompaniment)
60 D (accompaniment)
61 C (trumpet)
62 C (accompaniment)
63 A# (accompaniment)

64 A# (trumpet)
65 G# (accompaniment)
66 F# (accompaniment)
67 G (trumpet; lowest note)
68 E (bass)
69 D (bass)
70 C (bass)
71 Bass drum and cymbal
72 E (trombone)
73 A# (bass)
74 G (trombone)
75 A (trombone)
76 F# (trombone)
77 C (trombone)
78 G# (bass)
79 D (bass)

The 78-key scale omits hole 79

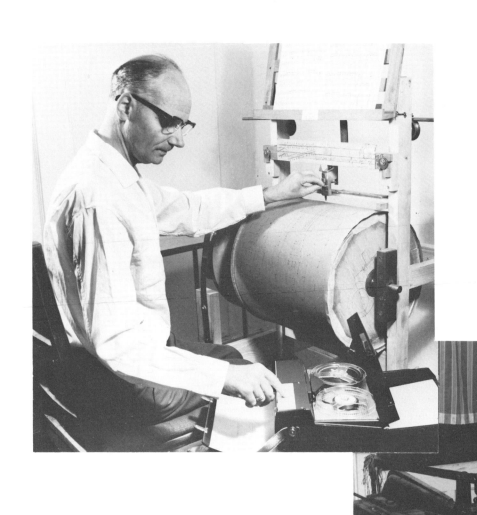

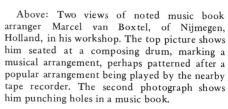

Above: Two views of noted music book arranger Marcel van Boxtel, of Nijmegen, Holland, in his workshop. The top picture shows him seated at a composing drum, marking a musical arrangement, perhaps patterned after a popular arrangement being played by the nearby tape recorder. The second photograph shows him punching holes in a music book.

Left: Among the instruments Mr. van Boxtel has arranged music for is this beautiful Style 36 Ruth organ (76 keyless). (Th. Koek Collection)

A. RUTH & SON
Band Organs

In the early 1840s Andreas Ruth established an organ works in Waldkirch, Germany. During the 19th century many different styles of cylinder-operated instruments were made.

In the 1900-1914 years many large book-operated instruments were produced. Large numbers of these were imported into the United States, where they found use on carousels, in skating rinks, and in other public places. Charles I.D. Looff, the famous carousel builder, brought many Ruth organs to the United States, including a number of the Style 38 models, and used them on large carousels.

Many Ruth organs bear a similarity to the Bruder products made in the same town. This was due to several factors, including the common use of facade carvers, the closeness of the firms, and (from the standpoint of similar catalogue illustrations) the common use of a printer, Aug. Faller.

Today, Ruth & Son organs are highly prized and are considered to be among the finest of their genre ever produced.

52-KEYLESS RUTH ORGAN SCALE
STYLE 33
217 mm. wide

6 Bass notes
4 or 5 Trombone notes
11 Accompaniment notes
20 Melody notes
11 Trumpet notes

1 C (trumpet; lowest note)
2 G (trombone)
3 C (trombone)
4 G (bass)
5 E (trumpet)
6 Snare drum
7 C (bass)
8 F# (trumpet)
9 E (bass)
10 E (2nd octave melody)
11 C# (2nd octave melody)
12 G (accompaniment)
13 B (2nd octave melody)
14 A (2nd octave melody)
15 A (accompaniment)
16 G (1st octave melody)
17 F (1st octave melody)
18 A# (accompaniment)
19 D (1st octave melody)
20 C (1st octave melody; high trumpet)
21 B (accompaniment)
22 A# (1st octave melody; trumpet)
23 C (accompaniment)
24 G# (1st octave melody, lowest note; trumpet)
25 Coupled trumpets off
26 C# (accompaniment)
27 A (1st octave melody; trumpet)
28 D (accompaniment)
29 B (1st octave melody; trumpet)
30 C# (1st octave melody)
31 E (accompaniment)
32 E (1st octave melody)
33 F# (1st octave melody)
34 F (accompaniment)
35 G# (2nd octave melody; lowest note)
36 A# (2nd octave melody)
37 F# (accompaniment)
38 C (2nd octave melody)
39 D (2nd octave melody)
40 G (accompaniment)
41 F (2nd octave melody)
42 Registers soft
43 F (bass)
44 G (trumpet)
45 D (bass)
46 Bass drum
47 F (trumpet)
48 A (bass)
49 D (trombone)
50 F (trombone)
51 D (trumpet)
52 A (trombone); blank in some organs

The five lowest melody holes also play trumpets, disconnected by hole 25.

56-KEYLESS RUTH ORGAN SCALE
STYLE 34

4 Trombone notes
7 Bass notes
12 Accompaniment notes
23 Melody notes
11 Trumpet notes

1 Bass drum
2 G (trombone)
3 D (trombone)
4 D (accompaniment)
5 D# (accompaniment)
6 D (trumpet)
7 E (accompaniment)
8 F (accompaniment)
9 F (trumpet)
10 F# (accompaniment)
11 G (accompaniment)
12 G (trumpet)
13 G (bass)
14 F# (2nd octave melody)
15 E (2nd octave melody)
16 C# (2nd octave melody)
17 B (bass)
18 B (2nd octave melody)
19 A (2nd octave melody)
20 G (1st octave melody)
21 D (bass)
22 F (1st octave melody)
23 D# (1st octave melody)
24 C# (1st octave melody)
25 F (bass)
26 B (1st octave melody; trumpet)
27 A (1st octave melody; trumpet)
28 Registers soft
29 G# (1st octave melody, lowest note; trumpet)
30 A# (1st octave melody; trumpet)
31 E (bass)
32 C (1st octave melody; trumpet)
33 D (1st octave melody)
34 Coupled trumpets off
35 E (1st octave melody)
36 F# (1st octave melody)
37 G# (2nd octave melody; lowest note)
38 C (bass)
39 A# (2nd octave melody)
40 C (2nd octave melody)
41 D (2nd octave melody)
42 F# (trumpet)
43 F (2nd octave melody)
44 G (2nd octave melody)
45 A (bass)
46 E (trumpet)
47 C# (accompaniment)
48 C (accompaniment)
49 B (accompaniment)
50 C (trumpet)
51 A# (accompaniment)
52 A (accompaniment)
53 G (accompaniment; lowest note)
54 C (trombone)
55 F (trombone)
56 Snare drum

Trumpets coupled to the melody are turned off by hole 34.

65-KEYLESS RUTH ORGAN SCALE
STYLE 35A
274 mm. wide

The Style 35A scale of 65 keys is similar to the following Style 35B scale except that holes 1 and 67 are omitted.

67-KEYLESS RUTH ORGAN SCALE
STYLE 35B
274 mm. wide

6 Trombone notes
8 Bass notes
36 Accompaniment, alto violin, and melody notes
15 Trumpet notes

1 Ocarina
2 Bass drum
3 D (trombone)
4 F (trombone)
5 A (trombone)
6 F (bass)
7 G (bass)
8 A (bass)
9 Band leader
10 B (1st octave melody)
11 A# (1st octave melody; trumpet)
12 A (1st octave melody; trumpet)
13 Registers loud (trumpet coupler on)
14 G# (1st octave melody; trumpet)
15 G (1st octave melody; trumpet)
16 Registers soft
17 F# (1st octave melody, lowest note; trumpet)
18 E (2nd octave melody)
19 C# (2nd octave melody)
20 B (2nd octave melody)
21 A (2nd octave melody)
22 F (trumpet)
23 G (2nd octave melody)
24 F (1st octave melody)
25 D# (1st octave melody)
26 C# (1st octave melody)
27 E (trumpet)
28 C (1st octave melody)
29 D (1st octave melody)
30 E (1st octave melody)
31 F# (2nd octave melody; lowest note)
32 D (trumpet)
33 G# (2nd octave melody)
34 A# (2nd octave melody)
35 C (2nd octave melody)
36 D (2nd octave melody)
37 C# (trumpet)
38 F (2nd octave melody)
39 F (accompaniment)
40 E (accompaniment)
41 D# (accompaniment)
42 C (trumpet)
43 D (accompaniment)
44 C# (accompaniment)
45 C (accompaniment)
46 B (accompaniment)
47 B (trumpet)
48 A# (accompaniment)
49 A (accompaniment)
50 G# (accompaniment)
51 A# (trumpet)
52 G (accompaniment)
53 F# (accompaniment)
54 F (accompaniment; lowest note)
55 A (trumpet)
56 E (bass)
57 D (bass)
58 G (trumpet)
59 C (bass)
60 B (bass)
61 A# (bass)
62 G (trombone)
63 E (trombone)
64 C (trombone)
65 Snare drum
66 Snare drum
67 Bells

High trumpet notes are coupled to the melody when turned on by 13. Holes 10 to 12, 14, 15, and 17 are for alto violins. In the preceding scale notes F (hole 38) and E (hole 18) may be reversed.

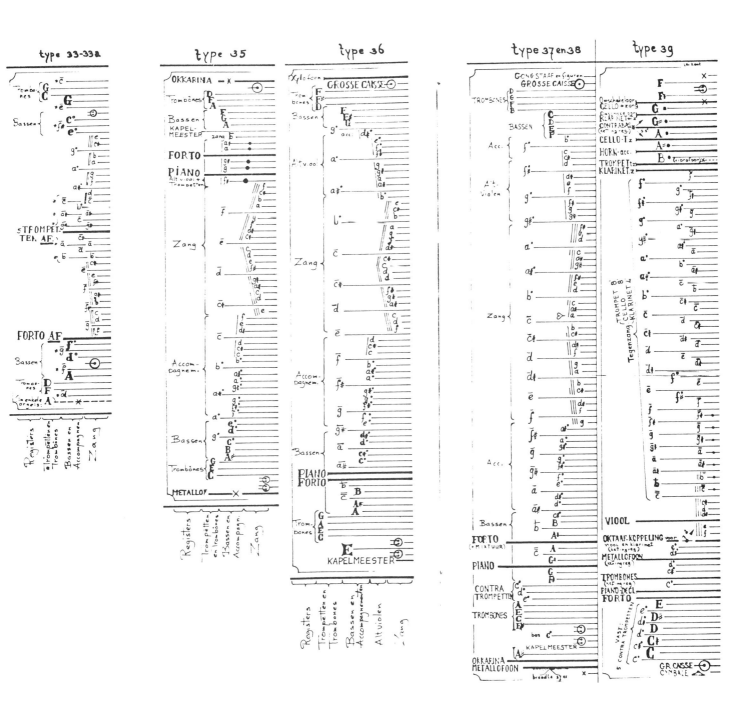

Scales for A. Ruth & Son organs, styles 33, 33a, 35, 36, 37, 38, and 39, are shown reduced in size. (From "Het Pierement," journal of the Kring van Draaiorgelvrienden ["Circle of Friends of the Hand-Cranked Organ"], the Dutch organization of mechanical organ enthusiasts)

78-KEYLESS RUTH ORGAN SCALE
STYLE 36
316 mm. wide

6 Trombone notes
6 Bass notes
18 Accompaniment notes
23 Melody notes
20 Trumpet notes

1 Bass drum
2 D (trombone)
3 F (trombone)
4 A (trombone)
5 F (bass)
6 G (bass)
7 A (bass)
8 Band leader
9 B (1st octave melody; trumpet)
10 A# (1st octave melody; trumpet)
11 A (1st octave melody; trumpet)
12 Accompaniment loud
13 G# (1st octave melody; trumpet)
14 G (1st octave melody; trumpet)
15 Accompaniment soft
16 F# (1st octave melody; lowest note)
17 E (2nd octave melody)
18 C# (2nd octave melody)
19 B (2nd octave melody)
20 A (2nd octave melody)
21 F (trumpet)
22 G (2nd octave melody)
23 F (1st octave melody; trumpet)
24 D# (1st octave melody; trumpet)
25 C# (1st octave melody; trumpet)
26 E (trumpet)
27 C (1st octave melody; trumpet)
28 D (1st octave melody; trumpet)
29 E (1st octave melody; trumpet)
30 F# (2nd octave melody; lowest note)
31 D (trumpet)
32 G# (2nd octave melody)
33 A# (2nd octave melody)
34 C (2nd octave melody)
35 D (2nd octave melody)
36 C# (trumpet)
37 F (2nd octave melody)
38 F (2nd octave accompaniment)
39 E (2nd octave accompaniment)
40 D# (2nd octave accompaniment)
41 C (trumpet)
42 D (2nd octave accompaniment)
43 C# (2nd octave accompaniment)
44 C (2nd octave accompaniment)
45 B (2nd octave accompaniment)
46 B (trumpet)
47 A# (2nd octave accompaniment; lowest note)
48 A (1st octave accompaniment)
49 G# (1st octave accompaniment)
50 A# (trumpet)
51 G (1st octave accompaniment)
52 F# (1st octave accompaniment)
53 F (1st octave accompaniment)
54 A (trumpet)
55 E (1st octave accompaniment)
56 D (1st octave accompaniment)
57 G (trumpet)
58 C (1st octave accompaniment)
59 B (1st octave accompaniment)
60 A# (1st octave accompaniment; lowest note)
61 G (trombone)
62 E (trombone)
63 C (trombone)
64 Snare drum
65 Snare drum
66 Xylophone (chain perforation?)
67 Piccolo on
68 Blank
69 Violin pipes on
70 Blank
71 Clarinet and flute on
72 Blank
73 E (bass)
74 General cancel
75 D (bass)
76 Swell shutters open (chain perforation?)
77 C (bass)
78 Blank

The high trumpets are coupled to low melody notes.

78-KEYLESS RUTH ORGAN SCALE
STYLE 36 (variation)
316 mm. wide

7 Trombone notes
11 Bass notes
12 Accompaniment notes
25 Melody notes
16 Trumpet notes

1 Bells on
2 Bass drum
3 F (trombone)
4 F# (trombone)
5 D (trombone)
6 F (bass)
7 G (bass)
8 G# (bass)
9 G (trumpet; lowest note)
10 D# (accompaniment)
11 E (alto violin; lowest note)
12 F (alto violin)
13 F# (alto violin)
14 A (trumpet)
15 G (alto violin)
16 G# (alto violin)
17 A (alto violin)
18 A# (alto violin)
19 A# (trumpet)
20 B (alto violin)
21 E (2nd octave melody)
22 C# (2nd octave melody)
23 B (1st octave melody)
24 B (trumpet)
25 A (1st octave melody)
26 G (1st octave melody)
27 F (1st octave melody)
28 D# (1st octave melody)
29 C (trumpet)
30 C# (1st octave melody)
31 C (1st octave melody; lowest note)
32 D (1st octave melody)
33 E (1st octave melody)
34 C# (trumpet)
35 F# (1st octave melody)
36 G# (1st octave melody)
37 A# (1st octave melody)
38 D (trumpet)
39 C (2nd octave melody; lowest note)
40 D (2nd octave melody)
41 F (2nd octave melody)
42 E (trumpet)
43 D (accompaniment)
44 C# (accompaniment)
45 C (accompaniment)
46 F (trumpet)
47 B (accompaniment)
48 A# (accompaniment)
49 A (accompaniment)
50 F# (trumpet)
51 G# (accompaniment)
52 G (accompaniment)

Style 35 Ruth organ as shown in a catalogue illustration of the 1912 period.

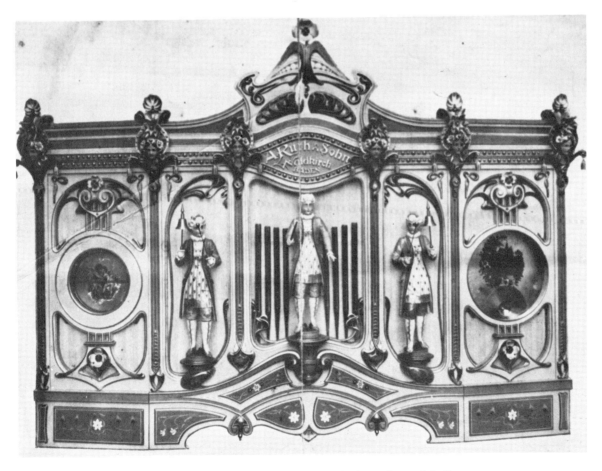

Style 36 Ruth organ as shown in an original sales catalogue of the firm.

53 F# (accompaniment)
54 G (trumpet)
55 F (accompaniment)
56 E (accompaniment; lowest note)
57 G# (trumpet)
58 D# (bass)
59 D (bass)
60 A (trumpet)
61 C# (bass)
62 C (bass)
63 A# (trumpet)
64 Registers soft
65 Registers loud
66 B (trumpet)
67 B (bass)
68 C (trumpet)
69 A# (bass)
70 A (bass)
71 G (trombone)
72 A (trombone)
73 E (trombone)
74 C (trombone)
75 Snare drum
76 E (bass; lowest note)
77 Snare drum
78 Band leader

Another 78-keyless Ruth scale lists bell ringer or figure at hole 1 and swell open at hole 78.

When the 76-keyless Bruder scale went out of popular use some of the Bruder organs were converted to play 78 Ruth Style 36 music. The two scales are similar, but the Ruth has two higher trumpets, and the dividing points between accompaniment / alto violin / melody differ.

92-KEYLESS RUTH ORGAN SCALE
STYLE 37
370 mm. wide

The 92-keyless Ruth scale is the same as the 96-keyless Ruth scale with the exception of holes 93 to 96 which are omitted.

96-KEYLESS RUTH ORGAN SCALE
No. 1
STYLE 38
385 mm. wide

9 Trombone notes
10 Bass notes
16 Accompaniment notes
5 Alto violin notes
23 Melody notes
23 Trumpet notes

1 Bell ringers
2 Bass drum
3 D (trombone)
4 G (trombone)
5 F (trombone)
6 B (trombone)
7 C (bass)
8 D (bass)
9 E (bass)
10 F (bass)
11 B (low accompaniment)
12 F (1st octave trumpet)
13 C (low accompaniment)
14 C# (high accompaniment; lowest note)
15 D (high accompaniment)
16 F# (1st octave trumpet)
17 D# (high accompaniment)
18 E (high accompaniment)
19 F (high accompaniment)
20 G (1st octave trumpet)
21 F# (high accompaniment)
22 G (high accompaniment)
23 G# (high accompaniment)
24 G# (1st octave trumpet)
25 F# (2nd octave melody)
26 E (2nd octave melody)
27 D (2nd octave melody)
28 A (1st octave trumpet)
29 C (2nd octave melody)
30 A# (2nd octave melody)
31 G# (1st octave melody)
32 A# (1st octave trumpet)
33 F# (1st octave melody)
34 E (1st octave melody)
35 D (1st octave melody)
36 B (1st octave trumpet)
37 C (1st octave melody)
38 A# (1st octave melody)
39 A (1st octave melody; lowest note)
40 C (2nd octave trumpet; lowest note)
41 B (1st octave melody)
42 C# (1st octave melody)
43 C# (2nd octave trumpet)
44 D# (1st octave melody)
45 F (1st octave melody)
46 D (2nd octave trumpet)
47 G (1st octave melody)
48 A (2nd octave melody; lowest note)
49 D# (2nd octave trumpet)
50 B (2nd octave melody)
51 C# (2nd octave melody)
52 E (2nd octave trumpet)
53 D# (2nd octave melody)
54 F (2nd octave melody)
55 F (2nd octave trumpet)
56 G (2nd octave melody)
57 A# (low accompaniment)
58 F# (2nd octave trumpet)
59 A (low accompaniment)
60 G# (low accompaniment)
61 G (2nd octave trumpet)
62 G (low accompaniment)
63 F# (low accompaniment)
64 G# (2nd octave trumpet)
65 F (low accompaniment)
66 E (low accompaniment)
67 A (2nd octave trumpet)

Above: Several listeners are enchanted by 96-key Ruth organ music as they sit and listen to one of the most magnificent instruments ever to be publicly exhibited in America. From the early 1960s until the late 1970s the organ toured with the Gooding Amusement Company shows headquartered in Columbus, Ohio.

Left: Style 36 Ruth organ (76 keyless) as exhibited during a European organ festival. (Verdonk Collection; photograph courtesy of Marcel van Boxtel)

68 D# (low accompaniment)
69 D (low accompaniment)
70 A# (2nd octave trumpet)
71 C# (low accompaniment)
72 B (bass)
73 B (2nd octave trumpet)
74 A# (bass)
75 Registers loud
76 A (bass)
77 C (2nd octave trumpet)
78 G# (bass)
79 Registers soft
80 G (bass)
81 F# (bass)
82 C (1st octave trumpet; lowest note)
83 D (1st octave trumpet)
84 E (1st octave trumpet)
85 A (trombone)
86 E (trombone)
87 C (trombone)
88 F# (trombone)
89 Snare drum
90 C (low accompaniment)
91 Snare drum
92 Band leader
93 A# (trombone)
94 Ocarina on (chain perforation)
95 Bells on (chain perforation)
96 Violin off? (If correct, this allows ocarina solos)

Holes 18, 19, 21-23 are for alto violin pipes; holes 82-84 are for contra trumpets. The 92-key Ruth scale is similar but omits the last four holes.

96-KEYLESS RUTH ORGAN SCALE
No. 2
STYLE 38
385 mm. wide
(From a B.A.B. Organ Co. description)

1 A (baritone)
2 Bass drum
3 B (baritone)
4 C# (baritone)
5 D# (baritone)
6 F (1st octave trumpet; lowest note)
7 F (accompaniment; lowest note)
8 C (trombone)
9 Band leader
10 G (accompaniment)
11 G (1st octave trumpet)
12 D (trombone)
13 A (bass)
14 A (accompaniment)
15 B (bass)
16 A (1st octave trumpet)
17 B (accompaniment)
18 E (trombone)
19 C (bass)
20 C# (accompaniment)

21 B (1st octave trumpet)
22 D (bass)
23 D# (accompaniment)
24 Trumpet off
25 C# (1st octave trumpet)
26 F (high accompaniment)
27 E (bass)
28 Baritone off
29 F (bass)
30 G# (3rd octave melody)
31 F# (3rd octave melody; lowest note)
32 D# (1st octave trumpet)
33 E (2nd octave melody)
34 D (2nd octave melody)
35 F (2nd octave trumpet; lowest note)
36 C (2nd octave melody)
37 A# (2nd octave melody)
38 Mixture off (or mixture soft)
39 G# (2nd octave melody)
40 F# (2nd octave melody; lowest note)
41 G (2nd octave trumpet)
42 E (1st octave melody)
43 D (1st octave melody)
44 A (2nd octave trumpet)
45 C (1st octave melody)
46 A# (1st octave melody)
47 B (2nd octave trumpet)
48 G# (1st octave melody)
49 F# (1st octave melody)
50 Blank
51 G (1st octave melody)
52 A (1st octave melody)
53 C (2nd octave trumpet)
54 B (1st octave melody)
55 C# (1st octave melody)
56 A# (2nd octave trumpet)
57 D# (1st octave melody)
58 F (1st octave melody)
59 G# (2nd octave trumpet)
60 G (2nd octave melody)
61 A (2nd octave melody)
62 Blank
63 B (2nd octave melody)
64 C# (2nd octave melody)
65 F# (2nd octave trumpet)
66 D# (2nd octave melody)
67 F (2nd octave melody)
68 E (1st octave trumpet)
69 G (3rd octave melody)
70 A (3rd octave melody)
71 F# (bass)
72 Blank
73 E (accompaniment)
74 D (1st octave trumpet)
75 D (accompaniment)
76 F (trombone)
77 G (bass)
78 C (1st octave trumpet)
79 C (accompaniment)
80 F# (trombone)
81 Blank
82 A# (1st octave trumpet)
83 A# (accompaniment)
84 G# (bass)
85 G (trombone)
86 G# (accompaniment)
87 G# (1st octave trumpet)
88 Registers loud
89 Snare drum
90 F# (accompaniment)
91 Snare drum
92 F# (1st octave trumpet)
93 E (baritone)
94 D (baritone)
95 C (baritone)
96 A# (baritone)

The preceding scale was deduced by studying two poorly-marked scale sticks. It is possible that the "trombone" section is actually part of another section of the organ.

96-KEYLESS RUTH ORGAN SCALE
STYLE 39
385 mm. wide

1 ?
2 F (bass)
3 Snare drum
4 F# (bass)
5 Cello on (M)
6 G (bass)
7 Clarinet on (CM)
8 G# (bass)
9 Contrabass
10 A (bass)
11 Cello on (CM)
12 A# (bass)
13 Horn - accompaniment
14 B (bass)
15 Trumpet on (CM)
16 Clarinet on (CM)
17 F (1st octave melody; lowest note)
18 F (countermelody; lowest note)
19 G (accompaniment)
20 F# (1st octave melody)
21 F# (countermelody)
22 G# (accompaniment)
23 G (1st octave melody)
24 G (countermelody)
25 A (accompaniment)
26 G# (1st octave melody)
27 G# (countermelody)
28 A# (accompaniment)
29 A (1st octave melody)
30 A (countermelody)
31 B (accompaniment)
32 A# (1st octave melody)
33 A# (countermelody)
34 C (accompaniment)
35 B (1st octave melody)
36 B (countermelody)
37 C# (accompaniment)
38 C (1st octave melody)
39 C (countermelody)
40 D (accompaniment)
41 C# (1st octave melody)
42 C# (countermelody)
43 D# (accompaniment)
44 D (1st octave melody)
45 D (countermelody)
46 E (accompaniment)
47 D# (1st octave melody)
48 D# (countermelody)
49 F (accompaniment; lowest note)
50 E (1st octave melody)
51 E (countermelody)
52 F# (accompaniment)
53 F (2nd octave melody)
54 High F (countermelody)
55 F# (2nd octave melody)
56 High F# (countermelody)
57 G (2nd octave melody)
58 High G (countermelody)
59 G# (2nd octave melody)
60 High G# (countermelody)
61 A (2nd octave melody)
62 High A (countermelody)
63 A# (2nd octave melody)
64 High A# (countermelody)
65 B (2nd octave melody)
66 High B (countermelody)
67 C (2nd octave melody)
68 High C (countermelody)
69 C# (2nd octave melody)
70 D (2nd octave melody)
71 D# (2nd octave melody)
72 Violin pipes
73 E (2nd octave melody)
74 High F (2nd octave melody)
75 Octave coupler

76 Low E (accompaniment)
77 Low D# (accompaniment)
78 Bells (chain perforation)
79 Low D (accompaniment)
80 Low C# (accompaniment)
81 Trombones (chain perforation)
82 Low C (accompaniment)
83 General cancel; registers soft
84 Registers loud
85 E (bass)
86 Contra trumpet E
87 D# (bass)
88 Contra trumpet D#
89 D (bass)
90 Contra trumpet D
91 C# (bass)
92 Contra trumpet C#
93 C (bass)
94 Contra trumpet C
95 Bass drum
96 Cymbal

Hole 9, "contrabass," is a chain perforation which adds the lower bass octave to holes 6, 8, 10, 12, and 14, extending the bass down to low G. Hole 75, "octave coupler," is a chain perforation which adds the upper octave to melody holes 55, 57, 59, 61, 63, 65, and 67, extending the melody up to high C.

101-KEYLESS RUTH ORGAN SCALE
(From a B.A.B. Organ Co. description)

1 A (1st octave primary note scale)
2 A# (1st octave primary note scale)
3 B (1st octave primary note scale)
4 D (1st octave primary note scale; 1st octave trombone and trumpet)
5 Bass drum
6 F (1st octave primary note scale; 1st octave trombone and trumpet)
7 Band leader
8 G (2nd octave primary note scale, lowest note; 1st octave trombone and trumpet)
9 Trombone and mixture off
10 A# (2nd octave primary note scale; 1st octave trombone and trumpet)
11 C (2nd octave unknown section)
12 C (2nd octave primary note scale; 2nd octave trombone and trumpet, lowest note)
13 Trumpet off
14 C# (2nd octave primary note scale; 2nd octave trombone and trumpet)
15 B (2nd octave unknown section)
16 A# (2nd octave unknown section)
17 D (2nd octave primary note section; 2nd octave trombone and trumpet)
18 A (2nd octave unknown section)
19 D# (2nd octave primary note section; 2nd octave trombone and trumpet)
20 G# (2nd octave unknown section; lowest note)
21 G (1st octave unknown section)
22 E (2nd octave primary note section; 2nd octave trombone and trumpet)
23 F# (1st octave unknown section)
24 F (2nd octave primary note scale; 2nd octave trombone and trumpet)
25 F (1st octave unknown section)
26 F# (2nd octave primary note scale; 2nd octave trombone and trumpet)
27 E (1st octave unknown section)
28 G (3rd octave primary note scale; lowest note)
29 D# (1st octave unknown section)
30 Registers loud
31 G# (3rd octave primary note scale)
32 A (3rd octave trombone and trumpet)
33 F# (5th octave primary note scale)
34 E (5th octave primary note scale)
35 Clarinet off
36 D (5th octave primary note scale)
37 C (5th octave primary note scale)
38 G# (3rd octave trombone and trumpet)
39 A# (5th octave primary note scale)
40 G# (5th octave primary note scale)
41 F# (4th octave primary note scale)
42 G (3rd octave trombone and trumpet)
43 E (4th octave primary note scale)
44 D (4th octave primary note scale)
45 F# (3rd octave trombone and trumpet)
46 C (4th octave primary note scale)
47 A# (4th octave primary note scale)
48 F (3rd octave trombone and trumpet)
49 A (4th octave primary note scale)
50 B (4th octave primary note scale)
51 E (3rd octave trombone and trumpet)
52 C# (4th octave primary note scale)
53 D# (4th octave primary note scale)
54 D# (3rd octave trombone and trumpet)
55 F (4th octave primary note scale)
56 G (5th octave primary note scale; lowest note)
57 D (3rd octave trombone and trumpet)
58 A (5th octave primary note scale)
59 B (5th octave primary note scale)
60 C# (5th octave primary note scale)
61 C# (3rd octave trombone and trumpet)
62 D# (5th octave primary note scale)
63 F (5th octave primary note scale)
64 High G (5th octave primary note scale)
65 Violin pipes off
66 C (3rd octave trombone and trumpet; lowest note)
67 G# (4th octave primary note scale)

68 G (4th octave primary note scale; lowest note)
69 D (1st octave unknown section)
70 F# (3rd octave primary note scale)
71 B (2nd octave trombone and trumpet)
72 F (3rd octave primary note scale)
73 C# (1st octave unknown section)
74 E (3rd octave primary note scale)
75 A# (2nd octave trombone and trumpet)
76 D# (3rd octave primary note scale)
77 C (1st octave unknown section)
78 D (3rd octave primary note scale)
79 A (2nd octave trombone and trumpet)
30 C# (3rd octave primary note scale)
81 B (1st octave unknown section)
82 C (3rd octave primary note scale)
83 G# (2nd octave trombone and trumpet)
84 B (3rd octave primary note scale)
85 A# (1st octave unknown section)
86 A (1st octave unknown section)
87 A# (3rd octave primary note scale)
88 G (2nd octave trombone and trumpet)
89 A (3rd octave primary note scale)
90 G# (1st octave unknown section; lowest note)
91 B (2nd octave primary note scale; 1st octave trombone and trumpet)
92 Xylophone
93 A (2nd octave primary note scale; 1st octave trombone and trumpet)
94 G# (2nd octave primary note scale)
95 F# (1st octave primary note scale; 1st octave trombone and trumpet)
96 Snare drum
97 E (1st octave primary note scale; 1st octave trombone and trumpet)
98 Snare drum
99 C (1st octave primary note scale; 1st octave trombone and trumpet, lowest note)
100 G (1st octave primary note scale; lowest note)
101 Key frame key?

This scale was taken from two B.A.B. Organ Co. scale sticks. Large organs such as this Ruth were nearly chromatic from the lowest bass note all the way up to the highest treble note, with various ranks of pipes overlapping each other along the way. The only melody rank marked on this scale is clarinet, which plays from A, octave 3, to F, octave 4. Note the overlapping bass, trombone, accompaniment, and low trumpet sections.

First Carousell in the U. S. at Coney Island, N. Y. 1876.

Charles I. D. Looff.

Charles I.D. Looff Scrapbook . . .

The following dozen pages are from the Looff family scrapbook and are reproduced by the courtesy of Wilda Looff Taucher, Charles' granddaughter. Born in Germany on May 2, 1852, Charles I.D. Looff came to America on August 14, 1870. After working as a carver in the furniture trade he installed his first carousel in Coney Island in 1876 (see above photograph). In 1880 he opened a factory in New York. By the 1890s, Looff carousels, many of which were very large and impressive, had achieved national fame. In August 1910 he set up a factory in Ocean Park, California. Later, this was moved to nearby Long Beach. Writing his own biographical sketch in 1917, Looff noted that he had facilities for carousel production on both coasts: in Long Beach, California and in Riverside, Rhode Island. He died in Long Beach on July 1, 1918.

Above: Charles I.D. Looff in 1915.

Left: Charles I.D. Looff with trained bears in Seattle, 1909.

Note: The authors express appreciation to Barbara Charles for technical data pertaining to the Looff illustrations on this and the following pages.

Above: This early photograph taken at Crescent Park, Riverside, Rhode Island, shows (from left to right) Charles I.D. Looff, Anna Dolle Looff, Charles Looff, Jr., Helen Looff, Emma Looff, William Looff, and Arthur Looff. Music for the carousel was provided by a large Ruth organ, possibly a Style 36. By 1980 Crescent Park had closed, but many facilities remained intact and were the object of a community preservation effort.

Left: This large band organ, of unusual facade style, was photographed as part of a Looff carousel in Santa Cruz, California, 1911.

Next page: A large Ruth organ, possibly a Style 35, in use on a Looff carousel in the 1905-1910 period.

Charles I.D. Looff was one of the main importers of A. Ruth & Son band organs during the early 20th century—hence the inclusion of this photographic scrapbook in the present volume. The above illustration shows a book-operated Ruth band organ with "CH. LOOFF, RIVERSIDE, R.I." carved on a cartouche at the top of the facade and was taken sometime after the unit's 1909 installation in Natatorium Park, Spokane, Washington. Later, the carousel was moved to downtown Spokane, where it was still operating in 1980. Note the ornately carved tiger in the foreground. It is embellished with the wings of an eagle and has a tiny monkey riding just above the tail. Today, Looff carousel animals are highly regarded by collectors. The National Carousel Association, a nationwide group of collectors and historians, seeks to preserve existing carousels and to study their history. Prominent in the association are Frederick Fried (author of "A Pictorial History of the Carousel") and Barbara Charles, both of whom provided information for the present book.

The Hippodrome and other attractions at Ocean Park, California were owned by Charles I.D. Looff. On September 3, 1912, fire struck and leveled what was once one of America's most popular amusement parks. The remnants of the Looff carousel are shown to the left.

Next Page: This superb Looff carousel was built in 1911 and installed in the Hippodrome at Ocean Park. Music was provided by a huge Style 38 Ruth band organ. This was one of Looff's finest installations. It was in service scarcely more than a year before it was destroyed in the 1912 conflagration.

Above: This Charles I.D. Looff carousel, shown in Lakeside Park (Syracuse, N.Y.) in 1903, used an ornate organ, probably a Ruth, with carved figures in niches at each side of the facade. Looff was very patriotic, and his carousels often had bunting of stars and stripes. The above unit is decorated with portraits of American presidents. Later, the carousel was moved to Goddard Park in Rhode Island. As of 1980 the ride was in storage.

Left: The Rivers of Venice and the similar Canals of Venice attractions were installed in several amusement parks by Charles I.D. Looff. The one shown to the left attracts patrons by means of a large roll-operated Welte orchestrion (shown to the right of the picture between the two flags). Welte was proud of this sale and featured the Rivers of Venice in several of its catalogues. Inside, patrons rode boats past plaster castles, palm trees, mosques, and other exotic scenery. These were set up in Riverside, Rhode Island and Seattle, Washington, among other places. The illustration here is of the installation in Crescent Park, Riverside, R.I.

Pages from the Looff scrapbook . . . (1) The top photograph shows a wooden bandshell-stage at Luna Park (Seattle). The back of the stage had doors which opened up to reveal an immense 96-key Ruth Style 38 organ which played concerts for the audience seated on rows of benches. (2) The center picture is of a Looff-built theatre operated by Fisher & Mantells at Luna Park. "High Class Musical Comedy" was the order of the day for just 10c (or 20c for reserved seating). (3) Looff's Hippodrome at Long Beach was one of Southern California's attractions when this photograph was taken in 1911.

INTERIOR OF LUNA PARK SEATTLE
O.T.PRASCH—304

LUNA PARK SEAT

Luna Park in Seattle was built by Charles I.D. Looff. In addition to the large Looff carousel (the building is at the above center), the park featured thrill rides, several theatres and shows, and other attractions.

Luna Park's carousel featured a large Ruth band organ with cherubs and other carved figures. Around 1915 it was moved to Chutes Park (San Francisco), which was later called Whitney's. The unit featured a large Ruth band organ with cherubs and other carved figures, possibly a 96-key Style 38.

This large Looff carousel, which bears a close resemblance to the Ocean Park (California) carousel shown earlier, uses a large Style 38 Ruth organ. No two Style 38s were precisely alike, and a comparison of photographs inevitably shows minor differences in the carvings, position and styles of the cherubs used, and other details. The Style 38, of 96-key specification, was the largest regular size in the Ruth line. Only three or four survive in America today.

The above unit was installed on the Santa Monica Pier. Later it was moved to Belmont Park (San Diego, Calfornia), and still later it was broken up.

Next Page: A view of the Santa Monica (California) Pleasure Pier, built by Looff and leased by him for a 20-year period beginning in 1917. The carousel building (with the "WELCOME" sign) was still in existence when this book was published in 1980 and featured a merry-go-round with a Wurlitzer Style 153 organ. In the prospectus for the Santa Monica Pleasure Pier Co., Looff was described as: ". . . a man who is known in amusement circles from coast to coast, enjoying a reputation for high ideals and clean sport that few men in the business, if any, can equal. In permanent amusement center parlance, the name of Looff is as familiar as those of Barnum, Sells and Floto, and Buffalo Bill are to the traveling show public. He invented, built, and operated in Coney Island in 1876 the first carousel in America, being one of the originators ს that famous pleasure resort. In 1880 he started the first amusement enterprise in Atlantic City. Mr. Looff owns and is interested in successful pleasure resorts in various parts of America today, such as: Crescent Park, R.I., Spokane, Washington, Dallas, Texas, and in California - San Francisco, Santa Cruz, Redondo Beach, Ocean Park, Long Beach, and Santa Monica. He is also an important manufacturer of amusement devices, having a large factory in Long Beach, California, and at Riverside, Rhode Island for the manufacture of carousels, circle swings, racing coasters, and water ride equipment and everything pertaining to the legitimate amusement and show business." The "first carousel in America" statement was hype, for historian Frederick Fried has traced a unit which was at Salem, Massachusetts in 1799 and another in Ohio in 1840.

SANTA MONICA PI
TAYLOR PH

The Calliaphone
PRONOUNCE IT "KA-LI-A-PHONE"

"Plays By Hand, or Automatic"

Model CA-43, Also Plays by Hand.

THE prettiest, sweetest toned instrument in the world. A tone decidedly different from all others. "The first new tone in 40 years." Small, light and compact. Floor space only 24x32 inches, height 59½ inches. Weight 350 pounds. Built practically of metal throughout, with metal pneumatic valves that are not affected by weather like organs. Plays ten-tune rewind rolls, $3.50 per roll. Pickled steel case, finished imitation walnut. Patented brass self-seating action valves. All parts interchangeable and standard 43, 53 or 58 whistles. Guaranteed 15 years. Our exclusive patented "Easy Pull" action. We do not use any action that "strikes" the keys down. Whistles made of special alloy tubing, special thickness and temper for pure sweet tones. A feature found on no other similar instrument. Operates with engine or motor. "The best—by test."

TANGLEY COMPANY

Built by Tangley Company, Muscatine, Ia.

During the 'teens and 'twenties hundreds of calliopes were made in America. The two main brands were Tangley and National, with Tangley far out front in the sales race. Also in the race, but a late starter (1928), was the Rudolph Wurlitzer Company with its Caliola.

The typical Tangley calliope, or Calliaphone, used regular 10-tune type A coin piano rolls, although some rolls were available with extended perforations (for sustaining pipe notes) and were intended specifically for use on such instruments. Playing "Entry of the Gladiators," "Stars and Stripes Forever," or other soul-stirring tunes, the loudly-voiced Calliaphone was just the thing to draw crowds to the midway of a carnival, circus, or traveling show. Such an instrument could be heard a quarter mile away. (Note: for additional information on the Tangley Calliaphone see page 147)

VERBEECK
Band Organs and
Dance Organs

The Verbeeck family, Pierre Verbeeck in Belgium and James Verbeeck in London, produced fairground, street, and dance organs during the early 20th century. In recent times the tradition has been continued by a family member.

Some early instruments were sold under the "Magic Orchestra" name, while certain later organs bore the designation "Verbekson" or had no particular trademark. Many of the 87-, 89-, and 92-key Verbeeck organs made during the early years were compatible with or related to Limonaire scales, although one "Verbeeck" organ examined by the authors had a Mortier chassis. Verbeeck may have remodeled early instruments of other makers. The 98-key size was the most popular large early model. The scale of this is similar to the 98-key Marenghi layout.

63-KEY J. VERBEECK ORGAN SCALE
(also known as 61-KEY J. VERBEECK)
23 cm. wide

1 Key frame key?
2 Registers loud
3 Carillon pipes on
4 to 11, Bass F, G, A, A#, B, C, D, E
12 Baritone on
13 to 22, Accompaniment G, A, A#, B, C, C#, D, E, F, F#
23 to 55, Melody G-D, E
56 Bass drum
57 Melody high F
58 General cancel
59 Snare drum
60 Violin pipes on
61 Harmonic flute on
62 Snare drum
63 Trombone on

75-KEY PIERRE VERBEECK STREET ORGAN SCALE
"THE ARAB"

8 Bass notes
10 Accompaniment notes
22 Melody notes
16 Countermelody notes

1 General cancel
2 Blank
3 Blank
4 to 11, Bass G, A, A#, B, C, D, E, F
12 to 21, Accompaniment G, A, A#, B, C, C#, D, E, F, F#
22 to 43, Melody G to E
44 Blank
45 Violin pipes on (M)
46 Triphone on (CM)
47 to 62, Countermelody E to G
63 Band leader
64 Vox celeste on (CM)
65 Loud violin pipes on (M)
66 Trombone on
67 Baritone on (CM)
68 Cello on (CM)
69 Blank
70 Bourdon celeste on (M)
71 Bass drum
72 Snare drum
73 Tremolo on
74 Snare drum
75 Bells on (M); play notes C-E from holes 27-43

A modern Verbeeck organ marked "VERBEKSON" which notes the firm has branches in Antwerp (Anvers in the French language) and London. This particular unit was installed in the "Bierstal," located at Klapdorp 8, Antwerp.

A large 98-key Verbeeck band organ is shown set up in the firm's London works before World War I. (Photograph courtesy of A.C. Upchurch)

GEBR. WELLERSHAUS
Band Organs

Gebr. Wellershaus (Wellershaus Brothers), located in Germany, was founded by August and Wilhelm Wellershaus. The firm was in business from the late 19th century until the factory was destroyed in a 1944 bomber raid.

Early instruments were of the pinned cylinder type. Later styles of larger format used folding cardboard books and employed the key frame system. Wellershaus organs were mainly distributed in Germany, Belgium, and Holland. Most had exceptionally ornate facades.

55-KEY WELLERSHAUS ORGAN SCALE

5 Bass notes
4 Trombone notes
9 Accompaniment notes
20 Melody notes
10 Countermelody notes

55 to 51, Bass C, D, F, G, A
50 to 47, Trombone F, G, D, C
46 to 38, Accompaniment E, F, F#, G, A, A#, B, C, D
37 to 18, Melody E, F, F#, G, A, A#, B, C, C# D, E to C, D
17 Registers loud
16 Registers soft
15 to 6, Countermelody B, C, C#, D, E, F, F#, G, A, A#
5 Bass drum and cymbal
4 Blank
3 Snare drum
2 Blank
1 Snare drum

43-KEYLESS WELLERSHAUS ORGAN SCALE

5 Bass notes
10 Accompaniment notes
23 Melody notes

1 to 5, Bass C, D, F, G, A
6 to 15, Accompaniment E, F, F#, G, A, A#, B, C, C#, D
16 to 38, Melody E, F, F#, G, A, A#, B, C, C#, D, E, F, F#, G, G#, A, A#, B, C
39 Bass drum
40 Register on
41 Snare drum
42 Register off
43 Snare drum

72-KEY WELLERSHAUS ORGAN SCALE

5 Bass notes
7 Trombone notes
20 Melody notes
17 Trumpet notes

1 to 5, Bass C, D, F, G, A
6 to 18, Accompaniment E, F, F#, G, A, A#, B, C, C#, D, E, F, F#
19 to 38, Melody G, A, A#, B, C, C#, D, E, F, F#, G, G#, A, A#, B, C, C#, D, E, F
39 Bass drum
40 Registers loud
41 Snare drum
42 Registers soft
43 Snare drum
44 to 46, Blank
47 to 53, Trombone C, D, E, F, F#, G, A
54 to 70, Trumpet C, D, E, F, F#, G, G#, A, A#, B, C, C#, D, E, F, G, A
71 Blank
72 Blank

Neueste Salon-Orgel-Werke.

No. 79.

This very ornate Wellershaus organ probably dates from about 1900 and is probably a cylinder-operated model. Note the jeweled electric "wonder light" at the top; an unusual feature.

FRITZ WREDE
Band Organs

Fritz Wrede (1868-1944) began the organ business in Hannover-Kleefeld, Germany at the age of 17. In 1890 the production of large cylinder type band organs commenced. Around 1900 his firm adopted the cardboard music system for larger organs, although production of small organs of the hand-cranked cylinder type continued.

After a production lapse during World War I, Wrede produced many fine band organs during the 1920s and 1930s, until production was halted in 1933. After financial problems forced reorganization, a limited number of organs were manufactured until March 28, 1944, when a bombing attack on Hannover killed Fritz Wrede and destroyed the factory.

Today Wrede organs are highly prized for their tonal quality and for the attractiveness of their facades. The distribution of surviving instruments indicates that most original sales must have been in continental Europe.

56/59-KEYLESS WREDE ORGAN SCALE
(Right to left)

      6 Bass notes
      12 Trumpet notes
      8 Accompaniment notes
         (Plus 6 Accompaniment notes overlapping with Melody)
      19 Melody notes

1 Blank
2 Blank
3 A (bass)
4 E (bass)
5 F (bass)
6 Snare drum
7 C (trumpet)
8 Snare drum
9 G (lowest accompaniment note)
10 A (accompaniment)
11 D (trumpet)
12 A# (accompaniment)
13 B (accompaniment)
14 E (trumpet)
15 C (accompaniment)
16 C# (accompaniment)
17 F (trumpet)
18 D (accompaniment)
19 E (accompaniment)
20 G (melody 3rd octave)
21 F (melody 2nd octave)
22 F# (trumpet)
23 D (melody 2nd octave)
24 C (melody 2nd octave)
25 A# (melody 2nd octave)
26 G (trumpet)
27 G# (melody 2nd octave)
28 F# (melody 1st octave)
29 E (melody 1st octave)
30 A (trumpet)
31 C# (melody 1st octave)
32 C (melody 1st octave)
33 D (melody 1st octave)
34 A# (trumpet)
35 F (melody 1st octave)
36 G (melody 2nd octave, lowest note)
37 A (melody 2nd octave)
38 B (trumpet)
39 B (melody 2nd octave)
40 C# (melody 2nd octave)
41 F (melody 2nd octave)
42 C (trumpet)
43 F# (melody 2nd octave)
44 A (melody 3rd octave)
45 F (melody; cello used for countermelody or continued accompaniment)
46 D (trumpet)
47 F# (melody; cello used for countermelody or continued accompaniment)
48 G (melody; cello used for countermelody or continued accompaniment)
49 A (melody; cello used for countermelody or continued accompaniment)
50 E (trumpet)
51 A# (melody; cello used for countermelody or continued accompaniment)
52 B (melody; highest accompaniment; cello used for countermelody or continued accompaniment)
53 Registers loud (forte)
54 Registers soft (piano)
55 Bass drum with cymbal
56 D (bass)
57 C (bass)
58 G (bass)
59 Band leader

69-keyless Wrede band organ, also in a travel trailer, restored and ready to entertain listeners. Wrede organs are remarkable for their facades decorated with many carvings. A cartouche on the front is incised "Fr. Wrede, Hannover." (Verlaan Collection; photograph courtesy of Marcel van Boxtel)

A beautiful 76-keyless Wrede band organ shown in its travel trailer. In Europe (in Holland and Germany in particular) festivals or gatherings of fairground organ owners are held, and instruments are brought in trailers from near and far. Arthur W.J.G. Ord-Hume, who went from his London home to Hannover, Germany to attend an organ rally, was told by a taxi driver on his arrival that it was indeed a shame that he had to pick this particular time to visit the beautiful city, for the streets were congested with organs! (Vermolen Collection; photograph courtesy of Marcel van Boxtel)

RUDOLPH WURLITZER COMPANY
Band Organs

The Rudolph Wurlitzer Company, founded in Cincinnati, Ohio in 1856, sold many pinned-barrel or cylinder organs imported from Europe during the late 19th century. Around 1897-1899 an arrangement was made with Eugene DeKleist, of North Tonawanda, N.Y., to sell DeKleist organs under the Wurlitzer name.

Most DeKleist-Wurlitzer organs of the first few years of the 1900-1910 decade were operated by pinned cylinders. The 1905-1912 period was one of transition; for many models the buyer had the option of the pinned cylinder or the paper roll system. Shortly after 1912 the paper rolls became standard, and the pinned cylinder instruments were deleted from Wurlitzer catalogues. For an in-depth discussion of DeKleist and Wurlitzer organs the reader is urged to refer to *The Encyclopedia of Automatic Musical Instruments,* beginning on page 930 of that reference.

Wurlitzer roll-operated band organs can be divided into two general groups: early (pre-1920) and late (1920s and 1930s). In the pre-1920 years, Wurlitzer band organs used many varieties of rolls. Most late-style band organs were designed to play either 125, 150, or 165 rolls, and many of the earlier organs were "modernized" to accept one of these standard roll styles.

Most of the early scales listed in the present book were furnished by Doyle Lane, who acquired them from Ralph Tussing (who for many years operated an organ repair and roll-cutting business in North Tonawanda), who earlier acquired them from the Wurlitzer Company. Some of the following scales were taken from early scale sticks which were labeled with an identifying number. Like the standardized B.A.B., North Tonawanda, and Artizan scales, the identifying number in many instances is two or three numbers smaller than the actual number of functional holes in the tracker bar. By studying early catalogue illustrations and specifications, it was possible in some cases to determine which roll was used on which style of organ. The scale stick label number is used here to identify each scale, with the organ style listed in parentheses.

WURLITZER 38 (A) BAND ORGAN ROLL
(Early scale for Style 120 organ)

    3 Bass notes
    8 Accompaniment notes
    14 Trumpet notes
    15 Piccolo notes

1 Snare drum
2 to 4, Bass G, C, D
5 to 10, Accompaniment, G, A, B, C, C#, D
11 to 24, Trumpet E, F, F#, G, A, B, C, C#, D, E, F, F#, G, A
25 to 39, Piccolo G, A, B, C, C#, D, E, F, F#, G, A, B, C, D, E
40 Bass drum
41 Rewind
    (From a Wurlitzer scale stick)

WURLITZER 38 (B) BAND ORGAN ROLL
(Early scale)

    4 Bass notes
    7 Accompaniment notes
    14 Clarinet notes
    13 Trumpet notes

1 Snare drum
2 to 5, Bass C, D, F, G
6 to 12, Accompaniment A, B, C, D, E, F, F#
13 to 26, Clarinet G, A, B, C, D, E, F, F#, G, A, B, C, D, E
27 to 39, Trumpet E, F, F#, G, A, B, C, D, E, F, F#, G, A
40 Bass drum
41 Rewind
    (From a Wurlitzer scale stick)

WURLITZER 44 BAND ORGAN ROLL
(Early scale for Style 110 organ)

    3 Trombone notes
    5 Bass notes
    6 Accompaniment notes
    15 Trumpet notes
    14 Piccolo notes

1 Snare drum
2 to 4, Trombone G, C, D
5 to 9, Bass C, D, E, F, G
10 to 15, Accompaniment A, B, C, D, E, F
16 to 30, Trumpet F#, G, A, B, C, D, E, F, F#, G, A, B, C, D, E
31 to 44, Piccolo G, A, B, C, D, E, F, F#, G, A, B, C, D, E
45 Bass drum
46 Rewind
    (From a Wurlitzer scale stick)

WURLITZER 48 (53) BAND ORGAN ROLL
(Early scale for Style 100 organ)

    5 Bass notes
    8 Accompaniment notes
    17 Clarinet notes
    18 Piccolo notes

1 Snare drum
2 to 6, Bass and trombone G, C, D, E, F
7 to 14, Accompaniment G, A, A#, B, C, C#, D, D#
15 to 31, Clarinet E-G, A
32 to 49, Piccolo C to F
50 Bass drum
51 Rewind
    (From a Wurlitzer scale stick)

WURLITZER 49 BAND ORGAN ROLL
(Early scale for styles 135 and 140)

    4 Trombone notes
    4 Bass notes
    8 Accompaniment notes
    16 Clarinet notes
    17 Trumpet notes

1 Snare drum
2 to 5, Trombone C, D, G, A
6 to 9, Bass G, A, C, D
10 to 17, Accompaniment G, A, B, C, D, E, F, F#
18 to 33, Clarinet G, A, B, C, C#, D, E, F, F#, G, A, B, C, C#, D, E
34 to 50, Trumpet G, A, B, C, C#, D, E, F, F#, G, A, B, C, C#, D, E, F
51 Bass drum
52 Rewind
    (From a Wurlitzer scale stick)

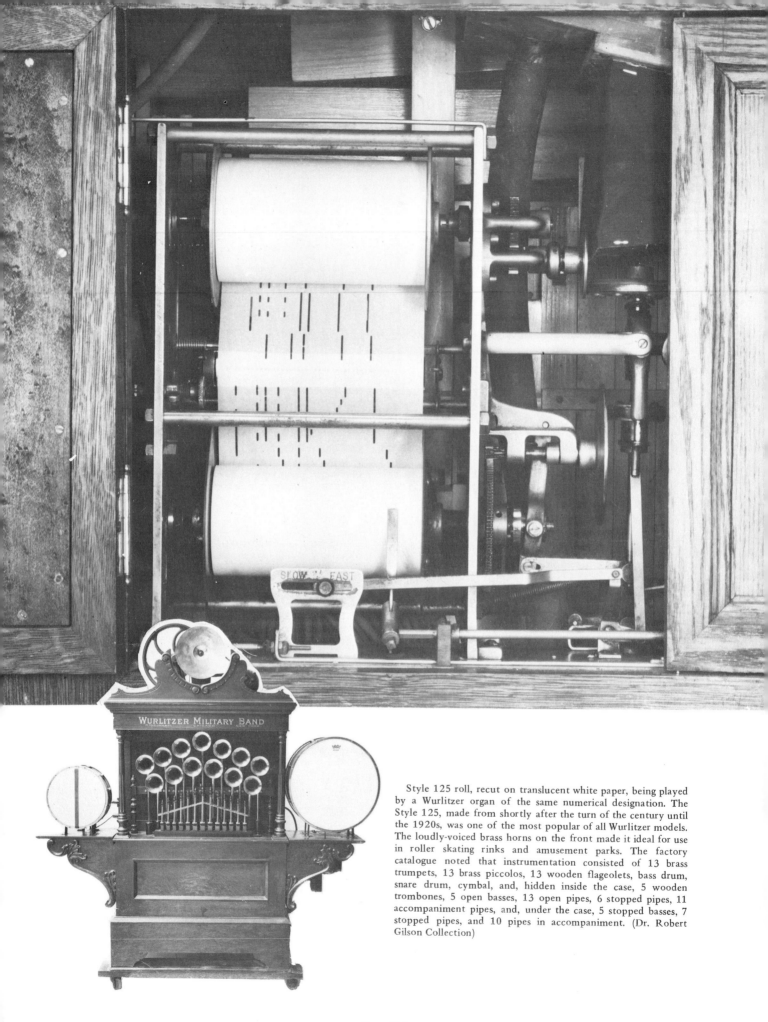

Style 125 roll, recut on translucent white paper, being played by a Wurlitzer organ of the same numerical designation. The Style 125, made from shortly after the turn of the century until the 1920s, was one of the most popular of all Wurlitzer models. The loudly-voiced brass horns on the front made it ideal for use in roller skating rinks and amusement parks. The factory catalogue noted that instrumentation consisted of 13 brass trumpets, 13 brass piccolos, 13 wooden flageolets, bass drum, snare drum, cymbal, and, hidden inside the case, 5 wooden trombones, 5 open basses, 13 open pipes, 6 stopped pipes, 11 accompaniment pipes, and, under the case, 5 stopped basses, 7 stopped pipes, and 10 pipes in accompaniment. (Dr. Robert Gilson Collection)

WURLITZER 59 BAND ORGAN ROLL

(Early scale)

3 Trombone notes
3 Bass notes
8 Accompaniment notes
16 Clarinet notes
13 Piccolo notes
15 Trumpet notes

1 to 3, Trombone G, C, D
4 to 6, Bass G, C, D
7 to 14, Accompaniment G, A, B, C, D, E, F, F#
15 to 30, Clarinet G-G, A, B, C,
31 to 43, Piccolo C, C#, D, E, F, F#, G, A, B, C, C#, D, E
44 to 58, Trumpet C, D, E, F, F#, G, A, B, C, C#, D, E, F, F#, G
59 Rewind
60 Bass drum
61 Snare drum
  (From a Wurlitzer scale stick)

WURLITZER 155 BAND ORGAN ROLL

(Early scale for the "Monster" organ)
10 7/16" wide; spaced 10 holes per inch

10 Bass notes
10 Trombone notes
11 Accompaniment notes
25 Melody notes
18 Piccolo notes
21 Trumpet notes

1 Shutoff
2 ?
3 Bass drum and cymbal
4 to 13, Trombone F, G, A, A#, B, C, D, E, F, F#
14 to 23, Bass C, F, G, A, A#, B, C, D, E, F
24 to 34, Accompaniment G, A, A#, B, C, C#, D, E, F, F#, G
35 to 59, Clarinet (Melody) E-D, E, F
60 to 77, Piccolo D to G
78 to 98, Trumpet G, A, A#, B, C, D, E-D, E-G
99 Snare drum
100 Rewind
  (From a Wurlitzer scale stick) One original Wurlitzer scale stick labels hole 1 "T.V." and hole 2 "N.T," the latter possibly for "Nickel Trip," or shutoff.

WURLITZER 160 BAND ORGAN ROLL

(Early scale for the "Mammoth" organ)

13 Trombone notes
16 Bass notes
13 Accompaniment notes
30 Melody notes
18 Piccolo notes
27 Trumpet notes

1 Shutoff
2 Bass drum and cymbal
3 to 15, Trombone F, G to F#
16 to 31, Bass C, D, E, F, G-F#
32 to 44, Accompaniment G to G
45 to 74, Clarinet (Melody) C to F
75 to 92, Piccolo E, F-A
93 to 119, Trumpet G to A
120 Tympani (reiterating?)
121 Snare drum
122 Rewind
  (From a Wurlitzer scale stick) Two incomplete Mammoth organs and one Monster organ known to exist were converted many years ago to play Wurlitzer 165 rolls, after the early-style 155 and 160 rolls were discontinued.

"Standardized" Wurlitzer Rolls
Styles 125, 150, 165

From the 'teens onward the three standard rolls used on most models of Wurlitzer band organs were the 125, 150, and 165. As noted previously, many earlier Wurlitzer organs were "modernized" to use these roll types as were organs of other manufacturers.

Generally, Wurlitzer organs made during the late 'teens and during the 1920s and 1930s which had style numbers up to and including 125 used Style 125 rolls, models with style numbers over 125 and up to 153 used Style 150 rolls, and models 157, 165, and 166 used Style 165 rolls.

WURLITZER 125 BAND ORGAN ROLL

6" wide; .1227" per space

5 Bass notes
9 Accompaniment notes
14 Melody notes
13 Trumpet notes

1 Shutoff
2 Snare drum
3 to 7, Bass G, C, D, E, F
8 to 16, Accompaniment G, A, B, C, C#, D, E, F, F#
17 to 30, Melody A#, G, A, B, C, C#, D, E, F, F#, G, A, B, C
31 to 43, Trumpet E, F, F#, G, A, B, C, C#, D, E, F, F#, G
44 Bass drum
45 Rewind

WURLITZER 150 BAND ORGAN ROLL

7" wide; .1227" per space

3 Bass notes
3 Trombone notes
9 Accompaniment notes
16 Melody notes
15 Trumpet notes

1 Swell shades open
2 Bells on
3 Piccolo and melody violin pipes on
4 Cancel
5 Shutoff
6 Snare drum
7 to 9, Trombone G, C, D
10 to 12, Bass G, C, D
13 to 21, Accompaniment G, A, B, C, D, E, F, F#, G
22 to 37, Melody G, A, B, C, C#, D, E, F, F#, G, A, B, C, C#, D, E
38 to 52, Trumpet C, D, E, F, F#, G, A, B, C, C#, D, E, F, F#, G
53 Bass drum and cymbal
54 Rewind

WURLITZER 165 BAND ORGAN ROLL

9 5/8" wide; .1227" per space

6 Bass notes
10 Accompaniment notes
22 Melody notes
14 Trumpet notes

1 Bass-bells on?
2 Brass trombone and brass trumpet on
3 Uniphone bells on (Melody)
4 Triangle
5 Swell closed

6 Chimes on (Melody)
7 Crash cymbal
8 Wood trumpet on
9 Violin and viola pipes on (Melody; loud)
10 Piccolo and flageolet on (Melody)
11 Snare drum
12 to 17, Bass C, D, E, F, G, A
18 Shutoff
19 to 28, Accompaniment G, A-D, E, F, F#
29 Rewind
30 to 51, Melody G-D, E, F
52 General cancel
53 to 66, Trumpet F-D, E-G
67 Bass drum and cymbal
68 Flute on (Melody)
69 Violin pipes on (Melody; soft)
70 Trombone on
71 Swell open
72 Castanets
73 Snare drum loud
74 Tympani
75 Violin pipes and prestant on (Melody)

The function of hole 1 is unknown. Uniphone bells (hole 3) have large resonators, so if these are present in an organ they should be connected to this hole. Wurlitzer usually referred to ordinary orchestra bells (glockenspiel or bell-lyre bells) as "chimes," so if an organ has these, they should be connected to hole 6.

WURLITZER 180 BAND ORGAN ROLL
14 1/8" wide; .1227 per space

1 Blank
2 Blank
3 Blank
4 Blank
5 Crash cymbal
6 Wood block
7 Rewind
8 Bass drum
9 Snare drum
10 Tympani
11 to 23, Bass F to F
24 Bass, clarinet, horn coupler on (bass, melody & accomp. loud)
25 to 37, Horn G to G (accompaniment)
38 to 55, Baritone, trombone F# to B
56 Trombone on
57 to 74, Clarinet, bells G to C
75 Clarinet extension
76 to 88, Piccolo G to G
89 Piccolo extension
90 to 102, Trumpet C to C
103 Trumpet extension
104 Shutoff
105 Swell open
106 Swell closed
107 Bells on
108 General cancel for 24, 56, 107
109 Blank
110 Blank
111 Blank
112 Blank

(From a Wurlitzer blueprint) The 180 roll uses multiplexing to play 30 clarinets from 18 holes, 25 piccolos from 13 holes, and 25 trumpets from 13 holes. Without the clarinet, piccolo, or trumpet extension holes punched, the note holes in the roll play the lower pipes in each of these sections. When an extension hole is punched, the upper twelve note holes in its section are switched over to the upper octave of pipes. The octave extension device stays on only as long as the extension hole is punched.

In one Wurlitzer band organ catalogue which describes the Style 180, the illustration is of a Style 166 organ, with the text

noting "the case design is similar to the cut shown above." The specifications include the statement: "playing notes, 88, with 36 additional notes controlled by couplers." These couplers are the aforementioned clarinet, flute, and trumpet extensions listed in the above tracker scale.

At least two of the five Style 180 band organs known to have been made were later converted by Wurlitzer to play Caliola rolls (or 65-Note Automatic Player Piano rolls). One of these organs uses Caliola rolls, has no automatic registers, and has numerous dummy (non-operative) pipes as well as having many fewer pipes than listed in the Wurlitzer catalogue. It is connected as follows:

7 to 27, A to F, 21 bass notes
19 to 31, A to A, 13 accompaniment notes
39 to 58, G to C, 30 melody notes
59 to 71, C# to C#, 13 piccolo notes (12 not used)
16 to 33, F# to B, 18 trombone notes
34 to 58, C to C, 25 trumpet notes

An original Wurlitzer scale stick labeled "Style 180 Organ change to 65-Note Piano" is similar to the above, but it is unclear concerning the wood bass and accompaniment sections.

Another 180 organ which was factory-converted to play Caliola rolls has major parts missing, making it impossible to tell how Wurlitzer tubed it.

Retubing a band organ to play Caliola or 65-Note Automatic Player Piano rolls was a compromise which sacrificed much of the musical capability of the instrument. When it seemed apparent that 180 rolls would be in exceedingly limited demand, and they would be too costly to make for the few organs which used them, Wurlitzer chose to convert instruments to play Caliola rolls in order to use as many of the pipes in the Style 180 as possible. A more "typical" and more musical "band organ sound" could have been produced by tubing a Style 180 to play Style 165 rolls, although many of the Style 180 pipes would have been unused.

WURLITZER CALIOLA ROLL
9 5/8" wide; .1227 per space
(Same scale as Wurlitzer 65-Note Automatic Player Piano rolls)
1 Shutoff
2 to 5, Blank
6 Snare drum
7 to 71, A to C#, 65 playing notes
72 and 73, Blank
74 Bass drum and cymbal
75 Rewind

The Wurlitzer Caliola, introduced in 1928, used rolls based on the same tracker scale as the Wurlitzer 65-Note Automatic Player Piano roll, but the Caliola arrangements were in a style more appropriate for calliope or organ music (with extended perforations for sustained notes). The Caliola was a moderate success, and during the next few years 62 instruments were built.

NEW PARK RIDING GALLERY. (Shown Without Tent.)
Seating capacity, 76 persons.

PARK RIDING GALLERY

THE illustration above shows our Gallery designed for Park and similar purposes. It has an outside diameter of 42 feet exclusive of tent, and carries 36 Galloping Horses, 4 large Chariots, and has a seating capacity of 76 adults.

This outfit is gotten up in a most elaborate style throughout, the center being composed of fourteen panels richly carved and handsomely decorated with oil paintings. Forming a part of and corresponding in design and finish with this center is a large Military-Band Organ. It is one of the finest instruments ever used for the purpose, having 47 keys, including brass trombones, trumpets, piccolos, and clarionets, besides the bass and snare drums and cymbals.

Massillon

Skating

Rink

MASSILLON,
OHIO,

S. BURD,   PROPRIETOR.

Massillon (Ohio) Skating Rink.

USING
ONE OF OUR

Monster
Military Band
Organs

WHICH IS
GIVING PERFECT SATISFACTION.

Mr. BURD'S WORDS OF APPRECIATION.

MASSILLON, O., July 21, 1905.
THE RUDOLPH WURLITZER CO., Cincinnati, O.

Gentlemen:

I received the Monster Military Band Organ and have installed the same in my rink, and must say that I am more than pleased with the same. My patrons like it very much, and many who do not skate come to hear the instrument. It is certainly a musical wonder. My rink was formerly an opera house and is

Mr. S. Burd.

56 x 130 feet. I have an incline in my rink that is about twelve feet wide and has a three-foot fall; it is the only one of its kind in the country. I have a gallery that will seat 200 people. The cost of the rink was $31,000. I give this slight description so you can see that the rink and the organ correspond in beauty.

Yours most respectfully,

S. BURD.

Wurlitzer (DeKleist) band organs in use during the first decade of the 20th century.

Style No. 146-A—Military Band Organ
49 Keys
PLAYED BY PAPER MUSIC ROLLS

Built in Oak Veneered Case, fancy white enamel carved front decorated with gold leaf and colors and hand painted panels.

INSTRUMENTATION

OUTSIDE, VISIBLE—Latest improved Bass and Snare Drum with spring tension and nickel-plated Cymbal.

INSIDE—3 Wooden Trombones; 3 Octave Stopped Basses; 15 Wooden Trumpets; 15 Stopped Flute Pipes; 16 Violin Pipes; 9 Open Pipes; 16 Open Flute Pipes.

BOTTOM—3 Open Bass Pipes; 9 Stopped Accompaniment Pipes; 16 Stopped Melody.

STOPS—1 for Trumpets; 1 for Stopped Flute and 1 for Inside Violin.

DIMENSIONS

HEIGHT to top of Scroll, 6 feet 1 inch. HEIGHT with Scroll down, 5 feet 4 inches. WIDTH, with Drums, 7 feet 2 inches, without Drums, 4 feet 3 inches. DEPTH, 2 feet 5½ inches. WEIGHT, packed for shipment, 900 lbs.

The Style 146-A was one of the most popular Wurlitzer styles of the 'teens and 1920s. The front is a close copy of a Bruder organ, leading to the speculation that early models (pre-1914) may have been imported from Bruder (of Waldkirch, Germany). The 146-A uses Wurlitzer 150 rolls.

Style No. 153—Duplex Orchestral Organ
54 Keys

For Three-Abreast Carouselles and Open-Air Dance Pavilions

With duplex long roll Tracker Frames, latest drums with self-tightening tension rods.

Oak Veneered Case; natural finish; fancy white enamel front; hand-carved scroll work in gold leaf and colors. Raised panels decorated with landscape and flowered designs.

INSTRUMENTATION

BASSES—3 Wooden Trombones; 3 eight-foot Stopped Diapason Pipes; 3 four-foot Open Diapason Pipes; 3 two-foot Stopped Diapason Pipes.

ACCOMPANIMENT—9 Stopped Flute Pipes; 18 Violin Pipes.

MELODY—16 Stopped Flute; 16 Octave Violin; 15 Wooden Trumpets; 15 Cello Pipes; 32 Violin; 16 Open Flute; 15 Stopped Pipes; 16 Bell Bars.

TRAPS—Bass Drum; Snare Drum and Cymbal.

AUTOMATIC STOPS—1 for Octave Violin; 1 for Open Flute; 1 for Cello Pipes; 1 for Stopped Pipes; 1 for Bell Bars; 1 for Swell Shutters.

DIMENSIONS

HEIGHT, with front, 7 feet 1 inch; without front, 5 feet 2 inches. WIDTH, with front, 8 feet 8 inches; without front, 4 feet 2½ inches. DEPTH, with front, 3 feet 8 inches; without front, 2 feet 7½ inches. WEIGHT, packed for shipment, 1,300 lbs.

The Style 153 organ, which uses 150 rolls, was one of the great workhorses of the Wurlitzer line. Many hundreds of these were produced for use on carousels, with traveling shows, and other attractions. Until they were sold in the late 1970s, the Gooding Amusement Company (Columbus, Ohio) had nearly twenty examples of this model.

**Two
Abreast
Portable**

ALLAN HERSCHELL CO., INC.

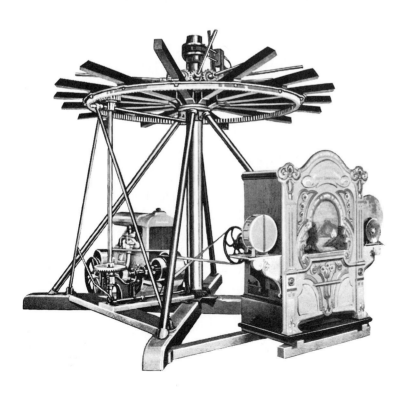

These two illustrations from an Allan Herschell Company (North Tonawanda, N.Y. amusement park outfitters) catalogue of the early 1920s show a Wurlitzer Style 146A (uses Style 150 rolls) band organ located at the center of a carousel. A similar instrument in the collection of Harvey and Marion Roehl was once used in this manner on a merry-go-round near Binghamton, New York,

Wurlitzer band organ prices, September 1st, 1927. Styles 103, 105, 125, 146-A, 153, and 165 were the standard models usually carried in stock at all times. Wurlitzer salesmen were encouraged to push these types. Among the larger organs listed here, styles 148, 157, and 180 were sold only in limited numbers

Net Price List
F. O. B. Factory

MILITARY BAND ORGANS

September 1st, 1927

Style	Catalog Page No.	Price
Style No. 103	5	$ 450.00
Style No. 104	6	700.00
Style No. 105	7	850.00
Style No. 106	8	950.00
Style No. 125 (Rink Organ)	9	1050.00
Style No. 146-A	10	1025.00
Style No. 146-A Duplex	00	1225.00
Style No. 146-B	11	1150.00
Style No. 146-B Duplex	00	1350.00
Style No. 148 (Rink Organ)	12	1250.00
Style No. 148 Duplex (Rink Organ)	00	1450.00
Style No. 153 Duplex	13	1900.00
Style No. 157 Duplex	14	2750.00
Style No. 165 Duplex	15	4250.00
Style No. 180 Duplex (Including Motor and Blower)	16	8000.00

Motors to operate organs are extra.

Not included in organ price list.

WURLITZER
N. Tonawanda, N. Y.

REVISED LIST OF

MUSIC ROLLS

For the

Artizan

and

North Tonawanda

Military Band Organ

STYLES
X-A, X-A1, X-A2, A, A1, A2

46 KEY ENDLESS

MANUFACTURED BY

The Rudolph Wurlitzer Mfg. Co.

NORTH TONAWANDA, N. Y.

ROLL NO. 441
1. Hail, Hail, the Gang's All Here .... Song
2. Let Me Call You Sweetheart .... Waltz
3. Fisher's .... Hornpipe

ROLL NO. 549
Blue Streak .... March

ROLL NO. 737
Our Director .... March

ROLL NO. 765
Flowers of the Orient .... Waltz

ROLL NO. 851
1. Our Director .... March
2. The Skaters .... Waltz
3. Blue Streak .... March

ROLL NO. 852
Stein Song .... Fox Trot

ROLL NO. 853
Where the Golden Daffodils Grow .... Fox Trot

ROLL NO. 854
It Happened in Monterey .... Waltz

ROLL NO. 855
1. Stein Song .... Fox Trot
2. It Happened in Monterey .... Waltz
3. Where the Golden Daffodils Grow ... Fox Trot

ROLL NO. 856
Ro-Ro-Rollin' Along .... Fox Trot

ROLL NO. 857
Whippoorwill .... Fox Trot

ROLL NO. 858
Because There's a Change in You .... Waltz

ROLL NO. 859
When It's Springtime in the Rockies ... Waltz

ROLL NO. 860
On the Sunnyside of the Street .... Fox Trot

ROLL NO. 861
Like a Dream .... Fox Trot

ROLL NO. 862
Down the River of Golden Dreams .... Waltz

ROLL NO. 863
Dancing with Tears in My Eyes .... Waltz

ROLL NO. 864
With You .... Fox Trot

ROLL NO. 865
I'm in the Market for You .... Fox Trot

ROLL NO. 866
1. Ro-Ro-Rollin' Along .... Fox Trot
2. Because There's a Change in You ... Waltz
3. Whippoorwill .... Fox Trot

ROLL NO. 867
1. On the Sunny Side of the Street ... Fox Trot
2. When It's Springtime in the Rockies . Waltz
3. Like a Dream .... Fox Trot

ROLL NO. 868
1. With You .... Fox Trot
2. Dancing with Tears in My Eyes ..... Waltz
3. I'm in the Market for You .... Fox Trot

At one time the Rudolph Wurlitzer Manufacturing Co. apparently had perforators for making Artizan and North Tonawanda Musical Instrument Works rolls, as the catalogue to the left indicates.

Style No. 165—Duplex Orchestral Organ
69 Keys

For largest type stationary Carouselles, Roller Coasters and other Park installations. Used with great success in Park Dance Pavilions

Case, Oak Veneered; finished natural, with highly decorated white enamel fancy front; wings detachable.

Equipped with Duplex Tracker Frame.

DIMENSIONS WITH FRONT ON—HEIGHT, 8 feet 5 inches. WIDTH, 12 feet 8 inches. DEPTH, 4 feet 4 inches.

DIMENSIONS WITHOUT FRONT—HEIGHT, 5 feet 10½ inches. WIDTH, 6 feet 5 inches. DEPTH, 3 feet.

WEIGHT, packed for shipment, 3,000 lbs.

Automatic rewind; stops off and cut-off for drums.

INSTRUMENTATION

BASSES—6 eight-foot Stopped Pipes; 6 eight-foot Open Pipes; 6 Wood Trombones.

ACCOMPANIMENT—10 Stopped Pipes; 10 Open Pipes.

MELODY—14 Wood Trumpets; 14 Wood Bassoons; 14 Wood Viola Pipes; 22 Flute Pipes; 22 Piccolo Pipes; 22 Flageolet Pipes; 22 Open Piccolos; 22 Loud Violin; 22 Soft Violin; 22 Bells.

TRAPS—Bass Drum; Cymbal; Crash Cymbal; Triangle; Snare Drum; Castanets.

Automatic Swell Shutters.

AUTOMATIC STOPS—1 for Trombone; 1 for Trumpets; 1 for Bells; 1 for Flute and Piccolo; 1 for Flageolet and Open Piccolo; 1 for Loud Violin; 1 for Soft Violin.

The Style 165 Duplex Orchestral Organ, which uses 165 rolls, was the largest regular band organ in the Wurlitzer line. The 165 roll was the largest Wurlitzer roll made in quantity (the larger 180 roll was made only in limited numbers). Although complete sales and production figures do not survive, the authors estimate that 100 to 200 were originally sold. Early models were imported from Gebr. Bruder (of Waldkirch, Germany). After 1914, Style 165 organs were made at North Tonawanda, N.Y., some with Bruder components ordered earlier from the German firm. The Style 165 saw use on large carousels, in roller skating rinks, and other locations desiring a large and rich volume of music.

The New Wurlitzer Caliola

For Amusement Parks, Rinks, Carouselles, Circus Riding Devices and Outdoor Advertising

The Wurlitzer Caliola, first shipped in 1928, was intended to compete with the Tangley Calliaphone and other calliopes. While some brass pipe Caliolas were made, most had wooden pipes. The Caliola uses Wurlitzer 65-Note Automatic Player Piano rolls or special Caliola rolls of the same tracker scale but with extended perforations for playing sustained pipe notes. The "crackle lacquer" finish was made by applying a base coat of black paint to the instrument, letting it dry, and then applying a red or green (usually) finish coat which had been mixed with a soap compound. When the outer layer dried it pulled apart in sections and gave a curious "alligatored" appearance, as the illustration shows.

Just the instrument enterprising amusement interests have been looking forward to for years—something to attract the crowds—an entirely new musical instrument with a beautiful tone and remarkable volume. It plays from rolls or may be played by hand, creating beautiful musical effects. No class of amusement can afford to overlook this opportunity, as it is ideal for Circuses, Parks, Rinks, Riding Devices—in fact every amusement. As an outdoor advertising feature for Truck, Show Wagon or Ballyhoo Platform, there is no other instrument comparable to this New Wurlitzer Caliola.

INSTRUMENTATION

44-note Flute Pipes, either Wood or Brass. Equipped with or without Keyboard Plays ten-tune 65-note, Automatic Player Piano Roll. Operated by ¼ H. P. Electric motor or 1½ H. P. Gas Engine. Worm Drive Countershaft attached to case. Equipped with loud or soft volume control. Instrument can be furnished with Bass and Snare Drums at an additional charge.

SPECIFICATIONS

HEIGHT TO TOP OF SCROLL, 5 feet, 4 inches. HEIGHT WITHOUT SCROLL, 4 feet, 8 inches. WIDTH, 3 feet, 7½ inches. DEPTH, 2 feet, 10 inches. WEIGHT, 435 lbs., with countershaft and drive wheel.

FINISH—Red or Green Crackle Lacquer with carvings in Gold. Hand Painted Picture on Panel and Screens.

"SKATE YOUR DATE" read the sign in front of Randall's Roller Rink in Chenango Bridge, New York, where this Wurlitzer Caliola was once located. The instrument was superbly preserved, and its original green crackle paint finish is almost like new. The tonal quality of the Caliola resembles a calliope (Tangley, for example), but the quality is not quite so harsh. The instrument uses Caliola rolls which are based on the Wurlitzer 65-Note Automatic Player Piano scale.

BAND ORGANS AND DANCE ORGANS
Various Manufacturers

In this section we list scales and information for band organs and dance organs not represented elsewhere in the book. The main part of the listing, however, consists of unattributed scales or scales which have been attributed but not with certainty. These scales have come from the B.A.B. Organ Company files, the Eugene DeRoy archives, and elsewhere and in some instances may represent one-of-a-kind scales or modifications of the scales of other manufacturers (such as Gavioli, Frati, et al).

The authors list these unattributed scales to whet reader interest and curiosity, knowing that the same space could have been devoted to listing more positively known scales (additional Mortier scales, for example, were available to the authors, but just selected representative ones were chosen for use in this volume). By the time you've read to this point, you, the reader, will have more knowledge of band organ and dance organ tracker scales than *any* music book or roll composer ever did in "the good old days." So it is perhaps fitting that we conclude this section with some mystery scales. Of course, if you solve the mystery and identify any of the scales as being a standard scale of a well-known organ maker, then in a future edition we'll delete it from this section and replace it in the correct location, and then we'll dig into our file of scale sticks and come up with another mystery layout.

94-KEY ALPHONSE STEENPUT STREET ORGAN SCALE "THE WINDMILL"

12 Bass notes
12 Accompaniment notes
25 Melody notes
20 Countermelody notes

1 to 12, Bass G to F#
13 to 24, Accompaniment G to F#
25 to 49, Melody G to G
50 to 69, Countermelody D to A
70 Triangle
71 Trumpet: D
72 Cymbal
73 Trumpet: G
74 Bass drum
75 Trumpet: A
76 Bass drum
77 Trumpet: B
78 Snare drum
79 Trumpet: D
80 Snare drum
81 Tambourine
82 Cancel melody registers
83 Trumpet on (M)
84 Violin pipes on (M)
85 Piccolo on (M)
86 Mixture on (M)
87 Bells on (M)
88 Cancel countermelody registers
89 "Baritone kast" (?)
90 "Baritone balk" (?)
91 "Alt" (?)
92 Clarinet on (CM)
93 Trombone on
94 ?

ALPHONSE STEENPUT ORGANS

57-KEY ALPHONSE STEENPUT ORGAN SCALE

6 Bass notes
9 Accompaniment notes
15 Melody notes
15 Countermelody notes

57 Blank
56 Baritone on (CM)
55 Flute 4' on (M)
54 Celeste on (M)
53 Cello on (CM)
52 Xylophone on (M)
51 Snare drum
50 General cancel
49 Snare drum
48 Violin on (M)
47 Trombone on
46 to 41, Bass G, A, B, C, D, E
40 to 32, Accompaniment G, A, B, C, C#, D, E, F, F#
31 to 17, Melody C-A, B, C, C#, D, E
16 Vox humana on (M)
15 to 1, Countermelody G-C, D, E, F, F#, G, G#, A, B, C

VAN DER BEKEN ORGANS

62-KEY VAN DER BEKEN ORGAN SCALE
23 cm. wide

1 Blank (or key frame key?)
2 Trombone on
3 General cancel
4 to 11, Bass G, A, A#, B, C, D, E, F
12 to 27, Accompaniment and trumpet G, A-B
28 Snare drum
29 to 57, Melody C to E
58 Snare drum
59 Trumpet on
60 Forte and xylophone on
61 Bass drum
62 Violin pipes on
    Xylophone and forte play from notes G to C, holes 36 to 53.

UNATTRIBUTED ORGAN SCALES
(or not attributed with certainty)

43-KEY UNKNOWN ORGAN SCALE

> 3 Bass notes
> 35 Accompaniment-melody-piccolo notes

1 Bass drum
2 to 4, Bass F, A#, C
5 to 11 Accompaniment f, g, a, a#, c, d, d#
12 to 24, Violin pipes (melody) e, f, g, a, a#, b, c, d, d#, e, f, g, a#
25 to 39, Piccolo c, d, d#, e, f, g, a, a#, b, c, d, d#, e, f, g
40 Snare drum
41 Registers loud
42 Snare drum
43 Registers soft

The dividing point between the accompaniment and the melody may be different from that given. The melody and piccolo may overlap.

44-KEY UNKNOWN ORGAN SCALE
11.5 cm. wide; spaced 4 holes per cm.

> 8 Bass notes
> 11 Accompaniment notes
> 20 Melody notes

1 Blank
2 Snare drum
3 Wood block
4 F (accompaniment)
5 F# (accompaniment; lowest note)
6 A (melody)
7 G (melody)
8 E (accompaniment)
9 F (bass)
10 F# (melody)
11 F (melody)
12 D (accompaniment)
13 E (bass)
14 E (melody)
15 D# (melody)
16 C# (accompaniment)
17 D (bass)
18 D (melody)
19 C# (melody)
20 C (accompaniment)
21 C (bass)
22 C (melody)
23 B (melody)
24 B (accompaniment)
25 B (bass)
26 A# (melody)
27 A (melody)
28 A# (accompaniment)
29 A# (bass)
30 G# (melody)
31 G (melody)
32 A (accompaniment)
33 A (bass)
34 F# (melody)
35 F (melody)
36 G# (accompaniment)
37 G (bass)
38 E (melody)
39 D# (melody)
40 G (accompaniment)
41 D (melody)
42 C (melody)
43 Bass drum
44 Blank

The note scale progresses from low to high in the following order: bass 37 up through bass 9, accompaniment 5, then accompaniment 40 through accompaniment 4, then melody 42 through melody 6.

45-KEY UNKNOWN ORGAN SCALE
(Marked "EIFLER")

> 5 Bass notes
> 9 Accompaniment notes
> 14 Melody notes
> 13 Trumpet notes

1 Snare drum
2 Shutoff
3 Snare drum
4 to 8, Bass G, C, D, E, F
9 to 17, Accompaniment g, a, b, c, c#, d, e, f, f#
18 to 31, Melody (flute) g, a, a#, b, c, c#, d, e, f, f#, g, a, b, c
32 to 44, Trumpet e, f, f#, g, a, b, c, c#, d, e, f, f#, g
45 Bass drum

Eifler, located at one time in Pennsylvania, seems to have been a carnival or amusement operator who used organs made by a variety of manufacturers.

48-KEY UNKNOWN ORGAN SCALE
(Marked "P.M")

> 10 Bass notes
> 12 Accompaniment notes
> 26 Melody notes

1 to 10, Bass D, E, F, F#, G, A, A#, B, C, C#
11 to 22, Accompaniment a to g#
23 to 48, Melody a to a, b

48-KEY UNKNOWN ORGAN SCALE
(Marked "G.M.D.B.")
(Related to Marenghi?)

> 8 Bass notes
> 9 Accompaniment notes
> 25 Melody notes

1 Triangle
2 Bass drum
3 to 6, Bass F, A, B, D
7 to 10 Accompaniment g, a#, c, d
11 to 23, Melody high to low: e, c#, b, a, g, f, d#, c#, b, a, g, f, e (lowest note)
24 to 34, Melody low to high: f#, g#, a#, c, d, e, f#, g#, a#; c, d
35 f?
36 to 40, Accompaniment d#, c#, b, a, f
41 to 44, Bass E, C, A#, G
45 Snare drum
46 Castanets
47 Snare drum
48 Castanets

48-KEY UNKNOWN ORGAN(?) SCALE
(Marked "MANDOLIN")
(An orchestrion or organ with mandolin section?)

> 9 Bass notes
> 12 Accompaniment notes
> 24 Mandolin(?) notes

1 to 9, Bass D, E, F, F#, G, A, A#, B, C
10 to 21, Accompaniment a to g#
22 Bass drum
23 to 41, Mandolins a to d#
42 Snare drum
43 to 47, Mandolins e to g, a
48 ?

49-KEY UNKNOWN ORGAN SCALE
(Marked "EIFLER")
(Related to Gavioli?)

> 3 Bass notes
> 10 Accompaniment notes
> 14 Trumpet notes
> 18 Piccolo notes

1 Snare drum
2 Shutoff
3 Snare drum
4 to 6, Trombone G, C, D
7 to 16, Accompaniment G, A, B, C, C#, D, E, F, F#, G
17 to 30, Trumpet E, F, F#, G, A, B, C, C#, D, E, F, F#, G, A
31 to 48, Piccolo G, A, B, C, C#, D, E, F, F#, G, A, B, C, C#, D, E, F, F#
49 Bass drum

The piccolo notes may also serve as the melody section.

51-KEY UNKNOWN ORGAN SCALE

> 4 Bass notes
> 10 Accompaniment notes
> 17 Melody notes
> 13 Countermelody notes

1 Cancel registers
2 Snare drum
3 to 6, Bass G, A, D, E
7 to 16, Accompaniment A, B, C, C# D, D#, E, F#, G, G#
17 to 33, Melody A to C#
34 and 35, Countermelody A, A#
36 Register on
37 Register on
38 to 48, Countermelody B to A
49 Snare drum
50 Register on
51 Bass drum

The melody plays on two ranks of violin pipes. The countermelody plays on flageolets and stopped flutes which are controlled by registers. The organ is evidently an earlier instrument modified into a small Dutch street organ.

52-KEY UNKNOWN ORGAN SCALE
(Marked "100 A")
(Related to Gebr. Bruder?)

1 Bass drum
2 Registers loud
3 F (1st octave)
4 F (3rd octave; lowest note)
5 G (3rd octave)
6 G (2nd octave)
7 F# (1st octave)
8 A (3rd octave)
9 F (5th octave)
10 F# (2nd octave)
11 D (4th octave)
12 G# (2nd octave)
13 F (2nd octave; lowest note)
14 C (4th octave)
15 A# (4th octave)
16 E (1st octave)
17 A (2nd octave)
18 G# (4th octave)
19 D# (1st octave)
20 F# (4th octave)
21 A# (2nd octave)
22 D (1st octave)
23 E (3rd octave)
24 D (3rd octave)
25 C# (1st octave)
26 B (2nd octave)
27 C (1st octave)
28 C (3rd octave)
29 B (3rd octave)
30 C (2nd octave)
31 B (1st octave)
32 C# (3rd octave)
33 D# (3rd octave)
34 F (4th octave; lowest note)
35 A# (1st octave)
36 C# (2nd octave)
37 G (4th octave)
38 A (4th octave)
39 A (1st octave)
40 D (2nd octave)
41 B (4th octave)
42 C# (4th octave)
43 E (4th octave)
44 G# (1st octave)
45 D# (2nd octave)
46 A# (3rd octave)
47 G# (3rd octave)
48 F# (3rd octave)
49 G (1st octave)
50 E (2nd octave)
51 Registers soft
52 Snare drum

The scale stick is not marked as to bass, accompaniment, melody, etc.

52-KEY UNKNOWN ORGAN SCALE
(Marked "CELLZON")

        4 Trombone notes
        4 Bass notes
        9 Accompaniment notes
        19 Melody notes
        10 Trumpet notes

1 Registers loud
2 Snare drum
3 Shutoff
4 Snare drum
5 to 8, Trombone F, G, C, D
9 to 12, Bass G, C, D, F
13 to 21, Accompaniment G, A, A#, B, C, D, E, F, F#
22 to 40, Melody G, A, A#, B, C, C#, D, E, F, F#, G, A, A#, B, C, C#, D, E, F
41 to 50, Trumpet F, F#, G, A, A#, B, C, D, E, F
51 Bass drum
52 Registers soft

Melody: clarinet and piccolo pipes. Registers soft = piccolo off.

54-KEY UNKNOWN ORGAN SCALE
(Marked "M")
(Related to Marenghi?)
(Right to left)

        8 Bass notes
        23 Accompaniment and melody notes
        14 Piccolo notes

1 Shutoff
2 Band leader?
3 "P" (register?)
4 "V" (register)
5 "D" (cancel?)
6 Castanets
7 Snare drum
8 and 9, Bass C and D
10 Snare drum
11 to 16, Bass E, F, G, A, A#, B
17 to 24, Accompaniment F, G, A, A#, B, C, C#, D
25 to 39, Melody D# to F
40 to 53, Piccolo C to C, D
54 Bass drum

Accompaniment and melody may overlap. Melody: violin pipes and trumpets.

58-KEYLESS UNKNOWN ORGAN SCALE

        7 Bass notes
        12 Accompaniment notes
        24 Melody notes

1 D (bass)
2 F (2nd octave melody)
3 G (bass)
4 C# (2nd octave melody)
5 "BA F" (register loud)
6 A# (2nd octave melody)
7 "MD" (mandolin off)
8 G (2nd octave melody)
9 G (accompaniment)
10 E (1st octave melody)
11 A# (1st octave melody)
12 C# (1st octave melody)
13 C# (accompaniment)
14 A# (1st octave melody)
15 E (accompaniment)
16 G (1st octave melody)
17 D (accompaniment)
18 F (1st octave melody; lowest note)
19 B (accompaniment)
20 G# (1st octave melody)
21 G# (accompaniment)
22 B (1st octave melody)
23 F (accompaniment; lowest note)
24 D (1st octave melody)
25 Shutoff
26 F (2nd octave melody; lowest note)
27 A (bass)
28 G# (2nd octave melody)
29 E (bass)
30 B (2nd octave melody)
31 Rewind
32 D (2nd octave melody)
33 Bass drum
34 "CF" (register)
35 "Pedal"
36 F# (1st octave melody)
37 D# (accompaniment)
38 A (1st octave melody)
39 C (accompaniment)
40 C (1st octave melody)
41 A (accompaniment)
42 D# (1st octave melody)
43 F# (accompaniment)
44 F# (2nd octave melody)
45 Triangle
46 A (2nd octave melody)
47 B (bass)
48 C (2nd octave melody)
49 F (bass)
50 E (2nd octave melody)
51 C (bass)
52 "MF"
53 "ME" (mandolin on?)
54 "M an Piano P"
55 Snare drum
56 "XD" (xylophone off)
57 "XE" (xylophone on)
58 "R"

59-KEY UNKNOWN ORGAN SCALE
(Related to Gavioli?)

       3 Bass notes
       3 Trombone notes
      19 Accompaniment and melody
      16 Trumpet notes
      14 Piccolo notes

1 Snare drum
2 Shutoff
3 Snare drum
4 to 6, Bass (or trombone) G, C, D
7 to 9 Trombone (or bass) G, C, D
10 to 28, Accompaniment and Melody G, A, B, C, C#, D, E, F,
  F#, G, A, A#, B, C, C#, D, E, F, F#
29 to 44, Trumpet C, C#, D, E, F, F#, G, A, A#, B, C, C#,
  D, E, F, G
45 to 58, Piccolo G, A, A#, B, C, C#, D, E, F, F#, G, A, B,
  C
59 Bass drum

60-KEY UNKNOWN ORGAN SCALE
"PICCOLO PAN"

      7 Trombone notes
     14 Bass and accompaniment notes
     20 Melody notes
     13 Trumpet notes

1 Bass drum
2 to 15, Bass and accompaniment C, D, E, F, F#, G, A, B, C, C#, D, E,
  F, F#
16 to 35, Melody G to D
36 Registers loud
37 to 43, Trombone F, G, A, B, C, D, E
44 Registers soft
45 to 57, Trumpet D, E, F, F#, G, G#, A, A#, B, C, D, E, F
58 Snare drum
59 Shutoff (or key frame key)
60 Snare drum

63-KEY UNKNOWN ORGAN SCALE

1 to 5, Bass G, C, D, E, F
6 to 30, Accompaniment and melody G, A, A#, B, C, C#, D, E, F, F#,
  G, A, A#, B, C, C#, D, E, F, F#, G, A, A#, B, C
31 to 33, Bells G, A, B
34 Bass drum
35 Bell C
36 Snare drum
37 ?
38 Bell D
39 Snare drum
40 to 42, Bells E, F, F#
43 Shutoff
44 to 63, Violin pipes C, C#, D, E to G, A

64-KEY UNKNOWN ORGAN SCALE
(of Belgian manufacture)

1 Bass (bass registers loud?)
2 Tremolo on
3 Xylophone on
4 Vox humana on
5 Baritone on
6 Cello on
7 to 11, Notes F, E, D#, D, C#(?)
12 Shutters open
13 to 17, Notes C, B, A, G, F#
18 General cancel
19 Reed on
20 and 21, Notes E, D
22 Bass drum
23 to 28, Notes E, D, C, B, A, G
29 Snare drum
30 Flute on
31 Cello on
32 to 44, Notes F#, G, G#, A, B, C, C#, D, E, F, F#, G, A
45 to 62, Notes G, A, B, C, C#, D, D#, E, F, F#, G, G#, A, B, C, C#,
  D, E
63 Snare drum
64 Violin pipes on

   23 through 28 may play the bass notes. Other sections are unknown.

65-KEY UNKNOWN ORGAN SCALE
(Related to a Waldkirch-built Gavioli?)

      7 Bass notes
     11 Accompaniment notes
     23 Melody notes
     18 Countermelody (baritone) notes

1 Shutoff (or key frame key?)
2 Snare drum
3 to 9, Bass F, G, A, B, C, D, E
10 Snare drum
11 to 16, Accompaniment F#, G, A, A#, B, C
17 Bass drum
18 to 22, Accompaniment C#, D, D#, E, F
23 to 45, Melody F#-D, E, F
46 Registers soft
47 to 64, Countermelody C, D-D, E, F, F#, G
65 Registers loud

65-KEY UNKNOWN ORGAN OR ORCHESTRION SCALE
(Marked "65 PIANO")

1 to 17, D to F#
18 to 29, G to F#
30 to 54, G to G
55 General cancel
56 "F" (loud?)
57 Snare drum
58 "P" (soft, or piano on?)
59 Snare drum
60 Violin pipes on?
61 Flute pipes on?
62 Triangle
63 ?
64 Cello on?
65 Cancel (shutoff, or key frame key?)

65-KEY UNKNOWN ORGAN SCALE
(Related to Frati?)

1 to 30, Piano G, C, D, E, F, G, A, A#, B, C, C#, D, E, F,
   F#, G, A, A#, B, C, C#, D, E, F, F#, G, A, A#, B, C
31 G B
32 A C
33 Snare drum
34 Bass drum
35 B D
36 Snare drum
37 Triangle
38 C E
39 Snare drum
40 D F
41 E G
42 Snare drum
43 Shutoff
44 to 63, Melody C, C#, D, E, F, F#, G, G#, A, A#, B, C,
   C#, D, D#, E, F, F#, G, A
64 F A
65 F# A#

   The holes with two notes listed are not marked as to clef on
the scale stick (from the B.A.B. Organ Co. files). If treble clef,
the first letter is correct; if bass clef, the second letter is correct.
The four snare drum holes are unusual. See the note in the
Gavioli section concerning a similar instrument in the Brabandt
Collection.

65/67-KEY UNKNOWN ORGAN SCALE
(Ruth converted to Gavioli-related music?)

       6 Bass notes
      10 Accompaniment notes
      21 Melody notes
      17 Countermelody notes

1 Band leader
2 Bass drum
3 Trombone on
4 General cancel
5 to 10, Bass G, A, B, C, D, E
11 to 20, Accompaniment F#, G, A, B, C, C#, D, D#, E, F
21 Violin pipes on (M)
22 Piccolo on (M)
23 Xylophone on (M)
24 to 44, Melody F# to A, B, C, C#, D, E
45 Saxophone on (CM)
46 Clarinet on (CM)
47 to 63, Countermelody D to D, E, F, F# G
64 Snare drum
65 Swell shutters open
66 Snare drum
67 Triangle

66-KEY UNKNOWN ORGAN SCALE
(Related to Gavioli?)

       5 Bass notes
       5 Trombone notes
     25 Accompaniment and melody notes
     13 Trumpet notes
     14 Piccolo notes

1 Snare drum
2 Shutoff
3 Snare drum
4 to 8, Trombone G, C, D, E, F
9 to 13, Bass C, D, E, F, G
14 to 38, Accompaniment and melody A, A#, B, C, D, E, F, F#, G, A,
   A#, B, C, D, E, F, F#, G, A, A#, B, C, D, E, F
39 to 51, Trumpet C, D, E, F, F#, G, A, A#, B, C, D, E, F
52 to 65, Piccolo G, A, A#, B, C, D, E, F, F#, G, A, A#, B, C
66 Bass drum

69-KEY UNKNOWN ORGAN SCALE
(Related to Limonaire?)

1 Vox humana on
2 Snare drum
3 Blank?
4 Snare drum
5 Blank
6 Castanets
7 Loud violin pipes on
8 and 9, Notes G, A
10 Trombone on
11 Soft violin pipes on
12 and 13, Notes B, C
14 English horn on
15 and 16, Notes D, E
17 Flageolet on
18 Bass drum
19 to 21, Notes D, E, F
22 Clarinet on
23 General cancel
24 to 30, Notes F#, G, A, B, C, C#, D
31 Xylophone on (bells?)
32 Cello on
33 Baritone on
34 to 49, Notes D#, E, F, F#, G, G#, A, B, C, C#, D, E, F, F#, G, A
50 Cymbal, bell ringer, or bells on?
51 to 68, Notes G, A, B, C, C#, D, D#, E, F, F#, G, A, A#, B, C#,
   D, E
69 Triangle

   The bass probably includes holes 7, 8, 11, 12, 14, and 15.

70-KEY UNKNOWN ORGAN SCALE
(Related to Marenghi?)

       8 Bass notes
     10 Accompaniment notes
     19 Countermelody notes
     21 Melody notes

1 Shutoff
2 Snare drum
3 and 4, Bass F, G
5 Castanets
6 and 7, Bass A, A#
8 Snare drum
9 and 10, Bass B, C
11 Bass drum
12 and 13, Bass D, E
14 Band leader
15 and 16, Accompaniment D, E
17 "B" (register - baritone or bells?)
18 to 21, Accompaniment F, F#, G, A
22 Forte T (trumpet on?)
23 to 26, Accompaniment A#, B, C, C#
27 Cornet P (trumpet off?)
28 FX (xylophone or bells on?)
29 to 47, Clarinet and baritone notes D, D#, E, F to G, A
48 to 68, Melody G, A, A# to E
69 General cancel
70 V (violin on?)

   Melody stops: piccolo, xylophone, violin, cornet.

73-KEY UNKNOWN ORGAN SCALE
(Related to Gavioli?)

8 Bass notes
11 Accompaniment notes
19 Countermelody notes
22 Melody notes

1 Shutoff
2 Violin pipes on (M)
3 Oboe on (CM)
4 Piccolo on (M)
5 Flute on (M)
6 Saxophone on (CM)
7 Cello on (CM)
8 Bass drum
9 to 16, Bass F, G, A, A#, B, C, D, E
17 to 27, Accompaniment G, A to F#
28 to 46, Countermelody C to F#
47 Triangle
48 to 69, Melody G to D, E, F
70 Trombone on
71 Snare drum
72 General cancel
73 Snare drum

80-KEY UNKNOWN ORGAN SCALE

15 Bass notes?
14 Accompaniment notes?
25 Melody notes
15 Countermelody notes

1 to 15, Bass D to E
16 to 29, Accompaniment F to F#
30 to 54, Melody G to G
55 General cancel
56 Register?
57 Snare drum
58 Piccolo on?
59 Register?
60 Violin pipes on?
61 Flute on?
62 Triangle (or bass drum?)
63 to 77, Countermelody E to F#
78 Register?
79 Shutoff (key frame key?)
80 Snare drum

The dividing point between bass and accompaniment is uncertain.

82-KEYLESS UNKNOWN ORGAN SCALE

9 Trombone notes
12 Bass notes
12 Accompaniment notes
25 Melody notes
14 Trumpet notes

1 A# (1st octave melody)
2 C (1st octave melody)
3 C (trombone)
4 A (bass)
5 Registers soft
6 A (high trumpet)

7 Snare drum
8 G (trumpet; lowest note)
9 A (1st octave melody)
10 F# (2nd octave melody)
11 E (trombone)
12 A# (bass)
13 Registers loud
14 G# (high trumpet)
15 Snare drum
16 B (bass)
17 D# (1st octave melody)
18 C (2nd octave melody)
19 F# (trombone)
20 A# (trumpet)
21 G (high trumpet)
22 E (2nd octave melody)
23 G# (bass)
24 Bell ringer
25 A (2nd octave melody)
26 F# (1st octave melody)
27 A (trombone)
28 C# (bass)
29 C# (2nd octave melody)
30 D (accompaniment)
31 C# (trumpet)
32 D (bass)
33 F (high 2nd octave melody)
34 G# (accompaniment)
35 B (accompaniment)
36 D# (bass)
37 G (1st octave melody)
38 Band leader
39 C (accompaniment)
40 D (trumpet)
41 D# (accompaniment)
42 F (accompaniment; lowest note)
43 D# (trumpet)
44 F# (accompaniment)
45 C# (accompaniment)
46 E (bass)
47 F (1st octave melody; lowest note)
48 G (accompaniment)
49 Bell ringer
50 B (trombone)
51 F (trumpet)
52 E (trumpet)
53 A# (accompaniment)
54 C (trumpet)
55 D# (2nd octave melody)
56 E (accompaniment)
57 A (accompaniment)
58 A# (trombone)
59 B (2nd octave melody)
60 F# (trumpet)
61 Register
62 C (bass)
63 G (2nd octave melody)
64 D (2nd octave melody)
65 B (trumpet)
66 G (trombone)
67 F (2nd octave melody; lowest note)
68 A# (2nd octave melody)
69 G (bass)
70 Register
71 C# (1st octave melody)
72 G# (2nd octave melody)
73 F# (bass)
74 F# (trombone)
75 B (1st octave melody)
76 E (1st octave melody)
77 A (trumpet)
78 Bass drum
79 G# (1st octave melody)
80 D (1st octave melody)
81 F (bass)
82 D (trombone)

Holes 61 and 70 apparently turn a register on and off. Holes 24 and 49 might turn bells on and off instead of operating bell ringers. The dividing point between accompaniment and melody is uncertain.

84-KEY UNKNOWN ORGAN SCALE

8 Bass notes
8 Trombone notes
42 Accompaniment, melody, and piccolo notes?
21 Countermelody notes

1 Bass drum
2 Snare drum
3 to 10, Trombone (or bass?) G, A, A#, B, C, D, E, F
11 to 18, Bass (or trombone?) G, A, A#, B, C, D, E, F
19 to 29, G, A, A#, B, C, C#, D, E, F, F# G
30 to 47, G#, A, A#, B, C, C#, D, E, F, F#, G, A, A#, B, C, C#, D, E
48 to 60, F, F#, G, A, A#, B, C, C#, D, E, F, F#, G
61 to 81 G, A, A#, B, C, C#, D, E, F, F#, G, A, A#, B, C, C#, D, E, F, F#, G
82 "D" (?)
83 "B" (bells ?)
84 Bells?

The dividing points between accompaniment, melody, and possibly piccolo are uncertain. Note the similarity between this scale and the B.A.B. "82" (or Artizan and North Tonawanda Style E) roll.

85/82-KEY UNKNOWN ORGAN SCALE
(Related to Gavioli?)

6 Bass notes
6 Trombone notes
9 Accompaniment notes
10 Melody notes
18 Piccolo notes
19 Countermelody notes

1 Bells on
2 Registers soft
3 Snare drum
4 Shutoff (or key frame key?)
5 Snare drum
6 to 11, Bass F, G, C, D, E, F
12 to 20, Accompaniment G, A, A#, B, C, D, E, F, F#
21 to 39, Melody G, A, A#, B, C, C#, D, E, F, F#, G, A, A#, B, C, C#, D, E, F
40 to 57, Piccolo E, F, F#, G, A, A#, B, C, C#, D, E, F, F#, G, A, A#, B, C
58 Bass drum
59 to 64, Trombone F, G, C, D, E, F
65 Band leader
66 to 84, Countermelody G, A, A#, B, C, C#, D, E, F, F#, G, A, A#, B, C, C#, D, E, F
85 Registers loud

The 82-key variation of the preceding omits holes 1, 2, and 85.

Melody = clarinet. Countermelody = saxophone and trumpet.

104-KEY UNKNOWN ORGAN SCALE

1 Xylophone on
2 Piano on
3 Tremolo on
4 Bass and accompaniment register
5 Viola on
6 Mandolin on
7 Viola on
8 II Medium loud
9 III Loud
10 I Soft
11 Castanets
12 Cymbal
13 Harmonic flute
14 Loud violin pipes on
15 Trombone on
16 Baritone on
17 to 20, Bass F to G#
21 Flageolet on
22 Cello on
23 to 26, Bass A to C
27 Trumpet on
28 Clarinet on
29 to 32, Bass C# to E
33 to 40, Accompaniment F to C
41 Soft violin pipes on
42 Snare drum
43 Accompaniment C#?
44 General cancel
45 to 69, Low note scale C to C
70 Snare drum
71 to 102, High note scale C to G
103 Triangle
104 Bass drum

Low note scale: clarinet, baritone, cello, flute, piano. High note scale: flageolet, violin pipes, trumpet, xylophone, mandolin, piano. The piano apparently plays all of the notes, including bass, accompaniment, and both note scales.

106-KEY UNKNOWN ORGAN SCALE

1 Snare drum
2 ?
3 Snare drum
4 E (1st octave reed)
5 D (1st octave reed)
6 F# (1st octave reed)
7 A# (1st octave reed)
8 C (2nd octave reed; lowest note)
9 D (1st octave main musical scale)
10 D (2nd octave reed)
11 F (1st octave main musical scale)
12 G (1st octave main musical scale)
13 E (2nd octave reed)
14 A (1st octave main musical scale)
15 B (1st octave main musical scale)
16 F# (2nd octave reed)
17 C (2nd octave main musical scale; lowest note)
18 C# (2nd octave main musical scale)
19 G# (2nd octave reed)
20 D (2nd octave main musical scale)
21 D# (2nd octave main musical scale)
22 A# (2nd octave reed)
23 E (2nd octave main musical scale)
24 F (2nd octave main musical scale)
25 C (3rd octave reed; lowest note)
26 F# (2nd octave main musical scale)
27 G (2nd octave main musical scale)
28 D (3rd octave reed)
29 G# (2nd octave main musical scale)
30 A (2nd octave main musical scale)
31 E (3rd octave reed)
32 A# (2nd octave main musical scale)
33 B (2nd octave main musical scale)
34 F# (3rd octave reed)
35 G# (3rd octave reed)
36 A# (3rd octave reed)
37 Swell II
38 Swell I
39 Trumpet on
40 Clarinet on
41 Cello on
42 General cancel
43 G (5th octave main musical scale)
44 F (5th octave main musical scale)
45 D# (5th octave main musical scale)
46 C# (5th octave main musical scale)
47 B (4th octave main musical scale)
48 A (4th octave main musical scale)
49 G (4th octave main musical scale)
50 F (4th octave main musical scale)
51 D# (4th octave main musical scale)
52 C# (4th octave main musical scale)
53 B (3rd octave main musical scale)
54 A (3rd octave main musical scale)
55 G (3rd octave main musical scale)
56 G# (3rd octave main musical scale)
57 A# (3rd octave main musical scale)
58 C (4th octave main musical scale; lowest note)
59 D (4th octave main musical scale)
60 E (4th octave main musical scale)
61 F# (4th octave main musical scale)
62 G# (4th octave main musical scale)
63 A# (4th octave main musical scale)
64 C (5th octave main musical scale; lowest note)
65 D (5th octave main musical scale)
66 E (5th octave main musical scale)
67 F# (5th octave main musical scale)
68 Soft violin pipes on
69 Loud violin pipes on
70 Flute on
71 Piccolo on
72 Mandolin on
73 Spare
74 B (3rd octave reed)
75 A (3rd octave reed)
76 G (3rd octave reed)
77 F (3rd octave reed)
78 D# (3rd octave reed)
79 C# (3rd octave reed)
80 B (2nd octave reed)
81 F# (3rd octave main musical scale)
82 F (3rd octave main musical scale)
83 E (3rd octave main musical scale)
84 A (2nd octave reed)
85 D# (3rd octave main musical scale)
86 D (3rd octave main musical scale)
87 G (2nd octave reed)
88 C# (3rd octave main musical scale)
89 C (3rd octave main musical scale; lowest note)
90 Registers loud (Grand jeux; forte)
91 A# (1st octave main musical scale)
92 F (2nd octave reed)
93 G# (1st octave main musical scale)
94 F# (1st octave main musical scale)
95 D# (2nd octave reed)
96 E (1st octave main musical scale)
97 C (1st octave main musical scale; lowest note)
98 C# (2nd octave reed)
99 B (1st octave reed)
100 G (1st octave reed)
101 A (1st octave reed)
102 F (1st octave reed)
103 C (1st octave reed; lowest note)
104 Cymbal
105 Bass drum
106 Spare

NEW SCALES
for
ORCHESTRIONS AND BAND ORGANS

In modern times collectors and researchers have had access to a wide variety of orchestrions, organs, and other old-time instruments in good playing condition, as exhibited in private collections, museums, and other locations. In addition, there are many phonograph records and tapes available of old-time instruments. As a result, comparisons of various instruments, their musical features, and their abilities can be made to a greater extent today than years ago.

Now and then, after being inspired by older instruments, a collector with musical ability becomes interested in trying his or her hand at producing an original automatic musical instrument. Sometimes this takes the form of an entirely new scale or tracker layout concept. Other times, an adaptation or modification of an earlier scale is made. The owners of some public museums have also built certain display instruments which maximize visual effects and which require specialized types of new rolls. The result is a growing list of new tracker scales, each of which is usually represented by just one instrument and by just a few music rolls. A few of these tracker scales are included here to demonstrate what was done during the 1970s and to preserve information so that a future owner of one of these specialized devices will know its musical layout and capabilities.

76-KEY BAND ORGAN SCALE
(Designed by Jack Hewes)

76 Spare
75 to 58, Countermelody G to C
57 Wood block
56 Triphone on (cm)
55 Wood block
54 Triangle
53 to 51 Same as 56-key Limonaire
50 Cello (cm)
49 and 48 Same as 56-key Limonaire
47 Bells on (m)
46 to 1 Same as 56-key Limonaire

With 8 bass, 11 accompaniment, 22 melody, and 18 countermelody notes.

MODIFIED SEEBURG H ORCHESTRION SCALE
(New scale)

All of the functions are the same as regular Seeburg H rolls, with the following exceptions:
A Multiplex switch on
43 Xylophone off; with switch on, tremolo off
45 Xylophone on; with switch on, tremolo on
46 Snare drum single tap; with switch on, wood block
49 Snare drum roll; with switch on, wood block
51 Tympani; with switch on, tambourine single tap
52 Tympani; with switch on, tambourine shake
B Multiplex switch off

Both wood block beaters play a single tap. Holes A and B are in the same positions as holes A and B in the MSR organ roll (related to the H roll). Modifications designed by Terry Borne and Art Reblitz.

T ROLL SCALE
(Modified OS roll scale)

All the functions are the same as regular OS organ rolls (used on the Reproduco organ), with the following exceptions:
A Bass hammer rail down
B Snare drum; with switch on, tambourine shake
C Play
D Bass drum and cymbal; with switch on, tambourine beater
E Bass hammer rail up

Holes 1 to 88, same as the OS roll

F Multiplex switch (chain perforation)
G Bass drum; with switch on, wood block
H Rewind
I Bass drum; with switch on, castanets
J Triangle

Preceding modification designed by Hal Davis.

92-KEYLESS MODIFIED MORTIER DANCE ORGAN SCALE
(Designed by Art Reblitz for House On The Rock)
11¼" wide; spaced 9 holes per inch

00 Play
0 Large bell
1 Low tom tom (loud)
2 Crash cymbal
3 High tom tom (soft)
4 Bell ringers
5 High tom tom (soft)
6 Tremolo on (ranks 58, 59, 60, 83, 86)
7 Snare drum
8 Bass violin pipes I and II on
9 Snare drum
10 Bass bourdon on
11 Tambourine
12 Tympani
13 Trombone on
14 Bass drum (without cymbal)
15 Tympani
16 General cancel
17 to 24, Bass notes A#, C, C#, D, D#, F, G, G#
25 to 34, Accompaniment notes A#, C, C#, D, D#, E, F, G, G#, A
35 to 56, Melody notes A# to G
57 Violin pipes and unda maris pipes on (melody section)
58 Bourdon celeste on (melody)
59 Trumpet on (melody)
60 Baxophone on (melody)
61 Carillon on (melody)
62 Xylophone on (melody)
63 to 82, Countermelody notes D# to A#
83 Bourdon celeste on (countermelody)
84 Violin celeste on (countermelody)
85 Cello on (countermelody)
86 Saxophone on (countermelody)
87 Gong crescendo
88 Gong crash
89 Shutoff
90 Rewind

63-KEYLESS BAND ORGAN SCALE
(Designed by Ken Smith)
23 cm. wide

A scale designed by Ken Smith, partially based on the 56-key Limonaire organ scale. With 8 bass, 11 accompaniment, 23 melody, and 13 countermelody notes.

63 Bass drum and cymbal
62 to 50, Countermelody, C to C
49 Violin pipes on
48 General cancel
47 Snare drum
46 Ocarina on
45 Snare drum
44 Trombone on
43 to 36, Bass G, A, A#, B, C, D, E, F
35 to 25, Accompaniment G, A to F#
24 to 2, Melody G to F
1 Registers forte

70-KEYLESS HOOGHUYS BAND ORGAN SCALE
(Designed by Mike Kitner)
Paper rolls; 8¾" wide; spaced 9 holes per inch

1 Blank
2 Swell open
3 Swell closed
4 Violin pipes on
5 English horn on
6 Violin celeste on
7 Harmonic flute on
8 Trumpet on
9 Vox humana on
10 Bells on
11 Trombone on
12 Rewind
13 Blank
14 Bass drum and cymbal
15 to 20, Bass notes F, G, A, C, D, E
21 to 30, Accompaniment G, A, A#, B, C, C#, D, E, F, F#
31 to 40, Countermelody (saxophone) G, A, A#, B, C, C#, D, E, F, F#
41 to 59, Melody G, A, A#, B, C, C#, D, E, F, F#, G, A, A#, B, C, C#, D, E, F
60 Wood block
61 to 66, High melody notes F#, G, A, A#, B, C
67 General cancel
68 Snare drum
69 Wood block
70 Snare drum

This is a hypothetical scale expanded from the 60-key Hooghuys scale which includes a countermelody-type saxophone rank which plays from the accompaniment note section and which has no countermelody section. The saxophone has a register but it is used for "accompaniment forte" rather than countermelody. Adding extra valves, a tracker bar interface, and paper music rolls would allow the organ to have an independent countermelody section while still enabling it to play its original cardboard music books.

DICTIONARY of TERMS

DICTIONARY OF TERMS

We list definitions of terms often encountered when reading key frame and tracker bar layouts. For a broader dictionary of terms relating to instruments in general, refer to *The Encyclopedia of Automatic Musical Instruments,* the source for many of the definitions given here. The definitions given are those which relate to automatic musical instruments and may differ from definitions for orchestra instruments and other non-automatic devices.

ACCELERATOR. Device which quickens the operation of an expression mechanism, altering a crescendo, decrescendo, or other volume level change from slow to fast or vice-versa. Used by Hupfeld, for example, in the Dea, Triphonola, and Pan.

ACCENT. To increase the loudness or intensity of a note or chord within a group of otherwise softer notes. Refer to the Apollo X scale, for example.

ACCOMPANIMENT. The part of music or section of an instrument which plays a subordinate part to the more prominent melody and countermelody sections. In German, Begleitung.

ACCORDION. A portable hand-held reed instrument with bellows which are expanded and contracted by arm movements and which is played by means of a keyboard or buttons. Variant spellings sometimes seen include accordian and, in Europe, accordeon.

AEOLINE PIPE. Delicate, bright string pipe used in pipe organs and in a few large European orchestrions (Hupfeld Helios, for example).

AMPLIFIER. Expression device which increases the pump vacuum level by decreasing the amount of atmospheric pressure normally bled into the system. Used in Ampico, Coinola, and certain other instruments.

AUTOMATIC ROLL CHANGER. Ferris-wheel type device (usually) which stores 2 to 12 perforated paper rolls and changes them automatically, usually in the sequence in which they are placed on the changer mechanism (or, if desired, a particular roll can be selected). Synonyms for automatic roll changers of this type: magazine system, revolver system. Several variations occur, including a device made by Philipps which incorporates extra roll-holding sections (usually a total of 12) which hang below the basic revolver-type mechanism; and a 10-roll cartridge-type changer unit, called a "10-roll magazine," by Popper & Co., but constructed on different principles from those used in standard revolver- or magazine-type mechanism. Perhaps the most sophisticated roll changing device was that developed by Hupfeld, which, in its most elegant form, consisted of two 10-roll changers arranged side by side (for a total selection of 20 rolls) and equipped with a device for selecting a desired roll from a distant control panel or wallbox. In America, the Wurlitzer Automatic Roll Changer (capitalized in Wurlitzer's usage) achieved fame, as did the Philipps-made roll changing device employed on many Wurlitzer Mandolin and Concert PianOrchestras. For use on a Hupfeld, Philipps, or Wurlitzer roll changer rolls were equipped with wood (Hupfeld) or metal rods in place of the normal tapered end and tab.

BAND LEADER. Or band master. A carved (usually) statue which stands on the facade of a band organ and which beats time with a small baton. Motion often governed by the bass drum key in the tracker or key frame scale. Also: Dirigent, Kapellmeister, kapellmeester.

BAND ORGAN. (Mainly American usage). Loudly-voiced self-contained automatic organ designed for skating rink, carousel, or outdoor amusement use. Models with brass trumpets and trombones are sometimes called military band organs. Synonyms: fairground organ, fair organ, carousel organ.

BARITONE. 1. Band organ pipe register sounding together two ranks: a rank of saxophone-type pipes and a rank of open flute pipes. 2. Large softly-voiced reed pipe which produces a humming, nasal sound. Also spelled barytone.

BARREL. Pinned cylinder, usually of wood, on which a musical composition is programmed for use in an organ, orchestrion, or piano. (Walze = barrel in German; hence Walzenorgel and Walzenorchestrion for barrel organ and barrel orchestrion.) Synonym: cylinder.

BARREL ORGAN. A loudly-voiced (usually) organ operated by a pinned wooden cylinder. Made for outdoor use. (Note: softly-voiced instruments for church and other indoor uses were also made, primarily in England.)

BARREL PIANO. Piano, usually without a keyboard, operated by a pinned wooden cylinder. Those used in streets are called street pianos or hurdy-gurdies (the latter being an incorrect usage from a historical viewpoint).

BASS. 1. The lower range of a musical scale (treble is the upper range). 2. General term (sometimes used in organ and orchestrion advertising) for pipes in the bass note range.

BASS DRUM. Large drum, usually 14" or more in diameter. Also: grosse Trommel, caisse, grosse caisse, groote trommel.

BASS HORN. Reed pipe rank used in large orchestrions, an example being the Hupfeld Pan Orchestra.

BASSOON PIPE. (Called orchestral bassoon in pipe organ literature.) A reed pipe, imitative of the bassoon sound, sometimes found as the bass octave of a clarinet or oboe rank. Used in certain photoplayers and large orchestrions. In band organs the bassoon pipe is often called fagott.

BAXOPHONE. Pipe rank, voiced somewhat like a saxophone, distinguished by having a large circular aperture at the center front of each pipe. Usually placed behind the xylophone on a dance organ. Invented by Guilliaume Bax of the factory of Th. Mortier, Antwerp, Belgium, and used extensively by Mortier.

BEATER. Striking stick or metal rod used to sound a percussion instrument such as a drum, cymbal, bell, etc.

BELL RINGER. A carved statue (sometimes used in pairs) standing on the facade of a band organ, which rings a small bell by striking it with a beater. Certain early organs with bell ringers controlled them with a special key or keys in the music scale. Later instruments often coupled the bell ringer to the bass drum hole. Seldom used after the 1910-1920 era, with the exception of certain Dutch street organs.

BELLS. Tuned metal bars or (rarely in pneumatic instruments) tuned cup-shaped saucer bells. Also called orchestra bells or glockenspiel in American literature. Foreign equivalents include: stalen platen, staalplaten, glokken, klokken, Glocken, Klangplatten.

BIRD WHISTLE. Metal organ pipe of special construction, often about 1½" in length, with an extension of the open end immersed in a container of oil, causing the pitch to warble in imitation of a canary. Used in certain theatre organs, photoplayers, and orchestrions for sound effect and novelty purposes.

BLANK. Unused. In a tracker scale, a hole or key which is not connected and/or serves no purpose. In some scales blank holes or keys were included to provide for additional pipe ranks or other effects which were planned for the future. In other scales a blank space represents a function originally planned but never used, or a function which was discontinued from an earlier scale layout.

BOMBARDON. In some band organs, trombone (large, bright-sounding bass reed pipes). In others, a separate more mellow rank of bass reed pipes. In a pipe organ, a reed rank brighter than the fagatto but not as brassy as a trombone.

BOOK MUSIC. Or music book. Long strip of stiff cardboard folded zig-zag fashion into a compact pile or "book." Music is scored lengthwise on the book by rectangular (usually) perforations. Book music is usually played on a key frame (to which refer) or a keyless frame. Most very large band organs and dance organs used cardboard music, one reason being that books were less susceptible to tracking problems than music rolls. Synonym: cardboard music. In the French language music books are called cartons.

BOURDON. In a pipe organ, a large dull flute, usually wooden. In a Dutch street organ, two ranks of loudly voiced melody flutes tuned to a strong celeste. Bourdon is often used generically to refer to stopped flute ranks in many types of organs and orchestrions.

CAFE ORGAN. Dance organ (to which refer).

CALLIOPE. Instrument with stopped flute-type metal (usually) pipes voiced on high pressure and intended for outdoor use. Barrel-operated steam calliopes, mostly made during the 19th century, used steam to blow the pipes. Most 20th century calliopes (e.g., the Tangley Calliaphone) are air-operated (via a pump or blower) and are properly called air calliopes. These devices were mainly used in America.

CANCEL. To discontinue a previous function. Also: off, aff, af, ab, Abschieber, afsluit, afsluiter, ausschalten, declan, declanche, declanchement, ferme jeux, uitschakeling, piano, D.

CARILLON. 1. In pipe organs, dance organs, and street organs a mixture of several ranks of open metal pipes, frequently sounding the octave, fifth and third above the fundamental note. Imitative of small church bells, especially when played staccato. 2. Set of bells, usually of 3 to 4 octaves in range, played from a keyboard or by a pinned cylinder or other automatic device. Used mainly in clock and church towers.

CAROUSEL ORGAN. Fairground organ used on a carousel or merry-go-round. Synonyms: band organ, fairground organ, military band organ.

CASTANETS. In an organ or orchestrion, small cup-shaped clappers made of Bakelite, hardwood, or other hard substance. Sound is produced by striking the clappers against each other or against a mounting board. Used to accent rhythm in dance organs and orchestrions.

CELESTA. Mellow-sounding instrument in which large felt hammers (resembling oversize piano hammers) strike tuned steel or aluminum bars. Refer also to chrysoglott.

CELESTE. Two or more ranks of pipes of which one or more ranks is tuned sharp or flat of the first rank. Celeste tuning, usually employed with ranks of identical tonal quality, gives an added fullness to the music.

CELLO GRAVE. Large 16' string pipes, usually made of metal, used in the countermelody section of Mortier, Gaudin, and certain other dance organs; used for very low, deep countermelody notes.

CELLO PIPE. String-toned pipe constructed in the manner of a violin pipe (usually with frein or harmonic brake), but of a deeper tone than a violin pipe. Often (e.g., in Popper & Co. descriptions) a single rank of violin-type pipes is described as having violin (highest treble section), viola, violoncello, and cello (lowest bass section) pipes, although violoncello and cello are synonymous from a strict usage viewpoint.

CHAIN PERFORATIONS. Closely-spaced (separated by narrow paper "bridges") perforations in a music roll. Instead of a long open perforation, the chain perforation is used to give added strength to the paper and to minimize tearing. The bridges are very small and do not interrupt the flow of air in the tracker bar hole. The result is a continuously-sounding or sustained note (or a sustained control function).

CHARLESTON CYMBAL. Term used in some European orchestrion and dance organ scales to indicate hi-hat cymbal (to which refer).

CHIMES. Tuned brass tubes, struck by mallets, with a tonal quality imitative of church bells. Also, tubular chimes. In some Wurlitzer factory scale sticks, the term chimes was used to designate orchestra bells (flat steel bars).

CHIMNEY FLUTE PIPE. Half-stopped flute pipe with a tubular "chimney" at the top. In some organs, jazz flutes are chimney flutes with strong tremolo (although Decap and others also had different types of jazz flutes). Synonym (in pipe organ terminology): rohrflute.

CHINESE BLOCK. Wood block (to which refer).

CHINESE CYMBAL. Crash cymbal (to which refer).

CHOIR. The division of a pipe organ usually controlled by the third manual, containing soft stops useful for accompaniment purposes.

CHORD. The simultaneous sounding of several tones, usually three or more.

CHROMATIC. Adjective used to describe the presence of all twelve different tones (including sharps). A chromatic scale has all twelve notes in succession, without any omissions. A non-chromatic scale (often seen in band organs) is one in which one or more notes is omitted from the chromatic 12-note scale.

CHRYSOGLOTT. Tuned percussion instrument having metal bars struck by large felt hammers. Used in theatre organs. Resembles a large scale celesta (to which refer) with electromagnetic action. The tone resembles that of the hand-played vibraharp.

CLARINET PIPE. Reed pipe with a cylindrical open resonator; imitative of the orchestral instrument. Used as a rank in pipe organs, band organs, photoplayers, and some large European orchestrions.

CLARINETTE. Variation of clarinet.

CLARIONETTE PIPE. Variation of clarinet.

CLARION PIPE. Octave trumpet pipe used in pipe organs at 4' on the manuals and 8' on the pedals.

CLAVIOLINE. A simple electronic organ used in some post-1940 Decap and Mortier/Van der Bosch dance organs, replacing one or more ranks of solo organ pipes.

CLOSED. Usually refers to the closing of a swell shutter or crescendo shutter. In German, zu.

COIN PIANO. Coin-operated piano, especially an electric coin-operated piano. Synonym: nickelodeon (modern usage; refer to nickelodeon definition).

COMBINATION. In a pipe organ a term which indicates a combination of registers or pipe ranks which are turned on or off simultaneously.

CONCERT FLUTE. Open wood pipe organ rank with tone somewhat louder and smoother than that of the orchestral instrument.

CONTRA BASS. The lowest-speaking rank of bass pipes in a large orchestrion or band organ, when controlled by a separate register.

CORNOPEAN PIPE. Moderately loud reed pipe, somewhat softer and less bright than a trumpet pipe. Used in pipe organs.

COUNTERMELODY. 1. An independent melody, subordinate to the melody in a piece of music, and played simultaneously with the melody. 2. A section of pipes in a band organ which usually plays countermelodies, long sustained chords, low melodies, or other parts.

CONSOLE. 1. Key desk or keyboard unit of a pipe organ. Contains one or more keyboards (manuals), control stops, and other devices for operating the organ. 2. Center or piano section of a theatre photoplayer or pit organ.

COUPLED. Describes two or more piano hammers or other sounding devices which are connected to play from the same hole in the music roll (or key in a key frame, etc.). In many coin pianos and orchestrions the bass piano notes are coupled for an additional octave (or more or less) to permit a better foundation of tone than would otherwise be possible from a 65-note music roll, for example.

COUPLER. Device, especially in a photoplayer or pipe organ, which permits the operator (or a music roll) to couple and uncouple at will additional pipe ranks or sections of the instrument. Specific couplers are called bass couplers, sub-bass couplers, octave couplers, etc. in pipe organs.

CRASH CYMBAL. Large-size cymbal (to which refer), usually with a bent-over rim or lip and sometimes (especially in modern dance organs) studded with metal grommets to provide additional harmonics. Struck with great force by a wooden or felt-padded beater. Synonym: Chinese cymbal.

CRASH DECRESCENDO. Fast decrescendo.

CRESCENDO. To become gradually louder. Also a term for swell shutters, louvers, or other mechanisms which control sound volume. Antonym: decrescendo: the gradual decreasing of volume or intensity of music.

CYLINDER. Wooden cylinder or barrel used in a barrel piano, organ, or orchestrion. Individual notes are represented by protruding metal pins or staple-like bridges.

CYMBAL. Plate-shaped metal disc, usually slightly concave, made of brass (stamped from a brass sheet, spun on a lathe, or wire-wound). Usually from 10" to 16" in diameter, although smaller cymbals are found on disc-operated pianos. Large cymbals are usually called crash cymbals or Chinese cymbals. Small- and medium-size cymbals are struck by wooden (usually) or metal beaters; large ones, by wood or by felt-padded beaters. A popular device for accenting the rhythm in an orchestrion or organ. Also: cymbale, Becken.

DAMPER. 1. In a piano, a felt pad which mutes the string after it has been sounded. Controlled by the sustaining pedal; when the sustaining pedal is "on," the dampers are lifted and the notes are sustained. 2. Any device which mutes or dampens the sound of a percussion instrument. Dampers are used on bells, drums, and certain other effects in large orchestrions and organs.

DANCE ORGAN. Self-contained player pipe organ, usually with an ornate facade, used in dance halls, cafes, and other locations, expecially in Belgium and Holland. Softly voiced (in comparison to band organs). Distinguished by the strongly accented rhythm of their music; the short and powerful chords of the accompaniment pipes maintain the dance rhythm. Usually of large size (8' to 20' or more in width) and fitted with a key frame system for playing cardboard music books. Later models (after about 1930) have novelty percussions, accordions, and other devices prominently displayed on the facades. Made by Bursens, Decap, Mortier, and others. Some modern models use electronic tone generators instead of organ pipes. Synonym: cafe organ.

DIAPASON. The basic tone of the church pipe organ; smooth, steady sounding pipes richer in tone than flutes but not as raspy as strings nor as bright as brilliant reed pipes.

DECRESCENDO. To become gradually softer.

DIAPHONE PIPE. A basic or foundation (not solo) pipe invented by Robert Hope-Jones. The tone is generated by supplying wind to the pipe in intermittent bursts or puffs, the frequency of which determines the pitch of the pipe. Unlike most types of organ pipes, the volume can be varied (without altering the pitch) by increasing or decreasing the wind pressure. Used in many theatre organs and in certain early roll-operated Wurlitzer photoplayers (e.g., certain models of Wurlitzer's Style L). Notable for quickness of speech in the low bass range. Synonym (slang): thunder pedal.

DIAPHONIC DIAPASON PIPE. Synonym for diaphone pipe (to which refer).

DIMINUENDO (often seen abbreviated as dim.) Same as decrescendo (to which refer).

DISC. Circular sheet of metal (for use on most types of disc music boxes), cardboard (for use on certain organettes), or composition

cardboard-metal (for certain organettes) on which a musical program is arranged—by perforations or by perforations extending from the underside. Almost always easily interchangeable, so that different tunes can be played on the same instrument. Also spelled as disk. Synonyms (not in popular usage with collectors today, however): record, tune sheet.

DISC MUSIC BOX. Or disc-type music box. Music box on which a disc causes a music comb to be plucked by means of intervening star wheels (usually) or levers. One of two main music box types (the other: the cylinder-type music box, which is not treated in the present volume). Popular during the 1890s and early 1900s. Made by Polyphon, Regina, Symphonion, and others.

DOPPEL. German for double. Doppelflute = double-mouthed flute. Doppelmechanik = double mechanism, etc.

DRAAIORGEL. A Dutch term for the hand-cranked organ, usually of the barrel or cardboard music type.

DREHORGEL. A German term for the hand-cranked barrel organ.

DULCIANA. A soft diapason-like pipe organ stop.

DUPLEX ROLL MECHANISM. Roll frame or spoolbox assembly in an electric piano, photoplayer, or orchestrion which accommodates two rolls, so that one roll can play while the other is rewinding. Made by Hupfeld, Seeburg (for photoplayers), Wurlitzer (photoplayers and band organs), and others. Also, duplex roll changer: two revolver mechanisms or automatic roll changers (to which refer) arranged side by side, with several rolls on each changer mechanism. These were made by Hupfeld and Philipps.

ECHO. 1. A separate division of a pipe organ located remotely from the main pipe chambers. 2. A soft form of an ordinarily louder pipe rank.

ELECTRIC PIANO. 1. Any electrically-operated piano (as opposed to a foot-pumped or hand-cranked piano). 2. Coin-operated piano, or coin piano. Term widely used by coin piano makers during the early 20th century. Synonym: nickelodeon (strictly modern usage; refer to nickelodeon definition).

END TAB. The end part of a piano roll, usually made of glue-backed cloth, to which an eyelet or hook is affixed for attaching the roll to the take-up spool.

ENDLESS ROLL. Roll type made by gluing the beginning and end of a roll together to form a continuous loop. As the roll passes over the tracker bar it is fed into a storage bin. Advantages: (1) The roll passes over the tracker bar at a constant speed, so no tempo compensation is needed from one part of the same roll to another part. 2. The mechanism is simpler as no rewind-to-play mechanisms are needed. 3. The music is continuous, with no silent pause for rewinding. Disadvantages: 1. Rolls take several minutes or more to change. 2. Rolls are easily damaged during the changing process. 3. A large amount of space is needed for the roll storage bin. 4. It is not possible to select tunes by a fast forward or reverse mechanism. Endless rolls were mainly popular during the 1900-1910 decade, although some manufacturers (such as Link and the North Tonawanda Musical Instrument Works) used them in later years. Supplanted by the more popular and convenient rewind-type roll (to which refer).

ENGLISH HORN. 1. A pipe organ rank imitative of the orchestral instrument. 2. Brilliant-voiced reed pipes used in some band organs. (Note: the English posthorn theatre organ rank is different.)

EXPRESSION. The varying of the volume or intensity of music. This is done by operating the controls of an instrument (e.g., the pedals of a piano), by opening and closing swell or crescendo shutters, by varying the vacuum level in a piano (low vacuum = soft music; high vacuum = louder music), and by other means. An instrument is said to have "expression" if the musical performance can be varied in one of these ways. A music roll or music book may have expression cut in it to operate such controls automatically, or they may be operated by hand (as with the expression shutter of an organette).

EXPRESSION PIANO. An automatic piano, usually electrically-operated, which has the pedals automatically controlled and which has limited vacuum-level variations (e.g., the Recordo piano, the Seeburg Style X). Synonym: Semi-reproducing piano.

FAGATTO: A pipe organ rank somewhat imitative of the orchestral bassoon.

FAIR ORGAN. Or fairground organ. Mainly English-usage term for a loudly-voiced self-contained automatic organ designed for skating rink, carousel, or outdoor use. Usually decorated with an ornate facade. Synonyms: band organ (American usage), carousel organ, military band organ (especially an instrument with brass trumpets and trombones; American usage).

FEEDER MOTOR. Motor which drives a paper roll mechanism. Term especially used by the Mills Novelty Company.

FLAGEOLET. 1. In band organs, a short loudly-voiced open wood pipe frequently used to supplement or augment the tone and volume of the piccolo. 2. In orchestrions, a short treble flute or a description of the highest one or two octaves of a flute rank.

FLAUTO TRAVERSO. Orchestral flute (to which refer).

FLUE PIPE. A pipe which produces its sound by the action of air against the edge of the pipe mouth in combination with the resonance of a column of air within an open or closed pipe. One of three basis families of pipes: (1) Flue, as just described. (2) Reed pipes, which produce sound by the vibrations of a free or beating reed, and (3) Diaphone pipes (rarely used), which produce sound by intermittent bursts of air introduced into the pipe. The flue pipe family encompasses many different popular types of pipes, including various flute, diapason, and violin varieties. Flue-type pipes, unlike reed pipes, require a minimum of attention and care and will stay in tune for relatively long periods of time. For this reason flue pipes (usually violin and flute) were the main types used in smaller styles of coin pianos and orchestrions.

FLUGELHORN. A solo reed pipe organ rank imitative of its orchestral counterpart. The tone is between that of a mellow horn and a brilliant trumpet.

FLUTE PIPE. Type of flue pipe (to which refer) often used in orchestrions, photoplayers, organs, and other instruments. Usually made of wood, the flute produces a clear tone relatively free of harmonics. Flutes in the high treble range are called piccolos; those in the bass range are called bass flutes or bourdons. Varieties of flutes include open flutes, stopped flutes (a stopped flute is equal in pitch or tonal length to an open flute of twice the length—when all other dimensions are equal), and harmonic flutes (with a small hole at the nodal point in the center front of the pipe). Double-mouthed flutes are called doppelflutes. Flutes are the easiest to maintain of all common types of pipes. For this reason they found wide use in automatic instruments.

FORTE. Loud. (As opposed to piano, or soft.) Forte is abbreviated as f. Fortissimo (very loud), as ff. Mezzoforte (moderately loud), as mf. Used in musical notation and in descriptions of instrument expression, especially reproducing pianos.

FORZANDO. Variation of sforzando (to which refer).

FOUNDATION. 1. Open pipe organ ranks, usually metal, having a strong fundamental tone with few harmonics. 2. Lowest musical tones in a band organ, large orchestrion, etc. A deep bass tone provided by bourdon, violoncello, or other bass-range pipes. Used as accompaniment for other pipes or instruments, never as solo. These bass pipes are sometimes referred to as foundation pipes. Synonyms: bass section, bass registers, etc.

FOX-TROT BELLS. Hupfeld's designation for tubular bells of relatively short length and with tuned resonators. The fundamental pitch is almost completely overpowered by the harmonics, resulting in a bright clanking sound similar to tuned cowbells. Used on the Hupfeld Symphony-Jazz orchestrion.

FREIN. A French term, used universally, describing the harmonic brake (to which refer) of a violin-type pipe.

FRENCH HORN. Reed-type pipe imitative of a French horn. Slightly less brilliant than a trumpet. In fairground organs has a brass resonator similar in appearance to a trumpet. In pipe organs, the French horn has a capped gray metal conical horn.

FRERES. The French word for brothers, as in Limonaire Freres. The term is listed here as it appears regularly in musical literature and is sometimes confused by the uninitiated. Interchangable with Gebruder (brothers in German). Bruder, the organ builder, gave the firm's name as Bruder Freres in its French-language catalogues and as Gebruder Bruder in its German-language catalogues, for example.

FUGARA. 4' string pipes of the gamba type with a bright penetrating tone.

FULL ORGAN. All ranks of an instrument (such as a photoplayer or pipe organ) playing at once.

GAMBA. A string-toned pipe with a moderately loud, clear, brilliant tone. Less imitative of the orchestral counterpart than the viol d'orchestre (VDO) pipe.

GEBRUDER. German for brothers. Usually abbreviated, as in Gebr. Bruder (Bruder Brothers). Included in this listing as the Gebr. term sometimes is confusing to the uninitiated. The Flemish word Gebroeders has the same meaning and was used by Decap, for example.

GEDECKT. Softly-voiced stopped flute used in pipe organs, large orchestrions, and photoplayers in combination with other ranks to enhance the fundamental tone.

GEMSHORN. Conical open metal flue pipe used for accompaniment.

GENERAL CANCEL. Mechanism in an automatic musical instrument which turns off several (or all) pipe ranks, other instruments, or functions simultaneously. Also see cancel.

GLOCKENSPIEL. See orchestra bells.

GREAT. A division of the pipe organ controlled by its own manual; includes louder stops such as diapasons. In church organs this division is frequently unenclosed. Related to other organ divisions such as swell, echo, and choir.

HAMMER RAIL. A long strip of wood in a piano action upon which the piano hammer shanks rest when not in play. Usually movable for soft and loud effects; controlled by the soft pedal. In German, Hammerleiste, schieb.

HARMONIC BRAKE. Metal strip, usually of brass and usually secured with two screws, placed at the mouth of a violin pipe to stabilize the tone and to enable it to speak more quickly. On large-scale violin-type pipes the harmonic brake is often made in the form of a wooden roller. Synonyms: harmonic bridge, frein.

HARMONIC FLUTE. Pipe, usually wooden, used in orchestrions, photoplayers, and organs. The harmonic flute is open at the top and has a small hole at the nodal point (of the sound wave) about at the center of the front of the pipe. This hole permits the pipe to sound the second harmonic tone (rather than the fundamental or basic tone) with more prominence. The harmonic flute is equal in tonal length to a regular (nonharmonic) open flute of half its length. Used in many types of instruments; some Seeburg coin pianos and orchestrions with flute pipes have harmonic flutes, for example.

HARMONIUM. 1. Reed organ. In Europe the designation harmonium is preferred to the American designation reed organ. 2. One or more sets of organ reeds used as an accompaniment or even a solo voice on certain photoplayers, orchestrions, and other automatic musical instruments. Usually each bank of reeds is assigned the name of an organ pipe rank such as cello, diapason, clarinet, French horn, oboe, etc.

HARP. 1. Instrument with 46 strings (usually) arranged vertically in a triangular frame. Played by plucking the strings. The Wurlitzer (made by Whitlock) Automatic Harp was popular during the early 20th century and is illustrated in this volume. 2. Metal plate or frame which bears the tension of the strings in a piano. Usually called a piano plate.

HARP EFFECT. 1. Specific term used by Philipps, Hupfeld, and other coin piano and orchestrion manufacturers to designate a special piano action which mounts above the treble piano hammers (usually for a two-octave range) in an automatic musical instrument. The hammers of the harp effect are made of hard wood or compressed-felt, are actuated by a rotating splined shaft, and strike the strings in a reiterating manner—producing a realistic mandolin-like ringing sound. Popular circa 1905-1925. The term was also used to describe a regular curtain-like mandolin attachment to a coin piano, so clarification is usually needed when the harp effect notation is encountered. 2. Large scale marimba struck with dense felt hammers. Used in pipe organs, particularly in theatre and residence organs. Somewhat imitative of the orchestral harp, especially when rapid arpeggios are played.

HI-HAT CYMBAL. A double cymbal; two cymbals spaced apart with the faces parallel. Also called double cymbal, clamp cymbal, pedal cymbal, charleston cymbal, dubbel becken, doppel Becken. Used in certain instruments of the 1920s and 1930s.

HURDY-GURDY. 1. Properly, a keyboard-type (usually) instrument in which the tuned piano strings are actuated by contact with a rotating rosin-covered wheel. Sometimes called the organistra or symphonia or (in French) the chifonie. Term also applied to lute-like stringed instruments whose strings are sounded by a rosined wheel. 2. (Popular usage; incorrect by historical standards.) Barrel-operated street piano. 3. (Popular usage; incorrect by historical standards.) Portable hand-cranked barrel organ; monkey organ.

INNER PLAYER. Term used circa 1900-1910 to describe a home player piano of the type with the pneumatic mechanisms built into the case (in contrast to the earlier push-up piano player type). Term not generally used by collectors today. (Inner-players are simply referred to as player pianos.)

JAZZ CYMBAL. In the Hupfeld Pan Orchestra an effect produced by a small reiterating metal rod which strikes near the edge of the crash cymbal. Possibly used in other orchestrions as well.

JAZZ FLUTE. In dance organs, a stopped flute pipe or chimney flute (rohrflute) made in a special manner with a special tremulant which consists of a pallet covering the outside opening of a small hole drilled in the back of the pipe, opposite the mouth. When a jazz tremolo effect is desired, the pallet opens and closes rapidly while the pipe is being sounded in the normal manner. The opening and closing of the hole temporarily sharpens the pitch each time and produces the characteristic jazz flute sound. (Also see vibratone, a related pipe.)

KETTLE DRUM. In an automatic musical instrument (especially a piano orchestrion) an effect obtained by alternately striking two small-size beaters to the left and right of the larger bass drum beater on a bass drum head. The term, which should be "kettle drum effect" as no separate drum is used, is found widely in orchestrion literature—nearly all of Seeburg's descriptions of large orchestrions and photoplayers, for example. Synonym: tympani.

KEY. 1. Finger-operated control lever used to sound a note on a keyboard instrument such as a piano, organ, or accordion. 2. Musical pitch of an instrument or music arrangement (e.g., the key of C). 3. Actuating levers, usually made of brass, used to operate organ reeds (as in a cylinder music box with reed organ attachment), organ pipes (such as in a large barrel orchestrion), or a pneumatic system (as in the key frame of a band organ). 4. Key(s): the number of playing notes plus the number of control stops (for changing registers, stopping the instrument, rewinding the roll, etc.) on an automatic musical instrument, especially a dance organ or band organ (such as 89-key Gavioli organ, 101-key Mortier organ, etc.). In German, Tasten, Tonstufen. In French, touche.

KEY FRAME. Device mainly used on band organs and dance organs but used on many other types of instruments as well. Contains a series of spring-loaded brass or steel levers. When one end of a lever pops up through a hole in a cardboard music book (to which refer), the other end of the lever or key opens an aperture which actuates a pneumatic action. The folding cardboard music book is pulled through the key frame by india rubber pinch rollers. A durable system capable of withstanding rugged use; one which is resistant to humidity changes. For these reasons most very large band organs and dance organs of European manufacture use the key frame system. (Compare to keyless frame, to which refer.)

KEYBOARD. A set of keys or levers, arranged in order of ascending pitch, which enables a piano or organ to be played by hand. Synonym (in pipe organ nomenclature): manual.

KEYBOARDLESS. Term used to describe a piano or organ of upright or vertical format and without a keyboard. Synonym: cabinet style.

KEYLESS FRAME. In a band organ or dance organ a music system which used paper rolls or cardboard music books and a regular tracker bar, rather than a key frame with spring-loaded metal keys. Such instruments are sometimes called keyless. (Term mainly used in Europe.)

KLAVIER. (German). Upright or vertical piano, usually of medium or large size (term never used to describe a grand piano; the latter is a Flugel in German). Small-size upright pianos are called Pianinos in German nomenclature. In addition, the term klavier sometimes is used to describe a keyboard, to which refer.

KRUMHORN. A sedate sounding 8' pipe organ reed rank useful in solo passages or in combination with other ranks.

LATCH RELEASE. Rewind, in Tel-Electric expression piano terminology.

LEADER. 1. Roll leader: the beginning or fore part of a music roll on which the tune title(s), tempo, and other information is printed and to which the end tab is affixed. 2. Band leader, to which refer.

LEAKER. Expression device used in Artrio-Angelus reproducing pianos and other instruments, which causes the piano to play more softly by bleeding atmospheric pressure into the vacuum system.

LIEBLICH GEDECKT. 1. Stopped wooden flute pipe, smoother and usually softer than the gedeckt. 2. An air pressure regulator connected to a rank of bass bourdon pipes in a pipe organ which allows that rank to double as a softer rank by lowering the air pressure. The pressure change is not so great as to cause a noticeable pitch alteration.

LIGHT(ING) EFFECTS. Decorative electrical effects such as blinking lights, wonder lights, motion picture effects, and other illuminated devices used on coin pianos, orchestrions, organs, and other instruments to create attention and to attract the public.

LOCK-AND-CANCEL. Descriptive of a control used to operate a pneumatic musical instrument. One short perforation locks the mechanism in the "on" position, in which position it remains until another perforation releases it to the "off" position. In this way an effect (a pipe register, for example) can be "on" for a long period of time without having to use an extended or chain-type perforation.

LOTUS FLUTE. Stopped flute pipes, usually of limited musical range, used in orchestrions (e.g., Hupfeld Pan Orchestra, Symphony-Jazz, and late Helios styles) and organs, mainly circa 1910-1930, but especially in the 1920s. Usually equipped with a tremolo device which, together with music arranged to "slide" (e.g., glissando effect) from one note to the next, imparts a haunting rising and falling tone to the music. Usually played as a solo effect using specially-arranged music rolls. Compare to the Swanee whistle, to which refer. In German: Lotos Flote.

LOUD. Having great intensity of sound. Musical notation from the Italian language: forte. Antonym, Italian: piano.

LOUD PEDAL. In a piano the sustaining pedal. (Popular usage, technically inaccurate.)

MANDOLIN. A mechanical device or curtain apparatus in a piano which, when turned on, produces a "tinny" or "rinky-tink" sound similar to that made by metal or wooden hammers hitting the strings. Sometimes made in the form of a cloth curtain with separate metal or wood studded tabs; sometimes in the form of small wooden or metal levers, studs, or hammers. A common attachment to coin pianos and orchestrions. Also: mandoline, Harfe, zither, banjo.

MANUAL. Keyboard, especially on a photoplayer or pipe organ.

MARACCA. Hollow gourd or wood rattle containing small pebbles or seeds; used as a percussion effect. Also: Rumba bus.

MARIMBA. Large scale xylophone with thin bars and tuned tubular resonators, producing a sound much mellower and more sustained than that of the xylophone.

MASTER ROLL. Roll used on a perforator to control the punches for making production rolls. Sometimes the master roll is several times the length of the final production roll in order to provide greater accuracy and easier synchronization with the reader or sensing mechanism.

MELODY SECTION. 1. Predominant part of music which is recognizable as the "tune." Technically, any succession of single notes (as contrasted to "harmony," which is the simultaneous sounding of several notes). 2. In a band organ, the section of pipes which frequently plays the melody or main melodic parts of the music. Other sections of a typical band organ are the countermelody, accompaniment, and bass.

MEZZOFORTE. Intensity or sound level of moderate loudness. In reproducing pianos, an intensity halfway between forte (loud) and piano (soft). Abbreviated as mf.

MILITARY BAND ORGAN. Mainly American usage to designate a fairground organ (to which refer) or band organ with exposed brass pipes on the front, although in the 1920s Wurlitzer used the military adjective to designate band organs without brass pipes. Synonyms: skating rink organ, trumpet organ (mainly used to describe early barrel-operated models).

MITERED PIPE. Pipe which has been mitered or cut (giving it a "bent" appearance), usually at a 90-degree angle, so that it will fit into a short space. So long as the interior or speaking length of the pipe remains the same, the pitch is unaffected by mitering.

MIXTURE. In a pipe organ two or more pipe ranks of the same basic tonal family (but differing in harmonic development) which are sounded together by a single register. Usually used in the treble range to achieve a greater volume (to balance the more powerful bass). High treble mixtures add great brilliance to the tone.

MONKEY ORGAN. Portable hand-cranked barrel organ, especially one employed by an organ grinder and used in the streets.

MORTUARY ORGAN. Paper-roll-operated piano and pipe organ combination unit (or sometimes an organ only, without piano) used to provide a musical background for mortuary services. The Seeburg Style MO is an example.

MULTIPLEX. The use of a single hole in a tracker bar (or key in a key frame, etc.) to perform multiple functions, usually in combination with other holes. Thus, for example, holes 1, 2, and 3 may have separate functions when used singly. 1 and 2 have yet another function when used at the same time; 1 and 3 have still another function; and 2 and 3 have still another function. Used in certain types of reproducing pianos, large orchestrions, and other instruments to reduce the number of holes needed in the tracker bar (and, consequently, the width of the roll) to perform a given set of functions. Examples of multiplexing can be found with the Hupfeld Pan Orchestra and Weber Maesto scales listed in this book, to cite just two of many examples.

MUSIC BOOK. See book music.

MUSIC BOX. Music box (mainly American usage; e.g., Regina Music Box Co.) or musical box (mainly British usage). A cabinet, usually made of wood, which contains a disc-type or cylinder-type music box movement. 2. General term used by the public (but not by collectors) to describe any type of automatic musical instrument.

MUSIC BOX COMB. Series of tuned metal teeth arranged adjacent to each other and fastened to a common bedplate. Used to produce sound in a cylinder or disc music box. Made in many varieties. Also called a musical comb.

MUSIC LEAF SYSTEM. Describes the use of a roll made of heavy manila paper and acted upon by a key frame. A term used by Imhof & Mukle.

MUSIC ROLL. Strip of thin paper (usually) on which music and control functions are arranged by a series of perforations. When played on a tracker bar the perforations cause a roll-operated instrument to perform. Two main music roll types were made: (1) rewind-type rolls (the most popular), to which refer; and (2) endless-type rolls, to which refer.

NICKELODEON. 1. An early theatre, mainly circa 1903-1914, which charged 5c admission. Nickelodeon = nickel + odeon (the Greek word for theatre). Also called nickelodeon theatre. 2. Term used to describe a coin-operated piano, orchestrion, or similar instrument. (Strictly modern post-1940 usage; never used earlier in this context. Such instruments were called electric pianos, orchestrions, etc. The nickelodeon term has become very popular and is in wide use among collectors and the public today.)

OBOE PIPE. Brightly-voiced reed pipe with a conical metal resonator. Used as a solo rank in certain large orchestrions or as a solo and ensemble stop in pipe organs.

OCTAVE. 1. A musical interval of eight notes. Every note has double the number of vibrations of its corresponding note an octave lower and half the vibrations of its corresponding note an octave higher. 2. Term popularly used to describe thirteen equally-tuned half steps (the notes at each end are counted; e.g., C to C), the twelve-toned equal temperament scale into which the octave is divided on the piano and in most pipe ranks. Sometimes called the chromatic scale. In original catalogues (e.g., Operators Piano Co. description of Coinola percussions) and in popular usage today a "two octave" set of xylophone bars would mean a 24-note chromatic set, for example. As noted, the 13-step terminology is also often used, especially in describing pipe ranks. 3. A 4' pipe organ rank of diapason tone.

OCTAVE COUPLER. Refer to coupler.

ON. To actuate a device or component. Also: an, aan, ein, einschalten, inschakeling, E.

OPEN. Not closed. In German, auf.

OPHICLEIDE. Loud, brilliant reed pipe organ rank, usually the most powerful in the organ.

ORCHESTRA BELLS. Bar-type bells (refer to bells definition). 2. In a theatre organ, bar-type bells played with a reiterating or repeating action. (When the same bells are played with a single-stroke action they are called glockenspiel in organ terminology.)

ORCHESTRAL FLUTE. Open wood or metal pipe organ rank imitative of the orchestral instrument, usually of harmonic length.

ORCHESTRAL OBOE. Pipe organ rank imitative of the orchestral instrument.

ORCHESTRION. Self-contained automatic musical instrument, especially a large one, equipped with several different instruments in imitation of an orchestra. Usually contains some percussion effects (e.g., drums, cymbal, triangle, etc.). Main types include: (1) Barrel orchestrion: usually without piano; with many ranks of pipes and with percussion effects. Softly voiced. Made for indoor use. Popular during the 19th century. (2) Keyboard-type piano orchestrion: built around an upright piano; with one or more chromatically-scaled extra instruments (e.g., a rank of violin or flute pipes, a xylophone, a set of bells) and with percussion effects. Paper-roll operated. Popular during the early 20th century. (3) Large keyboardless piano orchestrion: contains a piano, several (usually) ranks of pipes, and many other effects, some of which are (usually) arranged to play solo melodies. Paper-roll operated. Popular during the early 20th century. (4) Small cabinet-style orchestrion: small cabinet, usually smaller than an upright piano, containing an abbreviated-scale piano, one or more chromatically-tuned extra instruments, and percussion effects. Popular during the 1920s, especially in America (e.g., Seeburg KT,

KT Special, etc.). Other uses of the orchestrion term (instruments which were designated as orchestrions by the original manufacturers, but which collectors today consider as part of other series) include the following: (5) Disc-operated piano of limited scale, sometimes with percussion effects (e.g., disc pianos made by Lochmann, Polyphon, and Symphonion). (6) Large disc-type music box, usually with 10 or 12 bells. (7) Mechanical (not pneumatic) piano of limited scale, plus percussion effects. Operated by a heavy manila paper roll (e.g., Regina Sublima Piano and related Polyphon products). (8) Barrel piano with limited percussion effects. (9) Mechanical zither or dulcimer (e.g., the so-called "Piano Orchestrion," also sold as the Piano Melodico). (10) Paper-roll organette (e.g., Orchestrion Harmonette). Instruments listed from 5 through 10 are not considered to be orchestrions by collectors today. The term orchestrion was applied to many other non-orchestrion instruments over the years. Synonyms: automatic orchestra, orchestra piano.

ORGAN. Generally, an instrument on which music is played by means of tuned pipes or reeds. Among automatic musical instruments the following main types are found: 1. Organette: small hand-cranked instrument which plays tuned reeds. 2. Player reed organ: large instrument, usually equipped with a keyboard, which plays tuned reeds. 3. Player pipe organ: large pipe organ, usually equipped with one or more keyboards or manuals, designed for providing music in a church, theatre, or residence. Usually not self-contained, but built in as part of a building. With paper-roll player built into the console or into a separate cabinet. 4. Portable hand-cranked barrel organ. 5. Band organ or fairground organ with loudly-voiced pipes and ornate (usually) front. 6. Street organ or pierement: loudly-voiced instrument mainly used in the streets of Holland. 7. Dance organ: softly-voiced instrument, usually with ornate facade and of very large size, used in dance halls, especially in Belgium and Holland. 8. Calliope: with a limited scale of flue-type pipes, played with extremely high wind pressure. 9. Serinette: hand-cranked softly-voiced scale of flute pipes; a popular parlor instrument of the 18th and 19th centuries. 10. Any attachment consisting of one or more ranks of pipes or sets of reeds attached to another instrument. Orgel = organ in German and Dutch. Orgue = organ in French.

ORGANETTE. Small hand-cranked (usually) reed organ, without keyboard. Usually of very limited scale (14 to 20 reeds). Synonyms (used circa 1880-1900, not used by collectors today except to describe specific instruments): organetta, organina, orguinette, and other terms intended to designate "little organ."

PEDAL. 1. A foot-actuated lever. 2. The division of a pipe organ containing large bass pipe ranks (together with auxiliary smaller ranks) and controlled by the pedal board (a series of levers in the shape of a large keyboard played by the feet).

PERCUSSION. Or percussion effect. Tonal effects produced by striking a device, usually of fixed pitch or tonal character (as opposed to tunable piano strings, etc.). Two types: (1) Chromatic percussions with a series of units, each tuned to a corresponding note in a piano or organ scale. Examples: xylophone, orchestra bells. (2) Non-chromatic percussions such as a cymbal, bass drum, snare drum, tambourine, tenor drum, triangle, wood block, etc. In automatic musical instrument terminology, chromatic-type percussions are usually listed individually. Non-chromatic types are often grouped together as "percussion" or "drum and trap effects."

PERFORATION. A hole in a music roll, music book, disc, etc. Perforations are arranged in a manner to produce a musical performance when used on an automatic musical instrument. Perforator: a machine which produces perforations, especially in a music roll.

PHILOMELA. 8' open wood pipe organ rank voiced with a clear, bright tone.

PHOTOPLAYER. Automatic musical instrument, usually consisting of a keyboard-type piano with one or two attached side chests which contain pipes, percussion instruments, and novelty sound effects. Usually with a single or duplex roll mechanism built into the piano case above the keyboard. Used to provide music and sound effects to accompany silent motion pictures. Seeburg and Wurlitzer photoplayers, for example, are illustrated in the present volume.

PIANISSIMO. Term of Italian origin used to designate very soft.

PIANO. In musical scales the term piano has several widely different meanings and variously refers to "soft," "off," or the stringed musical instrument. To eliminate confusion, it is only used in this book to refer to the musical instrument. The related word "klavier" is not used, for it variously means piano (the musical instrument) or keyboard.

PIANO ACTION. The devices or connecting links, hammers, and related hardware between the keyboard and the strings of a piano; the piano hammers and their actuating devices.

PIANO-PIPE ORGAN. Name sometimes given to a piano with two or three (usually) ranks of pipes built into the same case (e.g., Reproduco, Nelson-Wiggen Selector Duplex Organ, Seeburg Style MO). Used in theatres and mortuaries in the 1915-1930 years.

PICCOLO. 1. Pipe rank in orchestrions; similar in appearance to a wooden flute pipe and used in the top one or two treble octaves of the musical scale. 2. In orchestrions the name sometimes given to the upper range of a rank of flute pipes. (A rank of flutes is sometimes elaborately described as being a rank of "bourdon, flute, and piccolo" pipes, bourdon and piccolo referring to the lower and upper ranges.) 3. In band organs, a metal (usually) pipe, usually of polished brass, which is blown transversely (across the bottom of the pipe, rather than into the pipe) at high pressure. Usually with a wooden acorn-shaped plug at the top of the pipe. 4. In theatre pipe organs, a 2' stop of brightly-voiced wood or metal flute pipes. 5. An adjective meaning "small." A piccolo flute is a little flute, a piccolo drum is a little drum, etc. (Terminology rarely used by collectors today.) 6. A coin piano or orchestrion (slang; southern United States usage).

PIEREMENT. Dutch street organ. (Term originally used only in Holland; now used by some collectors in other parts of the world.)

PIFFARO. Or piffero. 1. Generic Italian term for instruments such as the fife, bagpipe, and others used by shepherds. 2. In band organs a term rarely used to describe a rank with a tone suggestive of one of these instruments.

PILOT. Term used by Skinner, Wurlitzer, and others to indicate a multiplex hole in the tracker bar which controls the connection of certain tracker bar holes to certain notes or functions in the organ.

PIPE. A tubular instrument which produces sound by the action of air against a reed or against the pipe mouth, in combination with the resonance of the air within the tube itself. Pipes are generally referred to as having a pitch or tonal length expressed in feet, such as 2', 4', 8', etc. Pipes are usually either open at the top or closed. Generally, the tonal length of a closed pipe is twice that of a comparable open pipe (the same pitch sounded by a 2'-long closed pipe would take a 4'-long open pipe to produce). Pipes used in automatic musical instruments are of two main types: (1) Flute pipes which produce their sound by the action of air against the edge of the pipe mouth in combination with a column of air; and (2) reed pipes which produce sound by the action of a vibrating reed (there are two types of reeds: free and beating); the reed sound is amplified by the upper part of the pipe which, on a reed pipe, is called a resonator or horn. A third type of pipe, the diaphone, produces sound by intermittent bursts of air which are rapidly introduced into the base of the pipe under high pressure (refer to diaphone definition). Used in theatre organs and a few large photoplayers.

Pipes are mounted on a pipe chest or windchest and are blown by air under pressure. Pipe pressure is measured in inches; the number of inches that a given pressure will force a column of water up an open glass tube. (Pressure for calliopes is sometimes measured in pounds per square inch—the amount of pressure that the air will exert against a one-inch square area.) Pipes are tuned by adjusting the reed or by changing the tonal length of the pipe by moving a tuning slide or stopper. Pipes are voiced to a specific wind pressure and cannot be interchanged with an instrument having significantly different pressure. Pipes are arranged in ranks and are controlled by registers or stops. Definitions of specific ranks are given in this section. Refer to flute, piccolo, etc. for additional information. Often fanciful names ("fanfare trumpet," for example) were used to describe basic ranks. When several ranks of similarly-tuned pipes are in the same instrument, care must be taken to separate the ranks sufficiently—otherwise the sound waves from two similarly-tuned ranks will cancel each other (this phenomenon is known as destructive interference). Celeste tuning (to which refer) mitigates this problem. Certain ranks in large orchestrions are called foundation or fundamental pipes.

These provide a rich bass sound which makes the treble pipes and solo pipes sound richer and fuller. Foundation pipes are never played alone but are always used in combination with other ranks. Solo ranks are those pipes with distinctive voicing which are used to play solo parts (or to carry the basic musical theme) while other ranks play accompaniment.

PIPE ORGAN. Musical instrument containing ranks of pipes (and sometimes other instruments) played by pressurized air and controlled by one or more keyboards (manuals) and (usually) a pedalboard. A player pipe organ is one fitted with a music roll attachment. A reproducing pipe organ plays special rolls which reproduce the playing of a human artist by automatically manipulating the stops, swell shutters, and other control devices as well as the keys and pedals.

PLAY. To operate, to commence producing music. Sometimes seen in notations as replay, marche avant, or the confusing term reverse. In a rewind music roll system the term play refers to the function which returns the roll to the playing direction when rewind is completed.

PLAYER PIANO. 1. Foot-pumped (usually) upright or grand piano with the pneumatic mechanisms built into the case (in contrast to the piano player, a device which contains the player mechanisms in a separate cabinet which is placed in front of the keyboard). Made for home use. Uses 65-note (early models) or 73-note (early European models) or 88-note (universally used after 1908) rolls. Hundreds of different makes were produced during the early 20th century. Synonym: inner-player (early usage). 2. Any type piano which uses a paper roll. Collectors designate roll-operated instruments by specific terms, including player piano (foot-pumped type), coin piano, orchestrion, etc.

PNEUMATIC. 1. Adjective describing a musical instrument which is operated automatically by the action of wind pressure or vacuum (as opposed to mechanical). 2. Small bellows, especially one used in a pneumatic stack.

PNEUMATIC ACTION. The vacuum- or air-operated series of pouches, valves, and other devices used to sense the paper roll (or music book, paper strip, etc.) and cause an instrument to play automatically. Definition sometimes used to include auxiliary systems as well: pump, blower, reservoir, etc.

PNEUMATIC STACK. A series of air-actuated pouches, valves, and bellows, especially in a piano or orchestrion, built as a coordinated unit and used to play a piano action automatically.

PNEUMATIC SYSTEM Complete system, including tracker bar (or key frame or other sensing mechanism), pump, reservoir, pneumatic stack, windchest, etc. of an automatic musical instrument which utilizes wind pressure or vacuum (or a combination of both) to operate the player mechanisms.

PRESTANT. Short diapason-like pipe in a band organ. Plays with a bright string-like tone. Also used in pipe organs.

PRODUCTION MASTER ROLL. Finished master roll, ready to use on a roll-duplicating perforator, as opposed to an incomplete master roll which is used in the preparation of a production master. An incomplete master sometimes has only the introduction, one verse, one chorus, and the ending. From this, a production master having repeated choruses is made.

PUMP. 1. Bellows-operated device used to provide vacuum or wind pressure to operate an automatic musical instrument. 2. Tracker bar pump. Usually a hand-held device which produces vacuum by means of a piston in a cylinder. Used to clean lint and dirt from the tracker bar.

PUSH-UP PIANO PLAYER. A cabinet-style device which contains pneumatic mechanisms and which is pushed up to the piano keyboard in order to play the piano automatically. Usually foot pumped. Synonyms: cabinet player, Vorsetzer (German).

QUINTADENA. A stopped metal flute pipe which produces a third harmonic which is nearly as loud as the fundamental. Widely used in mortuary organs, photoplayers, pipe organs, and very large European orchestrions.

RANK OF PIPES. Single row of pipes, arranged in musical order and of the same type or tonal character. Sections of a single rank may be given individual names. For example, a single rank of violin-type pipes may be called "violin, viola, and violoncello," violin pertaining to the treble part, viola to the middle range, and violoncello to the bass. In orchestrion and organ nomenclature a listing of such terms usually does not correspond to the actual number of ranks of pipes in the instrument. Note: do not confuse with register. A register is a device for controlling one or more ranks of pipes or even a portion of a single rank.

REED. 1. Vibrating metal tongue which produces sound in a harmonium or reed organ. 2. Type of organ pipe: 2a. Free reed: a metal tongue which moves in and out of its aperture (called a shallot) freely as it vibrates. Used in reed organs and harmoniums, organettes, and in certain types of organ pipes, especially those of soft of medium voicing. 2b. Beating reed: a carefully curved (according to principles of voicing) tongue covers the shallot opening (but is too large to enter it) and then springs back again as it vibrates. Mainly used for loudly-voiced pipes. Generally, imitative beating reed pipes such as clarinet, trumpet, etc. (used in band organs and pipe organs) are more realistic than free reed pipes (used in large European orchestrions) which, despite their resonators, tend to sound more like harmonium reeds.

REED ORGAN. An organ containing from one to many sets of tuned free reeds. Small reed organs have one manual (keyboard), while larger ones have two manuals and pedals like a pipe organ. Refer also to harmonium.

REGISTER. Control for operating one or more ranks of pipes in an organ or automatic instrument. Synonyms: stop, organ stop.

REGISTRATION. The selection of stops to be used while playing a pipe organ.

REITERATING. Constantly repeating. The repetition or repeated striking of a single note by means of a special mechanical or pneumatic action built for this purpose or by means of closely-spaced holes in a music roll or music book. When an extended hole appears in the music roll (or when a staple-like bridge pin occurs in a pinned cylinder arrangement) the reiterating action will constantly repeat the note until the perforation has ended. Synonym: repeating.

REPEATING. Reiterating, to which refer.

REPLAY. Synonym for play, to which refer.

REPRODUCING PIANO. Automatically-played piano which, by means of special rolls, re-enacts a recording artist's performance, including different levels of intensity (independently controlled for bass and treble sections of the keyboard) in addition to the musical notes and the pedal action. Distinguished from an expression (or semi-reproducing) piano by having multiple intensity levels. Rolls, called reproducing piano rolls or artists' rolls, are made from master rolls produced on a special recording piano which captures the nuances, idiosyncrasies of techniques, and the attack of the performing pianist. The result is a very realistic performance when a reproducing piano is properly regulated. Reproducing pianos were made in upright, grand, and cabinet styles. Leading types produced circa 1905-1930 were Ampico, Duo-Art, and Welte-Mignon. Certain large orchestrions (e.g., Hupfeld Pan Orchestra) incorporated reproducing-type mechanisms. Synonyms (used years ago, not by collectors today): artistic piano, re-enacting piano, master-playing piano, recording piano, reperforming piano. Note: In original advertising such terms as "artistic" and "uses artists' rolls" were often used to describe regular (non-reproducing) types of automatic pianos.

REPRODUCING PIPE ORGAN. Pipe organ which used rolls recorded by organists and incorporating expression effects. The Aeolian Duo-Art Organ and the Welte Philharmonic Organ are examples.

REVERSE. In twin-tracker instruments (such as the Nelson-Wiggen Selector Duplex Organ and the Empress Twin Tracker Solo Expression Piano) in which a double-wide roll has half the tunes perforated in one direction and the other half in the opposite direction, reverse actuates the mechanism which reverses the direction of the roll after the tunes on one side are finished, and switches over to the other half of the tracker bar.

REWIND. When a rewind-type roll reaches the end of the playing notes a special reroll (or rewind) perforation causes the roll frame to shift to the reroll position. The pneumatic mechanisms which actuate the playing notes are disengaged so that no notes will be played when the roll is rewinding. Rerolling is done at high speed. When the leader of the roll reaches the tracker bar, a rewind-to-play hole in the tracker bar (or, in some instruments, a mechanical device fitted to the take-up spool) actuates a mechanism which shifts the roll frame from reroll to forward. The roll is then ready to play another performance or to be taken from the instrument. Also: reverse, retour, retour rouleau, Ruckroller, Ruckrollen, zuruck, zuruckrollen, terugloop, terugspoelen.

REWIND-TYPE ROLL. Standard and most-used type of paper roll for pianos, organs, and orchestrions. Wound on a spool. The end tab of the roll is attached to a take-up spool which pulls the end over a tracker bar as it plays. When the performance ends, the roll is rewound on the original spool. When rewinding is completed, the same performance can be heard again, or the roll can be exchanged with another. (Compare to endless-type roll, to which refer.)

RHUMBA. In a dance organ a term synonymous with maracca, to which refer.

ROHRFLUTE PIPE. Chimney flute pipe, to which refer.

ROLL. 1. Perforated paper roll as used on a player piano, orchestrion, organ, etc. Can be of the endless or rewind type. 2. Sustained or reiterating striking action, particular on a drum (as in snare drum roll).

SALICET. 4' pipe organ rank resembling salicional (to which refer).

SALICIONAL. Small scale metal 8' or 16' pipe organ rank having a bright string tone. Often used with celeste rank on pipe organs for voix celeste.

SAXOPHONE. 1. In an orchestrion or band organ a reed-type pipe similar to a clarinet, but larger. 2. In an orchestrion, a reed-type pipe with a 4-sided inverted pyramidal wooden resonator, open at the large end. A popular addition to jazzband-type orchestrions of the 1920s. 3. In a dance organ a visible but non-musical saxophone is sometimes mounted on the front. Behind the saxophone and concealed from view is a rank of saxophone pipes. When a saxophone pipe is played, a corresponding key on the display instrument is opened by means of a wire connected to a pneumatic. 4. Name given to the bass part of a clarinet rank in an orchestrion.

SCALE. 1. Musical range of an instrument. Description or number of notes from the lowest playing bass note to the highest playing treble note. (This may differ from the actual number of piano notes; for instance, a 65-note piano roll is played by using only 65 notes of an 88-note piano). 2. The number of playing notes plus the number of holes necessary to perform register changes and other functions. Thus an instrument may be described, for example, as having a 130-note scale. Synonym: key (definition 4, to which refer). 3. Layout or diagram of the function of each hole in a tracker bar, key in a key frame, etc.

SCALE STICK. Long narrow strip of cardboard, wood, or other material marked with the scale of a tracker bar or key frame. Used by roll and book arrangers as a guide for the correct placement of marks on a master roll.

SCHLAGWERK. German term for the percussion (non-chromatic) section of an automatic musical instrument, especially of an orchestrion or organ.

SELECTOR. Automatic tune selector used in certain Marquette (Cremona), Western Electric, and other instruments.

SFORZANDO. Or forzando. 1. The sharp accenting of single notes or groups of notes. 2. In an organ or photoplayer the pedal which, when depressed, will bring into play one-by-one all (or nearly all) ranks of the instrument. Synonyms: crescendo pedal, full-organ pedal.

SHUTOFF. To cease operating. Also: off, stop, coin trip, contact, Kontakt, Auslosung, arc, fine, arret.

SINGLE STROKE. Type of pneumatic or mechanical action which causes a beater or hammer to strike just once when a note is sustained in a music arrangement. Compare to reiterating (to which refer).

SIREN. Mechanical device which produces a slowing rising and falling wailing tone. Incorporated as part of certain photoplayers and theatre organs as a novelty sound effect for accompanying silent films.

SKATING RINK ORGAN. Band organ, often with visible brass pipes, used to provide music in a skating rink. Synonyms: military band organ, trumpet organ (if cylinder-operated).

SLEIGH BELLS. Tuned sleigh bells, usually with one to six bells per note, mounted to a board which is shaken. Found in certain European band organs and in many theatre organs. Tuned sleigh bells = grelotphone in French.

SNARE DRUM. Small two-headed (usually) drum with "snares" (tightly stretched pieces of gut or wire) which rattle against one drum head when the other drum head is struck. A popular addition to automatic instruments, especially orchestrions, band organs, and dance organs. Also: side drum, tambour, Trommel, kleine Trommel.

SNARE DRUM BRUSH. Several dozen wires bound together with a handle; used for soft drumming effects. Also: borstel.

SOFT. Having a small volume of sound. Opposite of loud. In this book the word piano (Italian designation for soft) is used only to mean the stringed instrument, to avoid confusion.

SOFT PEDAL. In an upright piano a pedal which, when depressed, brings the piano hammers closer to the strings, thus causing them to strike more softly. In a grand piano the pedal shifts the keyboard laterally to cause a piano hammer to strike just 2 strings instead of 3 on a 3-string note, etc. In this book, the soft pedal is designated as the hammer rail in upright instruments.

SOLO INSTRUMENT. Solo section. In an orchestrion, organ, or other instrument a chromatically-tuned (usually) extra instrument (such as a rank of pipes, set of xylophone bars, or bells) which, on occasion, play the main theme or solo part while the other sections of the instrument play accompaniment. In a fairground organ, a brightly-voiced rank of pipes may play a solo part while other pipes in lower octave ranges provide accompaniment.

STOP. In an organ or other instrument with pipes, a register for controlling one or more ranks of pipes. In a pipe organ or reed organ manually-operated stops are located above the keyboard and are called draw-stops or draw-knobs.

STREET ORGAN. Specially-constructed loudly-voiced organ designed for use on a hand cart. Used mainly in Holland. Synonyms: Dutch street organ, pierement.

STREET PIANO. Hand-cranked barrel piano, usually mounted on a cart, used to play music in city streets, especially during the 19th century.

SUSTAINING PEDAL. In a piano a pedal which, when depressed, lifts the dampers (to which refer) from the piano strings, causing the vibrations to be sustained or continued until they fade naturally or until the sustaining pedal is released.

SWANEE WHISTLE. Patented (in 1924) pneumatically-actuated slide whistle. The pitch rises and falls as the bottom slide or stopper is moved in and out. Sometimes called a lotus flute (although lotus flute refers to another style of pipe). Popular addition to jazzband-type orchestrions of the 1920s.

SWELL. A division of the pipe organ controlled by its own manual and contained in a box fitted with swell shutters for expression purposes.

SWELL SHADES. Synonym for swell shutters.

SWELL SHUTTERS. Louvered shades which open and close to vary the volume of sound which can be heard. Also: swell shades, swell, shutters, G. Werk, zwelblinden, crescendo.

TAKE-UP SPOOL. In a roll-operated instrument, the powered cylinder to which the end tab of the roll is affixed. The take-up spool pulls the roll over the tracker bar.

TAMBOURINE. Wooden hoop with a drum-like head on one end. The hoop is inset with small metal discs or jingles which rattle when the instrument is shaken. A popular addition to orchestrions, photoplayers, etc.

TASTEN. German word for keys on a piano or organ keyboard or metal keys in an organ key frame.

TEMPERAMENT. 1. Term denoting a system of tuning in which the various intervals are tempered or adjusted. The errors inherent in the chromatic scale of twelve half-steps are distributed among the intervals in such a way that each interval has a small error but none sounds offensive. 2. Loosely, that octave of 13 notes in a piano, organ, or tuned percussion instrument which is first tempered during the tuning procedure. From this octave of notes all other notes are directly or indirectly tuned.

TEMPLE BLOCK(S). Tuned gourd-like hollow blocks, usually with a horizontal slit at the end, used as percussion effects in certain dance organs. Usually seen in sets of three or four. Also: kloppen.

TENOR. High bass notes, roughly in the octave immediately below middle C. Frequently used for countermelody parts or to reinforce the melody.

TENOR DRUM. Small drum, usually under 12" diameter, without snares. (Compare to bass drum.)

THEATRE ORGAN. Pipe organ made for use to accompany silent films in a theatre. Loudly-voiced (usually with 15" and 25" pressure for certain pipe ranks). Contains pipes imitative of orchestra instruments. Contains tibia pipes as a main foundation rank. Unified control system by means of which functions assigned to a particular keyboard or manual can be shifted to another by means of pneumatic or electrical connections, and for this reason sometimes called a unit organ or unit orchestra (the latter being a Wurlitzer trademark: Wurlitzer Hope-Jones Unit Orchestra). Usually with a horseshoe-shaped console with stop tabs arranged in semicircular rows.

THEME. 1. The subject part of a musical composition; the main melody (as opposed to the accompaniment). 2. Mechanism in Duo-Art and other reproducing, expression, and player pianos which accents a note or chord.

TIBIA. In a church organ an open wood 8' flute pipe. In a theatre organ a large scale stopped flute considered to be a foundation rank.

TIBIA CLAUSA. Huge-scale stopped flute pipe having almost no harmonics. Used widely in theatre organs.

TIERCE. A rand of pipe organ foundation pipes sounding two octaves and a third above the key being depressed. Synonym: seventeenth.

TRACKER BAR. In a roll-operated instrument the device containing a series of spaced openings through which air passes in order to actuate a pneumatic mechanism (or to directly sound a note, in the case of paper-as-a-valve organettes). Synonyms: tracker board (term rarely used), keyless frame (in band organ and dance organ terminology only; mainly European usage).

TRACKER BAR LAYOUT. Or tracker bar scale. Diagram or listing of the function of each hole in a tracker bar.

TRANSPOSE. To shift music into a higher or lower key without making any other changes.

TRANSPOSING DEVICE. Device which enables the tracker bar, especially of a piano, to shift laterally for up to several notes so as to transpose the music arrangement to a higher or lower range for use in accompanying a singer. Not generally used in instruments with non-musical perforations (i.e., control perforations) in the tracker bar, for transposing the tracker bar would confuse the controls (exception: some very late Duo-Art reproducing pianos in which only the note-playing portion of the tracker bar shifts).

TRAPWORK. Term denoting non-tuned percussion instruments and sound effects in a large orchestrion or dance organ. Also: traps.

TREBLE. The upper range of the musical scale (as opposed to bass). Diskant in German.

TREMOLO. Rapidly repeated variation in the loudness of music. Achieved in several ways: 1. In certain pipe organs, by "shaking" the pressure supply. 2. In certain pipe organs and orchestrions, by beating repeatedly against the outside of a pressure reservoir (this also causes a slight variation in the musical pitch). 3. In dance organs and certain band organs by: 3a. interrupting the wind supply and thus supplying air to the pipes in short puffs, or 3b. by arranging the music in an intermittent fashion so that a sustained pipe note sounds fully, then begins to die away, and then sounds fully again. 4. In certain orchestrions and organs by putting a butterfly valve in the main wind line. The valve opens and closes rapidly. 5. In reed organs, by placing a rotating paddle over the opening from a reed chest. Synonyms: tremulant, vibrato (popular usage but incorrect technically; refer to vibrato definition).

TREMULANT. Tremolo, to which refer.

TRIANGLE. Round steel bar bent into a triangular shape. The ends are close but do not touch. Suspended from a cord and sounded with a metal striker. Widely used in automatic instruments.

TROMBONE PIPE. Brightly-voiced reed pipe made of wood or metal. Mainly used in band organs, sometimes as the bass part of a trumpet rank. Imitative of the trombone sound. Also: bombardon, posaune.

TROMBONE CHANT. Trombone rank in the melody section of a band organ, large Gavioli instruments for example.

TRUMPET PIPE. In a band organ, a brilliantly-voiced reed pipe, made of wood or metal (usually brass), and imitative of a trumpet. Usually used with a bass accompaniment of trombones.

TUBULAR CHIMES. See chimes.

TUTTI. In orchestral music a term used to denote full orchestra passages (as opposed to solo passages). In certain pipe organ scales the term is synonymous with "full organ on."

TWELFTH. A pipe organ foundation rank sounding an octave and a fifth above the keys which are depressed. Synonyms: nazard, octave quint.

TYMPANI. Kettle drum or kettle drum effect (made by smaller beaters on a bass drum). Also: Pauke, Pauken.

UNDA MARIS. Literally, "waves of the sea." Two ranks of celeste-tuned string pipes used in dance organs and street organs. The unda maris pipes produce a characteristic undulating sound from which the "waves of the sea" name (in Latin) is derived.

UNIFICATION. Or unified system. System used in most theatre organs and in some smaller instruments (such as certain mortuary organs made by Seeburg and Operators) whereby a large rank of pipes extending over many octaves from bass to treble can be drawn or used at any desired pitch. To be played from the same position on the keyboard (or tracker bar) a section of flute pipes, for example, can be selected at 2' pitch (a treble section of the pipe rank), 4' pitch, or 8' pitch (the bass section). Or, by setting the 2', 4', and 8' stop tabs all at once, the same key will play three pipes—the same note at three different pitches. On multiple-keyboard organs a given rank can be switched from one keyboard to another.

UNIPHONE BELLS. Or unifon bells. Bar-type bells, usually with a scooplike depression in the center, with a closed-end tubular resonator behind each bar. Used in certain fairground organs, in certain varieties of the Cremona Orchestral J orchestrion, and in a few other instruments.

UNIVOX. Simple electronic organ used in some Decap and Mortier/Van der Bosch dance organs built in modern times.

VIBRATO. A device which causes a rapid and repetitive change in pitch (e.g., a vibrato effect is achieved in the Mills Violano-Virtuoso by shaking the tail piece). Compare to tremolo.

VIBRATONE. Also vibraton. Jazz flute pipe (to which refer) with a thin diaphragm of metal, plastic, or other substance mounted in a circular hole in the front of the pipe. When the pipe sounds, the diaphragm resonates and produces a buzzing kazoo-like sound. Usually fitted with a jazz tremolo mechanism.

VIENNESE FLUTE. Synonym for orchestral flute.

VIOL D'ORCHESTRE. Often abbreviated as VDO. Pipe organ rank imitative of an orchestral violin.

VIOLA DA GAMBA. Pipe organ string-toned rank of delicate tone, imitative of the stringed instrument from which it derives its name.

VIOLA PIPE. Organ pipe of 8' or 16' pitch, imitative of the orchestral viola; somewhat smoother sounding than the violin pipe.

VIOLIN. Treble-pitched 4-stringed instrument played with a rosined horsehair bow. The two commercially successful automatically-played violins were the Hupfeld Phonoliszt-Violina and the Mills Violano-Virtuoso.

VIOLIN CELESTE. Celeste violin pipe ranks. Also: vox celeste, voix celeste.

VIOLIN PIPE. Flue-type pipe of raspy violin-like quality popularly used in coin pianos, orchestrions, and organs. The tonal quality is regulated by a distinctive-appearing harmonic brake (to which refer). Bass-voiced violin pipes are called cello or violoncello pipes, middle range pipes are called violas, and treble range pipes are called violin pipes.

VIOLONE PIPE. Organ pipe voiced between a diapason and string tone.

VOIX CELESTE. Violin celeste.

VOICING. 1. The process by which the tonal quality of the pipe is regulated (as opposed to tuning, which regulates the pitch). 2. Term used to describe the loudness, softness, or the harmonic or tonal character of a pipe. 3. The process by which the hardness of the felt piano hammer head is adjusted or regulated.

VORSETZER. A German-origin term which is generally used by collectors today. 1. An electrically-operated (usually) cabinet-style player containing a reproducing mechanism which uses reproducing piano rolls. The cabinet is equipped with felt-covered "fingers" and is pushed up to the keyboard of an upright or grand (usually) piano. The fingers and corresponding pedal mechanisms then automatically play the keyboard and pedals of the piano. Vorsetzer = sitter-in-front-of in German. Vorsetzers with reproducing mechanisms made by Hupfeld, Welte, and others. (This definition, a vorsetzer with a reproducing mechanism, is the one generally used by collectors today.) 2. Any push-up piano player or device which is placed in front of a piano or organ keyboard to play it. Synonyms: cabinet player, piano player, push-up piano player.

VOX HUMANA. Pipe rank of the reed family, usually with a capped metal resonator. Literally, "human voice." Used in photoplayers and in several types of organs.

WALDFLUTE. Moderately loud open wood flute pipe.

WOOD BLOCK. Hardwood block, usually hollow or with a cavity, which is struck by a beater. Also: Chinese block, Indian block, Holz Trommel, wood drum.

WOODWIND. 1. Family of musical instruments, including the piccolo, flute, clarinet, oboe, bassoon, and other instruments (as opposed to the brass, string, and percussion families). 2. Term used by the Estey Organ Company to denote certain ranks in their pipe organs.

XYLOPHONE. 1. Set of tuned wooden bars. From the Greek language: xylo = wood; phon = sound. (When equipped with resonators, a xylophone is called a marimba, to which refer.) Synonym: marimbaphone (used by the Link Piano Co., not general usage). 2. Careless description of orchestra bells (which are of metal and thus by logical definition of the word, cannot be a xylophone).

BIBLIOGRAPHY
and SUGGESTED READING

BIBLIOGRAPHY
and
SUGGESTED READING LIST

Apel, Willi. *Harvard Dictionary of Music.* Harvard University Press; Cambridge, Massachusetts. Various dates.

Barnes, William H. *The Contemporary American Organ.* J. Fischer & Bro.; New York, New York. Various dates.

Boston, Canon Noel and Langwill, Lyndesay G. *Church and Chamber Barrel-Organs.* Lyndesay G. Langwill; Edinburgh, Scotland. 1967.

Bowers, Q. David. *The Encyclopedia of Automatic Musical Instruments.* The Vestal Press; Vestal, New York. 1972.

Bowers, Q. David. *A Guidebook of Automatic Musical Instruments, Vol. I and II.* The Vestal Press; Vestal, New York. 1967.

Bowers, Q. David. *Put Another Nickel In.* The Vestal Press; Vestal, New York. 1965.

Buchner, Dr. Alexander. *Mechanical Musical Instruments.* Batchworth Press; London, England. No date (circa 1955).

Clark, John E.T. *Musical Boxes—A History and Appreciation.* George Allen & Unwin, Ltd.; London, England. 1961.

Cockayne, Eric V. *The Fairground Organ.* David & Charles; Newton Abbot, England. No date (circa 1970).

deWaard, Romke. *From Music Boxes to Street Organs.* English language edition by The Vestal Press; Vestal, New York. 1962.

Faust, Oliver C. *A Treatise on the Construction, Repairing, and Tuning of the Organ.* Tuners Supply Co.; Boston, Massachusetts. 1949.

Fried, Frederick. *A Pictorial History of the Carousel.* A.S. Barnes & Co.; New York, New York. 1964.

Givens, Larry. *Rebuilding the Player Piano.* The Vestal Press; Vestal, New York. 1963.

Givens, Larry. *Re-enacting the Artist.* The Vestal Press; Vestal, New York. 1970.

Hall, Ben M. *The Best Remaining Seats.* Bramhall House; New York, New York. 1961.

Helmholtz, Hermann. *The Sensations of Tone.* Reprint of 1885 edition by the Dover Press; New York, New York. 1954.

Irwin, Stevens. *Dictionary of Pipe Organ Stops.* G. Schirmer, Inc.; New York, New York. 1962.

McTammany, John. *The Technical History of the Player.* Musical Courier Co.; New York, New York. 1915. Reprinted by the Vestal Press, 1971.

Michel, N.E. *Michel's Piano Atlas.* Published by the author; Pico Rivera, California. Various dates.

Mosoriak, R. *The Curious History of Music Boxes.* Lightner Publishing Corp.; Chicago, Illinois. 1943.

O'Kelley, Connie. *San Sylmar.* Notes on musical instruments by Q. David Bowers. Published by Merle Norman Cosmetics; Los Angeles, California. 1978.

Ord-Hume, Arthur W.J.G. *Barrel Organ.* A.S. Barnes and Company; South Brunswick, New Jersey. 1978.

Ord-Hume, Arthur W.J.G. *Collecting Musical Boxes and How to Repair Them.* Crown Publishers; New York, New York. 1967.

Ord-Hume, Arthur W.J.G. *The Mechanics of Mechanical Music.* Published by the author; Chiswick, London, England. 1973.

Ord-Hume, Arthur W.J.G. *Player Piano.* A.S. Barnes and Company; New York, New York. 1970.

Reblitz, Arthur A. *Piano Servicing, Tuning, and Rebuilding.* The Vestal Press; Vestal, New York. 1976.

Roehl, Harvey N. *Player Piano Treasury.* The Vestal Press; Vestal, New York. 1961.

Scholes, Percy A. *The Oxford Companion to Music.* Oxford University Press; London, New York, and Toronto. Various dates.

Silver Anniversary Collection. An anthology of articles from the publications of the Musical Box Society International. Musical Box Society International; Summit, New Jersey. 1974.

Webb, Graham. *The Cylinder Musical Box Handbook.* Faber & Faber; London, England. 1968.

Webb, Graham. *The Disc Musical Box Handbook.* Faber & Faber; London, England. 1971.

Weiss-Stauffacher, Heinrich and Bruhin, Rudolph. *The Marvelous World of Music Machines.* Kodansha International; Tokyo and New York. 1976.

Periodicals

"The AMICA." News bulletin of the Automatic Musical Instrument Collectors Association.

"The Bulletin of the Musical Box Society International." Periodical of the Musical Box Society International.

"The Key Frame." Journal of the Fair Organ Preservation Society.

"The Music Box." Journal of the Musical Box Society of Great Britain.

"Het Pierement." Journal of the Kring van Draaiorgelvrienden.

Note: For a listing of current addresses of collectors' organizations worldwide send a request to the Vestal Press, publisher of the present volume.

INDEX and
EASY FINDING LIST

INDEX AND EASY FINDING LIST